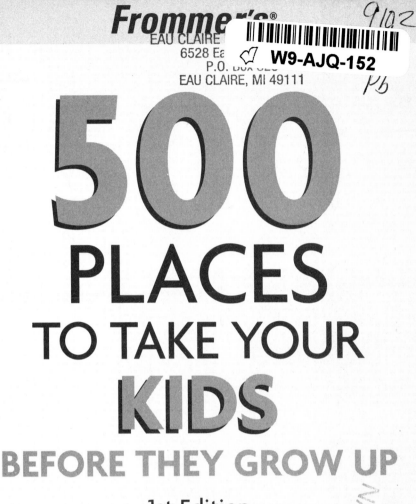

Frommer's®

9/02

EAU CLAIRE
6528 Ea
P.O. Box
EAU CLAIRE, MI 49111

W9-AJQ-152

Pb

500
PLACES
TO TAKE YOUR
KIDS
BEFORE THEY GROW UP

1st Edition

by Holly Hughes

WITHDRAWN

EAU CLAIRE DISTRICT LIBRARY

WILEY

Wiley Publishing, Inc.

T 141483

Contents

About This Book . . . vii

chapter 1　**Taking in the Scenery** 1
Awesome Vistas . . . 2
Seven Beautiful Bridges . . . 12
Drives . . . 20
Train Rides . . . 32
Boat Rides . . . 41

chapter 2　**Cities Great & Small** 51
One-of-a-Kind Cityscapes . . . 52
The Big City Buzz . . . 61
Postcards across America . . . 69

chapter 3　**Weird & Wonderful** 81
Otherworldly Landscapes . . . 82
Atmospheric Places to Explore . . . 97
A Touch of Kitsch . . . 104
Caves & Waterfalls . . . 119

chapter 4　**Walk with the Animals** 127
In the Wild . . . 128
Zoos . . . 146
Aquariums . . . 155

chapter 5　**Lost in the Mists of Time** 166
Fossils . . . 167
Early Humans . . . 176
The Ancient World . . . 187

chapter 6　**Windows on History** 218
Positively Medieval . . . 219
Historic Restorations . . . 238
Native Americans . . . 252
Settling America . . . 260
Black American History . . . 271

chapter 7　**War & Peace** 282
Bloody Battlegrounds . . . 283
History at Sea . . . 295
World War II & the Cold War . . . 305

chapter 8 **For Budding Scientists** 316
Science Museums . . . 317
The History of Flight . . . 328
Inventions & Industry . . . 334
Stargazing . . . 341

chapter 9 **Holy Places** 348

chapter 10 **A Dose of Culture** 371
Masterpieces of Art . . . 372
Music . . . 382
Theater & the Movies . . . 391

chapter 11 **Historic Homes** 398
Castles & Mansions . . . 399
Famous Homesteads . . . 416
U.S. Presidents . . . 427

chapter 12 **Out & About** 437
Hiking & Backpacking . . . 438
Cycling . . . 454
In the Saddle . . . 461

chapter 13 **On the Water** 468
Paddling Away . . . 469
Swimming . . . 482
Snorkeling & Diving . . . 485
Beaches . . . 491

chapter 14 **Calling All Sports Fans** 499

chapter 15 **Rides & Thrills** 524
Adrenaline Rushes . . . 525
Carousels & Ferris Wheels . . . 532
Roller Coasters . . . 537
Theme Parks . . . 543

Alphabetical Index 553

Geographical Index 561

Published by:

Wiley Publishing, Inc.

111 River St.
Hoboken, NJ 07030-5774

ISBN-13: 978-0-7645-9588-2
ISBN-10: 0-7645-9588-1

Editor: Margot Weiss
Production Editor: Heather Wilcox
Cartographer: Guy Ruggiero
Photo Editors: Richard Fox & Margot Weiss (with special thanks to Jack Brink)
Interior book design: Melissa Auciello-Brogan
Production by Wiley Indianapolis Composition Services

Front cover photo: Top row left to right: Egypt, Giza: The Great Sphinx; Utah, Arches National Park: Turret Arch viewed through North Window; Massachusetts, Cape Cod: Girl Jumping off dock. Bottom row left to right: Japan, Mt. Fuji scenic, meadow with wildflowers in foreground; Chile, Easter Island: Rano Raraku, Moai statues.
Spine: South Dakota: Mount Rushmore; Santa Cruz Island, Galapagos Islands: Giant Tortoise with head extended; Greece, Athens: Parthenon Temple on the Acropolis.
Back cover photo: New York: Statue of Liberty closeup of head; Maine, Cape Elizabeth: Portland Head Lighthouse, surf in foreground.

For information on our other products and services or to obtain technical support, please contact our Customer Care Department within the U.S. at 800/762-2974, outside the U.S. at 317/572-3993 or fax 317/572-4002.

Wiley also publishes its books in a variety of electronic formats. Some content that appears in print may not be available in electronic formats.

Manufactured in the United States of America

12 11 10 9 8 7 6

About the Author

Holly Hughes has traveled the globe as an editor and writer—she's the former executive editor of Fodor's Travel Publications, the series editor of Frommer's Irreverent Guides, and author of *Frommer's New York City with Kids*. She's also written fiction for middle graders and edits the annual *Best Food Writing* anthology. New York City makes a convenient jumping-off place for her travels with her three children and husband.

Acknowledgments

Many thanks to all my fellow parents whose brains I picked for travel suggestions over the past two years. You were so generous with your trip memories, I almost felt in some cases as if I had traveled there with you. And to all the other parents who had to listen to my enthusiastic ramblings by the coffee urns at PTA meetings and on the soccer field sidelines—thank you for never letting your eyes glaze over as I raved on and on about yet another far-flung destination they really should visit.

I've also relied on the devoted corps of Frommer's writers to supply me with phone numbers, addresses, and recommendations of their own favorite family destinations. Your descriptions have been invaluable—you're the real experts in your various parts of the world, and I'm beholden to you.

I've had the extreme good fortune to work with Margot Weiss, an incredibly patient and sympathetic editor, who played the role of midwife with wonderful good humor and good sense. And I am always indebted to Mike Spring, who's not only the publisher on this project but who first inspired me to become a travel writer many years ago.

And finally, I have to thank my husband and children, who not only put up with having Mom disappear into her office for hours at a time but who are the best travel companions I could ever ask for. I've been blessed with three children who are great travelers—they love getting up before dawn to catch an early plane, they know how to amuse themselves on long flights, they can negotiate a crowded train platform, they don't need to be pacified with videos on long car trips, and they are excited every time we check into a new hotel. They make travel an adventure to look forward to.

—Holly Hughes

An Invitation to the Reader

In researching this book, we discovered many wonderful places. We're sure you'll find others. Please tell us about them, so we can share the information with your fellow travelers in upcoming editions. If you were disappointed with a recommendation, we'd love to know that, too. Please write to:

Frommer's 500 Places to Take Your Kids Before They Grow Up, 1st Edition
Wiley Publishing, Inc. • 111 River St. • Hoboken, NJ 07030-5774

An Additional Note

Please be advised that travel information is subject to change at any time—and this is especially true of prices. We therefore suggest that you write or call ahead for confirmation when making your travel plans. The authors, editors, and publisher cannot be held responsible for the experiences of readers while traveling. Your safety is important to us, however, so we encourage you to stay alert and be aware of your surroundings. Keep a close eye on cameras, purses, and wallets, all favorite targets of thieves and pickpockets.

Other Great Guides for Your Trip:

Frommer's New York City with Kids
Frommer's Chicago with Kids
Frommer's Las Vegas with Kids
Frommer's San Francisco with Kids
Frommer's Washington, D.C., with Kids
Frommer's Family Vacations in the National Parks
The Unofficial Guide to California with Kids
The Unofficial Guide to Florida with Kids
The Unofficial Guide to the Mid-Atlantic with Kids
The Unofficial Guide to New England & New York with Kids
The Unofficial Guide to the Southeast with Kids
The Unofficial Guide to Walt Disney World with Kids

Frommer's Icons

We use **four feature icons** to help you quickly find the information you're looking for. At the end of each review, look for:

 Where to get more information

✈ Nearest airport

🚆 Nearest train station

🛏 Recommended kid-friendly hotels

Frommers.com

Now that you have the guidebook to a great trip, visit our website at **www.frommers. com** for travel information on more than 3,000 destinations. With features updated regularly, we give you instant access to the most current trip-planning information available. At Frommers.com, you'll also find the best prices on airfares, accommodations, and car rentals—and you can even book travel online through our travel booking partners. At Frommers.com, you'll also find the following:

- Online updates to our most popular guidebooks
- Vacation sweepstakes and contest giveaways
- Newsletter highlighting the hottest travel trends
- Online travel message boards with featured travel discussions

About This Book
Why These 500 Places?

The obvious question just about everybody asked me when I told them I was writing this book: "Have you been to all 500 places?" I regret to say I haven't—not yet—but I've been to a surprising number of them over the past few years. If not, I've talked to other families who have generously shared their travel memories with me. Immersed in writing this book, at times I almost imagined we *had* been everyplace. But I have to say, now that it's written, I'm glad we haven't seen it all and done it all yet—we still have a few traveling years ahead of us as a family, and now we've got a thicker file than ever of thrilling trips to look forward to.

Of course, choosing a destination is only part of the challenge. Knowing what it's like to travel with youngsters, I've tried to give you the tools you need to make these trips unforgettable. I've dug up tidbits of history or other background, so you can look like experts when you're leading your children around a site. It's not enough just to go to a place—you've got to imagine how the people of this distant era lived, why one army won this battle and not the other, what makes this park different from that one, which animals thrive where. You do it to keep the kids interested, and then somehow you find yourself having a richer experience of the place, too. Awakening that sense of wonder is what travel is all about, for adults as well as children.

I've also suggested strategies for certain destinations—whether or not to hire a tour guide (some enrich the experience, others bog you down in boring details); whether to drive, walk, or take the tram; whether to dawdle over a museum's every exhibit or zero in on a few key displays. With the proper strategy, you'd be surprised how much even young children can delight in these destinations. Don't sell them short! The payoff is all cumulative – the more your children travel, the more they'll observe and appreciate on further trips, and the more intriguing trips you'll be able to plan.

Of course, you are the experts when it comes to knowing your own family's interests—whether that be history, culture, nature, outdoor adventure—so rather than follow a geographic scheme, I've organized this book in groups of destinations with a similar emphasis, spread around the globe. After a successful trip to one destination, I hope you'll consider planning new trips to others in that category—chances are you'll like them too.

The geographic index in the back will help you match nearby destinations, so you can take in a whole cluster of sights on one vacation.

Hotels

I wish I'd had space to give you full-blown hotel reviews, but you can rely on these choices being the most family-friendly lodgings in the area. Traveling with a family is not cheap, so I tended to recommend moderately priced hotels rather than the most expensive lodgings. (You don't need my help in finding the poshest hotel in town—what's hard to find is the small hotel with no advertising budget.) I also recommend modern, plainly furnished hotels rather than antique-laden B&Bs, which, for all their charm, may not welcome children. The other criteria I look for: kitchenettes, room service, room layouts that accommodate extra beds, TVs in the room, and the trump card, a swimming pool (give us a good pool and my kids will accept almost anything). **Price ranges** of course are relative. The three price ranges I note—$$$ (expensive), $$ (moderate), and $ (inexpensive)—don't conform to one set of dollar equivalents, but reflect the local market. A $125-per-night motel room in South Dakota would seem expensive, but if you can find something clean and safe at that price in London, SNAP IT UP. For fuller descriptions (and other useful travel info), please consult the corresponding Frommer's guides for these destinations. Note that any **phone numbers** listed are what you'd dial from within that country—to dial from overseas, add the appropriate country code.

Age Ranges

For each destination, I've also indicated an **age range** for children. When I say "All ages," that means you could bring a baby or young toddler in a stroller and not feel out of place. I'm not saying the 6-month-old would get much out of the experience (!), but at least you could take older siblings there without the baby being a hindrance. In a few cases, I've upped the age range on a destination if it somehow poses challenges handled best by older kids. I admit that these recommended age ranges are subjective—for lack of a more objective test, I've based them on what my own children would have been interested in at what age. My kids have become good travelers over the years. Yours can be too.

They're only young once, so see the world through their eyes—you won't regret it!

Chapter 1   Taking in the Scenery

Awesome Vistas . . . 2
Seven Beautiful Bridges . . . 12
Drives . . . 20
Train Rides . . . 32
Boat Rides . . . 41

Sequoia National Park.

Monument Valley
The Iconic Wild West Landscape
Ages 6 & up • Kayenta, Arizona, USA

WHEN MOST OF US THINK of the American West, this is what clicks into our mental Viewmasters: A vast, flat sagebrush plain with huge sandstone spires thrusting to the sky like the crabbed fingers of a primeval Mother Earth clutching for the heavens. Ever since movie director John Ford first started shooting westerns here in the 1930s, this landscape has felt familiar to millions who have never set foot here. We've all seen it on the big screen, but oh, what a difference to see it in real life.

If you possibly can, time your visit to include sunset—as the sheer walls of these monoliths capture the light of the setting sun, they truly seem to catch fire. There are three ways to tour the area, which is also a Navajo reservation: driving the 17-mile Valley Drive; hiking with a guide; or on horseback. Guides are usually local Navajos, born and bred to this barren landscape. If you drive, you can take your own car; but it is a rocky, rutted dirt road, so I personally would opt for a **jeep or van tour.** (Hold out for one that visits backcountry areas that are otherwise off-limits to visitors, including close-ups of several **natural arches** and Ancient Puebloan **petroglyphs.**)

Sticking to the **Valley Drive** takes you to **11 scenic overlooks,** once-in-a-lifetime photo ops with those incredible sandstone buttes for backdrop. Often Navajos sell jewelry and other crafts at the viewing areas, or even pose on horseback to add local color to your snapshots (a tip will be expected).

John Wayne—John Ford's favorite leading cowboy—roamed these scrublands on horseback, and seeing it from a Western saddle does seem like the thing to do. Local outfitters run everything from a guided 1-hour trail ride to an overnight campout. One of the most comprehensive tour companies (jeeps, hikes, horses, you name it) is **Sacred Monument Tours** (© **435/727-3218;** www.monumentvalley. net), but plenty of other operators can be booked from the visitor center. Although most of the park lies in Arizona, it is right on the state border, and you enter it from Utah. Just outside the park, **Goulding's Museum and Trading Post** is furnished as it was in the 1920s and 1930s when the moviemakers first discovered the area; there are also displays about the many films that were shot here.

Be sure to get a map so the kids can learn the eccentric rock formations' names—imaginative names like The Mittens, Three Sisters, Camel Butte, Elephant Butte, the Thumb, and Totem Pole. And as you stare at them, take an extra moment to imagine the forces of nature that have sculpted the soft desert stone into these incredible shapes. It's an only-in-America panorama that the kids won't ever forget.

Monument Valley.

ⓘ U.S. 163, 30 miles north of Kayenta (☎ **435/727-5870;** www.monumentvalley online.com).

✈ Flagstaff Pulliam, 200 miles.

🛏 $$$ **Goulding's Lodge,** Monument Valley, UT (☎ **435/727-3231;** www. gouldings.com). $$ **Hampton Inn-Navajo**

Nation, U.S. 160, Kayenta, AZ (☎ **800/ HAMPTON** or 928/697-3170; www. hampton-inn.com).

WHY THEY'LL THANK YOU: Just like the movies—only more so.

Awesome Vistas

The Redwood Forests of California

All ages • Crescent City, California, USA

Iᴛ's ʜᴀʀᴅ ᴛᴏ ᴇxᴘʟᴀɪɴ the feeling you get in the old-growth forests of **Redwood National and State Parks.** Everything seems big, misty, and primeval—flowering bushes cover the ground, 10-foot-tall ferns line the creeks, and the smells are rich and musty. It's so *Jurassic Park* you half expect to turn the corner and see a dinosaur.

The scientific name for these massive conifers is *Sequoia sempervirens,* cousins of the giant sequoias (see Sequoia National Park ❸). Sheathed in rough reddish bark, miraculously fire-resistant, their stout straight trunks shoot up 100 feet or more before a canopy of branches begins; they often reach a total height of more than 300 feet. Among the planet's most ancient individuals—the oldest dated coast redwood is more than 2,200 years old—they only grow in temperate rainforests, meaning nowhere but the U.S. Pacific Coast. In 1968, the federal government created Redwood National Park (nowadays combined with three state redwood parks) to protect what's left of this seriously endangered species. The relative isolation of this stretch of coast helped the forests survive intact, but it also makes for a long drive.

The most spectacular display is along the **Avenue of the Giants,** a 33-mile stretch of U.S. 101 through the Humboldt Redwoods State Park (☎ **707/ 946-2263;** www.humboldtredwoods.org).

Environmentalists bemoan the tacky attractions along this route, but youngsters love 'em—from south to north, hollow **Chimney Tree,** where J. R. R. Tolkien's Hobbit is rumored to live; **One-Log House,** a small dwelling built inside a log; and the **Shrine Drive-Thru Tree.** More dignified landmarks include **Founders Grove,** honoring those who started the Save the Redwoods League in 1918; and the 950-year-old **Immortal Tree.** Don't settle for looking at all this out your car window—from many parking areas you can ramble on short loop trails into awesome redwood groves.

The other cluster of parks begins another 100 miles or so farther north, threaded along U.S. Highway 101. The most scenic drive parallels 101, along the **Newton B. Drury Scenic Parkway,** passing through redwood groves and meadows where Roosevelt elk graze, and **Coastal Drive,** which has grand views of the Pacific. But again, the truly spine-tingling experience requires getting out and hiking through these soaring perpendicular woods. Pick up a park map to find your way to **Tall Trees Trail,** a 3¼-mile round-trip to a 600-year-old tree often touted as the world's tallest (get a permit at the Redwood Information Center in Orick); the self-guided mile-long **Lady Bird Johnson Grove Loop;** the short, very popular **Fern Canyon Trail;**

or, for the littlest hikers, the quarter-mile-long **Big Tree Trail,** a paved trail leading to—what else?—a big tree.

ⓘ 1111 Second St. (✆ **707/464-6101,** ext. 5064; www.nps.gov/redw).

✈ Crescent City.

🛏 $ **Curly Redwood Lodge,** 701 Redwood Hwy. S. (U.S. 101), Crescent City

(✆ **707/464-2137;** www.curlyredwood lodge.com). $$$ **Lost Whale Bed & Breakfast,** 3452 Patrick's Point Dr., Trinidad (✆ **800/677-7859** or 707/677-3425; www.lostwhaleinn.com).

WHY THEY'LL THANK YOU: Seeing the redwoods before they're gone.

Awesome Vistas **3**

Sequoia & Kings Canyon National Parks
Giant Trees of the Sierras
All ages • Visalia & Fresno, California, USA

ONLY 200 MILES BY ROAD from often-overrun Yosemite National Park **393**, Sequoia and Kings Canyon national parks still feel like untrammeled wilderness. Only one road, the **Generals Highway,** loops through the area, and no road traverses the Sierra here. High-altitude hiking and backpacking are what these parks are really all about; some 700 miles of trails traverse this terrain of snowcapped Sierra Nevada peaks (including **Mount Whitney,** which at 14,494 ft. is the highest point in the lower 48 states), high-country lakes, and alpine meadows. For families, though, there's one main attraction: the largest groves of giant sequoias in the Sierra Nevada.

Though they are two separate parks, Sequoia and Kings Canyon are contiguous and managed jointly from the **park headquarters** at Ash Mountain—you hardly know when you're leaving one and entering the other.

Of the 75 or so groves of giant sequoias in the parks, the two most convenient to visit are Grant Grove (in Kings Canyon near the Big Stump park entrance), and Giant Forest (in Sequoia, 16 miles from the Ash Mountain entrance). In **Grant Grove,** a 100-foot walk through the hollow trunk of the **Fallen Monarch** makes a fascinating

side trip. The tree has been used for shelter for more than 100 years and is tall enough inside that you can walk through without bending over. In **Giant Forest,** the awesome **General Sherman Tree** is

Sequoia National Park.

considered the largest living thing in the world; single branches of this monster are more than 7 feet thick. Other trees in the grove (each of them saddled with names like General Lee or Lincoln) are nearly as large, creating an overall effect of massive majesty. Giant Grove has some 40 miles of intersecting footpaths to wander; the 6-mile **Trail of the Sequoias** will take you to the grove's far eastern end, where you'll find some of the finest trees.

While Sequoia's raison d'être is those incredible trees, Kings Canyon encompasses the deepest canyon in the United States: Drive to **Road's End** on the Kings Canyon Highway (open late May to early Nov) to stand by the banks of the Kings River and stare up at granite walls rising thousands of feet above the river.

ⓘ **Ash Mountain entrance,** CA 198 from Visalia. **Big Stump entrance,** 180 from Fresno, CA (✆ **559/565-3341;** www.nps. gov/seki, www.sequoia-kingscanyon.com, or www.visitsequoia.com).

✈ Fresno-Yosemite, 53 miles.

🛏 $ **Dorst Campground,** in Sequoia near Giant Forest (✆ **800/365-2267**). $$ **Wuksachi Village & Lodge,** 64740 Wuksachi Way, Lodgepole (✆ **888/252-5757** or 559/565-4070; www.visit sequoia.com).

WHY THEY'LL THANK YOU: The redwoods' awesome (and even more endangered) cousins.

---

④ Awesome Vistas

The Columbia River Gorge
Mighty Old River
All ages • Troutdale to The Dalles, Oregon, USA

Gouging out the jagged border between Washington and Oregon, just east of Portland the mighty Columbia River bores through the Cascade Range in one of the most beautiful river gorges in the world. The Grand Canyon's stark red-stone chasms may be more primeval and powerful looking, but I have a special fondness for the Columbia River Gorge, where the awesome panoramas come carpeted in lush dark-green forest and spangled by crystalline waterfalls.

I-84 runs beside the river on the Oregon side (WA 14 follows the Washington shore), but it's well worth getting off I-84 at Troutdale to wind along U.S. 30, the Historic Columbia River Highway, for 22 miles at the west end of the 70-mile-long Gorge (it also parallels I-84 for 15 miles at the east end). You'll sweep close to sheer waterfalls—there are no fewer than 77 in the Gorge—and rise to breath-catching vistas. Stop at **Vista House** at Crown Point (✆ **503/695-2230;** www. vistahouse.com) for a spectacular view of Beacon Rock, an 800-foot-tall monolith across the river in Washington. A few miles east are the gorge's tallest falls, the 620-foot-high **Multnomah Falls.** When U.S. 30 leaves the river, continue on I-84 past the **Bonneville Lock and Dam** (in June and Sept you can see migrating salmon climb a fish ladder to bypass the locks) to the **Bridge of the Gods,** where Indian oral tradition claims a natural rock bridge once existed. Cross the bridge to Washington to visit the excellent **Columbia Gorge Interpretive Center,** 990 SW Rock Creek Dr., Stevenson (✆ **800/991-2338;** www.columbiagorge.org).

Showstopper views are great, but the gorge is even more fascinating as a unique natural phenomenon. At the end of the last Ice Age, huge glacial ice dams in Montana (which still has glaciers—see the Going-to-the-Sun Road ㉒) burst and sent 1,000-foot-high floodwaters racing along the river toward the ocean, dragging ice chunks and rocks that carved a steep-walled gorge. Tributaries that had once meandered down gentle valleys were suddenly plummeting down to the river in dramatic cascades. The volcanic Cascade Range then began to rise *around* the gorge, making it even more dramatic. Call the kids' attention to the contrast between the rainforest west of the Cascades and the sagebrush scrublands to the east, caused by moist air condensing into rain and snow as it hits the western slopes, leaving the east side high and dry in what is called a rain shadow.

On the Oregon bank in Cascade Locks you can board the stern-wheeler

Columbia Gorge (✆ **800/643-1354;** www.sternwheeler.com) for a cruise on the Columbia; if trains are more your style, hop aboard the **Mount Hood Railroad,** 110 Railroad Ave. (✆ **800/872-4661;** www.mthoodrr.com) and chug up the Hood River Valley in vintage rail cars.

ⓘ ✆ **541/386-2333;** www.fs.fed.us/r6/columbia.

✈ Portland International, 30 miles.

🛏 $$ **Columbia Gorge Hotel,** 4000 Westcliff Dr., Hood River, OR (✆ **800/345-1921** or 541/386-5566; www.columbia gorgehotel.com). $$$ **Dolce Skamania Lodge,** 1131 SW Skamania Lodge Way, Stevenson, WA (✆ **800/221-7117** or 509/427-7700; www.skamania.com).

WHY THEY'LL THANK YOU: Marveling at each curve in the road.

Awesome Vistas **5**

Uluru (Ayers Rock)
Australia's Red Rock Center

Ages 6 & up • Uluru-Kata Tjuta National Park, Northern Territory, Australia

Iт's A BIT OF A MYSTERY why people trek from all over the world to gawk at Ayers Rock. For its size? Hardly—nearby Mount Conner is three times as big. For its shape? Probably not—most folks agree the neighboring Kata Tjuta (the Olgas) is more picturesque. And yet, undeniably, a faint shiver goes up the spine when you gaze on its serene, hulking mass.

People used to believe that Uluru (Ayers Rock's proper Aboriginal name) was a meteorite, but we now know it was formed by sediments laid millions of years ago in an inland sea and thrust aboveground by geological forces (there's twice as much again underground, it's thought). On photos it may look like a big smooth blob, but face to face it's dappled with holes and overhangs, with curtains of

stone draping its sides, with little coves hiding water holes and Aboriginal rock art, all of it changing color dramatically depending on the slant of the sun. The peak time is sunset, when oranges, peaches, pinks, reds, and then indigo and deep violet creep across its face as if it were a giant opal. At sunrise the colors are less dramatic, but many folks enjoy the spectacle of the Rock unveiled by the dawn to bird song.

Aborigines refer to tourists as *minga*—little ants—because that's what we look like crawling up Uluru, which to them is sacrilege. And yet despite this, and despite ferocious winds, sheer rock faces, and extreme temperatures, visitors still feel compelled to scramble up the rock, taking anywhere from 2 to 4 hours; the views from the top are amazing, but is it worth it? There are plenty of other options. The paved 9km (5.6-mile) **Base Walk** circumnavigates Uluru, with time to explore water holes, caves, folds, and overhangs; an easy kilometer (.6-mile) round-trip trail from the **Mutitjulu** parking lot visits a pretty water hole with rock art near the Rock's base. On the free daily 90-minute **Mala Walk,** a ranger, who is often an Aborigine, discusses the Dreamtime myths behind Uluru and explains the significance of the rock art and other sites you see. Another peaceful way to see the Rock is on hour-long camelback forays through the red-sand dunes with **Frontier Camel Tours** (*℃* **1800/806 499** in Australia, or 08/8956 2444; www.cameltours.com.au). If it's aerial views you want, several local companies do scenic flights by light aircraft or helicopter over Uluru and other local landmarks.

With a glorious sunset viewing of Uluru your goal, start your day at Kata Tjuta (the Olgas), 50km (31 miles) west of the Rock. *Kata Tjuta* means "many heads," an apt name for this monolith of 36 momentous red domes bulging out of the earth like turned clay on a potter's wheel. The Olgas are more important in Dreamtime legend than Uluru, and many modern visitors find they're even more spiritual. Good hikers may do the challenging 7.4km (4.6-mile) **Valley of the Winds** walk among the domes; there's also an easy 2.6km (1.6-mile) **Gorge** walk.

ⓘ **Uluru-Kata Tjuta Cultural Centre** (*℃* **08/8956 3138**). **Ayers Rock Resort** (see below).

✈ Ayers Rock (Connellan) airport.

🛏 $$$ **Emu Walk Apartments** or $$ **Outback Pioneer Hotel and Lodge,** Yulara Dr., Ayers Rock Resort (*℃* **08/8957 7888;** www.voyages.com.au).

WHY THEY'LL THANK YOU: Getting in touch with Dreamtime.

Lake Titicaca: Jewel of the Andes

Ages 6 & up • Copacabana, Bolivia & Puno, Peru

FACE IT: The kids will talk a lot about their upcoming trip to Lake Titicaca—they just won't be able to resist saying the name. But that's okay. Once they get there and see this huge deep-blue freshwater lake sitting in its cup of mountain peaks, an awesome 3,600m (11,811 ft.) above sea level, they'll stop snickering.

To locals, measuring the altitude is irrelevant: Lake Titicaca is a mysterious and sacred place. Here, in the midst of the lake, Manca Capac and Mama Ocllo—the Adam and Eve of the Incas—were supposedly born on the Isla del Sol (Sun Island), which you can visit on a day trip from the picturesque lakeside town of Copacabana, Bolivia. (A 3-hr. bus ride from La Paz, **Copacabana** is also known for its Moorish-style cathedral, with a deeply venerated miracle-working statue of the Virgin inside.) On Sun Island, you'll visit the ruins of **Chinkana,** a huge stone labyrinth built as a seminary for Inca priests. The path back to the town of Challapampa passes the sacred rock, shaped like a puma, from which Manco Capac and Mama Ocllo first stepped; farther on, you can look down and see the two huge footprints the sun is said to have made when it landed on earth to give birth to them. Tours also stop at Isla de la Luna (Moon Island), site of an ancient convent where the Virgins of the Sun performed ceremonies honoring the sun.

On the Peruvian shore (several local tour packages include both sides of the lake), the main town of Puno is not nearly as lovely as Copacabana, but the kids will want to come here to take a boat tour to the **Uros islands.** Since the time of the Incas, the local Uros Indians have lived on these tiny floating islands built on soft patches of reeds. Walking on the springy islets is truly a strange sensation. Some Uros wait for the tour boats to arrive so they can hawk their handmade textiles and reed-crafted items, but many others keep to their thatched huts, far from the snapping cameras, fishing and catching birds and continually repairing the reed underpinnings of their islets. Full-day trips also include stops at Taquile and Amantani islands, serene and rustic natural islands with **Inca ruins** to explore.

Other Andean peoples subscribe to a different myth: that Viracocha, the creator deity, called up the sun, moon, and stars to rise from icy Lake Titicaca to lighten the dark world. Powerful spirits still live in this amazing sky-high lake, they say. Gliding over the calm blue surface, you may find yourself staring down into the water's cold depths to connect with them. But you don't need to believe in these ancient legends to sense the magic of Lake Titicaca.

ⓘ **Puna tourist information,** Plaza de Armas (✆ **051/36-5088;** www.peru.info).

✈ Manco Capac, Juliaca, Peru, 45km (28 miles) from Puno.

🛏 $$ **Hotel Rosario del Lago,** Rigoberto Paredes and Av. Costanera, Copacabana, Bolivia (✆ **0102/862-2141;** www.hotel rosario.com/lago). $$$ **Sonesta Posada del Inca,** Sesquicentenario 610, Sector Huaje, Peru (✆ **051/364-111;** www.sonesta.com).

WHY THEY'LL THANK YOU: Gazing up at a star-spangled sky from the stars' birthplace.

The Cliffs of Moher
Where Ireland Plunges into the Sea
All ages • Lahinch, County Clare, Ireland

SOMETHING AS SPECTACULAR as the Cliffs of Moher could never go undiscovered by the tourist throngs. They are County Clare's foremost natural wonder, 213m (700 ft.) high and 8km (5 miles) long, a series of sheer rock faces plummeting to the crashing Atlantic surf below. The views from here are truly panoramic, especially from 19th-century **O'Brien's Tower** at the northern end. On a clear day you can see the Aran Islands up to the north in Galway Bay. It's a dramatic place, with the roar of the waves crashing below and the call of circling seagulls. Daredevils might venture onto a forbidden area of north-facing cliffs which have been half-heartedly fenced off, but there's plenty enough room on the main cliffs, with their well-paved path and lookout points; the heights are awesome without feeling perilous (and believe me, I'm borderline acrophobic). Because the cliffs jut out into the sea on a headland, you can gaze clearly over the sea to the north, west, and south.

Talk about the middle of nowhere—the Irish country road R478 meanders down from the **Burren** 80 and Galway, with little along the roadside and very few cars in sight. Then suddenly you round a curve and there's an immense parking lot filled with cars and tour buses and you've arrived at the Cliffs of Moher. Proximity to Shannon Airport means that this is often

Loop Head Lighthouse at the Cliffs of Moher.

a tour group's first stop upon hitting Ireland, so don't be surprised if you see a lot of folks staring out to sea with the glazed eyes of jet lag. There's no admission fee

per se, although you'll have to pay to get into the parking lot, and some tacky souvenir stalls are set up along the footpath to the cliffs. Just shepherd the children past it all and head uphill.

And while you're here, explore further along the craggy Clare coastline, where you'll find many off-the-beaten-path delights with intriguing names like Pink Cave, Puffing Hole, Intrinsic Bay, Chimney Hill, Elephant's Teeth, Mutton Island, Loop Head, and Lover's Leap. The tour buses won't follow you, that's for sure.

(i) R478, 7 miles north of Lahinch (© **065/ 708-1171;** www.county-clare.com).

✈ Shannon International, 48km (30 miles).

⊨ $$ **Aran View House,** Doolin (© **065/ 707-4061**). Closed Nov–Mar.

WHY THEY'LL THANK YOU: Nothing between you and America but sea.

The Giant's Causeway
Hero's Footsteps in Black Rock
All ages • Bushmills, Northern Ireland

OFTEN CALLED THE EIGHTH WONDER of the world, the Giant's Causeway is a one-of-a-kind **natural rock formation** that captures the imagination as few others do. It doesn't take much effort for children to imagine the striding giant who purportedly left these immense stone footprints in the sea off of Northern Ireland.

A World Heritage Site, the Causeway consists of roughly 40,000 tightly packed basalt columns that extend for 5km (3 miles) along the North Antrim coast. The tops of the columns form a dense honeycomb of stepping stones that sprawl outward from the cliff foot and eventually disappear under the sea. They're mostly hexagonal, about 30cm (12 in.) in diameter, and some are as tall as 12m (40 ft.). How

did they get there? Scientists estimate that they were formed 60 or 70 million years ago by a series of volcanic eruptions and cooling lava. In the surrounding cliff faces you can see dark stripes of volcanic basalt interrupting the sheer red rock.

But all that is the scientific explanation; the ancients, on the other hand, believed the rock formation to be the work of giants. Another even more romantic legend claims that the Causeway isn't natural at all, but the handiwork of Finn MacCool, the great Ulster warrior and commander of the king of Ulster's armies, who built it as a highway over the sea to bring his girlfriend from the Isle of Hebrides.

Tourists have come here to marvel over the Causeway since the late 17th century, and there were many years when visitors were forbidden to walk out onto the stones, or had to pay extra to do so. Thankfully today they are open to the public. Watch your footing as you scamper over the uneven surface, traipsing from stone to stone. Delicate flowers and mosses grow in the crevices, and all sorts of seabirds nest in the nearby cliffs. To reach the causeway, follow the path from the visitor center's parking area. Along the way you'll pass plenty of other extraordinary volcanic rock formations, amphitheaters of stone and striated columns and formations with fanciful names like Honeycomb, Wishing Well, Giant's Granny, King and His Nobles, and Lover's Leap. From the causeway, a wooden staircase climbs up Benbane Head and back along the **cliff-top walking path,** where you'll get spectacular views of the North Antrim coast. Or, to get a bird's-eye view, book a spectacular helicopter ride over the coast through **The Helicopter Center,** Newtownards Airfield (✆ **028/9182-0028**).

ⓘ Causeway Rd. (✆ **028/2073-1855;** www.giantscausewayofficialguide.com).

✈ Belfast, 121km (75 miles).

🛏 $$ **Marine Hotel,** 1 North St., Ballycastle (✆ **028/2076-2222;** www.marine hotel.net).

WHY THEY'LL THANK YOU: Myths written in monumental stone.

Awesome Vistas **9**

Les Calanches: Going Coastal in Corsica

Ages 4 & up • Corsica, France

L'*ILE DE BEAUTÉ,* CORSICA IS CALLED—"island of beauty"—and rightly so. This mountainous Mediterranean island combines rugged landscapes with stunning vistas of the sea, while native herbs and flowers perfume the air with an unforgettable fragrance. Although Corsica is technically a French possession, the island is in fact much closer to Italy (you can practically swim to Sardinia from Corsica), and everything here seems to have an Italian accent. You're lulled into thinking it's simply a fragment of the Riviera that worked itself loose from the mainland—and then you drive through a landscape that looks as though it fell from Mars: Les Calanches.

Ferries from Marseilles arrive at Corsica's main city, **Ajaccio,** birthplace of Napoleon Bonaparte, a Riviera-like town with palm trees and promenades. Up the western coast from here, driving or cycling along coastal D81, you curve around a headland to the tranquil village of **Piana,** with its red-tiled roofs rising 440m (1,444 ft.) above the azure sea. But beyond Piana, you enter an altered reality: The granite landscape to either side of the twisting road begins to turn red and become strangely striated and crumpled. The highway seems hacked out of the mountainside, and it zigs and zags crazily to cling to the corrugated rock faces. And so it goes, all the way along the southern end of the **Gulf of Porto,** from Piana over to Porto.

Les Calanches remind me of the buttes of Monument Valley ❶, but smaller and more eccentric, crabbed like the figures of arthritic old crones. And then, of course, there's that dynamite seaside backdrop setting it off, the hazy blue of the Mediterranean contrasting dramatically with the sharp-focused red rocks. As you drive along, ask the children to try to decide what these oddly shaped boulders remind them of—a rearing stallion? A fire-breathing dragon? A stegosaurus? Patches of green pine scrub, snarls of gray thorn, and bursts of dark red and yellow flowering shrubs decorate the creased red-granite spires here and there, and the shoulder of the road drops with heart-stopping suddenness to the waters below. The road bends so sharply you can't see beyond the next curve—honk to warn oncoming drivers of your presence before you pull around to the next dizzying view.

Several **walking paths** have been laid out through this tortured landscape—park your car and get out to take a short scramble over the rocks. (Trail maps are available from the Piana tourist office.) From Porto, you can go on a **boat tour** to view the spiky red rocks from the water; contact **Nave Va** (✆ **04-95-21-83-97;** www.naveva.com). And I'm sure

I don't need to tell you that sunset is the most glorious time of all to view Les Calanches, especially one of those lingering summer sunsets that the Mediterranean does so well.

ⓘ D81, between Piana and Porto (www. corsica.net).

✈ Ajaccio, 74km (46 miles).

🛏 $$ **Hotel Restaurant Beau Sejour,** Quartier Vaita, Porto (✆ **20-71-08-11-33**). $$$ **Les Roches Rouges,** Piana (✆ **04-95-27-81-81;** www.lesrochesrouges.com).

WHY THEY'LL THANK YOU: Spotting the shapes in the rock piles.

---

⑩ Awesome Vistas

Phang Nga Bay
Thailand's Secret Caverns
Ages 8 & up • Phuket, Thailand

THE JAMES BOND MOVIE *The Man with the Golden Gun* was filmed here, on this gorgeous bay north of the well-developed Thai resort island of Phuket. It's a stunning backdrop, with limestone karst towers jutting precariously from the water's glassy turquoise surface, creating more than 120 small islands that look like something out of a Chinese scroll painting. Kids, of course, are notorious for not appreciating beautiful scenery; what they will appreciate is the unique way you get to explore this craggy seascape—lying down in small canoes to slip inside secret caves. It lives up to every pirate fantasy they've ever had, and then some.

An arm of the Andaman Sea, its warm waters edged with white beaches, red mud banks, and tropical stands of mangrove trees, **Phang Nga Bay** is a national park 1½ hours' drive north of Phuket Town. Two-passenger kayaks, with an experienced paddle guide at the helm, dart around the bay's distinctive craggy

island rocks; you'll be told to lie flat in the boat to slip through tight cave openings. Once inside, magnificent chambers open up above the internal lagoons (called *hongs,* which is Thai for "rooms"), where it's believed pirates once hid their operations—or, if you're James Bond, secret agents hid their evil devices.

Touristy as it is, it's something you've got to do, especially with kids. The **day-long tours** include transport to and from Phuket Town, a cruise to the part of the bay where the islands cluster, a paddle guide, a bright-yellow inflatable kayak, and lunch. Once you've finished the tricky maneuvering around the caves, the guide may even let you paddle a bit yourself. The premier operator for these trips is **Sea Canoe,** Box 276, Muang Phuket 83000 (✆ **07621-2252;** www.seacanoe.net).

Of course, if you want to do things the cushy way, you can just cruise around this lovely tropical bay on a restored Chinese sailing junk, the ***Bahtra*** (contact **East**

Kayaking in Thailand.

West Siam in Patong, 119 Rat-U-Thit 2000 Year Rd.; (*C* **07634-0912**). You won't get inside those caves, but you'll still feel plenty pirate-y.

(i) www.phuket.com/island/phangnga.htm.

✈ Phuket International.

🛏 $$$ **Dusit Laguna Resort,** 390 Srisoontorn Rd., Cherngtalay District (*C* **067632-4320;** www.dusit.com). $$ **Karon Beach Resort,** 51 Karon Rd., Tambon Daron (*C* **07633-0006;** www. katagroup.com).

WHY THEY'LL THANK YOU: Hoping to find pirate treasure.

Seven Beautiful Bridges

11

The Ponte Vecchio
Where Dante Crossed the Arno
All ages • Florence, Italy

Florence, Italy, owns the bragging rights as fountainhead of the Renaissance, and no landmark is more steeped in its history than the **Ponte Vecchio.** The name means "old bridge," and this triple-arched stone bridge, lined with shops in the medieval custom, is indeed old, dating from 1220. The Arno is prone to devastating floods, one of which had washed away the Roman-era wooden bridge at this crossing point. But the stone bridge was built to survive, and so it has, against all odds.

Back then, Florence was just beginning to develop into a great city-state. In 1290, a crenellated stone palace, the **Palazzo Vecchio** (where today you can visit the **Uffizi Gallery 332**), was built near the foot of the bridge on the north bank, and work began on Florence's famous cathedral, the **Duomo,** with its distinctive geometric

bands of white, green, and pink marble. Florence's greatest poet, Dante Alighieri, lived between the Palazzo Vecchio and the Duomo and crossed the Ponte Vecchio often, as he mentions in his 1292 poem *La Vita Nuova*.

Another flood came in 1333; the bridge endured, though it was significantly redesigned afterward. The cathedral continued to take shape through the 1400s, adding its great red-tiled dome and the sculpted bronze doors of its Baptistery, while the bridge became the precinct of butcher shops (no doubt it was handy to toss scraps out the window into the Arno).

A century later, in 1540, with the Renaissance in high gear—Michelangelo had sculpted his *David,* Leonardo had painted the *Mona Lisa*—the second Cosimo de Medici moved into the Palazzo

Ponte Vecchio.

Vecchio, and it suddenly became essential to have a classy bridge leading over the Arno to the Medicis' new **Pitti Palace** (with kids, you may skip the Pitti's extensive art galleries, but don't miss a romp in the hillside **Boboli Gardens** behind it). Cosimo hired the prominent artist Giorgio Vasari to add a private bypass, a windowed corridor over the shops, where the Uffizi Gallery today displays portraits by such masters as Bronzino, Rubens, Rembrandt, and Ingres. Half a century later, Ferdinand de Medici, still not satisfied, banned butchers, allowing more refined tradesmen, goldsmiths and jewelers, to move in. (Crossing the bridge, you'll pass a bust of celebrated goldsmith and sculptor Benvenuto Cellini.)

Fast-forward to 1944, when the Nazis were beating a desperate retreat through Italy. As they came through Florence, they planted explosives to blow up the bridges and cut off their Allied pursuers. Someone in command, though—allegedly Hitler himself—was an art lover, for only the Ponte Vecchio was spared. It was endangered again in 1966, when the flooding Arno swept over it, washing away a fortune in jewelry from the goldsmiths' shops. But again the bridge survived.

Today the restored Ponte Vecchio is closed to vehicular traffic but its cramped shops continue to sell expensive Florentine gold and silver. Walking across the Ponte Vecchio from the Duomo and the Uffizi Gallery to the Pitti Palace, stop at the arched opening halfway over—and commune with the spirits of Dante, Michelangelo, and those wicked, wicked Medicis.

(i) **Tourist office,** Via Cavour 1r (© **055-290-832;** www.firenzeturismo.it).

🚃 🛏 See Uffizi Gallery **332**.

WHY THEY'LL THANK YOU: A time capsule of the Renaissance.

Le Pont Neuf: Spanning the Heart of Paris

All ages • Paris, France

As the river Seine winds its way through Paris, any number of bridges arch over it, connecting the Right Bank with the Left Bank. My kids demanded we take one of those touristy boat rides just for the fun of gliding under the bridges, whooping underneath each one to hear their voices echo off the vaulted stone. With a wonderful sort of Gallic illogic, the oldest and most venerable is the Pont Neuf—literally, New Bridge. At the tip of the Ile de la Cité, just downstream from **Notre Dame 316**, the Pont Neuf links the Right Bank's 1st arrondissement (home of the **Louvre 334**) with the Left Bank's 6th arrondissement (home of the Sorbonne and the Luxembourg Gardens), so just about every visitor to Paris walks across this historic bridge at one time or another. But I often wonder how many of them really see it, or

how many stop to contemplate what a marvelous structure it is.

Erected in 1578 (King Henry IV laid the first stone), the Pont Neuf was radical when it was built. For one thing, it was not weighed down with houses and shops (like old London Bridge or the Ponte Vecchio **11** in Florence); its few original shops were removed in a 1606 reconstruction. For another thing, it featured innovative raised pavements for pedestrians—that is, sidewalks—and soon became a favorite spot for leisurely strolls, especially because its rounded bays, like castellated balconies over the river, were perfect for rendezvous. At 28m (92 ft.) wide, it was for a long time the widest bridge in Paris, and it still carries lots of traffic, including automobiles, which had not even been dreamed of when it was designed. A statue of Henry IV on horseback stands mid-bridge on the

Le Pont Neuf.

island; the original was torn down and melted in the French Revolution.

For 4 centuries, the Pont Neuf has withstood all the floods that washed the older bridges away—an impressive feat, considering that the original wooden posts still support the foundation. With 12 gracefully proportioned arches, it's the longest bridge in Paris, combining a seven-arch section between the Right Bank and Ile de la Cité and a five-arch section from the island on to the Left Bank. (Yes, my kids insisted on counting the arches, as well as the pairs of ornate iron lampposts between them.) Even now, with the Pompidou Expressway roaring under its northernmost arch along the Right Bank, the Pont Neuf presides over the river with a majestic, calm elegance.

In 1985, the artists Christo and Jeanne-Claude used the Pont Neuf for a famous public art piece, wrapping it in silky golden cloth for 2 weeks. That will never happen again, but you can create your own Pont Neuf moment. Look at it from the quays, especially at night, when it is brilliantly lit and the dark river laps dreamily at its arches. Or stand on it in the daytime, gazing at Notre Dame in one direction, the Eiffel Tower in the other—with all of Paris at your command.

(i) For general information on Paris, plus airport and lodging, see **54**.

WHY THEY'LL THANK YOU: An old bridge called New Bridge that was ahead of its time.

13 Seven Beautiful Bridges

The Covered Bridge Tour
A Vermont Sampler of Classics
All ages • Bennington, Vermont, USA

WONDERFUL 19TH-CENTURY RELICS, New England's covered bridges evoke a rustic era of horses and buggies, quilting bees, and barn raisings. What you may not know is that bridges were covered not to shelter travelers from rain or to give courting couples a place to smooch—although they certainly did that—but to protect the bridge's timbers from weather damage. Most of them are painted red, for the simple reason that red paint, colored with iron oxide, was cheap to make. In southeastern Vermont, an easy and scenic half-day drive takes in five covered bridges. Remember: only one car at a time can drive through, so watch for oncoming traffic.

Begin in the town of Bennington with the **Vermont Covered Bridge Museum,** West Rd. at Gypsy Lane (© **802/442-7158;** www.vermontcoveredbridge museum.org), which explains the what,

where, when, who, and why of covered bridges; if the kids get overwhelmed with details, at least they'll be diverted by the working train layout. Then it's time to hit the road, beginning on Route 67A across from the entrance of Bennington College, with the **Silk Road Bridge** over the Wallomsac River. Built about 1840 by Benjamin Sears, it's the shortest bridge on this route, 88 ft. long. Sears's son built the next bridge over the Wallomsac, 5 miles west along Route 67A, the **Paper Mill Village Bridge.** Originally named for a 1790 paper mill, this 125 ft. bridge has good parking nearby if you want to get out and snap a photo, and there's a picturesque waterfall below.

Proceed on 67A to Murphy Road for the next Wallomsac bridge, **Henry Bridge,** named after Elnathan Henry, who also built the nearby B&B the Henry House. This 117-ft.-long bridge dates from 1840. Go north on Route 7A about 13 miles to the town of Arlington; turn east on E. Arlington Road and go 2 miles to the 1870 **Chiselville Bridge,** named for a former chisel factory. It was also called the Roaring Branch Bridge because it crosses Roaring Branch Brook, and luckily was built high enough to survive the 1927 flood that wiped out many other Vermont covered bridges. Go back to Arlington and proceed west on Route 313 4 1/2 miles to the **West Arlington Bridge** over the Battenkill River, popular with canoeists, kayakers, and fly fishermen. This is a real crowd-pleaser to end the tour with; a white steepled church is next door, and the Inn on Covered Bridge Green B&B, where artist Norman Rockwell once lived is also nearby.

Don't assume that the country's only covered bridges are in New England. Parke County, Indiana, about an hour's drive east of Indianapolis, has an even greater concentration of them tucked away on backcountry roads. For a driving map, contact the **Parke County Tourist Information Center,** 127 S. Jefferson St., Rockville, IN (*C* **765/569-5226**).

ⓘ www.bennington.com/chamber/Bridges.

✈ Boston, 190 miles.

🏨 $ **Paradise Motor Inn,** 141 W. Main St., Bennington (*C* **802/442-8351;** www.theparadisemotorinn.com).

WHY THEY'LL THANK YOU: A crossing that bridges centuries.

Seven Beautiful Bridges **14**

The Brooklyn Bridge
New York Icon
All ages • New York, New York, USA

AS THRILLING A SIGHT as this beautiful brown-hued East River bridge is from afar, with its Gothic-style towers and lacy mesh of cables, the view from the bridge is even more thrilling. A boardwalklike **pedestrian walkway** goes all the way across, raised slightly above the car traffic. One mile long, it should take about half an hour to traverse—except you'll be tempted to stop more than once to ooh and ahh at the vision of Manhattan's skyscrapers thrusting upward, with the great harbor and Verrazano Bridge beyond.

The Brooklyn Bridge took 16 years to build, from 1867 to 1883, and for a while, it seemed to be cursed—original designer, John A. Roebling, died from tetanus contracted when his foot was crushed while surveying the site, and his son, Washington, who took over the job, fell ill with the bends after diving into the

river to supervise the workmen laying the pilings. A virtual invalid afterward, Washington Roebling watched the bridge going up through a telescope from his house in nearby Brooklyn Heights, while his wife actually supervised much of the completion of the project.

Why has the Brooklyn Bridge captured the popular imagination more so than other New York City bridges? Well, for one thing, it was the first steel-wire suspension bridge in the world when it opened in 1883. (Until then, the only way to get from Manhattan to Brooklyn was via ferry). Ever since, the Brooklyn Bridge has become a byword in New York lore. The standard old joke defines a con artist as a guy trying to sell rubes the deed to the Brooklyn Bridge. Cocky teenage hoodlums have proved their bravado by shinnying up its cables, and suicides with a flair for the dramatic have plummeted to their deaths from those same cables into the tidal currents below. The bridge has appeared in countless movies and TV shows, its outline practically synonymous with New York City.

From Manhattan, the **entrance ramps** are along Centre Street just south of Chambers Street on Park Row; pedestrian ramps on the other side empty out into Brooklyn's downtown—a bit of a wasteland on weekends, but not a far walk from **Brooklyn Heights,** one of the loveliest brownstone neighborhoods you'll ever see. Go armed with a map. If your kids aren't hardy urban trekkers, walk halfway to get the view and then double back to Manhattan. Be aware that things get awfully windy once you're above the water!

(i) For information on New York City, including airport and lodging, see **56**.

WHY THEY'LL THANK YOU: It's one thing to see a landmark, another to walk across one.

Seven Beautiful Bridges

15

Tower Bridge
Thames Gateway to London
Ages 6 & up • London, England

NATURALLY, WHEN THEY GO TO LONDON, the kids will ask to see London Bridge. But what they're really thinking of is this, a grand drawbridge spanning the Thames with a pair of Gothic-style towers that echo Westminster's spires. It's one of the world's most celebrated landmarks, and possibly the most photographed bridge on earth. This is the bridge they see in all those London establishing shots in movies and on TV—you can almost hear the matching musical cue of *Rule Britannia*.

The original London Bridge, the one from the nursery rhyme, was a medieval structure loaded with houses and shops that tumbled down long ago; the current London Bridge, just upriver from this, is an ugly letdown, just like its predecessor, which was bought in the 1960s and shipped off to Arizona where it disappoints thousands of tourists every year. However medieval it looks, Tower Bridge was actually built in 1894, next to the **Tower of London** **360**, and it was an engineering wonder in its time. An **exhibition** inside the bridge, well worth the admission fee, commemorates its history with lots of appealing modern gadgetry—animatronic characters, video, and computers. It takes you up the north tower to high-level

Tower Bridge.

walkways between the two towers with **spectacular views** of St. Paul's, the Tower of London, and the Houses of Parliament. You're then led down the south tower and on to the bridge's original engine room, with its Victorian boilers and steam-pumping engines that used to raise and lower the bridge (Tower Bridge is London's only drawbridge, which is why the central span is so high, although with dwindling river shipping trade it's only raised a few times a week now).

From the bridge's walkways, stop to admire the loopy course of the Thames River. London wouldn't have existed if it hadn't been for the Thames: Early Saxons settled near a conveniently shallow fording place near Westminster Bridge; Roman occupiers built a fort near today's London Bridge; William the Conqueror strategically positioned his White Tower here; and the docklands farther east

became the great port that made England a world power. The Thames is narrow enough and shallow enough to be spanned by plenty of handsome bridges, which you may have been crossing already without knowing their names. Along one great horseshoe curve heading west from here, they are London Bridge, Southwark Bridge (by the Globe Theatre), Blackfriar's Bridge (St. Paul's Cathedral), Waterloo Bridge (convenient for West End and South Bank theaters), Westminster Bridge (flanking the Houses of Parliament), Lambeth Bridge, and Vauxhall Bridge (near the Tate Gallery).

(i) (c) **020/7403-3761;** www.towerbridge.org.uk.

✈ ⊨ See London **55**.

WHY THEY'LL THANK YOU: Nothing says London better.

Seven Beautiful Bridges **16**

Sydney Harbour Bridge
Panorama, Australian-Style

Ages 6 & up • Dawes Point to Milson's Point, Sydney, Australia

AUSTRALIANS, with typical deprecating wit, call it "The Coathanger," this mighty steel arch soaring over Sydney Harbour. With a 503m (1630 ft.) central span, it isn't the longest single-arch bridge in the world but it's the largest, thanks to its 49m-wide (160-ft.) deck bearing eight lanes of car traffic, two railway lines, a bike lane, and a pedestrian walkway. The bridge is certainly longer than its arch rival, the Tyne Bridge in Newcastle, England, with its strikingly similar design (the Tyne bridge was finished first but its design was submitted later—draw your own conclusions). Sydney's opened in 1932, 5 years before the Golden Gate Bridge **17**, but like the Golden Gate this was a vital Depression-era public works project, creating jobs for some 1,400 workers over 8 years; construction costs weren't even

paid off until 1988. It's the focal point of the classic Sydney postcard view, with its high-rise skyline backdrop, the water below bustling with ferries, barges, tall ships, and yachts, and the **Sydney Opera House** looking like a fleet of white sails caught mid-billow over Sydney Cove. Call (c) **02/9250 7250** for guided tours; www.sydneyoperahouse.com. Sydneysiders deemed the Opera House a monstrosity when it opened in 1973, 40 years after the bridge, but today it seems like the perfect finishing touch to this glorious harborscape.

Surprisingly few tourists do the obvious and walk across the Harbour Bridge. It's free, it only takes about half an hour from one end to the other (return on a ferry or a CityRail train), and the views are breathtaking. Reach the bridge walkway

Walking the Sydney Harbour Bridge.

from the Rocks, the historic district west of Circular Quay, by heading down Cumberland Street to the stairs underneath the bridge on your right. Partway across, you can enter the **Pylon Lookout** (☏ **02/9247 3408**), one of four massive support pylons faced with Australian granite. Climb up 200 steps and you'll be 89m (292 ft.) above the water, with 360-degree views. For the really big thrill, however, go all the way to the summit of

the main bridge arch, 134m (440 ft.) over the water, with **BridgeClimb,** 5 Cumberland St., The Rocks (☏ **02/9240 1100** or 02/8274 7777; www.bridgeclimb.com). BridgeClimb organizes 3-hour climbs for ages 12 and over, heading out onto the steel catwalks in small groups every 10 minutes, wearing "Bridge Suits" and harnessed to a line. It's not cheap, but it's the sort of vertigo-inducing experience you'll never forget.

Of course, it's also fun to see the bridge from the water. Just hop on a regular passenger ferry from the wharf at Circular Quay to **Darling Harbour** (where you can visit the **Sydney Aquarium** ❶⓮❼ and the **Powerhouse** ❷⓼❾), chugging right under the Harbour Bridge. Thrill-hounds can pay more to board a high-speed tour with **Harbour Jet** (☏ **1300/887 373;** www.harbourjet.com), departing from Darling Harbour, or **Oz Jet Boat** (☏ **02/9808 3700;** www.ozjetboating.com), from the Eastern Pontoon at Circular Quay.

ⓘ **Sydney Visitor Centre,** 106 George St., The Rocks (☏ **02/9240 8788;** www.sydney visitorcentre.com).

✈ Sydney International.

🛏 $ **Bernly Private Hotel,** 15 Springfield Ave., Potts Point (☏ **02/9358 3122;** www.bernlyprivatehotel.com.au). $$$ **The Stafford,** 75 Harrington St., The Rocks (☏ **02/9251 6711;** www.rendezvous hotels.com).

WHY THEY'LL THANK YOU: Soaring over the harbor.

Crossing the Golden Gate Bridge
Ages 6 & up • San Francisco, California, USA

WARN THE KIDS ahead of time that the Golden Gate Bridge is not golden at all, but a flaming orange. (As toddlers, my kids thought it was going to be made of actual gold.) Once past that surprise, though, they cannot fail to be bowled

over by this glorious bridge spanning the Pacific Ocean where it meets San Francisco Bay. In all lights it has a magical quality—brightening at dawn, glowing at sunset, glittering at night, or blazing proudly through the city's trademark fog.

It's one of those quintessential U.S. landmarks, familiar from dozens of movies. Cars roll over it, boats cruise under it, and airplanes buzz overhead, but this bridge is best experienced while walking.

This deeply gouged strait was named the Golden Gate after the area's golden brown hills, yet it is a triply apt name when you also consider San Francisco's boom in the 1849 Gold Rush and its role as America's western gateway for immigrants. Though it echoes the East Coast's Brooklyn Bridge, built 54 years earlier, the West Coast bridge has a streamlined Art Deco look, with its gracefully swung single span, spidery bracing cables, and subtly tapering twin towers. Given the strong tides and depth of the strait, skeptics had claimed for years that a bridge could not be built here—that it would buckle in a gale wind or collapse in an earthquake. Nevertheless, construction began in May 1933, creating jobs for thousands for 4 years at the height of the Depression, and was completed at the then-colossal cost of $35 million. (Its East Bay sibling, the 8¼-mile-long Oakland Bay Bridge, was completed the year before.) With only one pier actually planted in the water, it features a single long central span, designed intentionally to sway in the strait's winds. At 1¾ miles long, it was for 27 years the longest suspension bridge in the world; its twin towers soar 746 ft., and its two main cables weigh 11,000 tons apiece.

On its opening day in 1937, some 200,000 pedestrians joined an inaugural walk across the bridge. To make your crossing, bundle up against the wind, then set out from the **Roundhouse** on the east side of the bridge. Be prepared: The traffic alongside the pedestrian walkway gets pretty noisy, and the bridge vibrates. Even if you only make it halfway, the experience is amazing; walk all the way to **Vista Point** in Marin County and you'll be rewarded with one of the most famous cityscape views in the world.

ⓘ Hwy. 101 N from San Francisco (www.goldengatebridge.org).

✈ ⊨ See the Cable Car Hills of San Francisco **68**.

WHY THEY'LL THANK YOU: A highwire walk they'll never forget.

Drives **18**

The Lighthouse Tour of Maine

All ages • Kittery to Castine, Maine, USA

Iᴛ's ᴏɴᴇ ᴏꜰ ᴛʜᴏsᴇ ᴄʟᴀssɪᴄ ɪᴍᴀɢᴇs of New England: the stalwart lighthouse, perched above crashing waves, sending out its beam to welcome home the fishermen. And nowhere is the concentration greater than in Maine. It's only natural—Maine's jagged coastline is so fringed with inlets and islands and carved-out bays, if a giant came along and pulled it straight it would be 5,500 miles long. You need a lot of lighthouses to navigate a shore that crazy, and driving from one to the next is a great connect-the-dots way to enjoy the state.

Start out north of Kittery, turning off Route 1 to York Beach. At the northern end of Long Sands Beach, postcard-perfect **Nubble Light** sits high on a peninsula, with its white Victorian keeper's house alongside. On a clear day, if you've got binoculars, you may also be able to see slim granite-gray **Boon Island Light** 10 miles out to sea—New England's tallest lighthouse, at 13 stories high. Just north of Kennebunkport, off Route 1 on Maine 208, the hamlet of Cape Porpoise has a lighthouse offshore on **Goat Island,** which has been used by the Secret Service detail to protect the senior President Bush when he's at his Kennebunkport home.

Nubble Light in Cape Neddick.

There are no fewer than five lighthouses in greater Portland—from south to north: the gracefully proportioned **Cape Elizabeth Light** at Two Lights State Park, featured in the paintings of Edward Hopper; the tapering white **Portland Head Light,** Fort Williams Park, 1000 Shore Rd., an active lighthouse since 1794 with a small museum in its former keeper's house; the granite-block **Ram Island Ledge Light** offshore from Portland Head; the fire-hydrant-shaped **Spring Point Light** on a breakwater at the end of South Portland's Broadway; and around the same point, the **Portland Breakwater Light,** nicknamed Bug Light for reasons the kids should be able to figure out.

Go north on I-95 to Brunswick, where Route 1 branches off east, running like a spine along the heavily indented coast. In Boothbay Harbor, ferries from the pier visit the stout white **Burnt Island Light,** which you can tour. In Bristol, there's the whitewashed stone **Pemaquid Point Light,** which now contains a fishing museum. In Port Clyde, the peaceful **Marshall Point Light,** which also contains a small museum, played a bit part in the movie *Forrest Gump.* Northeast of here, the Penobscot Bay area has a host of lighthouses, including a pair on either side of Rockland harbor, the quirky **Rockland Harbor Southwest Light,** North Shore Rd., growing out of a wood-shingle house, and the red-brick **Rockland Breakwater Light** on the north side of the harbor. Another 50 miles or so on Route 1 will take you around the top of the bay to Castine, where the privately owned rough, conical **Dice Head Light** sits at the end of Route 166.

ⓘ **Maine Office of Tourism** (✆ 888/624-6345; www.visitmaine.com).

✈ Portland International, 45 miles from Kittery, 140 miles from Castine.

🛏 $$$ **Sebasco Harbor Resort,** Rte. 217, Sebasco Estates, near Brunswick (✆ 800/225-3819 or 207/389-1161; www.sebasco.com). $$ **Topside,** 60 McKown Hill, Boothbay Harbor (✆ 877/486-7466 or 207/633-5404).

BEST TIME: Spring, or fall, when you can enjoy the foliage. In summer Rte. 1 backs up for miles.

WHY THEY'LL THANK YOU: Watching the beacon light wink on and off.

19 Drives

The Skyline Drive & Blue Ridge Parkway
Driving the Appalachians
All ages • Virginia, North Carolina & Tennessee, USA

Aɴᴄʜᴏʀᴇᴅ ᴀᴛ ᴇɪᴛʜᴇʀ ᴇɴᴅ by national parks—Shenandoah National Park at one end, Great Smoky Mountains National Park at the other—this 574-mile stretch of Appalachian mountain-crest highway is stunning any time of year. In May, wildflowers bloom along with dogwood and mountain laurel, and in summer these mountain reaches stay refreshingly cool and green. We drove it in early fall, missing the vivid foliage of mid- to late October but experiencing an amazing sight: a blizzard of monarch butterflies stubbornly plowing into oncoming traffic, refusing to veer off of their hard-wired migration route. In the winter, whenever snow and ice close some parts of the parkway, you can even cross-country ski here.

Tell the kids that all those trees releasing hydrocarbons into the atmosphere creates the mountains' distinctive haze—blue along the Blue Ridge, slightly grayer (and therefore "smoky") in the Smoky Mountains. Both parkways are mileposted, which makes counting down the distances fun for kids, and there are walking trails marked continually (look for signs bearing a rifle-and-powderhorn symbol). We also played Spot the Scenic Overlook, keeping watch for the next pulloff area where we could jump out and really drink in those hill-and-valley vistas. Another thing to do is to count the tunnels—there's only one in Virginia but 26 in North Carolina, most of them in the hilly section below Asheville.

The 105-mile Skyline Drive, which has an entry fee, begins at Front Royal, Virginia, and slices southwest through long, skinny Shenandoah National Park. Around Waynesboro, the road's name changes to the Blue Ridge Parkway (469 miles in total), and the surrounding greenery becomes the Jefferson National Forest. You'll cross the border into North Carolina

and roll through the Pisgah National Forest (my kids love that name), reaching higher elevations as you angle west past Asheville to the Great Smoky Mountains park, which spills west into Tennessee.

You can take a break at several sites en route: At the Blue Ridge Parkway milepost 5.8, Humpback Rocks, the **Mountain Farm** trail meanders through a cluster of 19th-century farm buildings; at milepost 85.9, the Peaks of Otter, a loop trail leads to the rural **Johnson Farm;** milepost 176.2 accesses picturesque **Mabry Mill,** along with a blacksmith shop, wheelwright's shop, and whiskey still; **Puckett Cabin** (milepost 189.9) was the home of a busy 19th-century mountain midwife; the **Jesse Brown Farmstead** (milepost 272.5) consists of a cabin, spring house, and a Baptist church. At milepost 292, **Moses H. Cone Memorial Park** offers a turn-of-the-century manor house. Since your drive should take at least 2 days, overnight in Boone, North Carolina, where the **Hickory Ridge Homestead Museum** (𝒞 828/264-6390) is a re-created log cabin furnished in 1780-era style.

(ⓘ) **Shenandoah National Park** (𝒞 540/999-3500; www.nps.gov/shen). Blue Ridge Parkway (𝒞 828/298 0398; www.nps.gove/blri).

🛏 $$ **Holiday Inn Express,** 1943 Blowing Rock Rd., Boone (𝒞 **800/HOLIDAY** or 828/264-2451; www.ichotelsgroup.com).

WHY THEY'LL THANK YOU: Backwoods trails and the Daniel Boone vibe.

Drives 20

The Cabot Trail
North America's Highland Wilds
All ages • Nova Scotia, Canada

NOVA SCOTIA IS LATIN for "New Scotland," and the name really fits blustery, craggy Cape Breton Island. The Scots who settled this part of Canada were generally Highlanders who'd rebelled against the English Crown, and I like to think that they immediately felt at home on these isolated uplands. **Cape Breton Island**

Cape Breton Island, Nova Scotia.

National Park is a starkly beautiful wilderness with a split personality: in the interior rises a melancholy plateau of wind-stunted evergreens, bogs, and barrens, a fitting home for druids or trolls; around the edges, the mountains tumble suddenly to the sea in a dramatic coastscape of ravines and ragged, rust-colored cliffs. The Scottish Highlands don't have a scenic coastal highway, but the North American version does: the Cabot Trail, a 300km (185-mile) loop built in 1939 to take advantage of those astounding sea views.

You'll get onto the roadway at **Baddeck,** a New England-y town where Alexander Graham Bell spent his summers (there's a good exhibit on his life and work on Chebucto St.), but things get more rugged as you swing north toward the park. The gateway to the park is the Acadian town of **Chéticamp,** the most French-speaking part of the island—notice the French names on local shops and restaurants—where the visitor center has some good natural history displays and a large-scale relief map to give the kids a geographic idea of where they're going.

The Cabot Trail circuit should take 6 to 8 hours to drive. Don't expect to make good time; the road has lots of brake-testing steep climbs and whooshing descents, and you'll also want to stop at many pullouts. The most gorgeous stretch is the 44km (27 miles) from Chéticamp to Pleasant Bay along the western coast. You'll lose the water views for a time after Pleasant Bay, as you cut across the headlands to Cape North, where English explorer John Cabot first set foot on the North American continent (although some Newfoundlanders claim he first landed in Newfoundland). Going down the eastern coast, you'll pass through a series of towns with Scottish names—Ingonish Centre, Ingonish Ferry, South Ingonish Harbour—and then make a precipitous climb to the promontory of **Cape Smokey,** where panoramic views explode on every side.

Stop and stretch your legs on some of the hiking **trails** that head inland from the road. The best ones for kids are the half-mile-long **Bog Trail,** which follows a boardwalk into the gnarled bogs of the tableland, and the half-mile **Lone Shieling loop,** which enters a verdant hardwood forest that includes 350-year-old sugar maples; a re-creation of a Scottish crofter's hut is a highlight of the trail. An 11km (6.8-mile) trail leads along the bluffs of Cape Smokey; even if you don't go all the way to the tip, it's worth walking partway just to feel the headland winds and taste the salt air.

ⓘ **Cape Breton Highlands National Park** (𝄐 **888/773-8888;** www.pc.gc.ca).

✈ Halifax 282km (175 miles).

🛏 $ **Cape Breton Highlands Bungalows,** Cabot Trail, Ingonish Beach (𝄐 **902/285-2000**). $$ **Inverary Resort,** Shore Rd, Baddeck (𝄐 **800/565-5660** or 902/295-3500; www.inveraryresort.com).

WHY THEY'LL THANK YOU: Scotland via French-speaking Canada.

Drives 21

San Juan Skyway: Million-Dollar Highway

All ages • Begins & ends in Durango, Colorado, USA

CLOSE TO THE FOUR CORNERS, where Colorado, Utah, Arizona, and New Mexico meet at right angles, this 256-mile loop of highway is one of the country's most spectacular drives, taking in the whole panorama of the Southwest—from ancient Native American cliff dwellings to Wild West towns to smart ski resorts, all against an incredible backdrop of 10,000-foot-high Rocky Mountain passes, canyons, waterfalls, and alpine meadows.

I prefer to follow the circuit clockwise from Durango, saving the most breathtaking scenery for the end. You can drive it in 1 day, but there are enough intriguing stops en route to make it worth 2 or 3 days. For example, the first (and, frankly, least scenic) 45 miles, along U.S. 160 west from Durango, takes you past **Mesa Verde National Park** 🔟, an

awe-inspiring archaeological site with thousands of Ancestral Puebloan cliff dwellings that deserves a full day on its own. Ten miles past the park, just before the town of Cortez, turn north on CO 145 up the Dolores River Valley, slicing into mountains thickly forested with green. Sixty miles past Dolores, the kids should be able to spot the startling rock spire that earned **Lizard Head Pass** its name. A few miles past here, you can detour 4 miles east to historic **Telluride.** This is where Butch Cassidy robbed his first bank, in 1889. The museum at 201 W. Gregory Ave. (© **970/728-3344**) displays loads of artifacts from the town's Wild West Days, and you get a distinct late 1800s vibe just from walking around the landmarked downtown streets.

Enjoying the Ouray Hot Springs Pool in Ouray, Colorado.

Colorado 145 goes west, following the San Miguel River Valley to Placerville, where you pick up CO 62 to head north over the Dallas Divide. You'll come next to **Ridgway,** a tiny old railroad town; go south on U.S. 550 to **Ouray,** another quaint Old West town to explore (a soak in the hot springs here makes a great break from driving). Past Ouray, you'll be driving the Million Dollar Highway, so named because millions of dollars passed over it in the great days of Colorado gold and silver mining. It's still worth a million dollars just for the views; the next 23 miles, over Red Mountain Pass to **Silverton,** are breathtaking, as the road shimmies up the sheer sides of a gorge, dives through tunnels, and passes cascading waterfalls. On the Red Mountain slopes around you, look for relics of mining equipment and log cabins. From Silverton, U.S. 550 climbs over two last passes,

the Molas Divide and the Coalbank Pass; south of Purgatory, you join the gorgeous route of the Durango & Silverton Narrow Gauge Railroad **28** as you head back to Durango.

ⓘ **Durango Area tourist office,** U.S. 160 & E. 8th Ave. (✆ **800/463-8726;** www. durango.org).

✈ Durango/La Plata, 14 miles.

⊨ $$ **New Sheridan Hotel,** 231 W. Colorado Ave., Telluride (✆ **800/200-1891** or 970/728-4351; www.newsheridan.com). $$ **The Strater Hotel,** 699 Main Ave., Durango (✆ **800/247-4431** or 970/247-4431; www. strater.com).

BEST TIME: Apr–Oct (passes may be blocked by snow in winter).

WHY THEY'LL THANK YOU: Million-dollar mountain vistas.

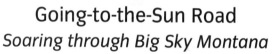

22 Drives

Going-to-the-Sun Road
Soaring through Big Sky Montana
All ages • West Glacier, Montana, USA

WHEN THE ICE AGE ENDED millennia ago, receding glaciers revealed a stunning valley they'd carelessly gouged out of what is now the state of Montana and lower Alberta, Canada. Majestic mountain crags loom on either side, their crevices hiding lakes and ponds that are really just melted glacial leftovers. The glaciers are still receding, in fact (the effect of global warming, some say); often in winter, avalanches heap over the scenic 50-mile road that bisects this valley. Climbing some 3,400 feet in a mere 32 miles, this breathtaking drive truly lives up to its poetical name: the Going-to-the-Sun Road.

The drive begins at West Glacier, the park entrance that meets U.S. Highway 2 near Columbia Falls, Montana. The first stretch of road traces the southeast shore

of **Lake McDonald,** the park's largest lake, with postcardlike panoramas of shimmering water backed by verdant mountains. Across from the Avalanche Campground ranger station, look for the marker for the Trail of the Cedars, a level quarter-mile nature boardwalk. Back on the road, you keep winding up into the mountains, getting a bird's-eye view of the surrounding peaks—be careful about looking out the car's side windows, because some of those drops are dizzying. There are three landmarks along this middle section: **The Loop,** an excellent vantage point for Heaven's Peak; **Bird Woman Falls Overlook,** where you can gaze across a sweeping valley to a waterfall; and, most kids' favorite, the **Weeping Wall,** a wall of rock that does, in fact, weep groundwater profusely. At the 32-mile mark, **Logan Pass** has a visitor center, open summers only, that sits right on top of the Continental Divide—which, as you no doubt remember from geography class, is the ridge of the Rockies from which all rivers flow either east or west. Downhill (east) from here is the turnout for **Jackson Glacier,** the most easily recognizable glacier in the entire park, followed by trailheads for short wildlife-viewing hikes to Sunrift Gorge and Sun Point. At the east end lies the St. Mary visitor center. If you'd rather not retrace the park road, complete the loop clockwise another 57 miles by following U.S. 2 south, west, and then north along park borders back to West Glacier. Along the way, the Two Medicine park entrance offers another fun short trail, the Running Eagle Falls trail (trailhead 1 mile west of the entrance), a third-of-a-mile stroll through dense forest to a large, noisy waterfall.

The whole loop can be done in 1 day with plenty of time for picnics, short hikes, and pulling off-road to enjoy the jaw-dropping vistas. To get the full effect, journey across the Going-to-the-Sun Road before 8:30am; you'll be astounded by the masterful job Mother Nature does of painting her mountains.

ⓘ **Glacier National Park** (✆ **406/888-7800;** www.nps.gov/glac).

✈ Kalispell 29 miles.

🛏 $$ **Glacier Campground,** 12070 U.S. 2 (✆ **888/387-5689** or 406/387-5689). $$$ **Lake McDonald Lodge,** on Lake McDonald (✆ **406/892-2525;** www.glacierparkinc.com).

BEST TIME: Early June to mid-Oct.

WHY THEY'LL THANK YOU: Straddling the Continental Divide.

Drives 23

The Pacific Coast Highway

California's Oceanside Spectacle

All ages • Los Angeles to San Francisco, California, USA

BEGINNING NEAR the old mission town of San Juan Capistrano, state highway 1 hugs the California coast all the way up to Leggett, in northern California—and I mean it *hugs* the coast, darting around coves and clinging to steeply shelving cliffs, with the Pacific Ocean almost always out your side window. It's not the most efficient route to take from southern to northern California (or vice versa). Travelers intent on getting there fast opt for inland I-5, or at least U.S. 101. No, if you're driving the **Pacific Coast Highway,** you're looking for scenery—and some of the most spectacular coastal scenery in the world it is.

While some consider the PCH the whole series of connected highways from the Mexican border to Canada, I define it as California Highway 1 (which sometimes overlaps with U.S. 101). At various points, this winding two-lane road may be called the Cabrillo Highway, after the Spanish explorer, or El Camino Real, the old Spanish road linking a chain of early settlements (see The Mission Trail 243). What really matters is its proximity to the Pacific.

We tend to skip the southern section, avoiding L.A.'s congestion, and start alongside the bleached sands of **Santa Monica Beach** 447. We usually break up the drive into 3 days so we can stop en route to walk on beaches, explore small towns, and so on. Along the way—say, around Cambria, near **Hearst Castle** 372—suddenly we're no longer in Southern

Wildlife along the Pacific Coast Highway.

California, and things get more rugged. Up near **Half Moon Bay** 119, there's a steep downward plunge of the road called **Devil's Slide** that the kids love. Past San Francisco, we cruise a lonelier stretch of Northern California coast, where we make a pilgrimage to the giant redwoods—depending on time, we may make it as far as Muir Woods or **Redwood National Park** 2.

The most dramatic stretches of the drive occur where the mountains crowd close to the ocean's edge—for instance, just north of Santa Barbara, where the Santa Inez peaks tumble precipitously to the beach, or the entire section from Morro Bay north to Carmel, where the sea nips at the toes of the Santa Lucia mountains. Each curve you whip around reveals another jaw-dropping vista, narrow strips of white foam-edged sand purling below you on one side, furrowed brown mountainsides beetling over you on the other. Surfers bob on their boards offshore—or are those seals?—and hawks coast dreamily overhead. It's beautiful at noon, with blue skies and bright sun; it's beautiful in a haunting fog; it's beautiful glowing at sunset; it's even beautiful in a wistful gray rain. It's just plain beautiful.

I've driven the Pacific Coast Highway twice with my kids, both times going south to north. Next time I plan to drive it north to south, which I suspect is even more thrilling. Maybe in a red convertible, with the Beach Boys' "Wouldn't It Be Nice" blasting from the car radio . . . ah, California.

(i) http://gocalif.ca.gov; www.us-101.com.

Los Angeles International. San Francisco International.

See Hearst Castle 372.

WHY THEY'LL THANK YOU: Riding the curves, watching the surf.

Haleakala Crater Road
Volcano Touring in Hawaii
All ages • Maui, Hawaii, USA

IF YOU REALLY WANT TO BE DULL, it's called Highway 378, and on the map it's such a wiggly line that you wonder what the road engineers were smoking when they laid it out. But when you drive the Haleakala Crater Road, you understand immediately: Every wiggle in that road is another steep switchback curve climbing up, up, up, right to the summit of the world's largest dormant volcano. It may take you over an hour to cover these 20 miles, with the weather changing every few miles as you pass through different climate zones. You'll run into patches of fog that turn out to be not fog at all, but drive-through cumulus clouds. Look out the window and you may see rare black-faced Hawaiian geese on the wing, right beside you. By the time you get to the top, the crater—a black hole so big it could hold Manhattan—is almost beside the point.

And then you get to drive back down (in low gear, please!).

Many visitors time their visit to Haleakala for sunrise or sunset, when the sun gilds the lunarlike landscape with colors so fiery, you can almost imagine that the lava beds have heated up again. Haleakala does mean House of the Sun, after all, and when you see the sun rise up out of the ocean, it's awe inspiring. With kids in the car, though, I hesitate to drive those curves in predawn or postdusk darkness. Besides, daylight lets them enjoy the views along the way, which can extend as far as 100 miles on a clear day. There are three scenic overlooks en route to the summit, essential stops not only for the views but to let the kids pop their ears and adjust to the thin air. At **Leleiwi Overlook,** about halfway up, you get your first full panorama of the crater above. When the clouds are low and the sun's in the right place, you can see your own shadows, ringed with a rainbow, reflected on the surface of the clouds below—a rare phenomenon indeed. Shortly before the summit, the **Haleakala Visitor Center** has great views of the moonlike volcanic landscape. But it's still a few miles to **Puu Ulaula Overlook,** where the **Haleakala Observatories** are located, 10,023 feet high. Often you can see all the way to the Big Island from here (look for the snowcapped peak of Mauna Kea **310**). On your way back down, stop at the **Kalahaku Overlook** to admire the only-in-Hawaii silversword plant, with its spiky silver spears and tiny purple flowers.

If your kids are older, several local operators will take you up the volcano in a van and then give you mountain bikes to coast down the winding road; try **Maui Downhill** (✆ **800/535/BIKE,** www.mauidownhill.com) or **Maui Mountain Cruisers** (✆ **800/232-6284;** www.mauimountaincruisers.com).

ⓘ **Haleakala National Park,** Hwy. 37 to 377 to 378 (✆ **808/572-4400;** www.nps. gov/hale).

✈ Kahului, 37 miles.

🛏 $$ **Banyan Tree House,** 3265 Baldwin Ave., Makawao (✆ **808/572-9021;** www. hawaiimauirentals.com). $$ **Olinda Country Cottages,** 2660 Olinda Rd., Makawao (✆ **800/932-3435** or 808/572-1453; www.mauibnbcottages.com).

WHY THEY'LL THANK YOU: Driving through the clouds.

The Ring of Kerry
Ireland's Wide Green West
All ages • County Kerry, Ireland

IRELAND'S GREATEST TOURISM CLICHÉ is the Ring of Kerry, a 177km (110-mile) route around the Iveragh Peninsula where scores of tour buses thunder every day in summer. But taking your own car makes all the difference: Follow the road clockwise (the buses go counterclockwise) and you'll have the road less traveled, with room to enjoy the postcard-perfect seacoast views that made the Ring a tourist draw in the first place.

Without stops, the circuit takes 4 hours; plan for twice that so you can stop and explore, not just snap photos out your window. Driving south from tourist-choked Killarney on N71, you'll enter spectacular **Killarney National Park,** where the mountain scenery has an almost Wild West grandeur. From the road you gaze north over the memorably named range of Macgillycuddy's Reeks; Ireland's tallest mountain, **Carrantuohill,** at 1,041m (3,415 ft.), crops up in the distance. Stop to savor it at Ladies View, a scenic overlook where Queen Victoria's ladies-in-waiting raved about the panorama on a royal vacation (thus launching Kerry's tourism industry). Detour south to **Kenmare,** a neat little town on Kenmare Bay, where a Bronze Age stone circle stands intact around a dolmen tomb. At Kenmare Pier from May to October, **Sea-Fari Cruises,** Kenmare Pier (✆ **064/83171;** www.seafariireland.com), runs 2-hour excursions to spot dolphins, sea otters, gray seals, and herons.

Wind on down the coast to charming **Sneem,** its houses painted in vibrant shades of blue, pink, yellow, purple, and orange. A few miles past Sneem, signs point to **Staigue Fort,** 3km (1¾ miles) off N70 on a narrow one-track road. A huge hit with my youngsters, this circular fort

was built around 1000 B.C. of unmortared rough stones, big enough to shelter an entire Iron Age clan. At the western end of the peninsula, **Waterville** is an improbably Mediterranean-looking resort town, where Charlie Chaplin often summered; there's a super beach here, a good (if windy) spot for a picnic. Detour from the main road to Portmagee, where a bridge leads to **Valentia Island** and **The Skellig Experience** (✆ **066/947-6306;** www.skelligexperience.com). Its displays and audiovisuals delve into local birds and plant life, in particular those of the two tiny offshore islands known as the Skellig Rocks. These are Skellig Michael, a rock pinnacle towering over the sea where medieval monks built an isolated monastery; and neighboring Little Skellig, where vast flocks of gannets and other seabirds nest in summer. Cruises out to the Skelligs are available from Valentia.

Continue on N70, with Dingle Bay on your right. On this north side of the peninsula, open bog land constantly comes into view, a terrain formed thousands of years ago from decayed trees. Local residents dig up the turf to burn in their fireplaces. The atmospheric **Kerry Bog Village Museum** in Ballycleave (✆ **066/976-9184**) was our favorite stop: a cluster of thatched-roof cottages showing what life was like in Kerry in the early 1800s, from the blacksmith's forge to the turf-cutter's house to the roof-thatcher's dwelling. The life behind the postcard views—that's what we were after, and we got it.

ⓘ **Ring of Kerry** (www.kerrytourist.com). **Killarney Tourist Office,** Beech Rd., Killarney (✆ **064/31633;** www.killarneytown.com).

✈ Kerry County Airport.

🚆 Killarney Railway Station.

🛏 $$ **Derrynane Hotel,** off N71, Caherdaniel (✆ **800/528-1234** or 066/947-5136; www.derrynane.com). $$

Killarney Great Southern, Railway Rd., Killarney (✆ **800/44-UTELL** in the U.S., or 064/31262; www.gsh.ie).

WHY THEY'LL THANK YOU:
Kodachrome views, Celtic history.

Drives 26

The Fairy-Tale Road
In the Bootsteps of the Brothers Grimm
All ages • Hanau to Hameln, Germany

CHILDREN HAVE LOVED the aptly named Grimm's fairy tales ever since these real-life brothers first published their children's stories in 1812. Central Germany is Grimm country, and the so-called **Fairy-Tale Road** (Märchenstrasse) rolls right through it, past half-timbered villages, towered castles, and gnarled forests where many a poor woodcutter toiled. From Hanau to Hameln, it's a 400km (250-mile) drive. While a few sites are worth a stop, the main thing is to gaze out the window at the *Shrek*-like landscape where Snow White or Rumpelstiltskin could dance out into the road at any moment.

The official starting point is a monument to the Grimms at Neustadter Markt-platz in **Hanau,** a suburb 20km (12 miles) east of Frankfurt. Jakob Grimm was born here in 1785, his brother Wilhelm a year later, but there's little 18th-century charm left in Hanau; for that, head north on B43 to **Steinau an der Strasse,** where the Grimm brothers spent their youth. A memorial fountain honors them in the main cobblestone square, and on weekends puppet shows enact fairy tales at the **Steinauer Marionettentheater,** Kumpen 2 (✆ **06663/245**). Continue north on B40, then B254 and along the Schwalm River, which the Germans call *Rotkäppchenland,* or Little Red Riding Hood country. Quaint towns like Fulda, Lauterbach, and Alsberg set the fairy-tale scene; Neustadt has a circular tower

where Rapunzel could have let down her golden tresses. A good stop for the night is **Kassel,** where the Grimms lived from 1798 to 1830; the **Bruder Grimm Museum** at Schone Aussicht 2 contains letters, portraits, and mementos.

After Kassel, go north on B3 and Route 80, following signs to Sababurg, where **Dornröschenschloss Sababurg,** in Hofgeismar (✆ **05671/8080**), was the setting of the Sleeping Beauty legend. Briar roses still bloom in the courtyard of this turreted Italianate castle, which is set in an old zoological garden and encircled by a wilderness of ancient oak and beech trees. North on Route 80 then 83, **Bodenwerder** was the birthplace of Lügen Baron von Münchhausen (1720–97), known as the "Liar Baron" because he told the biggest whoppers in Germany; his tall tales became a popular children's book. In the Rathaus, or town hall, the **Münchhausen-Erinnerungszimmer** (Münchhausen Memorial Room) displays mementos of his life (closed Nov–Mar).

Then it's northwest on Route 83 to picturesque **Hameln,** site of the Pied Piper legend. When the stingy citizens refused to pay an itinerant rat-catcher who rid the town of rats, in revenge he played a bewitching tune on his flute and lured Hameln's children out of town, never to be seen again. Frescoes in the restaurant of **Rattenfängerhaus** (Rat-Catcher's House), Osterstrasse 28 (✆ **05151/3888**),

illustrate the legend; Hameln shops sell rat figures of every conceivable material, including candy.

ⓘ **Hameln tourist office,** Deisterallee1 (ⓒ **05151/957823;** www.hameln.com).

✈ Frankfurt.

🛏 $$$ **Mercure Hotel Hameln,** 164er Ring 3, Hameln (ⓒ **05151/7920;**

www.dorint.com). $$ **Schloss Hotel Wilhelmshöhe,** Schlosspark 8, Kassel (ⓒ **0561/30880** or 0561/3088428).

WHY THEY'LL THANK YOU: Rapunzel's tower, Sleeping Beauty's castle, and a rat for the Pied Piper.

27 Drives

The Great Ocean Road
Awesome Aussie Wonder

All ages • Torquay to Warrnambool, Victoria, Australia

THERE'S NO QUESTION that coastal roads pack a scenic wallop, but even among coastal roads, the Great Ocean Road stands out. If you want the kids to understand Australia's raw power, this drive is essential. Running along the southern coast for 106km (66 miles), it offers the expected sheer cliffs, sea vistas, and beaches, but then there's the Aussie difference: patches of lush rainforest and some incredible rock formations created by the pounding seas of the Southern Ocean.

Some tour operators offer 1-day loops from Melbourne, but it makes a lot more sense to rent your own car and take a leisurely 2 days. Where you stop, of course, depends on the kids' special interests. We associate Australia with surfers, and the eastern section of the drive, starting with **Torquay,** home of world-famous Bells Beach, is called the Surf Coast. The **Surfworld Museum,** Beach Road, West Torquay (ⓒ **03/5261 4606**) has interactive exhibits on surfboard design and surfing history and video of the world's best surfers. In Lorne, another surfing town, stop at the **Ozone Milk Bar** on Mount Joy Parade, a classic Australian milk bar—a kind of down-market cafe that sells everything from shakes and pies to newspapers. From **Lorne** to

Apollo Bay is a thrilling stretch of road, as the pavement narrows and twists along a cliff edge. The **Angahook-Lorne State Park** along here has many marked rainforest walks; about 13km (8 miles) past Apollo Bay, just off the main road, you can stroll on the **Maits Rest Rainforest Boardwalk.** The road cuts inland through the Otway National Forest; past Beauchamp Falls, head south on an unpaved road for 15km (9⅓ miles) to the windswept headland and the historic **Cape Otway Lighthouse,** built by convicts in 1848. Five kilometers (3 miles) southwest of the old timber town of Lavers Hill, small **Melba Gully State Park** lets you walk on trails through rainforest ferns to find one of the last giant gum trees, some 27m (89 ft.) in circumference; it's thought to be over 300 years old. By now you're on the Shipwreck Coast, so named because there were some 80 wrecks along here in just 40 years. You'll reach the water's edge again just past Princetown, where you can see what a treacherous shore this is: Along a 27km (17-mile) stretch through **Port Campbell National Park** are the **Twelve Apostles,** a series of rock pillars standing just offshore; the **Blowhole,** which throws up huge sprays of water; the **Grotto,** intricately carved by the waves; **London**

Australia's Great Ocean Road.

Bridge, which looked like the real thing until the center crashed into the sea in 1990; and the **Loch Ard Gorge.** The scenic road ends in Warrnambool, another of those evocative Australian names. There's a faster road back to Melbourne from here—faster, but not nearly so much fun.

ⓘ **Great Ocean Road Visitors Centre,** Stead Park, Geelong (ℂ **03/5275 5797;** www.greatoceanrd.org.au).

✈ Melbourne, 93km (58 miles).

🛏 $$ **Great Ocean Road Cottages,** Great Ocean Rd., Lorne (ℂ **03/5289 1070;** www.greatoceanroadcottages.com). $ **Macka's Farm,** Princetown Rd., Princetown (ℂ **03/5598 8261;** www.mackasfarm. com.au).

WHY THEY'LL THANK YOU: Surfing and shipwrecks.

Train Rides **28**

Durango & Silverton Narrow Gauge Railroad
Classic Steam Train
All ages • Durango, Colorado, USA

Ever since it was built in 1882, this little train has been puffing along the Rio de las Animas Perdidas (that's Spanish for the River of Lost Souls, a haunting name indeed), traveling 45 miles through the mountains and San Juan National Forest to the town of Silverton and back. When it was first built, Silverton was, as its name suggests, a silver-mining town, and the train's business was to bring precious ore back down to the railroad hub of Durango. When the United States went on the gold standard in 1893, the price of silver dropped dramatically, throwing this region's economy into a tailspin. Many local railroads went belly up, but this one survived because of its incredible scenic views. Nowadays it's tourists that trundle along those tracks, in strings of restored gold-colored Victorian-era coaches.

Traveling at around 18 mph, you'll climb 3,000 feet, past relics of the area's mining and railroading activities; elevations en route range from 8,000 feet at the passes to 14,000 feet on the peaks you'll see from the train windows. White puffs of smoke trail from its coal-powered steam locomotives—a fireman shovels about 6 tons of coal per day to power these locomotives. If you look at the tracks, they're only 3 feet apart (standard train tracks are 4 ft. 8½ in. wide), which makes it easier to navigate sharp mountain curves. In this train's case, the narrower tracks also meant workers had fewer inches to cut out of the sheer granite cliff face of the Animas Gorge. It was such a risky job that the railroad's president, William Palmer, constructed the route in secret so that his board of directors at the Denver & Rio Grande Railroad wouldn't veto the plan before he'd safely completed it.

This is a full-day excursion—it takes 3½ hours to ride from Durango to Silverton, you're given 2 hours to poke around picturesque Victorian-era Silverton, and then it's another 3½ hours back down to Durango. The best thing to do with your time in Silverton is to tour an actual mine; you can buy a combination ticket with the railroad ride that includes a visit to the

Old Hundred Gold Mine (✆ 800/872-3009 or 970/387-5444; www.minetour.com) in Cunningham Pass, just outside of Silverton (this only works with the 9:30am train departure). The tour takes you a third of a mile deep into Galena Mountain on an electric mine car, where miners demonstrate historic mining equipment and techniques. There's also gold panning, and box lunches are included in the deal.

Before getting on the train in Durango, spend half an hour or so in the **Durango & Silverton Narrow Gauge Railroad Museum,** right beside the train depot (✆ **970/247-2733**). Even if you have no train fanatics in the family (we do), the exhibits on the steam-train era will help set the scene for you, and kids enjoy climbing onto the restored locomotive and railroad cars.

ⓘ 479 Main Ave. (✆ **888/872-4607;** www.durangotrain.com).

🛏 See the San Juan Skyway **21**.

WHY THEY'LL THANK YOU: Clinging to the cliff face.

---

29 Train Rides

The Cumbres & Toltec Scenic Railroad
Mountain Train of the Wild West
All ages • Cumbres, Arizona, to Antonito, New Mexico, USA

Bᴀᴄᴋ ɪɴ ᴛʜᴇ 1880s, the Rocky Mountains were laced with little railroad lines, laid down to haul precious metal ore out of remote mines. Weaving through the San Juan Mountains, zigzagging along the New Mexico–Colorado border, the Cumbres & Toltec narrow-gauge railroad is the most classic example of these vintage lines. Along its 64 miles, it passes through a postcard-perfect mountain landscape of wildflower meadows, rustling stands of pine and aspen, and bristling rocky outcrops. It rumbles through two tunnels,

over 100-foot-high trestles, and along the magnificent Toltec Gorge of the Rio de los Pinos. And when it crests at the 10,015-foot Cumbres Pass, you're riding higher than any other passenger train in the States.

The Cumbres & Toltec began service in 1880, making it 2 years older than its sister Denver and Rio Grande branch line, the Durango & Silverton Railroad **28**. Although the route doesn't climb quite as steeply as the Durango-Silverton line, its entire course is high country—beginning at nearly 8,000 feet, about as high as the Durango train gets at its top passes. Narrow-gauge lines were better suited to mountain terrain, but there was one glitch: They couldn't interchange trains with standard-gauge lines. Finally the Denver and Rio Grande began the expensive job of converting its narrow-gauge routes in the 1890s. This branch line simply wasn't a candidate for conversion—the silver mines it served had shut down with the collapse of silver's value, and the area was otherwise remote and unpopulated. Traffic dwindled to a trickle by the 1920s, chugging along behind archaic coal-fired steam locomotives, the only engines that still fit on narrow-gauge rails. In 1969 the D&RG abandoned the route and began to rip up its tracks. A band of railroad preservationists scrambled to stop the demolition before the route's most scenic stretch, between Chama, New Mexico, and Antonito, Colorado, was lost forever, and the two states cooperated to open it as a tourist attraction (not to mention a bit of a movie star—it's appeared in films from *The Missouri Breaks* to *Indiana Jones and the Last Crusade*).

There are two ways to do the route: You can ride the full 64 miles, changing trains halfway through the route at Osier, Colorado, or you can do a day round-trip from either end, returning by train to your starting point. Either way, you're given time to stretch your legs and enjoy a buffet lunch beside Osier's old water tank and stock pens. If you do the through trip, van service is available to complete the loop. You can pay extra to ride in a luxurious parlor car; all passengers can sample sitting in the **open-air gondola,** which the kids shouldn't miss—it's the quintessential wind-in-your-face experience.

(i) ℂ **888/CUMBRES** or 505/756-2151; www.cumbresandtoltec.com

✈ Albuquerque, 160 miles. Santa Fe, 91 miles.

🛏 $$ **River Bend Lodge,** 2625 U.S. 64/285, Chama, NM (ℂ **800/288-1371** or 505/765-2264; www.chamariverbend lodge.com).

BEST TIME: Late May to mid-Oct.

WHY THEY'LL THANK YOU: When the whistle blows to shoo a high-country steer off the tracks.

Train Rides

30

The Rocky Mountaineer
Canada's Train of Wonders
All ages • Vancouver, British Columbia, Canada

WHEN THE OPERATORS of this **luxury train** through the Canadian Rockies call it "the most spectacular train trip in the world," the marketing hyperbole for once turns out to be true. This sleek blue-and-white train has an incredibly panoramic itinerary, clicketyclacking past churning waterfalls, shimmering glaciers, craggy snowcapped peaks, and galloping mountain streams. You won't have the vintage cars you'd get on the more historic trains

above, but there's something to be said for modern luxury coaches and upscale onboard dining. And while I for one love the romance of snuggling into a sleeping berth overnight, there's just too much unmissable scenery along this route to risk sleeping through any of it—the train tours make overnight stops at proper hotels, where you can get rested up for tomorrow's jaw-dropping sights.

There's no question these tours are pricey, though many meals are included,

The Canadian Rockies.

and you can tweak the price by choosing different levels of luxury, both on the train and in your overnight hotels. The company offers several vacation packages of different lengths and destinations, but the triangle from Vancouver to Jasper to Banff and back again is the one I'd opt for. The first leg goes from **Vancouver** to the picturesque resort town of Jasper, Alberta, angling north through the **Yellowhead Pass,** along scenic valleys rich in wildlife, including elk, bears, and scrappy mountain goats. **Jasper National Park** is rugged and back-woodsy, with activities like hiking and river rafting to get you into the wilderness. Motorcoaches then take you on the 285km (177-mile) trip from Banff to Jasper along the incredibly scenic **Icefields Parkway** (see The Columbia Icefields **72**), along the way stopping at the jewel-like resort town of **Lake Louise,** set on a vivid turquoise lake cupped in a dramatic bowl of glaciers (the greenish color of the lake results from sunlight refracted off the minerals deposited by glacier melt). From then it's a short drive down to **Banff,** the Canadian Rockies's other great national

park, where family float trips and short day hikes make it a snap to get into the great outdoors. The town of Banff has more ski-resort chic than Jasper, with boutiques and trendy cafes lining its turn-of-the-century streets; as a tourist, you're practically obligated to take the 8-minute gondola ride to the top of **Sulphur Mountain,** and to cruise **Lake Minnewanka** in a glassed-in motor launch—the scenic vistas make it worth the long lines. Reboarding the train in Banff, you'll glide in style back to Vancouver over the **Kicking Horse Pass,** following the original transcontinental rail line that united the vastness of Canada from east to west. There's no better way to appreciate how big—and how beautiful—North America is.

ⓘ 1150 Mountain St. (© **877/460-3200;** www.rockymountaineer.com).

✈ Vancouver International.

🚢 See Vancouver Aquarium **146**.

WHY THEY'LL THANK YOU: The pampered traveler's way to explore the mountain wilderness.

Chihuahua al Pacífico Railway
Climbing through the Copper Canyon
Ages 8 & up • Los Mochis to Chihuahua, Mexico

CROSSING MEXICO'S RUGGED Sierra Madre range, the Chihuahua al Pacífico Railway climbs from coastal Los Mochis, near the Sea of Cortez, up nearly 2,425m (7,956 ft.) northeast along the rim of the fabled Copper Canyon before descending to the city of Chihuahua. If you just rode the train straight through, it would take 15 hours to cover 644km (400 miles), rattling through 86 tunnels and across 39 bridges through some of Mexico's most magnificent scenery—thick pine forests, jagged peaks, and shadowy canyons. And it would all be a blur to the kids.

Instead, spread the trip out over 5 days; stay overnight in various towns en route, where your hotels can arrange side trips—horseback riding, hiking, or jeep rides to caves, waterfalls, old missions, Tarahumara Indian settlements, or quaint mining towns hidden in the many tributary canyons. The Copper Canyon is so big, it could engulf four Grand Canyons—why whiz through it in a single day?

I recommend starting at the western end, Los Mochis, which the train leaves at the eyelid-propping hour of 6am. Take a snooze until the first stop, cobblestoned colonial **El Fuerte,** on the coastal plain before the foothills of the Sierra Madre. Beyond El Fuerte, you enter the most dramatic part of the train ride, snaking steeply up the Pacific Palisade to **Bahuichivo,** the first stop in canyon country. If you overnight here, you'll stay in **Cerocahui,** built around a sweet-looking mission church. It's little more than unpaved streets and 100 or so houses, but it has a stunning view of the mountains; and several excursions make this a good overnight choice. Take the train onward to

Barrancas and then, 3km (1¾ miles) farther, **El Divisadero,** the same Continental Divide you can straddle up in Montana (see Going-to-the-Sun Road **22**). A 20-minute stop allows passengers to walk to a lookout to gape at the most breathtaking panorama of the canyon along the whole train route. The next-to-last stop is at **Creel** (rhymes with "feel"), a rustic logging town with access to lots of fabulous side trips.

You must buy tickets for a particular date, point of departure, and destination, so design an itinerary to book in advance or sign up for a packaged tour (several leave from El Paso or Tucson; **Sierra Madre Express** in Tucson [📞 **800/666-0346**] does a 1-week tour that runs its own deluxe trains through the canyon). Just don't expect trains to stick to the official timetable—they won't. Take it in stride and the kids will too.

ⓘ www.mexicoscoppercanyon.com.

✈ Los Mochis and Chihuahua.

🛏 $$$ **Hotel Posada Barrancas Mirador,** El Divisadero (📞 **800/896-8196** in the U.S, or 635/578-3020). $$ **Hotel Posada del Hidalgo,** Hidalgo 101, El Fuerte (📞 **800/896-8196** in the U.S., or 698/893-1194 in El Fuerte). $ **Motel Parador de la Montaña,** Av. López Mateos s/n, Creel (📞 **614/410-4580** or 635/456-0023; www.hotelparadorcreel.com). $$$ **Paraíso del Oso,** Cerocahui (📞 **800/884-3107** in the U.S., or 614/421-3372 in Chihuahua; www.mexicohorse.com).

WHY THEY'LL THANK YOU: Going deep into the canyons.

Train Rides

32

The Mountain Railways of North Wales
Vintage Excursions up the Welsh Peaks
All ages • Llanberis & Porthmadog, North Wales

LACING AROUND THE MOUNTAIN FASTNESSES of **Snowdonia National Park** **405** in North Wales are a number of intriguing little 19th-century railways, built by ingenious engineers to haul the "gray gold"— slate—out of that rugged terrain for shipping all over the world. All of them are delightful, but what's really amazing is the number of them in a compact area. In 2 or 3 days your family can take no fewer than six different train rides, each of them different.

One starting point is Llanberis, nestling between Lake Padarn and Lake Peris.

The **Snowdon Mountain Railway** (*℡* **0870/458-0033;** www.snowdon railway.co.uk) runs 8km (5 miles) from Llanberis to within a few yards of the top of the Snowdon peak at about 1,085m (3,560 ft.). The only rack-and-pinion train in Britain, it is also the steepest train ride (lasting 1 hr. each way), and the view from the top platform, where the train stops, is one of the most panoramic in the country—it's possible to see some 160km (100 miles) into Ireland, spying the Wicklow peaks on a clear day. The much tamer **Llanberis Lake Railway** chugs 8km (5 miles) along the dreamy shore of Lake Padarn (1 hr. round-trip).

Down on the coast, the town of Porthmadog offers the **Ffestiniog Railway** (*℡* **01766/516024;** www.festrail.co.uk), a steep and twisting 22km-long (14-mile) narrow-gauge railway with steam locomotives. It's the only link between the two main train

lines in North Wales, so many regular passengers use it, not just tourists. Its endpoint is Blaenau Ffestiniog, a gloomy slate-mining village up in the mountains, its surrounding rock face dramatically ravaged by mining. From the coastal town of **Caenarfon,** where there are a splendid castle ruin and an excavated Roman fort, a narrow-gauge railway runs 13km (8 miles) or so uphill into Rhyd Ddu, where walkers can reach hiking trails up Snowdon.

And if those haven't quenched your thirst for narrow-gauge railways, the **Bala Lake Railway** (*℡* **01678/540666;** www. bala-lake-railway.co.uk) is a 7km (4⅓-mile) stretch along Llyn Tegid (Bala Lake), a glacial lake mirroring the mountains in the inland town of Bala. From the coastal village of **Tywyn,** yet another train steams 11km (6¾ miles) up to Abergynolwyn, with five stations en route leading to waterfalls and mountain walking trails. Contact the **Talyllyn Railway** (*℡* **01654/ 710472;** www.talyllyn.co.uk).

ⓘ **Lllanberis Tourist Information Office,** 41B High St. (*℡* **01286/870765**).

🚃 Bangor, 14km (8¾ miles) north of Llanberis.

🛏 **Royal Victoria Hotel,** Llanberis (*℡* **01286/870253**).

BEST TIME: Trains run May–Oct.

WHY THEY'LL THANK YOU: The thrill of puffing up sheer mountainsides.

Zermatt to St. Moritz: The Glacier Express

All ages • Switzerland

THE NAME "EXPRESS" IS A BIT MISLEADING—it takes 7½ hours for the Glacier Express to get from Zermatt, in the southwestern Swiss Alps, over the Oberalp Pass to St. Moritz in the southeast. Along the way you'll cross 291 bridges, many trestled high above gorges, and duck through 91 tunnels. But every bit of that time, you'll have your noses pressed to the glass, gaping at the panoramas of hazy blue peaks and deep valleys around you, whether mantled in sparkling snow or carpeted in wildflowers. Seven-and-a-half hours may seem too short—even normally restless youngsters will be entranced.

Zermatt, at the base of the Matterhorn (in French, Mont Cervin), still has the atmosphere of a village. Though originally better known for mountain climbing (the **Alpine Museum** in town details the race to climb the Matterhorn, scaled first in 1865 by Edward Whymper), today it's a full-bore ski resort. In fact, Zermatt gets so much snow every winter that high-altitude skiing continues through the spring and early summer. A bewildering number of cable cars, gondolas, and cog railways ascend various peaks around town; if the kids are game, try a day out on the **Gornergrat,** the highest open-air railway in Europe.

St. Moritz, on the other hand, is probably *the* most fashionable ski resort in the world, a magnet for jet-setters, movie stars, tycoons, and aristocrats. It became a winter destination in the mid–19th century, when the first skiers ventured onto its slopes (locals thought they were nuts). Today there are five ski complexes, a bobsled run, curling rinks, even winter golf and horse racing on the frozen lake. In summer, golf and windsurfing are popular, and of course the spas still operate year-round. Expect chic shopping, posh restaurants, and sky-high prices.

When this track was first laid in 1928, some of the mountain bridges had to be dismantled for blizzards every winter, but in 1982 a new tunnel through the Furka mountain enabled the route to stay in operation year-round. There's at least one train a day, with a second one added in summer. Coaches are comfortably upholstered, with dining cars and panoramic observation coaches; both first- and second-class service is available, and though it's a pricey trip, substantial discounts are

The Glacier Express.

offered for children. Advance reservations are essential.

(i) **The Matterhorn-Gotthard Railway** (www.glacierexpress.ch). **Rail Europe** (✆ **800/438-7245;** www.raileurope.com).

🚃 Zermatt, narrow-gauge from Visp or Brig, 4 hr. from Geneva. St. Moritz, 2 hr. from Chur.

🛏 $$ **Hotel Riffelberg,** Zermatt-Umgebung (✆ **027/966-65-00;** www. zermatt.ch/riffelberg). $$$ **Hotel Waldhaus am See,** Via Dimlej 6, St. Moritz (✆ **081/ 836-60-00;** www.waldhaus-am-see.ch).

WHY THEY'LL THANK YOU: Counting the tunnels and bridges.

34 Train Rides

El Teleférico
Venezuela's Cable Car to the Skies
Ages 6 & up • Mérida, Venezuela

Sᴇᴛ ʙᴇᴛᴡᴇᴇɴ ᴛᴡᴏ sɴᴏᴡᴄᴀᴘᴘᴇᴅ ʀɪᴅɢᴇs ᴏꜰ ᴛʜᴇ Andes, the picturesque colonial town of **Mérida** is a lot like college towns everywhere, with cafes and bookstores and crowds of students roaming its narrow streets, thanks to the Universidad de los Andes. The **Sierra Nevada National Park** is next door, so there's always a crew of backpackers tramping around too. But one thing Mérida has that other college towns don't: the world's highest and longest cable car, running for 13km (8 miles) to the top of Pico Espejo.

The cable car begins in Plaza Las Heroínas, on the edge of downtown near the border of Sierra Nevada National Park. It's incredibly popular, so buy your tickets in advance and come early in the day (coming early may also mean clearer skies, though this high, there are no guarantees). Cars depart for the top only in the mornings; you'll be back down by midafternoon. The cable car usually runs Wednesday through Saturday, and maybe fewer days of the week in low season, so be sure to check ahead. Don't forget to dress warmly in layers, as the temperature will change several degrees on the way up. Remember, too, that the air is thinner up here—you'll really feel it, so don't overexert yourself.

The tramway consists of four individual stages. At each intermediate station, you have a brief break to walk around and enjoy the views before heading up the next one. Not everyone makes it all the way to the top—fourth-stage tickets are only sold up at Loma Redonda, the end of the third section. Up until then you ride in canary-yellow enclosed cars, but for the final stage, the cars are fire-engine red. The whole trip takes about an hour; you won't wear out children's attention spans.

The trip begins with a quick and high crossing over the **Río Chama,** a mountain river, then a steep ascent over **lush forests.** On the second stage, you'll notice the montane forest turning to cloud forest as you gain altitude, with forests supplanted by the scrub pines and distinctive velvety-leafed frailejones of the paramo. By the final stage, you've left the paramo and are above the tree line, swinging over barren mountainside with traces of snow on the highest peaks around you. At the top, a serenely beautiful white statue of the **Virgen de las Nieves** (Virgin of the Snows) presides over the peak. If the clouds permit, you can get a great view of **Pico Bolívar,** the highest mountain in Venezuela, crowned with a statue of its namesake hero.

Another popular option is to get off at Loma Redonda and hire a **mule** for the 4- to 5-hour round-trip ride to Los Nevados, a tiny, isolated Andean mountain village. Mule-packing in the Andes—how many of their friends have done that?

(i) Plaza las Heroínas (℗ **0274/252-5050;** www.telefericodemerida.com).

✈ Mérida.

🛏 $$$ **Hotel & Spa La Sevillana,** Sector Pedregosa Alta (℗ **0274/266-3227;** www.andes.net/lasevillana). $ **Posada Luz Caraballo,** in front of Plaza Milla (℗ **0274/ 252-5441**).

WHY THEY'LL THANK YOU: Switching from the yellow cars to the special red ones.

Train Rides
35

Kuranda's Scenic Skyways

Ages 4 & up • Cairns to Kuranda & back, Australia

THE QUEENSLAND COAST OF AUSTRALIA has not one but two world-class natural wonders: the Great Barrier Reef 438 and the Wet Tropics Rainforest. From a base at Cairns, one day you can go snorkeling on the coral cays, and the next head inland to the mountain village of Kuranda, an exotic retreat of cool mountain air and mist-wrapped rainforest. Some people drive up the winding 25km (16-mile) mountain road, but why remain earthbound when you can glide with the kids over the rainforest canopy in a cable car?

The **Skyrail Rainforest Cableway** is the world's longest gondola cableway, a 90-minute climb 7.5km (4⅔ miles) upwards in six-person gondolas. Get an early start and you'll have fine morning light for photographs, but don't cancel if it's raining—a silvery layer of mist only adds haunting beauty to the panorama. From the Skyrail terminal, in the northern Cairns suburbs (Captain Cook Hwy. at Kamerunga Rd., Caravonica Lakes), the view of the coast as you ascend is breathtaking. Rising over the foothills of the coastal range, watch the lush green of the rainforest take over beneath you; as the foliage gets thicker, you can spot ferns and orchids and the brilliant blue butterflies of the region.

Seeing Queensland by rail.

There are two stops, at Red Peak and Barron Falls, where you must change gondolas; take the time to stroll around the boardwalks at the intermediate stations for ground-level views of the rainforest.

Once you're in Kuranda, getting close to nature is very easy. You can walk through either of two aviaries—**Birdworld,** behind the Heritage markets off Rob Veivers Drive (© 07/4093 9188), or **The Aviary,** 8 Thongon St. (© 07/4093 7411)—or the outstanding **Australian Butterfly Sanctuary,** 8 Rob Veivers Dr. (© 07/4093 7575; www.australianbutterflies.com). The butterflies will land on you if you wear pink, red, and other bright colors. If you have time, the 40-hectare (99-acre) **Rainforestation Nature Park,** Kennedy Highway (© 07/4085 5008; www.rainforest.com.au), offers visitors a 45-minute narrated ride into the rainforest on a World War II amphibious Army Duck; you can also see a performance by Aboriginal dancers, throw a boomerang on the Dreamtime Walk, or have a photo taken cuddling a koala in the wildlife park.

In the afternoon (2pm or 3:30pm), hustle back to the fern-draped Kuranda railroad station and get on the **Kuranda Scenic Railway,** which snakes 34km (21 miles) through the magnificent vistas of the Barron Gorge National Park, past gorges and waterfalls, and through 15 tunnels back down to Cairns Central rail station. Two spectacular rides in 1 day—what lucky children!

(i) **Skyrail Rainforest Cableway** (© 07/4038 1555; www.skyrail.com.au). **Kuranda Scenic Railway** (© 07/4036 9249; www.ksr.com.au).

🛏 $$$ **Hotel Sofitel Reef Casino,** 35–41 Wharf St., Cairns (© 1800/808 883 in Australia, 800/221-4542 in the U.S. and Canada, 020/8283 4500 in the U.K., or 07/4030 8888; www.accorhotels.com). $$ **The Reef Retreat,** 10–14 Harpa St., Palm Cove, Cairns (© 07/4059 1744; www.reefretreat.com.au).

WHY THEY'LL THANK YOU: Seeing the rainforest canopy from above.

---

36 Boat Rides

The Seattle-Victoria Ferry
Sailing the High-Speed Puget Cats

All ages • Seattle, Washington, USA, to Victoria, British Columbia, Canada

CROSSING THE U.S.-CANADA BORDER is generally a fairly routine experience—but not if you sail across it on a **high-speed catamaran** from Seattle, Washington, to Victoria, British Columbia. The trip takes only 3 hours, just enough time for the kids to roam around the boat, get a bite to eat, and stare out the windows at the gorgeous northwest coast. Exciting as open water is, it soon gets monotonous for children; one of the glories of this trip for kids is that most of the ride is on glacier-carved **Puget Sound,** where land can be viewed on either side, the rugged conifer-mantled highlands of the Olympic Peninsula on one side and the rural Skagit Valley on the other.

You leave from Seattle's busy ferry port, Pier 69, with the futuristic Space Needle lifting its curious head over the downtown Seattle skyline and majestic Mount Rainier visible to the south, snow-capped even in summer. Working your way past Seattle harbor's sailboat and kayak traffic, you'll enter convoluted Puget Sound, with the mountains of the Olympic Peninsula gradually rearing their peaks on your left. Coming out of Puget Sound near Port Townsend, you'll see the lovely San Juan Islands on the right (the same company runs ferries to the San Juans, including some whale-watching excursions). Then it's across the Strait of

The Seattle-Victoria ferries.

Victoria's pride and joy is its rose gardens, particularly the spectacular **Butchart Gardens,** 800 Benvenuto Ave., Brentwood Bay (✆ **250/652-4422;** www.butchartgardens.com). If you can't sell your kids on visiting a garden, there's plenty to see around the charmingly restored Inner Harbour: **Miniature World** in the Fairmont Empress Hotel, 649 Humboldt St. (✆ **250/385-9731**), with loads of small-scale dioramas from history and literature, the glass-enclosed views of harbor creatures in the **Pacific Undersea Gardens,** 490 Belleville St. (✆ **250/382-5717**), and the **Victoria Butterfly Gardens,** 1461 Benvenuto Ave., Brentwood Bay (✆ **250/652-3822**), which are exactly what the name says.

Juan de Fuca, the first stretch of open water on your voyage so far.

On the far side of that strait lies Vancouver—Vancouver Island, that is, which is not the same thing as the mainland city of Vancouver. What is on Vancouver Island is British Columbia's capital, Victoria, which is like a little slice of Victorian England served up on the northwest coast of North America. Ferry schedules are organized to make a day trip perfectly doable, with plenty of time to explore Victoria before heading back to Seattle. The mild Pacific climate is beautifully suited to horticulture, and

ⓘ ✆ **800/888-2535** or 206/448-5000 or 250/382-8100; www.victoriaclipper.com.

✈ Seattle-Tacoma International, 23km (14 miles). Victoria International, 26km (16 miles).

🛏 $$ **Admiral Inn,** 257 Belleville St., Victoria (✆ **888/823-6472;** www.admiral. bc.ca). $$$ **The Edgewater,** Pier 67, 2411 Alaskan Way, Seattle (✆ **800/624-0670;** www.edgewaterhotel.com).

WHY THEY'LL THANK YOU: Gliding up the fjord in time for tea and scones.

Boat Rides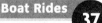
37

Cruising the Mighty Mississippi
A River Ride through the Heart of America
All ages • Various locations along the Mississippi River, USA

THE NATIVE AMERICANS LIVING ON ITS SHORES called it the Messipi, or "big river," but in American lore the Mississippi River is so much more. Yes, it is long—at 2,350 miles, it's the third-longest river in the world—but as it surges north to south down the middle of America, it gives this continent a heartbeat that is essentially, uniquely ours.

I vividly remember the thrill of crossing it for the first time, at age 13, on a nighttime train, with a momentous feeling of Heading West. To ride its majestic brown waters, for whatever stretch of the river, is to feel connected to West and East and North and South all at once. And if you're going to do it, do it the right way, on a

steam-powered paddle boat with lacy white fretwork and fluted smokestacks and the whole banjo-strumming shebang.

Several river towns offer 1- or 2-hour paddle-wheel cruises to give you a taste of what it feels like to be out on that great river—St. Paul, Minnesota; La Crosse, Wisconsin; St. Louis, Missouri; Tunica Resort, Mississippi; and New Orleans, Louisiana all have sightseeing paddle-wheelers. From LeClaire, Iowa, you can even book a 2-day cruise on the *Riverboat Twilight* along the Upper Mississippi to Dubuque and back ((800/331-1467; www.riverboattwilight.com). To really give the kids that old-timey thrill, though, a longer trip is the way to go, to see how the river changes character over its course. The headwaters begin up in Minnesota at Lake Itasca, but the Mississippi is merely a small stream at that point; after it meets the Minnesota River at St. Anthony Falls, it widens significantly, with steep bluffs on either side. Just above St. Louis it joins up with the Illinois and then the Missouri rivers, becoming truly huge and fast-moving. As it rolls down into Arkansas and Louisiana, the softer soil of the Delta creates a mazy, loopy river course, with many islands and a lazy majesty all its own. By the time it

reaches New Orleans, the Mississippi has really *been somewhere.*

The **Delta Steamboat Company** rules the river when it comes to these extended journeys: It has three vintage paddle-wheelers with sleeping cabins, theaters, dining rooms, and even a swimming pool; a "riverlorian" on board tells stories of the river, and young passengers can hang out in the pilothouse and earn a cub pilot's license. Itineraries vary according to which river ports you choose, from Minneapolis to St. Louis to Memphis to New Orleans. The boats dock at charming river towns along the way, with guided tours arranged; between ports, take along a copy of *Huckleberry Finn* or *Life on the Mississippi* and plunk yourself down in a deck chair while the kids scamper around the ship. A week on the river—it's a great way to see America in microcosm, exploring it at the pace of another century.

(i) (800/338-4962; www.mississippiriver cruises.com.

✈ Depends on port of embarkation.

🛏 Onboard.

WHY THEY'LL THANK YOU: Rolling down the river.

---

38 Boat Rides

Scouting Alaska's Inside Passage
Ferries to the Glacier
All ages • Juneau, Alaska, USA

EVERY SUMMER, boatloads of tourists crowd onto luxury cruise ships to be pampered on their way through Alaska. But that's not my idea of a rugged wilderness experience—not when you can still travel in comfort on the swift, well-outfitted ferries of the **Alaska Marine Highway System,** with the option of planning your own itinerary to suit your family's interests.

Officially designated an All-American Road, the Alaska Marine Highway covers 3,500 nautical miles from Bellingham,

Washington, out to the Aleutian Islands. A fleet of sleek blue-hulled ferries steams its entire length, but I think the most interesting segments are those of the Inside Passage, that crazy network of inlets and channels around the countless islands of the Alaskan Panhandle. Squeezed between the Canadian Yukon and the Gulf of Alaska, this little strip of southeast Alaska—a breathtaking mix of dense green northwest rainforest and pristine white glaciers—stretches 500 miles from Ketchikan to Yakutat.

In the middle is Juneau, Alaska's capital city and where you'll probably arrive by plane. Before leaving Juneau, trundle the kids off to see the **Mendenhall Glacier,** Glacier Spur Road (𝄢 **907/789-0097**), where you can stand in front of a wall of blue ice and feel its chilly breath. The two destinations that most interest my kids are in opposite directions from Juneau: **Ketchikan,** a spruced-up logging town with the world's largest collection of totem poles that's 17 hours south by ferry; and **Sitka,** an exotic mix of Russian and Tlingit cultures that's 8¾ hours north of Juneau by ferry. The beauty of taking the ferries? Using Juneau as a base and making separate excursions to Ketchikan and Sitka just takes planning. If you schedule it right, you may even be able to hit every town at an hour when the cruise mobs are gone and the locals relaxed.

Spending several hours on these ferries is no problem. These are handsome modern craft, with restaurants, gift shops, and in some cases even movie theaters on board, not to mention solariums and observation lounges where you can park yourselves to watch the scenic coast roll past. Naturalists often come along for the ride to talk about Alaska's wildlife and geology with passengers; some ships have small video arcades or play areas for toddlers. For overnight journeys, you can reserve two- to four-berth cabins (book several months in advance for summer voyages), although you are also free to roll out your sleeping bags on the comfy reclining seats in the lounges. Hey, that counts as roughing it in my book.

ⓘ 6858 Glacier Hwy. (𝄢 **800/642-0066** or 907/465-3941; www.ferryalaska.com).

✈ Juneau International.

🛏 $$ **The Driftwood Lodge,** 435 Willoughby Ave., Juneau (𝄢 **800/544-2239;** www.driftwoodalaska.com). $$$ **Goldbelt Hotel Juneau,** 51 E. Egan Dr., Juneau (𝄢 **888/478-6909;** www.goldbelt tours.com).

WHY THEY'LL THANK YOU: Waking up to see a glacier slide past your window.

Boat Rides   **39**

Pirate Cruising in the Caribbean

Ages 6 & up • The Bahamas or the Cayman Islands

Eᴠᴇʀ sɪɴᴄᴇ Dɪsɴᴇʏ's *Pirates of the Caribbean* movie came out (yar, that Johnny Depp), the pirate franchise has gotten a new lease on life; I know several 6-year-olds who won't leave the house without their eye patches and cutlasses. Entrepreneurs from Clearwater, Florida, to Bath, Maine, have launched pirate-themed harbor tours, but if you're going to do it, do it the right way: in the warm blue waters of the Caribbean.

The most elaborate outing is **Beyond Boundaries**'s 4-day pirate cruise, on a Windjammer tall ship departing from Miami and ending up in Nassau, The Bahamas. After all, with its scattered islands and secret coves, the Bahamas was a hornet's nest of pirate action back in the day. While at sea, the crew teach passengers sword fighting; pirate movies are projected onto the ship's big white sails; buried treasure is dug up on a deserted island; and a general goofy shipboard atmosphere reigns. Once you arrive in Nassau, there's a dinner at the interactive **Pirates of Nassau,** Bay Street (𝄢 **242/356-3759;** www.pirates-of-nassau.com), and a sightseeing tour of Nassau led by a pirate storyteller. (Even if you don't do the cruise, these Nassau attractions are good for pirate parents to know about.) Book ahead to get the right cabin configuration, before other families snap up the big cabins. There's a 9-day option if you want to continue on to Jamaica, where the pirate activities are more historic and less interactive.

In the Cayman Islands, a shorter option is a 2-hour coastal cruise out of Grand Cayman on the **Jolly Roger,** a rakishly decorated blue boat that is a two-thirds replica of Christopher Columbus's flagship, the *Nina.* The troupe of buccaneer actors on board perform all the standard pirate shtick, conscripting kids to haul the mainsail and swab the deck; there's also a swim stop for some snorkeling and splashing about. This colorful outing feeds on the Caymans's history as a Caribbean pirate hideout—many present-day Caymanites are descendants of the original pirates. Every October, Grand Cayman holds a weeklong **Pirate Heritage Festival** that's tons of swashbuckling fun—though, with most kids in school that time of year, it degenerates into a rum-soaked adult party, quite in keeping with the moral character of pirates.

(i) **Beyond Borders Adventure Travel** (℡ **800/487-1136;** www.potcfantrips.com). *The Jolly Roger* (℡ **345/945-SAIL;** www.jollyrogercayman.com).

✈ Miami International. Grand Cayman.

🛏 $$ **Harbour Heights,** W. Bay Rd., Grand Cayman (℡ **809/947-4660**). $$$ **Ramada Treasure Island Resort,** W. Bay Rd., Grand Cayman (℡ **809/949-777;** www.ramada.com).

WHY THEY'LL THANK YOU: Scrambling like monkeys up the rigging.

---

40 Boat Rides

Punting on the Cam
Ages 6 & up • Cambridge, East Anglia, England

PUNTING ON THE RIVER CAM in a wood-built, flat-bottomed boat (which looks somewhat like a Venetian gondola) is a traditional pursuit of students and visitors to Cambridge University, one of England's two venerable universities (see also Oxford **199**). Wafting your way downstream, you pass along the ivy-covered "Backs" of the colleges, their lush gardens sweeping down to the Cam. It's one of the best ways an outsider can glimpse student life at this university, whose illustrious graduates include everyone from Isaac Newton to Charles Darwin to Stephen Hawking.

Cambridge, founded in the early 13th century, is a conglomeration of some 31 colleges. The most famous of them you'll pass as you head downstream are St. John's, founded 1511, with its Bridge of Sighs arching over the river; Trinity College, founded by King Henry VIII in 1546 and the alma mater of Isaac Newton and Lord Byron; King's College, founded 1441, with its exquisite medieval Chapel (be sure to go visit it on foot after punting); and the lovely Queen's College, dating from 1448, just before the river splits at Sheep's Green.

People sprawl along the banks of the Cam on a summer day to judge and tease you as you maneuver your punt with a pole about 4.5m (15 ft.) long. The river's floor is muddy, and many a student has lost his pole in the riverbed shaded by the willows. If your pole gets stuck, it's better to leave it sticking in the mud instead of risking a plunge into the river.

About 3km (1¾ miles) upriver lie the meadows of **Grantchester,** immortalized by poet Rupert Brooke (the town lies about a mile from the meadows). When the town clock stopped for repairs in 1985, its hands were left frozen "for all time" at 10 minutes to 3, in honor of Brooke's famed sonnet "The Soldier."

Scudamore's Boatyards, Granta Place (✆ **01223/359750**), by the Anchor Pub, has been in business since 1910. You rent boats by the hour, and there's a maximum of six persons per punt; the place is open year-round, although March through October is the high season. If you'd rather not attempt punting yourself, you can hire a "chauffeur" for a (hefty) additional fee.

ⓘ **Cambridge Tourist Information Centre,** Wheeler St. (✆ **01223/457577**).

🚌 Cambridge, 1 hr. from London.

🛏 $$$ **Cambridge Garden House Moat House,** Granta Place, Mill Lane (✆ **01223/ 259988;** www.moathousehotels.com).

WHY THEY'LL THANK YOU: Rolling, rolling, rolling on the river.

Boat Rides

41

Cruising the Fjords
Ages 6 & up • Norway

IT TOOK, OH, 3 MILLION YEARS OR SO to carve out the dramatic furrows and fissures that make the Norwegian coast look like nowhere else on earth. At some points these deeply indented fjords become so narrow that a boat can hardly wedge between the steep mountainsides. Waterfalls spill down their cliffs, brightly painted storybook villages nestle in their creases, rags of mist trail around rocky coves. To glide up these crystal-clear waters by ship is an unforgettable experience.

The scenic city of **Bergen,** a quarter of the way up Norway's coast, is often called the gateway to the fjords; north of here, the coast suddenly fragments and crumbles dramatically into scattered archipelagoes and inlets. Elegantly appointed steamers travel north from Bergen along this breathtaking coast, taking 5 or 6 days to round Scandinavia's northern tip and reach Kirkenes. The round-trip journey circles around and sails back south, timing things so that you'll see in the daytime anything you missed while sleeping in your berth on the way up. Though these are luxury cruise vessels—and you'll pay cruise prices to travel on them—the ships are also transport for locals, stopping at 34 ports en route, with enough time for passengers to hop off for shopping and shore excursions. Among the major stops are **Trondheim,** a city with a remarkably well-preserved timbered medieval district;

Bødo, the first port north of the Arctic Circle; **Tromsø,** site of the world's northernmost planetarium (see Tromsø **311**); the fishing port of **Hammerfest,** where you may see local Lapps with their reindeer; and **Honningsvåg,** the world's northernmost village and terminus of the Midnight

One of Norway's dramatic fjords.

Sun Road, where you can take an excursion to the stark Nordskapp plateau, the "top of Europe," with its dark cliffs dropping precipitously into the Arctic Ocean. But it's not the sights onshore that the kids will remember in the end—it's the day after day of those stunning fjord views, with the northern light sparkling off the waters and each new turn revealing another dramatic forested chasm.

(i) **Bergen Line** (✆ **800/323-7436** or 212/319-1300). **Norwegian Costal Voyages** (✆ **800/334-6544;** www.cruisenorway.com).

✈ Bergen.

🛏 Sleeping quarters provided onboard. $ **Minotel Dreggen,** Sandbrugaten 3, Bergen (✆ **55-31-61-55;** www.hotel-dreggen.no). $$ **Quality Edvard Grieg Hotel and Suites,** Sandsliåsen 50, Bergen (✆ **55-98-00-00;** www.choicehotels.com).

BEST TIME: Summer June–July, when the sun barely sets.

WHY THEY'LL THANK YOU: When you cross the Arctic Circle—and keep on going.

Boat Rides

42

Crisscrossing Lake Como

All ages • Como, Italy

BACK AND FORTH WE WENT, trying to decide which of northern Italy's romantic lakes to visit: Garda? Maggiore? Como? We finally chose Lake Como because it's the smallest, only 4km (2½ miles) across at its widest point, with the far shore always visible, and therefore easier for our toddler son to scope out. (It's also closest to Milan, about 48km/30 miles away). I've heard the other two are spectacular, but I don't see how they could out-enchant Lake Como, its shimmering deep-blue waters bordered with flowery gardens and aristocratic villas of soft golden

stone. And even though we had a rental car, we soon realized the best way to enjoy Lake Como is to crisscross it on ferries, sitting in the balmy open air with other travelers instead of enclosed in a steel cocoon.

Lake Como is incredibly long and skinny, with its most charming towns clustered mid-lake. Starting from the town of Como at the southwest tip, we headed north along the western shore 5km (3 miles) to **Cernobbio,** a chic haven dominated by the celebrated Villa d'Este (see the hotel recommendation below),

Lake Como.

originally built in the 16th century. After a stroll in its lush gardens, it was north another half-hour to **Tremezzo,** where the landscaping is surprisingly tropical—citrus trees, palms, cypresses, and magnolias—and as we stood on its panoramic lakeshore we felt our urban anxieties begin to dissolve. Leaving the car behind, we hopped a ferry to **Bellagio,** a tony resort town as gracious as its Vegas namesake is garish. Clinging to a promontory at the lake's fork, Bellagio has steep cobblestone streets to climb, as well as arcaded shops, smart cafes, and a blossoming lakeside promenade.

Our next ferry took us to picturesque **Varenna,** which still has a certain fishing-village quaintness despite a stock of resort hotels. Here we investigated Italy's shortest river, the Fiumelatte, a mere 250m (820 ft.) long. It only appears in summer, rushing frothy and milk-white down a rock face to crash into the lake. Leonardo da Vinci once tried to determine the water's source, but neither he—nor anyone else—has ever found it. We boarded another ferry (by this time it was like a game to our son) and crossed back west

to **Cadenabbia** to see 19th-century **Villa Carlotta** (✆ **0344-40405**), or at least its gardens, with exotic flowers and banks of rhododendrons and azaleas. (There's a fine art museum, too, but we had a toddler to amuse.) A mile south and we were back at Tremezzo to reclaim our car.

Lake Como is definitely a summertime destination—the boat service operates only Easter to September, and many hotels close November to March. But under a blue sky, when the sun shines and the flowers bloom, it's like heaven on earth.

ⓘ **Società Navigazione Lago di Como,** Lungo Lario (✆ **031-304060** or 031-579211). **Como tourist office,** Piazza Cavour 17 (✆ **031-269712;** www.lakecomo.org).

🚆 Como, 40 min. from Milan.

🛏 $$$ **Grand Hotel Villa d'Este,** Via Regina 40, Cernobbio (✆ 031-3481; www.villadeste.it). $$ **Hotel Du Lac,** Piazza Mazzini 32, Bellagio (✆ **031-950320;** www.bellagiohoteldulac.com).

WHY THEY'LL THANK YOU: Hopping a ferry like it was the local bus.

Boat Rides **43**

Gliding down the Danube
From Vienna to Budapest in Style
All ages • Vienna, Austria, to Budapest, Hungary

Vɪᴇɴɴᴀ ᴀɴᴅ Bᴜᴅᴀᴘᴇsᴛ are two of Europe's most romantic cities, and two of my personal favorites, so the idea of linking them with a boat trip up the beautiful blue Danube was impossible to resist. Though the Danube doesn't have the majestic Wagnerian chasms and castles of the Rhine, I love the way it waltzes sweetly through green forests and farmlands, through eastern Austria, past Bratislava and along the Slovakia/Hungary border, and then down through the lush Hungarian lowlands. The water may be more brown than blue these days, but the Danube is still beautiful.

Vienna and Budapest make a natural pairing: Both have a 19th-century look and pace, great for strolling aimlessly, lingering in coffeehouses (where the pastries are fabulous!), and listening to schmaltzy music. Their grandest churches are both dedicated to St. Stephen—Vienna's **Gothic Domkirche St. Stephan** and Budapest's domed **St. Stephen's Basilica.** Vienna has the **Prater** (home of the **Ferris Wheel** ⑭⑧⑤); Budapest, the **zoo** and amusement rides in **City Park.** Budapest has medieval **Buda Palace** ⑧⑥, Vienna the baroque Habsburg palace of Schönbrunn.

Budapest still bears traces of its years under Communist rule, but less so than other former Iron Curtain capitals.

River steamers make a day of this journey, leaving Vienna at 6am and making stops in **Komaron,** site of a famous Austro-Hungarian fortress, and **Esztergom,** with its massive neoclassical cathedral. You'll arrive in Budapest late that night, ready to find your hotel and set off sightseeing the next morning. To make a round-trip in 1 day, you can travel via **hydrofoil,** which takes only 5½ hours to get from Vienna to Budapest or vice versa; you can opt to take the train back that night, which gives you an extra 3 hours for sightseeing in Budapest. There are three downsides to the hydrofoil option: The spray raised by the boat's jets obscures some details of the scenery, there are no sightseeing stops along the way, and it runs only April through October. But still.

Another (considerably cheaper) option is just to do the Hungarian section of the river, departing from and returning to Budapest. This particularly scenic stretch of the river, called the **Danube Bend,** is overlooked by tall forested hills; there's a dramatic horseshoe bend at Visegrád, known as the Elbow of the Danube, and stops can be made at several charming riverside towns. Leisurely boat rides up the Danube bend are run April through September by MAHART, the state shipping company (✆ **1/318-1704;** www.mahartpassnave.hu). From Budapest to Esztergom takes 5 hours.

ⓘ **DDSG Blue Danube Shipping Co.,** Friedrichstrasse 7, Vienna (✆ **01/588800;** www.ddsg-blue-danube.at).

✈ Vienna International. Ferihegy Budapest.

🛏 $$ **Hotel Erzsébet,** V. Károlyi Mihály u. 11-15, Budapest (✆ **1/889-3700;** www.danubiusgroup.com). $$ **Hotel-Pension Suzanne,** Walfischgasse 4, Vienna (✆ **01/5132507**).

WHY THEY'LL THANK YOU: A dreamy glide into Europe's old-fashioned heart.

Riverboating up the Amazon
Songs of the Rainforest
Ages 8 & up • from Manaus, Brazil

IF YOUR KIDS ARE LIKE MINE, they've raised money in school for saving the rainforest—but do they really know what it is that they're saving? Before they grow up, at least once they should encounter the world's biggest forest, this amazing tropical wilderness that accompanies the world's largest river on its mighty course through Brazil to the Atlantic Ocean. Indeed it is endangered, indeed we ought to save it—and, properly inspired, your children and mine can do it.

Thanks to the rise in eco-tourism, rainforest outings are much more accessible than they used to be. The usual starting point for visiting the Amazon basin is Manaus, the largest city in the region, located on the shores of the Rio Negro. Numerous operators run boat trips out of Manaus, usually on a double-decked riverboat that serves as your home base. These package tours generally include certain common elements: nature-spotting excursions in canoes up the smaller channels, sunset and sunrise tours, wildlife-watching walks under the leafy canopy of the rainforest, caiman spotting, piranha fishing, and a visit to a *caboclo* (river peasant) settlement with houses built on stilts. But when you're not on an excursion, you're moving on the wide brown river, its green shores slipping away to either side. There is always something to see, even if it's just the vastness of the river itself. **Viverde** (℮ **092/248-9988;** www.viverde.com.br), a local travel company, handles a range of tours; **Amazon Clipper Cruises** (℮ **092/656-1246;** www.amazonclipper.com.br) has three old-style Amazon riverboats which make regular 3- and 4-day trips; **Swallows and Amazons** (℮ **092/622-1246;** www.swallowsandamazonstours.com) runs a variety of adventure-tour itineraries on traditional wooden riverboats.

The most amazing thing to see around Manaus is the Meeting of the Waters (Encontra das Aguas), where the dark, slow waters of the Rio Negro meet the fast, muddy brown waters of the Rio Solimões. Because of differences in velocity, temperature, and salinity, the two rivers don't immediately blend but carry on side by side for miles. If the boat trip you're signed up for doesn't pass through this phenomenal juncture, try booking a flight-seeing tour over it—and actually, come to think of it, that's the best way to see how its contrasting colors gradually mix and mingle, from up on high.

ⓘ **Manaus Tourist Center Tourist Service Center** (℮ **092 3231-1998;** www.amazonastur.am.gov.br).

✈ Eduardo Gomes in Manaus 16km (10 miles).

🛏 Included in boat tours.

WHY THEY'LL THANK YOU: Either the piranhas or the parrots—depends on the kid.

One-of-a-Kind Cityscapes . . . 52
The Big City Buzz . . . 61
Postcards across America . . . 69

The rooftops of Paris.

Atlantic City's Monopoly Streets

All ages • New Jersey, USA

SINCE CASINO GAMBLING ARRIVED in the 1970s, this once-proud Victorian seaside resort 60 miles east of Philadelphia has been reborn as the Vegas of the East Coast—decidedly a mixed blessing for families. The ghost of the old Atlantic City is still here, though, especially on the mile-long wooden **Boardwalk** that curves along the uncrowded white-sand beach. Food stands and arcades survive between the hulking casino properties, and visitors can take a nostalgic ride in old-fashioned rolling chairs. And to get kids interested, Atlantic City has a unique hook: It's one giant Monopoly® board.

This is the city that the "creator" of Monopoly, Charles Darrow, had in mind when patenting his game board in 1933. Actually, Darrow stole the game from an Atlantic City woman named Ruth Hoskins, who had invented it to play with friends (hey, it was the Depression, and Darrow was hungry). Hoskins had put her hometown's street names on her game board, and they're still here today. Atlantic City's street-naming scheme is fairly simple—parallel to the Boardwalk, avenues are named after seas and oceans (going inland, Pacific, Atlantic, Arctic, then low-rent Baltic and Mediterranean), while the cross-streets that connect them are named after states. Walk down the Boardwalk east to west from Vermont Avenue to Indiana Avenue and you may feel like you have turned into a shoe, or an iron, or a top hat, or one of the other classic Monopoly game tokens.

Along the way, you can sample Atlantic City's most kid-oriented attractions: the **Absecon Lighthouse** at Rhode Island Avenue (228 steps to a great shoreline view at the top); carnival rides and games at the renovated **Steel Pier** at Pennsylvania Avenue; a **Ripley's**

Believe It Or Not at St. James's Place; and, farther west, the **Ocean One** shopping mall at Arkansas Avenue, and a **mini-golf** course at Mississippi Avenue. Let the busloads of gamblers crowd inside the claustrophobic casinos: You're outside walking along the ocean, with sunshine, salt air, sea breezes, and a box of saltwater taffy. It's a fun and funky day at the shore.

We were puzzled, though, that we couldn't find Ventnor Place or Marvin Gardens—but that's because they aren't in Atlantic City at all, but in Margate, two towns south. (On your way, drive by **Lucy the Elephant,** 9200 Atlantic Ave., a huge wooden roadside curiosity from the 1880s.) Marvin Gardens was Charles Darrow's hasty misspelling of **Marven Gardens,** a charming 1920s-era subdivision off the 7400 block of Ventnor Avenue. It

Lucy the Elephant in Margate.

took a bit of detective work to drive down here and find those two missing streets, but that made our Atlantic City Monopoly quest all the more special.

(i) **Tourist Office,** 2314 Pacific Ave. (*C* **888/AC-VISIT;** www.atlanticcitynj.com).

✈ Atlantic City, 10 miles.

🛏 $$ **Atlantic City Hilton,** Boston Ave. & Boardwalk (*C* **800/257-8677** or 609/347-7111; www.hiltonac.com). $$ **Holiday Inn Boardwalk,** Chelsea Ave. & Boardwalk (*C* **800/548-3030** or 609/348-2200; www.atlanticcity.holiday-inn.com).

WHY THEY'LL THANK YOU: Finding Marvin Gardens.

One-of-a-Kind Cityscapes

46

Las Vegas: Cruising the Strip
Ages 6 & up • Nevada, USA

CALL IT THE SEVENTH WONDER of the Artificial World—in its own way, Vegas is every bit as amazing as the Grand Canyon. After a brief flirtation with being a family-friendly destination, Las Vegas has lapsed wholeheartedly back into its Sin City image, but even so, it's such an outrageous phenomenon, every kid should at least see it once.

Drink in the bizarre panorama first by cruising up and down Las Vegas Boulevard South, aka The Strip—traffic generally crawls, which should make it easy to see everything; if you don't have a car, view it from the new monorail, which will eventually run the length of the Strip. Do it once by day, spotting all the outlandish architecture; do it once again by night, when the competing dazzle of neon signs is simply breathtaking. Time things right so you can catch the Strip's free outdoor spectacles: the **dancing fountains** at the Bellagio, 3600 Las Vegas Blvd. S; the **exploding volcano** at the Mirage, 3400 Las Vegas Blvd. S., and the nightly **pirate battle** at Treasure Island casino, 3300 Las Vegas Blvd. S.

Several of the casino-hotels' lobbies are like mini-amusement parks, with stage-set scenery and themed shops and cafes: Just guess what cities are re-created at **Paris Las Vegas,** 3655 Las Vegas Blvd. S.; **The Venetian,** 3355 Las Vegas Blvd. S.; and **New York–New York,** 3790 Las Vegas Blvd. S. At the pyramid-shaped **Luxor,**

3900 Las Vegas Blvd. S., there's a full-scale reproduction of King Tutankhamen's tomb, authentically handcrafted in Egypt; or, for all-out kitsch, visit the talking statues in the Forum Shops at the Roman Empire–themed **Caesars Palace,** 3570 Las Vegas Blvd. S. The **MGM Grand,** 3799 Las Vegas Blvd. S., has a multilevel glass enclosure where you can watch lions frolic; the **Mirage** has a minizoo of exotic cats and elephants owned by Siegfried & Roy, as well as a dolphin habitat; the **Imperial Palace,** 3535 Las Vegas Blvd. S., has a world-class car collection, many of them formerly owned by celebrities; and there are even theme-park rides built into some casinos (see **Las Vegas In-House Thrill Rides 492**). Most of these attractions are free, and even the ones that charge admission charge only a small amount.

There are fabulous shows to see at night, and splendiferous pool areas to lounge around. You can make day trips into the desert to the **Hoover Dam 302** and the **Grand Canyon 480**. But when all is said and done, what the kids will remember is that nighttime view of the Strip. It's brilliant, it's brash, it's exotic, it's truly one of a kind. No city can out-Vegas Vegas.

(i) **Tourist office,** 3150 Paradise Rd. (*C* **877/VISITLV;** www.vegasfreedom.com).

✈ McCarran International.

🛏 $$ **Mandalay Bay,** 3950 Las Vegas Blvd. S. (© **877/632-7000** or 702/632-7000; www.mandalaybay.com). $$ **MGM Grand,** 3799 Las Vegas Blvd. S. (© **800/929-1111** or 702/891-7777; www.mgmgrand.com).

WHY THEY'LL THANK YOU: Getting that neon fix.

Munich's Marienplatz
Inside the Music Box
All ages • Germany

MORE THAN MOST GERMAN CITIES, Munich can still show off its historic center—the Altstadt, or Old City—a picturesque remnant of its days as capital of the independent country of Bavaria. Time your visit to arrive a few minutes before 11am or noon (also before 5pm in summer) and join the crowd growing in the flagstoned square, facing north toward the Gothic-style facade of the Neues Rathaus (New City Hall). As the crowd thickens, you may need to hoist smaller children onto your shoulders. On the hour, the 32 enameled copper figures poised in the niches of the hall's ornate stone tower whirr and jerk into action, while the carillon plays jaunty music (sadly, an off-key tape nowadays). Okay, the show only lasts a few minutes, and the figures' stilted mechanical movements can't compare to the sophisticated animatronics that modern kids are used to. But to me, that's part of the glockenspiel's charm, like an old-fashioned music box.

The **glockenspiel** itself isn't all that old—it was only built in 1903—but the scenes it commemorates are plenty dated. The top "stage" depicts an actual 1568 wedding feast, complete with knights jousting in a tournament, and the bottom shows guild members dancing in a 1517 celebration of the end of the Great Plague. My kids marvel that this 19th-century building is the "new" city hall (its pinnacles and arcades are pure Gothic revival, much like London's Houses of Parliament); notice the much plainer Gothic tower on the **Altes Rathaus** (Old City Hall), to its right—and even that is only a 15th-century reconstruction of an earlier city hall that burned down.

Once the glockenspiel has done its thing, climb the 55 steps to the top of the **Rathaus tower** (an elevator is also available) for a city overview before exploring nearby sights. South of the square is the oldest church in Munich, copper-spired **St. Peter's,** and a couple streets farther south is the umbrella-shaded **Viktualienmarkt,** where Munichers have gathered since 1807 to gossip, browse, snack, and buy fresh produce. Walk 3 blocks east from Marienplatz to see the sole remaining tower from Munich's old city walls, the **Isartor (Isar Gate).** To the north of Marienplatz lies the **Residenz,** Max Joseph-Platz 3 (© **089/290671**), 130 rooms full of historic furniture, paintings, sculpture, ceramics, and other treasures of former Bavarian rulers; just beyond that lies the 17th-century formally planted **Hofgarten** royal park. It may be a fairy-tale view of this otherwise busy modern city, but aren't fairy tales what kids remember?

ⓘ **Munich Tourist Information Office,** Neues Rathaus, Marienplatz (© **089/ 2330300;** www.muenchen.de).

✈ Munich International, 27km (17 miles).

🛏 $ **Hotel Jedermann,** Bayerstrasse 95 (© **089/543240;** www.hotel-jedermann.de).

$$ **Hotel Splendid-Dollmann im Lehel,** Thierschstrasse 49 (② **089/238080;** www.hotel-splendid-dollmann.de).

WHY THEY'LL THANK YOU: That creaky old glockenspiel.

One-of-a-Kind Cityscapes

48

Brussels's Grand-Place
A Town Square for the Ages
All ages • Belgium

WHEN YOU WALK FROM a narrow cobbled street into the Grand-Place, your perspective suddenly zooms wide. Sunlight flashes off of gilded facades and gold-fili-greed rooftop sculptures; it's a dazzling sight indeed, a harmonious assemblage of ornamental stepped gables, stone-carved emblems, and heraldic banners draped under diamond-paned casement windows. To me, it's the essence of Old World Europe—and beautiful as it is in the daytime, be sure to come back on a summer evening when it's all lit up, with a synchronized colored light show the kids are sure to find magical.

As you circle the car-free square, paved with sparkly stone blocks, imagine the Renaissance guildsmen vying to establish their power by building the most richly embellished guild halls. No. 9, now an elegant restaurant named **Le Cygne (the Swan),** was originally head-quarters of the butcher's guild; by coincidence, Karl Marx lived here when he wrote the *Communist Manifesto*. No. 10, **L'Arbre d'Or (Gold Tree),** was the brewers' guild headquarters; there's a Brewery Museum here today. Nos. 13–19 is a set of seven mansions known as the **Maison des Ducs de Brabant,** decorated with busts of 19 dukes of the Brabant dynasty. No. 26, known as the **"Pigeon,"** also was once home to a famous writer, Victor Hugo, during his exile from France after antagonizing Napoleon III.

Perhaps the square's masterpiece, though, is the Town Hall, **Hôtel de Ville,**

built in 1402. Challenge the kids to pick out their favorites from the dozens of little sculptures on its busy gray facade—the drunken monks, a sleeping Moor and his harem, or maybe St. Michael slaying a female devil. Point out the tower, which is just slightly off-center—legend has it that when the architect discovered his mistake, he jumped from the tower to his death. Now see if they can find the other

Manneken Pis.

Gothic building on the square (hint: look for pointy arched windows)—the 19th-century Gothic Revival **Maison du Roi.** The name means "king's house," but no king ever lived here; it's now the Museum of the City of Brussels, which is worth paying to visit. The cool things to see are historic scale models of the city center and, on the third floor, a display of more than 650 costumes that have been donated over the years to cover up Brussels's most famous statue, **Mannequin-Pis.** You'll definitely want to take the kids 2 blocks south of Grand-Place, to rue de l'Etuve at rue du Chêne, to see this small bronze statue of a naked peeing boy. You

have to love a city that has something like this as its mascot.

ⓘ **Tourist office,** Town Hall, Grand-Place (ℂ **02/513-89-40;** www.brussels international.be).

✈ Brussels International, 14km (8⅔ miles).

🛏 $$ **Arlequin,** Rue de la Fourche 17–19 (ℂ **02/514-16-15;** www.arlequin.be). $$$ **Radisson SAS,** Rue du Fossé-aux-Loups 47 (ℂ **800/333-333** or 02/219-28-28; www.radissonsas.com).

WHY THEY'LL THANK YOU: It sets the gold standard for town squares.

One-of-a-Kind Cityscapes   **49**

Stockholm: City of Islands
All ages • Sweden

Sᴛᴏᴄᴋʜᴏʟᴍ ɪs sᴘʀᴇᴀᴅ ᴏᴠᴇʀ a huddled cluster of 14 islands—the heart of a 24,000-island archipelago that goes all the way to the Baltic Sea. Here you always sense the murmuring lap of water upon some nearby shore. Hopping ferries and crossing bridges is all part of the daily routine here, and kids quickly slip into the game of skipping from island to island, each with its own distinct flavor.

Drink in an aerial overview of the whole layout from the observation deck of **Kaknästornet,** a 152m (499-ft.) radio and television tower in eastern Stockholm. Heading back to the center of town, get into a Viking mindset at the **Historiska Museet,** Narvavärgen 13–17, which has some amazing artifacts, including an entire underground chamber of silver and gold Viking jewelry. Then cut down to Strandvågen and stroll west along the water to Stockholm's atmospheric Old Town, or **Gamla Stan**—the medieval "city between the bridges." Before you cross over the Norrbro, though, prep the kids with a visit to the **Museum of Medieval Stockholm,** Strömparterren, where you

can pore over artifacts such as excavated fragments of medieval city walls and the 16th-century ship *Riddarsholm.* When you reach Gamla Stan, you'll soon see the **Royal Palace,** Kungliga Husgerådskammaren, which, granted, is more baroque than medieval, but it's not every day you can visit the residence of a living monarch. Portions of the state apartments can be toured, though the kids may be happy just to see the crown jewels in the Treasury and gilded coaches and coronation costumes in the Royal Armory. Then wander around the maze of narrow cobblestone streets south of the palace, like a time warp to the Middle Ages. End up on the west side of Gamla Stan to cross to another island—**Riddarholmen,** or "island of the knights"—with its landmark church, founded in the 13th century as a Franciscan monastery. Almost all the monarchs of Sweden are buried here.

Set aside another day to explore Stockholm's other most-visited island, the forested **Djurgården** (Deer Park)—a good excuse to take a bracing ferry ride,

Stockholm in winter.

from Skeppsbron on Gamla Stan. The chief attractions on Djurgården are the magnificent 17th-century warship at **Vasamuseet** ❷❻❼ and the 75-acre open-air history park of **Skansen,** full of historic windmills and manors and cottages and an old town where costumed craftsmen demonstrate their trades. Also on Djurgården, there's the **Gröna Lunds Tivoli** amusement park, the local version of Copenhagen's Tivoli Gardens ❺❶❶. Or opt for a more leisurely ride, on a **Stockholm Sightseeing** (✆ 08/587-140-20) cruise around Djurgården's labyrinthine

network of canals, a lovely way to spend a long dreamy Swedish summer afternoon.

ⓘ **Tourist office,** Drottninggatan 33 (✆ 08/ 789-24-00; www.stockholmtown.com).

✈ Stockholm Arlanda, 45km (28 miles).

🛏 $$ **Radisson SAS Royal Viking Hotel,** Vasagatan 1 (✆ 800/333-3333 or 08/506-54000; www.radissonsas.com). $$ **Sheraton Stockholm Hotel,** Tegelbacken 6 (✆ 800/325-3535 or 08/412-34-00; www.sheratonstockholm.com).

WHY THEY'LL THANK YOU: Island-hopping around the maze.

50   **One-of-a-Kind Cityscapes**

The Canals of Venice

All ages • Italy

Wᴴɪʟᴇ ᴏᴛʜᴇʀ ᴄɪᴛɪᴇꜱ ʜᴀᴠᴇ ᴄᴀɴᴀʟꜱ, Venice out-does them all—it has only canals (more than 150 of them) and no streets, just walkways. Cars are useless; motor launches and anachronistic black gondolas are the way to get around town—that and

walking, which usually means getting lost in a maze of narrow stone lanes, echoing *palazzo* walls, high-arched bridges, and sudden vistas of church towers. Set on 118 separate islands, dredged out of a polluted lagoon, Venice is sinking about 2½ inches

57

per decade. It might not be there for our children's children—all the more reason to see it as soon as you can.

Water lapping against stone, a faint scent of decay, and a certain softness in the air make Venice a truly magical place. It's expensive, no question, and the major tourist sites are jammed in high season (when it's also wicked hot and the canals begin to reek). And yet my kids loved Venice. While many tourists do it in a day or two, we spent a full week there, and every day was a delight.

The layout is perplexing: The **Grand Canal** snakes through the city, crossed by only three bridges—the white marble **Ponte Rialto,** the wooden **Ponte Accademia,** and the stone **Ponte degli Scalzi**— so if you wind up on the wrong side of the canal, you'll have quite a walk to get back. There's nothing like a logical grid, or even any main thoroughfare; streets twist, turn, and dead-end unexpectedly. Get a good map and prepare to get lost anyway.

Most tourists simply mill around the colonnaded **Piazza San Marco**— arguably the loveliest public space in the world—where we too did our duty and saw the main sights: **St. Mark's Basilica,** a wondrous Byzantine church, all mysterious dark interior and glittering gold mosaics; and next to it the exotic **Doge's Palace,** with its Arabian Nights facade. We waited to see the two mechanical Moors chime the hour at the piazza's **Clock Tower.** Then we explored the watery streets by *vaporetto,* cruising the length of the Grand Canal, lined solidly with Venetian Gothic *palazzi;* we took another out to the island of **Murano** to see the glass blowers, and another to the crowded **Lido beach,** where we spent an afternoon bobbing in the bathtub-warm Adriatic sea. We even took a gondola— *once* (the fare is outrageous).

But after that we abandoned ourselves to strolling around the city, popping into churches (a great way to escape the brutal sun), lighting candles, sitting in pews, and enjoying the paintings and statues without learning the artists' names (though many are by famous artists indeed). We turned the city into a scavenger hunt, looking for winged lions (St. Mark's symbol), stray cats, laundry hung out of upper stories, greengrocers, pharmacies, and *gelateria*

One of Venice's canals.

(ice cream shops). We bought sandwiches and sat outside to eat, tossing bread crusts to the ubiquitous pigeons. We loved Venice. You will too. Go now.

ⓘ **Azienda di Promozione Turistica,** San Marco 71/F (📞 **041-5298711**).

✈ Aeroporto Marco Polo.

🛏 $$$ **Locanda Ai Santi Apostoli,** Strada Nuova, Cannaregio (📞 **041-5212612;** www.locandasantiapostoli.com). $$ **Pensione Accademia,** Fondamenta Bollani, Dorsoduro (📞 **041-5237846;** www.pensione accademia.it).

WHY THEY'LL THANK YOU: Streets of water.

---

51 **One-of-a-Kind Cityscapes**

The Canals of Amsterdam
Rings within Rings
All ages • The Netherlands

IT LOOKS LIKE A SPIDER WEB, my daughter pointed out on the map, the concentric rings of 17th-century canals in Holland's greatest city. Amsterdam has streets as well, but after a maddening hour in the historic core, frustrated by one-way streets and missing turns onto narrow humped bridges, we parked the car and vowed we'd spend the rest of our time on foot, on canal boats, or on beat-up bikes (the Dutch call them *omafiets,* or grandmother bikes) the way the Amsterdammers do. From then on, steering around the spider's web was a lark.

Venice's canals seem designed to get you lost; Amsterdam's, however, are much more user-friendly, laid out in a tidy pattern that suits the trim gabled houses that line them. We soon memorized the order of the chief circling canals—Singel, Herengracht, Keizersgracht, and Prinsengracht, with another two, Lijnbaansgracht and curvy Singelgracht, a few streets farther out—which are then crossed at right angles by streets, a few radiating canals, and the Amstel River. On the Singel at Muntplein, the **Flower Market** blossomed in front of us with its rafts of brilliant tulips, the very essence of Holland. On Herengracht and Keizersgracht, we toured a pair of 17th-century merchants' homes, **Museum Willet-Holthuysen** at

Herengracht 605, near the Amstel; and **Museum Van Loon,** Keizersgracht 672, near Vijzelstraat, just so we could imagine the insides of all those other lovely private homes we passed. The house we visited on Prinsengracht was more modern, and more sobering—the **Anne Frank House** 382. Then we found our way to the Eastern Dock, where all the canals peter out and two spectacular museums beckon children: **NEMO,** Oosterdok 2 off Prins Hendrikkade, a super, hands-on science museum; and the **Maritime Museum,** Scheepvaartmuseum, Kattenburgerplein 1, a trove of replica ships, models, charts, and navigational instruments that celebrate the seafaring prowess that once made this tiny nation a colonial power. Farther east, we continued to explore that colonial connection at the **Tropenmuseum,** Linnaeusstraat 2, where walk-through model villages and city-street scenes capture daily scenes in India, Indonesia, and other tropical locales.

We intended to take a narrated cruise on one of those glass-roofed boats we saw gliding along the canals. We didn't even do the **Museumboot,** which departs from Centraal Station and sails in a loop with jump-on–jump-off stops near major attractions—I'm sure it would have been a lovely way to go when we visited the **Rijksmuseum & Van Gogh Museum** ❸❸❻. We should have rented canal bikes, those nutty little four-person paddle boats we saw other folks pedal beneath the bridges. But we were too busy just wandering around the canals, peeking in windows, stopping in cafes, watching cats sleep on scrubbed stone doorsteps . . . well, there's always next time. And we loved Amsterdam, so I know there'll be a next time.

ⓘ **Tourist office,** Stationsplein Perron 2B 15 (✆ **020/201-8800;** www.visitamsterdam.nl).

✈ Amsterdam Schipohl, 13km (8 miles).

🛏 $ **Amstel Botel,** Oosterdokskade 2–4 (✆ **020/626-4247;** www.amstelbotel.com). $$ **Estheréa,** Singel 303–3009 (✆ **020/624-5146;** www.estherea.nl).

WHY THEY'LL THANK YOU: 200 canals, 1,200 bridges.

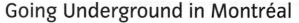

One-of-a-Kind Cityscapes

52

Going Underground in Montréal

All ages • Montréal, Canada

THERE'S MORE TO THE CITY OF MONTRÉAL than meets the eye, and in this case I mean that literally—down underneath the historic 18th- and 19th-century streets of Vieux Montréal and the office towers of modern Montréal lies **Montréal Souterrane,** a sprawling underground zone with some 1,600 shops, 200 restaurants, 6 hotels, 30 cinemas, and 10 Métro stations. It's like a lively parallel universe, a maze of corridors, tunnels, and plazas that simply cries out for children to explore.

Given the long Canadian winters and humid Québec summers, it makes perfect sense this climate-controlled underground "city" would have evolved, rising almost spontaneously in the early 1960s beneath several major downtown developments—Place Ville-Marie, Place Bonaventure, Complexe Desjardins, the Palais des Congrès, and Place des Arts. There was no master plan at work, but as these businesses flourished, other developers jumped on the trend, even when they had to build zigzag tunnels to bypass existing buildings. Even venerable Christ Church Cathedral was jacked up so that a new shopping complex could be buried beneath it. The opening of the Métro in 1966 was a huge plus—now people could

be whisked from one section to another on the subway. (Not all of the underground districts connect with pedestrian walkways, but all are linked via Métro.) Natural light streams in through skylights and atriums, eliminating that claustrophobic feeling of similar buried malls (like the one beneath Rockefeller Center in New York City, the original inspiration for La Ville Souterrane). Today there are no fewer than 32km (20 miles) of underground passageways—brightly lit, spanking clean, and always hopping with activity.

Exploring its tunnels, you'll run across all sorts of surprises. Under Place Montréal, a **fountain** sends up a 46m (151-ft.) geyser every 5 minutes; under 1000 de la Gauchtiére there's a big **ice-skating rink;** under the World Trade Centre, a section of the **Berlin Wall** is on display; under the Stock Exchange Tower, an interactive media installation called **Ars Natura** gives visitors a taste of the city's four science attractions (the Biodome, the Botanical Garden, the Insectarium, and the Planetarium). The immense **Mövenpick restaurant** at 1 Place Ville Marie is practically like a theme park, with more than a dozen cafeteria-style stations where you can buy food from around the world, everything from sushi to pastas to crêpes. Passageways lead you to Montréal's **main train station,** which has wonderful murals and a big food court; they also connect to **Bell Centre,** site of Montréal Canadiens games and big rock concerts. Not only are there several big works of **public art** underground, but the city's most prominent museum, the **Musée des Beaux-Arts,** has underground galleries. Get a map, follow the purple directional signs, or just wander at will—getting lost is half the fun.

ⓘ **Tourist office** (📞 **877/266-5687** or 514/873-2015; www.tourism-montreal.org).

✈ Montréal-Pierre-Elliott-Trudeau International, 23km (14 miles).

🛏 $$ **Delta Centre-Ville,** 777 rue University (📞 **800/268-1133** or 514/879-1370; www.deltahotels.com). $$$ **Fairmont Le Reine Elizabeth,** 900 bd. René-Lévesque oust (📞 **800/441-1414** or 514/861-3511; www.fairmont.com).

WHY THEY'LL THANK YOU: Navigating the maze.

Viva La Roma: The Eternal City

All ages • Italy

ROME IS LIKE THREE CITIES IN ONE: a sunbaked site of classical ruins; an art-saturated capital of popes and Renaissance princes; and a Fellini-esque tangle of Vespas and Fiats and *la dolce vita.* Whichever Rome you have come to see, you cannot miss the others, for all the layers of history commingle at every jog in the Roman streets.

Take, for example, the Capitoline Hill, a sacred site ever since the Etruscans built a temple to Jupiter here. After visiting the nearby **Colosseum** 🔟 , you may pop into the **Capitoline Museum** and **Palazzo dei Conservatori** to look at all their great classical sculpture. But to get there you walk through a High Renaissance masterpiece, **Piazza del Campidoglio,** the perfectly proportioned square atop the hill that was laid out by none other than Michelangelo. Also near the Colosseum, the church **San Pietro in Vincoli,** Piazza San Pietro in Vincoli 4A, off Via degli Annibaldi (📞 06-4882865), was built way back in the 5th century to house the chains that bound St. Peter in Palestine (they're preserved under glass), but its real draw is a Renaissance decoration: the tomb of Pope Julius II, with Michelangelo's famous

sculpture *Moses.* Just west of the Pantheon, **Piazza Navona** is a beautiful ocher-colored baroque plaza sitting on top of the ruins of the Stadium of Domitian (ancient Rome's main chariot-racing track); medieval popes flooded this same piazza to stage mock naval battles. In its center, Bernini's baroque **Fountain of the Four Rivers (Fontana dei Quattro Fiumi)** features four stone figures personifying great rivers on four continents: the Ganges, Danube, della Plata, and Nile. (Challenge the kids to figure out which is which.)

Speaking of fountains, join the crowds milling around the **Trevi Fountain,** another baroque gem in Piazza di Trevi, this one dominated by a triumphant Neptune bestriding a shell chariot drawn by winged steeds and a pair of Tritons. Another spot where you simply must take pictures of each other is at the flower-banked **Spanish Steps,** leading off of Piazza di Spagna.

After exploring the **Vatican** 🔟 , you can go on to **Castel Sant'Angelo,** Lungotevere Castello 50 (📞 06-6819111), for centuries Rome's chief citadel and dungeon. Built in the 2nd century as a tomb

Rome's Forum.

for Emperor Hadrian (he of Hadrian's Villa ③⑤⑦), in the Middle Ages it became a papal residence (an underground passage connects it to the Vatican). Its lushly

decorated Renaissance apartments contrast vividly with the dank prison cells where Cesare Borgia (illegitimate son of Pope Alexander VI) tortured his enemies.

Just remember: Part of enjoying Rome is slowing down and letting the cacophony swirl around you. Check out the **open-air food markets** weekday mornings in Campo de Fiori or Piazza Vittorio Emanuele, or just stop in a cafe for a cappuccino or a gelato. Drink in the experience with each of your five senses, and imagine all the generations that have made Rome their own.

ⓘ **Azienda Provinciale de Turismo,** Via Parigi 5 (𝄐 **06-36004399;** www.roma turismo.it). **Comune di Roma,** Stazione Termini (𝄐 **06-48906300**).

✈ Leonardo da Vinci International Airport (Fiumicino), 30km (19 miles).

🛏 $$$ **Hotel de Russie,** Via del Babuino 9 (𝄐 **800/323-7500** in North America, or 06-328881; www.roccofortehotels.com). $ **Hotel Grifo,** Via del Boschetto 144 (𝄐 **06-4871395**).

WHY THEY'LL THANK YOU: The glory that was—and is—Rome.

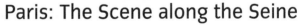

Paris: The Scene along the Seine

All ages • France

WHILE CONVENTIONAL WISDOM LABELS PARIS a city for lovers, in our experience it's even better for families. For one thing, it's a great walking city, with vibrant street life and a cool subway system. My kids love scoping out its layout, with numbered *arrondissements* and the duality of the bohemian Left Bank and bourgeois Right Bank. But the biggest surprise was how friendly those famously snooty Parisians are when you're traveling with *les enfants*. Who'd have thought?

Many of Paris's most famous sights are just that—postcard sights you can look at

without spending a franc. Take the **Eiffel Tower,** the symbol of Paris—at 317m (1,040 ft.). It can be seen over the rooftops for miles, though of course it's also fun to pay to go up its lacy iron framework, at least to the second landing, for a panoramic view. The same is true of the **Arc de Triomphe,** that grand Napoleonic boast in sculpture-laden stone at the western end of the Champs-Elysées, plopped in the middle of an impossibly frenetic traffic hub. (If you want to go inside, cross via the underground passage.) The Gothic cathedral of **Notre Dame** ③⑯ is best appreciated from outdoors, across the Seine, where you can admire its flying buttresses and sprouting gargoyles. Or you can simply roam Paris's great formal gardens, full of flowers and statuary and strolling Parisians of all ages—the **Jardin des Tuileries** on the Right Bank by the **Louvre ❸❹**, and the **Jardin du Luxembourg** on the Left Bank, where you'll also find the city's best playground.

And then there are atmospheric neighborhoods to ramble around. On the Right Bank, the narrow streets of **Le Marais** feature trendy bistros and boutiques amidst 17th-century aristocratic mansions, and **Montmartre,** the turn-of-the-century artists' quarter (think *La Boheme*), offers hilltop vistas from the Byzantine-style white basilica of **Sacré-Coeur,** place St-Pierre (✆ 01-53-41-89-00). On the Left Bank, you can visit such storied bohemian neighborhoods as the **Latin Quarter,** so named by Rabelais because students and professors from the nearby Sorbonne conversed in Latin on the streets; **Montparnasse,** where expatriate artists like Hemingway, Fitzgerald, and James Joyce enjoyed a cafe lifestyle; and **St-Germain-des-Prés,** the postwar haunt of Sartre and Camus.

My kids are fascinated by the French Revolution, so we had to visit **place de la Bastille** (the ancient prison stormed by the mob on July 14, 1789, is gone, but they like the column topped by a winged God of Liberty in the square); the **Conciergerie** prison, 1 quai de l'Horloge (✆ 01-53-40-60-93; www.monum.fr), where Marie Antoinette awaited her trial and beheading; and, at the eastern end of the Champs-Elysées, **place de la Concorde,** formerly known as Place de la Révolution, where the guillotine sliced off heads daily in front of bloodthirsty crowds. Your tastes may be different—but in Paris, there's something for everyone.

ⓘ **Paris Visitors Bureau,** 25–27 rue des Pyramides (✆ **08-92-68-30-00;** www.paris-touristoffice.com).

✈ De Gaulle, 23km (14 miles). Orly, 14km (8⅔ miles).

🛏 $$$ **Hotel de Fleurie,** 32–34 rue Grégoire-de-Tours (✆ **01-53-73-70-00;** www.hotel-de-fleurie.tm.fr). $$ **Residence Lord Byron,** 5 rue de Chateaubriand (✆ **01-43-59-89-98;** www.escapade-paris.com).

NEARBY: Le Pont Neuf ⓬, Paris Opera ❸❹❸, Notre Dame ❸❶❻, Cite des Science ❷❾❷, Catacombs & Sewers of Paris ❽❺, Fontainebleau ❸❻❻, and Versailles ❸❻❼.

WHY THEY'LL THANK YOU: They'll always have Paris.

55 **The Big City Buzz**

London: Britannia Rules

All ages • England

LONDON IS MY FAVORITE CITY in the world, and I have no idea why. It's expensive, crowded, polluted, completely illogical—and every time we plan a vacation, I vote for London first. My kids tease me about my fixation, but I've noticed they readily give in. As many times as we've gone, they still haven't exhausted its charms.

Visiting with kids, you're practically obligated to ride a red double-decker bus, take a black taxicab, and travel at least once on the Underground. But walking is our preferred way to explore London's densely packed sprawl. In half a day, you can stroll past all the major postcard sights, starting with **Trafalgar Square,** a plaza full of sculpture and pigeons around a towering column honoring British naval hero Admiral Nelson. The **National Gallery,** on the square's north side, is a superb art museum, but my children prefer the **National Portrait Gallery** around the corner at St. Martin's Place (℡ 020/7306-0055; www.npg.org.uk), a chronological series of portraits of kings, statesmen, authors, and scientists (a good place to brush up on British history). Swing north to see **Piccadilly Circus,** London's equivalent of Times Square; then head back down Haymarket and follow the Mall to **Buckingham Palace** (the bearskin-helmeted guards change shift at 11:30am daily in summer, alternate days rest of the year; we prefer not to battle the crowds for this hokey event). Double back through green **St. James Park** to Parliament Square, where you can see the famous brown Gothic revival towers of **Westminster Palace,** where Britain's Parliament sits. (Big Ben, by the way, isn't the name of the tower, or its huge four-faced clock, but its massive chiming bell, which sounds the time every 15 min.) **Westminster Abbey** (℡ 020/7654-4900; www.westminster-abbey.org), where most British monarchs have been crowned and many buried, is across Parliament Square. If you're lucky, the kids will linger over the tablets honoring great British writers in Poet's Corner.

Another day, you could roam around **Hyde Park,** Henry VIII's former deer-hunting ground laid out like a rolling patch of English countryside smack dab in the middle of the city (in adjoining **Kensington Gardens,** we love the spritely statue of Peter Pan alongside the Long Water), then go south into the Knightsbridge neighborhood to shop at **Harrod's** department store with its awesome Food Halls. Animal lovers can devote a day to the venerable **London Zoo,** Regent's Park (℡ 020/7722-3333; www.londonzoo.co.uk) or the **London Aquarium,** Westminster Bridge Road (℡ 020/7967-8000; www.londonaquarium.co.uk). We're partial to the shops, stalls, and pubs of the old open-air market **Covent Garden,** where the kids enjoy the **Transport Museum,** Covent Garden Piazza (℡ 020/7379-6344; www.ltmuseum.co.uk), and the **Theatre Museum,** 1 E. Tavistock St. And if you must, do the cheesy tourist things: **Madame Tussaud's** wax museum at Marylebone Road (℡ 0870/400-3000; www.madame-tussauds.com) and the ghoulish **London Dungeon,** 28–344 Tooley St. (℡ 020/7403-7221; www.thedungeons.com).

ⓘ **Visit London Tourist Board,** Stag Place, Victoria, London (℡ **020/7932-200,** or 090/6866-3344 in the UK; www.visitbritain.com).

✈ Heathrow, 24km (15 miles).

🛏 $$ **Hart House Hotel,** 51 Gloucester Place, Marylebone (℡ **020/7935-2288;** www.harthouse.co.uk). $$ **Vicarage Private Hotel,** 10 Vicarage Gate, South Kensington (℡ **020/7229-4030;** www.londonvicarage hotel.com).

NEARBY: The British Museum **183**, Tower of London **360**, The Science Museum & Natural History Museum **290**, Tower Bridge **15**, Imperial War Museum/Cabinet War Rooms **274**, Geffrye Museum **214**, Shakespeare's Globe Theatre **352**, The *Golden Hinde* **266**.

WHY THEY'LL THANK YOU: London still swings.

Big Ben & the Palace of Westminster.

Manhattan
A Kid-Sized Slice of the Big Apple
All ages • New York, New York, USA

I WAS 13 THE FIRST TIME I VISITED NEW YORK CITY, and I fell I love with it at once, its quirkiness and energy and the sheer size of it. I'd walk around staring up at the impossibly tall buildings, gaping at images I'd seen in countless movies and TV shows. I couldn't wait to move here. But it wasn't until I had kids that I got to know the other New York, the one where *Spider-Man* fades out and *Stuart Little* takes over. This is the Manhattan I now know and love—let me give you the key to this city.

One of the secrets is not to spend your entire time in crowded, pricey Midtown. There are three must-see sights in Midtown: the view from the top of the **Empire State Building,** Fifth Avenue & 34th Street; the sunken plaza of **Rockefeller Center,** Sixth Avenue & 47th–50th streets, where an immense gold statue of Prometheus lounges over twirling ice skaters in winter and umbrella cafe tables in summer; and **Times Square,** 42nd Street & Broadway, with its dizzying razzmatazz of neon signs and theater marquees. (A fourth must-see if you've got 'tween girls: the **American Girl Place** doll store/theater/restaurant at 609 Fifth Ave.) But after that, get out into the neighborhoods.

New York is so densely packed, there's always something interesting on the next block, and then the next. Downtown is an example—once you've started your day with the ferry trip to **The Statue of Liberty and Ellis Island** 61, it's an easy stroll through the skyscraper canyons of **Wall Street** to the historic ships and shops of **South Street Seaport,** 12 Fulton St. Let yourselves wander ever northward, through the exotic scramble of **Chinatown,** the 19th-century tenements of **Little Italy,** the hipster loft district of **Soho,** then the leafy brownstone streets of **Greenwich Village.** Who needs to pay to go into tourist attractions, when you can shop and snack and explore a kaleidoscope of cultures?

The heart of New York for kids is **Central Park,** an 840-acre island of green between the apartment buildings of the Upper West Side and the Upper East Side. For one thing, it's bookended by New York's two greatest museums—the **American Museum of Natural History** 283 and the **Metropolitan Museum of Art** 338, across the park from each other at 79th Street. Between museum visits, roam this brilliantly landscaped park, a seemingly natural countryside plunked down in the middle of the city. Near 65th Street on the east side, you can ride a vintage **carousel** and visit the **Central Park Wildlife Center;** midpark at 72nd Street is the **Lake,** with that elegant Bethesda Terrace you've seen in the movies. You'll see New York families jogging, biking, flying kites, throwing Frisbees, roller-skating, sledding, walking their dogs, playing in the playgrounds. Come join them.

ⓘ **Tourist office,** 810 Seventh Ave. (© **800/NYC-VISIT;** www.nycvisit.com).

✈ John F. Kennedy International, 15 miles. Newark Liberty International, 16 miles. LaGuardia, 8 miles.

🛏 $$ **Excelsior Hotel,** 45 W. 81st St. (© **800/368-4575** or 212/362-9200; www.excelsiorhotelny.com). $$$ **Le Parker Meridien,** 118 W. 57th St. (© **800/543-4300** or 212/245-5000; www.parkermeridien.com).

WHY THEY'LL THANK YOU: Seeing New York as New Yorkers do.

Chicago: City of the Big Shoulders

All ages • Illinois, USA

As a Midwestern teenager, Chicago was my ideal of The Big City: classic skyscrapers packed in a full-tilt downtown business district; a grand boulevard of luxury department stores and boutiques; immense museums stuffed to the gills with rarities and wonders; lavish restaurants and huge rambling hotels; trains rattling overhead on the El; and best of all, that silvery lake stretching to the horizon, pulling a wide vista of water and sky into the picture.

Now I'm a mom, and Chicago is still my ideal of The Big City—perhaps even more so now. Most of its major museums are absolutely kid-friendly—the **Shedd Aquarium** ⑭, the **Field Museum** ㉘, the **Museum of Science and Industry** ㉗, and the **Art Institute** ㉝— and three out of the four are handily located in **Grant Park,** just east of the Loop, Chicago's primary business district. (So is the **Adler Planetarium,** 1300 S. Lake Shore Dr., which has fantabulous sky shows and exhibits on the cosmos.) There's another whole cluster of attractions at **Navy Pier,** which thrusts out from the lakeshore just north of the Loop: It has many typical mall stores, but also the engaging **Chicago Children's Museum,** a flotilla of sightseeing boats, a small ice rink, an atrium of palm trees, and a 15-story Ferris wheel, a replica of the original built by George Ferris for the 1893 Chicago World's Fair. And we usually set aside a full day for rambling around Lincoln Park, which runs for miles along Lake Michigan and includes the **Lincoln Park Zoo,** 2200 N. Cannon Dr. at Fullerton Parkway, and the **Peggy Notebaert Nature Museum,** Fullerton Avenue and Cannon Drive, a hands-on environmental museum built into the slope of an overgrown sand dune. Just south of Lincoln Park is our favorite offbeat museum, the **International Museum of Surgical Science,** 1524 N. Lake Shore Dr., a gross-out experience that my teens lap up eagerly.

But beyond all this—and of course the obligatory excursions to **Wrigley Field** ㊌ and the **Brookfield Zoo** ⑬— we love just walking around Chicago. The Loop is like an open-air museum of classic skyscraper architecture, where we wander with necks craned, peering upward; Michigan Avenue is my absolute favorite shopping street in the world, with its prosperous wide sidewalks and great range of stores. My daughter, of course, insists we stop at **American Girl Place,** 111 E. Chicago Ave., while the boys demand **Niketown,** 669 N. Michigan Ave. One last special place for us: the Gothic-style **Tribune Tower** at the foot of Michigan Avenue, with 138 chunks of stone from famous buildings around the world plastered into the facade at street level. I don't know why we always have to visit this spot, but it makes us happy.

So Chicago has that going for it, which is nice.

ⓘ **Tourist office** (✆ **877/CHICAGO** or 312/744-2400; www.cityofchicago.org).

✈ O'Hare International, 15 miles.

🛏 $$ **Homewood Suites,** 40 E. Grand St. (✆ **800/CALL-HOME** or 312/644-2222; www.homewoodsuites chicago.com). $$ **Hotel Allegro Chicago,** 171 N. Randolph St. (✆ **800/643-1500** or 312/236-0123; www.allegrochicago.com).

WHY THEY'LL THANK YOU: The child-friendliest Big City I know.

Hong Kong: The Old Crown Colony

Ages 6 & up • China

I'VE ALWAYS THOUGHT OF HONG KONG as a sort of magic portal into the Far East. This former British Crown colony is a great place to let children dip a toe into Asian culture, with English spoken everywhere and modern creature comforts at hand. In this compact, teeming metropolis, wooden boats bob in the harbor beside ocean liners, crumbling tenements lean against modern high-rises, and rickshaws trundle past gleaming Rolls-Royces. For sheer assault on the senses, it's a unique and unforgettable experience.

There are a handful of tourist attractions here that kids will adore: over on the Kowloon peninsula, the **Hong Kong Space Museum,** in the waterfront Hong Kong Cultural Complex, 10 Salisbury Rd.; the hands-on **Hong Kong Science Museum,** 2 Science Museum Rd.; and the **Hong Kong Museum of History,** 100 Chatham Rd., a dynamic series of dioramas, replicas, scale models, and reconstructions that draw kids into the multilayered chapters of Hong Kong's history. You'll score big points for taking them to **Ocean Park,** on the southern shore of Hong Kong Island, a marvelous combination amusement park and aquarium—where you can see a giant panda, ride a looping roller coaster, and follow a glass tunnel through a tank of sharks all in the same afternoon.

But to get at the essence of Hong Kong, there are three activities you should not pass up. The classic is the green-and-white **Star Ferry,** a 5-minute ride between Kowloon and Hong Kong Island's Central District that surveys a glorious panorama of bustling Hong Kong Harbor. On Hong Kong Island, take the 8-minute ride on the **Peak tram**—the world's steepest funicular railway—to the top of Victoria Peak, where there are

spectacular views of the city below. The modern **Peak Tower** has a viewing terrace, as well as the obligatory set of tourist traps—a Madame Tussaud's, Ripley's Believe It or Not!, and the motion-simulator theater Peak Explorer. Don't leave without also walking around the lush cliffside footpaths. Victoria Peak is an exclusive residential enclave, where the expat British vibe is still strong; for more exotic Asian atmosphere, ride the rickety old **double-decker trams** around the northern end of Hong Kong Island. From your upper deck seats, you'll see laundry hanging from second-story windows, signs swinging over the street, markets twisting down side alleys. Jump off at Des Vouex Street and Morrison Road to browse the atmospheric shopping streets of the Western District—Hillier Street, Bonham Strand, Man Wa Lane. At Des Vouex Road and Queen Victoria Street, the kids will get a kick out of taking a zigzagging series of escalators to the Mid-Levels of Victoria Peak; it takes 20 minutes to go up, but be prepared to walk back down!

(i) **Tourist office,** Causeway Bay MTR station (near Exit F; © **852/2508 1234;** www.discoverhongkong.com).

✈ Hong Kong International, 32km (20 miles).

🛏 $$ **BP International House,** 8 Austin Rd., Kowloon (© **800/223-5652** or 852/ 2376 1111; www.bpih.com.hk). $ **The Salisbury YMCA,** Salisbury Rd., Kowloon (© **800/537-8483** or 852/2268 7000; www.ymcahk.org.hk).

WHY THEY'LL THANK YOU: Dim sum meets afternoon tea.

Tokyo: Feeling the Pulse of the Far East

Ages 6 & up • Japan

VISITING TOKYO IS A YIN-YANG SORT OF EXPERIENCE: One day you're steeped in an ancient culture of shoguns and samurai, the next day you're plunged into the rhythms of a high-tech modern metropolis. But kids don't experience it as a clash of cultures—they've seen enough anime to feel right at home with that half-ninja/half-Nintendo sensibility. Follow their lead and you'll find it endlessly fascinating.

For vestiges of old Tokyo—known as Edo—stroll around the **Asakusa district.** Enter through a bright-red torii gate and walk up Nakamise Dori, a pedestrian lane lined with traditional shops; at the lane's end is the revered **Sensoji Temple,** which dates back to 628, though today's version is a reconstruction of the original, destroyed by bombing in 1945. Through the red-and-gold pagoda on the left of Nakamise Dori you can enter the hidden **Demboin Garden,** a peaceful oasis. The old shogun-era Edo Castle is on the grounds of the **Imperial Palace,** Hibiya Dori Avenue, Chiyoda-Ku, home of Emperor Akihito, 125th emperor of Japan. Most of the palace grounds are closed to the public, but a camera shot from the southeast side of Nijubashi Bridge will catch the moat and the palace turrets above the trees.

Head for the Harajuku district to see the venerated **Meiji Jingu Shrine,** 1–1 Kamizono-cho, Yoyogi, with two immense torii built of ancient cypress. But the kids will be more intrigued by the nearby shopping streets, packed—especially on Sunday afternoons—with teenagers shopping for trendy clothes, where fractured English mottoes and cartoon icons express a global teen-speak. Another mandatory destination for older kids is Odaiba, a tract of reclaimed land in Tokyo Bay connected to the mainland by the colorful Rainbow Bridge. Top stops here

are the technology playground **Megaweb** at 1 Aomi, the **Ferris wheel** next door, and the **National Museum of Emerging Science and Innovation,** 2–41 Aomi (✆ 03/3570-9151; www.miraikan.jst.go.jp), a fabulous hands-on exploratorium of cutting-edge science and technology, full of robots, touch-screen displays, virtual-reality rides, and a planetarium.

You could spend a full day at Ueno Park, a museum mecca in northeast Tokyo. Its **Tokyo National Museum** (✆ 03/3822-1111; www.tnm.jp) bursts at the seams with old kimono, samurai armor, priceless swords, Buddhist sculptures, lacquerware, woodblock prints, calligraphy, ceramics, even an Egyptian mummy; kids also love Ueno's **National Science Museum** (✆ 03/3822-0111; www.kahaku.go.jp/english), with its dinosaur displays, hands-on discovery room, re-created nature habitats, an exhibit illustrating 4 billion years of evolution, and an entire arena of 100-some stuffed animals from around the world. The small 17th-century **Toshugu Shrine** honors Tokugawa Ieyasu, founder of the shogunate that made Edo the most important city in Japan; Ueno also contains the 17th-century **Kiyomizu Kannon-do Temple,** where mothers have left hundreds of dolls as symbols of their children, asking for protection from the goddess of childbirth and child-raising. The **Ueno Park Zoo** is small but popular.

Spread-out Tokyo is tricky to navigate—I advise you to get acquainted with Tokyo's swift, ultramodern subway system. A few other only-in-Tokyo experiences: a nighttime look at **Shibuya Crossing,** where the signs are even more dazzling than in Times Square or Piccadilly Circus; **sumo** matches, January, May, and September at the Kokugikan,

Tsukiji Fish Market.

1–3–28 Yokoami, Sumida-ku (✆ **03/ 3623-5111**); and an early-morning expedition to the cavernous **Tsukiji Fish Market,** 5–2–1 Tsukiji, Chuo-ku, where a dizzying variety of seafood, fresh and glistening right off the boats, is bought and sold from 4:40 to 6:30am. Men in black rubber boots rush wheelbarrows through the aisles, hawkers shout, knives chop and slice—it's an almost hallucinatory experience.

ⓘ **Tourist Information Center,** 2–10–1 Yurakucho (✆ **03/3201-3331;** www.jnto. go.jp).

✈ Narita International, 63km (39 miles).

🛏 $$$ **Imperial Hotel,** 1–1–1 Uchisaiwaicho, Chiyoda-ku (✆ **800/223-6800** in the U.S. and Canada, or 03/3504-1111; www.imperialhotel.co.jp). $ **Sakura Ryokan,** 2-6-2 Iriya, Taito-ku (✆ **03/3876-8118;** www.sakura-ryokan.com).

NEARBY: Edo-Tokyo Museum **218**, Ghibli Museum **356**.

WHY THEY'LL THANK YOU: Something old, something new.

60 Postcards across America

Boston Common
New England's Ultimate Town Green
All ages • Massachusetts, USA

THE OLDEST PUBLIC PARK in the United States, **Boston Common** (bordered by Beacon, Park, Tremont, Boylston, and Charles sts.) is a multilayered slice of history, nestled in the shadow of skyscrapers at the heart of one of America's first great cities. Standing on this sloping, tree-strewn 45-acre space, imagine what it looked like when the town fathers purchased it in 1634, when their settlement was just 4 years old and most folks needed a spot to graze their household cows and sheep. The occupying British army encamped here in the restless months leading up to the outbreak of the Revolutionary War; public gallows stood here until 1817; Martin Luther King, Jr., and Pope John Paul II both spoke here. It's Boston's living room, pulsing with the life of the city.

Many visitors confuse the rambling Common with its neighbor, the more sprucely landscaped **Public Garden,** the country's first botanical garden, where the famous swan boats glide over a man-made pond and a popular set of bronze statues commemorate the classic children's book *Make Way for Ducklings*. The Public Garden is lovely, yes, but there's something quintessentially American about Boston Common, despite the occasional bald patches of ground. It's always lively with picnickers, Frisbee and softball games, kite flyers, and busking musicians. The Frog Pond, where there really were frogs at one time, makes a pleasant spot to splash around in the summer and skate in the winter. At the Boylston Street side, the **Central Burying Ground** contains the grave of famed portraitist Gilbert Stuart; free concerts and plays are held at the bandstand. The aristocratic brick town houses of **Beacon Hill** overlook the Common along its north side, and the gold dome of the State House presides over the east end (note the eccentric codfish weather vane on top). On the Beacon Street edge of the Common, across from the State House, a stunning **memorial** designed by Augustus Saint-Gaudens honors Bostonian Col. Robert Gould Shaw and the Union Army's 54th Massachusetts Colored Regiment, the first American army unit made up of free black soldiers, celebrated in the 1989 movie *Glory*. And lest we get too historic, we should also mention the irresistibly touristy **Cheers,** 84 Beacon St. (*©* **617/227-9605;** www.cheers boston.com), originally the Bull & Finch Pub; the kids may recognize its exterior from Nick at Nite reruns of *Cheers* (a replica of the TV set is at Faneuil Hall Marketplace).

The Common is, appropriately enough, the starting point for the **Freedom Trail** (*©* **617/357-8300;** www.thefreedom trail.org), a historic 3-mile walking route (follow a red line painted on the sidewalks); maps are available at the **visitor information booth** on Tremont Street. My kids enjoy its connect-the-dots approach to sightseeing every bit as much as I did as a child. A hard-core history fiend can easily spend 4 hours along the trail, but a family with restless children can easily do it in less—especially since you can quit at any point. (Just don't miss the **Paul Revere House,** at 19 North Square, one of my childhood favorites.)

(i) **Greater Boston Convention & Visitors Bureau,** Two Copley Place (*©* **888/SEE-BOSTON** or 617/536-4100; www.boston usa.com).

✈ Boston's Logan Airport.

⊨ $$ **Doubletree Guest Suites,** 400 Soldiers Field Rd. (*©* **800/222-TREE** or 617/783-0090; www.doubletree.com). $ **The MidTown Hotel,** 220 Huntington Ave. (*©* **800/343-1177** or 617/262-1000).

NEARBY: Black Heritage Trail ❷❹❺, Boston Aquarium ❶❹⓿, Old Ironsides ❷❻❽, Fenway Park ❹❺❸.

WHY THEY'LL THANK YOU: Picnic and frolic in the shadow of 3½ centuries of history.

The Paul Revere House.

The Statue of Liberty & Ellis Island
Gateway to America
Ages 6 & up • New York, New York, USA

THE ICON TO END ALL ICONS, New York City's awe-inspiring Statue of Liberty is recognizable around the world as the symbol of American freedom. What's more, this is the city's greatest two-for-one deal: The same ferryboat takes you to the Ellis Island Immigration Museum, which turns out to be the real kid pleaser of the pair.

The Statue of Liberty (or, as she is officially known, Liberty Enlightening the World) is impressive enough from across the harbor, but close up—man, this chick is BIG. Don't be surprised if your young ones feel overwhelmed; even adults can get vertigo staring up her stately toga-clad physique. Lady Liberty weighs in at 225 tons of hammered copper, oxidized as planned to a delicate pale green, and her nose alone is 4½ feet long. Given to the United States by France, she has presided over the harbor since 1886. At present visitors cannot climb up inside the statue, but **ranger-led tours** (📞 **866/782-8834** or 212/269-5755 from outside U.S.; www.statuereservations. com) explore the promenade or go to the 10th floor observatory for fascinating historic exhibits and a peek through a glass ceiling into her ingenious steel skeleton, designed by Gustave Eiffel of Eiffel Tower fame. Even if you don't have a tour reservation, it's worth the trip to stroll around Liberty Island and gaze out over the harbor.

From the mountain of ragtag luggage stacked right inside the front doors, upstairs to the cramped dormitories and medical examination rooms (cough the wrong way and you could be sent right back to Europe), to glass cases crammed with the family heirlooms immigrants brought with them, the **Ellis Island Immigration Museum** brings history to life. Prepare to be awed by the second-floor Registry Hall, its soaring vaulted ceiling faced with white tile, where new arrivals shuffled along in tediously long lines to be interviewed by immigration officials. (Cue up the theme from *The Godfather, Part II.*) On the Wall of Honor outside, some 420,000 immigrants' names are inscribed in steel. There are hands-on exhibits, films, live plays, computer stations where you can examine ship manifests—2 hours is barely enough to do this place justice.

Both sights are free, though you'll have to pay for the boat over. Ferryboats make frequent trips, running a 35-minute loop from Battery Park to Liberty Island to Ellis Island and back to Battery Park (from New Jersey you can board ferries in Liberty State Park).

ⓘ **Statue of Liberty,** Liberty Island (📞 **212/363-3200;** www.nps.gov/stli). **Ellis Island** (📞 **212/363-3200;** www.ellisisland. org). **Ferry** (📞 **855/STATUE4;** www. statuereservations.com).

✈ ⇌ See Manhattan ❺❻.

WHY THEY'LL THANK YOU: America's beacon to the world still shines here.

Philadelphia: Cradle of Liberty

All ages • Pennsylvania, USA

IT'S NO EXAGGERATION to call this the most historic square mile in America, the very place where the Declaration of Independence was signed and the Constitution of the United States hammered out. The look is tidy and stereotypical, steepled red-brick buildings with neat white porticos. Yet there's nothing tidy about what happened here—it took enormous courage for these British colonists to leap off this cliff—and when you see your child's eyes light up, realizing that these were real people and not just Faces on the Money, that's when you'll be glad you came to Philadelphia.

The focal point of Independence National Historical Park is **Independence Hall,** Chestnut Street between 5th and 6th streets, where in a chamber known as the Pennsylvania Assembly Room, the Second Continental Congress convened in May 1775. Virginian Thomas Jefferson was assigned to write a document setting forth the colonists' grievances (Jefferson worked on it while boarding at **Graff House,** nearby at 7th and Market sts.), and by July 4, 1776, the Declaration of Independence was ready to be signed by the Congress—in Independence Hall you can even see the silver inkwell they used. You can also see the Rising Sun Chair that George Washington sat in 11 years later to preside over the Constitutional Convention, as President of the new United States. In a glass pavilion next door rests the 2,000-pound **Liberty Bell,** which was rung in 1776 at the first public reading of the Declaration; circle around it to find the famous crack up its side, which has been there since it was cast in 1751. At the northern end of grassy Independence Mall, the modern **National Constitution Center,** 525 Arch St., is so darn interactive, the children may not even notice how educational it is—you can take your own Presidential Oath of Office or try on a Supreme Court robe. In Signers Hall, bronze life-size statues depict the delegates who signed the Declaration—putting faces to those famous signatures was enormously satisfying.

A couple blocks east of the Mall, **Franklin Court,** Chestnut Street between 3rd and 4th streets, has some lively multimedia exhibits on the life and career of Philadelphia's most famous citizen, scientist/publisher/inventor/philosopher Benjamin Franklin. (You'll find more of the same out at the science museum **The Franklin Institute 286.**) But the most evocative colonial home here is the tiny **Betsy Ross House,** 239 Arch St., where a widowed Quaker seamstress supposedly sewed the first American flag. No one knows for sure if she really sewed it, or if this was even her house, but it makes a great story; and the house is so quaint, you'll want to believe it.

ⓘ **Visitor Center,** 6th and Market sts. (ⓒ **800/537-7676** or 215/965-7676; www.independencevisitorcenter.com).

✈ Philadelphia International.

🛏 $$ **Best Western Independence Park Inn,** 235 Chestnut St. (ⓒ **800/624-2988** or 215/922-4443; www.independenceparkhotel.com). $$$ **Rittenhouse Hotel,** 210 W. Rittenhouse Sq. (ⓒ **800/635-1042** or 215/546-9000; www.rittenhousehotel.com).

WHY THEY'LL THANK YOU: Imagine John Hancock, dipping his quill pen in that inkwell.

Washington, D.C.
Having a Ball on the National Mall
All ages • USA

WHEN CONGRESS HIRED Frenchman Pierre L'Enfant to design a capital city for the new United States, he came back with a supremely rational plan: a grid of numbered and lettered streets laced with diagonal avenues (named after states) and punctuated with circular plazas. In a stroke of genius, L'Enfant laid at the heart of it all the National Mall, a 2½-mile-long, 300-foot-wide plain lined with neoclassical government buildings—one unbroken sweep from the dome of the Capitol to the back lawn of the White House. What I wonder is this: Did L'Enfant foresee what a great place this Mall was going to be for children?

Most buildings along the Mall these days are museums, many of them run by the Smithsonian Institution, which means free admission; you can give restless kids a chance to stretch their legs between visits to the **National Museum of the American Indian 226**, the **National Museum of Natural History 285**, or the **Air and Space Museum 296**. We also love the **National Museum of American History,** Constitution Avenue NW between 12th and 14th streets, where you can see everything from the original Star Spangled Banner to gowns worn by various First Ladies, to Julia Child's kitchen and Archie Bunker's armchair. The Rotunda of the **National Archives,** Constitution Avenue between 7th and 9th streets, displays three incredibly important (and rare) original documents: the Declaration of Independence, the Constitution, and the Bill of Rights. If admission

Detail of the Capital Dome in Washington.

© Washington, DC Convention & Tourism Corporation (WCTC)/JakeMcGuire.com hadn't been free, we'd never have coaxed the kids into the **Freer Gallery of Art,** 1050 Independence Ave. SW, where we skipped the vast collection of Asian art just to see the amazing Peacock Room designed by James Whistler.

The Mall's diversions include a 19th-century **carousel** at Jefferson Drive and the **pool** in the National Gallery's Sculpture Garden at 7th Street, where kids can splash their feet in summer and ice-skate in winter. Vendors sell ice cream and soft pretzels; families jog, bike, and fly kites. What could have been a grandiose ceremonial space becomes instead a happy picnic ground.

Visiting the **U.S. Capitol,** the Mall's eastern landmark, requires some effort; line up early at the visitor center at 1st and Independence for your timed-admission ticket for a free half-hour tour. Visiting the **White House,** at the other end, requires even more effort, beginning with a call to your congressperson 6 months in advance. But seeing the stately monuments that lie to the west requires

nothing more than hopping onto a narrated **Tourmobile** tram (② **888/868-7707** or 202/554-5100; www.tourmobile.com) and hopping off again whenever you please. We were content to do a drive-by of Lincoln's, Washington's, and Jefferson's, but we were glad we got off for the **Vietnam Memorial** to be deeply moved by endless ranks of soldiers' names, simply etched in smooth black granite.

ⓘ **Tourist office** (② **800/422-8644** or 202/789-7000; www.washington.org).

✈ Ronald Reagan Washington National, 5 miles. Dulles International, 26 miles. Baltimore-Washington International, 30 miles.

🛏 $$ **Embassy Suites Hotel Downtown,** 1250 22nd St. NW (② **800/EMBASSY** or 202/857-3388; www.embassysuitesdcmetro.com). $$$ **Hilton Washington,** 1919 Connecticut Ave. NW (② **800/HILTONS** or 202/483-3000; www.washington.hilton.com).

WHY THEY'LL THANK YOU: Seeing the national treasures.

Niagara Falls: The Big Spill

All ages • New York, USA & Ontario, Canada

EVERYONE'S SEEN A KODACHROME PHOTO of Niagara Falls, that stupendous curve of cascading water that lies between the United States and Canada. It's one of those sites, however, that postcards never do justice to: To stand on a viewing platform and see, really see, how big it is, to hear the thunder of falling water, to feel the mist spritzing your face is another thing altogether. This is a natural wonder kids love and should see.

There are actually two waterfalls here, both of them doozies: the American Falls and Horseshoe Falls. Both are around 175 feet high, although Horseshoe Falls, at 2,500 feet wide, is more than twice as wide as its sibling. The Canadian shore

has the real panoramic view; both falls can be seen from the American side, but not together (Prospect Point for the American Falls, Terrapin Point for Horseshoe Falls). The Canadian side tends to have better hotels and more attractions. No matter where you stay, you can easily visit both, by crossing the Rainbow Bridge, preferably on foot—it's only the length of a couple city blocks. Bring a passport (or a driver's license and birth certificate).

On the U.S. shore, head for **Niagara Falls State Park** (② 716/278-1796; www.niagarafallsstatepark.com) to explore the falls: An **Observation Tower** overlooks the river, and **Cave of the Winds** (② 716/278-1790) takes you down

Niagara Falls.

by elevator onto boardwalks where you can walk around the base of the American Falls. Canada's 775-foot-high **Skylon Tower,** 52 Robinson St. (☏ 905/356-2651; www.skylontower.com), has a revolving restaurant on top, and the **Journey Behind the Falls** (☏ 905/354-1551; www.niagaraparks.com), allows you to descend via elevator to tunnels punctuated with portholes that look out through the blur of water right behind Horseshoe Falls. The coolest way to see the falls, of course, is the classic *Maid of the Mist* boat ride (☏ 716/284-8897; www.maidofthemist.com), which plays no favorites; it departs from either shore. You'll chug upriver toward the American and Horseshoe Falls, sailing right up the base of both (don't worry, blue slickers are provided to keep you dry).

Want more of an adrenaline rush? Book a 10-minute helicopter ride over the cascades with **Niagara Helicopters** (☏ 905/357-5672; www.niagarahelicopters.com) or **Rainbow Air** (☏ 716/284-2800), or crash through the white waters of the Niagara gorge with **Whirlpool Jet Boat Tours** (☏ 888/438-4444 in the U.S., or 905/468-4800 in Canada; www.whirlpooljet.com). The **Great American Balloon**

Company, Rainbow Boulevard South, Niagara Falls, New York (☏ 716/278-0824) offers a gentler sky-borne view.

This being a major tourist destination, there's a ton of other attractions around, from historic old forts and botanical gardens to aquariums and amusement parks. But overdeveloped as it may be, the spectacular Falls are still there.

ⓘ U.S. (☏ **800/338-7890** or 716/282-8992; www.niagara-usa.com). Canada (☏ **800/563-2557;** www.niagarafalls tourism.com).

✈ Buffalo Niagara International Airport, 34km (21 miles).

🛏 $$ **Courtyard by Marriott,** 5950 Victoria Ave., Niagara Falls, Ontario, Canada (☏ **800/321-2211** or 905/358-3083; www.nfcourtyard.com). $$$ **Red Coach Inn,** 2 Buffalo Ave., Niagara Falls, NY, USA (☏ **800/282-1459** or 716/282-1459; www.redcoach.com).

BEST TIME: May–Oct.

WHY THEY'LL THANK YOU: Roaring water, mist, and rainbows galore.

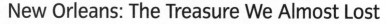

New Orleans: The Treasure We Almost Lost

All ages • Louisiana, USA

FOR SOME PEOPLE, it took a hurricane for them to realize they should have visited New Orleans. Here was a true original among American cities, a place where people danced with parasols at funerals, ate beignets and po' boys, believed in voodoo and vampires, and threw plastic beads off parade floats. Despite its raunchy Bourbon Street reputation, it was always a great family destination. Even in the Mississippi Delta heat (and every time I've been there it was sweltering hot), something about New Orleans always seemed laid-back and incredibly cool, darlin'. And Hurricane Katrina *nearly wiped it off the face of the earth.*

Luckily, the reports of New Orleans's demise were premature—though damaged, New Orleans is still very much with us, and open again for business. You've been given a second chance. Take it *now.*

The part of New Orleans least affected by the disaster was its prime tourist area: the **French Quarter,** one of the few areas that had been built above river level and escaped heavy flooding. The French Quarter—or as local signs have it, the Vieux Carré—is, despite the name, a Spanish-flavored fantasy of wrought-iron balconies and tiny flower-filled courtyards and alluring louvered windows, its center-piece being gardenlike Jackson Square. Just walking around here is entertain-ment, but several attractions are espe-cially appealing to families: the touristy-but-fun **Historic Voodoo Museum,** 724 Dumaine St.; the kitschy **Musée Conti Wax Museum,** 917 Conti St.; the **Old U.S. Mint,** 400 Esplanade

Ave., which despite the name is all about New Orleans jazz history and Mardi Gras traditions; and the open-air **French Mar-ket,** Decatur Street, from Jackson Square to Esplanade Avenue, where you can buy snacks like gator on a stick. Really.

By the time you read this, the historic St. Charles Streetcar will probably be clanking along again; it goes from the Quarter to the **Audubon Zoo** at 6500 Magazine St., which displays 1,800 ani-mals among lush subtropical plantings and a replica of a Louisiana swamp (dig the white alligator). Right on the banks of the Mississippi, the **Audubon Aquarium of the Americas,** 1 Canal St., is a world-class facility with exhibits of penguins, sharks, a coral reef, a rainforest, and a swamp. And though Mardi Gras itself may be overwhelming to children, they can get an eyeful of floats and larger-than-life character sculptures at **Blaine Kern's Mardi Gras World,** 223 Newton St., Algiers Point; they can even try on some fabulous costumes.

ⓘ **Tourist office,** 2020 St. Charles Ave. (✆ **800/672-6124** or 504/566-5011; www.neworleanscvb.com).

✈ Louis Armstrong New Orleans Interna-tional, 15 miles.

🛏 $$ **Hotel Monteleone,** 214 Rue Royale (✆ **800/535-9595** or 504/523-3341; www.hotelmonteleone.com). $$$ **Omni Royal Orleans,** 621 St. Ouis St. (✆ **800/ THE-OMNI** or 504/529-5333; www.omni royalorleans.com).

WHY THEY'LL THANK YOU: They'll know what it means to love New Orleans.

The Gateway Arch: Threshold to the West

All ages • St. Louis, Missouri, USA

AMERICA'S TALLEST MONUMENT, this graceful rainbow of stainless steel soars 630 feet above downtown St. Louis, right beside the Mississippi River. This great muddy river has always symbolized the divide between East and West in America, and crossing the Mississippi was a momentous step for pioneers heading west in the 1800s. Today, jetting effortlessly from coast to coast, we tend to forget the effort it took to settle this enormous continent. Standing here on the west bank of the Mississippi, poised between two bridges, Eero Saarinen's tapering curve of steel beckons dreamers westward all over again.

You can chug to the top of the Arch for incredible views, riding a **tram** system that's a marvel of engineering in itself (just think about it: no ordinary elevator could climb this curving shaft). You could fit two Statues of Liberty **61** on each other's shoulders beneath the arch, and if the Presidents on Mount Rushmore **95** had bodies to match their giant heads, they could still walk under it without stooping.

Order tickets in advance online or buy them early in the day to save a long wait at peak seasons; while you're hanging around waiting for your assigned tram, browse through the **Jefferson National Expansion Memorial** underground below the Arch, with IMAX films and exhibits about the Lewis and Clark expedition and frontier settlement—highlights include a Native American teepee and a typical Great Plains sod house. A pair of paddle-wheel **riverboats** (named Tom

Sawyer and Becky Thatcher, naturally) leave from a dock beside the Arch for 1-hour river tours.

St. Louis is a great city for families, with many free sights to visit. Downtown's **Union Station** was once the nation's busiest rail hub, a gateway to the west for the railroad era. It has been restored into a bustling mall with over 80 shops and even a small lake with paddle boats. West of downtown in huge Forest Park, site of the 1904 World Fair, there are a fine **zoo** (© **314/781-0990**; www.stlzoo.org) and the **St. Louis Science Center,** 5050 Oakland Ave. (© **800/456-7572** or 314/289-4444; www.slsc.org). Southwest of town is **Grant's Farm,** 10501 Gravois (© **314/843-1700**; www.grantsfarm.com, open mid-Apr to Oct), once farmed by Ulysses Grant himself and now owned by the Busch family, which means there's a stableful of Clydesdales along with a zoo, animal shows, and an exotic game preserve.

ⓘ 707 N. 1st St. (© **877/982-1410**; www.gatewayarch.com).

✈ Lambert–St. Louis International, 13 miles.

🛏 $$ **Drury Inn Union Station,** 201 S. 20th St. (© **800/378-7946** or 314/231-3900; www.druryinn.com). $$$ **Embassy Suites,** 901 N. 1st St. (© **800/362-2779** or 314/241-4200; www.embassysuites.com).

WHY THEY'LL THANK YOU: The West starts here.

San Antonio River Walk: Southwest Fiesta

All ages • Texas, USA

JUST A FEW STEPS BELOW THE STREETS of downtown San Antonio—Texas's most-visited city, if not its biggest—lies another world: River Walk, a cobblestoned 3-mile promenade along a horseshoe loop of the San Antonio River, landscaped with flowers and shaded by native cypresses, oaks, and willows. If, as some say, San Antonio preserves the soul of Texas, then River Walk is the soul of San Antonio. Walking along it, the Southwest vibe is irresistible.

Funny to think that River Walk almost was wiped out; in the 1920s the city considered paving over the San Antonio River to eliminate flooding. Other flood-control plans prevailed, however, and after the 1968 HemisFair exposition, celebrating the 250th anniversary of San Antonio's founding, a spruced-up River Walk proved so popular that the city fathers pushed for further beautification. Since then commercial development may have jumped the shark somewhat, turning stretches of the River Walk into a slick festival mall. Tour boats, water taxis, and floating picnic barges ply the river from its docks, and revelers crowd its banks and arched bridges in high season, especially during San Antonio's annual Fiesta (the third week in Apr). But kids tend to like this sort of hustle and bustle, and if they do go on overload, you're only a short walk away from riverbank oases of calm.

One of River Walk's obvious pluses is its proximity to San Antonio's top historic attraction, **The Alamo** ❷❻❷. For families, another plus is sprawling **HemisFair Park,** east of Alamo Street behind the convention center, where there are water gardens and a playground and the observation deck of the Tower of America. Turn up Navarro and Alamo streets and you'll get an adobe-styled look at the city's early-19th-century Spanish past, in **La Villita National Historic District.** Though trendy boutiques, crafts shops, and restaurants now occupy these villagelike blocks, their shaded patios, plazas, brick-and-tile streets, and original adobe structures make it a good place for the kids to absorb a little historic atmosphere.

River Walk has its share of packaged commercial attractions, too—the **Rivercenter Mall,** with an IMAX theater and 130 stores; a cluster of chain tourist draws including Ripley's Believe It or Not and a Guinness World Records Museum at **Alamo Square;** and plenty of restaurants, shops, and clubs. There's no shortage of things to do, and places to spend your money. And of course, the kids will beg you to drive out to **Sea World,** 10500 SeaWorld Dr. (✆ **800/700-7786;** www.seaworld.com) and/or **Six Flags Fiesta Texas,** 17000 I-10W and Loop 1604 (✆ **800/473-4378** or 210/697-5050; www.sixflags.com/parks/fiestatexas).

ⓘ ✆ **210/227-4262;** www.thesanantonio riverwalk.com.

✈ San Antonio International, 13 miles.

🛏 $$ **Crockett Hotel,** 320 Bonham St. (✆ **800/292-1050** or 210/225-6500; www.crocketthotel.com).

WHY THEY'LL THANK YOU: That fiesta atmosphere is contagious.

The Cable Car Hills of San Francisco

All ages • California, USA

MAYBE IT WAS ALL THOSE RICE-A-RONI® COMMERCIALS from my childhood, but I get a thrill when I hear the clang-clang of a **San Francisco cable car.** These beloved wooden icons, the only moving landmarks in the National Register of Historic Places, are absurdly impractical; San Francisco had nearly torn up all the tracks in 1947 until a public outcry saved the last three lines. And now, whaddya know, they are San Francisco's most iconic attraction, the one must-do for every visitor.

San Francisco's steep hills are notorious; it's a great location for filming car chases (remember *Bullitt*?) but a challenging place for everyone else. In 1869 engineer Andrew Hallidie watched a team of overworked horses pulling a heavy carriage up a rain-slicked San Francisco hill and resolved to invent a mechanical device to replace the beasts; in 1873 the first cable car traversed Clay Street. They really are ingenious: An electrically powered steel cable under the street constantly moves at 9½ mph, which each car clamps onto with an underground grip to get hauled along (operators are thus called "grippers," not drivers). Listen for the distinctive underground clickity-clack of the cable. Daredevils choose to ride in the open-air sections, not the enclosed seating areas, standing up and hanging onto a strap, which at under 10 mph isn't as perilous as it sounds.

Two cable car routes start at the intersection of Powell and Market

streets: The **Powell-Hyde line** ends at the turnaround in a waterfront park by Ghirardelli Square, and the **Powell-Mason line** meanders through North Beach to end on the east side of Fisherman's Wharf. The Powell-Hyde line has the steepest climbs and drops, if that's what you're interested in; take it from Market Street north, past crooked Lombard Street on your right before heading down Russian Hill with a breathtaking vista of **Alcatraz** **89** and the San Francisco Bay. The **California Street line** runs east–west from Market and California streets over Nob Hill to Van Ness Avenue. Queues to board the Powell Street cars at either end seem endless, but there are strategies to avoid them: Ride at less-popular night hours, jump on at an intermediate stop (this is iffy in high season, when cars get so full that they can't pick up passengers en route), or board at Powell and Market rather than the crowded turnarounds near Fisherman's Wharf (for the California line, the Van Ness end is less crowded). But we waited for over an hour at the Ghiradelli Square terminus and actually had fun— street musicians played, tourists swapped travel tips, and we could watch three or four cars pivot grandly around on the turntables. After that long wait, the ride seemed surprisingly short, but no one in my family complained.

ⓘ **San Francisco Municipal Railway** (𝄢 **405/673-6864;** www.sfmuni.com).

A San Francisco cable car.

Convention & Visitors' Bureau, 900 Market St. (© **415/391-2000;** http://onlysf.sfvisitor.org).

$$$ **The Argonaut,** 495 Jefferson St. (© **866/415-0704** or 415/563-0800; www.argonauthotel.com). $$ **Cartwright Hotel,** 24 Sutter St. (© **800/227-3844** or 415/421-2865; www.cartwrighthotel.com).

WHY THEY'LL THANK YOU: The San Francisco treat.

Chapter 3 Weird & Wonderful

Otherworldly Landscapes . . . 82
Atmospheric Places to Explore . . . 97
A Touch of Kitsch . . . 104
Caves & Waterfalls . . . 119

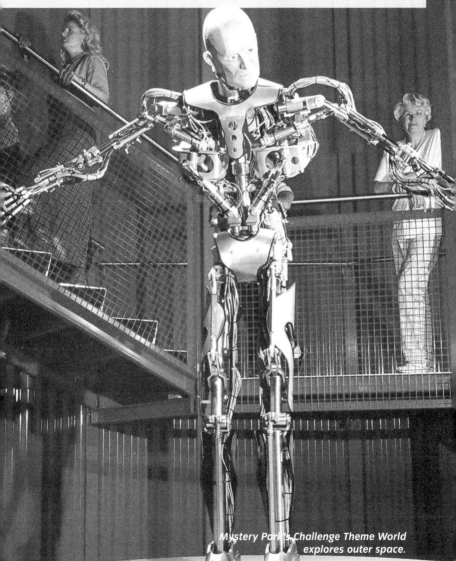

Mystery Park's Challenge Theme World explores outer space.

Devil's Tower
Something Strange in Wyoming
All ages • Devil's Tower, Wyoming, USA

I KNEW MY KIDS WOULD LOVE THE SCENE in *Close Encounters of the Third Kind* when Richard Dreyfuss starts sculpting Devil's Tower out of mashed potatoes. Spielberg sure picked the right natural landing pad for his alien spaceship to make contact with earthlings—there *is* something otherworldly about this stark monolith rising out of the Wyoming pines and prairies. The Northern Plains Indians called it Bears Lodge, and it has sacred meanings for them too. Even seeing a picture of it is unforgettable, but visiting Devil's Tower in person—well, that's more special than you'd imagine.

Time for a geology lesson. Devil's Tower is what's known as an igneous intrusion, meaning that it's a column of rock hardened by molten lava that seeped long ago into a vein of sedimentary rock. A shallow sea once covered this part of the Great Plains, and most of the rock is soft sedimentary stuff like red sandstone and siltstone, with a thin shale mixed in. The flat-topped cone that became Devil's Tower used to be under that sea, but once the waters had receded, centuries of erosion gradually wore away the softer rock around the igneous cone, leaving it exposed. Today the cone thrusts 1,267 feet above the surrounding pine trees and prairie grasslands. That flat top no doubt gave Spielberg the idea of an extraterrestrials' spaceport; a parachutist did land on top in 1941, drawing great publicity—especially since he then had to figure out how to get down! Vertical cracks groove the sides of the tower in almost parallel columns, giving it its distinctive furrowed look. It's well-nigh irresistible for climbers, although you must register at the visitor's center before attempting to ascend and follow strict regulations about bolts and drills. In deference to the Native American reverence for this sacred place, the park's staff urges climbers to voluntarily forego climbing in June, a month with many religious ceremonies for the local tribes.

For most of us, the best way to experience Devil's Tower is to take the 1.3-mile paved **Tower Trail** that circles around the base. It's very kid-friendly, being mostly flat (after a steep climb at the start) with benches and interpretive stations along the way. Take your time walking so that you can examine this rugged pinnacle from every angle and in different lights. Bring sketchbooks and try to draw its stern majesty. And don't be surprised if the kids start mounding their mashed potatoes at dinner that night, tracing ridges on the sides with their forks . . .

While you're here, kids shouldn't miss the **prairie dog towns** on the park's east road, where black-tailed prairie dogs scamper about, popping in and out of their subterranean condos. You came out here to see the West—well, this is about as Western as it gets.

Devil's Tower.

ⓘ Off U.S. 14 (ⓒ **307/467-5283;** www. nps.gov/deto).

✈ Gillette Airport, 40 miles.

🛏 See Mount Rushmore & Crazy Horse **95**.

WHY THEY'LL THANK YOU: An icon of the West with mystical power.

70 **Otherworldly Landscapes**

Arches National Park: Sculpted by Nature

All ages • Moab, Utah, USA

MORE THAN 2,000 imposing natural stone arches punctuate this sandstone plateau, almost as if it were one gigantic pop-up book. These are natural formations, the result of cycles of freezing and thawing rain and snow which continually dissolve the "glue" that holds together the sand grains of the stone, chipping away at them bit by bit over time. And yet knowing that the scientific process doesn't detract from the marvel of it, a seemingly endless variety of shapes and delicate colors, as if some giant sculptor were deliberately trying to make each arch more fantastic than the one before.

It's a place to let your imagination go wild. Is Delicate Arch really so delicate, or would its other nicknames (Old Maids Bloomers or Cowboy Chaps) be more appropriate? And what about those tall spires? You might imagine they're castles, the towering masts of stone sailing ships, or the petrified skyscrapers of some ancient city. Be sure to pick up a map at the visitor center, because half the fun is matching up the formations with the fanciful names that have been given to them. On the 18-mile scenic drive from one end of the park to the other, you'll pass such features as **Park Avenue,** a solid rock "fin" that reminded somebody of the Manhattan skyline; the **La Sal Mountains,** which early explorers thought looked like piles of salt; **Courthouse Towers,** with such monoliths as Sheep Rock, the Organ, and the Three Gossips; and the **Tower of Babel.** A side road leads to **The Windows, Turret Arch,** and the **Cove of Caves,** where erosion is

even now slowly making a new arch out of the largest cave. Detour onto **Wolfe Ranch Road** for a brief hike to see a 100-year-old ranch and some Ute pictographs.

Along the drive, stop to venture onto the various walking trails, many of them short and easy enough for even young children. A .3-mile walk lets you circle **Balanced Rock,** a 3,000-ton boulder perched on a slowly eroding pedestal; a .5-mile there-and-back trail leads past the **Parade of Elephants** to **Double Arch;** and another .3-mile walk goes to **Sand Dune Arch,** with an irresistible sandy hollow beneath that the kids can play in.

Hiking in Arches National Park.

83

(i) U.S. 191 ((C) **435/719-2299;** www.nps. gov/arch).

✈ Grand Junction, CO, 125 miles. Salt Lake City, UT, 230 miles.

🛏 $ **Arch View Camp Park,** U.S. 91 & U.S. 313 ((C) **800/813-6622** or 435/259-7854; www.archviewresort.com). $$ **Bowen**

Motel, 169 N. Main St. ((C) **800/874-5439** or 435/259-7132; www.bowenmotel.com).

WHY THEY'LL THANK YOU: Waiting for Balanced Rock to topple.

Going to the Moon
Craters of the Moon National Monument
All ages • Arco, Idaho, USA

HERE'S ONE APTLY NAMED NATIONAL PARK: Bring the children here and they will feel as though they've gone to the moon. Three lava fields, with some 60 distinct lava flows and 25 volcanic cones, cover nearly half a million acres on the Snake River Plain, a haunting black basaltic landscape 60 miles wide with deposits that may lie up to 10,000 feet deep. You may not know the difference between slabby pahoehoe and spiny pahoehoe (hint: they're both types of lava flow), but you'll know that this desolate landscape is one of the strangest sights you'll ever see.

The lava fields at Craters of the Moon were formed as long as 15,000 years ago, though much of it is quite young, formed only 2,000 years ago. At the visitor center, the kids will learn about such weird volcanic features as volcanic bombs (clumps of spewing lava that hardened in the air before falling to rest on the surface), lava tubes (underground tunnels hollowed out by receding flows of molten lava), and tree molds (the shapes of trees encased in lava before they decomposed). They'll learn the difference between steep-sided spatter cones and pock-marked cinder cones. Look for these as you drive the park's 7-mile scenic drive, with various spurs leading to intriguing features like 700-foot-high **Big Cinder Butte,** one of the world's tallest cinder

cones, or the curiously colored **Blue and Green Dragon lava flows.** A half-mile hike will take you through the **Devil's Orchard,** where lava fragments stand like wraiths upon a sea of cinders; another half-mile hike lets you explore several **lava tubes** such as the Boy Scout Cave (bring a flashlight) and the Indian Tunnel. Because it is situated along the Great Rift volcanic zone, you'll see deep fissures in the earth, collapsed pits and craters, and ridges built by magma oozing upward through old cracks.

This is by no means a dead landscape; if they pay attention, the kids will discover plenty of hardy flora and fauna that has adapted to this environment. Big patches of sagebrush grasslands and islands of grass (kipukas) have sprouted wherever they could find enough soil; on the lacy surfaces of cinder cones, wildflowers, shrubs, and even twisted little limber pines have managed to get a foothold. The mountains at the north end of the park have Douglas fir forests and groves of quaking aspens that look downright lush in contrast. In the daytime, you may see ground squirrels, lizards, chipmunks, and hawks; at dawn and dusk, coyotes, porcupines, and jackrabbits steal forth; and if you were here at night, you'd see wood rats, bobcats, and bats.

ⓘ Hwy. 20/26/93, near Arco (☎ **208/527-3257;** www.nps.gov/crmo).

✈ Hailey, 60 miles. Twin Falls, 90 miles.

🛏 $ **Arco Inn,** 540 W. Grand Ave., Arco (☎ **208/527-3100**). $$ **Best Western**

Kentwood Lodge, 180 S. Main St.,Ketcham (☎ **800/805-1001** or 208/726-4114; www. bestwestern.com).

WHY THEY'LL THANK YOU: Discovering life on the moonscape.

Columbia Icefields: Back to the Ice Age

Ages 4 & up • Alberta, Canada

CHILDREN WHO LOVED THE ANIMATED MOVIE *Ice Age* will look around this natural wonder and feel as if they're back in the movie all over again. Spreading over the eastern face of the Canadian Rockies, it's the world's largest nonpolar ice cap, a massive dome of glacial ice and snow straddling the top of the North American continent. And the drive to get here is equally spectacular: The 286km (178-mile) **Icefields Parkway,** a majestic stretch of highway between Banff and Jasper national parks (see The Rocky Mountaineer **30**), climbs through deep river valleys, beneath soaring, glacier-notched mountains, and past dozens of hornlike peaks shrouded with permanent snowcaps.

The Icefields Parkway can be driven in 3 hours, but plan on a full day so you can enjoy scenic stops en route. Past Lake Louise, you'll see **Bow Lake** at the foot of **Crowfoot Glacier;** farther north, a short hike from the road takes you to startlingly blue-green **Peyto Lake,** vividly colored by minerals dissolved in the glaciers, and, then, after a dramatic incline, to 3,490m (11,450 ft.) **Mount Athabasca** at Sunwapta Pass. The ice tendrils of the Columbia Icefields creep close to the road here, though it's only a glimpse of the massive amounts of century-old ice and snow tucked in around these peaks, covering 518 sq. km (200 sq. miles) and lying up to 760m (2,493 ft.) thick in some spots. There are a restaurant at the Columbia Icefields Centre lodge, an information center, and the ticket office for **Brewster**

Snocoach Tours (☎ **403/762-6735**), where you can book a 90-minute ride onto the surface of the glacier in a specially designed bus with balloon tires. The tour gives you an opportunity to hike on the glacier, but make sure the kids walk carefully—a tumble into a crevasse can easily break a leg.

After that, the road begins to plunge downward into the Athabasca River valley, and the rivers have to plunge downward

Columbia Icefields.

too, which means—hooray!—waterfalls. The best one to visit is **Athabasca Falls,** where you can walk on a mist-covered bridge over the chasm and follow walking trails to other scenic overlooks. The road rolls on past mountain meadows and lakes until it reaches the town of Jasper.

Keep an eye out and you may see bighorn sheep, mountain goats, elks, and maybe even mama black bears with their cubs. Don't try to get close to them though, and by no means try to feed them. Unlike animated animals, these can be dangerous!

(i) Hwy. 93, **Information center,** Sunwapta Pass (℃ **780/852-7030**).

✈ Calgary, 257km (160 miles).

🚃 Jasper.

🛏 $$ **Becker's Chalets,** Hwy. 95, Jasper (℃ **780/852-3779;** www.beckerschalets. com). $$$ **Columbia Icefields Center,** Sunwapta Pass (℃ **780/852-7032**).

WHY THEY'LL THANK YOU: Going back to the Ice Age.

Otherworldly Landscapes **73**

Petrified Forest & Painted Desert
Trees of Stone, Stones of Color
All ages • Near Holbrook, Arizona, USA

F**ROM THE NAME**, the children may expect to see standing trees of stones, leaves and branches and all. Well, a better name for the Petrified Forest might be the Petrified Pile of Logs, with its fossilized hunks of ancient trees scattered like kindling across the arid scrubby landscape. But these richly colored petrifications are plenty impressive close up, and the other half of the park, the Painted Desert, more than lives up to its name, in glowing pastel beauty.

Start at the **Rainbow Forest Museum,** the visitor center at the southern entrance to the park, where the displays will teach the kids how those petrified logs got petrified in the first place. These 225-million-year-old conifers date from the late Triassic age, when this area was an equatorial tropical forest. The trees fell, were buried in sediment, and then overlaid with volcanic ash, which gradually deposited silica in the trees that replaced their cells with quartz crystals. This unique set of circumstances left a profusion of these immense fossils in the area, which were sliced up and sold

for souvenirs at such a rate that in 1906 the government stepped in to preserve what was left in this park. A short walking trail behind the visitor center winds around a hillside strewn with logs (4–5 ft. in diameter), giving the children a first chance to examine them up close; across the road a 1.5-mile loop takes you to Agate House, a ruined pueblo fashioned out of colorful petrified wood.

Once you're back in the car, head north on the park's 27-mile scenic road. Several overlooks highlight wonders such as the **Crystal Forest** (unfortunately, tourists pried the quartz and amethyst crystals out of these logs long ago); the **Jasper Forest,** petrified trees with their roots still attached; and **Agate Bridge,** a natural bridge formed by a petrified log. In the hazy blue badlands of the **Blue Mesa,** chunks of petrified wood teeter on mounds of soft clay that are eroding away beneath them. **The Teepees** are a lovely set of hills striped with different colors. At **Newspaper Rock** you can gaze upon ancient Native American petroglyphs,

The Painted Desert.

with the ruined pueblos of their creators at nearby **Pueblo Parco.**

Across I-40, you'll be fully in the Painted Desert section of the park, where a series of eight overlooks let you admire the breathtaking desert colors, which were caused by various minerals in the mudstone-and-clay soil—iron, manganese, and others—which oxidized at different rates as they were exposed by erosion. It's a dreamscape of pastels washing over dramatically eroded buttes and mesas, one of nature's best special effects ever.

ⓘ U.S. 180, 20 miles east of Holbrook (② **928/524-6228;** www.nps.gov/pefo).

✈ Flagstaff, 90 miles. Phoenix, 180 miles.

🛏 $$$ **La Posada,** 303 N. Second St., Winslow (② **928/289-4366;** www.laposada. org). $ **Wigwam Motel,** 811 W. Hopi Dr., Holbrook (② **928/524-3048;** www.galerie-kokopelli.com/wigwam).

WHY THEY'LL THANK YOU: If the rock logs don't get them, the Kodachrome mesas will.

Saguaro National Park
A Forest of Classic Cactus
All ages • Tucson, Arizona, USA

Aꜱᴋ ᴄʜɪʟᴅʀᴇɴ ᴛᴏ ᴅʀᴀᴡ ᴀ ᴅᴇꜱᴇʀᴛ and they'll fill it up with green cacti, copying the image they've seen a gazillion times in cartoons: prickly treelike cacti with straight ribbed trunks and uplifted round arms. But it isn't until you stand next to one of these giants that you realize how awesome they truly are. When I say giant, I mean *giant*, some of them standing 50 feet tall and weighing up to 10 tons. The funny thing is, the only place these "typical" cacti grow is right here in the Sonoran Desert. "Of course," the kids say as they gaze

over this sun-bleached scrubland—"*this* is a desert."

Big as they are, these saguaro are sensitive to frost and fire, and incredibly slow to mature—they may live as long as 150 years, but they only grow an inch or two in the first 8 years of their lives, when they depend upon being in the shade of a "nurse tree"—look carefully underneath the paloverde or mesquite trees around here and you may be able to spot a tiny cactus seedling. (The nurse trees eventually are killed off as the saguaros—those ungrateful children—begin to come into their own power.) They don't begin to produce their bursts of cream-colored flowers until they are 35 years old, and their first branches don't appear until they are 50 to 70 years old. To protect the saguaro population, which grows too slowly to be easily replenished, this preserve was formed in 1933. Or perhaps I should say two preserves—there's one section west of the city (Tucson Mountain District) and one east of the city (Rincon Mountain District). The western section, **Tucson Mountain,** has the most impressive stands of saguaros, as well as a **water hole** near the information center where, at dawn and dusk, you may see animals attracted by the sweet fruit of the saguaro—coyotes, foxes, squirrels, and javelinas. Its scenic **Bajada Loop Drive** has several panoramic vistas and good hiking trails. The east section, **Rincon Mountain,** has an older set of cacti and, with fewer roads, is great for hikers and mountain bikers (the paved scenic loop road is also good for road bikes).

A flowering cactus in Saguaro National Park.

(i) **Tucson Mountain visitor center,** 2700 N. Kinney Rd. (© **520/733-5158**). **Rincon Mountain visitor center,** 3693 S. Old Spanish Trail (© **520/733-5153**). www.nps.gov/sagu.

✈ Tucson.

🛏 $$$ **Loews Ventana Canyon Resort,** 7000 N. Resort Dr. (© **800/234-5117** or 520/299-2020; www.loewshotels.com). $$ **Smuggler's Inn,** 6350 E. Speedway Blvd. (© **800/525-8852** or 520/296-3292; www. smugglersinn.com).

BEST TIME: Nov–Apr.

WHY THEY'LL THANK YOU: The shape is familiar, but who knew they were this BIG?

Pinnacles National Monument
Lost Pieces of a Mojave Jigsaw Puzzle
All ages • East of Salinas Valley, California, USA

Picture hundreds of towering crags, spires, and hoodoos, ferociously jabbing up out of the rolling brown California hills. These are the Pinnacles, the world's most dramatic demonstration of plate tectonics. Those rocky spikes are fragments of a

23-million-year-old volcano in the Mojave Desert that was split in two by the San Andreas Fault. One half of the volcano stayed in the Mojave; this is the other half, carried 195 miles north by shifting geologic plates. Okay, it got a little shattered and jumbled en route, and over the centuries the jagged remains were further sculpted and scoured by wind and erosion. It's a unique and unforgettable sight.

Those crags and spires beg to be climbed, so it's no surprise that this is one of the most popular weekend climbing spots in central California, with its mild winter climate (spring is also a good time to visit, when wildflowers carpet the chaparral). Located only 80 miles south of San Francisco, the Pinnacles get a lot of visitors—some weekends it seems every spire and monolith has a climber clinging to its surface. Most visitors arrive via CA 25 at the eastern entrance, where you can get an eyeful of dramatic spires right away, from the Bear Gulch picnic ground. For a moderately strenuous half-day hike, take the **Condor Gulch Trail** uphill from the visitor center; within 2 miles you'll be amid clusters of spires, which are much larger up close than they look from the parking lot. Switch to the **High Peaks Trail** to get a dramatic view: the Salinas Valley to your west, the Pinnacles below, and miles of coast to the east. After traversing the high peaks (including stretches of footholds carved in steep rock faces) for about a mile, the trail drops back toward the visitor center via a valley filled with eerie-looking hoodoos.

One intriguing feature of this jumbled rockscape is the talus caves, which are basically narrow stream canyons roofed over with tumbled boulders. Bats love these caves—in fact, **Bear Gulch Cave,** only a short walk from the picnic ground (take the Moses Spring Trail), only allows visitors in half the cave because rare Townsend's Big-Eared Bats occupy the other half; it's closed entirely mid-May to mid-July to protect newborn bat babies. If you enter the park from the west, there's a 2-mile loop trail from the Chaparral parking lot to visit **Balconies Cave,** another talus cave. Flashlights are required to explore either cave.

Along with the bats, the Pinnacles—which sit at an intersection of two ecosystems—have an incredible 400 species of bees buzzing around their chaparral and grasslands, and half a dozen extremely rare California condors were successfully released to the wild here. Keep your eyes open and you never know what you'll see.

(i) **Bear Gulch Visitor Center** ((C) 831/389-4485; www.nps.gov/pinn).

✈ Monterey Peninsula Airport, 58 miles.

⌂ $ **Pinnacles Campground,** off CA 25 near the eastern entrance ((C) 831/389-4462; www.pinncamp.com).

WHY THEY'LL THANK YOU: Mountains that migrate.

---

76 Otherworldly Landscapes

Hawaii Volcanoes National Park
Where Hot Lava Still Flows
Ages 6 & up • Volcano, Hawaii, USA

HAWAII VOLCANOES NATIONAL PARK beats out all the other U.S. national parks on two scores: It has the only tropical rainforest, and it has the only active volcano. Since 1983, the Big Island's Kilauea volcano has been erupting regularly, although these

are "quiet'" eruptions, with gas escaping slowly instead of exploding violently. Its slow-moving red lava oozes over the landscape, sometimes even over the park roads. The kids may wish they could see volcanic fireworks, but once they're here,

Desolation Point in Volcanoes National Park.

feeling the soles of their sneakers getting gummy from the heat below, they'll realize this is spectacular enough.

This is not a tame volcano, not by any means. Over the past 2 decades, some $100 million worth of property has been destroyed by the eruptions, though the lava flow has also added 560 acres of new land. On many days, the lava flows right alongside accessible roads, and you can get as close as the heat will allow; sometimes, however, the flow is in underground tubes that spill out miles away.

Near the visitor center, you can get your first look at **Kilauea Caldera,** a 2½-mile-wide, 500-foot-deep pit with wisps of steam rising from it. Going counterclockwise on Crater Rim Road, you'll drive past the **Sulphur Banks,** which smell like rotten eggs, and the **Steam Vents,** fissures where trails of smoke, once molten lava, escape from the inner reaches of the

earth. At the **Thomas A Jaggar Museum** there's a viewpoint for Halemaumau Crater, which is half a mile across but 1,000 feet deep; walk right to the rim to gape at this once-fuming old fire pit, which still gives off fierce heat from its vents. Near the Iki Crater, the .5-mile **Devastation Trail** is a sobering look at how a volcanic eruption wreaked havoc in 1959. Another intriguing stop is the **Thurston Lava Tube,** a cool underground hole in a lush forested bowl that somehow escaped the lava flow.

By now you won't be surprised to learn that the volcano goddess, Pele, was an important deity to ancient Hawaiians— you definitely wanted to be on the right side of this lady. At the 15-mile mark down Chain of Craters Road, you can see **Puu Loa,** an ancient site sacred to the Hawaiians, where a .5-mile boardwalk loop trail will show you thousands of mysterious Hawaiian petroglyphs carved in stone.

If the volcano is actively erupting, call the visitor center for directions to the best locations for night viewing—it's quite a sight, watching as the brilliant red lava snakes down the side of the mountain and pours into the cold sea, hissing and steaming ferociously. Of course, the ultimate view is from the sky: **Blue Hawaiian Helicopter** (✆ **800/745-BLUE** or 808/886-1768; www.bluehawaiian.com) runs several tours right over the bubbling caldera, for a bird's-eye view you'll never forget.

ⓘ Hawaii Belt Rd. (Hwy. 11; ✆ **808/985-6000;** www.nps.gov/havo).

✈ Hilo, 29 miles.

🛏 $$ **Killauea Lodge,** Old Volcano Rd., off Hwy. 11. (✆ **808/967-7366;** www.kilauea lodge.com). $ **Volcano House,** inside Hawaii Volcanoes National Park (✆ **808/967-7321;** www.volcanohousehotel.com).

WHY THEY'LL THANK YOU: Red-hot magma.

The Monteverde Cloud Forest
A Mountaintop Jungle
Ages 6 & up • Monteverde, Costa Rica

MONTEVERDE MEANS "GREEN MOUNTAIN," and that's exactly what you'll find at the end of the steep, rutted dirt road that leads to Costa Rica's Monteverde Biological Cloud Forest Reserve. Passing through mile after mile of dry, brown pasture, you may wonder if you're in the right place—where's the cloud forest? Well, this land used to be forest, until humans entered the picture. All the more reason to appreciate what has been saved when you finally hit the top of the mountain: a lush, tangled swath of greenery, where orchids and ferns trail from the treetops while monkeys chatter, tree frogs croak, and hummingbirds hum. Walking here in the early-morning mist with the susurration of leaves and disembodied birdcalls all around can be an almost out-of-body experience.

Cloud forests are always on mountaintops, where moist, warm air sweeping up the slopes from a nearby ocean condenses swiftly in the higher elevation, forming clouds around the summit. The clouds, in turn, condense moisture on the forest trees, giving rise to an incredible diversity of life forms—Monteverde boasts more than 2,500 plant species, 400 bird species, and 100 different mammal species. Monteverde is no secret, and its main trails are often crowded with eco-tourists, all gaping (generally without any luck) to see rare and elusive species like the quetzal with its 2-foot-long tail feathers. The density of the cloud forest, however, makes it possible to feel you've escaped the crowds, once you branch off the central paths. I suggest booking a **guided tour** through your hotel, which will also reserve your admission (only 120 people at a time are allowed inside the

reserve); the guide will be able to identify far more of the flora and fauna than you could spot on your own.

The option older kids will be dying to try is a **canopy tour,** where you can zip around harnessed to an overhead cable, going from platform to platform high above the forest floor in the treetops, where two-thirds of the species live. Two good operations are **Sky Trek** (✆ **645-5238;** www.skytrek.com) and **Selvatura Park** (✆ **645-5929;** www.selvatura.com), both located outside the reserve near the town of Santa Elena.

Slightly less crowded than the Monteverde Reserve but with much the same flora and fauna, the **Santa Elena Cloud Forest Reserve** (✆ 645-5390) can be a good alternative; the 3.5km (2.2-mile) **Bajo del Tigre Trail** in the town of Monteverde is a great bird-watching option. Other related attractions in Monteverde are the **Butterfly Garden** (✆ 645-5512), the **Monteverde Serpentarium** (✆ 645-5238; www.snaketour.com), the **Frog Pond of Monteverde** (✆ 645-6320; www.ranario.com), and the **World of Insects** (✆ 645-6859).

ⓘ ✆ **645-5122;** www.cct.or.cr.

✈ Juan Santamaria International, San José, 160km (99 miles).

🛏 $$ **Hotel El Establo,** PO Box 549-2050, San Pedro (✆ **645-5110;** www.hotel elestablo.com). $$ **Monteverde Lodge,** 5km (3 miles) outside the reserve near Santa Elena (✆ **257-0766** in San José, or 645-5057 in Monteverde; www.costaricaexpeditions.com).

WHY THEY'LL THANK YOU: Getting your head in the clouds.

The Blue Mountains

Ages 6 & up • Katoomba, Australia

THE TERM "MOUNTAINS" may be a bit of exaggeration when you're talking about these bush-shrouded hills north of Sydney, Australia, but there's no question they're spectacular, with deep river valleys, waterfalls, craggy cliffs, and dense exotic forests. It won't take you long to notice the blue haze that gives them their name—explain to the kids that it's caused by light striking the droplets of oil that evaporate from the leaves of the ubiquitous eucalyptus trees.

The gateway to the Blue Mountains is the town of **Katoomba.** The Blue Mountains Tourism office on Echo Point Road (✆ **1300/653 408** in Australia, or 02/4739 6266) is an attraction itself, with glass windows overlooking a gum forest, and cockatoos and lorikeets feeding on seed dispensers. Echo Point is an excellent spot to see the rock formations known as the **Three Sisters,** probably the Blue Mountains's best-known photo op. From

the ticket office in Katoomba at 1 Violet Rd. you can try out another Blue Mountains essential, riding the **Scenic Railway,** the world's steepest. Basically a carriage on rails that is lowered 415m (1,362 ft.) into the Jamison Valley at a maximum incline of 52 degrees, it's *very* steep and quite a thrill. The trip takes only a few minutes; at the bottom are some excellent walks through ancient tree ferns. Return on the **Skyway,** a cable car that travels 300m (984 ft.) above the Jamison Valley.

If your kids are into hiking, try the Australian variety, bush walking. There are some 50 walking trails in the Blue Mountains, ranging from routes you can cover in 15 minutes to 3-day tramps. Seven kilometers (4½ miles) east from Katoomba, in the town of **Wentworth Falls,** after you view the spectacular 281m-high (922-ft.) falls, try taking the National Pass Walk to the base of the falls, a superb hike cut into a cliff face with overhanging rock faces on one side and sheer drops on the other. (Walking back up, of course, takes a bit more work.) In **Blackheath,** 14km (8⅔ miles) northwest of Katoomba, the highest town in the mountains, the 2-hour Cliff Walk from Evans Lookout to Govetts Leap offers great views of both the Three Sisters and their Blackheath siblings, the Three Brothers.

ⓘ ✆ **02/4787 8877;** www.npws.nsw.gov.au.

✈ Sydney International, 114km (71 miles).

🛏 $$ **The Carrington Hotel,** 15–47 Katoomba St. (✆ **02/4782 1111;** www.the carrington.com.au). $ **Katoomba Mountain Lodge,** 31 Lurline St. (✆ **02/4782 3933;** www.katoombabackpackers.com.au).

WHY THEY'LL THANK YOU: A wild blue yonder.

Discovering Australia's Blue Mountains.

Rotorua: Land of Mists

Ages 4 & up • North Island, New Zealand

YOU'LL SMELL ROTORUA long before you see it, a peculiar sulphuric aroma that may provoke a loud "Euww! Who *farted?*" from the back seat. But then you draw closer, and they start to see the steam hissing out of fissures in the landscape, the scattered lakes and waterfalls, the volcano peak of Mount Tarawera in the hazy distance, and—who cares about the smell?

Geothermals are what make Rotorua special, so head first for the **Whakarewarewa Thermal Reserve,** Hemo Road (✆ **08000/494-252** or 07/348-9047; www.nzmaori.co.nz), a rocky landscape full of mud pools and the prolific Pohutu Geyser, which shoots up hot water 16 to 20m (52–66 ft.) 10 to 25 times a day. It also has a replica of a Maori village—the population of Rotorua is about one-third Maori (New Zealand's aboriginal peoples), and exhibits of Maori culture are one of the bigger tourism draws here. The other must-do in town is in Ngongotaha, a suburb halfway up Lake Rotorua's western shore: **Skyline Skyrides,** Fairy Springs Road (✆ **07/347-0027;** www.skylineskyrides.co.nz) hauls you on a gondola up Mount Ngongotaha, then offers all sorts of thrilling ways to descend, from a chairlift to a bone-rattling luge track.

There are more geothermal sites south of town, a whole valley of steamy activity: I'd choose **Waiotapu,** a half-hour drive south on Highway 5, where you can see the Lady Knox Geyser (she erupts daily at 10:15am) and all sorts of intriguing pools, from the beautiful Champagne Pool to the arsenic-tinted Devil's Bath to New Zealand's largest bubbling mud pool.

The small village of **Te Wairoa,** Buried Village, Tarawera Road (✆ **07/362-8287;** www.buriedvillage.co.nz), is Rotorua's version of Pompeii, an excavated townscape dug out of the lava that destroyed

it when Mount Tarawera erupted in 1886. Lots of artifacts discovered in the excavations are displayed at the museum onsite, but what'll really bring this place alive for the kids is going from one excavated dwelling to another on a meandering pathway along a stream.

Since the 19th century, tourists have been coming to "take the waters" in the geothermal spas and springs. The elegantly restored Art Deco **Blue Baths** in Government Gardens now includes the **Rotorua Museum,** where a multimedia cinema re-creates the experience of a volcanic eruption. The **Polynesian Spa,** Hinemoa Street (✆ **07/348-1328**), has lots of luxury soaking experiences, including a Family Spa section, where kids can frolic in the warm freshwater pool while adults relax in two adjacent hot mineral pools.

Hell's Gate in Rotorua.

(i) **Information center,** 1167 Fenton St. (© **07/348-5179;** www.rotorua.co.nz).

✈ Rotorua.

🛏 $$ **Rydges Rotoua,** 272 Fenton St. (© **0800/367-793** or 07/349-0900; www.rydges.com). $$ **Wylie Court Motor**

Lodge, 345 Fenton St. (© **08000/100-879** or 07/347-7879; www.yellowpages.co.nz/for/wyliecourt).

WHY THEY'LL THANK YOU: Like one giant hot tub.

The Burren: Ireland's Moonscape

All ages • County Clare, Ireland

In the heart of Ireland's green and rural County Clare lies an amazing landscape of rock and stony outcroppings, a limestone weirdness that looks as if you have just stepped onto the moon. It's called the Burren, from the Irish word *boirreann*, which means "a rocky place." What an understatement.

This strange 260 sq. km (100-sq.-mile) region of naked carboniferous limestone once lay under a prehistoric tropical sea; over the next 300 million years, decaying shells and sediment hardened into rock, thrust to the surface, and lay exposed to pelting Irish rains and scouring winds. Today you can drive around and gaze over massive sheets of rock, jagged boulders, caves, and potholes, punctuated with tiny lakes and streams as well as ancient Stone Age burial monuments. Get out of your car to explore and you'll see that something is always in bloom, even in winter, from fern and moss to orchids, rock roses, milkwort, wild thyme, geraniums, violets, and fuchsia. The Burren is also famous for its butterflies, which thrive on the rare flora. The pine marten, stoat, and badger, rare in the rest of Ireland, are common here.

A good place to begin your exploration is at the **Burren Exposure** (© **065/707-7277**) on Galway Road 4km (2½ miles) north of the Galway Bay village of Ballyvaughan. This 35-minute multimedia exhibition tells you all you need to know about the extraordinary natural wonders and historical legacy of the Burren. If you're coming from the south or west, however, it is more efficient to get your introduction at the **Burren Centre,** R476 to Kilfenora (© **065/708-8030**), which has less sophisticated, though authoritative, audiovisuals, landscape models, and displays on geology, flora, and fauna. Drive along corkscrewing R480 between Corofin and Ballyvaughan through the heart of the landscape, or better yet, hike a portion of the 26-mile **Burren Way** footpath signposted from Ballyvaughan to

Corcomroe Abbey, the Burren.

Liscannor, near the **Cliffs of Moher** ❼. A wide swath of the area bordered by Corofin, Lahinch, Lisdoonvarna, Ballyvaughn, and Boston has been designated the **Burren National Park;** it has no official entrance, so find a place to park and begin rambling around the limestone terraces and shale uplands. The area is particularly rich in archaeological remains from the Neolithic through the medieval periods—dolmens and wedge tombs (approximately 120), ring forts (500), round towers, ancient churches, high crosses, monasteries, and holy wells. It's an eerily different sort of place that the kids will remember forever.

ⓘ www.county-clare.com.

🚌 Ennis or Galway.

🏨 $ **Carrigann Hotel,** Lisdoonvarna (ⓒ **065/707-4036;** www.gateway-to-the-burren.com). Closed Nov–Feb.

WHY THEY'LL THANK YOU: A trip to the moon without a rocket.

---

81 **Otherworldly Landscapes**

Volcanoes of the Auvergne

Ages 6 & up • Montlosier, Aydat, France

WHEN YOU THINK OF FRANCE, you may not automatically think volcanoes. Yet in one 385,000-hectare (950,000-acre) region, no fewer than 90 extinct volcanic cones—known in French as *puys*—rise dramatically and eerily above the pine forests. Their symmetrical shapes, formed over centuries of successive eruption and cooling, are cloaked with the vivid green grass of the region; peat bogs and lakes, formed by glaciers, are tucked in between. The peaceful rural calm of this region, where few tourists venture, seems at odds with the violent geological activity that blasted craters out of the mountaintops 5,000 to 6,000 years ago; nowadays villages and farms are interspersed with the volcanoes, where farmers tend the cows and goats responsible for the Auvergne's luscious cheeses.

The highest and oldest peak, **Puy-de-Dôme,** has been used as a worship site since prehistoric times by the Gauls and the Romans. In 1648, Pascal used this mountaintop to prove Torricelli's hypothesis that altitude affects atmospheric pressure; in 1911, aviator Eugène Renaux landed here after a nonstop flight from Paris in just over 5 hours. You can reach its summit via shuttle bus or car; on a clear day you'll have a panoramic view as far east as Mont Blanc.

Les Puys (also known as Monts Dômes) are a minichain of 112 extinct volcanoes (some capped with craters, some with rounded peaks) packed densely into an area 4km (2½ miles) wide by 31km (19 miles) long. Each dome is different: Some were built up by slow extrusions of rock; others were the source of vast lava flows. This rectangle of extinct volcanoes traces one of the most potentially unstable tectonic areas in France, the San Andreas Fault of the French mainland.

This is a super area for **hiking and biking.** The hills may look dramatic, but they're gentle; and the quiet country roads and footpaths through the park have little or no traffic, yet you're never far from civilization. Throughout the region, even in the simple farmhouses, look for blocks of black stone formed by ancient volcanic deposits, with roofs of overlapping tiles of dark gray volcanic schist. A prime example is in the Auvergne's capital, Clermont-Ferrand, the Romanesque **Eglise Notre-Dame-de-Paris.** It's just another way the bizarre beauty of the old volcanoes has been tamed and embraced by the people of the Auvergne.

ⓘ ℂ **04-73-65-64-00;** www.parc-volcans-auvergne.com or www.franceguide.com.

✈ Clermont-Aulnat, 4km (2½ miles).

🛏 $$ **Hotel Le Kyriad,** 51 rue Bonnabaud, Clermont (ℂ **04-73-93-59-69**).

$$$ **Mercure Centre,** 82 bd. François-Mitterrand, Clermont (ℂ **04-73-34-46-46**).

WHY THEY'LL THANK YOU: Dead volcanoes, like slumbering green giants.

Otherworldly Landscapes 82

Blyde River Canyon: Great Green Gorge

Ages 4 & up • Graskop to Blydepoort, Mpumalanga, South Africa

IF YOUR MENTAL PICTURE OF A CANYON is an arid sandstone gorge (as in, say, the Grand Canyon or Mexico's Copper Canyon), South Africa's immense Blyde River Canyon will turn your head around. It's a land of heavy mists and high rainfall, precipitated by hot air rising over the canyon wall, giving the upper plateau lush grasslands, the riverbanks dense dark forests, and in between them, pockets of subtropical rainforests tucked into the creases of the ravines. Each level has its own wildlife, too: mountain reedbuck up on the escarpment, dassies on the canyon walls, hippos and crocodiles in the Blyde Dam, and impala, kudu, blue wildebeest, waterbuck, and zebra on the lowveld plain near the canyon's mouth. If you're going from Pretoria to the **Kruger National Park** ⑫⑥, take an extra day to drive along R532—the Panorama Route, as it's called for obvious reasons.

The starting point is the town of Graskop, where you head north on R532, though almost immediately you'll loop east onto R534 to stop at **God's Window,** your first amazing vista of the whole 33km (21-mile) canyon. Back on R532, head north to see **Berlin Falls,** a crystalline 48m (157-ft.) cascade. Several miles farther north, where the Blyde River meets the Treur River, **Bourke's Luck Potholes** ℂ **013/761-6019**) are bizarre swirly holes scooped out of the rock with mysterious dark pools of water inside; the lichen walking trail here is easy and good for children. A few miles farther, the **Three Rondawels** is an amazing outlook

above a heart-stopping sheer drop down to the Blyde River some 1,600m (5,250 ft.) below. The name refers to three massive spiral outcrops, topped with green hats, across from the viewpoint—I like the other name for them, the Three Sisters, because they look like hoop-skirted old biddies to me.

Near the Blydepoort Dam, turn east on R531 for two great options for exploring the landscape: a 90-minute boat ride on the Blyde Dam (look for the turnoff from R531 to **Aventura Swadini** (ℂ **015/795-5141**), where you can see the mouth of the canyon and look back up at the escarpment you were just driving on; or continue on to R40 and cut north to the

Blyde River Canyon.

Hoedspruit Research and Breeding Center for Endangered Species (☎ 015/793-1633), where you can take a 90-minute drive through a plains preserve to spot cheetahs, wild dogs, rhino, and various bird species. Head back to Graskop on the R40, then the R533; the total drive is only 159km (99 miles), but oh, what a ride.

ⓘ R532, Graskop to Blydepoort. **Graskop information,** Spar Center, Pilgrim's way

(☎ 013/767-1833; www.wildadventures. co.za).

✈ Hoedspruit.

🛏 $$$ **Casa do Sol,** off the R536, Hazyview (☎ 013/737-8111; www.casado sol.co.za). $$ **Rissington Inn,** off R40, Hazyview (☎ 013/737-7700; www.rissington. co.za).

WHY THEY'LL THANK YOU: That view at the Three Rondawels.

Atmospheric Places to Explore

83

The Catacombs of Rome
Ages 10 & up • Rome, Italy

OF ALL THE ROADS THAT LED TO ROME, **Via Appia Antica** (built in 312 B.C.) was the most famous, stretching from Rome to the seaport of Brindisi, where rich cargoes from Greece and the East flowed into the Empire. Along the road's initial section in Rome, patrician Romans erected great monuments and family tombs. Beneath the surface, however, was another story. Beginning in the 2nd century A.D., early Christians carved miles of narrow tunnels out of the soft tufa stone, using them both as burial places and as refuges for celebrating rites during spates of persecution. Today visitors can wander, guided by a priest or monk, through mile upon mile of musty tunnel, past burial niches gouged into walls—long shelves that held two to three bodies each. The dank, dark grottoes are creepily fascinating, but more than that, they are a powerful reminder that even Christianity was once an outlaw sect.

Just outside the city walls, as many as 50 catacombs were dug out over 300 years; together they contain some 20 million graves. If these tunnels were straightened and laid end to end, they'd be as long as Italy itself. Perhaps the most popular are the extensive **Catacombs of St. Callixtus,** the first cemetery of the Christian community of Rome, stretching for nearly 19km (12 miles) on five levels,

about 20m (65 ft.) underground. Sepulchral chambers and almost half a million tombs of early Christians are decorated with paintings, sculptures, and epigraphs (look for such repeated symbols as the fish, anchor, and dove). Sixteen popes from the 3rd century are buried here, along with St. Cecilia, early Christian martyr and patron of sacred music. The bodies of Sts. Peter and Paul, not to mention that of St. Sebastian, were at one time buried in the **Catacombs of St. Sebastian,** where the tunnels and mausoleums are full of mosaics and graffiti from centuries even before the time of Constantine. But kids may prefer the shorter and more dramatic tours of the **Catacombs of St. Domitilla,** the only catacombs where you'll still see bones in the tomb niches. Entering through a sunken 4th-century church adds a touch of mystery, too.

ⓘ **Catacombs of St. Callixtus,** Via Appia Antica 170 (☎ 06-51301580), closed Feb. **Catacombs of St. Sebastian,** Via Appia Antica 136 (☎ 06-7850350), closed mid-Nov to mid-Dec. **Catacombs of St. Domitilla,** Via d. Sette Chiese 280 (☎ 06-5110342), closed Jan.

✈ 🛏 See Viva la Roma ❺❸.

WHY THEY'LL THANK YOU: Hide-and-seek.

The Beehive Houses of Apulia, Italy

All ages • Alberobello, Italy

NOBODY ELSE EVER BUILT HOMES quite like these—beehive-shaped cottages with whitewashed limestone walls and conical fieldstone roofs. If you saw just one you might think it was some modern architect's fantasy, but when you see several dotting the rugged Apulian landscape, or entire neighborhoods—as in the town of **Alberobello,** which has some 1,000 of these houses—you really sit up and take notice. Known as *trulli,* they're like something out of a storybook, and children are instinctively attracted to such curvy, cozy dwellings.

Apulia, the high heel of Italy's boot, is a land of gritty survivors, invaded over the years by everyone from ancient Greeks to Goths, Byzantines, Saracen pirates, and Turks. *Trulli* were built as early as the 13th century, by peasants scavenging whatever materials came easily to hand. What's amazing, when you take a close look, is the craftsmanship involved: The stones fit together in such a way that not a speck of mortar was needed. This allowed medieval peasants to dismantle the structures quickly if a king came to inspect the district. For such provisional dwellings, they sure have lasted a long time.

Trulli-packed Alberobello is Italy's most fantastical village, but it can be a tourist trap, with tacky souvenirs on sale everywhere, even in converted *trulli* (the kids may pester you to buy a cunning miniature model, crafted in the same type of stone). From Alberobello's main square, Piazza del Popolo, turn left on Largo Martellotta, which will take you to the edge of the *trulli* neighborhood, a maze of curving cobbled lanes with the round houses on every side. There's no danger of missing it, as hordes of day-trippers descend on Alberobello every day to gawk at the structures. The best-known is the **trullo sovrano** (sovereign *trullo*) at Piazza Sacramento, 15m (49 ft.) tall, the only true two-story *trulli.* It is, however, a 19th-century creation, built as headquarters for a religious confraternity and Carbonari sect. To experience *trulli* living, you might want to book a night at the **Hotel Dei Trulli** (see the hotel recommended below), a cluster of 19 *trulli,* each its own mini-apartment of one, two, or three cones wedged together.

ⓘ **Tourist office,** Piazza Ferdinando IV (✆ **080-4325171**).

🚌 Alberobello, 1¾ hr. from Bari.

🛏 $$ **Hotel Dei Trulli,** Via Cadore 32 (✆ **080-4323555;** www.hoteldeitrulli.it).

WHY THEY'LL THANK YOU: Snug homes to curl up in.

Under the Sidewalks of Paris
Touring the Sewers & the Catacombs

Ages 8 & up (Sewers); 10 & up (Catacombs) • Paris, France

PARIS MAY BE THE CITY OF LIGHT, but it has its dark side too, and nothing is more gruesome than these two underground attractions. For older kids with a well-developed Goth sensibility—or at least a gross-out sense of humor—descending

The catacombs of Paris.

into the sewers and the catacombs of Paris will be an unforgettable memory.

Immortalized by Victor Hugo in Jean Valjean's thrilling subterranean escape in *Les Misérables*, the **Parisian sewer system** was begun in 1370, replacing the foul street-level open sewers that had done so much to help the Black Death decimate the population. In the early 1800s, extensive tunnels began to be bored beneath the cobblestone streets, a process accelerated when the Industrial Revolution brought mass-produced iron pipes and power-operated digging tools. Famous French city planner Baron Haussman designed a state-of-the-art system for channeling drinking water separately from sewage (now *there's* a valuable concept) and it's been growing ever since. Today Paris has 2,093km (1,300 miles) of meticulously laid-out tunnels bearing water mains, pipes, cables, and pneumatic tubes, such an impressive engineering accomplishment that the kids will forget all they wanted to see was a tunnel of poop.

Tours of Les Egouts (the sewers) begin at Pont de l'Alma on the Left Bank, where a stairway leads into the nether regions of the city; it's incredibly popular, and there's often a half-hour wait. Although most of the tour involves a film and exhibits, eventually you'll be led down for a brief foray into the echoing maze itself (which is in fact well-lit and not nearly as stinky as you may have anticipated).

If the sewers are not quite as gross as the kids hoped, never fear, the **catacombs** will live up to expectations. Not as ancient as the Catacombs of Rome **83**, those of Paris date from the eve of the French Revolution, when in 1785 city officials decided to convert a set of abandoned medieval quarries near Montparnasse—some 1,000 yards of subterranean tunnels—into a burial space to relieve the overcrowded cemeteries. The remains of seven million persons were subsequently moved here, and in 1810 they were opened to the public, with ghoulishly arranged piles of bones touted as an "empire of the dead." After a brief vogue, in 1830 the prefect of Paris closed down the whole operation, calling it obscene and indecent, and there the bones rotted until World War II, when French Resistance forces literally went underground to use the catacombs as their secret headquarters.

You enter the catacombs through a couple of narrow stone passages, electric-lit but still spooky. I found myself wondering what those 18th-century workers felt as they systematically piled femur bones in tidy shoulder-high stacks, then artfully displayed skulls on top.

(i) **Sewers,** Pont de l'Alma on the Left Bank ((C) **01-53-68-27-82**). **Catacombs,** 1 place Denfert-Rochereau ((C) **01-43-22-47-63; www.carnavalet.paris.fr**).

✈ ⊨ See Paris **54**.

BEST TIME: Sewers closed Nov–Apr.

WHY THEY'LL THANK YOU: If they're not creeped out by this, nothing will get them.

Atmospheric Places to Explore **86**

Buda Castle's Labyrinth: The Great Maze

Age 8 & up • Budapest, Hungary

SPANNING THE DANUBE, the twin cities of Buda and Pest—united in 1873 into one capital named Budapest—survived World War II and the Iron Curtain with a surprising amount of their charm intact. Hungary's medieval greatness is still embodied in Buda Palace, rising above old Buda on Castle Hill, which today contains three museums—the **Hungarian National Gallery,** the **Ludwig Museum of Contemporary Art,** and **Budpesti Történeti Museum** (Budapest History Museum). But it's what lies beneath the castle that I find most fascinating—a 10km (6¼-mile) network of tunnels, snaking underneath the cobblestone streets of the Castle District.

These began as natural caves, hollowed out by hot springs in the porous tufa rock of Castle Hill; people lived here way back in prehistoric times. It wasn't until the Middle Ages, however—perhaps as early as the 11th century—that underground passages were cut to connect the caves in a vast labyrinth. Many of the houses on Castle Hill apparently had their own private entrances into this interconnected maze, which provided them with wells, storage cellars, and possibly a secret escape route for the king. In World War II it became a rambling bomb shelter; during the Cold War years, the Soviet-controlled Hungarian communist government turned it into a secret military installation.

Since the fall of the Soviet empire, various efforts have been made to transform this hideaway into a tourist attraction. This latest incarnation presents the labyrinth as a walk through Hungarian history. After a cave filled with copies of famous prehistoric cave paintings, a series of stage-lit sculptural displays in successive caves represent: ancient shamans, the Magic Deer that was the totem of the nomadic Magyar people, the invading Huns, St. Stephen (who established the first Christian kingdom here in 1000), the invading Tartars in 1241, the Renaissance leader King Mathias who set up his court in 1485, and the invading Ottomans in 1526. These somewhat abstract sculptures, carved out of soft golden tufa stone, are a lot less hokey than the wax museum that was previously installed down here. It's not long on historical detail, but it is an effectively poetic evocation of the dramatic sweep of Hungary's past.

For those who aren't afraid of the dark, there's also a **"Personal Labyrinth,"** a maze of unlit tunnels that visitors can wander around in the dark (although bringing your own flashlight to explore this section is perfectly okay).

(i) Uri utca, 9 ((C) **1/212-0207;** www.labirintus.com).

✈ Ferihegy International.

🛏 $$ **Hotel Erzsébet,** V. Károlyi Mihály u. 11–15 (℃ **1/889-3700;** www.danubius group.com). $$ **Hotel Papillon,** II. Rózsahegy u. 3/b (℃ **1/212-4750**).

WHY THEY'LL THANK YOU: Underground through the ages.

87

The Mysterious Souk of Marrakesh
Ages 10 & up • Marrakesh, Morocco

IF CREATURE COMFORTS ARE HIGH ON YOUR LIST of travel requirements, don't bother coming to Marrakesh. If, however, you like to sample the exotic and have a bit of adventure, take the Marrakesh Express right now.

This Moroccan city of half a million people is dirty, noisy, smoggy, and smelly, and a continual whirl of activity. Marrakesh has always been a trading city, ever since this date-palm oasis at the foot of the Atlas Mountains first became a

crossroads for North African caravans, and so perhaps it makes sense that the heart of the city is its market—or souk, as they say in Morocco. Find your way first to **Djemaa El Fna Square,** the huge teeming plaza that is the center of activity in Marrakesh, with its throngs of food stalls, snake charmers, fortunetellers, jugglers, henna painters, and all sorts of charlatans trying to snare a few coins from tourists. (Let the kids watch, but do

The souk of Marrakesh.

not be intimidated into paying for anything you haven't bought.) The souk is a rabbit-warren of narrow streets leading off the north side of the square, a maze of tin-roofed alleys lined with stalls. You'll see rug merchants hanging their carpets on the walls of adjacent buildings; legume and spice sellers pile their goods, from orange lentils to dusty green mint to golden saffron, on thin blankets right on the pavements; and mounds of marinated olives, dates, and chickpeas gleam in bowls. Brass pots, ceramics, caftans, slippers, leather goods, and fabrics are displayed in a jumble of stalls, while some smaller vendors simply squat on the ground with their merchandise at their feet. At the northern end of the souk, the **workshops** of various craftsmen are open, where the kids may watch them do their leather tooling or slipper embroidering. (Try to avoid the Rahba Kedima section if you don't want to see dead animals or be pestered to buy love potions.)

Expect to be dogged by young men offering to be your guides (don't accept—you can't really get lost in this bazaar,

only a square kilometer in area). Expect to bargain vociferously (start out by offering one-third of the price first quoted to you), using lots of hand gestures, for any item you're interested in buying, and accept that you won't be paying the same price as a local would. Better yet, don't touch any wares, keep strolling, and don't make eye contact with vendors. You're not really here to purchase anything, but to soak up the atmosphere. Make sure you don't get separated from the kids; hold their hands casually, looking as nonchalant as you can. Your clothes will mark you as a tourist, but your body language will mark you as an intrepid one.

(i) **Tourist office,** Angle 31 rue Oued Fès et avenue Abtal (© **37/681-531;** www.tourism-in-morocco.com).

✈ Marrakesh.

🛏 $$$ **Le Meridien N'Fis,** Avenue Mohammed VI (© **24/339-400;** www.starwoodhotels.com).

WHY THEY'LL THANK YOU: A truly bizarre bazaar.

The Taj Mahal: A Love Poem in Stone
Ages 6 & up • Agra, India

NOTHING CAN PREPARE YOU FOR THE BEAUTY of the Taj Mahal. Yes, you've seen it a million times, on travel posters, in coffee-table books, even on the "It's a Small World" ride at Disneyland. You think you know that graceful center dome, the symmetrical white marble building with its pointed arches, the four punctuating minarets, the serene reflecting pool—but you cannot imagine how intricate it really is, how ethereal. Children generally assume it's a palace, until they learn the eerie truth: It's an over-the-top mausoleum.

Children always like a sight with a good story, and there's none better than the story behind the Taj. It was built by the

grieving Shah Jahan, the fifth emperor of the powerful Mughal dynasty, to fulfill a deathbed promise to his favorite wife, whom he called Mumtaz Mahal ("Elect of the Palace"). He placed it beside the Yamuna River (where flooding is always a danger), next to the bustling market of the Tajganj, where it is said he first saw Mumtaz selling jewels in a market stall. Work started in 1641, and it took 20,000 laborers 22 years to complete. When Shah Jahan himself died, his cenotaph was placed beside his beloved Mumtaz's, somewhat spoiling the perfect original symmetry of the mausoleum chamber.

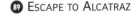
A red-sandstone gate-house divides the Taj Mahal's tranquil gardens from the crowded city outside. What I always thought of as a sugar-cube white building is in fact a bejeweled box, with exquisite detailing covering the marble inside and out—a technique called *pietra dura,* which came from either Italy or Persia, depending on which scholar you read. As you stroll around, study these intricately carved floral bouquets, inlaid with precious stones—agate, jasper, malachite, turquoise, tiger's-eye, lapis lazuli, coral, carnelian. Notice how the panels of **calligraphy,** inlaid with black marble, are designed to get bigger the higher they are placed, so the letters all appear the same size to a beholder on the ground level. Past the central pool rises the arched octagonal building containing the tombs, its white dome ringed by four minidomes. Inside, the two tombs are surrounded by delicate filigreed screens carved from a single piece of marble. Two red mosques flank the mausoleum on

The Taj Mahal.

either side, one of them required by the Muslim faith, the other a "dummy" built for the sheer love of symmetry.

Open from dawn to dusk, the Taj changes color depending on the time of day. There used to be nighttime hours for visiting by moonlight, no doubt the most shimmering hour of all. But even at high noon, the Taj Mahal will not disappoint you, not any of you.

(i) Tajganj ((C) **0562/233-0496**). Closed Mon.

✈ Agra, 35 min. flight from Delhi.

🛏 $$ **Jaypee Palace Hotel,** Fatehabad Rd. ((C) **0562/233-0800;** www.jaypeehotels. com). $$$ **WelcomHotel Mughal Sheraton,** 194 Fatehabad Rd., Taj Ganj ((C) **0562/233-1701;** www.welcomgroup.com).

WHY THEY'LL THANK YOU: An eternal symbol of love.

Atmospheric Places to Explore

89

Escape to Alcatraz
America's Most Famous Prison
Ages 8 & up • San Francisco, California, USA

WHAT DO YOU DO WITH the most notorious hardened criminals in the federal prison system? In 1934, at the height of the gangster era, the government had a brainstorm: wall them up in a converted military fort on an island in San Francisco Bay surrounded by sheer cliffs, frigid waters, and treacherous currents. Just let them *try* to escape from there. Thus was the **Alcatraz Island federal penitentiary** born, a maximum-security prison whose infamous inmates included Al Capone, "Machine

Gun" Kelly, and Robert Stroud (the Birdman). You may recognize its impregnable profile, lit by an ominous domed beacon tower, from such movies as *The Birdman of Alcatraz, Escape from Alcatraz,* and *The Rock;* it hasn't held a prisoner since 1963, but the vibe is still eerie—and therefore irresistible to youngsters.

These days it's harder to get into **Alcatraz** than it is to get out of it, thanks to

Alcatraz Island.

the popularity of National Park Service tours to the island; call at least a month in advance to reserve tickets. You'll take a ferry from Fisherman's Wharf and explore the famous prison with a slide show and audio tour, which includes fascinating stories told by former guards and inmates. As you listen to the audio narration and the grim anecdotes delivered by park rangers, you get a chilling sense of what it was like to be isolated in the middle of the bay—with winds blustering through the barred windows and armed guards pacing the gun galley—yet so achingly close to the beautiful city of San Francisco.

By declaring Alcatraz to be "inescapable," the government was almost daring prisoners to break out. Officially, no one ever did, although there were 14 audacious attempts over the

years: 23 fugitives were caught, 6 were shot, 2 drowned, and 5 others were missing and presumed drowned.

The ferry ride across the bay is fun, but you'll want to wear jackets, even in summer—and wear comfortable shoes, because there are many stairs to climb. Older kids who want to ratchet up the tour's already-somber tone may opt for the spooky "Alcatraz After Hours" tour. Hey, if you're going for creepy, you might as well go all the way.

(i) Pier 41, at Fisherman's Wharf ((C) **415/ 773-1188** for info, 415/705-5555 for reservations; www.nps.gov/alcatraz).

✈ ⊨ See San Francisco Cable Cars **68**.

WHY THEY'LL THANK YOU: Appreciating the sweet taste of freedom.

A Touch of Kitsch **90**

The Great New Jersey Diner Hunt
All ages • I-95, I-80 & the Garden State Parkway, New Jersey, USA

Gleaming roadside restaurants of chrome and brightly colored enamel, where you can chow down at a Formica counter lined with swiveling stools—this is the all-American diner experience, and there's nowhere

better to track it down than in highway-laced New Jersey, which has more diners than any other state in the country. Not more diners per capita, or more diners per square mile—more diners period.

Right across the Hudson River from New York City (take the Holland Tunnel), Jersey City has two classic diners worth seeking out. At the juncture of U.S. 1 and Manhattan Ave., **White Mana,** 470 Tonnele Ave. (℡ 201/963-1441), with its distinctive circular counter around the grill, was built for the 1939 World's Fair as the "diner of the future," and it does look somewhat like a red flying saucer just landed on Earth. From here, follow Route 1 to Culver Avenue and then West Side Avenue to find the neon-lit chrome-sided **Miss America Diner,** 322 West Side Ave. (℡ 201/333-5468), built in the 1950s. For New Jersey's oldest diner, take I-95 north to I-280 west and get off in Harrison for the red-and-white barrel-roofed **Max's Grill,** 731 Harrison Ave. (℡ 973/483-2012). Get back on I-95 and zip north to I-80 west, where you can stop off in Hasbrouck Heights to see the 1947 **Bendix Diner,** State Road 17 and Williams Street (℡ 201/288-0143), an Art Deco gem so picture-perfect that it was used not only in the 1982 film *Diner* but also the 1995 Drew Barrymore movie *Boys on the Side.* Take Route 17 farther west to Hackensack to see White Mana's sister diner, **White Manna,** 358 River St. (℡ 201/342-0914), dating from the late 1930s, all chrome

and glass blocks and hard-to-miss-from-the-road red signs. The petite burgers known as sliders are even better here than at the Jersey City location.

Down near the Jersey Shore—Bruce Springsteen's old Asbury Park stomping grounds—are three more beauties worth a visit. The **American Diner** in Shrewsbury, 1160 Route 35 (take exit 109 from the Garden State Pkwy.; ℡ 732/542-1658), may be a 1997 replica, but it was built by Kullman, one of the classic diner manufacturers; and it has the vintage look down pat, with lots of neon and chrome and glass-block walls. The bright and flashy **Broadway Diner** in Red Bank, 45 Monmouth St., just west of Route 35 (℡ 732/224-1234), is more authentic, built circa 1957, and a good breakfast stop—the pancakes here are excellent. Farther west in Freehold, the 1947 **Freehold Grill,** 59 E. Main St. (℡ 732/431-8607), has a particularly great period neon sign out in front and a long, sleek counter inside.

ⓘ www.njdiners.com.

✈ 🛏 See Manhattan **56**.

WHY THEY'LL THANK YOU: Landmark architecture served with a burger and a shake. You want fries with that too?

---

91 A Touch of Kitsch

Stone Mountain National Park
Where the South Rises Again
All ages • Stone Mountain, Georgia, USA

MOUNT RUSHMORE? A mere pipsqueak compared to this massive memorial to heroes of the Confederacy. It's the world's largest sculpture, and any Northerner who thinks the South lost the Civil War may find this Deep South rewriting of history a mite unsettling—but hey, if General Sherman had mercilessly burned and pillaged your hometown, you'd be pretty slow to forgive, too.

Mount Rushmore's sculptor, Gutzon Borglum, actually began with this sculpture, back in 1923, but after 10 years the project soured and he went out to South Dakota, where he could do things his way. It wasn't until 1963, when the state purchased the mountain and its lovely woodland surroundings for a park, that work resumed under Walter Kirtland Hancock and Roy Faulkner. The memorial was finally completed in 1970. Standing 90 feet high and 190 feet wide, hewn in bas-relief out of the side of a gray granite mountain, it depicts Confederate leaders **Jefferson Davis** (President of the break-away Confederate States of America), **Robert E. Lee** (top general of the South's armies), and **Stonewall Jackson** (a beloved general who died at Chancel-lorsville in 1863) galloping on horseback throughout eternity. At the on-site museum, the kids can stand next to rep-licas of various features from the statue and understand how truly enormous those figures are. The best view of the sculpture is from below, but you can climb a walking trail up its moss-covered slopes, especially lovely in spring when they're blanketed in wildflowers, or take the narrated tram ride to the top.

A highlight at Stone Mountain is **Laser-show,** a spectacular display of laser lights and fireworks with animation and music, every summer night at 9:30pm. And unlike Mount Rushmore, which sits in the middle of badlands, Stone Mountain is surrounded by a host of other park attractions that are tremendously appealing to kids: the **Stone Mountain Scenic Railroad,** which chugs

around the 5-mile base of Stone Mountain; the **Scarlett O'Hara,** a paddle-wheel river-boat that cruises 363-acre Stone Mountain Lake; and the **Antique Auto & Music Museum,** a jumble of old radios, juke-boxes, nickelodeons, Lionel trains, carousel horses, and classic cars. The 19-building **Antebellum Plantation** is a major sight-seeing attraction in itself, displaying an authentic 1830s country store, clapboard slave cabins, a smokehouse, a doctor's office, and three restored homes, from the 1790s, 1845, and 1850. And yes, there are mini-golf, a lakefront beach with water slides, 20 acres of wildlife trails, bicycle rentals, even a petting zoo.

ⓘ U.S. Hwy. 78 E. (𝒞 **800/317-2006;** www.stonemountainpark.com).

✈ Atlanta.

🛏 $$$ **The Georgian Terrace Hotel,** 659 Peachtree St., Atlanta (𝒞 **800/651-2316** or 404/897-1991; www.thegeorgian terrace.com). $$ **Marriott Stone Mountain Park Inn,** 1058 Robert E. Lee Dr. (𝒞 **770/ 469-3311;** www.marriott.com).

WHY THEY'LL THANK YOU: Getting in touch with Dixie pride.

A Touch of Kitsch 92

Coral Castle
One Big Florida Roadside Souvenir
All ages • Homestead, Florida, USA

Tʜᴇʀᴇ'ꜱ ᴘʟᴇɴᴛʏ ᴏꜰ ᴄᴏᴍᴘᴇᴛɪᴛɪᴏɴ, but Coral Cas-tle is probably the strangest attraction in Florida. Hewn by one solitary folk artist out of some 1,100 tons of pastel-tinted coral rock, this prehistoric-looking roofless "castle" harks back to an earlier age of Florida tourism—a time when the weirder and wackier a roadside attraction was, the better.

Like all such curiosities, this one has a story behind it. In 1923, a Latvian immi-grant named Edward Leedskalnin—

suffering from unrequited love for his 16-year-old fiancée, Agnes Scuffs, who had left him at the altar—moved to South Miami, after having knocked around Canada and California and Texas for a few lonely years. He spent the next 28 years of his life carving huge boulders of coral rock into this collection of outdoor sculp-tures, including such odd features as a moon fountain, a rocking chair, a table shaped like a heart, and another table shaped like the state of Florida. He began the thing in Florida City, his first home in the Miami area, but later spent 3 years moving the gigantic work-in-progress to his new home in Homestead, using a friend's tractor to haul it on his small trailer. In 1940 he erected a coral-rock wall around it and began charging visitors 10¢ to see it.

You don't come to see the Coral Castle so much for the artistic quality—in fact, the carving is blocky and crude—as for the mystery of it. It seems impossible that Edward Leedskalnin, who was only 5 feet tall and weighed no more than 100 pounds, could have done all this, using only tools he'd made himself from junk parts. Scores of affidavits on display from neighbors swear it happened . . . although nobody ever actually saw Ed working on it. Ed himself, being from a

family of stone masons in Latvia, claimed that he worked at night using secret techniques passed down through the ages, the same techniques that allowed slaves to build the Great Pyramids. Hmmm.

(i) 28655 S. Dixie Hwy. ((C) **305/248-6345;** www.coralcastle.com).

✈ Miami International, 40 miles.

🛏 $$ **Indian Creek Hotel,** 2727 Indian Creek Dr., Miami Beach ((C) **800/491-2772** or 305/531-2727; www.indiancreekhotel. com). $$$ **Sonesta Beach Resort Key Biscayne,** 350 Ocean Dr., Key Biscayne ((C) **800/SONESTA** or 305/361-2021; www.sonesta.com).

WHY THEY'LL THANK YOU: Deciding whether or not this was a hoax.

---

93 A Touch of Kitsch

Holland in America

All ages • Holland, Michigan, USA

THIS DUTCH-THEMED TOWN in southern Michigan balances on the knife-edge between serious cultural attraction and all-out kitsch-fest. Yes, the women painting blue-and-white Delft designs on pottery at the **DeKlomp Wooden Shoe & Delft Factory,** 12755 Quincy Ave. ((C) **616/399-1900**), are legitimate craftspersons you can watch making fine objects—but do they have to wear those starched white winged caps? And yes, 36-acre **Windmill Island,** 7th Street at Lincoln Avenue ((C) **616/355-1030**), has a real 240-year-old windmill transported in 1965 from the Netherlands, from which you can gaze over a garden of 150,000 vivid tulips in spring, canals and dikes, a miniature Netherlands village, and a hand-painted Dutch carousel—but do they have to hire young girls to stage klompen dances around the central plaza?

On the other hand, it could be so much worse. The **Dutch Village** theme park, for example, at 12350 James St. ((C) **616/396-1475;** www.dutchvillage.com), could

have installed roller coasters and thrill rides to accompany its replica Dutch architecture and gardens, but it stuck with old-fashioned options like a carousel and a swing ride, maintaining the flavor of an attraction opened in the late 1950s, soon after Walt Disney invented the theme park idea. Way back in 1928, Holland went for its share of the nascent tourism industry, launching an annual **Tulip Time** weekend in early May that's still going strong, with parades and concerts and a crafts fair. The vast **Veldheer Tulip Farm,** 12755 Quincy ((C) **616/279-1900**), remains what it is, a tulip farm, where you can buy flowers in the spring and bulbs in the fall. Holland's cobblestone downtown streets are lined with Dutch-themed cafes and shops in gabled old buildings, but they are appealingly quaint. Of course you can buy corny gifts here—but a tiny pair of wooden shoes is not such a bad souvenir.

Tulip season in Holland, Michigan.

who fled religious oppression and economic depression in the Netherlands to build a town that now numbers 112,000 people in its metropolitan area. Yes, tourism is a part of the economic mix, but they've also got the Heinz pickle factory, so there. If Holland, Michigan, falls into the kitsch category, so be it—it's clean and wholesome and picturesque enough to make kids perk right up.

ⓘ **Tourist information,** 76 E 8th St. (✆ **800/506-7299** or 616/394-0000; www.holland.org).

✈ Grand Rapids, 31 miles.

🛏 $$ **Best Western Kelly Inn,** 2888 W. Shore Dr. (✆ **800/528-1234** or 616/994-0400; www.bestwestern.com). $$ **Hampton Inn,** 12427 Felch St. (✆ **800/HAMPTON** or 616/399-8500; www.suburbaninns.tv).

BEST TIME: Tulip season, obviously, in late spring.

WHY THEY'LL THANK YOU: A little slice of Holland.

At the **Holland Museum,** 31 W. 10th St. (✆ **616/392-9084;** www.hollandmuseum.org), you can learn the history of that first intrepid band of settlers in 1847,

---

A Touch of Kitsch   **94**

Paul Bunyan: A North Woods Odyssey

All ages • Bemidji, Minnesota, USA

As a friend of mine from St. Paul pointed out, it seems that every town in Minnesota's beautiful lake-dotted center has some plaster animal on a pole outside of town—a rainbow trout, a beaver, a moose—to proclaim itself to visitors. But why mess around with a mere animal when you could have the North Woods's most enduring legend—the King of the Lumberjacks, Paul Bunyan, and his big blue ox, Babe?

You really know you've hit the North Woods when you arrive in **Brainerd,** Minnesota, and see the new 11½-foot-tall fiberglass Paul Bunyan statue beside the tourist information stand on Highway 371

just south of town. It's too realistic for my taste; the town commissioned this statue when it couldn't acquire the much larger seated Paul Bunyan figure from the now-defunct Paul Bunyan Center. That statue wound up at **This Old Farm,** 17553 Hwy. 18, Brainerd (✆ **218/764-2524**), a delightful mishmash of attractions including a restored 1940s farm, a corn maze, an arcade (where Paul sits), and a small ho-hum amusement park.

Some 70 miles farther upstate, in the town of **Akeley,** on Main Street you'll find the next Paul Bunyan statue, a really big one—he'd be 25 feet tall if he stood up. Instead he crouches down, resting his axe beside him, with his hand cupped to hold tourists for photo ops. The black beard on this one is seriously impressive. Beside the statue is the Paul Bunyan Historical Museum, which has nothing to do with Paul Bunyan but recounts the area's logging history.

Forty miles north, you come to **Bemidji,** where the granddaddy of all Paul Bunyan statues stands downtown, next to the tourist office, on the pine-edged shore of Lake Bemidji. Eastman Kodak once named this America's second-most-photographed roadside icon, a classic piece of Americana erected in 1937 by the Bemidji chamber of commerce. This rather crude Paul Bunyan figure (instead of a beard, he has a Snidely Whiplash–like handlebar mustache) stands 18 feet high and weighs 2½ tons. Next to him is his companion, Babe the Blue Ox, who weighs in at 5 tons. The site

chosen for the statues is purportedly Bunyan's actual birthplace (yeah, sure, tell us another). Other legends claim that Lake Bemidji itself was created by one of Paul's footprints. There's also a **Paul Bunyan Amusement Park** beside the statues, and south of town is the **Paul Bunyan Animal Farm,** 3857 Animal Land Dr. (② **218/759-1533**), a small petting zoo. It might as well cash in on the name—everybody else up here does!

ⓘ ② **218/759-0164;** www.visitbemidji.com.

✈ Grand Forks, ND, 113 miles.

🛏 $$ **AmericInn,** 1200 Paul Bunyan Dr. NW (② **800/634-3444** or 218/751-3000). $$$ **Hampton Inn,** 1019 Paul Bunyan Dr. S. (② **800/HAMPTON** or 218/751-3600; www.hamptoninn.com).

WHY THEY'LL THANK YOU: A tall man to match the tall tales.

A Touch of Kitsch

95

Mount Rushmore & The Crazy Horse Memorial

All ages • Keystone & Custer, South Dakota, USA

WHEN YOU THINK ABOUT IT, Mount Rushmore is one of the oddest monuments ever: Gigantic chiseled faces of four Presidents—why four? Why those four (Washington, Jefferson, Lincoln, and . . . Theodore Roosevelt?)? And why in the South Dakota badlands, miles away from most U.S. citizens? But crazy as it is, darned if another group didn't raise money to carve another mountain nearby with an even bigger sculpture, depicting American Indian chief Crazy Horse.

Mount Rushmore was the passion of one individual: Gutzon Borglum, a Danish-American sculptor from Idaho, who was hired by South Dakota to make a memorial to draw visitors to the Black Hills. Borglum—who had previously been hired

to carve Stone Mountain **91** in Georgia, until negotiations broke down—chose this peak because it was hard granite, the highest in the area, and it faced southeast, where it would catch good daytime light. He also picked which Presidents to portray: Teddy Roosevelt made the cut because he'd lived in South Dakota and was a conservationist (also because Borglum had already done a bust of TR for the U.S. Capitol). The project was conceived in 1923; sculpting began in 1927 and puttered along through the Depression. Washington was unveiled in 1934, Jefferson in 1936, Lincoln in 1937, and Roosevelt in 1939. Borglum died in 1941, and though his son Lincoln continued for

Mount Rushmore.

7 months, the work halted for good when the U.S. entered World War II.

Visit the **museum** under the amphitheater to learn about Borglum's innovative engineering. A 1-mile **Presidential Trail** leads to viewing terraces at the base of the mountain; take a guided tour so the kids can learn all the curious history. It's great to catch Mount Rushmore by the dawn's early light, or at least as soon as the park opens at 8am. In summer, a nightly lighting ceremony at 9pm (8pm in Sept) makes another splendid viewing op.

To many Native Americans, Mount Rushmore is a sacrilege, an intrusion on sacred landscapes, so the Lakota tribe initiated their own project 17 miles away, hiring sculptor Korczak Ziolkowski, who'd briefly worked with Borglum on Mount Rushmore. He began to hew the image of Chief Crazy Horse astride a thundering stallion in 1948; 50 years later—16 years after Ziolkowski himself had died—only the chief's nine-story-high face was completed. Millions of tons of rock have been blasted from the mountain face, though,

and even kids should be able to trace the form emerging from the granite; nightly laser shows in summer project the finished design onto the rough-hewn rock. When finished, Crazy Horse will be so big that all four heads on Mount Rushmore can fit inside it—641 feet long and 563 feet high. At the base of the mountain, the **Indian Museum of North America** focuses on the tribal history of numerous Native American cultures.

(i) **Mount Rushmore National Memorial,** Mt. Rushmore Rd., Keystone (© **605/574-2523;** www.nps.gov/moru). **Crazy Horse Memorial,** U.S. 385, north of Custer (© **605/673-4681;** www.crazyhorse.org).

✈ Rapid City, 35 miles.

🛏 $$ **Alex Johnson Hotel,** 523 6th St., Rapid City (© **800/888-2539** or 605/342-1210; www.alexjohnson.com). $$ **Sylvan Lake Lodge,** S. Dak. 87 & S. Dak. 89 (© **605/255-4521;** www.custerresorts.com).

WHY THEY'LL THANK YOU: Giant statues for American giants.

The Corn Palace: Harvest Gone Wild

All ages • Mitchell, South Dakota, USA

ON THAT CLASSIC COAST-TO-COAST See-America-First drive in the family truckster, once you hit the Great Plains things begin to seem a little slow—it's just such a long way between cities. That's the appeal of The Corn Palace, sitting squarely on South Dakota's long east–west stretch of I-90. You have to get off the road somewhere, and when you do, it might as well be somewhere that makes you blink your eyes in wonder.

Turning onto Mitchell's main street downtown, you can't miss The Corn Palace, a gaudy, multicolor riot of onion domes and turrets. It was originally built in 1921 as the main exposition hall for this agricultural market town, but in a way the Corn Palace is built new every year. Every spring, a different artist announces a theme and sets to work, creating a set of **murals** to cover the outside of the Corn Palace—murals made out of *corn*. Yes, that's right, kernels and husks of real corn are applied to the facade, a custom that goes back to the 1890s when the first Corn Palace was opened. Actually, it still seems bizarre, no matter how long they've been doing it. But that's why the Corn Palace looks as though it's made out of corn, though underneath the building is mere reinforced concrete.

Concerts, stage shows, and sports events take place in and out of the hall, and still the artists work to complete their design, using thousands of bushels of native South Dakota corn, grain, and grasses. Come here in the summer and you'll still see a work in progress.

Now that you're off the interstate, Mitchell has another worthy sight across the street—the **Enchanted Doll Museum,** 615 N. Main St. (✆ **605/996-9896**), which has more than 4,000 dolls, many of them collectors' items, arranged in vignettes and dioramas.

ⓘ 604 N. Main St. (✆ **866/273-CORN;** www.cornpalace.org).

✈ Rapid City, 35 miles.

🛏 $$ **Days Inn,** 15–6 S. Burr (✆ **800/ 329-7466** or 605/996-6208; www.daysinn. com).

WHY THEY'LL THANK YOU: It's beyond corny.

Wall Drug: The Power of Advertising

All ages • Wall, South Dakota, USA

AT THE OTHER END of South Dakota's I-90 corridor from The Corn Palace **96**, Wall Drug is a one-of-a-kind phenomenon—a wayside stop that just kept growing and growing. It all began in the Depression, when nearby Mount Rushmore was still under scaffolding, years away from attracting travelers to this middle-of-nowhere burg. Desperate for business, Wall Drug's owners, Ted and Dorothy Hustead, put up signs on the highway advertising free ice water to thirsty travelers. Motorists poured in.

Now convinced of the power of advertising, the Husteads planted more and more billboards, until they even began to appear in foreign countries. The Highway Beautification Act of the 1960s severely limited Wall Drug's billboard campaign, but still the tourists came; and over the years the Husteads (who still own the place, though it's now in the hands of the third generation) have added more and more popular features to draw them in.

Some 20,000 people a day, it's estimated, pull off the road to mill around this shambling low-slung complex, so extensive that it scarcely seems like a drugstore anymore. (There is a replica of the original small pharmacy inside, however.) Along with a "mall" of 26 little shops, Wall Drug has a restaurant, a vast postcard store, a gallery selling Western art, displays of Native American artifacts, a mechanical diorama of an American Indian village, and a mocked-up main street of a Western town. But wait! There's more! Animated figures tucked into every available niche "speak" to the customers, including a roaring T-Rex. Out in the back yard stand king-size plaster figures of a bucking bronco, a rabbit, and the mythical jackalope, and an 80-foot-long green brontosaurus statue benignly casts its shade over the children's play area.

Nothing defines "tourist trap" better than Wall Drug. That's why you must visit.

ⓘ 510 N. Main St. (ⓒ **605/279-2175;** www.walldrug.com).

✈ ⇌ See Mount Rushmore **95**.

WHY THEY'LL THANK YOU: Classic roadside Americana.

Watts Tower: One Man's Mania

Ages 6 & up • Los Angeles, California, USA

THE ONLY REASON MOST TOURISTS VENTURE into this gritty inner-city neighborhood is to view Watts Towers, the largest piece of folk art created by a single person. That person was Simon Rodia, an immigrant Italian tile setter who for 33 years worked patiently in his spare time on this quixotic project. Nine intricate cement-and-steel structures gradually rose to the sky from the tiny yard of his cottage by the streetcar tracks. They startle the eye and disturb the mind—which is why kids love them.

Rodia began the towers—which he himself called Nuestro Pueblo, or Our Town—sometime in the early 1920s. As the years passed and the surrounding area deteriorated, the childless bachelor grew more and more reclusive, compulsively devoting himself to the art project. Neighbor children threw rocks over the surrounding wall, and during World War II it was even rumored that the towers might be transmission antennae for sending secret information to the Japanese. Rodia abruptly quit the project and moved out in 1954, offhandedly leaving his cottage—and the towers in its yard—to a neighbor. After changing hands several times, they were "discovered" by art lovers and opened to the public in 1960. Rodia claimed to have lost all interest in this creation that had once so consumed him, and he would not give interviews, except to say, "I had in mind to do something big and I did it." We'll never know what inspired him to undertake this extraordinary effort.

Though Rodia had no engineering degrees and used the simplest of tools, he was a skilled craftsman with an old-world pride in his handiwork, and the towers are surprisingly strong (they survived the 1994 Northridge Earthquake with very little damage). They are topped with futuristic-looking spires, skeletal webs of interlaced steel. The tallest is 99 feet high. They are all encrusted with a zany profusion of brightly colored mosaics, created out of anything that came to hand—bottles, seashells, cups, plates, pottery, ceramic tiles, you name it. Ask the kids to look for chips of green glass (which came from old 7-Up bottles) and blue glass (from Milk of Magnesia bottles). Rodia's day job was at the legendary Malibu Potteries, so it seems likely that many fragments of valuable Malibu tile are embedded in the Towers. A few other fanciful structures, like a gazebo and a birdbath, are placed around the towers. **Tours** are offered every half-hour on a first-come, first-served basis.

(i) 1727 E. 107th St. ((C) **213/847-4646**).

✈ 🛏 See Hooray for Hollywood **355**.

WHY THEY'LL THANK YOU: Seeing what 33 years can produce.

A Touch of Kitsch

99

Winchester Mystery House
Monument to Paranoia
Ages 4 & up • San Jose, California, USA

Truth can be stranger than fiction, and no theme-park attraction could be any stranger than this actual house in San Jose, an hour's drive south of San Francisco. This quirky mansion, set in acres of meticulous gardens, was obviously the handiwork of a madwoman. Walking through it on any of the various guided tours, you'll be astonished at its weird mix of luxury, good taste, and utter craziness.

Begun in 1884, the Winchester Mystery House is the legacy of Sarah L. Winchester, a 44-year-old widow. Her husband was the son of the famous rifle manufacturer Oliver Winchester, maker of the fabulously successful Winchester repeater rifle—sometimes called the "Gun That Won the West." After both her husband and her baby daughter died, the disconsolate Mrs. Winchester consulted with a seer, who proclaimed that the family lay under a special curse—targeted by the unhappy spirits of people who had been killed with Winchester rifles. Gullible Mrs. Winchester bought the idea, and that's when her personal tragedy took a peculiar twist. The medium told her those unquiet souls could be appeased by only one thing: perpetual construction on the Winchester mansion. (Makes you wonder if she got a kickback from the contractor.) Convinced that she'd live as long as building continued, Mrs. Winchester—who happened to have a fortune to spend on this scheme—went through most of her $20-million inheritance over the next 38 years, as construction work went on 24 hours a day, 7 days a week, 365 days a year.

As you can probably guess, this is no ordinary home. With **160 rooms,** it sprawls across half a dozen acres, a red-roofed Victorian mansion with extra turrets and gables sprouting randomly. There was never any master blueprint; Sarah Winchester herself designed the additions, often drawing them on a scrap of paper or a tablecloth whenever a new idea seized her. It has some 40 bedrooms, 47 fireplaces, and 5 kitchens, and a number of high-tech features for its time—elevators, forced-air heating, and gas light fixtures that could be turned on with the press of a button. Her favorite flower was the daisy, and it's fun to look for the **daisy motif** repeated in room after room.

Still, what kids undoubtedly remember most are the many disturbing features: a

Winchester Mystery House.

staircase leading nowhere, a Tiffany window with a spider-web design, a window in the floor, and doors that open onto blank walls. Superstitious Mrs. Winchester harped on the number 13, hoping thereby to confound the vengeful spirits—there are 13 bathrooms, 13 windows and doors in the old sewing room, 13 palms lining the main driveway, 13 hooks in the séance room, and chandeliers with 13 lights. Did the perpetual renovation plan work? Well, eventually Sarah Winchester did die, but not until the ripe old age of 82—with the house still unfinished, of course.

ⓘ 525 S. Winchester Blvd. (I-280 at Highway 17; © **408/247-2101;** www.winchester mysteryhouse.com).

✈ San Francisco International, 45 miles.

🛏 See San Francisco Cable Cars **68**.

WHY THEY'LL THANK YOU: Realizing that even grown-ups get out of control sometimes.

A Touch of Kitsch **100**

Santa's Village
Where St. Nick Gets His Reindeer
Ages 4 & up • Lapland, Finland

WHILE THERE ARE Santa Claus–themed attractions around the world—many of them open year-round—when you think about it, it's obvious that this must be the real one. It's on the Arctic Circle, and Mr. and Mrs. Claus, as well as their elves, need to live at least that far north.

And where else do reindeer come from if not from Lapland?

Whatever you call him, Santa Claus or Father Christmas or St. Nicholas or Kris Kringle, the jolly man in the red suit appears in his grotto, **Santa's Office,** daily year-round, and "elves" at the **post** office across the way stamp letters with an authentic postmark. Even older children who don't "believe" anymore can find the low-key charm in this quaint-looking Finnish theme park (though it is certainly sophisticated enough to attract half a million visitors a year). **Santa House** (✆ **16/356-15-13**), set in a traditional Lapp log house, offers a historical exhibit about how various nations' Yuletide traditions developed. The nearby **Napipiri Reindeer Park** has a herd of 30 to 50 reindeer browsing around its corral; in winter they pull sleigh rides, and in the summer you can see spindly-legged calves tottering around the corral. Another kilometer south is **Santa Park** (✆ **16/333-000;** www.santapark.com), the only part of the development that gets a mite too cute—inside a glamorous stage-set "cave," children can join the elves in baking or toy making, sit on Santa's lap, and watch a film or a show, all for an extra admission fee.

Although winter seems at first the obvious time to go see Santa's Village, remember that this Arctic Circle region is dark continually during the winter (though brightly lit!). Even the Northern Lights—which don't appear as often here as they do at Tromsø **311**—may not be compensation enough. In summer, however, the sun shines around the clock, and Santa will still be here.

ⓘ Hwy. 4, 8km (5 miles) north of Rovaniemi (✆ **16/356-20-96;** www.santa clausvillage.info).

✈ Rovaniemi.

🛏 $$$ **Lapland Hotels Sky Ounasvaara,** Ounasvaara (✆ **16/335-33-11;** www. laplandhotels.com).

WHY THEY'LL THANK YOU: Whether or not they believe, the charm of the story wins through.

---

101 A Touch of Kitsch

Mystery Park: Alpine Sci-Fi

Ages 10 & up • Interlaken, Switzerland

WHEN YOU FIRST SEE THIS FUTURISTIC THEME PARK plopped down outside picturesque Interlaken, the "town between the lakes" in Switzerland's Bernese Oberland, you may think, "Wha-?" Topped with its silver-skinned geodesic globe, it looks like a space port straight out of *2001: A Space Odyssey,* despite the snow-powdered alpine peaks in the background. But it all makes sense when you learn that this oddity sprang from the brain of local writer Erich von Däniken, the controversial Swiss author of *Chariots of the Gods* and other books about ancient alien visitors to Earth. Whether or not you find von Däniken a crackpot—and most scientists and archaeologists do—there's a sort of *Outer Limits* spookiness that builds up the longer you roam around this attraction

that's wildly popular with visitors from all over the globe.

Radiating from the central pavilion, a ring of covered walkways lead to seven different "theme worlds," each offering a multimedia presentation exploring another mystery about man's contact with the alien universe. Several of them are housed in simplified replicas of ancient landmarks: "Nazca" explores the Nazca Lines **166** from Peru; "MegaStones" explores Stonehenge **163**; "Maya" explores the intricacies of the Mayan calendar as seen at Chichén Itzá **191**; "Orient" examines the Great Pyramid of Giza **169**. (As Däniken points out, very few tourists will ever travel to all these far-flung places, so he's collected them all in one spot.) Other pavilions in more abstract buildings explore phenomena such as

Mystery Park's Universe exhibit makes visitors feel as though they are surrounded by millions of stars.

outer space flights, cargo cults (accounts of humans being abducted by aliens), and the early mentions of flying machines in Eastern literature such as the *Mahabharata* and the *Rig Veda*. Within the central pavilion are a games arcade, submarine and space-capsule motion simulators, and a cafe.

The video game–like graphics and portentous music of the pavilions' shows speak a language that kids—or at any rate adolescent boys—automatically respond to. Even skeptical adults will enjoy seeing just what outrageous theories the von Däniken school is pushing. Several scholarly associations have assailed this site as flagrantly inaccurate (not to mention an obvious self-promotion for Däniken himself), but that's part of what I find so fascinating about it.

(i) Obere Bönigstrasse 100 (℅ **033/827-57-59;** www.mysterypark.ch).

Interlaken, 2 hr. from Zurich.

$ **The Swiss Inn,** Général Guisanstrasse 23 (℅ **033/822-36-26;** www.swiss-inn.com). $$$ **Victoria-Jungfrau Grand Hotel,** Höheweg 41 (℅ **800/223-6800** or 033/828-28-28).

WHY THEY'LL THANK YOU: Spotting the holes in the controversial argument.

Hundertwasser's Architecture Run Riot

Ages 6 & up • Vienna, Bad Blumau & Bärnbach, Austria

IMAGINE THIS: trees bubbling out of rooftops, tilting floors, mad yellow and white towers topped with onion domes, colorful facades jigsawed with black outlines, patches of mosaic seeming to sprout organically from the corners of windows. It's the sort of architecture your own kids might dream up on a sugar high, if you gave them a shovel, a bucket of Legos, permanent markers, and a blowtorch. But in this case, the child was artist Friedensreich Hundertwasser (a name he invented, meaning "Peace-Kingdom Hundred-Waters"), Austria's version of Antoni Gaudí (see The Gaudí Cathedral **323**). In just 2 days, you could easily see all three major buildings in Austria designed by this brilliant, eccentric architect: **Hundertwasser Haus** in Vienna, the spa at **Bad Blumau,** and the **Hundertwasserkirche** in Bärnbach.

Hundertwasser Haus is a low-income housing project in a rundown district of Vienna; you can only see it from the outside, but the whacked-out exterior definitely stands out on this drab working-class street—all the irregular windows, sudden eruptions of color and mosaic, and rambling black lines crisscrossing the facade. Hundertwasser—who considered straight lines and right angles to be "the devil's tools"—reportedly designed this building for free, just so that nothing ugly would be built in its place.

A 90-minute drive south of Vienna is the spa hotel at **Bad Blumau** in Styria, a region of Austria known for its hot springs. Offbeat as it looks, this is in fact a working spa, and a fairly upscale one, with New Age-y therapies, saunas, and thermal pools. Hundertwasser's love of nature really kicks into high gear here, with grass-covered roofs, curving pools, and gardens, the property erupting with joyous bright pavilions, bridges, and pergolas. Inside you can see how Hundertwasser's ideas extended to interior design, and you can even spend the night—the guest rooms are comfortable, though the suites have about the only level floors in the place ("an uneven floor is a melody to the feet," Hundertwasser once wrote).

In 1987, in a coal town southwest of Graz named Bärnbach (about a 90-min. drive from Bad Blumau), Hundertwasser renovated the 1948 St. Barbara's church, turning it into the stunning **Hundertwasserkirche.** He blithely stuck a gold onion dome on its clock tower and ornamented the modest white plaster exterior with bold mosaics of major religious symbols, not just of Christianity but of all world religions. Go inside to see the huge mosaic crucifix and, best of all, a glowing window with a stained-glass spiral. No matter your faith, it's a religious experience.

ⓘ **Hundertwasser House,** Löwengasse and Kegelgasse 3, Vienna (www.hundertwasser haus.at/HwH/en_main.htm). **Bad Blumau,** A8283, Bad Blumau (www.blumau.com). **Hundertwasserkirche,** Tiberstrasse 15, Bärnbach (www.baernbach.at).

✈ Vienna.

🛏 $$$ **Rogner-Bad Blumau Spa & Hotel,** A8283 Bad Blumau (✆ 43/ 338351009445; www.blumau.com).

WHY THEY'LL THANK YOU: An artistic vision kids will understand.

103 A Touch of Kitsch

The Wasserspiele
A Bishop & His Bad Jokes
All ages • Hellbrunn, Austria

JUST 20 MINUTES SOUTHEAST OF SALZBURG, the square yellow baroque palace of **Schloss Hellbrunn** was built as a summer retreat for the Prince-Archbishop of Salzburg back in the early 17th century. Being the Prince-Archbishop of Salzburg was a very important job—and certainly Markus

Sittikus was an adept politician and power broker. But after a walk through the gardens of Hellbrunn, we will forever think of him as one of history's most incorrigible practical jokers.

We hurried through the audioguide tour of the 18th-century interior, keen to get on to the **palace garden,** one of the oldest baroque formal gardens in Europe. A live tour guide leads the garden tours, for reasons that soon became clear: You need a human being to push buttons to activate the water-powered automata and so-called "water jokes." These were high-tech status symbols in the early 17th century, but only Hellbrunn's have survived.

Passing through the gardens, you'll see water-powered mechanical scenes set in small grottoes, and a truly remarkable mechanical theater of an entire baroque city, with some 250 moving figures. There's a grotto where the walls, ceiling, and even floors are covered with seashells; in the **Neptune Grotto** an immense leering mask sticks out his tongue repeatedly at you. And just when you least expect it, you get drawn into the action. Lean over to peer closer at a statue in a grotto? You get a spurt of water in your eye. Walk down a staircase

between a pair of stately stone urns? You get pelted with spray from both sides. There's even a stone dining table set out in the garden where all but one of the stone seats is rigged with a water jet; sitting safely upon the blank seat, the Prince-Archbishop could nod to a servant and have a spurt of water sent up the backside of any guest he chose to torment. Punked again!

(i) Fürstenweg 37 (℃ **0662/8203720;** www.hellbrunn.at).

✈ Salzburg-Mozart Regional.

🛏 $ **Altstadthotel Wolf-Dietrich,** Wolf-Dietrich-Strasse 7 (℃ **0662/871275;** www.salzburg-hotel.at). $$ **Hotel Mozart,** Franz-Josef-Strasse 27 (℃ **0662/872274;** www.hotel-mozart.at).

BEST TIME: Closed Nov–Mar.

WHY THEY'LL THANK YOU: The 17th-century palace; the timeless sense of humor.

A Touch of Kitsch **104**

Museo de los Momias
A Mexican Day of the Dead
Ages 12 & up • Guanajuato, Mexico

MY CHILDREN'S FAVORITE HISPANIC HOLIDAY—in fact, one of their favorite holidays of all—is the Dios de los Muertos, or Day of the Dead, Mexico's ghoulish version of Halloween. Well, it's Day of the Dead every day at the Museo de los Momias, where real **human mummies** are displayed in glass cases. It's not for the squeamish, and it's the only graveyard I know of that has souvenir stands, selling skulls made out of sugar and tiny effigies of the mummies.

Over the course of a century, from 1865 to 1985, corpses were taken out of the ground in this *pantéon* (cemetery) to make room for newcomers, a typical custom in Mexico where graveyards have

limited space. What to do with them? Put them on display, of course. At least that's the solution reached here in the beautiful regional city of Guanajuato, where a unique combination of dryness and the earth's gases and minerals in the town's municipal cemetery halted the decomposition of the bodies that were dug up. The mummies are propped up or laid out in their display cases, some of them still wearing the rags of their centuries-old clothing—they almost seem to be grinning, choking, or staring out of their hollow eye sockets, their long teeth clenched in a rictus of life beyond the grave. If you speak Spanish well enough to follow the tour guides' macabre stories, you'll learn creepy stories about the fates of some of the deceased. Are they true? Who knows? But there's no mistaking the pregnant woman with her collapsed stomach, and there are way too many babies here for my taste. Don't come here unless you've got a decided taste for the gruesome—and even so, be prepared to have nightmares.

(i) Esplanada del Pantéon (© **473/732-0639**).

✈ Léon-Guanajuato, 27km (17 miles).

🛏 $$ **Méson de los Poetas,** Positos 35 (© **473/732-6657** or 473/732-0705; www. mexonline.com/poetas.htm). $$$ **Parador San Javier,** Plaza Aldama 92 (© **473/732-2222** or 473/732-0626).

WHY THEY'LL THANK YOU: Uncovering secrets of the graves.

---

105 Caves & Waterfalls

Howe Caverns & Secret Caverns
The Story of the Dueling Caves
Ages 6 & up • Upstate New York, USA

THE CLOSER WE GOT TO HOWE CAVERNS, the vintage upstate New York tourist attraction, the more billboards for it we passed— "VISIT BEAUTIFUL HOWE CAVERNS, ONLY 6 MILES AWAY!"—nostalgic throwbacks to an earlier era of roadside advertising. And a few yards past every Howe Caverns sign stood another more gaudy sign, hand-painted in a psychedelic style reminiscent of Grateful Dead album covers, luring visitors instead to Secret Caverns. Naturally, we had to visit both.

Howe Caverns is the granddaddy of American underground attractions—discovered in 1842 by farmer Lester Howe, it really took off in 1929, when walkways, lighting, and elevators were installed, and it still has a sweet, wholesome sort of Depression-era charm. While caves such as Mammoth Cave **106** and Carlsbad Caverns **107** are bigger and more spectacular, Howe Caverns doesn't try to gussy things up with laser lights and animatronics—you're underground, it's chilly and damp and echo-y, it's gosh-darn spooky, and that's enough. Eighty-minute **guided tours** lead you through its various chambers, including a wedding chamber (yes, many couples have chosen this spot to tie the knot) and a quarter-mile boat ride on the underground Lake of

Venus. Above-ground there are some other touristy activities like gemstone mining and pony rides, and the on-site restaurant has panoramic views from its big plate-glass windows. My kids thought

Howe Caverns.

119

it was totally cool . . . until we drove on down the road to Secret Caverns.

Secret Caverns is even smaller and more anticlimactic—a long stairway down to one passageway with a 100-foot waterfall. No big deal. The reason to come here is to revel in its roadside kitsch. The extravagant painting and tongue-in-cheek humor of its billboards are a good indication of the wackiness to be found at Secret Caverns. A supersized bat is painted over the entrance, and droll exhibits within include the "mummified remains" of a tour guide and goofy accounts of its 1928 discovery by a pair of cows. The guided tour often devolves into an improv routine, with the guides making up outrageous names for the rock formations they pass (often different names on the way down and back up). It's a fairly bald sendup of Howe Caverns, but then, Howe Caverns gets all the tourists—let Secret Caverns have all the fun.

(i) **Howe Caverns,** 255 Discovery Dr., Howes Cave (✆ **518/296-8900;** www. howecaverns.com). **Secret Caverns,** Off Route 7, east of Cobleskill (✆ **518/296-8558;** www.secretcaverns.com).

✈ Albany, 35 miles.

🛏 $$ **Howe Caverns Motel,** on the Howe Caverns grounds (✆ **518/296-8950**).

WHY THEY'LL THANK YOU: Spelunking with a sense of irony.

Caves & Waterfalls **106**

Mammoth Cave
Kentucky's Subterranean Supremo
All ages • Cave City or Park City, Kentucky, USA

GROWING UP IN INDIANA, I remember driving down back roads past ramshackle barns with fat yellow letters emblazoned on their roofs:  SEE MAMMOTH CAVE. It always beckoned to us kids like some kind of exotic Shangri-La, or maybe the Eighth Wonder of the World, thanks to this old-timey advertising campaign.

In many ways Mammoth Cave *is* the eighth natural wonder of the world—it's the planet's longest system of caves, stretching for more than 360 underground miles (and that only counts the parts explored so far!) and going as deep as 379 feet below the surface. There's so much to see here that it can't be viewed all at once, so park rangers have developed many **tours,** ranging in duration from half an hour to 6 hours. While one quarter-mile loop is suitable for small children and the elderly, at the other end of the spectrum lies a tour for teens and adults that requires strenuous climbs and crawling through narrow passages. You could do more than one, since there's little overlap—some focus on the geology or biology of the caves, while others explore its history from prehistoric dwellers to 19th-century tourists to tuberculosis patients to present-day environmentalists; others switch off the electric lights and roam the dark caves with kerosene lanterns. Reservations are essential in summer—all the tours book up quickly.

Kentucky is geologically ripe for caves, with a vast subterranean drainage system that bored through its limestone bedrock. Draining water leaves behind not only the stalagmites and stalactites kids learn about in science, but also rippled formations like flowstone and dripstone. Embedded in the walls you'll see fossils—blastoids, crinoids, gastropods—left from the days when this region was a vast shallow sea. The ceiling soars 192 feet over

Mammoth Cave.

Mammoth Dome; the floor sinks 105 feet below the walkways in the Bottomless Pit.

I loved the fanciful names given to various "chambers," such as Fat Man's Misery, Giant's Coffin, Frozen Niagara, and the Snowball Room.

We were glad to find that the surface landscape—53,000 acres of lovely hardwood forests—offers loads of other fun activities: hiking, horseback rides, birdwatching, or canoeing along more than 30 miles of river.

ⓘ **Visitor Center/Park Headquarters,** South Entrance Rd. (✆ **270/758-2328;** www.nps.gov/maca).

✈ Louisville and Nashville are both about 1½ hr. away.

🛏 $$ **Jellystone Park RV/Cabin Resort,** 1002 Mammoth Cave Rd., Cave City (✆ **270/773-3840;** www.jellystone mammothcave.com). $$ **Mammoth Cave Hotel,** within the park (✆ **270/758-2225;** www.mammothcavehotel.com).

WHY THEY'LL THANK YOU: A whole world underground.

Caves & Waterfalls
107

Carlsbad Caverns
Colossal Underground Refuge
Ages 6 & up • Carlsbad, New Mexico, USA

NATIVE AMERICANS ALWAYS KNEW there was a giant cave system snaking around under the porous limestone reef of the Guadalupe Mountains. But white settlers only stumbled upon it a century ago, after noticing vast hordes of bats swarming out of a hole in the ground every summer day at sunset. Some 100 caves lie within today's park, an underground world of pale limestone where every fantastic and grotesque shape imaginable (and unimaginable) has been sculpted by natural forces—from frozen waterfalls to strands of pearls, soda straws to miniature castles, draperies to ice-cream cones. Above all, what is impressive here

is the sheer size of the cave, a constantly cool (56°F/13°C) refuge from the 100°F (38°C) heat outside in the Chihuahuan Desert.

The main cave open to the public, the immense Carlsbad Cavern, offers several options. With smaller kids, you may just want to take the elevator from the visitor center down 750 feet to the **Big Room,** which is a pretty understated name for this jaw-dropping rock chamber whose floor covers 14 acres. If you're more ambitious, follow the traditional explorer's route from the historic natural entrance, winding down for a mile into the depths through a series of underground rooms to the same Big Room. A self-guided tour from here runs 1¼ miles over a relatively level path, taking about an hour. Rangers along the path point out some of the more evocative formations, demonstrating the still-growing dome stalagmites and the daggerlike stalactites jabbing down from the ceiling.

Tours of other sections of Carlsbad Cavern range from the easy **Left Hand Tunnel,** a half-mile lantern tour, to the difficult **Hall of the White Giant** tour, which requires you to crawl long distances, squeeze through tight crevices, and climb up slippery flowstone-lined passages. The 2½-hour tour of **Slaughter Canyon Cave** is a far more strenuous cave hike from a different cave mouth altogether. And if the kids don't like being underground too long, they can still join one of the most popular activities at the caves, a sunset gathering at the natural entrance (May–Oct) to watch a quarter-million Mexican free-tailed bats flap out of the cavern to wheel out over the desert for a night of insect feasting. After all, that's how the Americanos found the joint in the first place.

ⓘ 3225 National Parks Hwy. (ⓒ **800/967-CAVE** or 505/785-2232; www.nps.gov/cave).

✈ El Paso, 150 miles. Cavern City Airport, 23 miles.

🛏 $$ **Best Western Cavern Inn,** 17 Carlsbad Cavern Hwy., White's City (ⓒ **800/CAVERNS** or 505/785-2291; www.bestwestern.com). $$ **Holiday Inn,** 601 S. Canal St. (ⓒ **800/HOLIDAY** or 505/885-8500; www.holiday-inn.com).

WHY THEY'LL THANK YOU: The Big Room.

Caves & Waterfalls **108**

Cheddar Gorge & Wookey Hole
Where Brits Go Underground
All ages • Cheddar & Wells, England

Sᴀʏ "ᴄʜᴇᴅᴅᴀʀ" and your kids will think of cheese, and indeed this Somerset village near Bath is the home of cheddar cheese. But it's also an area rich in underground caverns, one of them within Cheddar Gorge, the other just outside the nearby cathedral town of Wells. These are hardly undiscovered caverns—they are commercially developed tourist sites, with some cheesy (pardon the pun) special features added—but the caves themselves are impressive, and I for one secretly like the goofy add-ons.

More than a million years old, the **Cheddar Caves** have some spectacular sections, including cathedral-like Gough's Cave and Cox's Cave, with its calcite sculptures and brilliant colors. The operators have jazzed things up with holograms and optical effects, such as the Crystal Quest, a dark walk "fantasy adventure" taking you deep underground. Britain's oldest complete skeleton, 9,000 years old, is gruesomely displayed in the Cheddar Man exhibit. Adults and children over 12 years of age who want even more can book an Adventure Caving expedition, which is pricey but intriguing; there are also rock-climbing classes. Away from the caves, you can climb 274-step Jacob's Ladder, which has been set up as a walking timeline of Earth history. At the top, Pavey's Lookout Tower offers grand Somerset views, on some days as far as Wales, and a 5km (3-mile) walking trail lets you explore the Mendip Hills.

Ten kilometers (6¼ miles) south of Cheddar, at the source of the Axe River, lies another set of caves with an irresistible name: **Wookey Hole.** It takes

2 hours to tour this extensive set of limestone caverns, which includes an underground lake. Prehistoric people lived down here at least 50,000 years ago; ancient legend maintains that a stony figure in the first chamber is the Witch of Wookey turned to stone. Wookey Hole has its share of tacky features like the Magical Mirror Maze and Pirate Adventure playroom, but the Edwardian penny arcade is worth trying out, a collection of antique game machines that are surprisingly fun to play, even for PlayStation addicts.

ⓘ **Cheddar Gorge** (✆ **01934/742343;** www.cheddarcaves.co.uk). **Wookey Hole** (✆ **01749/672243;** www.wookey.co.uk).

🚆 Bath, 1½ hr. from London.

🛏 $$ **The Crown,** Market Place, Wells (✆ **01749/673457;** www.crownatwells.co.uk).

WHY THEY'LL THANK YOU: Cheddar Man and the Witch of Wookey, unforgettably bizarre.

---

109 Caves & Waterfalls

The Caves of Majorca
Journey to the Center of the Earth
Ages 6 & up • Majorca, Spain

THE MEDITERRANEAN RESORT ISLAND of **Majorca** is a place of sand, sun, and fun, wildly popular with European vacationers and a quick flight from Barcelona, Spain. Part of the Balearic archipelago, tourism has been Majorca's raison d'être for the past couple of centuries, after being popularized by 19th-century artistic types like George Sand, Frederic Chopin, and, later, Robert Graves. In those days, visitors would never dream of coming to Majorca without touring the spectacular caves on its east coast. Two of the most amazing are an easy drive from Palma, Majorca's main town.

Rich in literary associations, **Cuevas de Artà** are said to be the inspiration for Jules Verne's 1864 tale *Journey to the Center of the Earth.* (Verne may have heard or read about the caves; it is not known if he ever actually visited them.) Formed by seawater erosion, the caves are about 32m (105 ft.) above sea level, and some chambers rise about 46m (151 ft.). In the entrance vestibule, notice the walls blackened by torches used to light the caves for tourists in the 1800s. The **Reina de las Columnas** (Queen of the Columns) rises about 22m (72 ft.) and is followed by a set of rooms named after the sections of Dante Alighieri's *Divine Comedy:* a grim, forbidding cavern called "Inferno," then a field of stalagmites and stalactites (the "Purgatory Rooms"), which eventually lead to "Paradise." The stairs in the cave were built for Isabella II for her 1860 visit; in time, such celebrities as Sarah Bernhardt, Alexandre Dumas, and Victor Hugo arrived for the tour.

The roof appears to glitter with endless icicles at **Cuevas del Drach** (Caves of the Dragon), a short drive from Cuevas de Artà. These Dragon Caves contain five subterranean lakes, including **Martel Lake,** 176m long (577 ft.), the largest underground lake in the world. It was named after E. A. Martel, the French speleologist who charted the then-mysterious caves in 1896. Boating on the lake, you can look up at the intricate formations and marvel anew.

ⓘ **Cuevas del Drach,** Porto Cristo (✆ **97-182-07-53**). Cuevas de Artà, Platja de Cañamel (✆ **97-184-1293**).

✈ Palma de Majorca, 8km (5 miles).

🛏 $$ **Hotel Bonsol,** Paseo de Illetas 30, Illetas (☎ **97-140-2111;** www.mallorca online.com). $$$ **Hotel Villa Hermosa,** Carretera Felantix-Portocolom Km 6,

Felantix (☎ **97-182-4960;** www.hotel-villahermosa.com).

WHY THEY'LL THANK YOU: Leaving the sun-worshipping hordes behind.

Caves & Waterfalls 110

Victoria Falls
Shades of Stanley & Livingstone
Ages 6 & up • Livingstone, Zambia, or Victoria Falls, Zimbabwe

IN 1855, BRITISH EXPLORER DAVID LIVINGSTONE first gazed in wonder upon these spectacular falls and promptly named them for his Queen. But their local name, *Mosi-Oa-Tunya*—literally, "the smoke that thunders"—is more apt. When on a clear day more than 9 million liters of the Zambezi River crash down into the Batoka Gorge, the veil of roaring spray can be seen from up to 80km (50 miles) away. Straddling the border between Zimbabwe and Zambia, Victoria Falls are the world's largest, spanning almost 2km (1¼ miles) and dropping some 100m (328 ft.), twice the height of Niagara Falls **64**. A sight this tremendous can't help but be Africa's number-one tourist destination.

Nourished by perpetual spray, a **rainforest** flourishes on the southern cliff opposite the falls, protected by the Victoria Falls National Park. This is the best vantage point for viewing the falls, and getting drenched is all part of the experience (rent raincoats or umbrellas at the park entrance). You don't need a guide, though many hopefuls stand near the entrances angling for business; a clearly marked trail runs through the lush and fecund rainforest, with side trails leading to good overlooks of the falls. Head down the steep stairs to Cataract View to see **Devil's Cataract;** the final viewpoint, nearest the Victoria Falls Bridge, is called **Danger Point,** where you can perch on a cliff edge and peer down into the abyss. When the moon is full, the park stays open later so that visitors can marvel at the lunar rainbow reflecting off the mist.

During high water (Apr–June), when the view is less obscured by spray, the Zambian side offers a spectacular vantage point (just purchase a visa at the bridge). Here the focus is on the main gorge and Eastern Cataract; you can also walk (or scramble, rather) across to a viewpoint called **Knife Edge,** to stand suspended above the churning waters of Boiling Pot. *Warning:* There are no fences on this side of the river.

Even cautious youngsters should enjoy riding a 1922 steam locomotive across the mighty Zambezi via the Victoria Falls Bridge, purposely placed close to the falls for a breathtaking view. Contact **Victoria Falls Safari Express** (☎ **263/13/42229;** www.steamtrain.co.zw).

ⓘ www.zimbabwetourism.co.zw or www.zambiatourism.com.

✈ Livingstone, Zambia side. Victoria Falls International, Zimbabwe side.

🛏 $$$ **Ilala Lodge,** 411 Livingstone Way, Victoria Falls, Zimbabwe (☎ **263/13/44737** or 888/227-8311; www.ilalalodge. com). $$$ **Victoria Falls Safari Lodge,** Squire Cummings Rd, Victoria Falls, Zimbabwe (☎ **263/13/32014** or 27/31/310-3333).

WHY THEY'LL THANK YOU: Getting all wet.

Iguazu Falls: Spilling through the Jungle

Ages 6 & up • Puerto Iguazú, Argentina

IT'S NOT JUST ONE SPECTACULAR WATERFALL but a whole series of them, 275 in all, plunging step by step through an incredibly lush jungle canyon. While Iguazú Falls doesn't offer one single knock-'em-dead postcard panorama, exploring this rippling sequence of individual falls can be mesmerizing in its own way—in fact, it will engage some children for hours as they hurry ahead, treasure-hunt style, to find the next one, and the next one, and the next . . .

Like Victoria Falls 🄫 and Niagara Falls 🄬, Iguazú Falls sits on the border between two countries, in this case Brazil and Argentina, though the main park is on the Argentina side. From the visitor center, a train trundles to the trail heads for the two well-signposted walking trails, the Upper and Lower Circuits. The 1km (.6-mile) **Upper Circuit** winds its way along the top of the canyon, where you

can walk right to the edges of at least five waterfalls and look over as they drop as much as 60m (197 ft.) to the next stage of the river below. But the best views are along the 1.8km-long (1-mile) **Lower Circuit,** where you'll walk past the feet of nine magnificent waterfalls (the kids may want to keep a checklist), crashing down before you in walls of silvery spray. The most awesome of all the falls is on this route, the furious avalanche of water and spray known as **Garganta del Diable** (Devil's Throat). Along this path, you can catch a free boat over to **San Martín Island,** where you'll be literally surrounded by an arch of waterfalls. Combining the two circuits, exploring the cascades will take about 4 hours—it's not so much the distance you'll walk but the many times you'll want to stop and gasp at the views.

While you're here, don't make it all about the waterfalls; the surrounding **jungle** is just as amazing. Orchids, butterflies, tree frogs, lizards, parrots, parakeets, and brown capuchin monkeys inhabit the dense canopy overhead, a teeming tangle of bamboo, ficus, fig, cupay, and ancient rosewood trees, and that's just the short list—within the national park live 200 species of trees, 448 bird species, 71 kinds of mammals, 36 types of reptiles, 20 species of amphibians, and more than 250 kinds of butterflies. Though you'll see a fair bit just on the Upper and Lower circuit trails, a tour with an experienced jungle guide is something too fascinating to pass up. The main local operator, **Iguazú Jungle Explorer** (✆ **3757/421-696**), offers a variety of surprisingly inexpensive options.

ⓘ **Visitor center,** Victoria Aguirre 66 (✆ **3757/420-722**).

✈ Cataratas del Iguazú.

Iguazú Falls.

🛏 $$$ **Hotel Cataratas,** Ruta 12 Km 4 (✆ **3757/421090;** www.hotelcataratas. com.ar). $$$ **Sheraton Internacional Iguazú Resort,** Parque Nacional Iguazú

(✆ **0800/888-9190** or 3757/491-800; www.sheraton.com).

WHY THEY'LL THANK YOU: Water, water everywhere.

Caves & Waterfalls

112

Angel Falls
A Strand of Crystal from the Sky
Ages 12 & up • Canaima, Venezuela

IN THE WILDS OF SOUTHERN VENEZUELA stands the world's tallest waterfall—a silvery wonder with one uninterrupted drop of 807m (2,648 ft.) and a total drop of 979m (3,212 ft.), which adds up to twice the height of the Empire State Building, or 15 times as high as Niagara Falls. Angel Falls isn't just some sight you tack on to another nearby destination—there is no other nearby destination, except for Venezuela's largest national park, a wilderness known as Canaima National Park. So once you decide to come here, do the kids a favor and make sure you get the full amazing experience.

This region is so wild, there are just about no roads—people get around primarily in motorized dugout canoes called *curiaras*. As a result, most tourists only see the falls out of the window of their airplane as they approach Canaima, and they're often disappointed—Angel Falls is located up a steep canyon that can easily be socked in with clouds, especially in the rainy season. Even when the falls are visible, you'll get only a fleeting glimpse. If you really want to see the falls, then, go there by river. One-day excursions involve heading upstream through rapids and canyons for about 4 hours, then finishing off with an hour-long uphill hike through tropical forest to reach the pools at the foot of the falls. The hike is strenuous and can be muddy, but your reward at the top is plunging right into those deliciously

refreshing jungle pools. And because it was such an arduous trek to get here, you won't have to battle mobs of photo-snapping bus tourists—you'll have that breathtaking view of Angel Falls practically to yourselves.

Almost all visitors come here as part of a package tour, which will include accommodations, airfare, local guide services, the works. Two reliable ones are offered by **Canaima Tours** (✆ **0286/962-0559;** www.canaimatours.com) and **Lost World Adventures** (✆ **800/999-0558** in the U.S., or 0212/577-0303 in Caracas; www.lostworldadventures.com). When to come here? It's a trade-off—the river waters are highest during the rainy season, in August and September, but although this feeds the falls with abundant water, expect frequent rainfall. June and July will be less wet. From January to May, the river level is too low to visit the falls by boat at all, although flyovers are still possible.

✈ Canaima.

🛏 $$ **Campamento Parakaupa** (✆ **0286/961-4963;** www.canaima.net). $$ **Waku Lodge** (✆ **0286/962-0559;** www.canaimatours.com).

BEST TIME: June–Nov.

WHY THEY'LL THANK YOU: Getting there like Indiana Jones.

Chapter **4**   Walk with the Animals

In the Wild . . . 128
Zoos . . . 146
Aquariums . . . 155

Giraffe mom and baby at the San Diego Wild Animal Park.

Assateague: Island of the Wild Ponies

All ages • Assateague Island, Virginia, USA

MISTY OF CHINCOTEAGUE is one of those books my daughter loved reading as much as I did—it's practically required reading for any girl in her Horse Phase. As every Misty lover knows, the book is about a **Chincoteague pony,** and the place you go to see Chincoteague ponies is . . . Assateague Island. Chincoteague comes into the picture because it's the neighboring island, sheltered from the ocean by the outlying barrier island of Assateague; every year in July, Chincoteague townsfolk row over to uninhabited Assateague, round up the wild ponies that live there, make them swim across the narrow channel separating the two islands, and sell the new foals to raise money for the local fire department. Everybody *knows that,* Mom.

The good news is that you don't have to be a pony-crazed girl to enjoy a trip to Chincoteague and Assateague. Like most of this region of Maryland and Virginia, known as the Eastern Shore, it's a tranquil, wind-ruffled shoreland with a lot of wildlife refuges and weather-beaten charm. You can drive right onto Chincoteague, an old fishing village that was settled by the English in the late 1600s, and from there take another causeway to Assateague, which was settled by wild horses at about the same time—legend has it that the ponies' ancestors swam ashore from a shipwrecked Spanish galleon, but more likely they were put there by the English settlers as a natural corral. Go early in the day, because there's a quota for how many cars can be on Assateague at one time. You'll have to wait until 3pm to be allowed to drive onto the paved 4½-mile **Wildlife Drive,** which runs through the marshes and is the best

Chincoteague ponies.

place to see these shaggy, sturdy little horses. (Earlier in the day, you can walk or bicycle around this flat, easy loop to your heart's content; narrated bus tours run all day.) Besides the ponies, there are an amazing number of birds to spot, and at the end of the main road lies a splendid unspoiled beach—the **Assateague National Seashore**—which has bathhouses and lifeguards and a visitor center. If you're into shell collecting, the southern spit of land called Tom's Cove yields pailfuls.

Back in Chincoteague, there's one more must-do for pony lovers: taking a ride at the **Chincoteague Pony Center,**

6417 Carriage Dr. (© **757/336-2776;** http://chincoteague.com/ponycentre/ pony). Who knows—the pony you ride might be one of Misty's many descendants!

(i) © **757/336-3696;** www.nps.gov/asis.

✈ Norfolk, 83 miles.

🛏 $$$ **Island Motor Inn Resort,** 4391 N. Main St., Chincoteague (© **757/336-3141;** www.islandmotorinn.com). $$ **Refuge Inn,** 7058 Maddox Blvd., Chincoteague (© **888/868-6400** or 757/336-5511; www. refugeinn.com).

WHY THEY'LL THANK YOU: Wild horses couldn't drag us away.

In the Wild

114

Crystal River: The Real Mermaids

Ages 4 & up • Crystal River & Homosassa Springs, Florida, USA

MANATEES, which early sailors may have mistaken for mermaids, love to spend their winters around the clear, warm waters of Florida's west coast, heading inland along spring-fed rivers where the temperature is generally a steady 72°F. On average, these gentle sea mammals are about 10 feet long and 1,200 pounds—their closest living relatives are elephants—and they move too slowly to get out of the way of boats; injuries due to speedboat collisions are one of the main reasons they are an endangered species. Their prime spot is in the protected warm-water natural springs of King Bay in the **Crystal River National Wildlife Refuge,** which was created especially to protect the few remaining West Indian manatees (a quarter of America's manatee population winters in this one refuge). Several local operators lead daily boat tours out into the manatees' favorite waters to let human swimmers interact with these endearingly ugly creatures. One of the largest is **American Pro Dive,** 821 SE U.S. 19, Crystal River (© **800/291-3483** or 352/563-0041; www. americanprodiving.com). The refuge is

only reachable by boat, so a guided excursion is almost essential. American Pro Dive also runs manatee swims from November to April, 7 miles south of Crystal River in the **Homosassa Springs Wildlife State Park,** where the waters are only 4 feet deep and thus reassuring even for young, inexperienced swimmers. The trusting manatees, who are absurdly nearsighted, come close enough for you to pet their sleek gray-brown skin and feel the whiskers on their droopy snouts. Tours begin early, at 7am, when the manatees are around in greatest numbers; you'll be back at the dock by late morning.

After your face-to-face manatee encounter, you may also want to go underwater in a floating observatory in Homosassa Springs Wildlife State Park, where you can watch manatees in action, with thousands of fresh- and saltwater fish darting around them. As you'll notice through the observation glass, this is a rehabilitation facility that nurses manatees that have been injured by boat propellers; the sight of their scarred bodies, missing fins, and truncated tails is a sad reminder of the threat of their extinction.

(i) **Crystal River** ((C) 352/563-2088; www.
fws.gov/crystalriver). **Homosassa Springs,**
4150 S. Suncoast Blvd. ((C) **352/628-5343;**
www.floridastateparks.org/homosassasprings).

✈ Tampa International, 70 miles.

🛏 $$ **Best Western Crystal River Resort,**
614 NW U.S. 19, Crystal River ((C) **800/**

435-4409 or 352/795-3171; www.crystal
riverresort.com). $$$ **Plantation Inn,** 9301
W. Fort Island Trail, Crystal River ((C) **3552/
795-4211;** www.plantationinn.com).

WHY THEY'LL THANK YOU: Save these
gentle giants.

In the Wild

115

Whale-Watching in Quebec

Ages 4 & up • Baie-St-Catherine & Tadoussac, Quebec, Canada

YOU EXPECT WHALE-WATCHING CRUISES out in the
ocean—around Cape Cod, for example, or
the California coast, or up in Washington
State's San Juan Islands. But whale-
watching on a river? Well, you can see
whales, and plenty of them, on the St.
Lawrence River north of Quebec City,
where the river widens considerably on its
way to becoming the Gulf of St. Lawrence;
in fact it's one of the world's best whale-
watching sites. The relatively small beluga
and minke whales live in these teeming
blue waters year-round, and from late
June through September, larger migratory
species like finback and blue whales join
them, making sometimes as many as 500
whales swimming around at a time. Ferries from St-Simeon to Rivière-du-Loup
sometimes get treated to the sight of one
of these majestic sea mammals, but you
don't want to disappoint the kids—book a
proper whale-watching cruise.

Half a dozen operators run such
cruises out of the towns of Baie-St-
Catherine (on the north side of the river,
near the Saguenay's estuary) and Tadoussac (on the south side of the river). The
entire purpose of these cruises is to
observe whales, so they will alter their
route based on where the whales happen
to be that day, and even offer a guarantee
that you will sight a whale. Most cruises
last 2 to 3 hours, so it's possible to do as
a day trip from Québec. Two leading
whale-watch operators are **Croisières**

AML ((C) **800/563-4643** or 418/692-2634;
www.croisieresaml.com) and **Famille
Dufour Croisières** ((C) **800/463-5250** or
418/692-0222; http://cruises.dufour.ca);
both of them operate large catamarans or
cruisers that carry up to 500 passengers,
with snack bars, inside seating, onboard
naturalists, and underwater cameras so
you can see what's going on underneath
the fluke-flipping surface.

However, Croisières AML has another,
more adventurous option for those so
inclined: agile little 10-to-25-passenger
powered inflatables called Zodiacs where
you're really out on the water, wearing life
jackets and waterproof overalls and extra
sweaters. The big ships just aren't as
maneuverable as the Zodiacs, which can
zip in closer to the whales as they playfully roll, spout, and breach in the chilly
Canadian waters. It's all a matter of taste,
but personally I'd give up the creature
comforts to get closer to the whale.

(i) **Quebec visitor information** ((C) **877
266-5687** or 514/873-2015; www.tourisme.
gouv.qc.ca).

✈ Jean-Lesage International, Québec City,
185km (115 miles).

🛏 $$$ **Château Mont Sainte-Anne,** 500
bd. Beau-Pré, Beaupré ((C) **888/824-2832** or
418/827-5211; www.chateaumontsainte
anne.com). $$$ **Fairmont Le Manoir
Richelieu,** 181 rue Richelieu, La Malbaie

Whale-watching in Quebec.

((*C* **800/441-1414** or 418/665-3703; www.fairmont.com).

WHY THEY'LL THANK YOU: Looking these ocean giants in the eye.

116 In the Wild

Aransas National Wildlife Refuge
Where Whooping Cranes Whoop It Up
Ages 4 & up • Austwell, Texas, USA

IN 1941, THERE WERE ONLY 15 whooping cranes left—an entire species, reduced to just *15 birds,* one small flock in this shoreline nesting ground along Texas's Gulf Coast. Today, thanks to a dedicated team of conservationists, their numbers are slowly growing, but this Texas flock is still the only natural population in the world, numbering just over 200 birds. It's an amazingly rich habitat for birds in general, but the Cinderella story of the whooping crane is what will grab the kids.

Whooping cranes are North America's largest birds, with a wingspan of 7 feet; an adult male stands 5 feet high. With the luxurious long legs and throat typical of shore birds, they have especially elegant plumage—solid white, with just a touch of black on the wingtips and around the eyes, like an artful dab of mascara, and a dashing red cap on the top of the head. The cranes migrate some 2,400 miles up to the Northwest Territories of Canada in the summer, but they faithfully return here every year from November through April, where they feed on blue crabs, crayfish, frogs, and wolfberries. Beginning in late winter, you may see their distinctive courtship ritual, a dance that includes whooping, wing flapping, head bowing, and leaps into the air.

A 16-mile paved loop road allows you to drive through a variety of habitats at the refuge; get out of the car to climb the 40-foot **observation tower** or to stroll the **boardwalk** that leads through a salt

131

marsh to the coast. Nine short walking trails are laid out, all between .3 and 1.25 miles. Among the species you may see, besides birds, there are American alligators, turtles, lizards, javelinas, wild boars, nine-banded armadillos, raccoons, white-tailed deer, and numerous snake species (only a couple of them poisonous). The excellent visitors center has plenty of exhibits; you can rent binoculars here.

To be sure of seeing whooping cranes, book a guided tour, which will cruise the shoreline in a shallow-draft boat past the birds' most popular waters. Call the **Rockport Chamber of Commerce** (© **800/826-6441** or 361/729-6445; www.rockport-fulton.org) for a list of operators. Most of them start out not from the refuge but from a dock in the nearby town of Fulton; tours last 3 to 4 hours.

ⓘ FM 2040 (© **361/286-3559;** http://southwest.fws.gov/refuges).

✈ Corpus Christi, 50 miles.

🛏 $$$ **The Lighthouse Inn,** 200 S. Fulton Beach Rd., Rockport (© **866/790-8439** or 361/790-8439; www.lighthousetexas.com). $$ **Village Inn Motel,** 503 N. Austin St., Rockport (© **8090/338-7539** or 361/729-6370).

BEST TIME: Nov–Apr.

WHY THEY'LL THANK YOU: Hearing them whoop.

Custer State Park: Bison on the Prairie

All ages • Custer, South Dakota, USA

As the Beatles once sang, somewhere in the black mining hills of Dakota lives young Rocky Raccoon. But Rocky has a lot of company up here: white-tailed deer, pronghorn antelopes, elk, mule deer, mountain goats, burros, coyotes, prairie dogs, eagles, hawks, and an awesome herd of 1,500 American bison. At Custer State Park, kids can see what the Great Plains once looked like, back in the days when bison filled the land as far as the broad horizon.

A smart place to start is the Wildlife Station visitor center in the southeast corner of the park, where exhibits will acquaint the children with the many species they are likely to see. Then turn out and drive on **Wildlife Loop Road,** an 18-mile circuit through open grasslands and pine-clad hills where those species roam. Early morning and evening are the best times, when the animals are most likely to venture close to the road. Drive slowly, or get out of the car and walk quietly down the short nature trails to get a good look. Just west of the center you'll notice a set of corrals where bison are held after the annual late September roundup, which thins the herd and keeps it healthy (the public is invited to watch the cowboys move 'em out).

The landscape is downright startling along **Needles Highway** in the northwest corner, a 14-mile expedition through spruce forests, meadows fringed with birch and quaking aspen, and giant granite spires that thrust up to the sky. Park the car and walk around—there are several marked trails, and these rock formations are fun to explore, with tunnels you can walk through and a unique shape called the "Needle's Eye." From the northeast corner, **Iron Mountain Road** leads to **Mount Rushmore** , sliding through tunnels that frame the four Rushmore sculptures strikingly as you approach.

Just south of Custer State Park, you can explore **Wind Cave National Park** (© **605/745-4600;** www.nps.gov/wica); of the guided tours, the most fun is the 2-hour Candlelight Tour, where you explore a section of the cave where lighting hasn't been installed. If you're a cave lover and it's summertime, though, definitely head west on U.S. 16 to **Jewel Cave National Monument** (✆ 605/673-2288; www.nps.gov/jeca), the third-longest cave in the world, with 133 miles of underground passages charted so far. Eroded by stagnant acidic water rather than underground streams, Jewel Cave has narrow, twisting passages whose walls sparkle with calcite crystals and delicate gypsum deposits.

(i) U.S. 16A (✆ **605/255-4515;** www.travelsd.com).

✈ 🛏 See Mount Rushmore/Crazy Horse **95**.

WHY THEY'LL THANK YOU: Shaggy bison, outnumbering the people.

Arizona-Sonora Desert Museum
All ages • Tucson, Arizona, USA

Dᴏɴ'ᴛ ʙᴇ ꜰᴏᴏʟᴇᴅ ʙʏ ᴛʜᴇ ɴᴀᴍᴇ—this is no dusty indoor museum with dead stuffed animals, but a wide-open wildlife park with real creatures prowling around their natural settings. And the word "desert" is misleading too, for the Sonoran Desert—a huge geographical area that extends from central Arizona down through northern Mexico and Baja California—contains not only arid desert lands but also forested mountains, springs, rivers, and streams. So while this attraction does limit itself to wildlife from the Sonoran Desert, you'll see a lot more than Gila monsters, tarantulas, and scorpions here, that's for sure.

After all, when you think *desert* you don't think *fish*—and yet there are 10,700 fish species exhibited here, from the razorback sucker to the Colorado River squawfish. You'll also see black bears and mountain lions, black-tailed prairie dogs, desert bighorn sheep, coatis, otters, beavers, gopher snakes, screech owls, and enough hummingbirds to fill an entire walk-in aviary. Endangered species that thrive here include Mexican wolves, thick-billed parrots, ocelots, and those mysterious black desert cats called jaguarundis, crouched menacingly on their stony ledges. Lizards sun themselves indolently on a rock massif just inside the entrance; coyotes and javelinas (peccaries) stalk around their compounds, surrounded by fences that are nearly invisible—you'll feel as if there's nothing between you and the animals.

Though technically the animals you see here aren't in the wild, they are in their native environment, which makes the whole thing seem less artificial. Whereas traditional zoos display a variety of exotic species, the Arizona-Sonoran Desert Museum trains its sights upon a single ecosphere, and the exhibits make a point of demonstrating the interrelation of plants and animals. Landscaping shows off a rich diversity of Sonoran plant life—a hillside of wildflowers, a mountainside pine-oak woodland, a grassland plateau, a red rock canyon, and the most amazing cactus garden you'll ever see. About 15% of the museum is indoor exhibits (a relief on those days when the Arizona heat climbs above 100°F), notably the Earth Sciences Center, which displays a load of gems, minerals, and fossils collected throughout the region.

(i) 2021 Kinney Rd. (✆ **520/883-2702;** www.desertmuseum.org).

✈ 🛏 See Saguaro National Park **74**.

WHY THEY'LL THANK YOU: Expanding their concept of "desert."

Arizona-Sonora Desert Museum.

The Wildlife of Half Moon Bay
Nature Fierce, Nature Fragile
Ages 4 & up • Half Moon Bay, California, USA

Surfers know California's crescent-curved Half Moon Bay as a West Coast surfing mecca; during Prohibition, rumrunners knew its Pillar Point Harbor as a choice smuggling spot. But nature lovers know this coastal area an hour south of San Francisco as a haven for rare wildlife— and not just fleeting glimpses, but long, satisfying views. Mother Nature couldn't have set up a better lab to turn kids on to marine biology.

With younger children, **Fitzgerald Marine Reserve** is the ideal choice. Call ahead to find out when the tide is due to ebb, because low tide reveals an amazing variety of coastal critters clinging to the shallow marine shelf. Perch silently near the shore rocks and wait for shy intertidal animals to emerge from this delicately colored, quiet refuge, with beachy scrub and marshland and Monterey cypress trees. You can touch the hermit crabs, limpets, chiton, sea anemones, sponges, sea stars, and starfish, but don't pick them off their rocks; gulls circle overhead, just waiting to swoop down on an unattached mollusk. If you move a rock, replace it seaweed side up so that the tiny creatures in the vegetation won't be crushed.

Wait until the kids are older to visit **Ano Nuevo State Reserve,** where the main attraction is a primal scene of sex, blood, and pain—namely, the annual mating and birthing of the great elephant seals. These 3-ton marine mammals (one look at their pendulous upper lips and you'll know why they're called elephant seals) live on the open sea for 10 months a year, then come ashore in November, females already pregnant, in such numbers that they carpet the beach. One bull seal protects a harem of females as a few bachelors hang hopefully on the fringes. You can only witness this spectacle on a guided walk, which should be reserved months in advance. It's not a sight for the squeamish: males clash in often-bloody mating battles, females give birth on the dunes, and they mate frankly on the open sands—all redeemed by the tender sight of mother seals cuddling their young. In March, adults swim back to sea, leaving weaned pups to mature; after April, the youngsters leave too and the beaches are open to the public again. In spring and summer, adults occasionally return to the beach to molt; if you're lucky you'll see some then, but it's nothing like the massed bodies of winter.

If you miss the elephant seals, you can still watch smaller California seals sun themselves year-round at **Seal Cove Beach;** in early spring and fall, look for migrating whales from the bluffs above Princeton-by-the-Sea. Birders know to hunt for rare loons, great blue herons, red-tailed hawks, and brown pelicans. Mother Nature sure outdid herself here.

ⓘ **Fitzgerald Marine Reserve,** California St. Moss Beach (✆ **650/728-3584). Ano Nuevo State Reserve,** New Year's Creek Rd, Hwy. 1, Pescadero (✆ **800/444-4445** or 650/879-0227; www.anonuevo.org).

✈ San Francisco International, 25 miles.

🛏 $$$ **Beach House Inn,** 4100 N. Cabrillo Hwy. (Hwy. 1; ✆ **800/315-9366** or 650/712-0220; www.beach-house.com). $$$ **Seal Cove Inn,** 221 Cypress Ave. (✆ **650/728-4114;** www.sealcoveinn.com).

BEST TIME: Breeding season at the Ano Nuevo State Reserve is Dec–Mar.

WHY THEY'LL THANK YOU: The sea stars and the seals.

El Yunque: Puerto Rico's Rainforest Gem

All ages • Rio Grande, Puerto Rico

Mᴏ CHILDREN HAVE BEEN SAVING the rainforest for years—what American child hasn't been pelted with this eco-message?—but they had never actually seen one. So they willingly gave up another day at the beach in San Juan to drive west of town to the El Yunque rainforest. Within seconds of stepping through its gate, we were enveloped in a lushness so profound, we knew at once that all those school recycling projects had been worth it.

Part of the Caribbean National Forest, El Yunque is the only tropical rainforest in the U.S. National Forest system, a 28,000-acre patch of virgin forest that looks pretty much the way it did when Columbus first sighted Puerto Rico back in 1493.

We spent a good hour first in the **El Portal Tropical Forest Center,** with its three pavilions setting forth the four separate forest microclimates that compose the park. The best exhibit of all, though, was simply the bridge leading to the center, set high up near the tree canopy, where we got our first close-up views of the forest's lively birds. At last we hit the walking trails through the forest, and by now we knew what to look for on our hike to the waterfalls, and what to listen for—the distinctive coqui peep of the tiny tree frogs that live here in the millions. We could spot orchids blooming in the treetops, and incredibly tall ferns swaying among the tree trunks. We hiked along the quiet signposted trail to **La Mina**

Falls, which announced itself through the trees as we drew closer, not only by the roar of tumbling water but also by the unmistakable salsa beat of picnicking families with portable sound systems. On this weekend day, every family in the park, it seemed, was at the falls, sitting waist-deep in deliciously cold water on the slippery, pot-holed rock shelf below the cascades.

The other trail in the park is longer and steeper: the El Yunque trail, which winds upward through forests of sierra palm and palo colorado, before descending into the dwarf forest of Mount Britton, which is often shrouded in clouds. There are great views here from various peaks, including Yunque Rock.

The weather looked overcast when we started out, and at one point a light rain shower began to spatter upon the canopy, barely enough to get us wet. Somehow, that seemed absolutely perfect. After all, what should you expect in a rainforest if not rain?

ⓘ Rte. 191 (Ⓒ **787/724-8774;** www.fs.fed. us/r8/caribbean).

✈ San Juan International, 40km (25 miles).

🛏 $$ **Comfort Inn,** Calle Clemenceau 6, San Juan (Ⓒ **800/858-7407** or 787/721-0170; www.comfortinn.com). $$ **Gallery Inn at Galeria San Juan,** Calle Norzagaray 204, Old San Juan (Ⓒ **787/ 722-1808;** www.thegalleryinn.com).

WHY THEY'LL THANK YOU: Hearing the coquis.

In the Wild **121**

Booby Pond Nature Reserve
Red-Footed Boobies & Caribbean Pirates
Ages 8 & up • Little Cayman, the Caribbean

EVERY EVENING AT TWILIGHT, the drama begins. A mass of red-footed boobies hovers above the Caribbean Sea offshore, eyeing their enemies, the magnificent **frigate birds.** Marauding pirates who love to steal other birds' food, the huge frigates circle hungrily, stretching their pointed black wings nearly 2.4m (8 ft.) wide. They know the boobies have been out over the ocean all day, filling their crops with food to take back to their chicks nested in the mangrove lagoon. Desperately, the boobies gather in large groups. Suddenly they spiral upward in a column, then wheel and dart like torpedoes toward shore. The magnificent frigate birds dart in to attack. Who will win this battle for survival?

This adventure is played out every evening in nesting season on Little Cayman Island, an isolated scrap of coral and sand barely 16km (10 miles) long, flung down in the middle of the Caribbean Sea due south of Cuba. About 5,000 pairs of red-footed boobies—the largest colony of this species in the Western hemisphere—nest every year in the saltwater lagoon of the 83-hectare (204-acre) Booby Pond Nature Reserve on Little Cayman. February is peak nesting season for the boobies, who perch in the mangroves and forest trees around the pond. The name alone is irresistible—is it even possible to say "red-footed booby" without laughing?—but the kids will be charmed by these water birds with their strange guttural screeches. The smallest species of booby, they're still good-sized birds, with a wingspan of nearly 1.5m (5 ft.). Adults are either buff-colored or white with dark wingtips and, of course, unmistakably bright red feet.

Booby Pond Nature Reserve.

Take your place on the lookout platforms built around the edges of the pond to witness this twilight battle; there are

also telescopes on the veranda of the visitor center, a traditional Caymanian gingerbread bungalow. During the day, other water birds visit the pond as well. Let the kids explore the drylands adjacent to the pond, too, where they may see 1.5m-long (5-ft.) **rock iguanas,** the largest population of these spiny gray-brown lizards in the Caribbean.

(i) Near Blossom Village (www.national trust.org.ky/info/rfboobies.html).

✈ Grand Cayman, charter from there to Little Cayman.

🛏 $$ **The Anchorage,** Seven Mile Beach, Grand Cayman (© **800/433-3483** or 345/945-4088; www.theanchoragecayman. com). $$ **Pirates Point Resort,** Preston Bay, Little Cayman (© **345/948-1010;** www.piratespointresort.com).

WHY THEY'LL THANK YOU: The sunset battle.

---

122 In the Wild

Sea Turtles on the Costa Rican Coast

Ages 8 & up • Tortuguero, Costa Rica

CHRISTOPHER COLUMBUS FIRST SET FOOT on this Caribbean shore in 1502, on his fourth and final voyage to the Americas, and promptly named the place Costa Rica, or "Rich Coast." Looking at its dense green jungle, you'll know what he was talking about. Even today, this undeveloped region's greatest richness is its wildlife; nature lovers and eco-tourists continue to arrive in ever-greater numbers. And perhaps the most sought-after wildlife experience in Costa Rica is watching giant sea turtles come ashore to lay their eggs.

The top turtle-nesting beach on the Caribbean coast is isolated **Tortuguero**—the very name refers to sea turtles, or *tortugas* in Spanish. It's quite an adventure to get to Tortuguero, which has no roads, only a labyrinthine series of rivers and canals linking it to the port city of Limón, 50 miles away. Gliding

on a boat through this dense rainforest populated by howler and spider monkeys, three-toed sloths, toucans, and great green macaws is almost like a minicruise up the Amazon. A number of lodges perch on the hills around the village of Tortuguero; generally visitors book a **package** from a lodge that includes rooms, meals, a boat trip from Limón, a bus from San José, and a guided 2- to 4-hour nighttime visit to the beach to watch sea turtles (the only way you can get on the beach at night). Four species of turtles nest on this desolate 35km-long (22-mile) stretch of black sand—the green turtle, the hawksbill, the loggerhead, and the world's largest turtle, the giant leatherback. Considering its great size (up to 2m/6½ ft. long and weighing as much as 454kg/1,000 lb.), the giant leatherback is truly a spectacular turtle to see if you get the chance (Mar–May), but it's more likely that you will spot green turtles. Although they're an endangered species, they arrive in Tortuguero by the thousands during their prime nesting period, July through mid-October. The small **Caribbean Conservation Corporation Visitor Center** in the village has detailed exhibits on local flora and fauna, especially the sea turtles.

A sea turtle in Costa Rica.

ⓘ ℂ **709-8091;** www.cccturtle.org/tortnp.htm.

✈ San José, 249km (155 miles).

🛏 $$ **Pachira Lodge** (ℂ **256-7080;** www.pachiralodge.com). $$$ **Tortuga Lodge** (ℂ **257-0766** in San José, 710-8016 in Tortuguero; www.costaricaexpeditions.com).

WHY THEY'LL THANK YOU: The cycle of life renews itself.

In the Wild

123

The Galápagos: Nature's Laboratory
Ages 8 & up • Galapagos Islands

THE DENIZENS OF THE GALÁPAGOS ISLANDS must be the world's most trusting wildlife—and why not, since they've never had to worry about predators? On the Galápagos, you don't have to creep silently behind a bush to observe wildlife: Young sea lions will show off their best moves as you snorkel among them, mockingbirds will peck at your shoelaces, and the blue-footed boobie will perform its famous two-stepped mating dance right under your nose. It isn't easy to get here, nor is it cheap, but it is definitely the wildlife-viewing experience of a lifetime.

An astounding number of unique species thrive on this isolated equatorial Pacific archipelago of 19 small volcanic islands (plus about 40 islets), a fact that led English scientist Charles Darwin—who visited in 1835 as ship's doctor on the *Beagle*—to develop his 1859 theory of evolution. The Galápagos have been famous ever since, though their extreme location discourages mass tourism. That's a good thing. Most of the islands are protected as a national park, and number of visitors is strictly limited; so you won't battle crowds. There's still a **Darwin**

Research Station in Puerto Ayora (ℂ **05/526146**) on Santa Cruz, the most populated island, where you can get an up-close view of the gentle giant tortoises that have captured public imagination ever since Darwin first wrote about them. But to see the astonishing variety of rare species that thrive on these islands, you'll need to get on a boat. A **cruise** to the Galápagos is an excellent option—departing from Guayaquil, you'll sleep and dine on the cruise boat and take small dinghies to the islands by day for naturalist-led hikes, climbs, kayak trips, or snorkel outings to the best wildlife viewing spots. (This is definitely an active vacation!) Otherwise, base yourselves on Santa Cruz and book day trips to various islands.

When choosing your itinerary, consider the following islands: Santa Cruz for the tortoises; Santiago, its rocky tide pools home to rare fur sea lions and many beautiful heron species; Española, home to albatrosses and blue-footed boobies; Fernandina, with its vivid marine iguanas and flightless cormorants; Isabela, where Galápagos penguins (the world's only tropical penguins) can be found in

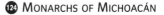

nest in the mangroves; or San Cristobal, where sandy Cerro Brujo beach is a good place to cavort with California sea lions, red crabs, and lava gulls.

ⓘ 966km (600 miles) off the west coast of Ecuador (✆ **05/526-189**).

✈ Baltra, near Santa Cruz Island.

🛏 $$ **Finch Bay Hotel,** Punta Estrada, Santa Cruz Island (✆ **05/5526-297;** www.finchbayhotel.com). $$$ **Royal Palm Hotel,** Via Baltra Km 18, Santa Cruz Island (✆ **800/528-6069** in the U.S., or 05/5527-409; www.royalpalmhotel.net).

CRUISE OPERATORS: $$$ **Ecoventura,** 6404 Blue Lagoon Dr., Miami (✆ **800/633-7972;** www.ecoventure.com). $$$ **KLEIN Tours,** Av. Eloy Alfaro and Caralina Aldaz, Quito, Ecuador (✆ **888/50-KLEIN** in the U.S.; www.kleintours.com).

WHY THEY'LL THANK YOU: Seeing the world as Darwin did.

Sea lions on the Galápagos.

underwater caves; Genovesa, where frigate birds puff up their red necks to attract mates and red-footed boobies

---

Monarchs of Michoacán

Ages 10 & up • Near Angangueo & Ocampo, Mexico

HIGH IN THE MOUNTAINS of northeast Michoacán, you're hiking up a mountain, no doubt fighting for breath in this altitude. Then you arrive in a grove of fir trees—and whatever breath you had left is truly snatched away. It's as if you had stepped into a kaleidoscope, with fragments of obsidian and gold flitting randomly around you. The branches on all sides sway under the weight of *butterflies,* massed millions of monarch butterflies, their gossamer wings whispering softly as the wind blows through the forest. This is what you came here to see—but the vision is so much more astonishing than you expected.

The monarchs have been coming here since time immemorial; the ancient Aztecs revered these poisonous black-and-orange butterflies, which they believed were the reborn spirits of fallen warriors,

dressed in battle colors. There are actually seven monarch nesting grounds in Michoacán (nesting season lasts from mid-Nov to Mar). Only two, however, are open to the public: **El Rosario** and **Chincua,** both reachable by day trip from the graceful colonial-era city of Morelia, which is about halfway between Mexico City and Guadalajara. Save the trip for a sunny day if you can—the effect is most dazzling with the benefit of a little sunshine.

It is possible for you to visit the sanctuaries on your own, but a licensed English-speaking guide is a worthwhile investment—they can answer the kids' scientific questions, transport you reliably over the back roads to the sanctuary, and steer you right to the nucleus of the butterfly colony, which constantly shifts around the mountain throughout the season. Guided butterfly excursions take 10 to 12 hours and usually provide lunch. While it varies, the hike through the mountain forest will probably take around an hour each way; it's often a steep walk, so wear sturdy shoes. One option at Chincua is to ride up on horseback; a local handler will lead the horse for you (facilities for renting are at the sanctuary gate). English-speaking guides can be contacted through a cooperative called **Mex Mich Guias** (www.mmg.com.mx).

(i) www.surf-mexico.com.

✈ Morelia.

🛏 $$ **Best Western Hotel Casino,** Portal Hidalgo 229, Morelia (© **800/528-1234** or 443/313-1328; www.hotelcasino.com.mx). $$$ **Villa Montaña,** Patzimba 201, col. Vista Bella, Morelia (© **800/223-6510** or 443/314-0231; www.villamontana.com.mx).

WHY THEY'LL THANK YOU: That dazzling grove.

The Cape Town Colony
March of the African Penguins
Ages 4 & up • Cape Town, South Africa

IT BEGAN WITH TWO AFRICAN PENGUINS, who showed up unexpectedly in 1985 on Foxy Beach, just south of Cape Town. They seemed unfazed by the human population close at hand; what they liked was the cluster of large granite boulders sheltering several tiny bays, where they could dig

The penguins at Boulder Coastal Park.

protected burrows in the sand and lay their eggs. The next year, a few more joined them, then more the next year. By now, there are over 2,500 African penguins in the breeding colony at the **Boulder Coastal Park,** which has been turned into a penguin reserve. With commercial fishing banned from False Bay, the nearby waters have plentiful fish for the penguins to eat. Still unfazed by the presence of humans, the penguins call the beach their own, but they'll let you share it with them. Heck, they'll even let you swim in "their" waters.

It's an experience not to be missed. African penguins return year after year to this haven, where they breed and nest from March through August. (Remember, in South Africa, that Aug is winter, though it never gets all that cold.) You can view them from a raised boardwalk overlooking Foxy Beach, observing their comical interactions as they defend their tiny bits of territory on the crowded rocks. Depending on the time of year you're there, you may be able to spot eggs in nests, tucked beneath beach vegetation or buried in the sand, or you'll see newly hatched chicks, still covered with fluffy gray down. Older penguin babies have blue-gray backs and white stomachs, in contrast to the adults' black and white with a black stripe across their chests. Even the tallest adults are only about 50cm (20 in.) tall.

A fence keeps humans away from the penguins' nesting area, but the penguins go wherever they like, including onto the adjoining public beach. The time to come is the late afternoon, when the seabirds have finished their day of ocean fish catching and return home to disgorge partially digested fish (yum, yum) into the mouths of their chicks. If you're out in the water, you can feel them whiz right past you, swimming at speeds up to 24kmph (15 mph). After watching how awkwardly they waddle on land, it's amazing to

sense their grace and power in the sea. Having finished their day's business, they may bask on the beach right near you, but cute as they look, don't let your kids chase the penguins. They have a right to be left alone—it's their beach, after all.

(i) Simon's Town (© **021/701-8692;** www. cpnp.co.za).

✈ Cape Town International.

🛏 $$ **British Hotel Apartments,** 90 St. George's St., Simon's Town (© **021/786-2213;** www.britishhotelapartments.co.za). $$ **De Waterkant Village,** 1 Loader St., De Waterkant (© **021/409-2500;** www. dewaterkant.com).

WHY THEY'LL THANK YOU: Feeling the whoosh of a penguin's depth-dive.

---

126 In the Wild

On Safari in Kruger National Park
Nature Red in Tooth & Claw
Ages 10 & up • Mpumaplanga, South Africa

SAFARI VETERANS BOAST of seeing the Big Five: lion, leopard, rhino, elephant, and buffalo. The kids will certainly have something to brag about at school after you visit vast Kruger National Park in South Africa, where many safari-goers spot four of the Big Five in 1 day (leopards are the most elusive). But going into the African bush is about so much more than spotting big game: Take a few days to explore this land, sensing the rhythms of its day from the first hungry stirrings to midday naps to twilight watering stops to nocturnal skitters and rustles. The graceful gallop of an antelope, the scuttling of a beetle, the wheeling flap of a heron (or vulture!), all have their own fascination once you're attuned to the African savanna.

Kruger covers 2.5 million hectares (6.2 million acres) from the Crocodile River in the north to the Limpopo River in the south, encompassing 16 distinct

eco-zones—though as you drive through, it may all look the same, a rolling plain covered with a large shrublike tree called mopane. You can drive the park roads by yourself—driving slowly, peering for animals that blend into the landscape, waiting patiently at the rivers and water holes that attract wildlife—but you're only allowed to get out at designated rest stops. Binoculars and cameras are a must. To increase your number of sightings, also book at least one **guided game drive,** led by experienced rangers in vehicles that seat from 10 to 46 people; the sunrise and early-morning drives usually offer the most animal encounters. It's surprising how close you may be able to get to the animals, who apparently don't associate the smell of gasoline with humans. To let the kids get a more intimate feel for the bush environment, also book a morning walk, a 3- to 4-hour

Even from the safety of a jeep, seeing a lion while on safari in Kruger is a thrill.

tramp where you won't see as much big game (in fact you'll hope you don't encounter anything too aggressive) but you will get closer to the trees, insects, and small animals, all part of the circle of life. Guided drives and walks are booked directly from rest camps, the lodgings offered within the park, which are hardly swanky—often tents or round thatched huts—but have an authentic safari flavor to them.

Flanking the park, there are also several private game reserves, wildly expensive once-in-a-lifetime experiences where you'll stay in luxury lodges, dine on gourmet cuisine, and be driven off-road in a jeep by your own expert tracker and ranger. Many of them won't even accept children under 12; two child-friendly options are **Umlani Bushcamp,** PO Box 11604 (✆ **012/346-4028;** www.umlani.com), and **Sabi Sabi,** PO Box 52665, Saxonwold 2132 (✆ **011/483-3939;** www.sabisabi.com).

✈ Kruger-Mpumaplanga International (near Hazyview). Eastgate (near Hoedspruit). Kruger Park Gateway (at Phalaborwa).

🛏 **Olifants** and **Lower Sabie** rest camps, apply through **South African National Parks,** PO Box 787, 6433 Leyds St., Muckleneuk, Pretoria (✆ **012/428-9111;** www.sanparks.org).

WHY THEY'LL THANK YOU: The drama of the watering hole at sunset.

In the Wild

127

Scotland's Bird Island: Foula
Ages 8 & up • Shetland Islands, Scotland

IN LOCAL DIALECT, *foula* means "bird island"—and no name could be more fitting. Foula is tiny—only 5km wide by 8km long (3 miles by 5 miles)—and geologically rugged, with five high peaks and towering sea cliffs, one of them Britain's second-highest cliff face, the Kame, 372m (1,220 ft.) high. Mostly treeless moors and marshes, it looks inhospitable, despite a profusion of wildflowers in midsummer. But it's exactly the sort of place you'd want to live if you were a **great skua,** and not surprisingly about 3,000 pairs of them, the world's largest colony,

nest here on the sheer face of the Kame. Locally known as "bonxie," these fierce seagulls are the mortal enemies of Arctic skuas, perennially fighting them for territory. The rock-climbing prowess of locals who go in search of gulls' eggs is the stuff of Shetland legend.

Foula isn't all about skuas; uncountable numbers of other birds haunt the isle too: kittiwakes, puffins, guillemots, razorbills, gannets, and red-throated divers, as well as grey heron, whooper swans, kestrels, golden eagles, ravens . . . the list goes on and on. Grey seals cavort onshore; killer whales swim offshore, and harbor porpoises playfully follow the ferryboat. Shetland ponies and the hardy local sheep roam freely on the bleak moors.

Sheep vastly outnumber humans on Foula; the population hovers at around 40 people, most of them crofters. With an instinct for survival, they built their own airstrip in the 1970s so that they wouldn't be dependent on the ferry anymore. Until the beginning of the 19th century, Old Norse was the language spoken, for although long-ago politics made the

islands Scottish territory, they are much closer in spirit to Scandinavia.

Scotland's Shetland Islands are remote already—even the Orkneys **164** are closer to the mainland. But once you've taken a plane or car ferry from Aberdeen to the main Shetland island—called, of course, Mainland—you'll have to take another plane or the weekly mail boat to far-flung Foula, 43km (27 miles) west of Mainland. Your best bet for visiting Foula may be on a daylong trip with **Cycharters Ltd.** (✆ **01595/693434**), which cruises past the bird cliffs so you can view them from the water. But if you're passionate about birds, this is a trip well worth the effort.

ⓘ www.visitshetland.com.

✈ Foula has 3 flights a week, summer months only, from Sumburgh airport on Mainland.

🛏 Mrs. Marion Taylor, Leraback, Foula (✆ **01595/753226**).

WHY THEY'LL THANK YOU: Totally for the birds.

Vestmannaeyjar's Great Puffin Rescue

Ages 6 & up • Heimaey, Vestmannaeyjar, Iceland

E<small>VERY</small> A<small>UGUST IN THE</small> W<small>ESTMANN</small> I<small>SLANDS</small> off the south coast of Iceland, a peculiar ritual takes place. After a summer of midnight sun, darkness is just beginning to return to the nighttime skies. And up on the sea cliffs, adult members of the world's largest Atlantic puffin colony—who have been dutifully feeding their babies tucked away in cliff-top burrows—suddenly stop bringing food. The curious young pufflings poke their colorful curved beaks and white faces out of their holes. Gathering the strength in their black wings, these penguinlike seabirds take to the skies to begin feeding themselves. Though they have never seen the night before, they instinctively know

how to fly in the dark, navigating by the moon.

And then they soar over Heimaey, the largest town in the Westman Islands. Confused by the city lights, the young birds get thrown off course. They waver; they crash into buildings. They fall to the pavement, stunned.

That's when the children of Heimaey jump into action. Allowed to stay up late in August just for this rescue work, they gently scoop up the dazed pufflings—chubby little creatures not quite 25cm (10 in.) tall, with webbed red feet—and carry them home in cardboard boxes to watch over them. Some kids may rescue as many as 10 a night. In the morning, they gather at the sea's edge, lift up the pufflings' glossy bodies, and fling them into the sky. Recovered, the pufflings flap their wings and head out over the open sea, where they will live for the next 2 years. Come here in August and your children can join in this thrilling rescue, a night they'll never forget.

From April through August, some 8 to 10 million puffins—60% of the world's total of this species—nest in the rugged volcanic Westmann Islands (in Icelandic, Vestmannaeyjar); the rest of the year they live out on the open ocean. On a 90-minute boat tour around Heimaey Island conducted by **Viking Tours** (© **488-4884;** www.boattours.is), you can study the puffin cliffs through binoculars, watching the adult puffins (who mate for life and use the same burrows year after year) disgorge fish from their

thick multicolored beaks to feed their young.

In town, also visit the local **Natural History Museum,** Heiðarvegur 12 (© **481-1997**), which has a fascinating little aquarium and several exhibits about the local seabirds. Just don't point out to the kids that the menus of local restaurants often feature a tasty dish called *lundi*—the Icelandic word for "puffin."

ⓘ www.icetourist.is.

✈ Heimaey.

🛏 $$ **Hotel Eyjar,** Bárustíg 2 (© **481-3636** or 895-8350; www.hoteleyjar.eyjar.is). $$ **Hotel Thórshamar,** Vestmannabraut 28 (© **481-2900**).

WHY THEY'LL THANK YOU: The rescue mission.

In the Wild **129**

Dolphin Discovery Centre
A Dolphin Float in West Australia
Ages 6 & up • Bunbury, Australia

Just 2½ hours down the scenic Old Coast Road from Perth is one of Australia's best-kept secrets: a bay where wild dolphins cruise into shallow waters to hang out with humans. No, this isn't the much-more-famous Monkey Mia Resort, which is a full day's drive north of Perth on the semideserted northwest coast. Dolphins swim to shore there, too, but there are often busloads of tourists waiting for them, strictly supervised and lined up like statues on the beach. At the Dolphin Discovery Centre, however, there's usually just a small and laid-back gang of visitors, who get to wade into the water and actually float with the dolphins.

There is a catch: Those sleek gray bottlenose dolphins only show up at Bunbury about two-thirds of the time (at Monkey Mia they show up pretty much every day).

However, I think it's worth the gamble to get a less crowded, more natural interaction with these fascinating cetaceans. Mornings are prime time for encountering dolphins, and they visit much more often in the summers (Nov–Apr, this being the Southern Hemisphere), less often in winter. An "interaction zone" has been marked off on the flat sandy beach in front of the discovery center, which has a cafe and a good little eco-display on the life cycle of the dolphin. (There are loggerhead turtles in the aquariums here, too.) The water is only waist-deep, so even young children can touch bottom. Volunteer guides in red shirts stand out in the water with you to make sure everybody is safe and respectful.

Just to make sure the kids aren't too let down if the dolphins don't show, also book a 90-minute dolphin-watch cruise from **Naturaliste Charters** (✆ **1300/361 351** or 08/9755 2276, no children under 4 years old). After all, there are about a hundred bottlenoses living in Koombana Bay, so once you get farther out from shore your chances of at least seeing dolphins is high. From November to April, the center runs 2-hour boat tours out into the deeper waters for stronger swimmers (ages 8 and over) to swim around near the dolphins. If they won't come to us, we'll go to them.

ⓘ Koombana Dr. (✆ **08/9791 3088;** www.dolphindiscovery.com.au).

✈ Perth, 241km (150 miles).

🛏 $$ **Abbey Beach Resort,** Busselton (✆ **08/9755 4600;** www.abbeybeach.com.au). $$ **Sanctuary Golf Resort,** Old Coast Rd., Bunbury (✆ **08/9725 2777;** www.sanctuary resort.com.au).

WHY THEY'LL THANK YOU: Dolphins whooshing past you.

Kangaroo Island
Unspoiled Australian Ecosystem
All ages • South Australia

WHEN KIDS THINK OF AUSTRALIA, what do they think of? Koalas and kangaroos. And sure, they're on display at wildlife parks and attractions all over Oz. But if you really want to see these iconic Australian marsupials in the wild, there's no place better than Kangaroo Island, just across the strait from Adelaide. Spend a few days here with the right guide and you can walk among sea lions, spot playful New Zealand fur seals, creep through the bush on the trail of wallabies or kangaroos, pick out clumps of koalas hanging sleepily on branches overhead—the list goes on and on.

Kangaroo Island has somehow managed to preserve its unique Australian ecosystem. No foxes or rabbits were ever introduced to prey on the native inhabitants; the island was also never colonized by the dingo (Australia's "native" dog, which probably was introduced from Asia some 4,000 years ago). About one-third of the island is unspoiled national park, with most of the rest devoted to sheep farms. Of the many preserves on the island, kids will score the most wildlife sightings at **Flinders Chase National**

Park on the western end of the island. Birders have recorded at least 243 species here; koalas are so common they're almost falling out of the trees (in fact, the government has had to take steps to reduce the koala population). Kangaroos, wallabies, and brush-tailed possums are so tame and numerous that a barrier was erected around the Rocky River Campground to stop them from carrying away picnickers' sandwiches. Platypuses have been seen, too, but they're elusive—you might need to wait next to a stream in the dark for a few hours. At Cape du Couedic, the southern tip of the park, the hollowed-out limestone promontory called **Admiral's Arch** is home to a colony of some 4,000 New Zealand fur seals that frolic in the rock pools and nap on the rocks.

Rangers at **Seal Bay Conservation Park** (✆ **08/8559 4207**), midway along the southern coast, lead guided tours along boardwalks through the dunes to a beach where you can walk through a colony of Australian sea lions. Up on the north coast, Lathami Conservation Park, just east of Stokes Bay, is a wonderful

It's hard to miss seeing koalas on Kangaroo Island.

place to see wallabies in the wild—just dip under the low canopy of casuarina pines and walk silently, keeping your eyes peeled. If you want to see penguins—tiny ones that stand about 30cm (1 ft.) high—the **National Parks & Wildlife South Australia** conducts tours of their colonies around Nepean Bay at both Kingscote and Penneshaw (✆ **08/8553 2381**).

ⓘ Howard Dr., Penneshaw, Kangaroo Island (✆ **08/8553 1185;** www.tourkangarooisland. com.au).

✈ Kangaroo Island, 25-min. flight from Adelaide.

FERRY PORT: Penneshaw, 40 min. from Cape Jervis.

🛏 $$ **Kangaroo Island Lodge,** Scenic Rd., American River (✆ **08/8553 7053;** www.kilodge.com.au). $$$ **Ozone Seafront Hotel,** The Foreshore, Kingscote (✆ **08/8553 2011;** www.ozonehotel.com).

WHY THEY'LL THANK YOU: Koala cuteness to the max.

Zoos **131**

San Diego Zoo: Panda-monium

All ages • San Diego & Escondido, California, USA

AS THE MOTHER OF A PANDA FANATIC, I knew we had to go to the San Diego Zoo, one of only three zoos in the U.S. with those black-and-white **giant pandas.** But the pandas are at the far end of the park, and as we worked our way there, many other creatures diverted us from our quest, all in a lush garden environment with swooping hillsides and curving paths the children were eager to explore. By the time we finally got there, the pandas could have been an anticlimax—but they weren't. They were spectacular.

More than 4,000 creatures live here, including rare species like the **Buerger's tree kangaroos** of New Guinea, **long-billed kiwis** from New Zealand, wild

Przewalski's horses from Mongolia, **lowland gorillas** from Africa, and **giant tortoises** from the Galápagos. Even better, we saw them in naturalistic habitats, brilliantly designed not only to make the animals comfortable but also to give zoo-goers some pretty close-up views. My favorite parts, actually, were the immense **aviaries,** where you could stand on a boardwalk and peer into a jungle canopy to spy parrots and lorikeets and other gaudy tropical birds. (My husband would vote for the **polar bears.** We had a *very hard time* getting him to leave that enclosure.)

San Diego's is a surprisingly old zoo for a West Coast institution: It was launched in 1916 by Dr. Harry Wegeforth, a shrewd zoologist who traveled around the world bartering native Southwestern animals like rattlesnakes and sea lions—a dime a dozen in California but glamorous overseas—for more exotic foreign species. He also brought back plants from every locale where animals were acquired, ensuring that their new habitations could be landscaped to feel like home. San Diego was one of the first zoos to separate animals from humans with moats instead of bars, and it has long been active in conservation efforts around the world, as well as breeding programs for endangered species. (Like the giant pandas, who had a 10-day-old new baby the day we were there.)

We were glad we invested in the value package, which allowed us to hop a ride on an express bus and take a cross-zoo trip on the cable car. But now I wish we'd had time for the two-in-one package that adds on the zoo's sister facility, the sprawling **San Diego Wild Animal Park,** 34 miles north of San Diego in Escondido at 15500 San Pasqual Valley Rd. (✆ **760/ 747-8702**). Here many of the animals roam freely in vast enclosures, allowing giraffes and ostriches to interact with antelopes and zebras, much as they would in Africa. Humans navigate the distances via monorail cars, walking tours, or pricey-but-unforgettable photo caravans (✆ **619/718-3050** for reservations). Grrr.

A panda at the San Diego Zoo.

ⓘ 2920 Zoo Dr., Balboa Park (✆ **619/ 234-3153** or 619/231-1515; www.sandiego zoo.org).

✈ San Diego.

🛏 $$$ **Catamaran Resort Hotel,** 3999 Mission Blvd. (✆ **800/422-8386** or 858/ 488-1081; www.catamaranresort.com). $ **Park Manor Suites,** 525 Spruce St. (✆ **800/ 874-2649** or 619/291-0999; www.parkmanor suites.com).

WHY THEY'LL THANK YOU: Black and white and fun all over.

132 Zoos

Brookfield Zoo
One-Day Trip around the World
All ages • Brookfield, Illinois, USA

WHILE THERE'S SOMETHING sweet and cozy about the Lincoln Park Zoo in town—which is, after all, the nation's oldest zoo— Chicago-area kids know that the real animal-watching takes place 14 miles west of the Loop (close enough you can get here by Metra train) at the Brookfield Zoo. With 216 acres to stretch out in, the zoo's thousands of animal residents have roomy naturalistic environments, with entire ecosystems set up for several species living together (or next door to each other, if they

A cuddly pig at the Brookfield Zoo.

are predator and prey). With all these exotic creatures around, I find it very easy to lose my bearings, to forget that I'm in the middle of the Illinois suburbs.

Brookfield always seems to be coming up with new **immersive exhibits.** One of the zoo's newest nooks is Wolf Woods, built for a pack of endangered Mexican gray wolves as part of a joint conservation effort with a number of other zoos. The Living Coast explores the western coast of Chile and Peru, including everything from a tank of plate-size moon jellies to a rocky shore where Humboldt penguins swim and nest as Inca terns and gray gulls fly freely overhead. The Fragile Kingdom is divided into two environments—one for the desert, where porcupines, meerkats, and sandcats scurry around, one for the equally fragile Asian rainforest, where clouded leopards and Amur tigers (the new name for Siberian tigers) prowl and slink around their enclosures, with binturongs, Prevost's squirrels, and small-clawed otters stashed safely across the way. The Habitat Africa exhibit alone

covers 30 acres, more than the entire Lincoln Park Zoo; okapis browse in a forest area, illustrating why stripes work for them better than the sun-dappled colors of their giraffe cousins stalking around the savanna section.

The minute you get to the zoo, buy your tickets to the perennially popular **dolphin show** at the Seven Seas Panorama. You'll also want to stop in at the muggy Tropic World, where you can walk at treetop level with mangabeys, mandrills, and gibbons chattering on either side, and the Australia House, where fruit bats flit around your head. Kids gravitate to Baboon Island, where a troupe of some 40 guinea baboons groom and grimace at each other.

(i) First Ave. and 31st St. (© **708/485-0263;** www.brookfieldzoo.org).

✈ ☞ See Chicago **57**.

WHY THEY'LL THANK YOU: Getting lost in Africa, not far from the Loop.

The Cincinnati Zoo
Celebrating the Circle of Life
All ages • Cincinnati, Ohio, USA

SURE, ALL THE MAJOR ZOOS are active in worldwide animal conservation efforts—but the Cincinnati Zoo is the one that really gets the point across to kids. Every one of its exhibits demonstrates the whole delicate balance of an ecosphere, the entwined roles of predator and prey, the interplay between plant and animal life (the zoo is also a lush botanical garden, with over 3,000 thriving plant species). An old Taj Mahal–inspired elephant house has been redesigned to demonstrate how dwindling habitats affect supersized species like the Asian elephant, the giraffe, and the okapi. But one of the most important buildings hasn't got a single animal inside: It's a vintage Japanese-style pagoda that's now a memorial to Martha, a passenger pigeon who died here in 1914, the very last of her once-ubiquitous species (the last Carolina parakeet also died here). Suddenly, protecting endangered species goes right to the top of a child's agenda.

The nation's second-oldest zoo (opened in 1875), the Cincinnati park has only 75 acres, but that makes it all the more walkable for younger children. With no room to expand, Cincinnati's designers have ingeniously packed as much as possible onto its acres, with 500-plus species housed in naturalistic environments. Among the endangered species here are white lions (courtesy of Las Vegas animal trainers Siegfried & Roy), fork-tongued Komodo dragons, shy red pandas, and lumbering manatees. The stars of the show, though, are the **Sumatran rhinoceroses,** glossy brown armored creatures (definitely the handsomest rhinos I've ever seen) that are the only ones of their species to successfully breed in captivity, a feat even more rare than the breeding of a giant panda cub.

One of the most popular parts of the **children's zoo** is the nursery, where kids crowd around to see the newest zoo babies being hand-fed by zoo staff. The Jungle Trails, a walk-through simulated rainforest, allows visitors to get a good look at orangutans, gibbons, and bonobos; outdoors there's a monkey island where you walk on a wooden bridge while acrobatic gibbons nonchalantly hoot and dangle on the wooden structure around you (it certainly puts the "jungle" into "jungle gym"). It's the only zoo I know of with an entire exhibit focusing on insects, from the emperor scorpion to the leafcutter ant—and why not? Insects, too, are part of the great chain of life.

(i) 3400 Vine St. ((C) **800/94-HIPPO** or 513/281-4700; www.cincyzoo.org).

✈ Cincinnati/Northern Kentucky International.

🛏 $$ **Millennium Hotel Cincinnati,** 150 W. 5th St. ((C) **800/876-2100** or 513/ 352-2100; www.millenniumhotels.com). $$$ **Westin Cincinnati,** 21 E. 5th St. ((C) **800/937-8461** or 513/621-7700; www.westin.com/cincinnati).

WHY THEY'LL THANK YOU: Saving the planet, one species at a time.

Zoo Atlanta: Babies, Babies, Babies

All ages • Atlanta, Georgia, USA

THE ZOOKEEPERS AT Zoo Atlanta have sex on the brain, and by that I mean animal reproduction. Their western lowlands gorilla clan has developed quite a family tree by now, and the pride of African lions includes a pair of half-grown lion cubs that were brought to the zoo on a sort of blind date, in hopes they will eventually mate. Everyone's waiting like impatient mothers-in-law for the black rhinos Bo and Rosie, and the Sumatran tigers Jalal and Sekayu, to produce offspring. In 1999 a pair of giant pandas, Lun Lun and Yang Yang, arrived on a 10-year loan from China with the usual expectation that they may be able to breed them here. And the zookeepers have got their eyes on a couple of glossy-maned golden lion tamarins and bright-orange Sumatran orangutans that may be lent out to other zoos for breeding purposes. The good news for kids is that there's nearly always some new baby to ooh and ahh over.

This delightful little zoo is also handy for families because it only covers 40 acres. **Flamingo Plaza** is the first habitat you'll see upon entering the zoo, greeting you with a blaze of color. Farther on, the 5-acre free-range **African Plains**—based on a habitat near Mzima Springs that happens to have the same red-clay soil as Georgia—houses

black rhinos, lions, bongos, zebras, Thompson's gazelles, and a trio of African elephants. The lushly landscaped **Ford African Rain Forest** centers on four vast gorilla habitats separated by moats, to keep family groups separate. A treehouse viewing platform lets you see the **Monkeys of Makokou** close at hand. Sumatran tigers (a highly endangered species), a languid cloud leopard, and gregarious orangutans live in the **Asian Forest** section, an Indonesian tropical rainforest with clusters of bamboo and a waterfall; nearby, you can get a good look at the grotesque Komodo dragon and a reclusive red panda. Kangaroos and wallabies hop around a mini-**Outback** across from the petting zoo.

By the time you've finished the main circuit, the kids may be ready for a little recreation, and there is a climbing wall, an animal-themed playground, and a carousel with hand-painted figures of endangered species that they can ride upon. And while this isn't an exhausting zoo to walk around, just for the fun of it you can take the scaled-down version of a Norfolk Southern steam train that toots around the park.

(i) 800 Cherokee Ave. (C) **404/624-5600;** www. zooatlanta.org).

✈ ⊨ See Stone Mountain National Park ⑨.

WHY THEY'LL THANK YOU: Calves, cubs, and pups.

Twin baby gorillas at Zoo Atlanta.

Beyond Pandas at the National Zoo

All ages • Washington, D.C., USA

FOLKS IN WASHINGTON are obsessed with the pandas at the National Zoo, and have been ever since 1972, when China gave the zoo its first pair after President Nixon's historic visit to China. It took a long time, but finally in July 2005 a giant panda cub, Tai Shan, was born at the Washington Zoo, and he's currently the biggest celebrity in the nation's capital. Well, panda schmanda—there's so much else to see up here, it'd be a shame to think it was all about the pandas.

One of the country's oldest zoos (established by Congress in 1889), the National Zoo is operated by the good folks of the Smithsonian Institution, which means that, like most Washington attractions, it's free of charge, and you can easily get here via the Metro. At 163 acres, it's not as dauntingly big as some of the other zoos in this section, but the site is a long crescent that slopes downhill from the entrance—eventually you'll have to hike back uphill again. Though it has 2,400 individual animals, they represent 400 species, the emphasis being on social groups rather than lone representatives of each species (better for breeding, for one thing). Two of the most popular exhibits are right by the entrance: the **giant pandas** and the **Cheetah Conservation Station,** where a successful breeding program has swelled the numbers of these amazingly speedy spotted cats. Strolling deeper into the zoo, I personally make a beeline for the **O-Line,** a set of cables strung above the Great Ape House for a playful

pack of orangutans. I also love **Lemur Island,** where a gang of irascible-looking ring-tailed lemurs scamper around; and **Within Amazonia,** a lushly landscaped walk-through South American rainforest, with free-ranging Goeldi's monkeys swinging on the vines, a two-toed sloth hanging motionless upside-down, and accents of color added by scarlet macaws and the intensely blue poison dart frog. A kid's farm at the far end lets younger children pet domestic animals. But on the route back, this being the National Zoo, I've got a soft spot for **Beaver Valley,** displaying such all-American icons as the beaver, the black-tailed prairie dog, and the shaggy dark American bison; a bald eagle lurks nearby, as well as the beautiful red-tailed hawk.

Other unusual specimens include a giant octopus, a wily African wildcat called the caracal, the huge-eared fennec fox, Sumatran tigers, a clouded leopard, a red panda, golden lion tamarins, kiwis and kookaburras, and the endangered Mexican gray wolf. And the **naked mole-rat,** you can't forget the naked-mole rat, one of the ugliest creatures my kids adore.

(i) 3001 Connecticut Ave. NW (© **202/ 673-4800** or 202/673-4717; www.si.edu/ natzoo).

✈ ⊨ See The National Mall **63**.

WHY THEY'LL THANK YOU: The cheetahs, the orangutans. And, okay, the pandas.

Going Ape at the Bronx Zoo

All ages • The Bronx, New York, USA

THE BIG KAHUNA of New York City's wildlife parks, the 265-acre Bronx Zoo is a world-class facility in every way, home to more than 4,000 animals from Siberian tigers and snow leopards to naked mole-rats and meerkats. Roaming its winding paths, it's hard to imagine that anything so urban as the Bronx is on the other side of that fence.

As befits the flagship zoo of the Wildlife Conservation Society, the Bronx Zoo accommodates most animals in extremely humane enclosures, outdoors if possible, in large environments re-creating as closely as possible the species' native habitats. This does mean that there are often long walks between exhibits, which may weary younger children. (Strollers can be rented at the entrance.) Study the zoo map as soon as you enter and plot which animals you want to visit and the simplest route to pass them. Operate on the assumption that you can't see everything in 1 day, even if your kids are good walkers. Relax, take your time, and enjoy yourselves.

From April to October, several rides help you navigate the park—an open-sided tram, the Skyfari cable car and the narrated **Bengali Express** monorail. Take advantage of the latter, which tours the Wild Asia section and shows off lots of exotic animals that can't be viewed any other way. The zoo's two star exhibits are the **Congo Gorilla Forest** and the **Butterfly Zone,** both of them fascinating—on a good day you can practically go snout-to-snout with our huge simian cousins through a wide glass window, or have immense tropical butterflies land on your outstretched hand—and **Tiger Mountain** gives you the same close-up access to the coiled power of its big striped cats. The **Children's Zoo** is surprisingly fun even for 8- or 9-year-olds, with lots of learn-by-doing exhibits (like a spider-web rope climb and a prairie dog burrow that kids can climb through).

Don't overlook the indoor exhibits, either: the deliciously creepy World of Darkness; the satisfyingly icky World of Reptiles; the chattering, capering denizens of the Monkey House; and my family's favorite, the extensive **Jungle World,** a lush, humid environment full of twittering birds and prowling cats and swinging monkeys. These make the zoo worthwhile even in winter, when many of the outdoor exhibits are closed.

(i) Bronx River Pkwy. and Fordham Rd. (© **718/367-1010;** www.bronxzoo.com)

✈ ⟞⟞ See Manhattan **56**.

WHY THEY'LL THANK YOU: Those great apes.

Toronto Zoo: Big as the Great Outdoors

All ages • Scarborough, Ontario, Canada

YOU WANT BIG? Then come to the zoo in Toronto, which meanders over no less than 287 hectares (709 acres). Opened in 1974, the Toronto Zoo never had to shoehorn naturalistic environments into a space originally conceived for cages and pens—from the very outset, the animals here have had *room to roam.* Five thousand animals live here, in four regions—Africa, Eurasia, the Americas, and the Canadian Domain—and if you wanted to see everything, you'd have to hike 10km (6¼ miles) of pathways, most of it in the open sun. Thank goodness there's a **zoomobile,** a jump-on-and-off tram which loops around the grounds (one full circuit takes 45 min.).

Even so, it pays to head first for the things you most want to see—which for most kids will be the **African Savanna** section. This creative exhibit re-creates a market bazaar and safari through Kesho (Swahili for "tomorrow") National Park, past such features as a bush camp, rhino midden, elephant highway, and several watering holes; kids can peer into a termite mound, stroke elephant tusks, and walk through a large baobab tree. It also includes the **Gorilla Rainforest,** the largest indoor gorilla exhibit in North America. But after this, the section I'd head for would be the Canadian realm, following the **Grizzly Bear Trail** down a steep hill. Here you'll find a full complement of iconic Canadian animals—moose, elk, bison, grizzly bear, cougar, lynx, and the Arctic wolf. I also like the outdoor section of the **Americas exhibit,** where a

replica of Mayan temple ruins provides a background for the jaguar, llamas, and spider monkeys. The **Australasia section** has all the exotic headliners: kangaroo, kookaburra, Komodo dragon, wombat, wallaby, and emu. If you decide to ride the tram instead of walk through any section, ride through the Eurasia exhibit—you should still be able to spot the Siberian tigers and snow leopard.

Another thing that makes Toronto Zoo special is the **kid's zone,** which is organized in biomes—the forest, the desert, the prairie, and a wetland—and ends up at a kids-only **water park.** It looks darned refreshing after all that walking—why do children get all the fun?

ⓘ Meadowvale Rd. (✆ **416/392-5900;** www.torontozoo.com).

✈ Pearson International, Toronto.

🛏 $$ **Delta Toronto East,** 2035 Kennedy Rd., Toronto (✆ **800/663-3386** or 416/299-1500; www.deltahotels.com). $$$ **Inn on the Park,** 1100 Eglinton Ave. W, Toronto (✆ **800/333-3442** in the U.S., 800/268-6282 in Canada, or 416/446-3308).

WHY THEY'LL THANK YOU: Trekking the savanna.

138 Zoos

Saved from Extinction at the Berlin Zoo

All ages • Berlin, Germany

Lɪᴋᴇ ᴍᴜᴄʜ ᴏғ Eᴀsᴛ Gᴇʀᴍᴀɴʏ, the Berlin Zoo has a phoenixlike history, all about rising from the ashes of World War II and the postwar division. **Germany's oldest zoo,** it was founded way back in 1844, building on a royal menagerie donated by King Friedrich Wilhelm IV. It was always beloved by Berliners, who knew many of its denizens by nickname. At the time World War II started, the zoo boasted thousands of animals; by the end of 1945,

only 91 had survived. Luckily the zoo was located in West Berlin, where economic prosperity allowed for a remarkable comeback. Today more than 13,000 animals live here, many of them in large, open habitats.

Entering through a colorful 1899 gate with Chinese-style roofs and elephant sculptures, you feel distinctly that you are in an old-world–style zoo, not a simulated safari plain or jungle. Many historic animal buildings have been retained, their varied architectural styles giving the impression of embarking on a round-the-world journey. It occupies a huge corner of Berlin's largest and most popular city park, the Tiergarten—once the private park of the electors of Prussia, and like the Zoo painstakingly rebuilt after being nearly devastated in World War II.

At one time the Berlin Zoo had the most species of any zoo in the world, although in accordance with reigning zoo philosophies, that number has been cut back to only 1,500 species (only!). What I find intriguing is that the animals here aren't exhibited in geological groupings, as they are at most zoos, but by species similarities—North American wolves next to African wild dogs, American bison next to gaurs and Asian buffalos—which allows kids to focus on biological characteristics instead of ecosystem niches. The most valuable residents are the black-and-white giant pandas (always my son's

favorites, wherever we go). The zoo also has Europe's most modern **birdhouse,** with more than 550 species.

The adjacent **aquarium** is pretty long-established itself—it's been around since 1913—and it is pretty impressive on its own, with more than 9,000 species, including a terrarium featuring crocodiles, Komodo dragons, and tuataras. Walking on a bridge over the reptile pit is creepy and cool, and the glass-roofed "hippoquarium" gives you a fascinating underwater look at those surprisingly buoyant river horses. You can buy separate admission to either the zoo or the aquarium but the combined ticket is a great two-for-one deal.

ⓘ Hardenbergplatz 8 (✆ **030/254010;** www.zoo-berlin.de).

✈ 🛏 See The Berlin Wall **281**.

WHY THEY'LL THANK YOU: New zoo in an old zoo.

Zoos 139

Schönbrunn Zoo
The Little Menagerie That Could
All ages • Vienna, Austria

AND NOW WE COME to the world's oldest zoo, and a sweet little gem it is: The Schönbrunn Zoo, set in the formal gardens of Vienna's Schönbrunn Palace. This was the summer palace during the reign of Empress Maria Theresia; in 1752 Maria's husband, Franz Stephan von Lothringen, set up a royal menagerie here, where Maria Theresia liked to have breakfast with her children. It still features the original baroque buildings, painted in the ocher color favored by the Hapsburg emperors, hands-down the loveliest historic buildings of any zoo anywhere.

Of course, theories of zookeeping have changed a lot since 1752, and this staid

little zoo was sadly behind the times—almost on the point of closing—when ambitious new management in 1991 decided to turn things around. What a Cinderella story it became, introducing such innovations as naturalistic environments, breeding programs, and ecosystem displays. Some 700 species inhabit this circumscribed site, and while many of them are small creatures like fish and reptiles and insects, there's a respectable number of the big animals—your crowd-pleasing lions, elephants, giraffes, and hippos.

Perhaps the most impressive of the new exhibits is the tropical **Borneo rainforest,** with orchids and mangrove forests—there's even a periodic stage-set storm, complete with pelting rain, cracks of lightning, thunder, and fog. Be sure to go up to the top level to walk at tree-canopy level with the flying foxes and bats. A nursery for exotic butterflies is connected to an aquarium that has a crocodile lagoon, an 80,000-liter (21,133-gallon) coral reef tank, and an underground glass tunnel (look up and you'll see stingrays) leading to a terrarium full of snakes and scorpions. In the **Big Cat House,** tigers and cheetahs now roam the outdoor areas where zoo-goers used to stand, while humans crowd into the interiors that once confined the cats. The **Polarium** is a popular stop, not only because it's cool inside in summer, but because visitors love to watch through a glass wall as penguins soar and dive; there are crowds every day for the sea lion feedings. The new **Desert House** took over an old Art Deco greenhouse outside the zoo proper to re-create a

desert ecosystem. An authentic antique Tyrolean farmhouse was transplanted stone by stone, timber by timber, to a hill at the back of the zoo, where a charming **petting zoo** was set up (as well as the best restaurant in the zoo). The final vindication for the zoo's rescuers: In 2003 China chose Schönbrunn Zoo to receive a pair of giant black-and-white pandas for a 10-year loan, an honor conferred only upon the most respected zoos. *Jawohl!*

(i) Schönbrunn Schlosstrasse (© **01/8779-2940;** www.zoovienna.at).

✈ Vienna International.

🛏 $$ **Hotel am Schubertring,** Schubertring 11 (© **01/717020;** www.schubertring.at). $$$ **Hotel Römischer Kaiser,** Annagasse 16 (© **800/528-1234** or 01/512775113; www.bestwestern.com).

WHY THEY'LL THANK YOU: Storm time in the rainforest.

---

140 Aquariums

The New England Aquarium
Four-Story Journey under the Sea
All ages • Boston, Massachusetts, USA

THE THING THAT ALWAYS GRABS MY KIDS when we visit the New England Aquarium is its centerpiece, the four-story, 200,000-gallon **Giant Ocean Tank.** A spiral ramp encircles the tank, which contains a replica of a **Caribbean coral reef,** its tropical colors glowing like neon in the intentionally low light of the aquarium's cool interior. An assortment of sea creatures coexist amazingly well in the tank, everything from tiny darting tetras to hulking sea turtles and swift sharks. Part of the reason for the peace might be that scuba divers subvert the food chain, feeding those predatory sharks twice a day; my kids press their noses against the glass, marveling at the divers nonchalantly hand-feeding the sharks while sea turtles glide placidly past.

A four-story spiral ramp encircles that great tank, and as you descend (we prefer to go to the top and work our way down), pry yourselves away from the giant coral reef to visit the nooks on the other side of the ramp, where the rest of facility's 15,000 creatures are displayed. Some tanks present freshwater specimens, others tropical sea creatures. Jellyfish shimmer in their own special tank, and denizens of the Amazon have a separate niche. There's even a thoughtful exhibit on the ecology of Boston Harbor, which lies just outside the aquarium walls. At the **Edge of the Sea** exhibit, visitors can touch the sea stars, sea urchins, and horseshoe crabs in the tide pool. The **Aquarium Medical Center** is especially involving—it's a working veterinary hospital.

We like the fact that this downtown Boston attraction is right by the harbor—you walk out onto the pier, in fact, to reach the floating marine mammal pavilion, **Discovery,** where sea lions cavort in several daily shows. Upon entering the main building, you can also buy tickets for the adjacent **IMAX theater** (℗ **866/815-4629** or 617/973-5206), but the really special treat is taking one of the naturalist-led **harbor tours** that teach science at sea; these are offered daily in the spring, summer, and fall. The city's best **whale-watching tours** (℗ **617/973-5206;** www.neaq.org/visit/wwatch/index.html) are run by the aquarium April through October; advance reservations are strongly suggested. It takes about 3½ to 5 hours to circle out and back to the whales' feeding grounds in the Stellwegen Bank. If you've never gone out onto the water to observe those great monarchs of the ocean, jump on the chance.

At busy times, the aquarium has an awful lot of people milling about on those dimly lit ramps—in July and August, try to make this your first stop of the morning, especially on weekends, for huge afternoon crowds can make getting around painfully slow.

ⓘ Central Wharf (℗ **617/973-5200;** www.newenglandaquarium.org).

✈ ⊨ See Boston Common **60**.

WHY THEY'LL THANK YOU: An entire coral reef in one tank—puts the home aquarium to shame.

Mystic Aquarium's Underwater Mysteries

All ages • Mystic, Connecticut, USA

IN A TRADITIONAL SEAFARING TOWN like Mystic, Connecticut, the locals have probably spent more time trying to catch fish than considering how to display them in big glass-sided tanks to entrance visitors—150 years ago, a whale was something to provide oil for lamps and bones for ladies' corsets, not something to watch at feeding times. Times and tastes change, however, and nowadays the Mystic Aquarium ties in beautifully to the town's maritime atmosphere, making a surprisingly natural complement to the **Mystic Seaport 272**.

One of things we like best about the Mystic Aquarium is that several of its exhibits are outside, a pleasant contrast to some urban aquariums where you spend the entire visit indoors. In the outdoor Alaskan Coast, five **beluga whales** squeal and twirl and otherwise perform for their trainers at feeding time. Next door is a facsimile of the Bering Strait's Pribilof Islands, home to **fur seals** and endangered Steller **sea lions,** and out back are **African black-footed penguins,** with underwater viewing windows. If you want to drop a bundle on a really special experience, phone well in advance of your trip and reserve a one-on-one session with a penguin ($62) or a whale ($162). I must say, I'll never forget what it felt like to stroke a whale's velvety fin and touch its tender tongue.

A re-creation of an **Amazon rainforest** definitely goes for the creep-me-out factor, featuring tarantulas, poison dart frogs, bats, stingrays, vampire tetras, and piranhas (the "misunderstood" piranhas, as the exhibit sympathetically explains). In the **Ray Touch Pool,** kids can touch cownose rays as they flutter, butterfly-like, in the shallows. Elsewhere, visitors go eye to eye with such creatures as sea horses, translucent jellyfish, and the pugnacious yellow-head jaw fish, which spends its hours digging fortifications in the sand.

The Mystic Aquarium.

What sets Mystic Aquarium apart is its collaboration with Dr. Robert Ballard of the Institute for Exploration, whose claim to fame (and it's a biggie) is that he discovered the submerged wreckage of the *Titanic*. As a result, the Aquarium now has museum-like exhibits on topics in **deep-sea archaeology**—the search for Noah's Ark; John F. Kennedy and *PT 109*—which actually make welcome diversions from looking at endless tanks of underwater wildlife.

Of course the **marine show** is wildly popular with kids; the frisky and engaging sea lions are real scene-stealers, and the show manages to be less gimmicky than similar commercial enterprises in Florida and California (I won't name names). It's also only 15 minutes long, which doesn't test the attention spans of very young visitors.

(i) 55 Coogan Blvd. ((C) **860/572-5955;** www.mysticaquarium.org).

✈ Providence, 45 miles.

🛏 $$ **Hilton Mystic,** 20 Coogan Blvd. ((C) **800/445-8667** or 860/572-0731; www. hiltonmystic.com).

WHY THEY'LL THANK YOU: Sea lion pups for the *ahh* factor, piranhas for the *eww* factor.

Aquariums

142

The National Aquarium
Getting Watery in Baltimore
All ages • Baltimore, Maryland, USA

ANCHORING ONE END of Baltimore's **Inner Harbor** 270 attractions, the National Aquarium lured us into its air-conditioned corridors on a steamy summer afternoon, when the idea of wandering past rippling tanks full of fish was too delicious to pass up. As we climbed from one level to another, we realized we weren't just

The National Aquarium's newest exhibit, Animal Planet Australia.

walking by wall tanks, we were walking through glass tunnels, immersed in the underwater experience. A few minutes ago, we'd been sweating; now we felt as if we'd just taken a refreshing swim.

Shoehorned onto its corner of pier, this brilliant aquarium makes a virtue of its vertically stacked location by giving each floor its own theme. It starts on the ground floor with a delightfully gruesome 250,000-gallon tank of dangerous-looking **stingrays and sharks,** hooking my sons instantly. The next level up handled the local Chesapeake ecosystem, tracing the course of the water cycle from a fresh-water pond down through tidal marshes (full of the famous Maryland blue crabs) out to the coastal beach, where long-distance currents wash some surprisingly tropical species past the Chesapeake. Level 3 could have been subtitled Freak Show of the Seas, where the kids hovered in fascination to see some of the ocean's most bizarre adaptations—the octopus, the electric eel, the ancient-looking sturgeon. Also on Level 3, we sampled a contrasting pair of exotic climes—frosty North Atlantic sea cliffs where adorable puffins scuttled around, and a long acrylic wall representing an **Amazon river forest,** full of odd creatures from the giant river turtle to the pygmy marmoset, the world's smallest monkey. (Hey, who said an aquarium was only for fish?)

For us, though, nothing could beat the top level's **rainforest exhibit,** where we wandered up and down steep terraces, basking in the humid heat and trying to spot the brightly colored birds, the shy iguana, and the sloth.

On the way back down to the lobby, we passed through the doughnut-shaped **Coral Reef,** where vivid tropical species flitted on all sides of us, and then the darkened **Open Ocean** tank, where sharks glided menacingly overhead. At feeding time in the coral reef, the divers always draw a crowd. A covered bridge leads from the main hall to the **Marine Mammal Pavilion,** where we could watch the obligatory dolphin "presentation" (the PC term for shows; reserve a seat when you pay your admission at no additional fee).

ⓘ 501 E. Pratt St. (✆ **410/576-3800;** www.aqua.org).

✈ Baltimore-Washington International, 10 miles.

⊨ $$$ **Baltimore Marriott Waterfront Hotel,** 700 Aliceanna St., Inner Harbor East (✆ **410/385-3000;** www.baltimoremarriott waterfront.com). $$ **Brookshire Suites,** 120 E. Lombard St. (✆ **866/583-4162** or 410/ 625-1300; www.harbormagic.com).

WHY THEY'LL THANK YOU: Getting lost in the rainforest.

Miami Seaquarium
Laid-Back Dolphins in the Lagoon
All ages • Miami, Florida, USA

DOWN IN **F**LORIDA, where it's shirt-sleeve weather year-round, you can slather on sunblock and enjoy your aquariums outdoors, with wide-open views of the real ocean just behind the exhibits. I'm not talking about the behemoth SeaWorld up in Orlando—I much prefer Miami's Seaquarium, which is more compact, is less grandiose, and doesn't gouge you for souvenirs and over-priced food every time you turn around.

Like SeaWorld, Seaquarium is big on **performing animal shows**—four theaters are the focal points of this 35-acre site; plan your visit to take in all four shows if you can. Having grown up with the TV series *Flipper* (the 1960s version, I must admit), I enjoyed the Flipper Show, which stars gray bottlenose dolphins in the very same lagoon used to film the 1990s series. The killer whale show was blessedly free of Shamu pomposity, and a pack of sea lions dove, barked, and clapped their hearts out for us in their own show. A handful of landscaped exhibits are clustered around the four theaters—you do a whole lot less hiking here than you do at Seaworld—from a pond full of flamingos to an indoor coral reef tank to a simulated mangrove forest to river shallows teeming with Nile crocodiles (oddly, not American alligators). The kids were suitably creeped out to stand surrounded by a circular channel full of swift sharks, but our favorite exhibit of all featured the **manatees**—Seaquarium is a leader in the campaign to save this endangered species.

People tend to have strong opinions about whether or not to go swimming with dolphins. If this is high on your list, reserve ahead (ℂ **305/365-2501**) to participate in a choreographed dolphin encounter in the Flipper Lagoon, at a stiff price. Children must be at least 52 inches tall.

My daughter and I added on a trip to **Parrot Jungle Island,** 1111 Parrot Jungle Trail (ℂ **305/372-3822;** www.parrotjungle. com), which in 2003 moved from its kitschy old coral-rock South Miami home to a new $46-million site on Watson Island, along the MacArthur Causeway near Miami Beach. Never having been to the old classic, we really enjoyed the new digs, 19 acres of protected bird sanctuary featuring trails, aviaries, a sepentarium full of reptiles and amphibians, and a boardwalk trail winding through a simulated Everglades landscape. Flying overhead are hundreds of parrots, macaws, peacocks, cockatoos, and flamingos. Continuous shows star roller-skating cockatoos, card-playing macaws, and numerous stunt-happy parrots—and you should know by now that my kids and I are suckers for that sort of thing.

ⓘ 4400 Rickenbacker Causeway (ℂ **305/ 361-5705;** www.miamiseaquarium.com).

✈ ⊨ See Coral Castle ⓽2.

WHY THEY'LL THANK YOU: Flipping for Flipper.

Shedd Aquarium: Splendor on the Lake

All ages • Chicago, Illinois, USA

THE SETTING IS MAGNIFICENT to start with—a Beaux Arts–style marble octagon right on the shore of Lake Michigan, at the south end of lovely Grant Park. But the Shedd is the world's largest indoor aquarium, and in this case size does matter. Thousands of fish, reptiles, amphibians, and marine mammals inhabit this lakeside palace, all gorgeously displayed. I can't rave enough about it.

Sure, you may be tempted to combine this with the two other great-for-kids attractions that share this shoreline tract, the **Field Museum of Natural History** ❷❽❹ and the Adler Planetarium, both a stone's throw away. But of the three (and I love them all), this is the one that deserves the most time, in my humble opinion, and you don't want to rush the kids through it. To hold its own against such stiff competition, the Shedd does offer a ticket that covers only the aquarium section, and of course it's worth every penny. The aquarium's centerpiece is a 90,000-gallon circular tank in the central rotunda, where vividly colored fish, sharks, and stingrays swirl around an immense replica of a **Caribbean coral reef.** An underwater camera and audio system pipe close-up views and sound effects out to eager crowds of spectators, which turn daily hand-feedings by a staff diver into an interactive show. It's hard to tear ourselves away from that reef, but we know by now that there are another 80-some tanks in adjacent rooms to peer into, all of them fascinating samples of marine habitats around the world, from Lake Tanganyika to the Red Sea to the nearby Fox River in Illinois. An entire exhibit focuses just on the dramatic seasonal fluctuations of the Amazon basin (look out for the **piranhas** and **anacondas**).

If you opt for the aquarium-only ticket, however, you miss my favorite part: the Oceanarium, a simply stunning re-creation of a rocky stretch of **Pacific Northwest coast,** backed by a wall of windows looking out onto the vast sparkling waters of Lake Michigan. My family is happy to sit here, dreamily gazing over the "coast," observing otters and seals and listening to the Pacific white-sided dolphins frolic in their holding pool. The other "extra" exhibit is the **Wild Reef,** a series of 26 interconnected habitats that house a Philippine coral reef patrolled by sharks and other predators. Floor-to-ceiling tank walls bring those menacing creatures up close, maybe too close (they even swim over your head at certain spots)—it's reassuring to find out how thick that acrylic wall is. Just making sure.

ⓘ 1200 S. Lake Shore Dr. (℗ **312/939-2438;** www.sheddaquarium.org).

✈ ⊨ See Chicago ❺❼.

WHY THEY'LL THANK YOU: That craggy coastline.

Monterey Bay Aquarium
Finding New Depths on the California Coast
All ages • Monterey, California, USA

MY PUNSTER SON DECLARED that he wanted to see a manta ray in Monterey—well, we didn't, but we saw stingrays, jaguar rays, bat rays, cownose rays, and a spider web ray, and we got almost giddy with the fun we were having. As a die-hard fan of big exhibit aquariums, I have to say this northern California stunner is probably my favorite.

Yes, it's huge, with more than 350,000 marine animals and plants on display, and it has two truly awesome big tanks you can gaze at for hours—the million-gallon **Outer Bay tank,** populated by yellowfin tuna, large green sea turtles, barracuda, sharks, giant ocean sunfish, and schools of bonito; and the three-story **Kelp Forest** with its stunning view of leopard sharks and other sea creatures lacing through the leaves of a towering kelp forest. But we all know size doesn't matter. What stirred me was how this glorious facility's displays highlight the sheer beauty of sea creatures—the feathery flutter of jellyfish, the supple grace of rays, the quicksilver flash of anchovies, sardines, and mackerel swimming in massive schools.

The site of this great aquarium was not chosen at random. It sits on the border of one of the largest underwater canyons on earth (wider and deeper than the Grand Canyon) and is surrounded by incredibly diverse marine life. One wing concentrates on the **Ocean's Edge,** exploring the kelp forest and coral reefs and other habitats of Monterey Bay—there's even a coastal aviary, reminding us that plovers and pipers and other shorebirds are part of the marine equation. **Touch pools**

Jellies at the Monterey Bay Aquarium.

abound here, along with the ever-popular penguin exhibit. The other wing focuses on the deep waters of the **Outer Bay,** where the fish get bigger, more colorful, and in some cases more predatory. It seems that at any given moment, there's a naturalist somewhere in the building leading a demonstration or narrating a feeding event, and on either end of the second floor are hands-on learning areas for younger children. Between the two wings, near the entrance, a few absolutely adorable sea otters frolic in a two-story habitat.

Consider adding an excursion to Moss Landing, 25 minutes north of Monterey on Calif. 1, to take Captain Yohn Gideon's **Elkhorn Slough Safari** (*(C)* **831/633-5555;** www.elkhornslough.com), a 2-hour

pontoon-boat tour of the Elkhorn Slough Wildlife Reserve. This experience is like jumping into a *National Geographic* special: Expect to see harbor seals, hundreds of waterfowl, and maybe even a raft of otters feet-up and sunning themselves.

(i) 886 Cannery Row (*(C)* **800/756-3737** or 831/648-4800; www.mbayaq.org).

✈ Monterey Peninsula Airport, 3 miles. San Francisco International, 100 miles.

🛏 $$ **Casa Munras Garden Hotel,** 700 Munras Ave. (*(C)* **800/222-2558;** 800/222-2446 in CA, or 831/375-2411; www.casamunras-hotel.com).

WHY THEY'LL THANK YOU: Cute otters, cool sharks.

Aquariums 146

Vancouver Aquarium: Baby Beluga in B.C.

All ages • Vancouver, British Columbia, Canada

VANCOUVER'S MOST ESSENTIAL SITE for families is **Stanley Park,** a 400-hectare (1,000-acre) peninsula of British Columbian rainforest, with hiking trails, beaches, a miniature train, a water park, and incredible ocean views on every side. But don't let yourselves get too distracted—be sure to set aside a good 2½ hours for the biggest attraction in the park, the Vancouver Aquarium. Looking at the ocean is one thing; at this aquarium you'll come to understand the ocean, which is another thing entirely.

The aquarium has been designed to be as hands-on as possible for children; rocklike stoops are provided for small folks to get a better view into fish tanks. Regal angelfish glide through a re-creation of an Indonesian coral reef; blacktip sharks scour the waters of the Tropical Gallery. The **Pacific Canada** exhibit is dedicated to indigenous sea life—you almost feel you can reach out and touch the sturgeon, wolf eel, rockfish, salmon, or the

thousands of flashing silvery herring that flit past. The stroll-through **Amazon Gallery** is another standout, a thickly planted humid environment with turtles, piranhas, tropical birds, leering crocodiles, an anaconda snake, the prehistoric-looking arapaima fish, and two-toed sloths dangling motionless from the trees.

On an outdoor terrace, rocky coves have been created for the popular Steller sea lions, harbor seals, sea otters, and beluga whales, who entertain aquarium visitors at periodic feeding times; stairs lead to lower levels where kids can get the underwater perspective on them. Very few children can resist pushing buttons to hear the sounds that whales, seals, bowheads, and walrus make in the wild. Plan in advance and you can arrange for a pricey private encounter with the beluga, or a somewhat more reasonably priced behind-the-scenes session with the sea otters or sea lions and their trainers.

The Vancouver aquarium's truly unique feature is the **BC Salmon Stream Project,** which consists of a channel running up from Coal Harbour to the aquarium, designed for salmon to return upstream from the open ocean to spawn. When it is completed, the salmon, guided by a special imprinted scent, should find their way home over thousands of kilometers and wind up in the salmon display pool inside the aquarium.

(i) Stanley Park ((C) **604/659-3552;** www.vanaqua.org).

✈ Vancouver International.

🛏 $ **Riviera Hotel,** 1431 Robson St. ((C) **888/699-5222** or 604/685-1301). $$ **Robsonstrasse Hotel,** 1394 Robson St. ((C) **888/667-8877** or 604/687-1674; www.robsonstrassehotel.com).

WHY THEY'LL THANK YOU: The underbelly of the beluga.

147 **Aquariums**

Sydney Aquarium
In the Swim, Down Under
All ages • Sydney, New South Wales, Australia

AUSTRALIA IS, AFTER ALL, an island continent, surrounded by oceans and seas, so it makes perfect sense that one of the world's best aquariums would be in Sydney. For kids, it's a no-brainer: Any child who's seen *Finding Nemo* knows that Sydney Harbour is an important place for fish, not to mention fur seals and gray nurse sharks; they know all about giant sea turtles riding the Eastern Current; and they'll feel right at home in the **Great Barrier Reef exhibit,** seeing the clown anemone fish and blue tangs zipping around their coral condos.

Still, this Darling Harbour attraction is even better than you'd expect, big and smart and totally absorbing. The route through its exhibits deals with four native Australian aquatic habitats, and right away, in the **Southern Rivers rooms,** the kids will see something truly exotic—what may be their first **platypus.** In the **Northern Rivers exhibit,** saltwater crocodiles edgily coexist with freshwater crocs. The **Southern**

Oceans exhibit has a fascinating section about Sydney Harbor, which is actually a drowned river and a unique mix of watery habitats, but chances are the kids won't let you linger to read all the information, because you're coming to the most appealing part of the aquarium—the display of perky little **fairy penguins** and the huge walk-through tank of big-eyed **fur seals** and **sea lions,** cavorting all around you. (This tank is actually a sanctuary, providing a home for rescued seals that for one reason or another can't be returned to open waters.) After the seal sanctuary, the **Open Ocean Oceanarium** presents the tougher, less cuddly side of ocean life, with sharks and stingrays and giant turtles gliding menacingly past the glass overhead. Then comes the *pièce de résistance,* the world's largest artificial **coral reef** exhibit—a magnificent re-creation of a section of the Great Barrier Reef, a 2.6-million-liter (687,000-gallon) tank with floor-to-ceiling walls of

A fairy penguin at the Sydney Aquarium.

163

glass. Darting around the intricate coral outcrops are thousands of colorful fish—triggerfish, blue and yellow tangs, angelfish, lionfish, and those bright striped clown anemone fish—along with the anemones and sponges that are all part of this amazing ecosystem. If you're planning to take the kids on up to Queensland to visit the **Great Barrier Reef** ⓭, this huge exhibit is the perfect introduction.

Like most aquariums, this one is a great place to learn about conservation efforts and the interplay between ecosystems. And like most children, yours may not focus on all the scientific facts. They will, however, come out with a renewed love for the life aquatic, which is just as wonderful Down Under.

ⓘ Aquarium Pier, Darling Harbour (✆ **02/ 9262 2300;** www.sydneyaquarium.com.au).

✈ ⊨ See Sydney Harbour Bridge ⓰.

WHY THEY'LL THANK YOU: Finding Nemo.

Aquariums **148**

Osaka Aquarium: Circling the Ring of Life

All ages • Osaka, Japan

Iꜰ ᴛʜᴇ ᴡᴏʀᴅ "ᴀǫᴜᴀʀɪᴜᴍ" simply means tank full of fish, then Osaka's immense waterfront attraction needs another name. In fact, its Japanese name—Kaiyukan—literally translated means "playing in the sea pavilion." Typical Japanese understatement. The kids will learn plenty about marine ecosystems here—and, of course, they'll enjoy themselves immensely, too.

After entering through a dramatic glass tunnel where colorful fish swim all around you, you are treated to a video of erupting volcanoes spewing fire and molten rock. *What does this have to do with water and fish?* the kids may wonder. Then you whiz up eight floors on an elevator and begin a journey down a spiraling corridor, starting out in—huh?—the daylight world of a Japanese forest. But as you pass through successive habitats along the spiral, the pieces begin to fit together. The entire Pacific Rim, you'll realize, is encircled by volcanic activity, a so-called "Ring of Fire" (apologies to Johnny Cash). But along with the Ring of Fire comes a Ring of Life, and in habitat after habitat, the profusion of life triumphs over the volcanic disruption and destruction.

Through huge acrylic glass windows, you gaze into 14 different **Pacific Rim** habitats, proceeding down the spiral past the Aleutian Islands, a kelp forest, Monterey Bay, an Ecuador rainforest, the Great Barrier Reef, the Tasman Sea, Antarctica, and other varied Pacific ecosystems, eventually winding up on the depths of the ocean floor, the domain of such weird creatures as an ethereal moon jelly and the Japanese giant crab with its incredible 3m (9¾-ft.) span. There's a staggering number of creatures to look at, 35,000 specimens representing 380 species, but seeing them in habitat groups, the kids will be able to make sense of it all, even if there's very little signage in English. The specimens aren't all fish, not by any means—there are mammals here, the usual sea otters, harbor seals, and sea lions, but also monkeys and squirrels and sloths. You'll see toucans as well as several varieties of penguins. Stars of the show include a **whale shark** (the world's largest fish), loggerhead sea turtles, bluefin tuna, the odd-looking ocean sunfish (which has the circumference of a truck tire but is flat as a pancake), and the ever-popular Pacific white-sided dolphins. When you've exhausted the charms of the aquarium, the surrounding Tempozan Harbor development has many other attractions to fill out your day—a festival market-place, harbor cruises on a replica of Columbus's ship *Santa Maria,* and one of the world's largest Ferris wheels.

ⓘ 1-1-10 Kaigan-dori, Minato-ku (✆ **06/6576-5501;** www.kaiyukan.com).

✈ Kansai International, Osaka.

🛏 $$ **Hotel Granvia Osaka,** 3-1-1 Umeda, Kita-ku (✆ **06/6344-1235**). $$$ **Westin Osaka,** 1-1-20 Oyodo Naka, Kita-ku (✆ **800/WESTIN-1** or 06/6440-1111; www.westin-osaka.co.jp).

WHY THEY'LL THANK YOU: Working your way to the ocean floor.

Chapter **5** Lost in the Mists of Time

Fossils . . . 167
Early Humans . . . 176
The Ancient World . . . 187

Luxor.

Dinosaur Valley
In the Tracks of the Dinosaurs
All ages • Glen Rose, Texas, USA

EVEN THE VERY YOUNGEST DINOSAUR LOVERS—and aren't preschoolers the biggest dinosaur fans there are?—can interpret the fossil record left in stone at Dinosaur Valley: The huge footprints in the rocks here are so unmistakable, it's easy to picture the prehistoric theropods and sauropods who made them 110 million years ago.

You'll find the prints beside the Paluxy River, a branch of the Brazos, which winds through this shady, lovely 1,500-acre park in Texas about an hour's drive southwest of Fort Worth. Late summer, when the river is low, is the best time to come. You can discern the footprints best when the rock is just slightly underwater, with the wetness darkening it. (Bring a whisk broom with you to clear any debris.) It's strikingly evident that two different types of dinosaurs walked in the moist limy mud that formed this rock. Many of the footprints (typically 15–25 in. long) show three toes and sharp claws, indicating a meat-eating dinosaur called **Acrocanthosaurus**. This guy stood 20 to 30 feet tall and walked on two legs. The even larger footprints (some more than 3¼ ft. long) were made by long-necked planteating dinosaurs, your basic sauropods (nicknamed **"brontosaurs"**). The kids can tell its front tracks from its back ones: The front feet were round with peglike toes, like an elephant's feet, while the back ones had large claws angling rearward. Most likely these were left by a 30- to 50-foot-long dinosaur named **Pleurocoelus**.

The tracks can easily be seen at two spots in the park: The main site is across the northwest parking lot and down some stone steps to the river; upstream is the Blue Hole, a sinkhole with many more brontosaur tracks (it's also a great place for swimming, so bring your suits). The kids will have no trouble imagining a scenario of the carnivorous Acrocanthosaurus stalking the gentle, slowmoving Pleurocoelus (originally a slab of tracks showed the meat-eater ambushing the plant-eater—to see that slab today, unfortunately, you'd need to be in New York City at the American Museum of Natural History **285**). But what's still here is graphic evidence indeed.

The **visitor center** has replicas, foot skeletons, murals, and diagrams to help kids visualize the dinosaurs. What's more, outdoors stand two immense fiberglass models, one of a brown T-Rex and the other of a green Apatosaurus—relics of the Dinosaur World exhibit at the 1964 New York World's Fair. Built by the Sinclair Oil Company (remember the old Sinclair gas station sign with its green brontosaurus?), these models are historic artifacts in their own right. Scientists still argue over what the head of the Apatosaurus should look like, but hey, we're all still learning.

(i) (C) **254/897-4588;** www.tpwd.state.tx. us/park/dinosaur.

✈ Dallas–Fort Worth International, 75 miles.

🛏 $ **Hotel Texas,** 2415 Ellis Ave., Ft. Worth ((C) **800/866-6660** or 817/624-2224). $$$ **Stockyards Hotel,** 109 W. Exchange Ave., Ft. Worth ((C) **800/423-8471** or 817/625-6427; www.stockyards hotel.com).

WHY THEY'LL THANK YOU: Dinosaurs walked here.

Agate Fossil Beds
A Ranch Full of Old Bones
Ages 4 & up • Harrison, Nebraska, USA

THEY WERE A YOUNG COURTING COUPLE, Kate Graham and James Cook, strolling on the buttes above the Niobara River on Kate's family's ranch in northwestern Nebraska in 1878. Young James had knocked around a bit as a sailor, a scout, a trapper, but like many frontiersmen he was a keen observer. Looking down, he noticed a peculiar glitter on a bone fragment by his feet; he picked it up and discovered it was a petrified animal leg bone, with tiny calcite crystals in the marrow cavity. By a stroke of luck, Cook had recently befriended a Yale University paleontologist roaming the West in search of fossils, and the ever-curious Cook had learned much about that exciting new science

from the professor (or "Man-That-Picks-Up-Bones," as Cook's friend Red Cloud, the Lakota Sioux leader, called him). Cook was just the man to sense that bone was something special.

It took over 30 years for James Cook to persuade paleontologists to study this isolated land—which he and Kate, after marrying, took over and named **Agate Springs Ranch.** But from 1909 on, the pair of high conical hills overlooking the river and grasslands became a beehive of activity. No fewer than six quarries were dug and combed through by scientists from several major universities; I can just imagine the fierce competition, each team of scientists protecting its own fossil trove. This is the world's best fossil deposit from the **Early Miocene Epoch,** filling in the missing links of many species from 20 million years ago—carnivorous beardogs, land beavers, the piglike Dinohyus, the gazelle-camel Stenomylus, and the short rhinoceros Menoceras. It tells the story of a severe drought hitting this savanna, and mammals converging upon the few last drinking holes to eventually die, leaving their bones in the soft sedimentary soil. Natural history museums all over the world are indebted to Agate Springs for the rare fossils unearthed here.

The visitor center has some dramatic **reconstructed skeletons** of those early mammals; kids can get a good sense of the process of paleontology from looking at a massive slab of stone with bones still embedded in it. There's also a fine exhibit of **Native American artifacts** given to James Cook over his years of friendship with local tribes. Computer touch-screens show you points of interests to look for when you go out on the park's two easy walking trails to various quarries. You can

Agate Fossil Beds.

also see the Bone Cabin, where paleontologists worked and stayed with the Cooks' son Harold, who himself became a paleontologist—growing up here, how could he become anything else?

ⓘ 301 River Rd. at Hwy. 29 (ℂ **308/668-2211;** www.nps.gov/agfo).

✈ Western Nebraska Regional, 50 miles.

🛏 $$ **Candlelight Inn,** E. Hwy. 26, Scottsbluff (ℂ **800/424-2305** or 308/635-3751; www.candlelightscottsbluff.com).

$$ **Hampton Inn Suites,** 301 W. Hwy. 26, Scottsbluff (ℂ **800/HAMPTON** or 308/635-5200; www.hamptoninn.com).

WHY THEY'LL THANK YOU: Seeing where the fossils came from.

151 Fossils

Florissant Fossil Beds
Fossil Snapshots of the Eocene
Ages 6 & up • Florissant, Colorado, USA

Sᴀʏ ᴛʜᴇ ᴡᴏʀᴅ *fossil* and a child thinks of dinosaurs, or maybe a sabertooth cat or woolly mammoth. But the fossils piled up at the Florissant Fossil Beds represent a whole other realm: millions and millions of bits of stone etched with fine impressions of **prehistoric spiders, flies, beetles,** and **ferns,** amazing in their intricacy and soft-shaded colors. While these teensy fossils may not look so impressive to children at first, to the paleontologists who first unearthed them in the late 19th century, they were a thrilling find—it's astonishingly rare to find something as delicate as insects so perfectly preserved. You'd expect a bone to leave its mark on the earth; but a tsetse fly?

Set in a quiet mountain valley just west of Pike's Peak, this national parkland tells a story 35 million years old: of a time when volcanic eruption left the land buried under unusually fine ash, trapping millions of plants and insects, as well as stands of prehistoric redwoods. The resulting depression in the earth eventually filled with water and

became a lake; the ash and all its organic matter settled as sediment, eventually hardening into rock, while mineral crystals grew in the cells of the redwood stumps, petrifying them. Then the lake dried up; the former lake bed heaved upward with the Rockies. Only in the late 19th century did a local rancher find the strange impressions in rock outcroppings. Paleontologists came from far and wide to obtain fossils here, but so did souvenir hunters, carting away massive quantities.

Several fossils are displayed at the **visitor center,** but after staring at the glass cases, urge the kids to go out and explore (a good excuse for tramping through this lovely Colorado landscape of wildflower meadow and Ponderosa pine forests). A .5-mile **self-guided trail** loop from the visitor center (grandly named Walk Through Time) lets you examine several petrified stumps, as well as an outcrop of shale still bearing many fossils. Another 1-mile loop branching off the short walk takes you past several more petrified trees and an historic excavation pit. The

A fossilized fern at the Florissant Fossil Beds.

hills are still full of these rare, minute fossils. Before you swat away that next mosquito, take a moment to ponder its ancient lineage.

ⓘ Teller County 1 (✆ **719/748-3253**; www.nps.gov/flfo).

✈ Colorado Springs, 35 miles.

🛏 $$$ **The Broadmoor,** Lake Circle, Colorado Springs (✆ **800/634-7711** or 719/634-7711; www.broadmoor.com). $$ **The Cliff House at Pike's Peak,** 306 Cañon Ave., Manitou Springs (✆ **888/212-7000** or 719/685-3000; www.thecliffhouse.com).

WHY THEY'LL THANK YOU: Seeing an entire creature, not just a bone.

Fossils **152**

Ghost Ranch: Haunted by Dinosaurs

Ages 4 & up • Abiquiu, New Mexico, USA

Yᴏᴜ ᴡᴀɴᴛ ᴏʟᴅ ᴅɪɴᴏsᴀᴜʀs? Try 215 million years old. You want complete skeletons? Ghost Ranch has those too, and in abundance. When an exposed cliff face on this dude ranch in northern New Mexico first yielded its fossil secrets in the late 1940s, the world of paleontology was turned upside down: Here, embedded in mudstone, was a mass grave of nimble two-legged Triassic carnivores named *Coelophysis. Hundreds* of them, and not just bones but compete intact skeletons—now that's a paleontologist's dream come true.

Ghost Ranch isn't a dude ranch anymore, but an education and retreat center set in a stunning Southwest landscape of colorful cliffs and eroded red hills. The adobe **dinosaur museum** on the grounds may be small but it's fabulous for kids. Its centerpiece is an 8-ton block of mudstone removed from that cliff, embedded with more than a thousand Coelophysis fossils; the children can inspect the fossil hoard at very close range and watch a paleontologist removing bones from the rock. This is still cutting-edge work: a **crocodilian skeleton** removed from Ghost Ranch slabs as recently as 2005 turned out to be an entirely new species, a 6-foot-long, two-legged reptile with tiny arms, a long neck, huge eyes, and a birdlike beak. (If any kids

drew something that weird, you'd be tempted to tell them they were just making it up.)

Other fossils on display include bones from the 100-foot-long **Seimosaurus** and the crocodile-like **Hesperosuchus,** two other early reptilians that were soon to be rendered extinct by the hollow-boned Coelophysis and its descendants. Once you're done with the museum, don't pass up the chance to hike around the buttes and mesas: A **walking trail** leads from the museum to a steep hill where many more Coelophysis skeletons were unearthed.

Visitors can drop in just to view the exhibits or can reserve slots in **paleontology workshops** at Ghost Ranch, some of which are designed specifically for parents and children or grandparents and grandchildren; there are also weeklong courses, more or less summer camps for the whole family (parents get their own activity program) utilizing the ranch's art studios, ropes courses, lake, hiking trails, and horseback riding. Semirustic lodging is available on-site, although in July and August it's usually filled with course participants.

ⓘ U.S. 84 (✆ **505/685-4333;** www.ghostranch.org).

✈ Santa Fe Municipal, 60 miles. Albuquerque, 120 miles.

🛏 $$ **El Rey Inn,** 1862 Cerrillos Rd. (© **800/521-1349** or 505/982-1931; www.elreyinnsantafe.com). $$ **Old Santa Fe Inn,**

320 Galisteo St. (© **800/745-9910** or 505/995-0800; www.oldsantafeinn.com).

WHY THEY'LL THANK YOU: New fossils still being found.

153 Fossils

La Brea Tar Pits: Oozing Ancient History

Ages 5 & up • Los Angeles, California, USA

Aɴ ᴏᴅᴏʀᴏᴜs sᴡᴀᴍᴘ of gooey asphalt oozes to the earth's surface in the middle of Los Angeles. No, it's not a low-budget horror-movie set—it's the La Brea Tar Pits, a bizarre primal pool on Museum Row where hot tar has been seeping to the surface from a subterranean oil field for more than 40,000 years. It's an incongruous sight in the middle of built-up Los Angeles; in this grassy patch of Hancock Park, you can walk right up to the abandoned asphalt quarry's slick black pool of oily water, inhaling its acrid scent and watching bubbles of methane gas bloop to the steamy surface. Suddenly the high-rise office towers of Wilshire and Fairfax boulevards seem to recede, and you can imagine a distant past when mammoths and saber-tooth cats prowled this fern-shaded landscape.

The **bubbling pools** have tempted thirsty animals throughout history—with fatal consequences.

Nearly 400 species of mammals, birds, amphibians, and fish, many of them now extinct, walked, crawled, landed, swam, or slithered into the sticky sludge, got stuck in the worst way, and stayed forever. For many years, their fossilized bones were pried out of hardened asphalt by the pit's owners, who were too busy extracting commercial tar to care about them. But as paleontology came of age in the early 20th century, in 1906 scientists began to study this prehistoric trove. Some 100 tons of **fossils** were eventually removed—ground sloths, giant vultures, mastodons, camels, bears, native lions, dire wolves, lizards, and relatives of today's super-rats—the world's largest collection of Ice Age remains.

Today those entombed specimens are displayed at the adjacent **Page Museum.** Some 30 complete skeletons, along with assorted skulls and other bones, are handsomely mounted with in-depth explanations; there are also a few animatronic figures flailing about, though nothing that would terrify young children. Advise them not to expect dinosaurs—these fossils are all from the Ice Age, but those are even rarer than dinosaur fossils. Until we came here, I never knew that there were native horses in prehistoric North America, which eventually became extinct. Archaeological work is ongoing; you can watch as scientists clean, identify, and catalog new finds in the Paleontology Laboratory.

This quarry has always been open to the public, and thankfully it hasn't been walled off and overcommercialized (the kitschy figures of struggling mastodons set outdoor in the pits are time-warp quaint). Poking around the park, I felt as much connected to the 1950s, when I first visited California, as I did to the Ice Age. Somehow in all my trips to L.A. I had never before made time for the La Brea Tar Pits. And now at last I was here, and it was so much cooler than the glitzy theme parks and Hollywood Boulevard attractions. I was thankful to be able to introduce it to my kids.

ⓘ 5801 Wilshire Blvd. (© **323/934-PAGE;** www.tarpits.org).

✈ 🛏 See Hooray for Hollywood 🔴**355**.

WHY THEY'LL THANK YOU: Mastodons checked in, but they never checked out.

The Jurassic Coast
Dinosaurs in Devonshire
All ages • Exmouth to Lulworth, England

YOU'VE HEARD OF *Jurassic Park;* well, here's the Jurassic Coast, a 153km (95-mile) stretch of English coastline in East Devon and Dorset that is so rich in fossils and dinosaur footprints, it's been named a World Heritage Site. Beachgoers normally seek out fine, soft sand, but in this area the prime spots are rocky shingle beaches, where fossils wash right up at your feet.

Passing along the cost, notice the changing color of the cliff faces: Red cliffs have no fossils, being from the Triassic period, when this area was desert; darker gray cliffs are from the swampy Jurassic Age, perfect for dinosaurs; white chalk cliffs were formed underwater in the Cretaceous era and have marine fossils, mostly ammonites.

The Jurassic Coast.

A good base is **Lyme Regis,** a charming sea resort. In 1810, 11-year-old Mary Anning discovered an articulated ichthyosaur skeleton here, and went on to become one of the first professional fossilists. You'll learn more about Anning and local geology at the **Lyme Regis Philpot Museum,** Bridge Street (✆ 01297/ 443370; www.lymeregismuseum.co.uk; open daily Apr–Oct, weekends the rest of the year), in an Edwardian brick building on the site of Mary Anning's girlhood home. Don't miss the Dinosaur Poo Table, inlaid with coprolites (fossilized dino spoor). At **Dinosaurland,** Coombe Street (✆ **01297/443541;** www.dinosaurland. co.uk), in a church where Anning was baptized, you can view fossils and sign up for fossil-hunting walks. At Monmouth Beach, children can examine a huge stretch of rocks with ammonites embedded in them. West of Lyme Regis, the lovely beach at **Seatown** is great for fossil collecting, and in Sidmouth, fossils and other excavated artifacts are displayed at the **Sidmouth Museum,** Church Street (✆ **01395/ 516139;** www.devonmuseums.net/ sidmouth), where you can book walking tours.

The beach at Charmouth, the next town east from Lyme Regis, has an even better beach for fossil hunters. Fossil-bearing rocks fall into the sea, where the waves break them up, exposing the fossils. The rocks then wash ashore at low tide, particularly after storms. At the **Charmouth Heritage Coast Centre** (✆ **01297/560772**), wardens explain what fossils are and how to collect them. Beautiful Lulworth Cove, east of Swanage, punctuated by a massive rock arch named Durdle Door, has a **Heritage**

Center with displays on the local geology (📞 01929/400587), especially the nearby Purbeck Beds, thick layers of limestone and clay containing many dinosaur footprints. Just east of the cove, a foot-path from the Wealden Cliffs leads to the Fossil Forest, full of fossilized tree stumps; it's on an Army range but can be visited on weekends (📞 01929/462721).

Inland at Dorchester is the Dinosaur Museum, Icen Way (📞 01305/269880), with life-size dinosaur reconstructions.

ⓘ Jurassic Coast (www.jurassiccoast.com). Lyme Regis Tourist Information, Church Street (📞 01297/442138).

🚂 Dorchester (2½ hr. from London) or Axminster.

🛏 $$ The Royal Lion Hotel, Broad St., Lyme Regis (📞 01297/445622; www. royallionhotel.com).

WHY THEY'LL THANK YOU: Fossil hunting with spectacular sea views.

155 Fossils

Newark Earthworks: Ancient Observatory

Ages 8 & up • Newark, Ohio, USA

THERE'S ALWAYS SOMETHING HAUNTING to me about ancient observatories—the very idea that supposedly primitive peoples could position standing stones or mounds of dirt in perfect alignment with heavenly bodies. The mounds in Newark, Ohio, are even more confounding because they are so huge, big enough to hold four Roman Colosseums and twice as accurate astro-nomically as Stonehenge **163**. But now here's the kicker: The Newark Earthworks have a golf course on top. Only in America, right?

To be fair, the Moundbuilders Country Club course was built in 1933, long before professors from Earlham College dis-covered in 1982 how precisely the ancient mounds aligned with the lunar cycle. The existence of the earthworks, however, has been charted since the 1840s. A viewing platform has been built near the golf club's parking lot, but you need to contact the Ohio Historical Society (see numbers below) to arrange to walk around the fair-ways. You can also play explorers and search out other preserved bits of the ancient earthworks around Newark—there's the Great Circle Earthworks, a ceremonial circle 1,200 feet in diameter set in a park (formerly Moundbuilders State Park) off State Road 79 between Parkview Drive and Cooper Street, and the

Wright Earthwork, a 50-foot section of mound wall just west of State Road 79, which you view from James Street.

At ground level, the Newark Earthworks appear simply like gentle grassy humps, 3 to 14 feet high; it's only when seen from the air that their geometric precision becomes evident. A huge octagon, span-ning 40 acres, is linked with a pair of paral-lel walls to an adjoining circle that encloses 20 acres; the opening of the octagon lines up perfectly with the moon when it is at the northernmost point of its 18.6-year cycle, and each of the octagon's eight cor-ners aligns with a different significant lunar event in the cycle. It's theorized that the prehistoric Hopewell Indians built these mounds around A.D. 250—perhaps to attract the attention of the moon divinity, or perhaps to predict lunar eclipses. Per-haps they also climbed atop the mounds to view the moonrise (certainly not to hunt for their balls in the rough!).

A prehistoric highway beginning at the octagon led southwest to Ohio's other major Hopewell site, 40 miles south of Columbus: Hopewell Culture National Park (Rte. 104, Chillicothe; 📞 740/774-1125; www.nps.gov/hocu). Otherwise known as Mound City, this immense rectangle of earthen walls encloses a number of burial mounds.

(i) 125 N. 33rd St. (© **800/600-7178** or 740/344-1919; www.ohiohistory.org/places/newarkearthworks).

✈ Columbus (30 miles).

🛏 $$$ **Cherry Valley Lodge,** 2299 Cherry Valley Rd. (© **800/788-8008** or 740/788-1200; www.cherryvalleylodge.com).

$$ **Courtyard by Marriott,** 500 Highland Blvd. (© **740/344-1800;** www.marriott.com).

BEST TIME: Late May to early Sept.

WHY THEY'LL THANK YOU: Discovering the ancient past right underneath our modern feet.

Fossils

156

Cahokia Mounds
Metropolis of the Ancient Mississippians
Ages 6 & up • Collinsville, Illinois, USA

IT WAS ONCE THE BIGGEST CITY north of Mexico, with somewhere around 20,000 residents—farmers, hunters, craftsmen, traders, priests—at its peak in A.D. 1100–1200. Archaeologists have named them the Mississippians, but we don't know what they called themselves, since they left no writings behind. An air of mystery hangs over this site, just across the Mississippi River from St. Louis. Who were these people and what was their world like? The answers are hauntingly elusive.

Exhibits at the site's visitor center show how archaeologists play detective with the ancient past. The variety of arrowheads dug up, for example, proves that these people were sophisticated enough to trade with tribes as far away as southern Minnesota and the Gulf Coast. Experts gather that the mounds were built by hand, with workers carrying dirt in baskets on their backs from so-called "borrow pits" to the mounds. Ordinary citizens apparently lived in simple houses with pole walls and thatched roofs, but they labored to erect these immense earthen structures—109 still exist, 68 of them in this park—for public ceremonies.

After viewing the center's model of the ancient city, you can take tours of three different sections of the 2,200-acre site—hour-long ranger-led tours, or 30- to 45-minute self-guided walks (maps and audiotapes available) of each area. You certainly can't miss **Monk's Mound,** a four-terraced platform mound that once held the home of the city's ruler; it's the biggest mound in the western hemisphere, covering 16 acres at its base and rising 100 feet. Climb the modern steps to its now-grass-covered flat top and you gaze over a huge leveled plaza, bounded by the city's 2-mile-long log stockade wall, bits of which have been reconstructed. From this vantage point, the kids can identify several mound shapes—flat-top, conical, ridge-top—which apparently had various purposes. Unlike other cultures, the Mississippians generally did not use mounds for burials, although in a few cases skeletons have been unearthed with all the trappings of a prince or chieftain; other skeletons found are mostly those of young women or men with hands and feet cut off, which suggests they were human sacrifices. (Mound 72 was particularly full of sacrificial burials.)

Once archaeologists started to dig, they found something even more amazing: the remains of an astronomical observatory, similar to Stonehenge **163** but built of red cedar logs instead of stones. Woodhenge, the scientists have

Monk's Mound.

named it. How did two prehistoric cultures on different continents each get the same idea? And why did this great Mississippian city die? Archaeologists keep on digging, for they still have a lot of questions to answer.

(i) 30 Ramey St. (© **618/346-5160;** www.cahokiamounds.com).

✈ 🛏 See St. Louis **66**.

WHY THEY'LL THANK YOU: Ancient mysteries, right in America's backyard.

157 Fossils

Effigy Mounds
Bears & Birds Rising from the Ground
Ages 6 & up • Harper's Ferry, Iowa, USA

THE KIDS CAN SEE INDIAN MOUNDS in many parts of the country, but only in the upper Mississippi valley can they see burial mounds that were actually sculpted in the shapes of animals.

Here on the riverside bluffs and flood plains of the upper Mississippi River, the eastern woodlands begin to give way to the western plains. As if drawn to the great river, ancient nomadic hunter-gatherers built rock shelters and burial mounds here as long ago as 500 B.C. Artifacts displayed in the visitor center—pottery, stone spearheads, clam shells

(highly valued by these tribes), and flat stones for grinding corn meal—demonstrate how their culture developed over the centuries. But as they grew more sophisticated, from A.D. 600 to 1300 the Indians of this region had the novel idea to put a little more spin on their mounds, shaping them to resemble their tribal totems—bison, deer, turtles, lizards, but especially bears, eagles, and falcons. Strung along the **walking trails** through this 2,500-acre park, the mounds (there are over 200 of them) are unmistakable.

They may rise only a yard or so above the surrounding ground, but the shapes are well-defined, edged with gravel paths or sprouting taller grass. The biggest one, **Great Bear Mound,** rises 3½ feet and is 70 feet wide at the shoulders and 137 feet long. Some mounds still bear traces of fire pits where the animal's head or heart or would be, suggesting that their purpose was highly ceremonial. There are three simple conical burial mounds right by the visitor center, but that's just a foretaste; an excellent 2-mile trail from the visitor center leads past 25 mounds, both conical mounds and effigy mounds, on the way to the **Fire Point overlook,** 300 feet above the river, for a truly stunning Mississippi River panorama. A longer hike, 4 miles round-trip from a parking area south on Highway 76, takes you to the park's biggest mound cluster, the **Marching Bear group,** which has 10 bears and three bird shapes.

The park is right off the scenic Great River Road in northeastern Iowa, just across the river from Prairie du Chien, Wisconsin. If the kids are eager to see more, **Pikes Peak State Park,** 15316 Great River Rd. (© **563/873-2341**), only 7 miles away in MacGregor, Iowa, has several effigy mounds along its walking trails as well.

ⓘ 151 Hwy. 76 (© **563/873-3491;** www.nps.gov/efmo).

✈ Dubuque, 80 miles.

🛏 $$$ **Best Western Quiet House & Suites,** Hwys. 18 & 35, Prairie du Chien, WI (© **608/326-4777;** www.quiethouse.com). $$ **The Frontier Motel,** 101 S. 1st St., Marquette, IA (© **888/681-0144** or 563/873-3497; www.thefrontiermotel.com).

WHY THEY'LL THANK YOU: Earth sculptures they can relate to.

Early Humans 158

Canyon de Chelly
Hanging Out with the Anasazi
Ages 8 & up • Chinle, Arizona, USA

For nearly 5,000 years, people have made their homes in this spectacular pair of narrow sandstone canyons of remote northeastern Arizona. The Navajos are the most recent guardians of this land; the Ancestral Puebloans (also known as the Anasazi) left their mark too, in the giant rock amphitheaters where they created caves, dwelling rooms, and ceremonial kivas. To explore the canyons is to see centuries unfold.

Ancestral Puebloan civilization reached its zenith between A.D. 1100 and 1300, but evidence suggests that these canyons may have been occupied as early as A.D. 300. In the nooks and crannies of the canyons you'll see ancient dwellings hollowed into the rock walls and the circular sacred rooms known as kivas; the largest

and most impressive ruins are the **White House Ruins** in Canyon du Chelly, which were inhabited between 1040 and 1275. You'll also see ancient tombs—the **Tomb of the Weaver** near the Antelope House ruins, and the **Mummy Caves,** both appropriately enough in Canyon del Muerto, or the Canyon of the Dead. While most tourists simply drive along the two scenic drives—the 15-mile North Rim drive, which overlooks Canyon del Muerto, and the 16-mile South Rim drive, which overlooks Canyon de Chelly (pronounced "duh *shay*")—hire a guide and you can take the kids right down into the canyons where they can poke around these fascinating ruins. Navajo guides or local tour companies will lead you either on foot or in a four-wheel-drive vehicle.

Canyon de Chelly.

The hike down is fairly demanding, so with kids you'll probably opt to drive—there'll still be a bit of walking to reach the various ruins.

Since you'll be seeing both Navajo and Ancestral Puebloan relics, make sure the kids learn the difference between the two kinds of rock art. Dark slick streaks on the walls of the canyon walls, where water seepage reacting with iron oxide created what's known as desert varnish. Ancestral Puebloans chipped away at the desert varnish to expose the lighter-colored rock underneath in pictorial designs we now call petroglyphs. Pictographs are similar designs made later by the Navajos, using colorful paints on the sandstone walls to commemorate important tribal events. Urge the kids to take time to decipher the stories told by the rock pictures—they're windows into an ancient way of life.

(i) Off Rte. 191 (© **928/674-5500;** www.nps.gov/cach).

✈ Flagstaff, 222 miles.

🛏 $$ **Holiday Inn Canyon de Chelly,** Indian Rte. 7 (© **800/HOLIDAY** or 928/674-5000; www.holiday-inn.com/ chinle-garcia). $$ **Thunderbird Lodge** (© **800/679-2473** or 928/674-5841; www.tbirdlodge.com).

WHY THEY'LL THANK YOU: Seeing pictographs *and* petroglyphs.

---

159 Early Humans

Mesa Verde
Ancient Colorado Condos on the Cliffs
Ages 4 & up • West of Cortez, Colorado, USA

Over 800 years ago—a.d. 500 to 1300—a native people we now call the Ancestral Puebloans began to settle in the canyons and mesas of the American Southwest, giving up their nomadic hunter-gatherer lifestyle for more permanent crop-tending communities. Faced with this mountainous terrain, the Ancestral Puebloans developed their own creative solution to the residential real estate question. Though the kids may come to Mesa Verde National Park thinking that our 21st-century high-rise cities are the ultimate in civilized living, they'll soon see that these mysterious ancients had the concept down centuries ago.

Start 10 miles north of Cortez, at the **Anasazi Heritage Center,** 27501 Colorado Rte. 184 (© **970/882-5600**), a fabulous hands-on place for the kids to learn about Ancestral Puebloan culture. Then head down to the park, which you enter via U.S. 160. Its three most awesome sites—Cliff Palace, Balcony House, and Long House—can only be visited on ranger-led tours, which must be booked at the Far View Visitor Center.

The largest site, **Cliff Palace,** is just that—a 151-room, four-story apartment house set under the rim of a cliff, with stepped-back roofs forming penthouse courtyards for the next level up. The 45-room **Balcony House** hangs above Soda Canyon, with stone stairs, log ladders, and narrow crawl spaces. **Long House** stretches across a long alcove in Rock Canyon, with 150 rooms and 21 kivas (subterranean chambers used for ceremonies and meetings) and a large public plaza for community gatherings.

Before or after your guided tour, there are plenty of other dwellings to visit—Mesa Verde is the largest archaeological preserve in the United States, with almost 5,000 archaeological sites. The 6-mile **Mesa Top Loop Road** has 10 stops where you can either view dwellings or walk a short distance to them. The **Chapin Mesa Museum** has dioramas and interpretive displays on Puebloan culture; behind the museum, a paved .3-mile trail leads down to **Spruce Tree House,** a 130-room dwelling set safe and snug inside an 89-foot-deep alcove. Or drive west to less-crowded Wetherill Mesa, where a half-mile hike takes you to **Step House;** to its left you'll find three even older homes, pit houses made by earlier Puebloans around A.D. 626. If the kids are seasoned hikers, try the **Petroglyph Point Trail,** which begins just past the Chapin Mesa Museum; it's almost 3 miles long, running along the rim of a stunning canyon to reach an impressive panel of rock art.

(i) Off U.S. 160, 10 miles west of Cortez (© **970/529-4465;** www.nps.gov/meve).

"Anybody home?" Exploring Mesa Verde.

🛏 $$ **Holiday Inn Express,** 2121 E. Main, Cortez (✆ **888/465-4329** or 970/565-6000; www.ichhotelsgroup.com).

BEST TIME: Late May to early Sept.

WHY THEY'LL THANK YOU: Chutes and Ladders come to life.

160 Early Humans

Valley of Fire: Ancient Art Gallery

Ages 10 & up • Overton, Nevada, USA

Oᴜᴛ ʜᴇʀᴇ in the desert, 55 miles from Las Vegas, the vistas are awesome—eccentric red rock outcroppings, sand dunes spiked with desert scrub and green creosote bushes—but it's hardly a hospitable place to live. And yet ancient peoples, such as the Ancestral Puebloans and the even earlier prehistoric Basket Makers, were drawn here to etch artwork onto the canyon walls and rock formations. Were they writing history, telling folktales, or creating sacred places to worship? No one knows for sure; maybe it was a little of each. But what I find most awesome about standing here is to sense, down through the centuries, the ineffable human passion to leave some permanent records of their doings, to communicate with eternity.

Two easily accessible sites in this state park display some of the most intriguing petroglyphs found anywhere. The first set is near the west entrance, at **Atlatl Rock,** where a 40-foot-high stairway leads up to an eroded red sandstone formation that looks as if one precariously balanced boulder is about ready to topple over. The park is full of such arresting formations, but this one shelters a smooth stone face etched quite clearly with pictures of ancient hunting or warfare—the drawings unmistakably depict an atlatl, a notched stick used to fling spears in an early precursor of a bow and arrow. Why is this weapon drawn so prominently? Some experts believe it was because this was considered a magic spot for warriors to

be healed from spear wounds. The weird thing is that the panel is angled to face east, to catch the sun's rays at sunrise; it's been angled so precisely that there must have been some ceremonial or religious intent.

Then there's an easy .5-mile loop trail through a small, twisty canyon that's been named **Petroglyph Canyon,** for obvious reasons: It just may be the world's most amazing place to see Ancient Puebloan rock art. Panel after panel of slick dark rock along the course of the canyon was etched by these ancient artists with astoundingly expressive figures—big-horned sheep, dancers (try to tell which ones were men and which ones were women), birds, suns. Trail markers point them out, but no one can say for sure what events these pictures narrate. Victory in a war against their neighbors? Celebrations of the end of a drought? Visits from aliens in spaceships? Encourage the kids to interpret the figures for themselves and tell their own versions of the stories. Hopefully at some point they'll shiver with awe, sensing the spirits of the ancients speaking to us still today.

ⓘ ✆ **702/397-2088;** www.parks.nv.gov/vf.htm.

✈ 🛏 See Las Vegas **46**.

WHY THEY'LL THANK YOU: Telling stories in stone.

The Caves of Lascaux
The Oldest Paintings in the World

Ages 6 & up • Montignac, France

IMAGINE WHAT WENT THROUGH the minds of four French boys hunting for a dog one afternoon in 1940, down in the Dordogne region of France, when they crawled into a cave and saw its walls daubed with hundreds of vivid paintings—majestic bulls, wild boars, stags, horses, and deer—astonishingly lifelike figures painted by Stone Age hunters 15,000 to 20,000 years ago.

Opened to the public in 1948, the **Caves at Lascaux** speedily became one of France's major tourist attractions, drawing a quarter of a million visitors annually—and causing such grave atmospheric changes that the precious paintings began deteriorating. The cave closed to the public in 1964, though qualified archaeologists can still apply to visit. But the kids don't have to be disappointed: A short walk downhill from the real caves, Lascaux II is an impressive reproduction of the original, molded aboveground in concrete, where some 200 paintings have been faithfully copied. Come early, because only 2,000 visitors are allowed in per day; from April to October, buy tickets at a kiosk by the Montignac tourist office (see below).

Also in Lascaux, up a hill from the caves, the intriguing site of a prehistoric bear cult has been preserved at **Site Préhistorique de Regourdou** (✆ **05-53-51-81-23**). Alongside the sepulchers and skeletons of a Neanderthal man and several bears, you can watch a pack of quite live semiwild bears roam around a naturalized habitat (off-limits to humans, of course), a charming way to bring visitors closer to their bear-worshipping ancestors.

Three other authentic caves can be visited here as well, but be sure to call up to a year ahead for reservations. **Grotte de Font-de-Gaume,** on D47, 1.5km (1 mile) outside Les Eyzies (✆ **05-53-06-86-00**), and **Grotte des Combarelles,** D47, 17km (11 miles) north of Bergerac (✆ **05-53-06-86-00**), feature Stone Age paintings, while **Grotte du Grand-Roc,** 48 av. Prehistoire (✆ **05-53-06-92-70**), has stalactites and stalagmites. The **Musée National de la Préhistoire** in Les Eyzies (✆ **05-53-06-45-45**) displays a hoard of prehistoric artifacts unearthed in local excavations.

ⓘ **Caves,** Off D706, 2km (1¼ mile) from Montignac (✆ **05-53-51-95-03**). **Montignac Office de Tourisme,** place Bertrand-de-Born (✆ **05-53-51-82-60;** www.bienvenue-montignac.com). **Les Eyzies Office de Tourisme,** 19 rue de la Préhistoire (✆ **05-53-06-97-05;** www.leseyzies.com).

🚌 Condat-Le-Lardin, 486km (302 miles) from Paris.

🛏 $$$ **Hotel Les Glycines,** Rte. De Périgueux, Les Eyzies-Tayac-Sireuil (✆ **05-53-06-97-07;** www.les-glycines-dordogne.com). $$ **Relais du Soleil d'Or,** 16 rue du 4-Septembre, Montignac (✆ **05-53-51-80-22;** www.le-soleil-dor.com). Closed Feb.

BEST TIME: Closed Jan.

WHY THEY'LL THANK YOU: Cave men rock.

Teotihuacán: Ghost City of Ancient Mexico

Ages 8 & up • San Juan Teotihuacán, Mexico

EVEN THE AZTECS WERE AWESTRUCK, naming these haunting ruins Teotihuacán (pronounced "teh-oh-tee-wa-*khan*"), or "place where gods were born." Gazing out upon the rough stone ruins, an easy day trip northeast from Mexico City, you can see why. Beneath these fragments—three pyramids, sacrificial altars, the remains of a few grand houses—lies the ghost of a great city that once covered 12 square miles, its temples and palaces painted with brilliant red frescoes. With a population of 200,000 at its zenith, Teotihuacán was the cultural epicenter of ancient Mesoamerica. Yet today it's one of history's great mysteries, for we know precious little about the people who lived here—what language they spoke, where they came from, or why they abandoned the place around A.D. 700, to vanish without a trace.

About the same time as the Romans were building the Colosseum and the Forum, the Teotihuacán people erected their own **Pyramid of the Sun,** still the third-largest pyramid in the world. Celestial observations were apparently vital to this culture—the movements of the planet Venus determined wars and human sacrifices—and the city was laid out accordingly. Climb 248 steps to the top of the pyramid to see its precision: The front wall of the Pyramid of the Sun is exactly perpendicular to the point on the horizon where the sun sets at the equinoxes, and the rest of the grand buildings lie at right angles to it. The first structure of the pyramid was probably built a century before Christ, and it was topped off with a temple about A.D. 300. When the site was discovered early in the

20th century, though, the temple had disappeared and the pyramid was an overgrown mass of rubble.

As you explore the site, set the kids on a treasure hunt for animal motifs. Walking up the main north–south street, the Calzada de los Muertos (Avenue of the Dead), look for a bit of wall sheltered by a corrugated roof: The fragment of a **jaguar painting** suggests what this street may have looked like with all its original paintings intact. Proceed to the **Pyramid of the Moon;** upon its plaza sits the **Palace of Quetzalpapalotl,** where figures of Quetzal-Mariposa (a mythical bird-butterfly) are painted on walls or carved in pillars; behind it, the **Palace of the Jaguars** has murals and frescoes of jaguars. At the south end of the Avenue of the Dead, in the immense sunken square named the Ciudadela (Citadel), there are the **Feathered Serpent Pyramid** and the **Temple of Quetzalcoatl;** point out to the kids the large serpents' heads jutting out from collars of feathers carved in the stone walls, as well as other feathered serpents carved on the walls.

ⓘ ✆ **59/4956-0276** or 59/4956-0052.

✈ Mexico City, 48km (30 miles).

🛏 $$$ **Hotel Four Seasons,** Reforma 500, Mexico City (✆ **800/332-3442** in the U.S., 800/268-6282 in Canada, or 55/5230-1818; www.fourseasons.com).

$$ **Hotel Imperial,** Paseo de la Reforma 64, Mexico City (✆ **55/5705-4911;** www.hotelimperial.com.mx).

WHY THEY'LL THANK YOU: Serpents, jaguars, and butterflies.

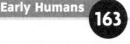
England's Standing Stones
Stonehenge & Avebury
Ages 6 & up • Wiltshire, England

ONE OF THE WORLD'S MOST MYSTERIOUS SITES, Stonehenge may be familiar to you from hundreds of photos and cartoons, but seeing it in person is still awe-inspiring—there's an aura about the place that can't be shrugged off. Stonehenge is distinctive because so many stones remain and they are capped by huge lintels across the top. Yet only 32km (20 miles) north there's another set of standing stones that originally was even larger than Stonehenge: Avebury.

No one knows who built **Stonehenge,** but scholars have determined that it was first laid out around 3100 B.C. as a circle of upright timbers. Around 2500 B.C. it was rebuilt using 5-ton bluestones floated on rafts from Wales; 2 centuries later, the ancient builders replaced the bluestones with 45-ton Sarsen sandstone blocks. Moving rocks this big is quite a feat; you can still see drag marks in the earth. How did ancient workers stand these rocks on end, much less haul the crosspieces to place on top? The biggest mystery, though, is why it was built at all. Archaeologists suggest that because the circle is perfectly aligned with the sun on the summer solstice, it was the site for some sun-worship ceremony. Over the

centuries, many stones fell over or were carted away by farmers, and visitors chipped off bits for souvenirs; immediate access to the stone circle has therefore been cut off to tourists—you'll have to circle around it on a walkway that never gets closer than 15m (50 ft.) to the actual stones.

Some visitors prefer **Avebury,** because it's not overrun with tour buses and you can walk right up and around the few remaining stones, bristling out of the ground around the edge of the village. More than 100 stones remain, although they are more worn down than the ones at Stonehenge. Avebury also has a tiny but significant archaeological museum on-site, the **Alexander Keiller Museum** (✆ **01672/539250**), displaying artifacts excavated not only from Avebury but from other nearby prehistoric sites.

Northeast of nearby Swindon, 2.5km (1½ miles) south of the village of Uffington (take the A420 to B4508), a mysterious chalk figure was laid out around 1000 B.C. on a northwest-facing hillside: the **White Horse of Uffington.** Some 114m (374 ft.) long, it's by far the largest hill figure in England. It may represent an ancient nature goddess, but one popular legend

Mysterious Stonehenge.

says it's not a horse at all but the dragon killed by St. George—a battle that supposedly took place on Dragon Hill, a low, flat-topped mound in the valley below, where the dragon's spilt blood supposedly burned a bare white patch where no grass can ever grow.

(i) **Stonehenge,** Junction of A303 and A344/A360, 3.2km (2 miles) west of Amesbury (© **01980/623108;**

www.stonehenge.co.uk). **Avebury,** A361, between Swindon and Devizes (same website).

🚆 Salisbury, 1½ hr. from London.

🛏 $$$ **Grasmere House,** 70 Harnham Rd., Salisbury (© **01722/338388;** www.grasmerehotel.com).

WHY THEY'LL THANK YOU: Ancient riddles without answers.

---

164 Early Humans

Ancient Stones of the Orkney Islands
Ages 8 & up • The Orkney Islands, Scotland

To visit the Orkney Islands, a sparsely populated archipelago some 6 miles north of the Scottish mainland, is to look at 1,000 years of history. It's virtually an archaeological garden, full of megalithic chambered tombs, stone chambers, and fortified Pict brochs (round stone towers). Don't expect slickly developed tourist sites—often you'll have to ask at a farmhouse for the key to a crumbling cairn, where you can poke around the eerie chambers by yourselves.

On the island called **Mainland,** the best stuff lies around the town of Stromness. The chambered cairn of **Maes Howe** (2700 B.C.) is a superb achievement of prehistoric architecture, constructed from single rock slabs 5.4m (18 ft.) long and 1.2m (4 ft.) wide. There's a passageway that the sun shines through only at the winter solstice. It also contains the world's largest collection of Viking rune inscriptions, the work of marauding Norsemen who broke in hunting for buried treasure. The Stonehenge-like **Ring of Brodgar** (1560 B.C.) is a circle of some 36 stones surrounded by a deep ditch carved out of solid bedrock; nearby are the remnants of an even older stone circle, the four upright **Stenness Standing Stones.** The remarkable **Unstan Chambered**

Tomb (© **01856/873-191**) is a burial mound 35m (115 ft.) across, dating from 2500 B.C., with a chamber over 2m (6½ ft.) high. Last occupied about 2500 B.C., **Skara Brae** (© **01856/841-815**) is a whole village of Neolithic stone-walled houses joined by covered passages, amazingly preserved after having been buried in the sands for 4,500 years.

Rousay island, off the northeast coast of Mainland, has nearly 200 prehistoric monuments, but the premier ones are on its southwest corner. On a stark promontory broods the Iron Age **Midhowe Broch and Tombs,** a 23m-long (75 ft.) cairn divided into a dozen compartments. When it was excavated in the 1930s, the graves of some two dozen settlers, along with their cattle, were found inside. The other major sight, the nearby **Blackhammer Cairn,** is a megalithic burial chamber from the 3rd millennium B.C. Between them is an old Norse grave site, **Westness;** from here there's a marked 1.6km-long (1-mile) archaeological trail past dusty-looking excavations on either side.

On southeast **Sanday Island** is one of the most spectacular chambered cairns in the Orkneys: the **Quoyness Chambered Tomb** (ask for the key at the Lady Village post office), dating from around 2900 B.C., its 4m-high (13-ft.) chamber twice as high as Unstan's. Over on **South Ronaldsay,** the **Tomb of the Eagles** (south of Windwick Bay; © 01856/831339) is a fine chambered tomb from 3000 B.C.

Warmed by the Gulf Stream, the Orkneys have a much milder climate than you'd expect; wildlife lovers can expect to see gray seals and an astounding number of bird species. Stay overnight to appreciate the awesome sunsets.

(i) **Orkney Islands** (www.visitorkney.com). **Kirkwall Tourist Office,** 6 Broad St.

(© 01856/872856). **Stromness Tourist Office,** Ferry Terminal (© 01856/850716).

✈ Kirkwall Airport, Mainland Orkney. Small airstrip on Sanday.

🛏 $$ **Stromness Hotel,** Victoria St., Stromness (© 01856/850298; www. stromnesshotel.com).

BEST TIME: May–July, when the midsummer sun remains over the horizon as long as 18¼ hr. a day.

WHY THEY'LL THANK YOU: The intense Indiana Jones vibe.

Early Humans **165**

Newgrange
Mysterious Mound of the Ancient Celts
Ages 6 & up • Slane, County Meath, Ireland

IT'S OLDER THAN ENGLAND'S STONEHENGE **163**, older even than the Great Pyramids in Egypt **169**—a **massive burial mound** dating back over 5,000 years, presiding serenely atop a hill near the Boyne River in Ireland. Newgrange is not only Ireland's best-known prehistoric monument, it's one of the archaeological wonders of western Europe, classified as a World Heritage Site by UNESCO.

Here are Newgrange's vital statistics: The mound rises 11m (36 ft.) tall and measures approximately 79m (260 ft.) in diameter. Inside, a passage 18m (59 ft.) long leads to a central burial chamber with a 6m (20-ft.) ceiling. The structure contains 200,000 tons of stone, including a 6-ton capstone; other stones weigh up to 16 tons each. It'd be impressive enough if it had been erected with modern engineering techniques, but when you remind the children what primitive tools were available to Newgrange's architects, they'll really be awed. Huge as the stones are, many of them were laboriously hauled from as far away as County Wicklow and the Mountains of Mourne.

What's more, each stone fits so perfectly in the overall pattern that the whole edifice is watertight, an amazing feat of engineering. And this is no mere utilitarian construction—the passage walls are carved with myriad decorative spirals, diamonds, and concentric circles.

Now here comes the really amazing part: Every year at the winter solstice, sunlight pierces the inner chamber with an orange-toned glow for about 17 minutes at dawn, from December 19 to December 23. Special **solstice viewing parties** are chosen by lottery months in advance; inquire at the visitor center, Bru na Boinne.

All tickets are issued at the visitor center; get there early to ensure getting on a **tour** (the last tour is at 4:30pm). In summer the site is extremely popular, so prepare to wait around for a while. You can purchase a combination ticket that also lets you tour **Knowth,** a slightly more recent megalithic passage tomb (begun in 3000 B.C.) a mile away. Underneath its grassy mound Knowth is more complex than Newgrange, with two main

burial chambers and 17 satellite tombs and a wealth of passage-tomb art, including some incredible calendar stones and lunar maps. A few miles inland, off the N3 road to Dublin, the **Hill of Tara** is the area's third important ancient site, and the youngest, built around 500 B.C.; there's little left here today on this high grassy mound, but at one time this was the fabled royal seat of the high kings of Ireland.

ⓘ Off N51, 3km (1¾ miles) east of Slane (ⓒ **041/988-0300**; www.knowth.com/newgrange.htm).

🚂 Drogheda, 48km (30 miles) from Dublin.

🛏 $$ **Conyngham Arms Hotel,** Main St., Slane (ⓒ **800/44-UTELL** in the U.S. or 041/988-4444; www.cmvhotels.com).

WHY THEY'LL THANK YOU: Prehistoric doesn't always mean primitive.

---

166 Early Humans

Secrets of Ancient Peru: The Nazca Lines

Ages 10 & up • Nazca, Peru

I**T'S AMAZING ENOUGH** to see ancient petroglyphs etched onto sandstone canyon walls—but what about geoglyphs, cut into the surface of the earth itself? Sprawling over nearly 1,036 sq. km (400 sq. miles) of the San Jose desert in southern Peru, the Nazca Lines are one of the most mysterious and awe-inspiring of ancient wonders: at least 10,000 lines forming **geometric designs**— trapezoids, zigzags, spirals—with another 300 **plant and animal figures** carved out of the barren earth beside them. And while you can see them from ground level, it wasn't until the age of airplanes that observers saw the pattern as it was meant to be seen—from the air. Which should lead kids to ask the obvious question: What did the prehistoric creators of these lines draw them for?

The Pan-American Highway rolls right through the Nazca Valley. Some of the biggest figures are 21km (13 miles) north of the town of Nazca. Experts believe they were constructed by the Nazca (pre-Inca) culture between 300 B.C. and A.D. 700, by removing dark surface stones to expose the pale soil beneath; the darker stones were then laid along the edge to sharpen the contrast. But why? There are lots of competing theories to explain

these lines: that they were an astronomical calendar; that they marked out underground sources of water; that they were pointers to direct the divine spirits of the nearby Andes mountains to bring rains to this desert; or perhaps even that they were landing strips for alien spacecraft. (There's no hard science to support that last theory, of course.) The animal shapes represent age-old Andean fertility symbols, particularly those associated with water. But it's still mind-boggling to imagine these ancient people going to all the trouble of designing a pattern they'd never be able to view in its entirety—let alone doing it so accurately.

One thing is sure: If you've come all the way down here to see the Nazca Lines, you should find a way to see them from the air. Various tour operators offer flyovers in small private planes from the town of Nazca; or you can cut to the chase and book a fairly pricey day trip from Lima offered by **AeroCondor,** Jr. Juan de Arona 781 (ⓒ **01/422-4214;** www.aerocondor.com.pe). From the window of an airplane, the kids will be able to identify specific shapes—a parrot, a hummingbird, a spider, a condor, a dog, a whale, a monkey—and they're huge: The spider is 50m (164 ft.) long, the monkey

100m (328 ft.) wide. The oddest of all is one humanlike figure with his hand raised in greeting, which almost inevitably has been named "the Astronaut." Cue up the *Twilight Zone* theme. . . .

✈ Lima, 346km (215 miles).

🛏 $ **Inkawasi Backpacker,** Alfredo Salazar 345 (𝄞 **01/422-7724**). $$$ **Sonesta Posada del Inca Miraflores,** Alcanflores 329 (𝄞 **800/SONESTA** or 01/241-7688; www. sonesta.com/peru_miraflores).

WHY THEY'LL THANK YOU: Seeing an ancient wonder as its makers never could.

Early Humans **167**

Easter Island: The Big Heads of Rapa Nui
Ages 8 & up • Chile

ON THIS TINY POLYNESIAN ISLAND—perhaps the most remote inhabited spot on Earth—stands an enigmatic horde of some 600 stone sculptures known as **moais,** 4-ton figures hewn from dark volcanic tufa rock. The faces are huge, with jutting brows and square jaws and startling white coral eyeballs. Though they were meant to be mounted on ceremonial stone platforms, many lie half-finished

Some of Easter Island's 600 maois.

in a quarry, tumbled carelessly on their sides, or abandoned mid-route to their pedestals. Why were they built? Even more baffling, how were such massive sculptures built by such primitive people?

It's a bit weird that Easter Island (Isla de Pascua) is part of Chile, considering that the coast of Chile is 4,000km (2,485 miles) away, but then Rapa Nui (as the islanders call it, meaning "Navel of the World") is no closer to anywhere else. Lan Chile flights and tour packages to the island generally depart from Santiago. Fossil evidence suggests that Rapa Nui was once covered with palm trees, which the original islanders carelessly cut down in a frenzy of statue building, spelling doom for this isolated population; the trees are being replanted, but it's still a shadeless place today. When the first Europeans visited the islands in 1722, the moais were upright; 50 years later, the next visitors found them knocked over, whether by desperate islanders or by hostile neighbors we'll never know. Empty platforms now stand ringed around the edge of the island, though curiously they face inland, rather than out to sea as you'd expect. Some of the figures have been reerected; you can see them standing in an inscrutable row, staring wordlessly over this volcanic blip in the middle of the vast Pacific.

Tourism is now Easter Island's main economic base; there are a handful of basic hotels and restaurants, along with tour guides, watersports operators (the island has some lovely white-sand beaches), and stables for horse trekking. Most people come on 3- or 4-day package tours, and everyone sees the same sights: a few ancient temples and ceremonial sites, cave paintings and petroglyphs, a lake-filled volcanic crater, but mostly the quarries and moais. The more you stare at them, the grander and more mystical they seem. Who needs any distractions from that?

ⓘ www.visit-chile.org.

✈ Mataveri, Easter Island.

🛏 $$ **Hotel Hanga Roa,** Av. Pont (📞 32/100299; www.hotelhangaroa.cl). $$$ **Hotel Iorana,** Ana Magoro (📞 32/100312; www.hoteliorana.cl/english.htm).

WHY THEY'LL THANK YOU: The silent statues keep their secrets.

The Egyptian Museum
Cairo's Treasure Chest
Ages 6 & up • Cairo, Arab Republic of Egypt

SOMETHING ABOUT ANCIENT EGYPTIANS really fires the interest of young children—is it the squiggly hieroglyphic writing? The anthropomorphic animals? The wigs and the jewelry and the streamlined elegance of their fashion sense? Who knows, but if you've come to Egypt to see the great desert monuments—and you'd be nuts to bring the kids here without seeing them—an essential first stop is in Cairo, at the world's largest collection of Egyptian antiquities. Some 120,000 pieces of priceless sculpture, painting, bas-relief, pottery, and jewelry have been crammed into two floors of a cavernous, dark, rather ugly neoclassical building. Unlike Western museums, the Egyptian Museum doesn't go to any trouble to make exhibits attractive or interesting, let alone interactive—displays are labeled with crumbling yellowed index cards typed in Arabic, French, and appalling English. What you see is what you get. But what you see is spectacular enough to make it all worthwhile.

Take, for example, the upstairs rooms dedicated to the **treasures of Tutankhamun** (14th c. B.C.). The enameled gold funerary mask, a remarkably lifelike and sensitive portrait of the teenage Pharaoh, always has a crowd of admirers around it; his solid-gold innermost coffin, displayed nearby, is a dazzling masterpiece of tasteful, restrained inlay and engraving. There's an extra charge to visit the **Mummy Rooms,** also upstairs, but it may be the highlight of the trip for the children: The remarkably well-preserved remains of Egypt's mightiest rulers exude much more personality than you'd expect. (Tutankhamun, by the way, is not here but rests once again in his Valley of the Kings tomb.) Gazing upon the features of three 19th Dynasty god-kings—Seti I and his son Ramesses II, the notorious oppressors of the Israelites, and Ramesses' son Merneptah, the Pharaoh of the Exodus—you get an undeniable impression of regal power and imperiousness, even though they are

The mask of Tutankhamun.

187

shriveled and stripped of all their royal paraphernalia.

This enormous, treasure-packed museum is not a place you can race through in an hour or even an afternoon. If you only have 2 hours, see the mummies and Tutankhamun. Take the other galleries at a child's pace, strolling past the glass cases until something catches your eye—something shiny, perhaps, or something very tiny and intricate, or something monumental and awesome. To interpret it all, try to get an **English-language guidebook** at the museum's gift shop, rather than investing in a guided tour (the Museum's tour guides are not really worth the fee).

ⓘ Midan al-Tahrir (ⓒ 02/578-2448; www.egyptianmuseum.gov.eg).

✈ Cairo International 19km (12 miles).

🛏 $$ **The Nile Hilton,** 1113 Corniche El-Nil (ⓒ **800/HILTONS** or 02/578-4446; www.hilton.com). $$$ **Semiramis Inter-Continental,** Corniche El-Nil (ⓒ **02/795-7171;** http://cairo.intercontinental.com).

WHY THEY'LL THANK YOU: Tutankhamun, mummies, animal-headed statues: What kid could ask for more?

The Pyramids of Giza
Ancient Wonders in the Desert
Ages 6 & up • Giza (Al-Jizah), Arab Republic of Egypt

THERE ARE OTHER PYRAMIDS scattered around the north of Egypt, but they're just shabby mounds of adobe compared to the Pyramids of Giza. This trio of stupendous tombs was one of the original Seven Wonders of the World—they're the only survivors of that ancient must-see list. And to sweeten the deal on this day trip from Cairo, there's a bonus: The kids can also see a bizarre statue right there guarding the Second Pyramid, a little monument they may know as the Sphinx.

Seeing the three Pyramids looming in the distance, you're struck by their apparent geometric perfection; up close, the thing that staggers you is their size—an estimated 2,300,000 stones in the Great Pyramid alone, weighing on average about 2.5 tons apiece (some stones weigh as much as 9 tons). They were built for three Pharaohs of the 4th Dynasty (about 27th c. B.C.): the **Great Pyramid of Cheops,** the slightly smaller **Second Pyramid of Chephren,** and the much smaller **Third Pyramid of Mycerinus.** Miniature pyramids nearby entombed the wives of these kings. The Great Pyramid is about 137m (450 ft.) tall—its missing pinnacle would have added another 9m (30 ft.)—and measures 230m (755 ft.) on each side; the four sides almost perfectly face the points of the compass. Originally the Great and Second Pyramids were faced with polished white limestone, though their facades today are jagged from centuries of thievery (you can still see a white bit at the top of the Second Pyramid). The Third Pyramid is faced with red granite. The eternal puzzler, of course, is how they were erected at all, given the primitive technology available. Obviously it took a lot of manpower, or rather slavepower. The Pyramids' shape was chosen to imitate the rays of the sun shining down from its desert zenith—the idea was that the buried king might ascend to heaven using his pyramid as a ramp.

The Second Pyramid of Chephren.

The **Great Sphinx,** Egypt's most mysterious symbol, has been repeatedly buried in sand and dug out again over the 4 millennia of its existence; 20m (66 ft.) tall and about 73m (240 ft.) long, it's a gargantuan likeness of King Chephren himself, dressed up as Harmachis, god of the rising sun. Ancient orange-red paint still clings in places to the battered face, which was vandalized by medieval Muslims. The Sphinx wasn't part of the original plan, but was improvised to get rid of a limestone knoll that blocked the king's view of his pyramid—maybe the most brilliant afterthought of all time. Its soft limestone, however, has required continual restoration over the ages. The royal "artificial beard," however, broke away in ancient times, beyond any hope of restoration (fragments are in the British Museum **183**).

✈ 🛏 See The Egyptian Museum **168**.

WHY THEY'LL THANK YOU: If the Pyramids don't wow them, the Sphinx sure will.

---

170 The Ancient World

The Valley of the Kings
Royal Tombs beneath the Desert Sands

Ages 8 & up • Across the Nile from Luxor, Arab Republic of Egypt

WITH ALL THEIR ROMANTIC ASSOCIATIONS of buried treasure and tomb robbers, the cavernous tombs of the Valley of the Kings have been a tourist magnet since Greco-Roman times. After centuries in which successive pharaohs' pyramids were plundered of their treasure, in the 16th century B.C. Tuthmosis I tried a new-and-improved method of royal burial: in underground chambers under a pyramid-shaped mountain across the river from Thebes (modern Luxor). Throughout the 18th, 19th, and 20th dynasties, over 60 personages (mostly royalty) followed Tuthmosis I's lead. In the end, of course, this elaborate necropolis was no more

thief-proof than the pyramids (only Tutankhamun's survived intact up to modern times). But while the pharaohs' buried riches are long gone, seeing the intricately decorated walls of these crypts is well worth the long trip up the Nile from Cairo.

Only about a quarter of these tombs are open to the public. The rules for touring them are strict: Photography is forbidden, visitors must be quiet and file in one by one, and the kids should be reminded not to touch *anything.*

Decorations on the smoothly plastered tomb walls were carved to raise designs out of the surface, then boldly painted.

Before you enter these narrow, mazelike passageways, ask the kids to imagine working down here, with only a guttering wick lamp to light the wall—it's amazing how much meticulous detail these anonymous artists accomplished under such odds. Certain themes are common: the king making offerings to the gods, or mystic encounters with bizarre deities in the Afterworld. Inside the **tomb of Horemheb** (14th c. B.C.), elegant figures pose against a gray background; the small but interesting **tomb of Ramesses I,** Horemheb's successor, has a vivid scene of the pharaoh consorting with hawk- and jackal-headed spirits. The **tomb of Ramesses VI** (12th c. B.C.) is worth seeing for its burial chamber, with magnificent ceiling paintings depicting the stars and other heavenly bodies as gods on a black background, with the sky goddess stretched out over all. Disappointingly, the tomb of King Tutankhamun has only one decorated chamber, and most of the treasures were moved long ago to the **Egyptian Museum** 🌑; but the kids will be dazzled by his quartzite sarcophagus, inside of which lies (under bulletproof glass) the gilded coffin that still contains Tut's mummy.

While you're here, don't miss the elegant columned **Temple of Hatshepsut,** just across the hill, or the jumbled ruins of the **Temple of Karnak,** with their elaborately incised round columns, just north of Luxor.

ⓘ **Tourist office,** Nile St., Luxor (✆ 095/382 215).

✈ Luxor International.

🛏 $$$ **Le Meridien Luxor,** Khaled Ben El Walid St. (✆ 095/2366 999; www.luxor.lemeridien.com). $$ **Luxor Hilton,** next to the Temple of Karnak (✆ 800/HILTONS or 095/237 4933; www.hilton.com).

WHY THEY'LL THANK YOU: Where the Pharoahs went to become gods.

The Ancient World **171**

The Acropolis
Hilltop Shrine of Ancient Athens
All ages • Athens, Greece

WE'VE ALL SEEN IT A HUNDRED TIMES on posters and postcards and cardboard coffee cups: the **Acropolis,** that hilltop rising boldly out of Athens with the famous columns of the **Parthenon.** But to actually be here, to walk around its crumbling stones, can be the experience of a lifetime. Ignore the crowds: We found a place to sit, gazed out over modern Athens sprawling below, and took time to muse about all who had been here before us.

This sheer rocky outcrop was an ideal defense against invaders, and people lived on the Acropolis as early as 5,000 B.C. In classical times, as Athens's population grew, citizens moved down from the Acropolis, but it remained a sacred site. Peer downhill at the houses in the Plaka to the northeast and the ruins of the Ancient Agora to the northwest, and you'll get the layout of the ancient city. The Acropolis's height couldn't protect it in 480 B.C., when Persian invaders destroyed most of its monuments, but Athenian statesman Pericles ordered the Acropolis rebuilt; almost all of what you see today comes from that era. Successive waves of invaders built other structures here, only to have them knocked down by the next invaders.

You enter the Acropolis through the Roman-era Beulé Gate, merely an

The Acropolis.

entrance to the real entrance—the monumental **Propylaia** arch. Just above the Propylaia, to the right, is the little, beautifully proportioned **Temple of Athena Nike;** to the left is the **Erechtheion,** the tomb of legendary Athenian king Erechtheus. Take time to study its delicate stone carving, especially the female figures (caryatids) holding up its pediments. (What you see are copies; the originals are in the nearby Acropolis Archaeological Museum.)

The real star of the show is the **Parthenon,** the great temple dedicated to Athena. Built of Pentelic marble, the Parthenon subtly changes color in the light—beige at dawn, golden at high noon, rose at sunset, ethereal white in the moonlight. Ask the children to imagine the Parthenon—along with most monuments here—decorated in a vivid paint scheme, as it was in antiquity. Ictinus, the Parthenon's architect, was a master of optical illusions: Big as it is, this temple seems light and graceful, with 46 slender columns (17 on each side, 8 at each end) ranged along the outsides. Its columns and stairs appear straight, yet all are minutely curved, with each exterior column thicker in the middle. The airy look of the Parthenon is also due to the

fact that it has no roof—in 1687, the Venetians, trying to capture Turkish-occupied Athens, blew it to smithereens. In the 19th century, British ambassador Lord Elgin carted off most of the remaining sculptures to London (see them in the British Museum **183**) for "safekeeping." The original sculptures on its triangular pediments portrayed the life of Athena, while a frieze around the tops of the columns depicted various battles. The message was the triumph of civilization—that is, Athens—over the barbarian forces of darkness. The barbarians came anyway (some say the bus loads of tourists are just the latest wave) but the Acropolis still rises above it.

ⓘ Dionissiou Areopagitou (☎ **210/321-0219**). **Athens Tourist Office,** Tsoha 24 (☎ **210/8707000**).

✈ Athens International, Spata, 27km (17 miles).

🛏 $$ **Athens Cypria,** 5 Diomias (☎ **210/323-8034**). $$$ **Hilton,** 46 Leoforos Vas. Sofias (☎ **800/445-8667** in the U.S., or 210/728-1000; www.hilton.com).

WHY THEY'LL THANK YOU: Socrates and Plato walked here.

National Archaeological Museum
The Great Hoard of Greek Antiquities
Ages 4 & up • Athens, Greece

IF WESTERN CIVILIZATION was born in ancient Greece, intervening centuries of war and invasion destroyed much of its heritage—or at any rate scattered it, for every new conqueror hoarded whatever Greek antiquities were available, a cache seen today in museums around the globe. But enough remained in Greece to fill Athens's rambling National Archaeological Museum with wondrous art and artifacts. While the **Acropolis** 171 is an open-air shrine to 5th-century Athenian culture, the museum's vast collection ranges all over the Greek isles and across centuries of Greek culture. With a few exceptions, it isn't individual pieces that'll impress the youngsters so much as the sweep of ancient history it brings to life.

Like magpies, we were attracted, of course, to the stunning **Mycenaean Collection,** blazing with gold masks, cups, dishes, and jewelry unearthed from the site of Mycenae by Heinrich Schliemann in 1876. We Trojan War fans stared open-mouthed at the majestic burial mask that Schliemann called the **"Mask of Agamemnon":** archaeologists have pretty much debunked that theory, but even if the mask belonged to an earlier, unknown monarch, it still has a haunting power, and all that gold testifies to the wealth and power that was Mycenae.

But as we passed through the museum's calm white galleries, we began to be more intrigued by the development of sculpture over time. We began with the **Cycladic figurines,** which date from about 2000 B.C., a collection of pale marble figures so simple and yet expressive (and adorable, my youngest declared), they reminded us of modern abstract art, like Henry Moore and Brancusi. With the Archaic period came stiffly posed **kouros** statues, carved from warm-colored stone, intricately detailed and yet less lifelike. By the **Classical period,** however, the Greeks had become such skilled sculptors, they could celebrate idealized physical beauty in bronze; probably the most awesome example is the 5th-century **Zeus of Artemision,** which many scholars contend is really a statue of Poseidon. The crucial question seems to be what this powerful-looking god originally was holding in his backward-flung hand, ready to hurl—if it was a thunderbolt, then this was Zeus; if it was a trident, Poseidon. In the **Hellenistic period** (323–31 B.C.) the statues finally become vivid individuals, like the coolly self-confident **Youth of Anticythera,** usually identified as Perseus (imagine his outstretched arm holding aloft a trophy head of Medusa), or the riveting statue of a small boy riding jockey on a powerful leaping horse. Before we came here, it was all Greek to us; 1½ hours later, we knew how much more we had to learn.

(i) 44 Patission ((C) **210/821-7724**).

✈ 🛏 See The Acropolis 171.

WHY THEY'LL THANK YOU: A thunderbolt or a trident—you decide.

Where the Gods Spoke to the Greeks

Ages 6 & up • Delphi, Greece

THE ANCIENT GREEKS BELIEVED THAT DELPHI, on the slopes of Mount Parnassus, was the center of the world, chosen by Apollo as the home of his most famous oracle. Pilgrims came from throughout the Greek world to ask Apollo's advice, on affairs of state or even small personal matters. The god's advice was often cryptic—"Invade and you will destroy a great empire," King Croesus of Lydia was told when he asked if he should go to war against Persia. So Croesus invaded, and destroyed a great empire—his own. Delphi, which is close enough to Athens for a long day trip, is one of Greece's loveliest sites, perched above a beautiful plain of olive trees stretching toward the Gulf of Corinth. Maybe it's just my imagination, but a mysterious aura still seems to hang over the ruins.

Originally the sanctuary was lined with outdoor sculptures; most have been moved inside to the **Delphi Museum.** The star of the museum, with a room to himself, is the 5th-century-B.C. *Charioteer of Delphi,* a larger-than-life bronze figure (his four-horse chariot, sadly, is long lost). Delicate eyelashes shade his enamel-and-stone eyes, and realistic veins stand out in his hands and feet.

The main attraction is the **Sanctuary of Apollo,** immediately beyond and just above the museum. You enter along the marble Sacred Way, trod by visitors for thousands of years, walking uphill past the remains of Roman stoas and a number of Greek treasuries. Cities built these small templelike buildings at Delphi to store riches and artworks dedicated to Apollo (ever vying to outdo their neighbors). Countless ancient inscriptions are incised on the treasury walls. The public can no longer go into the massive 4th-century-B.C. Temple of Apollo, but peer inside where three Pythian priestesses were always on duty, one of them delivering "Apollo's" pronouncements from a room deep within the temple. No one knows for sure how the priestesses, who often spoke in tongues, come up with their predictions—they may have inhaled hallucinatory fumes or chewed mind-altering herbs, such as the laurel leaf sacred to Apollo.

Delphi was also the site of the once-every-4-years Pythian Games, the most famous festival in Greece after the Olympics (see Olympia **462**), held up a steep hill from the temple at the remarkably well preserved 4th-century-B.C. **theater** and **stadium.**

Follow the Arakova-Delphi road toward the fragmentary ruins of the **Sanctuary of Athena,** who shared the honors here with Apollo. As a writer, I halt midway at the **Castalian Spring,** where legions of poets came to drink in hopes of finding inspiration. Above are the rose-colored cliffs known as the **Phaedriades** (Bright Ones), which almost magically reflect the sun's rays. It's no longer possible to drink from the springs, but inspiration wells up regardless.

ⓘ **The Sanctuary of Apollo & Delphi Museum** (✆ 22650/82-313).

✈ Athens 177km (110 miles).

🛏 $$$ **Amalia Hotel,** signposted on the Delphi-Itea Rd. (✆ **22650/82-101;** www. amalia.gr).

WHY THEY'LL THANK YOU: We have fortune cookies and horoscopes; the Greeks had an oracle.

Knossos: Daedalus's Ancient Labyrinth

All ages • Iraklion, Crete

THOUGH TODAY IT'S PART OF MODERN GREECE, the island of Crete long ago was home to its own powerful Minoan civilization, named after the famous king Minos. In Greek mythology, King Minos's palace at Knossos was notorious for its labyrinth, designed by the ingenious Daedalus and containing a grotesque monster, the Minotaur. Half-bull and half-man, the Minotaur devoured young victims purposely lost in the labyrinth. Finally the hero Theseus navigated the maze safely (with the help of Minos's daughter Ariadne) and slew the Minotaur. To punish Daedalus for revealing the secret to Ariadne, Minos imprisoned Daedalus and his son Icarus in the labyrinth. Daedalus built them wax wings to fly out, but Icarus, like any reckless adolescent, flew too near the sun, melted his wings, and fell to his death. It's a particularly vivid myth for youngsters, and rambling around the haphazardly laid-out ruins of Knossos, they'll feel it come thrillingly to life.

Arriving in Iraklion, Crete's gateway city, it's a good idea to look at the Minoan antiquities in the **Archaeological Museum,** 1 Xanthoudidou (© **2810/226-092**) before heading out to Knossos. These artifacts cover every phase of Crete's checkered history, from the first settlement by humans (around 6000 B.C.) to the emergence of a distinctive Minoan culture (2500 B.C.), the intrusion of Mycenaean Greeks (1500 B.C.), Roman occupation (starting in 67 B.C.), and conquest by Venetians in the 13th century. The original frescoes from Knossos are kept here for preservation (the frescoes now at Knossos are copies).

About 5km (3 miles) south of Iraklion, **The Palace of Knossos** is one of the world's great archaeological sites, the remains of not one but two major palaces from about 2000 B.C. to 1250 B.C. This was not just a royal residence but also the Minoans' chief religious-ceremonial center, as well as their administrative headquarters. Until archaeologist Arthur Evans began excavations in 1900, little was known about the Minoans, but the wealth of artifacts allowed archaeologists to virtually reconstruct an entire culture. While many ancient sites present only authentic ruins, Evans took a different tack, using every available clue and remnant to rebuild large parts of the palace—walls, floors, stairs, huge timber-framed windows to let in the Mediterranean sunlight, and wooden columns painted red and black. Copies of the original frescoes brighten the walls; stairways lead tantalizingly to long-gone upper stories. Look for King Minos's **stone throne,** dating from the 15th century B.C., in the throne room, a brilliant **fresco of leaping dolphins** in the queen's apartments, and **pictures of bulls** in numerous friezes and murals. This palace was so luxurious, it even had running water and flush toilets (and we're talking B.C.-era plumbing). For children especially, such aggressive restoration makes it easier to imagine the lives of ancient Minoans, Minotaur and all.

ⓘ Knossos Rd. (© **2810/231-940**).

✈ Iraklion 5km (3 miles).

🛏 $$$ **Candia Maris,** Amoudara, Gazi (© **2810/377-000;** www.maris.gr). $$ **Xenia-Helios,** Kokkini Hani (© **2810/761-502**).

WHY THEY'LL THANK YOU: Getting caught up in the labyrinth.

In the Footsteps of Alexander the Great

Ages 8 & up • Pella, Vergina & Dion, near Thessaloniki, Greece

THESSALONIKI, GREECE'S SECOND CITY, is known for its Byzantine churches and atmospheric Turkish quarter, but we came here to explore Alexander the Great country. When it comes to heroes, they don't get much more heroic than Philip of Macedonia and his son Alexander. When Philip was born in 382 B.C., most Greeks thought of Macedonians as a rude northern tribe of barbarians; by 338 B.C., he had conquered all of Greece. Two years later, Philip was dead, leaving his empire to his untested son Alexander, and many wondered how the youth could run Macedonia, let alone Greece. By the time he died at age 33, he was known as Alexander the Great and ruled most of the known world, as far east as India.

Both Philip and Alexander were born in **Pella,** a great seaport (now silted up) 40km (25 miles) west of Thessaloniki. On the hilltop north of the archaeological site, you can peer over a wire fence at the ruins of a vast palace complex (closed to the public), birthplace of both Philip and his son Alexander, and also where Aristotle tutored the young Alexander. In Pella's small **museum** (📞 **23820/31-160** or 23820/31-278; closed Sun), look for a mosaic of a lion hunt—some scholars suggest that it depicts an incident in which a friend saved Alexander from a lion. Compare it to the marble bust of Alexander in the museum and decide for yourself.

Another 20km (12 miles) south in **Vergina,** Philip had another immense **palace,** with a huge inner courtyard, a long colonnaded veranda, and an impressive theater where, walking to a play one fatal day in 336 B.C., he was assassinated. (Some scholars think Alexander was behind the foul deed.) Driving across the rolling plain, you'll see hundreds of **burial mounds.** In 1977, Greek excavators opened the marble gates of an unidentified tomb to find a solid gold ossuary: Inside, a pile of charred bones were still stained royal purple from the cloth in which they had been wrapped. Could it be Philip's tomb? It has never been fully proven, but alongside the bones were gold wreaths, little ivory portraits of Philip and Alexander, and an unmatched pair of bronze shin guards (an early injury had left one of Philip's legs shorter than the other). Inside the **Royal Tombs Museum** (📞 **23310/92-347**), a passageway leads into an area where five templelike tombs, their facades beautifully painted, can be viewed through a protective glass wall.

Some 78km (48 miles) south of Thessaloniki are the ruins of **Dion,** once Macedonia's most important religious sanctuary. Both Philip and Alexander established military camps here. (Check out the site's museum for models that help you visualize the Dion of Philip and Alexander.) It was here that 8-year-old Alexander first saw Bucephalos, a handsome black stallion that neither Philip nor any of his men could tame. Alexander asked if he could try, and, turning Bucephalos so that he could not see his shadow, the boy leaped on his back and galloped away. When the prince returned from his ride, Philip said, "My son, look for a kingdom equal to you. Macedonia is too small." There's a great deal to see at Dion, but leave time to picnic under the shade trees, imagining Alexander, at age 22, mounting Bucephalos and setting off to conquer the world.

ⓘ **Tourist office,** Aristotelous Sq., Thessaloniki (📞 **2310/271-888**).

✈ Thessaloniki.

🛏 $$$ **Electra Palace Hotel,** 9A Aristotelous Sq., Thessaloniki (📞 **2310/ 294-000;** www.electrahotels.gr). $$ **Philippion,** Seih-Souh hill, Thessaloniki (📞 **2310/ 203-321;** www.philippion.gr).

WHY THEY'LL THANK YOU: Where Alexander became Great.

The Ruins of Ancient Troy
Where the Iliad Comes to Life
Ages 10 & up • Hisarlik, Turkey

SITE OF HOMER'S EPIC BATTLE between the Trojans and the Greeks, not to mention archaeological in-fighting in the 19th century, the ruins of ancient Troy aren't very large, or very complete. But to my mind, Troy *should* look like a bereft ruin—wasn't it in flames when the victorious Greeks sailed away?—and it should have a tantalizing air of mystery. Though all you can see today is a hodgepodge of stony debris dug out of a windswept Turkish flood plain, it's still exciting to feel that you've stepped into one of the greatest stories of all time.

Thanks to the dogged archaeology of an obsessed German named Heinrich Schliemann, the foundations of this ancient city—lost for so long that many thought Homer had made it up—were uncovered in the 1870s on the Biga Peninsula of Turkey, where a silted-up bay had once connected to the Scamander River. Schliemann, however, unscrupulously removed significant amounts of treasure for his own personal gain, and some scholars (miffed no doubt by Schliemann's unorthodox behavior) dispute whether this buried city was actually Troy. Still, there's no question there was a major city here—in fact, several major cities: Archaeologists have defined at least nine different layers of construction dating back to 3500 B.C. The seventh layer down is assumed to be Homer's Troy, which evidence shows was destroyed by fire around 1200 B.C. (1184 B.C. is the date traditionally assigned to the events of the *Iliad*). Rebuilt 400 years later, Troy became an important city again during the Roman period—Augustus Caesar, Marcus Aurelius, and Hadrian all slept here.

A **guided tour** is a wise idea—experienced guides will be able to tell the kids a lot more about what they're seeing than you could possibly cull from a guidebook. Half-day tours are available from Çanakkale, or overnight tours from Istanbul (which include a visit to the tragic World War I battlefield of Gallipoli right across the straits). One experienced operator is **Hassle Free Travel Agency,** Cumhuriyet Cad. 61, in the Anzac House in Çanakkale (© **0286/217-5482;** www.anzachouse.com). Archaeologists estimate that the ruins of Troy actually extend 10 times farther than the 165 sq. m (1,776 sq. ft.) they've uncovered so far. A few structures have been reconstructed on the site, including a temple of Athena, a sacrificial altar, a Roman theater, a Senate building, and a graveyard of homeless marble columns. And of course there's a very satisfying model of the **Trojan Horse,** with steps so the kids can climb up inside.

ⓘ www.kultur.gov.tr.

NEAREST FERRY PORT: Çanakkale 16km (10 miles).

🛏 $$$ **Kolin Hotel,** Kepez (© **0286/218-0808;** www.kolinhotel.com). $$ **Tusan Hotel,** Güzelyali (© **0286/232-8746;** www.tusanhotel.com).

WHY THEY'LL THANK YOU: Walking in the steps of Achilles.

Ephesus: A Bit of Rome in Anatolia

Ages 8 & up • Near Selçuk, Turkey

WHILE THE EXCAVATIONS AT TROY are worth visiting for their literary value, the ones at Ephesus will simply take your breath away. It's one of the best-preserved ancient cities on the Mediterranean, a once-bustling Roman town that served as the capital of the Asian provinces. Built on the slopes of Panayir Dagi (Mt. Pion), the archaeological site requires only 1.6km (a mile) of walking, but it'll take 2 or 3 hours to wander through, there's so much to see—mosaic floors, arched colonnades, roads paved with marble, and layers upon layers of frescoes.

Entering at the top of the hill, walk first through the **Upper Agora,** the official part of town, full of temples and monuments and fountains, a town hall, and the Odeon, where the government council met. Sloping away from it is **Curettes Way** (curettes were a class of priests)—point out to the kids the pockmarks on the pavement made by thousands of horses' hoofs over the centuries. You'll pass a **Gate of Hercules** (that's Hercules wearing the skin of the Nemean Lion he slew) and the two-story **Trajan's Fountain** on your way to the **Temple of Hadrian,** with its glorious Corinthian columned porch. Behind it are a grand set of baths (the **Baths of Scholastika**). Across Curettes Way is a colonnaded shopping street with a fine mosaic floor, and above it the section that kids will probably enjoy the most: the **Terraced Houses.** This is where the richest citizens of Ephesus lived, and it's a great window into their sophisticated lifestyle—running water, heating systems, private inner courtyards, and a rich decor of mosaics

and frescoes. You'll see the **Library of Celsus,** with its fine two-tiered facade and three levels of niches for storing scrolls or books; the **Marble Way** (paved in real marble) leads from there to the **Great Theatre,** a hillside amphitheater that could seat 25,000—St. Paul delivered sermons here to the Ephesians in the early Christian era. Ephesus was an important Christian center as the religion spread throughout the Empire; Jesus' mother, Mary, lived here after his death, accompanied by St. John. Her house, now a church that's always crowded with pilgrims, is another couple miles to the southwest in Meryemana.

Make sure you leave enough time to see a few sights in **Selçuk,** the nearby city you'll use as a base: the **Ephesus Museum** at the intersection of Aatür Cad. and the park, for spectacular statues and friezes removed from the ruins; the ruined **St. John's Basilica** (off of Atatürk Cad.), built by Emperor Justinian over the tomb of St. John; and the forlorn single column that's all that remains of the **Temple of Artemis** (off the road to Kuşadasi), once one of the Seven Wonders of the Ancient World.

(i) www.kultur.gov.tr.

✈ İzmir 80km (50 miles).

🛏 $$ **Hitit Hotel,** Tariş Yani-Şarapçi Kuyu Mevki P.K. 66 (© **0232/892-6920;** www.kusadasihotels.com). $$ **Hotel Kalehan,** İzmir Cad. (© **0232/892-6154;** www.kalehan.com).

WHY THEY'LL THANK YOU: Imagining their daily lives.

The Colosseum & The Pantheon
Glories of the Roman Empire
All ages (Colosseum), 6 & up (Pantheon) • Rome, Italy

Pᴇʀʜᴀᴘѕ ɴᴏ ᴄʟᴀѕѕɪᴄᴀʟ Rᴏᴍᴀɴ ʀᴜɪɴ evokes the excesses of the late Empire like the **Colosseum.** In ᴀ.ᴅ. 80, the opening event at this 50,000-seat elliptical arena was a weeks-long bloody combat between gladiators and wild beasts. Later shows kept upping the ante: Vestal Virgins from the temple screamed for blood, ever-more exotic animals were shipped in to satisfy jaded curiosities, the arena floor was flooded for not-so-mock naval battles. Really big events like chariot races were held at the Circus Maximus, on the other side of the Palatine hill, but today it's a formless heap of ruins. The Colosseum, though—a kid can stand here and really imagine the whole scene.

Over the years the Colosseum has been damaged by earthquake, stripped of its rich marble facing, and begrimed by exhaust from cars whipping around the vicious traffic circle outside. But to modern eyes, its time-ravaged shell has its own haunted grandeur. On one side you can still see the original four-tiered design (each level has a different style of column, like a textbook illustration of Doric, Ionic, and Corinthian). You can stand center stage where the fighters stood before they met a bloody death or glory in the ring, or wander underneath where elephants, lions, and wild animals waited to be hoisted up in cages to the arena floor. It's simply amazing.

The Colosseum.

Across from the Colosseum are the **Roman Forums,** the center of Roman life in the days of the Republic. Traversed by the Via Sacra (Sacred Way), the vast public ground of the Forum lay between the Palatine and Capitoline hills. When it came to praising Caesar, purchasing a harlot, sacrificing a naked victim, or just hashing over the day's events, the Roman Forum was the place to be. By day, the columns of now-vanished temples and triumphal arches, not to mention the stones from which long-forgotten orators spoke, are mere shells fringed with wild grass and weeds. But at night, when the Forum is silent in the moonlight, it isn't difficult to imagine Vestal Virgins still guarding the sacred temple fire. Up Via dei fori Imperiali, the **Imperial Forums** are more recent, built in the 1st century A.D. by Julius Caesar when the older forums began to get overcrowded.

A few streets northeast of the Forums, the most intact ancient Roman building is **The Pantheon,** built in 27 B.C. by Marcus Agrippa and reconstructed by Hadrian in the 2nd century A.D. This remarkable temple to all the Roman gods had a stunningly simple design: a perfect sphere resting in a cylinder. Up until the 20th century, its massive hemisphere of cast concrete was the biggest pile of concrete ever constructed; another ribbed dome of cantilevered brick was laid on top and gilded for show. Animals were sacrificed and burned in the center, the smoke escaping through a 5½m (18-ft.) aperture at the top. Michelangelo studied its dome before designing the cupola of St. Peter's (whose dome is .5m/1⅔ ft. smaller). Since 609 it has been a Catholic church, where no less a star than the Renaissance painter Raphael was buried.

ⓘ **Colosseum,** Piazzale del Colosseo, Via dei Fori Imperiali (✆ **06-7004261**). **Pantheon,** Piazza della Rotonda (✆ **06-68300230**).

✈ 🛏 See Rome ❺❸.

WHY THEY'LL THANK YOU: *Gladiator* comes to life.

Paestum
Where Ancient Greece & Rome Collided
Ages 6 & up • Italy

Mᴀɢɴᴀ Gʀᴀᴇᴄɪᴀ ɪꜱ ᴀ ᴄᴏɴᴠᴇɴɪᴇɴᴛ ᴛᴇʀᴍ ꜰᴏʀ ɪᴛ, a network of settlements founded around the Mediterranean by voyaging ancient Greeks. Who would have thought that so near the luxe resorts of the Amalfi coast, you could wander around a Greek colony founded in 600 B.C.? Abandoned for centuries, the ruins of Paestum began to attract archaeologists in the mid–18th century, shortly after the discovery of Pompeii ❶❽❶ up the coast. An easy day trip from anywhere in Campania—Naples is 100km (62 miles) northwest, Salerno only 40km (25 miles) away (see the Amalfi Drive ❹❼❽)—it may be the oldest place the children will ever visit.

What fascinated us most about Paestum is that it's really two ruined cities atop each other. The first is the Greek city of Poseidonia, named after patron god Poseidon. A vigorous trading center, it thrived for 2 centuries as the northernmost Greek colony in Italy, only a few miles from the Etruscan border. Then the Romans took over in 273 B.C., and renamed the city Paestum. Curiously, the Greek ruins are more completely preserved, for even though the Romans rudely set up shop right on top of the Greek town, they could not bring themselves to knock down the three mighty temples of Poseidonia. The Roman remains are less awesome, but they'll give the kids a sense of a living town—the foundation stones of its shop-lined forum, a gymnasium, and an amphitheater.

Even the ancients wrote about the roses of Paestum, which bloom twice a year, splashes of scarlet perfectly complementing the salmon-colored Greek temples. The largest is the 5th-century **Temple of Neptune.** It's arguably the best-preserved Greek temple in the world, rivaled only by Athens's Temple of Hephaestus. Much of it is still standing—six columns in front, crowned by a massive entablature, and 14 columns on each side. But that's relatively young for Paestum: Both the **Temple of Hera** and the **Temple of Athena** date way back to the 6th century B.C. The Temple of Hera is Italy's oldest Greek temple, and it's surprisingly intact, with 9 chunky Doric pillars in front and 18 on the sides. The Temple of Athena (also known as the Temple of Ceres) has 34 stout Doric columns, along with ragged bits of its triangular pediment and a large altar for sacrifices to the gods.

Across from the Temple of Athena, the **National Archaeological Museum of Paestum,** Via Magna Grecia 917 (© **0828-811023**), displays some metopes removed from the Temple of Hera and some fine tomb paintings from the 4th and 5th centuries B.C.; don't miss the beautiful paintings of the Diver's Tomb.

ⓘ **Tourist office,** Via Magna Grecia 887 (© **0828-811016;** www.infopaestum.it or www.enit.it).

🚆 Paestum, 30 min. from Salerno.

🛏 $$ **Strand Hotel Schuhmann,** Via Marittima (© **0828-851151;** www.hotel schuhmann.com).

WHY THEY'LL THANK YOU: Gigantic columns, all in a row.

The Ancient World **180**

Under the Volcano
The Buried Town of Pompeii
Ages 8 & up • Pompeii & Ercolano, Italy

YES, POMPEII WAS THE SITE of a natural disaster when it was buried in volcanic ash and mud after Mount Vesuvius erupted in A.D. 79. But while the kids may pick up a melancholy aura about this ghost city, they'll soon see that Pompeii is exciting not because it was destroyed, but because it was saved—preserved by the very same volcanic debris, like a fly caught in amber, as it was 2,000 years ago. In other cities, a few large and important classical buildings survived, but Pompeii is an entire town: There's no better place to imagine the daily life of the ancient Roman Empire. It's a convenient day trip from Naples on the Circumvesuviana railway. If you're energetic enough,

you can also stop at neighboring Herculaneum, buried by the same eruption.

Not every artifact of ancient Pompeii remains on-site: The Pompeiians themselves (those who escaped alive) returned once the ashes had cooled to grab a few treasures before abandoning the town. The buried city was rediscovered in 1599, and once serious excavation began in the mid–18th century, several of the most precious mosaics and frescoes were taken up to Naples, where you can see them in the **National Archaeological Museum,** Piazza Museo Nazionale 18–19 (© **081-440166**). Still, there is plenty left on-site to see. Be aware that the Pompeiians had a different attitude toward sex than we do; you may prefer to distract

The ruins of Pompeii.

the kids from erotic images in some frescoes and mosaics (most of the really scurrilous stuff was moved to Naples).

Highlights include the **House of the Vettii**'s black-and-red dining room with its frescoes of delicate cupids; the spectacular frescoes in the **House of the Mysteries,** outside the city walls; and the imposing **House of the Faun,** with no fewer than four dining rooms and two spacious peristyle gardens. In the center of town is the **forum,** the heart of Pompeiian life, surrounded by a basilica, the Temple of Apollo, the Temple of Jupiter, and the Stabian Thermae (baths), where you'll even see some skeletons. (The other baths in town have some pretty graphic frescoes.) The open-air **Great Theater** could hold 5,000 spectators at its bloodthirsty battles between wild animals and gladiators. The main thing, though, is to walk these paved streets between largely intact buildings and visualize citizens going about their daily routines on that August day, just before an exploding cloud blotted out the sun.

Herculaneum, one-fourth the size of Pompeii, was found in 1709, but it still hasn't been completely dug out—it was more heavily buried than Pompeii, and being an upper-class resort, its buildings are more complicated and thus harder to unearth. You can get a good idea of how aristocrats lived at the **Casa dei Cervi** (House of the Stags). In the end, the wealthy were smothered under the ash just as permanently as the poor—there's another lesson learned at Pompeii.

(i) **Ufficio Scavi di Pompeii,** Via Villa dei Misteri 1, Pompeii (© **081-8610744**). **Ufficio Scavi di Ercolano,** Corso Resina, Ercolano (© **081-7390963**).

✈ Aeroporto Capodochino in Naples.

🛏 $$ **Hotel Britannique,** Corso Vittorio Emanuele 133, Naples (© **081-7614145;** www.hotelbritannique.it). $$$ **Hotel Excelsior,** Via Partenope 48, Naples (© **081-7640111;** www.excelsior.it).

WHY THEY'LL THANK YOU: Ancient lives trapped in midstride.

Arles: Roman Ruins in Old Provence

Ages 6 & up • Arles, France

Few places in France wear the marks of Roman occupation as clearly as Arles, on the banks of the Rhone in Provence. Yes, this is where Vincent Van Gogh painted *Starry Night* and *Sunflowers* (and cut off his left ear); and yes, this is where Frederick Barbarossa was crowned in 1178 at the church of St-Trophime. But in Arles, where layer upon layer of history overlap, it's fun to see the Roman past keep popping up—a crumbling column here, an ancient sarcophagus there—not set apart as an archaeological site but incorporated into a living town.

The Greeks founded Arles in the 6th century B.C., but Julius Caesar, that great empire builder, really put it on the map. By the time of Constantine the Great, in A.D. 306, it was the empire's second capital, known as "the little Rome of the Gauls." At the heart of the town, tree-shaded Place du Forum is built over the old **Roman forum**—look for two Corinthian columns and fragments from a temple embedded in the facade of the Grand Hotel Nord-Pinus. The courtyard of the **Muséon Arlaten,** Hôtel du Laval, rue de la République, contains an ancient Roman temple. West of here stands a crumbling stretch of the old **Roman city walls,** as well as two relics from the 1st century, when Augustus was emperor: the semicircular open-air **Théâtre Antique,** rue de Cloître (✆ **04-90-49-36-25**), and the **Amphitheater** (Lés Arènes), rond-point des Arènes (✆ **04-90-49-36-86**). The Amphitheater, an oval arena with two tiers of round arches, is surprisingly intact and still can seat a crowd of almost 25,000 on its worn stone benches; bullfights are held here in summer. Even bigger than the arena was the **Roman circus,** with a circular track so wide that 12 chariots could race side by side. Fragments of the circus are preserved beside the **Musee de l'Arles Antique,** Presqu'île du Cirque Romain (✆ **04-90-18-88-88**), an archaeological trove of exquisitely carved sarcophagi and intricate floor mosaics that supply rich detail for those ruins you've seen outdoors.

Near the river, the **Baths of Constantine,** rue D. Maisto, were probably the largest baths in Provence, dating from the later days of the Empire (note the use of concrete, a high-tech marvel at the time). Perhaps the most memorable sight is **Les Alyscamps,** Rue Pierre-Renaudel (✆ **04-90-49-36-87**), an ancient Roman necropolis that became a Christian burial ground in the 4th century (it was mentioned in Dante's *Inferno*). Though only a few of its empty marble sarcophagi remain on-site, this poplar-shaded spot is a favorite refuge for Arlesians.

ⓘ **Arles Office de Tourisme,** esplanade Charles-de-Gaulle (✆ **04-90-18-41-20;** www.tourisme.ville-arles.fr).

🚄 Arles, 4½ hr. from Paris.

🛏 $$$ **Grand Hotel Nord-Pinus,** 14 place du Forum (✆ **04-90-93-44-44;** www.nord-pinus.com). $$ **Hotel Jules Cesar,** 9 bd. des Lices (✆ **04-90-52-52-52;** www.hotel-julescesar.fr).

WHY THEY'LL THANK YOU: A scavenger hunt for tokens of the classical past.

Trier: Mini-Rome on the Mosel

Ages 4 & up • Germany

ITS ROMAN NAME WAS AUGUSTA TREVERORUM, founded under Augustus in 16 B.C. on the site of an ancient Assyrian colony from 2000 B.C.—even in European terms, that's *old*. Soon folks were calling this prosperous provincial capital Roma Secunda, the second Rome. Although the last Roman prefect departed in about A.D. 400, Trier today has an impressive set of monuments from its Roman era, their ancient stones meticulously cleaned and neatly landscaped.

The city's oldest Roman building is the **Amphitheater,** Amphitheaterplatz (🕾 **0651/73010**), dating from A.D. 100, where an audience of 20,000 could sit on three circles of stone seats, today carpeted with grass. Its acoustics are still impeccable; open-air performances are held here from time to time. Little doors in the arena walls lead to underground chambers where gladiators were imprisoned and wild animals chained before being set loose in the ring. The handsome **Porta Nigra** (Black Gate; 🕾 **0651/75424**) earned its name from the soot that covered it in medieval times. It's the best-preserved Roman structure in Germany, the only surviving section of the great wall that once surrounded Trier. Its huge sandstone blocks, assembled without mortar, were held together with iron clamps—the marks can still be seen. My boys also admired its cunning design, a secret courtyard between double arches, where armed defenders could surprise would-be invaders.

Today it's a Protestant church, but the **Basilica,** Basilikaplatz (🕾 **0651/72468**), was once a Roman palace, an imposing symbol of imperial might. The huge hall that still stands is believed to have been the throne room, a grand affair with two tiers of windows within high-rising arches; it looks even longer than it actually is, an optical illusion created by narrower arches in the center. Most of its interior decoration was destroyed by Frankish invaders in the Dark Ages; but traces of the original wall paintings still cling to the stone, and you can see the hypocaust heating system in its hollow floor. To get an idea of what filled these shells of buildings, stop in the nearby **Rheinisches Landesmuseum,** Weimarer Allee 1 (🕾 **0651/9-77-40**), a treasure house of Roman antiquities—mosaics, frescoes, ceramics, glassware, and funerary monuments. Just past the nearby Palastgarten park are the remains of a huge complex of **Imperial Baths,** Kaiserthermen (🕾 **0651/ 44262**), built in the early 4th century under Constantine I. Though never completed, these were among the largest in the Roman Empire. Wandering around its subterranean labyrinth, we could just imagine ourselves as fastidious Roman subjects, being soaked, scrubbed, and plucked before a feast at the Basilica or a show at the Amphitheater.

ⓘ **Tourist information,** An der Porta Nigra (🕾 **0651/97-80-80;** www.trier.de).

🚌 Trier.

🛏 **$$ Hotel Petrisberg,** Sickingenstrasse 11 (🕾 **0651/46-40**). **$$$ Villa Hugel,** Bernhardstrasse 14 (🕾 **0651/3-30-66;** www. hotel-villa-huegel.de).

WHY THEY'LL THANK YOU: Glimpses of a real toga party.

The British Museum's World of Treasure

Ages 8 & up • London, England

ONE OF THE BIG PERKS of having one of the world's most powerful empires is scarfing up treasures from around the world and then building a huge columned museum to show them all off. You could get lost in the grand echoing marble galleries of the British Museum, gazing in wonder at all the Stuff acquired in the name of the Empire. Here are the six coolest things to see:

The Rosetta Stone: Dug up by Napoleon's soldiers while conquering Egypt, this obelisk honoring pharaoh Ptolemy V from 146 B.C. holds a fascinating code, deciphered in 1821 by French scholar Jean-François Champollian. Look at the carved letters covering its surface; they are written in three languages— ancient hieroglyphics at the top, the demotic language used by everyday Egyptians in the middle, and classical Greek at the bottom. The art of reading hiero- glyphics had died out centuries earlier, but when they were compared to the same words in demotic Egyptian and Greek, the hieroglyphics were finally deciphered.

The Elgin Marbles: The British Museum has taken a lot of flak for holding onto these beautiful 5th-century-B.C. Greek artworks, which Greece would very much like back. However, the Brits do have a case. Lord Elgin, the British Ambassador to Constantinople (now Istanbul) in 1801–05, was given permission by the Ottoman Empire to take away bits of ancient statu- ary in Athens, which was under Turkish rule at the time. The Turks were merely using the Acropolis to store gunpowder, which Lord Elgin thought a shame, so he quietly removed a fair amount of the Parthenon and Erechtheon to preserve them for posterity—and England's still got 'em, a classical case of finders keepers. The centerpiece is a stunning 75m-long (247-ft.) frieze that once decorated the Parthenon, unfolding like a long comic

The Rosetta Stone at the British Museum.

strip starring all your favorite Greek gods and goddess.

The Reading Room: This domed rotunda in the central courtyard was the original Reading Room of the British Library (recently relocated to its own site), where scholars and writers as diverse as Mark Twain, Karl Marx, and Oscar Wilde researched and wrote some of their most famous books.

Sutton Hoo: Dug up in 1938 in an earth- ern mound in Suffolk, this funeral hoard of an ancient British warrior-king, heaped in the rotted remains of an old wooden boat, includes a scepter, silver bowls, a gold belt buckle, jeweled shoulder clasps, and a fear- some helmet covered with animal carvings.

Lindow Man: For connoisseurs of the creepy, regard the mummified corpse of a Druid human sacrifice, dating from the 1st century A.D.

The Mummy of Henutmehyt: This gold-encased mummy of an aristocratic woman is one of the most dramatic items in the museum's stellar Egyptian collection. Note the protective wings of the sky-goddess Nut on her coffin case, and in her armpits the watchful eye symbols to ward off danger in the afterlife.

ⓘ Great Russell St. (℗ **020/7323-8299;** www.thebritishmuseum.ac.uk).

✈ 🛏 See London **55**.

WHY THEY'LL THANK YOU: It's like one giant time machine.

---

184 The Ancient World

Hadrian's Wall
Roman Britain Ends Here
Ages 8 & up • Carlisle to Newcastle-upon-Tyne, England

STRETCHING FOR 117KM (73 MILES) across the north of England, from the North Sea to the Irish Sea, Hadrian's Wall marks the line where civilized Britain—that is, the part ruled by Rome—ended and the land of the barbarians began. One of Europe's best Roman ruins, the wall represents the farthest-flung point of the great Roman Empire.

The wall was built in A.D. 122–128 after emperor Hadrian, on an inspection tour of his empire's frontiers, sensed that his British territories were vulnerable to invasion, and ordered legionnaires to build a defensive wall across the island. Sections were originally made of turf, but eventually the whole thing was done in stone, with a fortified "castle" every mile and sentry turrets in between. The wild and forbidding landscape of the Cheviot Hills has always made a pretty effective buffer between England and Scotland, but Hadrian wasn't taking any chances.

The wall exists today as a series of fragments, many of them within **Northumberland National Park.** The most complete section runs for 16km (10 miles) starting west of Housesteads, near Bardon Mill; the lower courses of the wall have been preserved intact, with the rest reconstructed in the 19th century using the original stones. From the wall, there are incomparable views north and south. A good place to start is 29km (18 miles) west of Hexham, at the **Roman Army Museum,** junction

A69 and B6318 (℗ **01697/747485**), where a barracks room depicts living conditions in the Roman army, with realistic life-size figures. A short walk away, you can scale one of the most imposing and high-standing sections of the wall, **Walltown Crags.** From here, working your way east, the fort of **Vindolanda,** 2.5km (1½ miles) off B6318 (℗ **01434/344277;** www.vindolanda.com), gives you a good idea of daily life in Roman times, re-creating the civilian settlement that lay outside fort walls. The **Housesteads Fort and Museum,** B6318, Housesteads (℗ **01434/344363;** www.english-heritage.org.uk), displays a partially excavated Roman fort, Vercovicium, one of several built along the wall to help maintain its defenses. It includes Britain's only example of a Roman hospital, though kids may be more intrigued by the latrines. **Chesters Roman Fort and Museum,** B6318 from Chollerford (℗ **01434/681379;** www.english-heritage.org.uk), has the most visible remains of a Roman cavalry fort, originally built astride Hadrian's Wall.

A **footpath** runs along the entire Wall, and many hikers do the whole route, checking out various bits and pieces along the way. With youngsters in tow, however, it may be easier to drive B6318, which more or less traces the wall, with signposts to major sites. From early May to late September a **bus service** visits important Hadrian's Wall sites, beginning and ending in Hexham (℗ **01434/652220**).

🛈 www.hadrians-wall.org.

🚂 Hexham or Haltwhistle, 4½ hr. from London.

🛏 $$$ **George Hotel,** Chollerford, Humshaugh, near Hexham (✆ **01434/ 681611;** www.swallow-hotels.com).

WHY THEY'LL THANK YOU: A border drawn on a map is one thing; a border built in stone quite another.

The Ancient World **185**

In Search of Roman Britain

Ages 8 & up • Cirencester, Chedworth & Bath, England

THE ROMAN OCCUPATION OF BRITAIN was a major period of its history; the Romans were there for almost 4 centuries, building cities and roads and co-opting local tribal chieftains to administer the Roman way of life. Amazingly, the Romans pushed as far north as Hadrian's Wall 🔢, but this western area, on the edge of the Cotswolds and down into Somerset, was where their culture really took hold.

Begin in **Cirencester,** known as Corinium in Roman days; five roads converged here and it was a major city, second only to Londinium. The **Corinium Museum** houses one of the country's finest collections of archaeological remains from the Roman occupation, including some amazing mosaics. Pottery, artifacts, and provincial Roman sculpture, including figures of Minerva and Mercury, provide a link with the remote civilization that once flourished here.

From Cirencester, head north on the A429 to Yanworth, almost to Cheltenham, to **Chedworth Roman Villa,** the remains of a 4th-century country home excavated in 1864. Set in a lovely wooded valley, this sizable villa—32 rooms, arranged around a central courtyard—was probably the home of a native Briton who had gained a position of authority with the Roman occupiers; some of the beautiful mosaic floors here depict clothing and animals that are definitely British, not Italian. Built around a natural spring, which still bubbles forth in the cistern, the villa had a

shrine where native Celts also had worshipped, but the extensive baths show how Roman customs had taken hold. My boys were fascinated by the exposed hypocaust, the underground hot-water heating system—much more necessary on a cold English night than it would have been back in Rome. Look at the worn steps, hollowed out by the sandaled feet of the Romans, and you'll get a real sense of these long-ago people.

An hour or so south on the A46 lies the elegant Georgian spa town of **Bath.** Founded in A.D. 75 by the Romans, the **Roman Baths** were dedicated to the goddess Sulis Minerva; in their day, they were an engineering feat. Even today, they're among the finest Roman remains in the country, and are still fed by Bath's famous hot-spring water. The site of the Temple of Sulis Minerva has been excavated and is now open to view. The museum displays many interesting objects from Victorian and recent digs (look for the head of Minerva). In the adjoining pump room, you may want to taste the mineral water, but be forewarned—it's hot and tastes horrible.

🛈 **Corinium Museum,** Park St. (✆ **01285/ 655611;** www.cotswold.gov.uk). **Chedworth Roman Villa** (✆ **01242/890256;** www. nationaltrust.org.uk). **Roman Baths,** Stall St. (✆ **01225/477785;** www.romanbaths.co.uk).

🚂 Cheltenham, 2¼ hr. from London. Bath, 1½ hr. from London.

The Roman Baths in Bath.

$$ **The Fleece Hotel,** Market Place, Cirencester (☎ **01285/658507;** www.fleece hotel.co.uk). $ **Number Ninety Three,** 93 Wells Rd., Bath (☎ **01225/317977**).

$$ **Pratt's Hotel,** S. Parade, Bath (☎ **01225/ 460441;** www.prattshotel.com).

WHY THEY'LL THANK YOU: Amazing that the Roman Empire reached this far.

186 **The Ancient World**

The Ancient City of Petra
Red Rock Wonder
Ages 8 & up • Wadi Mousa, Jordan

Yᴏᴜ ᴀᴘᴘʀᴏᴀᴄʜ ɪᴛ ᴛʜʀᴏᴜɢʜ ᴛʜᴇ Sɪǫ, a deep, narrow sandstone gorge winding for a mile through the southern Jordanian desert. You come to the last turning—and there before you, just visible in the gap, is a dramatic columned temple cut *right out of a cliff face.* The fierce desert sun highlights its columns and pediments and mythological figures; you catch your breath in wonder. And that's just the beginning of Petra, a magical desert fortress whose very name means simply "Rock."

Petra sprang up between 400 B.C. and A.D. 100, a Nabataean city set squarely on important caravan routes. As camels laden with incense crossed the Wadi Araba desert, they paid heavy duties to the tax collectors of Petra, whose wealth gave rise to a grand cityscape chiseled out of the living rock. Deep in this natural stronghold, the Nabataeans were conquered by no one, though many tried; not until Red Sea shipping bypassed caravan routes did a diminished Petra finally fall

The desert fortress of Petra.

under control of Rome. Its ancient buildings may have been eroded by desert sand and wind, but because they were gouged out of the cliffs rather than free-standing, they haven't toppled like many buildings of similar eras. Their facades' original plaster and paint has worn off, but the city still glows with the natural color of the rose-red rock.

The city really begins at that first famous view from the **Siq of the Khazneh,** or Treasury. (The kids may recognize it from shots in the movie

Indiana Jones and the Last Crusade.) Beyond lie the spectacular **royal tombs,** which became more than just burial places—they were 1st-century architectural fantasies, picking up an eclectic mix of elements from cities like Alexandria and Rome, their ornate facades completely out of proportion to the small chambers within. Strangely, considering how many of Petra's buildings are tombs, no bodies have ever been found here.

As you explore Petra's various temples and shrines, remember what an international city this trade hub was: Temples built to Nabataean deities were later adapted to Roman gods, and possibly to Christian saints in the Byzantine era. On a summit behind the yellow-sandstone **Temple of Dushara** (one of Petra's few extant free-standing buildings), there's even the remains of a **fort** built by 12-century Crusaders. Another climb to the cliff top will take you to the **High Place of Sacrifice,** a circular ceremonial arena set up explicitly for gruesome acts of blood sacrifice—and also killer views of the site and the surrounding desert.

ⓘ www.visitjordan.com.

✈ Amman 225km (140 miles). Aqaba 150km (93 miles).

🛏 $$$ **Golden Tulip,** King's Way (ⓒ 03/215-6799; www.goldentulip.com). $$$ **Marriott Petra,** Queen Raina Al Abdullah St. (ⓒ 03/215-6407; www.marriott.com).

WHY THEY'LL THANK YOU: Desert surprise.

Masada: Fortress by the Dead Sea

Ages 8 & up • Israel

MASADA IS TO ISRAELIS WHAT MOUNT FUJI ③⑨⑦ is to the Japanese—national pride requires every citizen to scale these heights at least once. But like much else in Israel,

the meaning of Masada is controversial. Does this mountaintop fortress symbolize raw courage, or does it glorify foolhardy political extremism? Whichever you believe, the kids will still be riveted by

Masada.

Masada's compelling tale of a small garrison that defied the Roman army.

The story begins with King Herod, who built a stout fortress and magnificent palace atop this nearly inaccessible desert plateau around 30 B.C. After Herod's death, a small Roman garrison occupied the mount; it was taken over by a band of Jewish zealots during the Jewish revolt in A.D. 66. Living off the vast stores of food left by Herod, they had more than enough arms with which to defend themselves. Finally, in A.D. 73, 3 years after the fall of Jerusalem, the Romans got fed up with this last pocket of resistance; they built a ramp to scale the rock—in itself a remarkable feat of engineering—and attacked Masada with 10,000 troops, pulling out all the stops: siege engines, flaming torches, rock bombardments, battering rams. It seemed only a question of time until the 900 defenders surrendered. After one brutal night attack set the fortress gates on fire, the Romans, seeing Masada now defenseless, decided to wait until dawn to storm the fort. That final night, the 900 Jewish men, women, and children inside chose to commit mass suicide rather than succumb.

The Romans, who had expected to fight their way in, were astonished in the morning by the Jews' lack of resistance—and impressed by their stoic courage.

From the parking lot at the foot of the mount you've got three choices—ride the **cable car** that carries you almost to the summit; **climb** the winding path on the Dead Sea side, which has great views but can take up to an hour; or **drive** to the Arad side and walk up the Romans' great ramp, which takes only 15 to 30 minutes. If you climb, especially in the summer months, be sure to start at the crack of dawn—the heat is murderous by midday.

Masada **excavations** have unearthed perhaps the most exciting ruins in all of Israel: the original palace, synagogue, casement walls, houses, straw bags, plaits of hair, pottery shards, stone vessels, cosmetics, cooking utensils, and important scroll fragments. Walk with the kids around the ruins of the **Roman siege encampments,** a virtual crash course in Roman military field strategy. Evidence of the Jewish defenders' lives includes **ritual baths** (mikvehs) used by observant Jews, and some *ostraca* marked with Hebrew names—perhaps the very lots cast by the defenders as they decided who would kill the others rather than let them fall into Roman hands.

(i) Dead Sea Hwy. ((C) **07/658-4207**).

✈ Jerusalem.

🛏 $$$ **Golden Tulip Dead Sea Hotel,** Ein Bokek (www.fattal-hotels-israel.com). $$ **Kibbutz Ein Gedi Resort Hotel,** Ein Gedi ((C) **800/844-4007** or 08/659-4222; www.ngedi.com/guest_house.htm).

WHY THEY'LL THANK YOU: Discussing what you'd have done in their place.

The Ancient World **188**

Dun Aengus
A Ruin & a Riddle in Gaelic Ireland
Ages 6 & up • Inis Mór, Aran Islands, Ireland

ON THE ARAN ISLANDS the locals are a hardy lot, living in stone cottages, speaking only Gaelic among themselves, and casting out to sea every day in small round *currachs* made of tarred canvas. In many ways life here hasn't changed much for centuries—and that's why it's such a time warp experience to take a day trip from modern Galway City to the great **Iron Age fort** of Dún Aengus.

On a clear day you can see the offshore Aran Islands from both the Cliffs of Moher ❼ and the coastline of Connemara ❹❶❽. Ferries from Galway land at **Kilronan,** the main town on the island of **Inishmore** (Inis Mór); at the docks you can rent bikes or hail a minivan or, even better, an old-fashioned jaunting cart to get around the island. Follow the tourist traffic 7km (4⅓ miles) west to the island's greatest draw, Dún Aengus (Dún Aonghasa), which sits on a 90m-high (300-ft.) western cliff brooding over the sea. Set against the impossibly green landscape, this rough-piled structure of dark gray stones looks almost as if it had grown organically out of the gray-and-red-blotched rocky headland.

The fort is of great significance—every scholar agrees on that—but what they can't agree on is what that significance is. When you walk up the hill (a 20-min. hike from the visitor center), you pass a zone where sharp stones jut out of the ground,

a primitive defensive measure known as a **cheval-de-frise.** Yet the design of the structure—three concentric semicircles opening to the sea—looks more like a theater than a fortress. True, the cliff behind it is so sheer that there would have been no need to fortify that side. (Look over carefully, and hold young children's hands—there's no guardrail.) The walls are certainly defensive, 6m (20 ft.) high in some places, and the thickest is 4.3m (14 ft.) thick. Yet if it was a fort, why are there no dwellings inside, and why is there no provision for bringing in water in case of siege? And within the centermost horse-shoe, what is the purpose of that large table rock, almost like a sacrificial altar? Even more vexing is the question of who built Dun Aengus. It could have been an ancient Celtic tribe called the Fir Bolgs, a few centuries B.C., or it could have been 8th- or 9th-century Danes. Whoever built it also felt the need to build several such structures nearby—leave the other tourists behind and visit **Dún Dubhchathair** 2km (1¼ miles) southwest, **Dún Eochla** the same distance northwest, and Dún Eoghanacht 7km (4⅓ miles) west-north-west. Though smaller than Dún Aengus, they have the same primitive power, the same sense of mystery. If only these stones could speak!

(i) ✆ 099/61008.

✈ Inis Mór. Galway City 37km (23 miles) from Rossaveal.

FERRY PORT: Kilronan, 40 min. from Rossaveal.

🛏 $$$ **Galway Harbour Hotel,** New Dock Rd., Galway (✆ **091/569466;** www. galwayharbourhotel.com). $$ **Kilmurvey House,** coast road, Inis Mór (✆ **099/61218**).

WHY THEY'LL THANK YOU: Trying to solve the riddle.

The Great Stupa of Sanchi
Enfolding the Peace of Buddha
Ages 4 & up • Sanchi, India

THERE'S SOMETHING HUGELY APPEALING about the Great Stupa of Sanchi, a plump domed Buddhist monument of rough-dressed stone, tucked away in the land-locked state of Madhya Pradesh. The stupa may once have held some ashes of the Buddha, who died in 483 B.C. (smaller stupas alongside, like satellites around a mother ship, contain ashes of his disciples). Set on a squat hill with lovely views of the surrounding countryside, this time-weathered religious complex doesn't overwhelm the worshipper—it's a low-rise site of gentle domes and spaces for contemplation. The peace of the centuries seems to settle upon it like the folds of a sari.

India's finest example of **ancient Buddhist architecture,** the Great Stupa complex was founded in the 3rd century B.C. by the Mauryan emperor Ashoka, who converted to Buddhism after massacring thousands in his military campaigns. Ashoka's wife was a devout Buddhist from nearby Vidisha, and the city's prosperous merchants became patrons as well. Isolated Sanchi thrived in its serene way for centuries, until a resurgence of Hinduism in the 13th century A.D., along with rising Islamic militancy, made Buddhism wither. The site lay deserted for more than 500 years until 1818, when—a typical story for India—a British military adventurer stumbled upon the ruins. Excavations have gone on for the past century, unearthing about 55 temples, pillars, stupas, and monasteries (check out **Monastery 51,** with its tiny sleeping cells for monks). The more they uncovered, the more excited the archaeologists grew, for Sanchi has proven to be a textbook of evolving Buddhist architectural styles, an unbroken continuum with every era gloriously represented.

The proportions of the Great Stupa are so harmonious, you're surprised when you get up close to see how big it actually is. At 17m (55 ft.) high, nearly eight stories, it anchors the center of the complex like a massive beehive, or maybe a flying saucer. Originally it was a smaller brick hemisphere; in the 2nd century B.C. a balustrade was added (notice its bamboo-like pattern) and the brick dome was enlarged considerably with a casing of unevenly cut sandstone. Four intricately carved **gateways** of finer-grained sandstone were added circa 25 B.C., facing the four points of the compass—urge the kids to try to "read" their story panels from the life of Buddha. (At that era, the Buddha was never pictured as a human—look for him instead as a lotus, a wheel, a bodhi tree, or a pair of feet.) Originally the dome and the plinth it sits on were coated with white lime concrete, the railways and gateway painted red, and the surface of the stupa painted with swags and garlands; the antenna-like spire on top would have been gilded. It must have been grand in its heyday.

(i) www.mptourism.com.

✈ Bhopal, 45km (28 miles).

🛏 $$ **Jehan Numa Palace,** 157 Shamla Hill, Bhopal (© **0755/266-1100;** www.hoteljehanumapalace.com).

WHY THEY'LL THANK YOU: In harmony with the spirit of Buddha.

The Ancient World **190**

The Warriors of Xí-ān
A Chinese Army of Stone
Ages 6 & up • Bīngmǎyǒng, China

ANY CHILD WHO'S EVER PLAYED with toy soldiers will thrill to this sight: Thousands upon thousands of life-size warriors, an entire army of ancient terra-cotta statues standing at attention in an underground trench, ready to march before their emperor into the afterworld. After The Great Wall **210**, Qín Shǐ Huáng's tomb at Bīngmǎyǒng is the sight most Western visitors look forward to seeing when they come to China—and this is one major sight that never disappoints.

The nearby town of Xi-ān was once the largest, most cosmopolitan city in the world—perfectly located to dominate the Silk Road trading routes, it served as capital of several dynasties, up through the Tang dynasty (A.D. 618–907). The stone soldiers buried at Bīngmǎyǒng, however, date from much earlier, in the 2nd century B.C. The ambitious, totalitarian Qín Shǐ Huáng, the first Emperor of China, was bent on ensuring his place in the afterworld, and so he hired a corps of 700,000 workers (more than twice the number used to build the Great Wall) to do no less than reproduce the entire universe under ground. Historians tell us that his many-chambered **burial complex** covered a full square mile, containing models of palaces, towers, and buildings. A ceiling was painted with the constellations, and the Yangzi and Yellow rivers flowed in mercury. Whale-oil lamps provided permanent lighting, and automatic crossbows were

set up to shoot grave robbers; the rafters were reportedly hung with pearls, jade, and green feathers. There was so much down here that historians of the time don't even mention the soldiers.

The main part of the tomb has not been opened, although most likely it was plundered long ago. Still, if the soldiers are any evidence, the craftsmanship throughout was amazing. In Bīngmǎyǒng's first pit, you'll see 11 passageways with four columns of warriors in each—about **6,000 infantry** lined up, battle ready. Though their bodies were mass-produced from molds, by using interchangeable parts—varying leg or shoulder shapes, which then were posed at different angles—the workmen produced a mind-boggling variety of individual figures. The heads were all handmade, and no two are the same—study their facial features, hairstyles, and headdresses and you'll see a surprising range of ethnic types. Every detail, from the rivets on their armor to the straps on their sandals, has been rendered as realistically as possible. The regular soldiers are 5 feet 11 inches tall; senior officers, laid in pit 3, are a little taller, as befits their rank (one general dug up from pit 2 is nearly 6½ ft. tall).

The sight of these lifelike ranks of terra-cotta men is simply astonishing—they go on and on, like a digitally dubbed cast of extras in a blockbuster movie, except these were individually created by hand. Qín Shǐ Huáng got his wish all

The terra-cotta warriors of Xí-ān.

right—he'll be eternally remembered for this grandiose mania, and for the stunning artworks that resulted.

ⓘ ☎ **029/391-1961.**

✈ Xí-ān.

🛏 $$$ **Sheraton Xí-ān,** Fēnghào Dōng Lù 262 (☎ **029/426-1888;** www.sheraton. com/xian). $$ **Wūyī Fàndiàn,** Dōng Dàjiē 351 (☎ **029/721-2212;** www.may-first.com).

WHY THEY'LL THANK YOU: Emperors have toy soldiers too.

---

191 The Ancient World

Chichén Itzá: Marvel of the Ancient Maya

Ages 6 & up • Near Pisté, Mexico

TO ME, THE BEST REASON for traveling to the Yucatan Peninsula is not to frolic on the beach at Cancun, but to commune with the spirits of the ancient Maya at Chichén Itzá. (And no, it doesn't rhyme with "chicken pizza"; accent the last syllables: chee-*chen* eet-*zah*.) This immense ruined city, raised out of the encroaching jungle, holds an undeniable glamour for kids, a mix of ornate pyramids, celestial imagery, and gory human sacrifice. Just stand at the top of one of its vast plazas and imagine it packed with people during frequent mass rituals—the mind simply boggles.

One of the most important buildings here was **El Caracol** (The Observatory), where astronomers peered through slits in a circular tower to chart

Chichén Itzá.

213

the approach of the all-important equinoxes and summer solstice. This celestial obsession is reflected in the design of the magnificent El Castillo pyramid. Four stairways leading up to the central platform each have 91 steps, making a total of 364; add the central platform and you've got 365, equal to the days of the solar year. On either side of each stairway are 9 terraces, equaling 18 on each pyramid face, the same as the number of months in the Maya calendar. The pyramid is precisely aligned to cast a moving shadow—said to be the spirit of the feathered serpent—on its northern stairway at sunset on the spring and fall equinox, an awesome twice-a-year event to witness.

Elsewhere around the site, kids will find riveting **murals** of 9th-century Mayan customs. In the **Juego de Pelota,** Chichén's main ball court, scenes carved on both walls show figures playing a jai alai–like game in heavy protective padding—spot the kneeling headless player, blood spurting from his neck, while another player calmly holds his head (legend has it that losing players paid with their lives). In the **Temple of Jaguars,** a mural chronicles a battle in a Maya village. In the **Temple of the Skulls,** where sacrificial victims' heads were displayed on poles, carved into the stone are pictures of eagles tearing hearts from human victims;

the **Platform of the Eagles** has carved reliefs showing eagles and jaguars clutching human hearts in their talons and claws. Most impressive of all is the **Temple of the Warriors,** named for the carvings of warriors marching along its walls; a figure of the god Chaac-Mool sits at the top of the temple, surrounded by columns carved to look like enormous feathered serpents. At **La Iglesia** (the Church), masks of Chaac decorate two upper stories, but look closely and you'll see other pagan symbols—an armadillo, a crab, a snail, and a tortoise—representing Maya gods.

Scholars quibble over whether Chichén Itzá was always a Maya site or whether it was taken over at one point by the Toltec, but the kids won't care—they'll just scamper up and down the pyramids and romp across the wide-open plazas. Plan to stay the night if you can—the kids will love the nightly sound-and-light show.

ⓘ www.mayayucatan.com.

✈ Merida, 121km (75 miles).

🛏 $$$ **Hotel Mayaland,** Zona Arqueológica (℃ **800/235-4079** or 985/851-0127; www.mayaland.com). $$ **Villas Arqueológicas Chichén Itzá,** Zona Arqueológica (℃ **800/258-2633** or 985/851-0034).

WHY THEY'LL THANK YOU: Human sacrifice and killer ballgames.

The Ancient World   192

Tulum: Walled City of the Maya
Ages 4 & up • Tulum, Mexico

I LIKE TO THINK OF TULUM AS the beach resort of the Maya—poised on a rocky hill overlooking the turquoise Caribbean, this well-preserved fortress-city has the best location of all the Mayan ruins, not to mention being within day-trip range of Cancún's high-rise hotels and busy beaches. Although later explorers named

it Tulum from the Maya word for "wall"—it's quite rare for an ancient Mesoamerican city to have walls like this—the original name was thought to be Zama, which means "dawn." Come here at daybreak, when the sun first kisses the Yucatan coast, and you'll see how perfectly that name fits.

Tulum may have existed as early as the 6th century A.D., but its heyday was later than Chichén Itzá's, in the 12th to 16th centuries A.D., when Maya civilization in general had begun to decline. Being on the sea made Tulum a natural seaport, and as a trade hub it was able to survive 70 years after the Spanish conquest (until disease brought by the Europeans decimated the population). Most of the inhabitants probably lived in wooden huts outside the walls, leaving the interior for the residences of governors and priests and ceremonial structures. As befits a seaside city, the primary god here seems to have been the **diving god**—ask the kids to pick out his curious, almost comical figure in the building's decorations, usually depicted as an upside-down figure above doorways.

For younger children, Tulum may be easier to comprehend than Chichén Itzá **191**—it's a smaller and more open site, and the walled fort layout is something they're familiar with. There are still plenty of intriguing **carvings and reliefs** on these gently eroded gray stone piles, but they're not as gruesome as the ones at earlier Maya sites. The center of interest in Tulum is a hulking stone building above the cliff called the **Castillo,** the tallest

building on the site, which has also been called the Lighthouse for its prominence on the cliff. Actually a temple as well as a fortress (look for the image of the plumed serpent on its upper story), it was once covered with stucco and painted bright red—in fact, the kids can go ahead and imagine the whole town painted bright red, as it once was. The **Temple of the Frescoes,** directly in front of the Castillo, depicts the head of the rain god in relief on its cornice—if you pause a slight distance from the building, you'll see the eyes, nose, mouth, and chin.

Because so many visitors descend upon Tulum, it's no longer possible to climb all of the ruins—in many cases you'll be asked to remain behind roped-off areas.

(i) www.travelyucatan.com.

✈ Cancún, 129km (80 miles).

🛏 $$ **El Pueblito,** Bulevar Kukulkán Km 17.5, Cancún (✆ **998/885-0422** or 998/881-8814; www.pueblitohotels.com). $$$ **Marriott Casa Magna,** Bulevar Kukulkán Km 14.5, Cancún (✆ **800/228-9290** or 998/881-2000; www.marriott.com).

WHY THEY'LL THANK YOU: Ruins with a view.

---

193   **The Ancient World**

Tikal: Temples of the Jaguar Clan

Ages 6 & up • Near Flores, Guatemala

NESTLED IN LUSH SUBTROPICAL JUNGLE, where parrots and toucans and monkeys chatter in the canopy overhead, the Mayan ruins of Tikal are the ace in Guatemala's tourist deck. Once ruled by a dynasty known as the Jaguar Clan lords (sounds to me like something out of an animé film), this immense temple complex is a fascinating look into the heart of an ancient culture.

Mayan civilization thrived here for 1,500 years, from about 600 B.C to A.D. 900. Covering 16 sq. km (6 sq. miles), the

Tikal complex was the ceremonial heart of a city of 100,000 people, who gathered on its plazas for everything from religious rites (often including human sacrifices) to ballgames (where the losers sometimes became human sacrifices). Though some 3,000 structures remain, the chief ones are half a dozen rectangular pyramids built of gray limestone, which long ago were probably painted a bold red. Notice how precisely cut and mortared the stones are, even though the Mayans had no iron tools. These pyramids go by names the kids will love, like the **Temple of the Masks, the Temple of the Jaguar Priest,** and (my personal favorite) the **Temple of the Double-Headed Serpent,** which at 65m (212 ft.) was the tallest building in North America until the late 1800s. It's quite a climb to its top plateau, but as you look out over the rainforest, try to imagine the ancient city, which covered five times the area of what's here today. For the Mayans, pyramid building was an act of devotion, to exalt their god/kings by setting them on man-made mountains. The exteriors are huge, with broad, steep ceremonial stairways leading solemnly to their peaks, but inside are only small chambers for ceremonial purposes. At public events, kings and nobles were seated grandly atop the pyramids; the acoustics are so perfect that you can speak at a normal volume from Temple I and be heard clearly on Temple II, all the way across the Grand Plaza.

The ancient Mayans were sophisticated mathematicians and astronomers; the section of ruins known as the **Mundo Perdido,** or Lost City (another cool name), seems to have been built for ceremonies based on the Mayans' obsessively detailed calendar. Hundreds of **standing stones** that dot the grounds minutely record historic events and long-dead kings, with either carved pictures or the glyph symbols that were the Mayans' form of writing.

✈ Flores, 64km (40 miles).

⊨ $$ **Jaguar Inn,** Tikal National Park (✆ **502/926-0002;** www.jaguartikal.com). $$$ **Jungle Lodge,** Tikal National Park (www.enjoyguatemala.com).

BEST TIME: Nov–Feb (June and Sept–Oct are rainy season).

WHY THEY'LL THANK YOU: Scaling the grand stairs to a royal seat.

The Ancient World **194**

Machu Picchu: Lost City of the Incas

Ages 8 & up • Near Aguas Caliente, Peru

IN THE 16TH CENTURY, Spanish conquistadors ravaged most of the fabled cities of the Incas, desperate for their gold. Only Machu Picchu escaped—the Spanish couldn't even find it, snuggled between two peaks cloud-high in the Andes. Of course, no one else could find it either. Abandoned by its own citizens, Machu Picchu lay silent in its mountain fastness, swallowed up by the jungle for 4 centuries. Today the jungle has been cleared away and it's South America's most popular tourist sight—but even floods of tourists can't diminish the majesty and mystery of this lost city of the Incas.

Scholars don't know why Machu Picchu's residents deserted it—civil war? drought?—and they aren't even certain whether the city was mainly a fortress, a temple complex, a market town, or an astronomical observatory. What they can tell, however, is that its buildings survived remarkably intact—as you walk around, look at how skillfully the stonemasons fitted walls together, and how intricate the decorative stonework was. From **Funerary Rock,** just inside the entrance, you can get an overview of how the Incan love of nature translated into architecture. Steep terraces, gardens, granite and limestone temples, staircases, and aqueducts all are integrated gracefully into the hillsides; the buildings' forms seem to echo the very shape of the mountains. Celestial observations were important to the Incas, too, as you'll see from the famous

Temple of the Sun, whose windows are perfectly aligned to catch the sun's rays at the winter solstice (which is in June down here) and focus them on the stone at the center of the temple.

Guides, many of whom speak English, can be hired fairly inexpensively on-site, and it is useful to have an expert point out the significant details. Two sights you can't miss are the baffling **Inntihuatana,** or "hitching post of the sun," a ritualistic carved rock that seems to have functioned as some sort of sundial or calendar; and the **Sacred Rock,** perhaps a communal meeting area or performance space. Both of these landmarks were sculpted to resemble specific neighboring peaks—have the kids try to guess which ones.

Getting here is all part of the spiritual journey, according to Inca beliefs, and the classic way to reach Machu Picchu is to hike the Inca Trail, the ancient royal highway. From Qorihuayrachina, a 4-day, 43km (27-mile) trek follows winding paths and hand-hewn stone stairs through cloud forest, mountain passes, and dozens of other ruins. With kids, however, you might opt for the 2-day version, beginning at Wiñay Wayna. Both treks arrive at Machu Picchu at dawn—and what a thrilling experience it is to watch the rising sun gild these granite stones row by row. If hiking's not your thing, the 4-hour train ride from Cusco is plenty spectacular too—stay the night before in nearby Agua Calientes and you can still get that brilliant sunrise view.

Machu Picchu.

ⓘ www.peru.info.

✈ Cusco, 111km (69 miles).

🛏 $ **Hostal Machupicchu,** Av. Imperio de Los Incas, Aguas Calientes (© **084/211-065**). $$$ **Machu Pichu Sanctuary Lodge,** next to the ruins (© **084/246-419;** www.orient-express.com).

WHY THEY'LL THANK YOU: Sunrise turning the lost city to gold.

Chapter **6** Windows on History

Positively Medieval . . . 219
Historic Restorations . . . 238
Native Americans . . . 252
Settling America . . . 260
Black American History . . . 271

Haying in Sturbridge Village.

195

Thingvellir: The First Parliament

Ages 8 & up • Thingvellir, Iceland

LONG AFTER THE DEMOCRACIES of ancient Greece and Rome had been lost to the Dark Ages, the chieftains of one rugged little North Atlantic island got the notion that a nationwide meeting to settle disputes and set laws would be a pretty good idea. In the year 903, they gathered at a central meeting place—a treeless lava plain bordered by a glacial lake and two deep chasms formed by geological faults. The conclave worked so well, they met again the next summer—and the next, and the next, for nearly 900 years.

To stand at ancient Thingvellir, its stark lava hills reflected in the pure chilled waters of Lake Thingvallavatn, is a moving experience indeed. The place name Thingvellir means "parliament plain"; Althing was the name of the parliament (which still meets today in Reykjavik, an hour's drive away). There are few historic buildings here—the 16th-century building for the upper council, or Lögrétta, is long gone, and only an Icelandic flag marks the probable site of the **Law Rock** (Lögberg), where the elected Speaker of the Law announced new rulings and took questions from the floor, so to speak. You can see grass-covered mounds that used to be merchants' booths for the temporary city that sprang up for 2 weeks each summer. You can also see a simple white frame **church** from 1859, the most recent of many at this site, where Althing members worshiped and sometimes met when the weather was harsh. Of course, the first chieftains who met at Thingvellir were pagans, descendants of the Vikings who settled the island (along with a few

Irish slaves they picked up on their way). But in the year 1000, with the assembly split between pagans and converted Christians, leaders of the two factions voted on a peaceable compromise: Christianity would prevail but pagans could freely practice their rites. There's proof that democracy works.

This mossy sheltered spot, perched bravely on a craggy volcanic landscape, has the hallowed stillness of a momentous place. I came here on an early July morning, the air hung with the usual sulphur-scented haze of Iceland, and I swear I could hear ghosts whispering. (Okay, maybe it was the nearby waterfalls—I'd just been up all night admiring the midnight sun.) I wish the new **visitor center** had been around then, with its interactive multimedia presentation on Thingvellir's fascinating history. I wish I'd had time to rent an **Icelandic pony** from Skógarhólar farm and ride past old abandoned farmsteads along the timeworn tracks the Althing members rode on their way here. But even so, I was bowled over by Thingvellir. Your family will be too.

(i) ℂ **482/2660;** www.thingvellir.is.

✈ Keflavik International, 96km (60 miles)

🛏 $$ **Hotel Bjork,** Brautarholt 22–24, Reykjavík (ℂ **511-3777;** www.keahotels.is). $$$ **Hotel Loftleidir,** Hlídarfótur, Reykjavík (ℂ **444-4500;** www.icehotels.is).

BEST TIME: May–Sept.

WHY THEY'LL THANK YOU: The commanding view from the Law Rock.

The Book of Kells
The Most Beautiful Book in the World
Ages 8 & up • Dublin, Ireland

THE BOOK OF KELLS is a 680-page illuminated manuscript of the four Gospels, hand-lettered by ancient Irish monks around A.D. 800. Okay, so it's one of Ireland's greatest cultural treasures—still, I'd never have expected it would be one of my children's favorite memories of Ireland. But they didn't just like it, they *loved* it.

Much of the credit goes to **Trinity College,** Dublin, which has done a great job of displaying this treasure. Visitors are led through several anterooms meticulously explaining medieval bookmaking techniques, the lives of the anonymous monks who labored over the manuscript, decorative motifs to look for, and the adventure tale of the book's lucky survival over so many centuries. By the time visitors reach a dramatically darkened room with the great glass case displaying the book itself (curators turn it to a different page every day so that no one page is exposed to light too frequently), they understand why it is so important and are prepared to appreciate it—every patient brush stroke of the scribe's lettering, every gold gleam in the dazzling decorative borders, every vivid splash of lapis lazuli blue in the illustrations.

This is the most majestic work of art to survive from the early centuries of Celtic Christianity, and has often been described as "the most beautiful book in the world." Its creators managed to combine new artistic influences from Eastern Christendom with the traditional interlace patterning of Celtic metalwork to produce what

Gerald of Wales, a 13th-century chronicler, called "the work not of men, but of angels." For most of the Middle Ages the monastery of Kells, in County Meath, possessed the book. Whether it was originally created in Kells is unknown; some historians think it might have been made in St. Columba's monastery on the Scottish island of Iona 320, since several monks from Iona, escaping Viking raids, fled to Kells in 807 to found a new center for Celtic Christianity.

I also didn't expect my children to be so fascinated by the library's **Long Room,** with its intricate dark woodworking, busts of famous Irish writers, and tottering shelves of rare books. As for strolling around the 40-acre Trinity College campus, with its cobbled squares, gardens, quadrangle, and 18th-century buildings—that I expected them to love, and they did.

(i) **Old Library,** Trinity College ((01/608-2320; www.tcd.ie).

✈ Dublin.

🛏 $$ **Jurys Inn Christchurch,** Christ Church Place ((800/44-UTELL in the U.S., or 01/454-0000; www.jurys.com). $$$ **Stephens Hall,** 14–18 Lower Leeson St. ((877/424-6423 in the U.S., or 01/638-1111; www.stephens-hall.com).

WHY THEY'LL THANK YOU: Who knew a book could be this awesome?

Chester: Medieval Walled City

All ages • England

NOT ALL MEDIEVAL PEOPLE LIVED IN CASTLES— throughout the era more and more came to live in cities, and there's no better place to see how this new urban lifestyle evolved than in Chester, England. Still beautiful, with its distinctive red sandstone buildings, Chester has been lucky enough to preserve it all—a cathedral, a castle, and a full 3km (1¾ miles) of fortifying city walls, not to mention a half-timbered shopping district. Compact and easy to explore on foot, Chester is the sort of historic town that children immediately get the point of.

Chester's heyday was in the 13th and 14th centuries, when it was a bustling port on the River Dee, and a strong guild system attracted craftsmen and the up-and-coming professional class. When the river eventually silted up and trade evaporated, Chester was left a quiet provincial town with no reason to tear down its medieval structures; even in Georgian and Victorian times, builders continued to copy the black-and-white timbered facades. Visitors can ramble at will on the walkway atop the **city walls,** passing from one towered city gate to another; kids love to run along the balconied second story of **The Rows,** extensive double-tiered Tudor arcades in the center of town where shops still thrive. Only a few steps away on St. Werburgh Street is a glorious **cathedral,** built in 1092 as a Benedictine abbey, with hushed cloisters, a soaring nave, and amazingly inventive woodcarvings in the choir section (my kids could have studied those for hours). Chester even has a town crier—a costumed fellow who materializes at City Cross, ringing a hand bell, at noon most

summer weekdays, shouting local news and jovially chaffing the crowd, a hokey promotional gimmick that still amuses kids.

Chester's story didn't begin in medieval times; a Roman legion founded the town as a defensive stronghold on the Dee in the 1st century A.D., and many Roman remains have been excavated in the past few years, including an impressively complete **Roman amphitheater.** The original Roman fortress lies buried underneath the city, but its story is told at the **Dewa Roman Experience,** Pierpont Lane, off Bridge Street (© **01244/ 343407;** www.dewaromanexperience. co.uk), with lots of hands-on exhibits and reconstructions.

After all this, **Chester Castle,** looming on a bluff over the river, is a letdown; originally built in 1069, when Chester was one of the final strategic spots to fall to William the Conqueror, it fell into decay during the Civil War and was knocked down and completely rebuilt in the early 19th century, with only one original three-story tower still standing. The only tourist attraction inside the castle is a military museum.

ⓘ **Tourist Information Centre,** Town Hall, Northgate St. (© **01244/402385;** www.chester.com).

🚂 Chester, 4km (2½ miles) from London.

🛏 $$ **Blossoms Hotel,** St. John's St. (© **01244/323186;** www.macdonald hotels.co.uk).

WHY THEY'LL THANK YOU: Meandering atop the city walls.

The Bayeux Tapestry
Telling the Tale of the Norman Conquest
Ages 10 & up • Bayeux, France

THESE DAYS, WE COMMEMORATE a historical event with a documentary film or massive monument; back in the 11th century, an anonymous crew of artists, usually women, celebrated an important chapter of history in the medium they knew best: embroidery. The fact that this narrow 70m-long (230-ft.) strip of linen has survived for nearly a millennium is awesome enough, but when you gaze upon its detailed panels, so faithfully recording events that shook their world, you come face to face with the Dark Ages.

The Bayeaux Tapestry is actually an embroidery on linen, depicting some **50 scenes.** In an age when few could read, a chronicle in pictures was the ideal way to preserve history. Given the limited number of dyes available in that era, only eight colors of thread were used—still enough to illustrate every episode. The tale told is the conquest of Britain by William the Conqueror, the local Norman hero who crossed the Channel and vanquished the Anglo-Saxon army at the Battle of Hastings ➁. Legend has it that the Bayeux Tapestry was made by Queen Mathilda, the Conqueror's wife, and it's an appealing notion—but most likely false. Commissioned across the Channel in Kent, probably by William's half-brother Bishop Odo of Bayeux, the tapestry was completed a mere 10 years after the Battle of Hastings by a team of needleworkers doggedly stitching day in and day out.

The tapestry is housed in a long climate-controlled Plexiglas case; stroll along its length to find scenes such as the coronation of Harold as the Saxon king of England, Harold returning from a visit to Normandy, Harold learning of an ill-omened comet, William donning his war armor, and the gruesome death of Harold. The end of the strip, showing the final episodes, was somehow cut off long ago. Stitched **captions** are in medieval Latin, and the soldiers' armor and weapons are so realistic, historians speculate that ex-soldiers must have helped design it. A key element in William's victory was his cavalry, and hundreds of powerful embroidered horses almost seem to spring from the cloth.

Remember that this was made by Norman craftspeople—some find it flagrant propaganda, justifying William's naked aggression against another nation; yet others point to scenes of Norman brutality to show the artists' sympathy for the vanquished Saxons. Don't let the kids rush past the panels—the more you study the tapestry, the more you enter its stylized and yet vividly familiar world.

ⓘ **Centre Guillaume-le-Conquérant,** 13 rue de Nesmond (✆ **02-31-51-25-50).**

🚆 Bayeux, 2½ hr. from Paris.

🛏 $$$ **Hotel d' Argouges,** 21 rue St-Patrice, Bayeux (✆ **02-31-92-88-86).** $$$ **Le Lion d'Or,** 71 rue St-Jean, Bayeux (✆ **02-31-22-15-64;** www.liondor-bayeux.fr).

WHY THEY'LL THANK YOU: The art of war via the art of needlepoint.

Oxford University
Great Halls & Secret Gardens
Ages 6 & up • Oxford, England

AFTER THE SORBONNE IN PARIS, Oxford University is the oldest university in the world, and it's still very much alive. Larger than its sister university, Cambridge, and in a more bustling commercial town, Oxford may seem less picturesque—but venture inside its walled colleges and you'll get an idea of how black-gowned scholars have pursued their studies for centuries.

Originally Oxford was a cluster of separate foundations for monks, and even today its colleges are independent of each other, although they share a common curriculum and examination system. An Oxford student belongs to one college with its own tiny walled campus. He or she lives there, dines there, and studies with an in-house professor called a "tutor" or a "don," preparing for the general university exams. There are some 40 colleges in Oxford today, most of which you can visit (opening times are posted at gatehouses). Here's a quick tour of the best known.

Christ Church on St. Aldate's Street, founded by Henry VIII, has the largest front quadrangle in Oxford, with a big clock tower housing a 9-ton bell (nicknamed Tom) and a grand fishpond. The stairway leading to its dining hall was the basis for the shifting staircases of Hogwarts in the Harry Potter movies. **Balliol** on Broad Street, built of a dour gray stone compared to the warm yellow of most Oxford colleges, is often said to be the most "intellectual" college. **Trinity College** on Broad Street, next to Balliol, is known for its lovely gardens. **New College** on Holywell Street, snuggled in the lee of the old city wall, has Oxford's oldest quadrangle—despite the name, it's actually one of the oldest colleges, founded in 1379.

Oxford University.

Magdalen College on High Street, pronounced "maudlin," sits on the banks of the Cherwell River and has a huge surrounding park with deer roaming in it. The Bodleian Library on Catte Street, which nowadays receives a copy of every book published in Britain, also has many old and rare books. Its centerpiece is a beautiful domed building called the Radcliffe Camera. On the same street, Hertford College is most famous for its Bridge of Sighs arching over a side street. Back on Broad Street, you'll pass the Sheldonian Theatre, with its crumbling busts of Roman emperors on the fence pillars; students receive their degrees here. Slip into St. John's on St. Giles to view its beautiful cloistered quadrangle—and while you're here, stop by the Eagle and Child pub at 49 St. Giles, a favorite hangout of Oxford dons C. S. Lewis and J. R. R. Tolkien and their circle.

ⓘ Tourist Information Centre, 15–16 Broad St. (𝄐 01865/726871; www.visit oxford.org).

🚊 Oxford, 1½ hr. from London.

🛏 $$ Eastgate Townhouse, 23 Merton St. (𝄐 0870/400-8201; www.macdonald hotels.co.uk).

WHY THEY'LL THANK YOU: Book learning rules.

Positively Medieval 200

Acre: Israel's Crusader City

Ages 8 & up • Akko, Israel

FOR 2 CENTURIES IN THE MIDDLE AGES, armies of Christian knights from Europe streamed eastward to "free" the Holy Land from Muslim rule. In those days before jet travel, their home countries were impossibly far away; the Crusaders needed a secure base in the eastern Mediterranean. They found it in an ancient seaport, Acre, which had been ruled by the Phoenicians, by King David, by Alexander the Great, by the Ptolemaic kings of Egypt. Modern Acre is an industrial town, and its walled Old City at first looks totally Arab, with romantic minarets and palm trees against the sky. But from 1104 to 1291, it was a European outpost in Arab lands, and the ghost of that medieval past is still there—you just have to go underground to find it.

The knights of the First Crusade took Acre in 1104, renaming it Saint Jean d'Acre and building a great sandstone fortress, complete with mighty sea walls (the base for the walls you see today). With a population that eventually reached 40,000, it was the largest city of the Crusader kingdom. Acre fell into Saladin's hands for 4 years; but Richard the Lion-Hearted of England took it back in 1191, and the Crusaders hung on until the late 13th century, when they were driven out by the Mamelukes. The fall of Acre spelled the end for the Crusaders' hopes of ruling the Holy Land.

During the Ottoman empire, the Turks built a new city on top of the Crusader city, but since the 1950s the knights' city has been gradually excavated from beneath the 38m-high (125-ft.) walls of Acre Citadel, a former Ottoman prison. (Today it houses the Museum of Heroism, 𝄐 04/991-8264, closed Fri–Sat, honoring Jewish underground fighters imprisoned by the British who staged a mass escape in May 1947.) A replica of the Crusaders' Enchanted Garden blooms beside the visitor center for this Hospitallers' Fortress, which was headquarters of the Knights Hospitallers, the powerful Crusader order. Four wings surround a central courtyard; the first hall is a clear example of the double construction—the bottom shows the Crusaders' arches, the top the Ottomans'. Two wings have vaulted Gothic

The Hospitallers' Fortress at Acre.

ceremonial halls with pointed arches and massive banded columns (picture them hung with banners and coats of arms), while others have smaller rooms that were probably barracks and storerooms—a medieval toilet was even uncovered. You can also visit the **Templars' Tunnel,** in the southeastern part of the Old City, on Haganah Street, a 350m-long (1,148-ft.) tunnel carved out of rock as a secret passage from the fortress to the port. Once you've meandered around these echoing chambers, climb up onto the broad city walls for a sweeping view of the bay.

(i) **Hospitallers' Fortress,** Old City (📞 **700/ 70-80-20**). **Tourist Information Office,** El Jezzar St. (📞 **04/991-1764**).

✈ Haifa, 22km (14 miles).

🛏 $$$ **Le Meridien Haifa,** 10 David Elazar St.(📞 **04/850-8888;** www.fattal-hotels-israel.com). $$$ **Palm Beach Hotel and Country Club,** Acre Beach (📞 **04/ 987-7777**).

WHY THEY'LL THANK YOU: The medieval toilet.

201 Positively Medieval

Rhodes
Stopping Point on the Crusade Trail
Ages 8 & up • Rhodes, Greece

WHEN THE CRUSADES ENDED IN 1270, the Knights Hospitaller—a military religious order also called the Order of St. John— didn't return home from the Holy Land like the other knights. Buoyed by the wealth they'd accumulated, they declared they would go on defending Christianity. The Pope granted them sovereignty, and in 1310 they conquered the eastern Greek island of Rhodes, where they maintained a powerful fleet to police the Eastern Mediterranean against Muslim encroachment. That turbulent medieval era is powerfully evoked today in **Rhodes' Old Town,** a superbly preserved historic quarter girded by a magnificent 2½-mile set of walls.

Walk down cobblestoned Ippoton, also called the Street of the Knights, and you'll pass a continuous series of abrupt stone facades, the "inns" where various nations' Knights took meals and lodged guests. Subtle details echo the architecture of their countries; the eight-pointed cross that symbolizes the order crops up continuously. At the bottom of the hill, **Spanish House** sits next door to the **Inn of the Order of the Language of Italy** (see the shield above the door). Then comes the **Palace of the Villiers of the Isle of Adam,** the ornate **Inn of France** with its fleur-de-lis shield, and across the street the **Hospital of the Knights,** now the Archaeological Museum (entrance on Museum Square). Across from the Archaeological Museum, the Byzantine Museum is housed in the **Church of Our Lady of the Castle,** the Roman Catholic Cathedral of the Knights. The church farther on the right, **Ayia Triada,** played no favorites, displaying three coats-of-arms: those of France, England, and the pope. Past the arch that spans the street, still on the right, is the **Inn of the Language**

of Provence, and on the left is the traditionally Gothic **Inn of the Language of Spain,** with vertical columns and a lovely garden in the back. Though you can't enter most of these inns, which are privately owned, you can get an idea of their luxe accommodations at the **Hospice of St. Catherine,** at the opposite corner of Old Town on the Square of the Jewish Martyrs. Built in the late 14th century by the Knights to house guests, it has beautiful sea-pebble and mosaic floors, carved and intricately painted wooden ceilings, and a grand hall and lavish bedchamber.

The Order of St. John is long gone from Rhodes—Sultan Suleiman the Magnificent drove them out in 1523—after which the Holy Roman Emperor took pity and gave them the island of Malta, their international base ever since (hence their other name, the Knights of Malta). The Order still exists, defending Christianity and helping the sick around the world—a centuries-old tradition.

(i) **Tourist office,** Plateia Rimini (© **22410/ 35-945**).

✈ Rhodes, 13km (8 miles).

🛏 $$ **Hotel Mediterranean,** 35 Kos St. (© **22410/22-410;** www.mediterranean.gr).

WHY THEY'LL THANK YOU: Where does a knight go after the Crusades?

In Search of Joan of Arc: Rouen & Orléans

Ages 8 & up • Rouen & Orléans, France

OF ALL THE MILITARY COMMANDERS in the Middle Ages, perhaps none is as intriguing as the sole female—a 15th-century provincial teenager who led the French army to victory. Joan of Arc's uncanny ability to inspire reinvigorated the French soldiers, their courage ignited by the unarmed girl's fearlessness in the throes of battle. Now

there's a role model for modern girls.

Not long after Henry V of England won the Battle of Agincourt, with France split by competing nobles, the French nation very nearly ceased to exist. Enter Jeanne d'Arc, a country girl born in 1412 in the village of Domrémy in Alsace-Lorraine. Claiming to hear the voices of saints and archangels, she convinced the heir to the French throne to put her at the head of his army—and against all odds, it worked. She won back the territory around Reims so that Charles VII could legitimately claim his throne in the cathedral where all French monarchs are crowned.

Although her birthplace in Domremy is a popular tourist site, I feel Joan's spirit is most alive in northwest France. In **Orléans** in 1429, 119km (74 miles) southwest of Paris, a 17-year-old Joan led a French army to free the besieged city from English attackers. Models and exhibits tell her story at the **Maison Jeanne-d'Arc,** 3 place de Gaulle, Orléans (✆ **02-38-52-99-89**), a reproduction of the half-timbered house where she stayed during the siege. A famous statue of Joan on horseback prances in town at place de Martroi.

The tragic final chapter of Joan's story is told in **Rouen,** 135km (84 miles) northwest of Paris. After someone at court eventually betrayed her, she was captured by the English in 1430 and brought to this English stronghold in Normandy. Corrupt clergy put her on trial, first on a charge of witchcraft, then of heresy (for wearing male clothing into battle). The **Musee Jeanne-d'Arc,** 33 place du Vieux-Marché, Rouen (✆ **02-35-88-02-70**), vividly lays out the details of her life with dioramas, waxworks, and exhibits; right outside its door is **place du Vieux-Marché,** where Joan was burned at the stake in 1431, the exact spot marked by a bronze cross.

Down the rue du Gros-Horloge, behind Rouen's Notre-Dame Cathedral (art lovers will recognize it from Claude Monet's evocative paintings) stand the ruins of the **Archbishop's Palace,** where Joan's mockery of a trial was held. This medieval building, like nearly half of Rouen, was bombed out in World War II; a forlorn fragment of broken arches and rosette windows is all that remains. Up rue de la République, the cemetery of the turreted **Eglise St-Ouen,** place du Général-de-Gaulle, is where Joan was formally sentenced to be burned at the stake unless she recanted. She did sign such papers, to have her sentence reduced to life imprisonment, but was tricked into putting her trousers and tunic back on, and the death penalty was reinstated. Many English soldiers wept the day this sincere, passionate young woman was burned at the stake, and her ashes were lovingly gathered up and scattered into the Seine.

(i) **Rouen tourist office,** 25 place de la Cathedrale, Rouen (✆ **02-32-08-32-40;** www.rouentourisme.com). **Orléans tourist office,** 8, rue d'Escures, Orléans (✆ **02-38-78-04-04;** www.tourismeloiret.com or www.tourisme.fr).

🚄 Orléans, 50 min. from Paris. Rouen, 70 min. from Paris.

🛏 $$ **Hotel Mercure Orléans,** 44–46 quai Barentin, Orléans (✆ **02-38-62-17-39**). $$ **Mercure Centre,** Rue de la Croix-de-Fer, Rouen (✆ **02-35-52-69-52**).

WHY THEY'LL THANK YOU: Joan of Arc proved what a girl could do.

203 Positively Medieval

Bruges: City of Guilds

All ages • Belgium

LET OTHER CITIES BOAST PALACES AND CATHEDRALS— the Flemish town of Bruges shows off guildhalls, exchanges, warehouses, and the homes of wealthy merchants. In the 15th century, Bruges was a center for the Hanseatic league, a confederation of merchant cities that knit Europe together in trade, and it became one of the wealthiest

The Renaissance Hall in Bruges.

cities in medieval Europe. It's still a fairy-tale mixture of gabled houses, magnificent squares, narrow cobblestone streets, and meandering canals full of swans.

Every quarter-hour, a magnificent 47-bell carillon peals out from the **Belfry** on the **Markt** (Market Square)—between rings, we hurried to the top (366 steps) for a panoramic overview of the surrounding countryside. The attached **Market Halls** were the heart of Bruges's commerce from the 13th to the 16th centuries. Things didn't always run smoothly, as we learned from the sculpture in the center of the Markt, depicting butcher Jan Breydel and weaver Pieter de Coninck, who led a 1302 uprising against the rich merchants and nobles who dominated the city's trade guilds. A few steps away is another public square, the Burg, site of the Gothic Stadhuis (Town Hall), built in

the late 1300s, which makes it the oldest Town Hall in Belgium. Upstairs, in the ornate **Gothic Room,** we pored over wall murals depicting Bruges's history. Across the Burg, the 18th-century Palace of the Liberty of Bruges, a former courtroom and administrative center, also has a great room: the **Renaissance Hall,** which has been restored to its original 16th-century condition—on the oak chimney piece, we grinned at the figures of various European monarchs, an open bit of flattery from Bruges's shrewd merchants.

To see how these merchants lived, stop by the **Gruuthuse Museum,** Dijver 17, the fancy Gothic mansion of Flemish nobleman and herb merchant Lodewijk Van Gruuthuse. At the other end of the economic spectrum, the **Stedelijk Museum voor Volksunde,** Balstraat 43, occupies the low whitewashed houses of the former Shoemakers Guild Almshouse, or charity home. Various rooms show daily life from times gone by—a primary school, a cooper's workshop, a spice store. As a city of craft guilds, Bruges shows off two of its top crafts at the **Kantcentrum** (Lace Center), Peperstraat 3A, and **Diamantmuseum** (Diamond Museum), Katelijnestraat 43B. We ended up at the most tranquil spot in Bruges, the **Begijnhof** on Wijngaardstraat, a retreat for religious women founded in 1245. Benedictine nuns live now in this cluster of 17th-century whitewashed houses, where you can step inside the courtyard and almost breathe the air of another century.

ⓘ **Toerisme Brugge,** Burg 11 (✆ **050/44-86-86;** www.brugge.be).

🚆 Bruges, 1 hr. from Brussels.

🛏 $$ **Dante,** Coupure 29 (✆ **050/34-01-94;** www.hoteldante.be). $$ **Relais Oud Huis Amsterdam,** Spiegelrei 3 (✆ **050/34-18-10;** www.oha.be).

WHY THEY'LL THANK YOU: The swans on the canals.

Santiago de Compostela
Making the Pilgrimage
Ages 4 & up • Spain

ALL ROADS IN SPAIN once led to the north-western city of **Santiago de Compostela**, where the Catholic faithful could visit the **tomb of St. James,** Spain's patron saint, hoping the effort would guarantee them a place in heaven. The pilgrimage route ran from Paris over the Pyrenees and along Spain's northern coast—an enormous distance even by car. (Some hardy souls still make the trek on foot.) Even if you only drive the last section, from Pamplona through **León 322** to Santiago de Compostela, you can imagine the joy of weary pilgrims arriving at last in front of this glorious Romanesque cathedral.

It all began in A.D. 813, when priests unearthed what were said to be the remains of St. James (Santiago, in Spanish). In the 11th century, this huge cathedral was built over his tomb, and a trickle of local pilgrims grew into an international flood. From the Praza do Obradoido, admire its three ornate towers and the wrought-iron enclosed staircase; in an arch inside the middle tower is a statue of St. James, dressed in traditional pilgrim garb (wide-brimmed hat and walking staff), since he traveled widely around western Europe spreading the gospel. Show the kids the rounded arches, thick walls, and small windows, different from the more familiar pointy Gothic architecture. The west door's **triple-arched front portico** is famous, with sculpted biblical figures representing the Last Judgment. Look for St. James, in the center beneath Christ. The carved column under him bears five grooves worn into the stone by centuries of pilgrims, leaning forward to place their hands on the pillar and knock foreheads with the carved face at the bottom—the

likeness of the portico's designer, Maestro Mateo. It's nicknamed **Santo dos Croques** (Saint of the Bumps).

In our age of jet travel, it's amazing to recall that most medieval folks spent their entire lives in one village, without TV or newspapers or the Internet to tell them about the rest of the world; the few who took a pilgrimage played a vital role in disseminating European culture. Inside, notice how wide the barrel-vaulted aisles are, built to accommodate hordes of pilgrims. On the altar is a huge golden **mollusk shell** that pilgrims traditionally kissed, as well as a great silver incense burner—the *botufumiero*—which purified the air at night while hundreds of pilgrims slept in the cathedral.

The remains of St. James are in a silver urn in the crypt. Hard as it is to believe, they went missing for almost 300 years, when, in the 16th century, with Sir Francis Drake (see The Golden Hinde **266**) raiding the coast, the church fathers hid them so well that they weren't found again until 1879. To verify their authenticity, a sliver of the skull of St. James was fetched from Italy—and it fit perfectly into the recently discovered skeleton.

(i) Praza do Obradoiro (✆ **98-158-35-48;** www.santiagoturismo.com).

✈ Santiago de Compostela.

🛏 $$$ **Hotel de los Reyes Católicas,** Praza do Obradoido 1 (✆ **98-158-2200**). $$ **Los Abetos Hotel,** San Lázaro (✆ **98-155-70-26;** www.hotellosabetos.com).

WHY THEY'LL THANK YOU: Those finger marks in the stone pillar.

The Leaning Tower of Pisa

Ages 8 & up • Pisa, Italy

How MANY CARDBOARD PIZZA BOXES across America carry a picture of the Leaning Tower of Pisa? It may be the most instantly recognizable building in the Western world, with the possible exception of the Eiffel Tower. A grayish-white stack of colonnaded rings with a neat top hat, it has a certain architectural élan, but the thing that really makes it famous—face it—is that rakish tilt, nowadays a whopping 4m (13 ft.) off the perpendicular. If it stood straight, it would be 55m (180 ft.) tall; but it doesn't stand straight. It's famous for *not* standing straight.

This eight-story free-standing bell tower for the cathedral at Pisa was begun in 1173, part of Pisa's campaign to show that it was wealthier and grander than its Tuscan rival Florence. But about the time the third story was completed, in 1198, it became obvious that the tower was leaning. The builders discovered that the site they'd chosen wasn't solid rock, as they'd thought, but water-soaked clay. The architect, Bonnano Pisano, disappeared, a few bells were stuck in the third story, and work halted for decades, while Pisa fought an on-again-off-again war with Florence, capped by a serious 1284 naval loss against Genoa. Considerably reduced in prestige, Pisa took up the project again, completing the tower in 1319; the bells were finally installed in the top in 1350 (although they are no longer rung, for fear the vibrations might rattle the tower). But by then, Pisa had lost its

power, and in 1392 it was annexed by Florence, the final humiliation.

Climbing the 294 steps to the top isn't nearly as tippy an experience as I expected, but looking at it from the outside, you almost want to hold your breath, it looks so ready to topple over onto the roof of the cathedral next door, like a medieval set of dominos.

For years, annual measurements showed the tower leaning a fraction of an inch farther every year, so recent restoration sought to arrest the tilt, with tons of soil removed from under the foundation and lead counterweights placed at the monument's base. But Pisans staunchly believe the tower will never fall, pointing out that several mild earthquakes, not to mention extensive bombing in World War II, have not done the trick. Besides, the Pisa city fathers have no vested interest in making it straight again. It never has been perpendicular, and it never will be. And after all these years, it's the one thing Pisa's got that Florence never will.

(i) Piazza del Duomo 17 (© 050-560547; www.duomo.pisa.it).

✈ Galileo Galilei Airport, Pisa.

🚂 Pisa, 1 hr. from Florence.

🛏 $$ **Royal Victoria,** Lungarno Pacinotti 12 (© **050-940111;** www.royalvictoria.it).

WHY THEY'LL THANK YOU: Catch me now, I'm falling.

206 Positively Medieval

San Gimignano: Medieval Skyscraper City

All ages • Italy

THE FORTRESSLIKE WALLED TOWN OF San Gimignano rises proudly out of the Tuscan plain, its 13 noble towers giving it a "skyscraper" skyline. Just imagine what it was like in its heyday, in the 13th and 14th centuries, when there were as many as 72 towers. My middle son, the *Lord of the Rings* fan, pictures Minas Tirith in Middle Earth as looking a lot like San Gimignano, and he's pretty much right. Bound inside its walls, the tiny town is like a medieval stage set, remarkably unchanged since the days when it was a prosperous player in Tuscany's turbulent Guelph/Ghibelline politics. Nowadays, San Gimignano lives off of the tourists, but slip out of the fierce Tuscan sun into a quiet courtyard or church, and you can still find beautiful art and an other-worldly peace.

The heart of San Gimignano is a connected pair of large paved squares, the **Piazza della Cisterna** (named for the 13th-century cistern in the middle), and the **Piazza del Duomo,** a beautiful composition of medieval towers and palaces. San Gimignano's Duomo (technically no longer a cathedral but a "collegiata" since the town's prestige dwindled and it lost its bishop) may look plain and austere, but that's just because its 12th-century facade was never finished; inside is a world of tiger-striped arches and a galaxy of gold stars. The main artist here was Bartolo di Fredi, who in the 1360s painted a number of remarkable murals and frescoes—look for one of *Noah with the Animals* and his gruesome *Last Judgment,* which shocked churchgoers with its distorted and suffering nudes. In the Chapel of Santa Fina, the life story of a local girl, Fina, the town's patron saint, is told in frescoes by Domenico Ghirlandaio, Michaelanglo's fresco teacher.

Also on the square, the town hall, **Palazzo del Popolo,** Piazza del Duomo 1 (② **0577-990312**), was designed in the 13th century; the civic museum inside preserves a room where Dante made an impassioned pro-Ghibelline speech in 1300, when he was Florence's ambassador to San Gimignano. (Two years later his faction fell from power and he was exiled from Florence, never to return.) The palazzo's **Torre Grossa,** built a few years later, was always the town's tallest tower (about 53m/174 ft. high); it's the only one you can climb today, to get a bird's-eye view of this most remarkable town.

It's tempting to idealize the past, but the Middle Ages was a time of cruel politics, as the kids will realize after visiting the **Museo della Tortura,** Torture Museum, Via del Castello 1 (② **0577-942243**). In this Tuscan chamber of horrors, some of the most horrendous instruments of torture are on display—items such as cast-iron

San Gimignano's towers.

chastity belts and the garrote, that horror of the Inquisition trials of the 1400s. Fittingly, this museum is housed in the Torre del Diavolo (Devil's Tower).

(i) **Tourist office,** Piazza del Duomo 1 ((C) **0577-940008**).

Pisa Centrale station, 80–90 min. from Florence, 100–110 min. from Siena.

$$$ **Relais Santa Chiara,** Via Matteotti 15 ((C) **0577-940701;** www.rsc.it).

WHY THEY'LL THANK YOU: A Tuscan time warp.

Positively Medieval

207

Heidelberg's Royal Ruins
Ages 10 & up • Germany

SITUATED IN THE PICTURESQUE NECKAR VALLEY, Heidelberg is one of the few German cities that wasn't leveled by air raids in World War II; as a university town, it also escaped heavy industrialization. Sometimes it's hard to get a handle on Germany's medieval history, fragmented among so many small kingdoms, but here in the compact **Altstadt** (Old City) of Heidelberg, we suddenly felt in touch with the late Middle Ages and early Renaissance of Germany.

As in most medieval cities, all things radiate from the **Marktplatz,** which is still filled on market days with stalls selling fresh flowers, fruit, and vegetables. And, typically, here sits the **Rathaus** (city hall) at one end, the main church—the late-Gothic **Heiliggeeistkirche,** built around 1400—at the other. A few steps north, we walked through the turreted baroque Bridge Gate onto the arched **Alte Brücke** (Old Bridge) to get a sweet view up and down the Neckar. Then it was back to the narrow pedestrian-only Hauptstrasse, lined with quaint shops, to go west through the university quarter. Knowing that Heidelberg University was founded as a monastic institution in 1386, we were vaguely

Heidelberg's Alte Brücke and Castle.

disappointed that most of the buildings here today date from the early 18th century, but it was fun to see the old **Studentenkarzer,** Augustinergasse 2, a jail where unruly students were locked up, its walls and ceilings covered with graffiti and drawings. The baroque palace at Hauptstrasse 97 is now the **Krupfälzisches Museum** (© **06221/543554**), which displays 6 centuries' worth of local paintings and sculpture; you may want to stop here just for the archaeology section, where one item really engrossed us—a cast of the jawbone of the 500,000-year-old Heidelberg Man, a major anthropological find excavated nearby.

There are two routes uphill, both ending up at the huge red-sandstone **Heidelberg Castle** that perches above the Altstadt (we chose the steeper route, a punishing half-hour climb). The castle is a dignified ruin today, but even so it's one of the finest Gothic-Renaissance castles in Germany. The stern palace of Friedrich IV,

built 1601–07, is the least damaged section; its rooms are almost completely restored, including a portrait gallery of German princes and kings since the time of Charlemagne. In the cellars of the castle, the kids may gape at the Great Cask, a barrel-like monstrosity built in 1751 that can hold more than 208,000 liters of wine.

ⓘ **Heidelberg CVB,** Ziegelhäuser Landstraße 3 (© **06221/14220;** www.cvb-heidelberg.de/index_eng.html.

✈ Frankfurt, 70km (44 miles).

🛏 $$$ **Heidelberg Marriott Renaissance Hotel,** Vanerowstrasse 16 (© **06221/9080;** www.marriott.com). $$ **Parkhotel Atlantic Schlosshotel,** Schloss-Wolfsbrunnen-Weg 23 (© **06221/60420;** www.park hotel-atlantic.de).

WHY THEY'LL THANK YOU: The student jail and the giant wine cask—is there a connection?

208 Positively Medieval

The Jewish Quarter of Prague
Ages 8 & up • Czech Republic

THE HISTORY OF CZECH JEWS is not a happy one—massacred by Crusaders in the 11th century, walled up in a ghetto in the 13th century, enduring a massive 1389 pogrom, forced to wear identifying caps or yellow stars of David. Even after Austrian emperor Josef I relaxed the prohibitions against them, in 1781, it turned out badly—once all the prosperous Jews were free to move out, the ghetto became such a slum it had to be razed in the 1890s, with only a few historic buildings preserved. The Nazi occupation and World War II literally decimated Prague's Jewish population, reducing it from 56,000 to about 5,000 or 6,000. And yet the Jewish quarter—**Josefov,** the northwest sector of Prague's beautiful Old

Town—survived, and today it's one of Prague's most popular tourist draws. Even if you have no Jewish ancestors, it's an inspiring place to visit.

You can sign up for an English-language guided tour at the **Jewish Museum,** Maiselova 10 (© **222-317-191;** www. jewishmuseum.cz), in the former Maisel Synagogue. The Jewish Museum has extensive historical exhibits, but the story behind them is chilling: Most of Prague's ancient Judaica was destroyed by the Nazis during World War II, except for what the Germans salvaged—thousands of objects such as Torah covers, books, and silver—to install in an "exotic museum of an extinct race."

The tightly packed gravestones in Prague's Old Jewish Cemetery.

Europe's oldest Jewish house of worship, the **Staronová synagoga** (Old-New Synagogue), Červená 3, got its name when built in 1270 to distinguish it from an older one that's long gone. Jews have prayed in this vaulted Gothic sanctuary continually for more than 700 years, except for 1941–45, during the Nazi occupation. Czech writer Franz Kafka had his bar mitzvah here. Kids are fascinated by the pink rococo **Jewish Town Hall** (Židovská radnice) for one feature: the clock face on its north side, which has Hebrew figures instead of numbers, and hands that run counterclockwise, just as Hebrew writing is read right to left. The 15th-century **Pinkas Synagogue** is now an affecting memorial to the Czech Jews killed by the Nazis, all 77,297 names inscribed around its walls. The **Old Jewish Cemetery** (U Starého hřbitova 3A), dating from the mid–15th century, is one of the world's most crowded cemeteries,

a jumble of gray tombstones marking more than 20,000 graves. Local governments of the time forbid Jews to bury their dead anywhere else, so they resourcefully dug graves deep enough to hold 12 bodies vertically. Brace yourself before entering the adjoining **Ceremonial Hall**—it displays heart-wrenching drawings by children held at the nearby Terezín concentration camp in World War II.

ⓘ **Tourist Information,** Main Railway Station (✆ **420 12 444;** www.prague-info.cz).

✈ Ruzyně Airport, Prague.

🛏 $ **Hotel Cloister Inn,** Konviktská 14 (✆ **224-211-020;** www.cloister-inn.cz). $$$ **Hotel Ungelt,** Štupartská 1 (✆ **224-828-686;** www.ungelt.cz).

WHY THEY'LL THANK YOU: The ghetto survived, against all odds.

209

The Kremlin: Moscow's Red Fortress

Ages 8 & up • Moscow, Russia

WHEN I WAS A KID, the name "the Kremlin" stood for the Soviet Union, in all its Cold War menace. The image of the fortress's tightly guarded gates and impervious outer walls—red brick, the very color associated with Communism—epitomized a closed totalitarian society. What a revelation, then, to discover that this 53-hectare (130-acre) compound is full of palaces and churches and czarist-era treasures. Curiosities like the world's largest bell, the 200-ton **Czar Bell** (which was never rung), and the 40-ton **Czar Cannon** (which was never fired) express the ambition and excess of these Russian princes. To visit the Kremlin is to sense the full operatic sweep of Russian history.

Here's the Kremlin story in a nutshell: It began as a palisaded wooden encampment in the 12th century; white stone walls went up in the 1360s, but then it was sacked by the Mongol Tatars in 1382; Ivan the Great defied the Mongols, declared Moscow's independence in 1480, and built the red-brick walls in the 1490s. During an uprising here, young Peter the Great watched his relatives impaled; he fled Moscow in 1710 to found a new capital in the swamps of St. Petersburg. Power did not return to the Kremlin until the Soviets settled in 1918.

At the heart of the complex is tranquil **Cathedral Square** (Sobornaya Ploshchad), dominated by the gilt-domed **Ivan the Great Bell Tower,** at 80m (262 ft.) the tallest building in Russia. The imposing white limestone **Cathedral of the Assumption,** with its chunky golden domes, was where the czars were crowned, the seat of the Russian Orthodox Church. Czars were christened and married in the **Cathedral of the Annunciation,** with its quintessentially Russian silhouette of tented gables; next to it is the **Red Staircase,** which czars traditionally mounted after coronation. Within the somber **Cathedral of the Archangel Michael,** you can see the tombs of Russia's rulers from 1328 to 1696. Behind the small **Church of the Deposition of the Robe** rises the 11-domed roofline of the **Terem Palace** (not open to visitors), where the czars lived.

Besides the churches, visit **The Armory Museum** (✆ 095/302-3776), which despite its name holds much more than guns—things like Boris Godunov's armor, Peter the Great's gold brocade robes, and the dazzling jeweled Fabergé eggs of Czar Nicholas II and Empress Alexandra. The other major site, which requires advance reservations, is **The Diamond Treasury** (✆ 095/229-2036), repository of the crown jewels. If you buy a special (and pricey) ticket, you can see the changing of the guard on Cathedral Square every Saturday noon.

ⓘ Purchase Kremlin tickets at Kutafya Tower in Alexander Gardens (✆ 095/203-0349). Closed Thurs and for state events.

✈ Moscow.

🛏 $$ **Cosmos,** 150 Prospekt Mira (✆ 095/234-1000; www.hotelcosmos.ru). $$$ **Sheraton Palace,** 19 1st Tverskaya-Yamskaya Ulitsa (✆ 095/931-9700; www.sheratonpalace.ru).

WHY THEY'LL THANK YOU: The Fabergé eggs.

The Great Wall of China

Ages 6 & up • Bejing to the Gobi Desert

THE FIRST QUESTION everyone will ask when you get back from China is whether you saw the Great Wall. Maybe it isn't so big you can see it from outer space, but it is still a mind-boggling edifice. To hike along its broad walkways, climbing flights of stairs as the wall zigzags over pleated green mountains, is to feel in touch with the ages.

The Great Wall deserves its name—it is as much as 10,000km (6,214 miles) long when you put together all the fragments. Standing 6m (20 ft.) wide at the base and between 6 and 9m (20 and 30 ft.) high, it is wide enough for five horses to ride abreast along the ramparts. Its origins lie way back in the Warring States Period (453–221 B.C.), when rival kingdoms built defensive walls against their enemies; over the centuries subsequent emperors connected the various bits and added more to keep out Huns and Mongols and other invaders. The Wall begins east of Beijing at Shan Hai Guan, on the coast of the Bó Hai Sea, and runs west to the Gobi Desert. The chief portion, however—the part most tourists visit, an easy day trip from Beijing—is clearly medieval, reconstructed during the Ming dynasty (1368–1644), with high slotted battlements *(duo kou)* on the outer wall, level parapets on the inner, and stout stone watchtowers every 70m (230 ft.). While the older sections of the wall were built of rammed earth, the Ming rebuilt this section with stone and brick. The most popular, and most developed, section is at **Bādálǐng,** only 70km (44 miles) northwest of the city, where you'll find a museum, theater, restaurants, souvenir stands, even a cable car. Its dramatic setting in a steep forested mountain range means you'll have tremendous views, once you hike beyond the tourist crowds. Even closer to Beijing is the recently restored section at **Jin Shan Ling,**

The Great Wall of China.

55km (34 miles) northwest of the city, which is often less crowded; there are a number of impressive Buddhist **bas-relief carvings** on the separate Yún Tái (Cloud Platform) built in 1342. If the kids are up for some more vigorous Wall hiking, go to **Jīnshānlǐng** (✆ 010/8402-4647), for which you'll need to hire a minivan from Mìyún. The hike from here to the Mìyún Reservoir is roughly 10km (6¼ miles) and takes 3 to 4 hours. The middle portion of the hike, where the number of fellow hikers begins to dwindle and you reach authentically crumbling parts of the Wall, can be truly sublime.

Many tour operators run day trips out to these Wall destinations, though if you're feeling resourceful, you can also take a city-sponsored tourist bus or even a taxi.

ⓘ www.thegreatwall.com.cn.

✈ Capital Airport, Beijing.

🛏 $$$ **Grand Hyatt,** Dōng Chāng'ān Jiē 1, Dōngchéng District (✆ 010/8518-1234; http://beijing.grand.hyatt.com). $$ **Red House,** Chūnxiù Lù 10, Cháoyáng District (✆ 010/6416-7810; www.redhouse.com.cn).

WHY THEY'LL THANK YOU: Peering through the arrow slits, imagining the Mongol hordes.

---

211 Positively Medieval

Kyoto: City of Samurai & Shoguns
Ages 6 & up • Japan

TOKYO IS AN EXCITING BIG CITY, but if you really want to say you've been to Japan, visit Kyoto. The capital of Japan from 794 to 1868, it is like a treasure box of history, so precious that during World War II, Allied bombers intentionally spared it from destruction. When you're in Tokyo, it's easy to overlook Japan's rich medieval heritage; when you're in Kyoto, it's impossible to forget.

Take its temples, for example. **Ryoanji Temple** (Goryoshita-cho) contains Japan's most famous Zen rock garden, laid out in the late 15th century—15 pristine rocks, set in waves of raked white pebbles. Then there's the awe-inspiring view at **Kiyomizu Temple,** with its grand wooden veranda hanging over a cliff overlooking Kyoto. Founded in 798, it was rebuilt in 1633 without a single nail. Its grounds are stunning during cherry-blossom season and when the maples turn color in fall. **Sanjusangendo Hall** (Shichijo Dori) is an overwhelming sight: 1,001 life-size cypress statues of the thousand-handed goddess Kannon, standing row upon row in the longest wooden building in Japan. (Each Kannon only has 40 arms, but

supposedly each hand has the power to save 25 worlds.)

In medieval Japan, feudal lords known as shoguns ruled the nation from Kyoto. The **Temple of the Golden Pavilion** (Kinkakuji-cho), built in the 1390s for Shogun Ashikaga Yoshimitsu, has a shamelessly luxurious three-story pavilion covered in gold leaf (and this at a time of famine, earthquakes, and plague). His grandson died in 1482 before completing its sequel, the **Temple of the Silver Pavilion** (Ginkakuji-cho)—ask the kids to imagine this beautiful wooden villa coated with silver as originally planned. Shogun Ieyasu Tokugawa built the moated **Nijo Castle** (Horikawa Dori & Nijo Dori) in 1603, an elegantly understated palace of Japanese cypress, with delicate transom woodcarvings and exquisitely painted sliding doors. All the doors on the outside walls can be removed in summer, a sort of medieval air-conditioning. One of the paranoid shogun's security measures was the "nightingale floors," special floorboards designed to creak so that sentries could hear enemies sneaking in.

Though not an authentic historic site, at **Toei Uzumasa Movieland** (10 Higashi-Hachigaokacho, Uzumasa, Ukyo-ku; ✆ **075/864-7718**), one of Japan's three major film studios, you can walk around feudal-era "village" sets lined with samurai houses and old-time shops. Besides the daily Ninja shows, kids can enjoy a special-effects show, a haunted house, a games arcade, and indoor rides.

ⓘ **Tourist Information Center,** Karasuma Dori (✆ **075/371-5649;** www.city.kyoto. jp/koho/eng/index.html).

🚄 Kyoto, 2½ hr. from Tokyo by bullet train, 75 min. from Kansai International outside Osaka.

🛏 $$ **ANA Hotel Kyoto,** Nijojo-mae, Horikawa Dori, Nakagyo-ku (✆ **800/ANA-HOTELS** in North America or 075/231-1155; www.anahotels.com/eng/index.html). $$$ **The Westin Miyako,** Sanjo Keage, Higashiyama-ku (✆ **800/WESTIN-1** in North America, or 075/771-7111; www. westinmiyako-kyoto.com).

WHY THEY'LL THANK YOU: Shogun showplaces.

Historic Restorations

Viking Days in Dublin
All ages • Ireland

IF IT HADN'T BEEN FOR VIKINGS RAIDING IRELAND in A.D. 795, Dublin might still be a quiet river ford with a minor monastery. Compared to the Irish kings, who were hunter-herders holed up in isolated mountain fortresses, the Vikings were cosmopolitan merchant-politicians who immediately grasped the importance of seaports. Dublin duly became the Viking capital, and 150 years of Viking rule put Ireland squarely on the medieval trade map, making Dublin Ireland's greatest city. No wonder Dubliners have whole-heartedly embraced this chapter of their heritage.

The perennially popular **Dublin's Viking Adventure,** Essex Street West, Temple Bar (✆ **01/679-6040**), is your starting point, a historical re-creation where costumed actors play citizens of Viking-era Dublin. Stroll from period house to period house interacting with the "Vikings," who resolutely refuse to admit they weren't born in the 10th century. You'll watch builders construct a house, chat with a silversmith, observe a feast in progress, and see a life-size replica of a longboat. The site includes a faithful reconstruction of Wood Quay, an excavated settlement along the Liffey

that's considered the most important Viking site of this kind outside Scandinavia. An almost irresistible add-on is the **Viking Splash Tour,** 64–65 Patrick St. (✆ **01/707-6000;** www.vikingsplashtours. com), 1¼-hour ride around Dublin in a reconditioned WWII amphibious vehicle called a "duck boat." The garrulous driver is dressed like a Norseman, passengers can wear horned helmets if they so choose, and everybody is urged to let out a lusty Viking war cry from time to time. After a drive-by of major sights such as Christchurch Cathedral, **Trinity College** ⑲⑥, the elegant houses of Merrion Square, and lushly planted St. Stephen's Green, you'll plunge into the Grand Canal Basin for a final 20 minutes on the Liffey. It's pricey, but memorable.

The final piece in the package is **Dublinia,** St. Michael's Hill, by Christchurch (✆ **01/679-4611;** www.dublinia.ie), which picks up the story from the arrival of the Anglo-Normans in 1170 until the 1530s. This living history lesson about medieval Dublin is more of a hands-on sort of place, where kids can don bits of armor, sample spices and medicines, write in a scribe's book, put their heads in the stocks (always a crowd pleaser), and tot up cargo values at the wharf—my kids were totally engrossed. But even Dublinia has gotten into the Viking act with its new section, Viking World, which does a good job of weaving the Viking era into the greater Dublin story.

(i) **Dublin Tourism Centre,** Suffolk St. (www.visitdublin.com).

✈ 🚊 See The Book of Kells **196**.

WHY THEY'LL THANK YOU: Kids and Vikings, wild kindred spirits.

Jorvik Viking Centre
Ghosts of the Norse Invaders
All ages • York, England

WITH SO MANY LAYERS OF HISTORY jostling each other in Great Britain, it's easy to forget that this country was also once a colony of the Vikings—who, far from being bloodthirsty rampagers, were often in fact solid Danish citizens eager to settle in new lands, plant crops, intermarry with the natives, and adopt local religions. Northwest England, just across the sea from their Scandinavian home base, was prime Viking territory, and their legacy is brought vividly to life in York, at the Jorvik Viking Centre.

Before the Viking era, York was a Roman stronghold, but the legions decamped around A.D. 400. York lay deserted until 597, when Christian missionaries built a bishop's church here (the basis of today's York Minster) to spearhead the conversion of the Saxons, and a center of learning and religion gradually evolved. Conquest-hungry Vikings abruptly arrived in 867 with an invincible army and captured the city. Permanent settlers followed a decade later. The area became its own kingdom, ruled by Viking kings for almost a century, until Eric Bloodaxe (what a name!) was expelled in 954.

Twentieth-century archaeologists discovered the **ancient Viking city** of Jorvik (easy to see how that evolved into York) many feet below present ground level and excavated it over 5 years between 1976 and 1981. They found 1.8m-high (6-ft.) wooden house walls, fence lines,

alleyways, and backyards, and dug up tens of thousands of objects, many of them perfectly preserved in the wet soils. Based on this wealth of evidence, the Jorvik Viking Center is a reconstruction of the old city as it stood in its heyday in 948, meticulously patterned after the excavated town. Riding in a so-called "time car," you travel back through the ages (stopping briefly in 1067, when Normans sacked the city) to visit a Viking street market, a family's house, and a waterfront where ship chandlers work and a Norwegian ship unloads its cargo. Sounds and even smells are piped in, and the faces of the modeled figures have been reconstructed from individual Viking skulls. At the end, you enter the **Finds Hut,** where thousands of real artifacts are displayed and explained by live costumed staff.

While you're here, of course, don't miss visiting the 13th-century **York Minster,** one of the world's most beautiful church buildings, with 100 stained-glass windows.

(i) Coppergate ($\textcircled{C}$ **01904/643211;** www.jorvik-viking-centre.co.uk).

🚆 York (2 hr. from London).

🚊 $$$ **York Moat House,** North St. ($\textcircled{C}$ **01904/459988;** www.moathouse hotels.com).

WHY THEY'LL THANK YOU: Brings the Dark Ages to light.

Living in the Past at the Geffrye Museum

Ages 8 & up • London, England

Lᴏᴏᴋ ᴀ ᴍɪᴄʀᴏᴄᴏsᴍ of British urban life over the past 4 centuries, this ingenious museum presents history in a manner that makes absolute sense to children—by showing how people lived in each era. It's a perfect antidote to all the palaces and stately homes you may have trooped them through, because these houses show how different classes lived—all in a relatively compact space, suited to shorter attention spans. Though it's in East London, out of the usual tourist areas, it's well worth the foray.

The main building is a chronological series of **period parlors,** each from a different era, starting with Elizabethan England. While the first few reflect the lifestyle of wealthy families, more middle-class interiors begin to dominate, all the way up through an Edwardian suburban villa and an Art Deco flat. You get a visceral understanding of how history evolved as you walk from dark Jacobean wood paneling into the pale walls of a early Georgian room, from the fuss and clutter of a Victorian parlor into the almost rustic simplicity of Edwardian Arts and Crafts style. The

connections between social history and decor trends are pointed out thoughtfully: For example, as English trade developed, more and more imported objects appear, and interior fashions also reflect changing foreign alliances, from late Georgian neoclassical simplicity to Oriental accents in the 1890s to Scandinavian modern in the 1950s. Fireplaces and candlesticks give way to gas grates and wall sconces, succeeded by electric heaters and table lamps.

Built in 1715, only a few years after the Great Fire of 1666 razed much of London, these architecturally distinctive houses by a stroke of luck survived Hitler's Blitz, when much of surrounding Shoreditch was reduced to rubble. As the icing on the cake, the **gardens** in front also show evolving tastes in gardening, including a walled herb garden.

ⓘ 136 Kingsland Rd. (𝄞 **020/7739-9893;** www.geffrye-museum.org.uk).

✈ ⊨ See London **55**.

WHY THEY'LL THANK YOU: A cavalcade of history, one room at a time.

Irish National Heritage Park
A Walk through Ancient Ireland

Ages 6 & up • Ferrycarrig, Ireland

Dᴏᴡɴ ᴏɴ ᴛʜᴇ sᴏᴜᴛʜᴇᴀsᴛ ᴄᴏʀɴᴇʀ ᴏғ Iʀᴇʟᴀɴᴅ, County Wexford was ripe territory for invaders—first the Vikings in the 9th century, then the Normans in the 12th century. Whereas western Ireland was mostly able to escape the scrutiny of the English

occupiers, Wexford chafed under nearby Britain's grip, and Wexfordmen early on were supporters of an Irish republic. If Dublin is your entry point into Ireland, drive down to Wexford before heading out to the rest of the country—this is the best introduction you could get to the many layers of ancient Irish history.

Set on 15 hectares (36 acres) along the River Slaney off N11, Irish National Heritage Park is laid out as a trail through many centuries of Ireland's past, with detailed reconstructions from successive periods, ending at the medieval period. Guided tours are included with admission, but you can also walk through it on your own; either way, plan on at least 2 hours.

You'll begin with a **Stone Age campsite,** a domelike tent covered with animal hides, then a later Stone Age settlement with wattle-and-daub huts topped by thatched roofs. The **Bronze Age** is represented by a stone circle, which couldn't have been built without that age's new sharp metal tools. If you tour more of Ireland later, you may see Celtic ruins that correspond to the reconstructions here—for example, the **hilltop ring fort** (like Staigue Fort on the Ring of Kerry **25**), or the **early Christian monastery** (like Clonmacnois **319**). There's even a **Fulacht Fiadh,** a Celtic version of a barbecue pit, where interpreters occasionally roast meats in the open air. Down by the river,

you'll find a Viking house and boatyard with a longboat moored (see Dublinia **212**). The Norman period is represented by a generic lime-washed white **castle,** where a Norman aristocrat might have lived, and an intriguing **crannog,** or artificial island, like those where Irish farm owners lived.

There's nothing Disneyfied or hokey about this place—the costumed interpreters and guides take things seriously. Archaeological purists may sniff at these sites because they're reconstructions, but kids won't care; they'd rather see whole buildings than ruins, and the furnishings that have been added bring them to life.

(i) ℂ 053/20733; www.inhp.com.

🚌 Wexford.

🛏 $$$ **Kelly's Resort Hotel,** Wexford-Rosslare Harbor Rd., Rosslare (ℂ **053/32114;** www.kellys.ie). $$ **Rosslare Great Souther,** Wexford-Rosslare Harbor Rd. (ℂ **800/44-UTELL** in U.S. 053/33233; www.gsh.ie).

WHY THEY'LL THANK YOU: Blows the dust off ancient times.

Bunratty Castle & Folk Park
Life on the Irish Manor
All ages • Bunratty, County Clare, Ireland

GET OFF THE PLANE IN SHANNON, IRELAND, and you may be disappointed to drive right onto a stretch of superhighway without a thatched cottage or a single-lane country road in sight. But never fear, traditional Ireland is not far away. In fact, you can get your first taste of it—and a very satisfying first taste at that—just off that highway at Bunratty Castle.

Nestled beside the O'Garney River, Bunratty Castle is Ireland's most complete **medieval castle.** Children may wonder at first what happened to the rest of it—this appears to be just one big tower with

a moat, not the sort of walled keep with a grand inner house that they may be familiar with. But in Ireland that other sort of castle belonged to the era of the Norman invaders; by the time Bunratty was built, in 1425, fortified towers were extremely popular among Ireland's wealthy families, built as "safe houses" to protect the inhabitants from their feuding neighbors. Walk across the stout drawbridge and you'll find a carefully restored ancient stronghold, full of authentic furniture, armorial stained glass, tapestries, weapons, and works of art.

On the 8-hectare (20-acre) property surrounding Bunratty Castle, Bunratty Folk Park shows visitors the more plebeian side of Irish life, and my family actually found this much more engrossing. An entire **19th-century Irish village** has been re-created, complete with outlying thatched cottages and farmhouses. The main village street has a school, post office, pub, grocery store, print shop, ice-cream store, and hotel—all open for browsing and shopping. Fresh scones are baked in the cottages, and craftspeople ply such trades as knitting, weaving, candle making, pottery, and photography. Up on a hill (with fabulous views of the countryside) sits the slightly larger home where a family of the minor gentry lived, socially distinct from both the grand folks at the castle and the village people.

At night, the castle's baronial Great Hall serves as a candlelit setting for a 3-hour **medieval banquet.** Guests are seated at long trestle tables, where platters of traditional dishes (made with modern Irish ingredients) are served, to be eaten in strictly medieval use-your-fingers style and washed down with mulled wine, claret, and mugs of the traditional honey-based drink called mead. Hokey, yes, but undeniably fun. As a counterpoint, the Folk Park offers an "at home" evening in a farmhouse cottage, with homey Irish stew and soda bread and trad music played on fiddle, flute, and bodhran.

ⓘ Limerick-Ennis Rd. (N18; ℂ **061/ 360788**).

✈ Shannon International Airport, 29km (18 miles).

🛏 $ **Bunratty Woods,** Low Rd., Bunratty (ℂ **061/369689;** www.iol.ie/~bunratty). $$$ **Dromoland Castle,** N18, Newmarket-on-Fergus (ℂ **800/346-7007** in the U.S., or 061/368144; www.dromoland.ie).

WHY THEY'LL THANK YOU: From castle to cottage, the whole authentic historic shebang.

Historic Restorations

Swiss Open-Air Museum
Walk into an Alpine Panorama
All ages • Ballenberg, near Brienz, Switzerland

Tucked into the German part of the Swiss Alps—the Bernese Oberland—the Swiss Open-Air Museum looks like a scene out of *Heidi,* with clusters of typical old farm buildings, tiny Alpine settlements, and gardens and fields being cultivated with traditional agricultural methods. It's a sprawling site, covering more than 809 hectares (2,000 acres)—prepare to do a lot of walking—set up like a mini-Switzerland, with 13 different geographic groupings from the Jura to the Valais. Fringed with stands of dark pine and wildflower-spangled meadows, it's a charming slice of Swiss countryside where kids can scamper and roam around in the fresh Alpine air.

The oldest building here is a rough timber farmhouse from 1336. Yes, of course you'll see brown wooden chalets with tiny-paned windows and window boxes of red geraniums, your classic Alpine homes straight off a jigsaw puzzle, but there are many surprising variations. Look out for the house from Ostermundigen with its fanciful Baroque roofline, the wooden facade painted gray to look like expensive stone. As you wander around (I'd plan for at least 3 hr. to see it all), ask the kids to note the different roof materials, from thatch to wood shingles to tiles, and to compare the half-timbered homes to weathered brown frame-and-plank construction, with white plaster walls appearing in some of the newer homes (if you can call the 17th c. new!). Notice how efficiently these Swiss ancestors made their homes play multiple roles, tucking in a threshing floor or a weaving cellar and attaching a barn (no doubt it was easier to milk the cows on a winter morning that way).

Children are also delighted to discover how many **farm animals** live on-site, some 250 of them—everything from bees and hens to pigs and horses, including a few nearly extinct breeds of goats and cattle, many of which the kids can pet. **Craft demonstrations** are scatted among the hamlets, showing not only common domestic skills like cheese making, bread baking, spinning, and weaving, but more specialized skills such as bobbin lace making and the woodcarving for which this region is famous. Don't miss the **Oberentfelden house,** where every

historic object is purposely laid out for kids to touch.

It's a handy day trip from Interlaken, past the resorts of Lake Brienz. Guided tours are available, for an extra fee (reserve ahead), but they aren't necessary—just roaming around is all the fun you'll need.

(i) (C) **033/952-10-30;** www.ballenberg.ch.

🚃 Brienz, 17km (11 miles) from Interlaken.

🛏 $ **The Swiss Inn,** Général Guisanstrasse 23, Interlaken ((C) **033/822-36-26;** www. swiss-inn.com). $$$ **Victoria-Jungfrau Grand Hotel,** Höheweg 41, Interlaken ((C) **800/223-6800** or 033/828-28-28; www.victoria-jung frau.ch).

WHY THEY'LL THANK YOU: Petting the goats.

Edo-Tokyo Museum
The Heritage of Old Japan
All ages • Tokyo & Koganei City, Japan

TOKYO IS UNFORTUNATELY SHORT on architectural heritage—between the 19th-century mania for Westernization, the 1923 Great Kanto Earthquake, and World War II air raids, few traditional Japanese buildings have survived. Enter the Edo-Tokyo Museum (Edo-Tokyo Hakubutsukan), a city government project to create a **3-D timeline of Tokyo** from its humble beginnings in 1590, the era of the first shogun, to the 1964 Tokyo Olympics. It was an ambitious plan indeed—and a huge success.

The main facility—and the easiest to get to—is on two floors of a spaceshiplike building near Asakusa. Starting on the sixth floor, you'll walk over a replica of Nihombashi Bridge, the starting point for all roads leading out of old Edo. Some of the exhibits are scale models, others lifesize re-creations of such buildings as a

late-Edo longhouse (cramped quarters for the commoners), a Kabuki playhouse, an 1870 newspaper office. As you move from the Edo Period displays to the modern era, you'll notice the creeping influence of Western architecture—there's even a Ford Model-A taxi parked in front of a house, from the days when Japan had no auto industry. One of the most intriguing rooms shows life during the WWII air raids, with taped windowpanes and blackout shades on the light fixtures.

As a fan of historic re-creations, though, I much prefer the outdoor half of this museum, even though it's out in Koganei, a half-hour's train ride from Shinjuku. This **open-air architectural park** is a vivid portrayal of the evolution of Tokyo. Some 30 original structures, many of them weathered by age, were moved here from around Japan and placed on small streets in chronological order. You can go inside and prowl around, comparing the 1742 thatched-roof farmhouse with its tatami floors and central fire pit with the modern kitchen of a 1920s-era home. You'll visit a 1929 bathhouse, all its tiles and faucets gleaming; an early Meiji tailor's shop; a 1933 store where bottles of soy sauce and sake line the shelves and a bright yellow 1960s streetcar waiting at its stop.

If the kids enjoy the Edo-Tokyo, you might also try the **Fukagawa Edo Museum,** 1–3–28 Shirakawa, Koto-ku (② **03/3630-8625**), a hangarlike building with 11 full-scale replicas of traditional houses, vegetable and rice shops, a fish store, two inns, a fire watchtower, and

tenement homes, re-creating an actual 19th-century neighborhood. The village even changes with the seasons—the trees sprout cherry blossoms in spring—and, every 45 minutes or so, undergoes a day's cycle from morning (roosters crow, lights brighten) to night (the sun sets, the retractable roof closes to make everything dark).

(i) **Edo-Tokyo Museum,** 1–4–1 Yokoami, Sumida-ku, Tokyo (② **03/3626-9974;** www.edo-tokyo-museum.or.jp). **Open Air Architectural Museum,** 3–7–1 Sakura-cho, Koganei City (② **02/388-3300**).

✈ ⊨ See Tokyo ⑤⑨.

WHY THEY'LL THANK YOU: Seeing what all those skyscrapers replaced.

Historic Restorations

219

Plimoth Plantation
The Pilgrims' Progress
All ages • Plymouth, Massachusetts, USA

Every American schoolchild knows about Plymouth—about how the Pilgrims, fleeing religious persecution, left Europe on the *Mayflower* and set up a settlement at Plymouth in December 1620. What you won't know until you visit is how small everything was, from the perilously tiny *Mayflower* to the landing point at Plymouth Rock. But rather than feel disappointed, children will probably be awed to realize just how difficult this venture was, and how brave the settlers were to attempt what they did.

The logical place to begin (good luck talking kids out of it) is at **Plymouth Rock.** This landing place of the *Mayflower* passengers was originally 15 feet long and 3 feet wide, though it has eroded over the centuries and been moved many times. The portico that protects the rock,

erected in 1920, makes it harder to imagine Pilgrims springing off the boat onto shore, but the atmosphere is still inspiring. ***Mayflower II,*** a Plimoth Plantation attraction berthed beside Plymouth Rock, is a full-scale replica of the type of ship that brought the Pilgrims from England to America in 1620; you'll be amazed that 102 voyagers survived a transatlantic voyage on a wooden vessel only 107 feet long. Costumed guides give first-person accounts of the voyage, and alongside the ship museum shops provide a stage set of early Pilgrim dwellings.

Having landed, now you're ready for the big attraction: **Plimoth Plantation,** an extensive re-creation of the 1627 Pilgrim village. Enter by the hilltop fort that protected the village and walk down to the farm area, visiting homes and gardens

The *Mayflov*

ONE OF OUR BEST FAMILY VACATIONS EVER
3-day getaway to Colonial William
one of those summer trips we
poned for years, waiting unt
kids were old enough to
history. The weather w
then pouring rain—
tered. Williamsb
levels, it's a sl
lot, but the
ever exp
It's
ho

constructe
toric detail. Plimoth has some of the most convincing costumed reenactors in the country, who chat with visitors while going about daily tasks as they were done in the 1600s. Sometimes you can join the activities—perhaps planting, harvesting, witnessing a trial, or visiting a wedding party.

Though the Pilgrims enjoyed friendly relations with the native Wampanoags (nearby **Hobbamock's Homesite** re-creates their village), the plantation Pilgrims still conduct daily militia drills with matchlock muskets, no doubt because boys like my sons so adore weapons demonstrations. You can buy a combination ticket with the *Mayflower II,* and admission is good for 2 days; so don't rush through the site—there's too much to see.

Two non-Plantation sites in town are worth a stop: **Pilgrim Hall Museum,** 75 Court St. (© **508/746-1620;** www.pilgrim hall.org), which displays original artifacts

Bradford's Bible, and
Wax Museum, 16 Carver St. (© **508/ 746-6468**), where more than 180 life-size figures in dioramas depict episodes in the Pilgrim story. On the hill outside is the gravesite of the Pilgrims who died that first winter—more or less half the original group, a sobering statistic indeed.

(i) Plimoth Plantation Hwy. (© **508/746-1622;** www.plimoth.org).

✈ Boston, 40 miles.

🛏 $$ **John Carver Inn,** 25 Summer St. (© **800/274-1620** or 508/746-7100; www.johncarverinn.com).

BEST TIME: Open Apr–Nov.

WHY THEY'LL THANK YOU: Makes Thanksgiving more than just a turkey dinner.

as a
sburg,
post-
all three
ake sense of its
as sweltering hot,
and none of that mat-
rg works on so many
m-dunk. The kids learned a
y also had more fun than we
ected.

also a relative bargain, considering
w much Williamsburg offers for the
oney. Rockefeller money underwrites the
301-acre site of Virginia's colonial capital,
sprucely maintaining its 88 original buildings (houses, shops, offices, inns, courthouse, jail, armory, Capitol, the works) and
hiring a top-notch staff to run things so
graciously, 21st-century hassles seem to
disappear. We bought a package pass that
admitted us to three Historic Triangle
sites—which we visited in chronological
order: Jamestown, Williamsburg, Yorktown—as well as nearby Busch Gardens
and Water Country USA. Staying on
Colonial Williamsburg property, we
could walk in and out of the historic area,
and at check-in we booked as many extras
as we could from a crowded activity
schedule. We had dinner in one of the taverns on-site (for reservations call Ⓒ **800/
TAVERNS**), eating surprisingly delicious
authentic dishes by candlelight with live
minstrels strolling around. We watched an
actor channel Patrick Henry for an hour,
deftly answering the audience's every
question. All the costumed interpreters
stationed around the site are amazingly
well-informed; some of them refuse to
admit they aren't living in 1770 (almost a
running joke with the visitors watching
them), but others are more relaxed, like

the cabinetmaker who jokingly asked us to
bring him some Dunkin' Donuts—and even
he had PhD-level knowledge of his era, not
just cabinetry but agriculture, the colonial
economy, and pre-Revolutionary politics,
and we were fascinated by our half-hour
chat while he turned chair legs on his
lathe.

Jamestown, the first permanent
English settlement in the New World,
was a great surprise: You can drive
around the actual site, with ruins of the
original buildings, but the kids got
more out of the Jamestown Settlement
reconstruction—they could really see the
alarmingly tiny ships that brought the settlers from England in 1607, and the primitive stockaded settlement, scarcely more
sophisticated than the replica Powhatan
Indian village nearby. At **Yorktown,** where
Washington won the final victory of the
American Revolution in 1781, we drove
around the battlefield route and explored a
replica army camp. Next time we'll skip
Busch Gardens, but **Water Country USA**
was a marvelous surprise, the perfect
goofy way to end our history-packed 3
days.

ⓘ **Williamsburg Visitor Center,** VA
132 south of U.S. 60 bypass (Ⓒ **800/
HISTORY** or 757/220-7645; www.colonial
williamsburg.com).

✈ Newport News, 14 miles.

🛏 $$ **Radisson Fort Magruder Hotel,**
6545 Pocahontas Trail (U.S. 60; Ⓒ **800/
333-3333** or 757/220-2250). $$ **Williamsburg Woodlands Hotel & Suites,** 105 Visi-
tors Center Dr. (Ⓒ **800/HISTORY** or 757/
229-1000; www.colonialwilliamsburg.com).

WHY THEY'LL THANK YOU: Being
extras in a history movie.

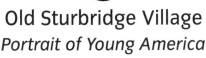

Old Sturbridge Village
Portrait of Young America
All ages • Sturbridge, Massachusetts, USA

Lᴇᴛ's ʙᴇ ʜᴏɴᴇsᴛ: Old Sturbridge Village is a fabricated tourist attraction, an early-19th-century village composed of authentic buildings moved here from other locations. The costumed docents around the site are only pretending to follow the pursuits of 170 years past. But Sturbridge Village is a careful, thoughtful re-creation, and my family warms to it because it depicts an ordinary farm village, and illustrates a period of time they haven't studied to death.

Only 1 of the more than **40 restored structures** in the complex stands on its original site—the Oliver Wight House, now part of the Old Sturbridge Village Motor Lodges (see below). The rest were transported here from as far away as Maine. But all are authentic buildings and they represent the living quarters and places of trade and commerce of a rural settlement of the 1830s. What struck us, in comparison to other historic re-creations, was that by the 1830s a more diversified economy was beginning to emerge; not only are there shops for traditional trades like blacksmithing and printing and coopering, but there is a shoe shop and a tinsmith's shop (tin ware had become a popular commodity by the era). At the edge of the village sits an industrial area with a gristmill, a sawmill, even a carding mill for the nascent textile industry. A professional class is starting to emerge by this time, too, with a lawyer setting up his tiny white frame office downtown and a country bank that issued its own currency to farmers, replacing the old barter system for local transactions. There's both a Quaker meetinghouse and a regular Congregational meetinghouse, showing the growth of religious diversity.

It's also a very kid-oriented attraction: Some of the village's "residents" include children who roll hoops and play games true to the period, and there's a **children's museum** where kids 3 to 7 can dress up in costumes and use their imaginations in a pretend farm kitchen and one-room school.

As opposed to Williamsburg **220** and Plimoth **219**, Sturbridge is not a place where historic events took place—it's just an ordinary hometown. And while we like open-air museums like Shelburne **224** and Bunratty **216** where different eras are dramatically juxtaposed, at Sturbridge you can look down the town common and, for a split second, imagine you really do live in the 1830s.

ⓘ **Old Sturbridge Village,** 1 Old Sturbridge Village Rd. **Visitors Center,** 380 Main St. (✆ **800/733-1830** or 508/347-3362; www.osv.org).

✈ Bradley International, 42 miles.

🛏 **Old Sturbridge Village Motor Lodges,** Rte. 20 (✆ **508/347-3327;** www.osv.org).

WHY THEY'LL THANK YOU: Everyday life is history, too.

Kidstory, a learning gallery for children at Sturbridge Village.

Charles Towne Landing
Carolina's Great Colonial Port
All ages • Charleston, South Carolina, USA

IN SOME WAYS all of Charleston, South Carolina, is a historic re-creation, full of stately homes and gardens and drawling Old South decorum. Like any city, however, it started as a village, and its humble beginnings are reconstructed today at Charles Towne Landing. It's refreshingly modest, with the real feel of a struggling settlement in a raw new territory.

Carolina was originally named for King Charles of England, who in 1663, strapped for funds, gave eight of his most generous supporters a huge chunk of North America (encompassing most of present-day North Carolina, South Carolina, and Georgia). These so-called Lords Proprietors had no interest in living there, but they recruited a crew of rice growers from Barbados to farm the land, who arrived on the banks of the Ashley River in 1670. Within a decade they had established Charles Towne—again named for the king—at the fine natural harbor where the Ashley and Cooper rivers meet. Bumper crops of rice and indigo (produced by slave labor, of course) soon made South Carolina the wealthiest of England's American colonies, and Charleston remained America's busiest seaport until well into the 19th century.

Today, 663 acres at the site of that first settlement has been turned into charming Charles Towne Landing. Exhibits showing the colony's history have been tucked underground; aboveground you'll see a re-creation of a small village, a full-scale reproduction of the 17th-century trading vessel *Adventure* (overseas trade was a key factor in Charles Towne's boom), and a replica of a 17th-century crop garden where the rice, indigo, and cotton were grown. There's no flashy theme-park atmosphere here: What you see as you walk under huge old oaks, past freshwater lagoons, and through the Animal Forest (with the same species that lived here in 1670, from bears to bison) is just what those early settlers saw. Costumed interpreters conduct hands-on learning projects, and you can rent a bike to explore 80 acres of gardens along the marsh and lagoons.

After touring the open-air park, you may also want to visit several of Charleston's historic homes, including the **Heyward-Washington House,** 87 Church St. (📞 **843/722-0354**), built in 1772 by the "rice king" Daniel Heyward, with its authentic 18th-century kitchen; and **Magnolia Plantation,** S.C. 61 (📞 **800/367-3517** or 843/571-1266; www.magnoliaplantation.com), where the Drayton family have lived since the 1670s, with its simple pre-Revolutionary house (not the original, but an authentic substitute).

ⓘ 1500 Old Towne Rd. (📞 **843/852-4200;** www.discoversouthcarolina.com).

✈ Charleston International.

🛏 $$$ **Ansonborough Inn,** 21 Hasell St. (📞 **800/522-2073** or 843/723-1655; www.ansonboroughinn.com). $ **Best Western King Charles Inn,** 237 Meeting St. (📞 **800/528-1234** or 843/723-7451; www.kingcharlesinn.com).

WHY THEY'LL THANK YOU: Wandering the old-fashioned forest.

Old Town State Historic Park
Spanish Village of Old California
All ages • San Diego, California, USA

IN CALIFORNIA, colonial history moves south to north—it was down in San Diego that the first Spanish missionary, Father Junipero Serra, came from Mexico in 1769 to begin converting the Native Americans, and he steadily moved north from there (see California Mission Trail 🔵243). While the mission building was soon moved up the hill, this scatter of adobe buildings was the nucleus of the original town of San Diego.

Old Town's buildings have been furnished to re-create the early life of the city as it was from around 1821 to 1872. This is where San Diego's Mexican heritage shines brightest—the stars and stripes weren't raised over Old Town until 1846. In the 1820s, the town's commercial center moved closer to the waterfront, giving rise eventually to the Victorian-era **Gaslamp Quarter** (which has also been outfitted as a tourist destination, with more commercial wallop); this area was no longer prime real estate, and thus escaped redevelopment. Seven of the park's 20 structures are original; the others were constructed to supplement them in the 1930s. Among the sites are an unbelievably tiny schoolhouse; a newspaper office; La Casa de Estudillo, a mansion built around a typical central courtyard, which depicts the living conditions of a wealthy family in 1872; and the high-raftered barn of Seeley Stables, named after A. L. Seeley, who ran the stagecoach and mail service in these parts from 1867 to 1871. Pick up a map at Park Headquarters, and while you're there check out the displayed model of Old Town as it looked in 1872.

What our family liked about Old Town was its lack of preciousness—it isn't walled off from the surrounding city, and its dusty wide main street feels like a lonely Wild West outpost. When you're here, it's hard to believe that something as slick as Sea World is only a few miles away. There isn't a nonstop program of stage activities, the way there is at Williamsburg 🔵220, although on Wednesday and Saturday costumed park volunteers reenact life in the 1800s with cooking and crafts demonstrations, a working blacksmith, and parlor singing. Every day there's a free 1-hour **walking tour;** but it's entirely possible to explore the site on your own, and it won't exhaust you. All around the historic complex are restaurants, some Mexican, some not. It's a relaxed, small-scale place, no hustle, no bustle—which, come to think of it, was probably just what that early settlement was like, too.

ⓘ 4002 Wallace St. (ⓒ **619/220-5422;** www.oldtownsandiego.org).

✈ 🛏 See San Diego Zoo 🔵131.

WHY THEY'LL THANK YOU: Settling America with a Spanish accent.

Shelburne Museum: American Hodgepodge

Ages 6 & up • Shelburne, Vermont, USA

MOST HISTORIC RESTORATIONS CHOOSE ONE ERA— sometimes even one specific year—and adhere to it scrupulously. The charming thing about the Shelburne Museum is that it hops from one time period to another. In the course of an afternoon, you can wander through an immense red round Shaker-style barn, a mahogany-paneled 1906 side-wheeler excursion steamer, and a quaint 19th-century farmhouse with stenciled walls. To add to the pleasure, the whole collection is scattered over 45 rolling acres of bucolic Vermont countryside, right by the shores of Lake Champlain.

Established in 1947 by Americana collector Electra Havemeyer Webb, the museum contains one of the nation's most singular collections of **American decorative, folk, and fine art,**

occupying some 37 buildings, transported whole to this site from around New England and New York. Like many historic collections, it has a blacksmith's shop, a print shop, a one-room schoolhouse, a brick meeting house, a stagecoach inn, and a settler's cabin with rough-hewn wood walls. But the mix also includes a lighthouse, a covered bridge, and a rail station, where the locomotive once used to pull the President's train sits on a siding. The **Circus Building** is a sure-fire child pleaser, with a vintage carousel outside and two spectacular hard-carved miniature circuses inside, one of them including no fewer than 35,000 tiny figures.

My two favorite spots here, though, are the re-created **Park Avenue apartment** of Electra Webb, furnished in 1930s

1950s kitchen at the Shelburne Museum.

elegance, with incredible Monets and Degases on the walls, and the **1950s ranch house,** with its Early American living room and yellow Formica kitchen, loaded with authentic items I recognized from that not-so-long-ago era. Suddenly the past seems truly alive when I enter those rooms (though it was sobering to realize that my kids still considered the 1950s house as "full of old stuff").

My preferred way to approach the Shelburne Museum in summer is to ride the **Lake Champlain car ferry** from Essex, New York (*©* **802/864-9804;** www. ferries.com). It's a pleasant glide across this beautiful lake, and we feel almost as if we've come from another country, into an odd and delightful place where you can wander randomly through time.

🛈 Rte. 7 (*©* **802/985-3346;** www.shelburne museum.org).

✈ Burlington, 15 miles.

🛏 $$$ **The Inn at Shelburne Farms,** Harbor Rd., Shelburne (*©* **802/985-8498;** www.shelburnefarms.org). $ **Smart Suites,** 1700 Shelburne Rd., South Burlington (*©* **877/862-1986**).

BEST TIME: Open May–Oct.

WHY THEY'LL THANK YOU: A time machine with lots of different buttons to push.

Greenfield Village
Henry Ford's History Lesson
All ages • Dearborn, Michigan, USA

AUTOMOBILE MAGNATE HENRY FORD had two passions: cars and history. No, make that three passions: cars, history, and philanthropy. (Plus he was really into clocks.) Once the phenomenal success of his Model T made him a multimillionaire, he could indulge all these passions by building a 90-acre indoor-outdoor museum complex. And Ford couldn't have spent his money any better.

Greenfield Village is more than just another historic re-creation; it's a glorious hodgepodge of actual homes transported here from around the United States (and even a few from Europe), most of them associated with specific individuals Ford admired. With money-is-no-object largesse, Ford acquired the home and bicycle shop of the Wright brothers, the farm where tire maker Harvey Firestone grew up, the workshop of botanist Luther Burbank, a courthouse where country lawyer Abraham Lincoln tried cases, the boyhood home where H. J. Heinz first bottled horseradish sauce. He snapped up the homes of poet Robert Frost and dictionary author Noah Webster, and a schoolhouse where educator William McGuffey taught. Ford's own birthplace is here, too. If he couldn't get the original, Ford had a meticulous replica made, as he did with George Washington Carver's log cabin birthplace (see ❷❹❽) and Thomas Edison's New Jersey invention complex (see ❸❶). Keeping these homes company are everything from a Cotswold stone cottage to a Cape Cod windmill to a set of Georgia slave quarters to a London clockmaker's mechanical glockenspiel to a fanciful 1913 carousel. You won't be able to imagine yourself into any single era, but you'll sure pick up vivid snippets of the past.

Once you've done Greenfield Village, there's yet more to see at the **Henry Ford Museum** next door, a 12-acre repository of Americana. With the same sort of acquisitive curiosity, Ford's staff assembled collections of historic airplanes (including the Fokker that Admiral Byrd used to explore the Arctic) and of course cars—everything from a 1901 Model T to one of the few existing '48 Tuckers to the limousine in which President John F. Kennedy was shot. My favorite things here are an original neon McDonalds sign, an unsolicited testimonial scrawled by bank robber Clyde Barrow ("I have drove Fords exclusively when I could get away with one"), and Buckminster Fuller's 1946 house of the future. From here, you can also take a tour of the famous **Ford Rouge Plant,** where you can see in action the factory assembly line process that made Ford's fortune. Two days is not enough time to see everything here.

ⓘ 20900 Oakwood Blvd. (✆ **313/271-1620;** www.hfmgv.org).

✈ Detroit Metropolitan, 10 miles.

🛏 $$$ **Dearborn Inn,** 20301 Oakwood Blvd. (✆ **800/228-9290** or 313/271-2700; www.marriotthotels.com). $ **Econo Lodge Dearborn,** 23730 Michigan Ave. (✆ **313/565-7250;** www.choicehotels.com.

WHY THEY'LL THANK YOU: History is made by individuals.

Native Americans 226

National Museum of the American Indian

Ages 6 & up • Washington, D.C., USA

Aᴍᴏɴɢ ᴛʜᴇ ꜱᴛᴀᴛᴇʟʏ ᴡʜɪᴛᴇ ꜱᴛᴏɴᴇ ᴘᴀʟᴀᴄᴇꜱ lining the National Mall, this Smithsonian branch really stands out: A burnt sand-colored exterior of kasota limestone wraps around undulating walls, echoing the pueblos and hogans of the Southwest tribes; with its bands of reflective windows peering out like eagle eyes, it also reminds me of some sort of Northwest tribal totem. Inside, a huge rotunda lobby is filled with celestial references, from the equinoxes and solstices mapped on the floor to the sky visible in the oculus dome, 120 feet overhead, and nature is brought in throughout the galleries—wonderfully appropriate for a museum celebrating Native peoples.

As one of the Smithsonian's newest branches, the American Indian museum shakes off the dusty approaches of the past, and has so much more than just exhibits in glass cases. Of course, it has an amazing number of artifacts to display, with its core collection of 800,000 **Native American artifacts** assembled by George Gustav Heyer—wood and stone carvings, masks, pottery, feather bonnets, and so on, representing some 1,000 Native communities through North and South America. Children can be lost for minutes, studying some of these intricate handmade objects. While there are many fine museums showcasing one tribal group or another, this one includes all the native populations of the Western Hemisphere, and many of the exhibits are organized around cross-cultural themes. (Never before had I noticed so many connections between North and South American tribes.)

The museum's designers also purposely made this a "living" museum, with Native peoples performing, storytelling, and displaying their own art alongside the historic exhibits—and that fabulous atrium entrance turns out to be perfect for **ceremonial dances.** Workshops include **demonstrations** of traditional arts such as weaving or basket making; a roster of **films** includes a number of animated shorts that retell nature legends and creation myths. Almost every exhibit, it seems, has a video of some tribe member explaining the significance of this or

National Museum of the American Indian.

that custom—a much easier way for kids to learn than reading blocks of text mounted on a wall. Again, how appropriate for a Native American museum to honor oral tradition.

Some of the exhibit themes are a bit too anthropological, or too politically complex, for children to follow, but just looking at the precious objects can be enough. A pair of traditional beaded moccasins alongside red high-top sneakers hand-painted with tribal motifs—that's the sort of thing kids intuitively get.

ⓘ 4th St. and Independence Ave. SW (ⓒ **202/633-1000;** www.nmai.si.edu).

✈ 🛏 See The National Mall **63**.

WHY THEY'LL THANK YOU: Seeing what life's like for children of the tribe.

Native Americans

227

Mashantucket Pequot Museum
A Forgotten Tribe's History Lesson
All ages • Mashantucket, Connecticut, USA

IN 1992, A NEARLY EXTINCT Native American tribe—the Mashantucket Pequots, only 520 individuals—was granted permission to open a gambling casino on their ancestral lands deep in the southeastern Connecticut woods. What began as a bingo parlor grew to a casino, which then needed a hotel, and—presto!—within 3 years they had the world's most profitable gaming operation, Foxwoods, on their hands. With their newfound wealth, the tribe poured $139 million into a museum dedicated to Native American arts and culture, opened in 1998. Whatever the locals think about their gazillionaire Indian neighbors, all agree on one thing: They sure got a fabulous museum for their money.

Thoughtful, not glitzy, the Mashantucket Pequot Museum delves into **Native American history** in 3-D—instead of tired beads and feathers

pinned behind a glass case, you can look at models, dioramas, and films; listen to oral histories (many in native languages, including the Pequots' Passamaquoddy tongue); and use interactive consoles. Beautiful murals have been painted by Native American artists (and not just Pequots—with so much money on hand, the tribe has done some significant reaching out to other less fortunate tribes).

These exhibits go way back in time, all the way to the Ice Age, as you descend into a re-created glacial crevasse, frigid temperatures, dripping water, and all. There's also a diorama of an **ancient caribou hunt.** To me, the most absorbing exhibit was the extensive life-size **Pequot Village re-creation,** which you can walk through: Sounds and even smells are wafted through the air as you pass wigwams, canoes, and fake campfires where costumed figures go about

253

their daily business, fishing, hunting, cooking, butchering animals, basket weaving, and pottery making. We loved the newlyweds building their first wigwam together. My teenage son appreciated the museum's frank discussion of conflicts between the Pequots and new Dutch and English settlers, culminating in a reconstruction of the 17th-century Pequot fort at Mystic, which was attacked in 1637 by European settlers. But the story doesn't end there; you see how Pequots lived on, fitting into the Connecticut community (a 2-acre outdoor farmstead is open spring through fall). The last

display is a trailer home, marking a sad chapter in a proud tribe's history. Of course we know that wasn't the end for the Pequots—just take a look down the road at Foxwoods.

ⓘ 110 Pequot Trail (✆ **800/411-9671;** www.pequotmuseum.org).

✈ Providence, 45 miles.

🛏 $$ **Two Trees Inn,** 240 Lantern Hill Rd. (✆ **800/369-9663** or 860/312-3000; www.foxwoods.com).

WHY THEY'LL THANK YOU: A culture resurrected.

Native Americans **228**

Indian City USA: Visit with the Tribes
All ages • Anadarko, Oklahoma, USA

Sʟɪᴄᴋ ɪᴛ ɪsɴ'ᴛ, but that's what I find appealing about Indian City USA. Located on 200 acres of flat plains carved out of the surrounding Kiowa, Apache, and Commanche reservations, this attraction presents seven authentic replica villages, representing several Southern Plains Indian tribes. Tours are led by actual tribe members, and the extensive gift shop (a great place to get Indian dolls, moccasins, drums, and the hatchets my sons crave) sells the work of tribal artists and artisans. It's been around since the 1950s, and it looks every bit its age; but if you're trying to catch the spirit of an ancient people, high-tech glitz seems beside the point, when you can get the story from the people themselves.

The **Navajo** village shows two different styles of circular hogans as well as an outdoor oven for baking bread. The **Chiricahua Apache** village shows several of the brush-covered wickiups that this nomadic tribe used, one of them being used as a sort of sauna. Women were the builders in the **Wichita** tribe, and their 40-foot-high Council Lodge is Indian City's most impressive structure, a

massive circular lodge of pine poles covered with willow branches and then swamp grass. The **Kiowa** Winter Camp, with its two travel-ready animal-hide tepees set inside a willow fence, is also typical of a Commanche or Arapaho camp, complete with a travois for hauling the tepee from site to site during hunting season. The wattle-and-daub homes of the **Apache Caddo** village, in contrast, are permanent dwellings for an agricultural people that stayed in one spot. Go inside the two **Pawnee** earth lodges to see how complex the interiors of these simple-seeming sod mounds could be. A neat **Pueblo** adobe home, which you can step inside, completes the collection. A large swath of the site has been turned over to a 140-acre Exotic Game Pasture.

Many artifacts of daily life have been installed in these residences—weapons, cooking utensils, drying racks for hides and meat—and even more are displayed in the museum in the visitor center lodge. To see still more Native artifacts, stop by the **Southern Plains Indian Museum,** 715 E. Central Blvd., or U.S. 62, just east of Anadarko (✆ **405/247-6221**). Check

Indian City's website before planning your trip, to see if you can time your visit to coincide with its periodic Indian ceremonials and dances.

ⓘ 311 E. Main St. (ⓒ **800/433-5661** or 405/247-5661; www.indiancityusa.com).

✈ Oklahoma City, 48 miles.

🛏 $$$ **Renaissance Oklahoma City Hotel,** 10 N. Broadway, Oklahoma City

(ⓒ **800/Hotels-1** or 405/228-8000; www.renaissancehotels.com). $$ **Wingate Inn,** 2001 S. Meridian Ave., Oklahoma City (ⓒ **800/228-1000** or 405/682-3600; www.wingateinns.com).

WHY THEY'LL THANK YOU: Hunters versus farmers—match the home to the lifestyle.

Knife River Indian Villages
Big Towns in the Dakotas
All ages • Stanton, North Dakota, USA

Wᴴᴇɴ ᴛʜᴇ Lᴇᴡɪs ᴀɴᴅ Cʟᴀʀᴋ ᴇxᴘᴇᴅɪᴛɪᴏɴ came through the Dakotas in 1804, they found three tribes of Northern Plains Indians living along the Missouri River in large, socially complex towns, a far more populous area than today. Having shifted to agriculture from their old nomadic lifestyle, these farming tribes flourished on the fertile Missouri flood plains, where there was also a lucrative trade in flint from the banks of the aptly named Knife River. This was where the white explorers met a French fur trader and his Shoshone captive wife, Sacagawea, who joined their expedition as interpreter and guide. The 1837 smallpox epidemic decimated the Hidatsa, Mandan, and Arikara tribes, but today their culture is honored at this lovely park along the Knife River, just before it flows into the Missouri.

Hands-on exhibits at the excellent **visitor center** explain tribal culture, but the thing you really want to see is behind the center: the **earth lodge,** a detailed reconstruction of a typical Hidatsa home. The men used tepees on bison hunts, but in this matriarchal society, women owned the lodges, and they were sizable permanent dwellings, 40 to 50 feet across, with timber supports and sod roofs. (The sod

houses built by early Great Plains pioneers were inspired by earth lodges.) A central fire pit was used for cooking, warmth, and curing leather; the floors are covered with bulrush mats, a shrine to ancient spirits sits along one wall, and an underground covered pit stores extra food. Weapons such as lances, shields, and war clubs hang ready from the rafters, but there are also toys, such as a hoop-and-stick game and a miniature tepee for dolls.

Ask to check out a **kids' discovery pack** at the visitor center before heading out on the nature trails; it comes with binoculars, a bird identification kit, and a magnifying glass. Naturalists see this site as a valuable link to the past, before dams altered the Missouri River's flow. Bottomlands beside the river are forested with cottonwood, willow, box elder, and other plants that thrive on being flooded every spring; an escarpment then rises above flood level, where the terrain is sturdy mid-grass prairie, a complex mix of grasses and wildflowers. Look sharp and the kids'll spot gophers, white-tailed deer, cottontail rabbits, and ground squirrels, as well as wild turkeys, pheasants, and sharp-tailed grouses.

If possible, come the last weekend in July for the **Northern Plains Indian Culture Fest,** a bustling 2-day event featuring artisans, storytellers, and costumed interpreters, bringing to life this traditional culture in fascinating detail.

(i) Country Rd. 37 (© **701/745-3300;** www.nps.gov/knri).

✈ Bismarck, 50 miles.

🛏 $$ **Best Western Ramkota Hotel,** 800 S. 3rd St., Bismarck (© **800/780-7234** or 701/258-7700; www.bestwestern.com). $ **Days Inn Bismarck,** 1300 E. Capitol Ave., Bismarck (© **800/329-7466** or 701/223-9151; www.daysinn.com).

WHY THEY'LL THANK YOU: That cozy earth lodge.

Native Americans **230**

The Hopi Reservations
Secret Ceremonies from Ancient Times
Ages 6 & up • Arizona, USA

FOR THE HOPI PEOPLE, this remote Arizona landscape of flat-topped mesas and barren plains is the center of the universe. They have lived for nearly 1,000 years on this grouping of mesas, completely encircled today by the Navajo Reservation. Here the Hopi preserve their complex ancient customs, including the famous masked kachina dances (Jan–July) and death-defying Snake Dances (Aug–Dec). Though these are generally closed to non-Hopis, you may be able to view social dances, held August through February— ask when you're on the reservation, and you might get lucky. Hopiland is not theme-park perfect—most villages on the reservation are straggles of modern homes scattered along roughly 20 miles of Ariz. 264—but that's one of the things I like about it.

At the top of First Mesa, tiny historic **Walpi** is the best place for visitors to learn more about life in the Hopi villages—1-hour tours are offered daily (sign up at the **Ponsi Hall Visitor Center;** © 928/737-2262). Small stone houses seem to grow directly from the rock of the mesa top, and ladders jut from the roofs of kivas; the view stretches for hundreds of miles. On Second Mesa you'll find the **Hopi Cultural Center,** Ariz. 264 (© **928/734-6650**), a combination museum, motel, and restaurant. On

the Third Mesa, the Hopi claim **Oraibi** is the oldest continuously occupied town in the United States—it dates from 1150. Today, Oraibi is a mix of old stone houses and modern cinder-block ones.

Across the reservation, small shops sell crafts and jewelry, including kachina dolls and some beautiful coil and wicker plaque baskets. The **Monongya Gallery** (© **928/ 734-2344**), on Ariz. 264 outside of Oraibi, has one of the largest selections of kachina dolls. Kachinas, either as dolls or as masked dancers, represent spirits of everything from plants and animals to ancestors and sacred places. According to legend, the kachinas lived with the Hopi long ago, but the Hopi people made them angry and the spirits left—after passing on how to perform their ceremonies. These ceremonies are believed to bring rain to water the all-important corn crop, but they also ensure health, happiness, long life, and harmony in the universe. As part of the kachina ceremonies, dancers often bring carved wooden kachina dolls to village children.

When visiting the Hopi pueblos, respect all posted signs; remember that photographing, sketching, and recording are prohibited in the villages and at ceremonies. Kivas (ceremonial rooms) and ruins are off-limits.

(i) **Hopi Office of Public Relations,** Box 123, Kykotsmovi, AZ 86039 ((C) **928/734-3283;** www.hopi.nsn.us). **Hopi Cultural Preservation Office** ((C) **928/734-3612;** www.nau.edu/~hcpo-p).

✈ Flagstaff, 150 miles.

🛏 $$ **Hopi Cultural Center Restaurant & Inn,** Second Mesa ((C) **928/734-2401;**

www.hopiculturalcenter.com). $$$ **Quality Inn Navajo Nation,** Main Street and Moenave Avenue, Tuba City ((C) **800/644-8383** or 928/283-4545; www.quality inntubacity.com).

WHY THEY'LL THANK YOU: The Kachinas.

---

231 Native Americans

The Indian Side of Artsy Santa Fe

Ages 4 & up • Santa Fe, New Mexico, USA

WITH ITS NARROW WANDERING STREETS, flat-topped adobe buildings, and dramatic clouds overhead, Santa Fe has always had an exotic aura, deeply imbued with the spirit of the local Indians and the Spanish settlers who took the land from them. On Santa Fe's central Plaza, Native Americans sell jewelry, pottery, and weaving under the portico of the Spanish-built **Palace of the Governors,** and even the New Mexico State Capitol building has an unusual twist—it's designed in the shape of a Zia Pueblo emblem, the only round capitol building in the U.S. It's impossible to ignore the Native American context of this city.

Santa Fe is an artsy city, with lots of galleries and museums, but two in particular open doors onto Native American culture. At the **Museum of Indian Arts & Culture,** make a beeline for the interactive exhibit *Here, Now, and Always,* which you enter through a tunnel that symbolizes the *sipapu,* the Ancestral Puebloan entrance into the upper worlds, with evocative piped-in sounds of trickling water, drums, and Native American music. The taped voices of Native Americans tell tribal legends as you step into a Navajo hogan dwelling, stroll through a trading post, and contrast a traditional Pueblo kitchen with a modern kitchen—a perfect way for kids to understand how oral tradition works.

Navajo culture is the specific focus down the street at the **Wheelwright**

Museum of the American Indian; its building resembles a Navajo hogan, with its doorway facing east (toward the rising sun) and its ceiling formed in the interlocking "whirling log" style. Even if your kids aren't interested in whatever Native artworks are on display, it costs nothing to pop into the museum store, which replicates the typical turn-of-the-century trading post on Navajo reservations; experts are usually around to teach you about the various baskets, jewelry, pottery, rugs, or figures on sale.

If you don't have time to go to **Taos Pueblo** 232, stop at one of the Tiwa pueblos closer to Santa Fe, with their ancient adobe architecture, ceremonial kiva rooms (which visitors cannot enter), and resident artisans demonstrating their crafts. **San Ildefonso Pueblo,** off NM 502 ((C) **505/455-3549**), is known for its matte-finish, black-on-black pottery; a fun ceremony to catch here is the Corn Dances, held in late August or early September, which celebrate fertility. The largest of the New Mexican pueblos, **San Juan Pueblo,** NM 74, off NM 68 north of Española ((C) **505/852-4400** or 505/852-4210), has trademark pottery that's a lustrous red ceramic incised with traditional geometric symbols. The annual San Juan Fiesta, June 23 through June 24, features buffalo and Comanche dances.

(i) Museum of Indian Arts & Culture, 710 Camino Lejo (**(C) 505/476-1250;** www.miaclab.org). **Wheelwright Museum of the American Indian,** 704 Camino Lejo (**(C) 800/607-4636** or 505/982-4636; www. wheelwright.org).

✈ Albuquerque, 60 miles. Santa Fe Municipal.

🛏 $$ **El Rey Inn,** 1862 Cerrillos Rd. (**(C) 800/521-1349** or 505/982-1931; www. elreyinnsantafe.com). $$ **Old Santa Fe Inn,** 320 Galisteo St. (**(C) 800/745-9910** or 505/ 995-0800; www.oldsantafeinn.com).

WHY THEY'LL THANK YOU: Learning the difference between a hogan and a pueblo.

Native Americans 232

Taos Pueblo: Following the Old Ways

All ages • Taos, New Mexico, USA

IT'S AMAZING THAT IN OUR FRENETIC WORLD, some 150 Taos Pueblo residents still live much as their Tiwa ancestors did 1,000 years ago, without electricity and running water. Their two main buildings—**Hlauuma** (north house) and **Hlaukwima** (south house)—are a rambling series of rooms piled on top of each other, built of straw and mud with distinctive flowing rooflines that echo the shape of Taos Mountain to the northeast. The adobe exterior blends in with the surrounding mud; bright blue doors are the same shade as the sky that frames the brown buildings. The kids will intuitively feel these people's connection to the natural world.

The village looks much the same today as it did when a regiment from the Spanish explorer Coronado's expedition first came upon it in 1540. Though the Tiwa were essentially a peaceful agrarian people, in 1680 they spearheaded the only successful revolt by Native Americans in history, driving the Spanish from Santa Fe until 1692 and from Taos until 1698—you can still see the old church ruined in that uprising. The Pueblo today is actually several individual homes built side by side with common walls. Some 1,800 other Tiwas live in conventional homes on the pueblo's 95,000 acres, but though 90% of them are practicing Roman Catholics, they often still practice ancestral rituals. The center of their world is nature;

women use hornos to bake their traditional bread, and most still drink water from the sacred Blue Lake nearby.

As you explore the pueblo, you can visit the residents' **studios,** sample homemade bread, look into the **San Geronimo Chapel,** and wander past the ruins of the **old church** and **cemetery.** Ask permission from individuals before taking their photos; some will request a small payment. Do not trespass into kivas (ceremonial rooms), private homes, and other areas marked as restricted. You can buy traditional fried and oven-baked bread for the kids to sample, as well as a variety of arts and crafts like moccasins, pottery, and jewelry. To try traditional feast-day meals, stop by the **Tiwa Kitchen,** near the entrance to the pueblo. Close to Tiwa Kitchen, the **Oo-oonah Children's Art Center** displays the creative works of pueblo children.

(i) Veterans Hwy. (**(C) 505/758-1028;** www. taospueblo.com).

✈ Albuquerque, 140 miles.

🛏 See Ghost Ranch **152**.

BEST TIME: Closed 10 weeks late winter or early spring (call ahead).

WHY THEY'LL THANK YOU: Real people, living ancient lives.

British Columbia's Native Peoples
Getting to Know the First Nations
Ages 8 & up • Vancouver & Victoria, Canada

THERE'S NOTHING LIKE A GOOD TOTEM POLE to grab a kid's interest. They're gargantuan, for one thing, with those huge-eyed beaky faces stacked atop each other, often with ghastly leering expressions. An air of ancient wisdom hangs about them, and you can't help but want to know more about the Native American people—referred to as the First Nations—who made these giant wood-carvings. But there's so much more to the First Nations than totem poles, as you'll learn at two top-notch museums in British Columbia.

Vancouver's **Museum of Anthropology** is a stunning building to begin with, echoing in concrete and glass the traditional post-and-beam buildings of the First Nations people; you enter through majestic doors that resemble a giant carved bent-cedar box. Artifacts from various coastal communities flank the ramp leading to the Great Hall's over-whelming series of great **totem poles,** with dramatic floor-to-ceiling windows behind them revealing a backdrop of the North Shore mountains and English Bay.

Although this anthropology museum mainly focuses on the aboriginal culture of British Columbian natives, the First Nations are by no means extinct, and tribute is also paid to **contemporary Native artists** who carry on the traditions. Kids can caress the cedar bear and sea-wolf sculptures at the Cross Roads by Haida artist Bill Reid; everyone seems to be enraptured by Reid's huge yellow cedar carving *The Raven and the First Men,* relating a creation myth in which the trickster god Raven coaxes humanity out of its birthplace in a clamshell. The kids will have fun pulling out the glass-topped drawers in the **Visible Storage Gallery,** where more than 15,000 artifacts—spears, native ornaments, utensils, toys, and games—are tucked away. And don't forget to walk around the grounds behind the museum, where two Haida long-houses stand, positioned authentically on a north–south axis, with 10 hand-carved totem poles alongside.

If you're up for a ferry ride—and I'd take any excuse to enjoy the 95-minute ferry ride to Vancouver Island—head over to Victoria (also covered in The **Seattle-Victoria Ferry 36**) to visit the **Royal British Columbia Museum.** It's a general-interest museum, with excellent natural history and modern history exhibits, but the showpiece of the museum is its out-standing **First Peoples Gallery** on the third floor. The artifacts displayed here include a full-size re-creation of a long-house and a hauntingly wonderful gallery of totem poles and masks. And the fun continues outside, in Thunderbird Park beside the museum, where you can watch a team of Native carvers working on new totem poles in a cedar longhouse.

(i) **Museum of Anthropology,** 6393 NW Marine Dr., Vancouver (*©* **604/822-5087;** www.moa.ubc.ca). **Royal British Columbia Museum,** 675 Belleville St., Victoria (*©* **888/447-7977** or 250/387-3701; www.royalbc museum.bc.ca).

✈ 🛏 See Vancouver Aquarium **146**.

WHY THEY'LL THANK YOU: Those inscrutable totem poles.

234

San Juan Fortress: New World Outpost

All ages • San Juan, Puerto Rico

As usual, we were feeling antsy 2 days into our beach vacation, yearning for some proper sightseeing. As we drove through Old San Juan, the Caribbean's biggest historic district, the boys leaned eagerly out the taxi windows, wondering what lay at the end of those thick city walls barricading the Atlantic seacoast. Then we came to the end of Calle Noragaray and saw it: El Morro, the staunch old fort commanding the rocky point at the entrance to San Juan Bay. A sweep of smooth green lawn (perfect for kite flying) sets it apart from the historic town it was built to protect; beyond the ramparts lies one of the most dramatic views in the Caribbean. Now there is a *fort*.

El Morro (the name means "headland") was built by Spanish colonists in 1540, long before any English settlers showed up in North America. Of course, it wasn't this big at first: Originally it was just one stout round tower, now encased in the seaward core of the fort. More walls and cannon-firing positions were added over the years, until by 1787 the citadel had filled out to the current plan, an intriguing labyrinth of dungeons, barracks, vaults, lookouts, iron grates, and bulwarks. Over the main entrance, as you cross a bridge over a dry grassed-in moat, notice the Spanish royal coat of arms carved in stone. The upper plaza, where soldiers drilled and officers were quartered, faces the city to defend the fort from land; go down a long, steep ramp, designed for

moving wheeled cannons, to the lower plaza and you're facing out to sea. (The enlisted men lived here, in cramped barracks.) Starting with an attack from Sir Francis Drake in 1595, this Spanish stronghold withstood many onslaughts over the centuries from both the English and the Dutch. The United States bombarded it in 1898 during the Spanish-American War—and by the end of that war, Puerto Rico had become a U.S. possession.

Although there are historical exhibits set up around the fort, little has been done to furnish its rooms—nothing to distract from the massive, impregnable battlements of sand-colored stone, and that's what my sons most remember about it. Nowadays it's run by the National Park Service as part of the **San Juan National Historic Site,** combining El Morro with Fort San Cristóbal, the newer (1634) and larger fort a mile to the east. The combined visitor center has a film and historic exhibits, set in a World War II strategic military base that's connected to San Cristóbal by tunnels.

ⓘ Calle Norzagaray (✆ **787/729-6777**).

✈ San Juan.

🛏 See El Yunque Tropical Forest **120**.

WHY THEY'LL THANK YOU: Standing on the mighty ramparts, looking out across the blue Caribbean.

Roanoke Island: The Lost Colony

Ages 4 & up • Near Manteo, North Carolina, USA

THE STORY HAS A CERTAIN *Twilight Zone* creepiness that kids adore. In 1587, on Roanoke Island, between the Outer Banks and the North Carolina mainland, an expedition of 120 men, women, and children landed to settle England's first permanent New World colony. Virginia Dare—granddaughter of their governor, John White—was born that year, the first child of English parents born in America. When White sailed back to England, he intended to return within the year. But a war with Spain kept White away from Roanoke for 3 years; what he found on his return in 1590 was a mystery. The rudimentary houses that he had helped build were dismantled, the entire area enclosed by a high fortlike palisade. At the entrance, crude letters hacked on a post spelled out the word CROATOAN. With no evidence of violence, White concluded that the settlers had joined the friendly neighboring Croatoan tribe—but circumstances forced him to sail for England before a search could be made. No trace of the "Lost Colony" was ever found.

The visitor center at the **Fort Raleigh National Historic Site** tells the colony's baffling story in exhibits and film; an oak-paneled replica of an Elizabethan room sets the historic era. Outdoors, all that's left of the fort is a silent mound of dirt, which I like—a reconstruction might have spoiled the site's sense of mystery. At the park's amphitheater, a replica of the palisade stands as a stage set for Paul Green's *The Lost Colony,* presented every night except Sunday from June through late August. This symphonic drama has been running since 1937; for tickets contact the **Waterside Theater,** 1409 National Park Dr., Manteo, NC 27954 (℗ **866/468-7630** or 252/473-3414; www.thelostcolony.org).

Evocative as the actual site is, the kids will fill in the details at the more commercial **Roanoke Island Festival Park** (℗ **252/473-1144**; www.roanokeisland.com) in Manteo. A 69-foot-long three-masted bark, the *Elizabeth II,* lies moored across from the waterfront—a composite 16th-century ship built for the 400th anniversary of Sir Walter Raleigh's first exploratory voyage to Roanoke in 1584. There's also a re-creation of the camp where the first English explorers stayed. In the summer, living-history interpreters around the park portray colonists and mariners; kids can putter around the hands-on exhibits in the on-site museum, learning about Raleigh's voyages to Roanoke, Outer Banks pirates, and the freed slaves who lived here during the Civil War.

ⓘ ℗ **252/473-5772;** www.nps.gov/fora.

✈ Norfolk International, 80 miles.

🛏 $$ **Cahoons Cottages,** 7213 S. Virginia Dare Trail, Nags Head (℗ **252/441-5358;** www.cahoonscottages.com). $$$ **The Tranquil House Inn,** 405 Queen Elizabeth St., Manteo (℗ **800/458-7069** or 252/473-1404; www.tranquilinn.com).

WHY THEY'LL THANK YOU: Whatever happened to Virginia Dare?

Frontier Culture Museum
Transplanting the Old World to the New
All ages • Staunton, Virginia, USA

SETTLED WELL BEFORE THE AMERICAN REVOLUTION, the Shenandoah Valley town of Staunton (pronounced "*Stan*-ton"), Virginia, was a major stop for pioneers on the way west, the starting point for a major mountain route west to the Ohio River Valley. But say "pioneers" to school kids, and they tend to assume these folks were all the same. Many pioneers, however, had freshly come from Europe, or were only one generation removed—in 1775, for example, a quarter of a million Americans were German, and the same number Irish. So while other historical restorations relocate old American buildings, the Museum of American Frontier Culture went all the way across the ocean to collect examples of the farms these early European immigrants had left behind.

There are **five farmsteads** now on this rambling site in Staunton, each nestled in its own tidy hollow, with outbuildings and livestock and gardens to match. The oldest is an English half-timbered farmstead from Worcestershire, the home of a prosperous yeoman who might have sent his sons or daughters to further the family name in the English colonies. The German farm, also half-timbered but considerably smaller and plainer, is a late-17th-century example from the Rhineland-Palatinate, one of the German regions that sent most emigrants to the Americas. As for the Irish farm, a cozy white plaster cottage with a thatched roof and unmortared stone wall, it hails from Ulster, the Protestant part of Ireland from which most early Irish Americans came. There's also a working blacksmith's forge from Ulster, the sort of forge that would have served several neighboring villages.

Different as these three farms appear, it all makes sense when you get to the last two farm homes, which were brought here from other parts of Virginia, one dating from 1773, the other from 1835. Though they're built of local materials such as logs and weatherboard and fieldstone, the floor plans and interiors freely borrow elements from all three European models, melding them into a new, and strikingly American, type of farm. Just ask the costumed docents "living" around the property—they'll point out the telling details, whether it be a brick hearth, a hayloft, or a split-rail fence. (They'll also let you watch them shoe a horse or spin a skein of wool—and they may even ask the kids to help hoe the garden, working like real pioneer children.) Suddenly it's easy to picture a new immigrant, looking upon this fertile, rolling Shenandoah Valley landscape and deciding to make it home.

(i) Richmond Rd. (U.S. 250; ✆ **540/332-7850;** www.frontiermuseum.org).

✈ Richmond, 92 miles.

🛏 $$$ **Belle Grae,** 515 W. Frederick St. (✆ **888/541-5151** or 540/886-5151; www.bellegrae.com). $$ **Regency Inn,** 268 N. Central Ave. (✆ **540/886-5330**).

WHY THEY'LL THANK YOU: Discovering the soul of each farm.

Conner Prairie Farm: Frontier Homesteads

All ages • Fishers, Indiana, USA

ALL RIGHT, TIME FOR A very embarrassing admission: I grew up in Indianapolis and yet I have never gone to Conner Prairie Farm. My old friends in Indy find this hard to believe; they are always going out there with their kids, on school field trips, Scout troop outings, and family Sunday excursions. I'm writing this book now so you don't put off the Conner Prairie Farm excursions in your own children's lives.

Conner Prairie Farm occupies 1,400 beautiful big-horizon acres nestled in a bend of the White River just north of Indianapolis, where in 1802 pioneer farmer John Conner snatched up a fertile patch of treeless prairie land to raise corn, rye, and oats. In 1934, pharmaceutical magnate Eli Lilly turned it into a model farm to investigate scientific agricultural methods; then in the late 1960s, it became a time capsule of **19th-century pioneer life.**

From my friends' accounts, the site is much more thoroughly developed now than it was when we were kids; there are five areas, each devoted to a different era, with costumed interpreters and authentic buildings moved here from all over Indiana. Refreshingly, instead of moving forward through time, these areas are arranged so you go backward in time, seeing the houses grow smaller and simpler, the crafts grow more rudimentary, life more primitive and strange.

Enter via a red covered bridge to reach an 1886 small Indiana town, with a one-room schoolhouse and a Quaker meeting-house; from there you go back to 1836, a prairie crossroads village with scattered cabins, a general store, a blacksmith shop, and another one-room school-house. The Conner home, built in 1823, was perhaps the first brick house in Indiana, a prosperous working farmstead with two barns, a loom house, spring house, and garden. From there you time-travel to 1816 to see the wigwams and trading post of the original settlers, the Lenape Indians. There are plenty of craft demonstrations everywhere, but kids will most enjoy the final section, where they can really get busy churning butter, carding wool, milking a cow, and building a split-rail fence. This was the part of pioneer life that appealed to me most as a kid—the fact that youngsters could be so useful with their hands—and I long to give my own kids that experience.

The best time to come, I'm told, is in summer, when on selected evenings you can take a picnic blanket and basket and listen to the excellent **Indianapolis Symphony Orchestra** play under the stars. We are so there next summer.

In costume at the Conner Prairie Farm.

(i) 13400 Allisonville Rd. ((C) **800/966-1836** or 317/776-6000; www.conner prairie.org).

✈ Indianapolis International, 40 miles.

🛏 $$$ **Omni Severin Hotel,** 40 W. Jackson Place, Indianapolis ((C) **800/ THE-OMNI** or 317/634-6664;

www.omnihotels.com). $$ **University Place Conference Center and Hotel,** 850 W. Michigan St., Indianapolis ((C) **800/ 626-270** or 317/269-9000; www.university place.iupui.edu).

WHY THEY'LL THANK YOU: Communities where every child mattered.

The Amana Colonies
Communal Living on the Iowa Plains
Ages 4 & up • Amana, Iowa, USA

WHO WERE THE INSPIRATIONISTS? No, not a doo-wop group from the early '60s; they were a German religious sect that emigrated to the United States and in 1855 settled along the Iowa River. The original colonists' descendants still live in the seven towns they founded—Amana, East Amana, Middle Amana, West Amana,

Simple white stone markers in Amana's cemeteries indicate that everyone is equal in God's eyes.

High Amana, South Amana, and Homestead. Although they voted to dissolve their strict communal lifestyle in 1932, the community they created still stands virtually intact, a landmarked district of some **500 historical buildings**—square, tidy brick houses, white rail fences, and gray wooden barns set amid rolling green hills. Many visitors come to shop for the handcrafted products still made by Amana artisans; but for children, there's a great history lesson here, in the tale of how an immigrant sect adapted to its new homeland.

The Community of True Inspiration, to give them their full name, chose this sparsely populated area not only for the fertile farmland but also for its distance from corrupting influences (the word *amana,* from the Bible, means "to remain faithful"). Like the Amish, they had strict rules about clothing and lifestyle (11 church services a week!), but the Inspirationists also had a firm utopian plan: All land and buildings were owned by the community, with families living in assigned quarters and every person over 14 assigned a job. Every village was provided with a store, a school, a bakery, a dairy, and a church. As you drive around, notice the communal town layouts, with barns and agricultural buildings clustered at the edge, homes in the middle, and craft workshops and factories in a group.

Whereas the Amish were chiefly farmers, the Amana folk shrewdly diversified with crafts and manufacturing, becoming known for woolens, furniture, and appliances. (Heard of Amana refrigerators? They're still made here.) The **Amana Heritage Museum** in Amana (✆ **319/622-3567;** www.amanaheritage.org) displays all sorts of crafts at which the community excelled, from tinsmithing to basket weaving. But children are fascinated by the museum's intricate dollhouses, made by community craftspeople to amuse the younger members; similarly, the **Mini-Americana Barn Museum** in South Amana (✆ **319/622-3058;** www.barnmuseum.com) is full of elaborate wooden miniatures made by woodworker Henry Moore. Also in South Amana, the **Communal Agriculture Museum** shows 19th-century farm techniques; in Middle Amana, you can visit an old **Communal Kitchen,** where assigned cooks put together group meals for several households.

Among other sites, there are also a **Store Museum** in Homestead, **Opa's Tractor Barn Museum** in West Amana, and the radically simple **Communal Church** in Homestead.

The children may be disappointed that today's Amana folk dress just like we do, at least on weekdays. But there's still an appealing small-town tranquility to these seven hamlets, even when tour buses line up outside the gift shops.

ⓘ **Welcome Center,** 622 46th Ave. (✆ **319/622-7622;** www.amanacolonies.com).

✈ Cedar Rapids/Iowa City, 25–30 miles.

🛏 $$ **Amana Holiday Inn & Water Park,** Exit 225 from I-80, Amana Colonies (✆ **319/668-1175;** www.ichotelsgroup.com). $ **Econo Lodge,** 2214 U Ave., Interstate 80, Williamsburg (✆ **319/668-2097;** www.choicehotels.com).

WHY THEY'LL THANK YOU: Community meant something here.

🔵 **239** **Settling America**

Amish Country
The Plain People of Pennsylvania
All ages • Lancaster, Pennsylvania, USA

Rolling hills, winding creeks, neatly cultivated farms, covered bridges—Lancaster County, Pennsylvania, has a bucolic beauty that would attract visitors anyway. But most tourists come here to see the Amish, dressed in their old-fashioned black clothes and driving buggies at a slow clip-clop along country roads. Yet these folks are not actors, they are real working people, and their strict customs are meant to separate them from the modern world, not to draw attention to it. The challenge of coming here with children is to discover the essence of the Amish community without falling into the tourist trap.

Begin in quaintly named Intercourse, Pennsylvania, at **The People's Place,**

3513 Old Philadelphia Pike (✆ **717/768-7171;** closed Sun), an interpretive center that will teach kids the subtle distinctions between three local sects: the Amish, the Mennonites, and the Brethern, who settled here in the early 18th century, drawn by William Penn's promise of religious tolerance. The children will learn, for example, not to take photos of the Amish; why Amish children attend one-room schoolhouses; and why they paint hex designs on their barns. Avoiding Intercourse's gaggle of Pennsylvania-Dutch-themed shops, head west to Bird-in-Hand (another quirky name) for a 20-minute jaunt in a horse-drawn buggy at **Abe's Buggy Ride,** Route 340, just east of Route 896 (℄ **717/295-5410;** closed Sun)—maybe this will help youngsters appreciate the slow pace of Amish life. Stop east of Lancaster for a guided tour of the 10-room **Amish Farm and House,** 2395 Lincoln Hwy. (℄ **717/394-6185**). Wind up at the **Central Market** downtown (just off Penn Sq., open Tues, Fri, Sat), the oldest farmers' market in the U.S., with its swirling fans, 1860 tiles, and hitching posts.

In summer, tourists clog the main roads around Lancaster, and horse-drawn vehicles can cause bottlenecks; get a good area map so you can venture onto quiet back roads, where you have a better chance of seeing Amish farmers in their daily rounds. Stop at local farm stands to buy their excellent produce, and you'll have a natural opportunity to exchange a few words. Perhaps the best way to get the flavor of Amish life is to stay with a farm family: The **Pennsylvania Dutch Convention & Visitors Bureau,** 501 Greenfield Rd. (℄ **800/PA-DUTCH** or 717/299-8901; www.padutchcountry.com), lists about 40 working farms that take guests. Expect simple lodgings, hall bathrooms, and filling family-style breakfasts.

ⓘ **Pennsylvania Dutch CVB,** above. **Mennonite Information Center,** 2209 Millstream Rd. (℄ **800/858-8320** or 717/299-0954).

✈ Philadelphia, 57 miles.

🛏 $$ **Country Inn of Lancaster,** 2133 Lincoln Hwy. E. (℄ **717/393-3413;** www.countryinnoflancaster.com). $$$ **Willow Valley Family Resort,** 2416 Willow St. Pike (℄ **800/444-1714** or 717/464-2711; www.willowvalley.com).

BEST TIME: Many Amish attractions are closed Sun.

WHY THEY'LL THANK YOU: Discovering that the Plain People are human too.

Settling America **240**

Fort Scott: Prairie Outpost

All ages • Kansas, USA

FORT SCOTT BEGAN WITH THE INDIANS and ended with the Indians. When it opened in 1842, this frontier garrison was entrusted with protecting the first few white settlers against local Indians, both the native Osages and other unhappy tribes who'd arrived under Andrew Jackson's harsh Trail of Tears resettlement scheme. By the time the fort closed in 1873, it had just safeguarded the construction of a railroad cutting across what was left of the Indian reservation lands. Over 31 dramatic years, as a policy of Manifest Destiny inexorably pushed America westward to California, it was up to Fort Scott to hold down the middle of the continent. Walk around its flat, no-nonsense parade ground and the nearby patch of tallgrass prairie and you can almost feel 19th-century America's growing pains.

Life was never easy at Fort Scott. Besides protecting local settlers, its soldiers formed escort parties for increasing numbers of wagon trains traveling the Santa Fe and Oregon Trails, and in 1849 a stampede of adventurers passed through on their way to join the California Gold Rush. Kansas became a territory in 1854, then a state in 1861; after 7 years fraught with such battles between anti- and pro-slavery forces, the army often had to intervene (earning the territory the name "Bleeding Kansas"). Its troops played a pivotal role in both the Mexican-American War (1846–48) and the Civil War (1861–65), when it was the army's chief supply depot for the Southwest and constantly in danger of attack from Confederate forces.

Twenty of Fort Scott's buildings still stand, now restored, with many of them historically furnished. One of the most interesting exhibits for kids is in the **Dragoons Barracks,** where displays illuminate the daily life of the first soldiers stationed on this tenuous frontier in the 1840s. The visitor center is set in the large hospital building, the region's major medical facility during the war. During the Civil War, Fort Scott had to build the two-story prison you'll see today, to incarcerate an overwhelming number of prisoners of war. The plain white frame buildings are arranged around a broad, grassy parade ground where the soldiers drilled and held inspections. When interpreters in period uniform march out to demonstrate their weapons, the fort seems to snap to attention all over again.

(i) Hwy. 69 and Hwy. 54 (© **620/223-0310;** www.nps.gov/fosc).

✈ Joplin, MO, 60 miles. Kansas City, KS, 90 miles.

🛏 See George Washington Carver Birthplace **248** or the Harry S. Truman Home **391**.

WHY THEY'LL THANK YOU: When Kansas felt like the end of earth.

Stockyards National Historic District
Where Cowpokes Cut Loose
All ages • Fort Worth, Texas, USA

Fort Worth sure does put the "cow" in "cowboys." When this town boomed in the 1890s, it was because it had the Southwest's biggest livestock market, where millions of cattle—as well as horses, mules, hogs, and sheep—were shipped north along the Chisholm Trail. That's how Fort Worth got the nickname "Cowtown," and the Stockyards are where the city's Old West heritage burns brightest.

Two miles north of downtown Fort Worth, the 125-acre Stockyards District, with its Spanish-flavored architecture, is still a lively place to hang out—only now it's tourists, not cattlemen, thronging the sidewalks along Exchange Street. Commercial it may be, but its robust Western vibe is infectious. Twice a day, at 11:30am and 4pm, duded-up cowhands drive about 15 head of longhorn steers down the red-brick street past the Stockyards. Former hog and sheep pens have been turned into **Stockyards Station,** a festival mall of Western-themed shops and restaurants, where the city's most authentic boots and Stetson hats are for sale; the old horse and mule barns have been turned into the **Texas Cowboy Hall of Fame,** 128 E. Exchange Ave., a magnet for rodeo fans. Inside the **Livestock Exchange Building,** 131 E. Exchange Ave., the nerve center of the old livestock business, the small Stockyards Museum displays artifacts such as guns, barbed wire, furniture, and clothing. Western music and movie stars like Gene Autry, Dale Evans, Roy Rogers, and Bob Wills are honored in bronze along Exchange Avenue's **Trail of Fame.**

Keeping the kids busy around here is no problemo. Across from Stockyards Station they can get lost in the **Cowtown Cattle Maze,** 145 E. Exchange Ave., a wooden labyrinth built to look like cattle pens. The **Grapevine Vintage Railroad** (© 817/410-3123; www.gvrr.com) runs two different daily routes from the

A cowpoke in Fort Worth.

Stockyards, one to downtown Fort Worth, the other out to Grapevine, Texas. The **Fort Worth Stockyards Arena & Livery** (℃ 817/624-3446) offers guided horseback rides from the Stockyards out along the Trinity River. On most weekend nights, there's rodeo action at the **Cowtown Coliseum,** 121 E. Exchange Ave. (℃ 817/888-COWTOWN; www. stockyardsrodeo.com), the world's first indoor rodeo arena. **Billy Bob's Texas,** 2520 Rodeo Plaza, known as the world's largest honky-tonk, offers line-dancing lessons every Thursday evening for families.

ⓘ 130 E. Exchange Ave. (℃ **817/625-9715;** www.fortworthstockyards.org).

✈ Dallas–Fort Worth International.

🛏 See Dinosaur Valley ⓲.

WHY THEY'LL THANK YOU: Yee-HAW! That durn cattle drive.

Settling America **242**

Wild West Relics: Tombstone & Bisbee

Ages 8 & up • Tombstone & Bisbee, Arizona, USA

Tombstone, "the town too tough to die," is a classic tourist trap kids love—especially when actors reenact the famous Gunfight at the O.K. Corral. But only 25 miles south is the much more authentic Bisbee, one of the best-preserved historic towns in Arizona. Within day-trip distance from Tucson, Tombstone's hokey attractions make a tempting lure for the kids; swing on down to Bisbee for the real deal.

Between 1880 and 1887, an estimated $37 million worth of silver was mined in Tombstone, and the town's historic district has several imposing buildings among the gussied-up saloons and former bordellos lining the main drag, Allen Street. Narrated tours, including several by stagecoach, can be picked up around

here. Daily at 2pm, there's a reenactment of the famous gun battle at the former livery stable known as the **O.K. Corral,** 308 E. Allen St. (℃ 520/457-3456), the very spot where, one fateful October day in 1881, Virgil, Morgan, and Wyatt Earp and their friend Doc Holliday took on the outlaws Ike Clanton and Frank and Tom McLaury. It's a totally kitschy (and sometimes downright rude) attraction that also includes **Tombstone's Historama,** a multimedia affair narrated by Vincent Price that rehashes Tombstone's "bad old days." More authentic sites are the **Wyatt Earp House,** a simple adobe cottage at 102 E. Fremont St. (℃ 520/457-3111), and the **Boot Hill Graveyard,** Highway 80, north of downtown (℃ 520/457-9344), where you can see the graves of Clanton and the McLaury brothers, who were killed in the shootout; the kids will get a kick out of reading various epitaphs, such as "Here lies Lester Moore, 4 slugs from a 44, No Les, no more." Gallows still stand in the courtyard of **Tombstone Courthouse State Park,** 219 Toughnut St. (✆ 520/457-3311), which also displays artifacts and photos of Tombstone's past. Staged gunfights, gold panning, a mock mine shaft and shooting gallery, and arcade games carry on the Wild West theme at **Helldorado Town,** 4th and Toughnut sts. (✆ **520/457-9035**); it's cheesy, sure, but that's Tombstone for you.

Built into the steep slopes of Tombstone Canyon on the south side of the Mule Mountains, Tombstone's neighbor Bisbee got rich on copper mining. Bisbee never became a bona fide ghost town, but it still looks like a slice of the past. Old Victorian buildings line narrow winding streets, and miners' shacks perch on the steep hillsides above downtown. For a good overview, hop on the **Warren Bisbee Railway,** Copper Queen Plaza (✆ 520/940-7212; www.bisbeetrolley. com), a narrated trolley tour that loops around town. The kids will love the **Queen Mine Tours,** Highway 80 interchange (✆ 866/432-2071 or 520/432-2071), which head underground into one of the old copper mines. Though Bisbee has been colonized by funky artists and boutique owners these days, on weekends when bikers rumble onto the downtown streets, the West still seems satisfyingly Wild.

ⓘ **Tombstone Visitor Center,** Allen and 4th sts. (✆ **888/457-3929** or 520/457-9317; www.tombstone.org). **Bisbee Visitor Center,** 2 Copper Queen Plaza (✆ **866/2-BISBEE** or 520/432-3554; www.discover bisbee.com).

✈ 🛏 See Saguaro National Park **74**.

WHY THEY'LL THANK YOU: The Wild West, clichés and all.

---

243 Settling America

California Mission Trail
The Priests Who Won the West
Ages 4 & up • San Diego to Sonoma, California, USA

WHEN CALIFORNIA FOURTH GRADERS study state history, acres of poster board get turned into maps showing **21 Franciscan missions** strung along the coast from San Diego to Sonoma. Field trips are a given, since there's a mission within driving distance of almost every school—that's how well the Spanish padres saturated old California. Founded from 1769 to 1823, the missions were built to convert Native Americans to Christianity, and though they've endured fires, earthquakes, and secularization, amazingly every site is still preserved for modern visitors. Driving up the California coast, you'll already be on the Spanish settlers' El Camino Real (Royal Road)—the valiant old missions make natural stopping places en route, just as they did then.

Begin in San Diego at **Mission Basilica San Diego de Alcala,** 10818 San Diego Mission Rd. (✆ 619/281-8449), the first mission, founded by Spanish missionary Junípero Serra in 1769, though it was soon moved from its original site in Old Town **223** to escape the corrupting influence of the local garrison. Next up the coast is **San Juan Capistrano,** Ortega Highway CA 74 (✆ 949/234-1300), known as the "Jewel of the Missions"

The California Mission Trail.

for its beautiful gardens. The legendary swallows are said to return here to nest each March 19 (in reality, you'll see the well-fed birds here all year round).

North of Los Angeles, the **Santa Barbara Mission,** Laguna and Los Olivos streets (℗ 805/682-4149), the "Queen of the Missions" with its graceful twin bell towers, sits on a hilltop overlooking the town of Santa Barbara and the Channel Islands. Farther up the Central Coast, **Mission San Luis Obispo,** 751 Palm St. (℗ 805/781-8220), was built of adobe by

native Chumash laborers; when hostile natives shot burning arrows into its thatched roof, Serra doggedly replaced it with California's first clay roof tiles. **San Carlos Borromeo de Carmelo** in Carmel, Basilico Rio Road (℗ 831/624-3600), with its magnificent stone church, was Serra's sentimental favorite—he is even buried here. Northeast of Carmel, **Mission San Juan Bautista,** 2nd and Mariposa streets, San Juan Bautista (℗ 831/623-4528), is supplemented today by an entire city plaza of restored historic buildings. Despite straddling the San Andreas fault, this mission's church—the largest in the chain—has been in continuous service since 1797. On up the coast, **Mission Santa Cruz,** Mission Plaza (℗ 831/426-5686), was known as the "bad luck" mission. It has survived fires, earthquakes—even a pirate attack. Its museum has excellent exhibits on the Native Americans it served.

Mission Dolores, 3371 16th St. (℗ 415/621-8203), formerly Mission San Francisco de Asis, is the oldest building in San Francisco. In the 1840s, it was a gambling den; Alfred Hitchcock used its graveyard as a location for *Vertigo*. It even survived the 1906 San Francisco earthquake—perhaps Father Serra was protecting it from heaven.

ⓘ www.parks.ca.gov.

✈ ⇆ See San Diego Zoo **131**.

WHY THEY'LL THANK YOU: One way the West was won.

California Gold Rush Country
Land of the Forty-Niners
Ages 6 & up • Hwy. 49 from Nevada City to Angels Camp, California

I*N A CAVERN, in a canyon, excavating for a mine/Lived a miner, Forty-Niner . . .* Rarely do state highway numbers have historical significance, but California state highway

49 does. Winding through the hills west of Sacramento, **Highway 49** is the main road through a string of Wild West towns that had their brief but dizzying heyday in

the California Gold Rush of 1849. As if frozen in time, their Main streets still have raised wooden sidewalks, buildings with double porches, saloons, and Victorian storefronts. Touring the Gold Country, the kids will feel transplanted to a movie western (hundreds of films have been shot here), to a time when the promise of an easy fortune lured thousands of adventurers to risk their all in a raw new territory. Soon enough the boom went bust—but not before it had jump-started the settlement of the whole West Coast.

It's about 100 miles along Highway 49 from Nevada City in the north to Angels Camp in the south; visiting the whole area could take several days. Here are the highlights: Start where the Gold Rush itself began—just north of Placerville in quiet, pretty **Coloma** at the **Marshall Gold Discovery State Historic Park**. Here, on the south fork of the American River, on January 24, 1848, carpenter James Marshall was building John Sutter's sawmill when he chanced upon a gold nugget. On Main Street, the largest building in town is a replica of the sawmill; exhibits at the **Gold Discovery Museum** lay out the story of the frenzy that ensued once the news got out. Notice the number of Chinese stores on Main Street, the remnants of a once-sizable community of Chinese who immigrated here to provide labor for the mines. Some 40 miles south of here, you can tour the **Sutter Gold Mine,** 13660 Hwy. 49, Amador City. You'll wear a hard hat, ride on a mining shuttle, and "tag in" just like a miner. Down in the shaft, you may be able to spot gemstones and gold deposits still embedded in the quartz of the Comet Vein. The other face of the Gold Rush shows at two nearby ghost towns— **Mokelumne Hill,** nowadays one street overlooking a valley with a few old buildings, and decrepit **Volcano,** which looks almost haunted with the dark rock and blind window frames of a few backless, ivy-covered buildings. Once it had a population of 8,000; today, it's more like 100. That's what happens when a boom goes bust.

Another 30 miles farther south, Gold Rush country's most popular site, **Columbia State Historic Park,** re-creates a boom town at its lively height. Kids love roaming around its dusty car-free streets, where they can take stagecoach rides or visit a newspaper office, a blacksmith's forge, a Wells Fargo express office, or a Victorian-era saloon.

ⓘ **Marshall Gold Discovery State Historic Park** (ⓒ **530/622-3470;** www.coloma.com/gold). **Sutter Gold Mine** (ⓒ **866/762-2837** or 209/736-2708; www.suttergold.com). **Columbia State Historic Park** (ⓒ **209/532-4301;** www.columbiacalifornia.com).

✈ Sacramento, 55 miles from Placerville.

🛏 $$ **City Hotel,** Main St., Columbia State Park (ⓒ **800/532-1479** or 209/532-1479; www.cityhotel.com). $$ **Imperial Hotel,** Main St., Amador City (ⓒ **209/267-9172;** www.imperialamador.com).

WHY THEY'LL THANK YOU: There's gold in them thar hills.

Black Heritage Trail

All ages • Boston, Massachusetts, USA

MANY TOURISTS DON'T REALIZE that Boston has not one but two Freedom Trails—the Revolutionary War trail, and the Black Heritage Trail, which celebrates Boston's antislavery movement. The latter runs 1.6 miles, through Beacon Hill, the center of the free black community in the years leading up to the Civil War. Walking around this neighborhood, you get a sense of how a close-knit black community gathered, gradually developing political savvy and spreading radical new ideas. The seeds of the Emancipation Proclamation were sown here on Beacon Hill. Walking the Trail is a great way to explore an era of American history that all too often takes a back seat in Revolutionary War–obsessed New England.

The 15 marked points on the trail start at the **Robert Gould Shaw Memorial** on Beacon Street across from the State House. Shaw was the white officer who led the 54th Massachusetts Regiment, the Union's first black regiment, celebrated in the 1989 film *Glory*, and this bas-relief sculpture by Augustus St. Gaudens is incredibly affecting. Other buildings you'll pass include the homes of George Middleton, an African-American Revolutionary War soldier; successful barber John J. Smith, a free black who hosted antislavery debates both at his shop and in his home; and Lewis Heyden, a freed slave whose boardinghouse was an early Underground Railroad stop. You'll see the Baptist church where church desegregation efforts began in the 1830s (years later, after the Civil War, the same church building became Boston's first African Methodist Episcopal church).

From Memorial Day to Labor Day, National Park Service rangers lead free 2-hour **guided tours** daily along the route; the rest of the year, contact the Park Service to arrange a tour. To go at your own pace without the commentary, pick up a brochure outlining the tour at the Boston Common and State Street visitor kiosks, or from the **Museum of Afro-American History,** 46 Joy St. (© **617/725-0022;** www.afroammuseum.org), which is where the Trail ends. The museum's site occupies the restored **Abiel Smith School** (1834), the first American public grammar school for African-American children, and the **African Meeting House** (1806), the oldest standing black church in the United States. William Lloyd Garrison founded the New England Anti-Slavery Society in this building, where Frederick Douglass made some of his great abolitionist speeches. Once known as the "Black Faneuil Hall," it also schedules lectures, concerts, and church meetings. The museum's displays employ art, artifacts, documents, historic photographs, and other objects—including many family heirlooms. Children enjoy the interactive touch-screen displays and multimedia presentations, and the patient, enthusiastic staff helps them put the exhibits in context.

ⓘ © **617/742-5415;** www.nps.gov/boaf.

✈ 🛏 See Boston Common **60**.

WHY THEY'LL THANK YOU: A second Freedom Trail, just as important as the first.

National Underground Railroad Freedom Center

Ages 4 & up • Cincinnati, Ohio, USA

IT WASN'T UNDERGROUND and it wasn't a railroad—don't let the kids come here expecting to see a subway museum. What is celebrated here is even more important: an organized secret network of homes, churches, and stores willing to harbor runaway black slaves on their desperate flight from Southern plantations to the North. It's fitting that Cincinnati, lying right across the Ohio River from Kentucky, should be the site of this museum, for once you had crossed that river you were technically free at last.

The Freedom Center sits handily between the Bengals stadium and the Reds's ballpark, but while it may share parking lots with those two venues, this is a much more serious attraction, a daringly inventive exhibit designed to change people's minds as much as to convey information. The focal point of the sleek modern lobby is a startlingly ramshackle gray wood building once used to warehouse slaves—human beings, penned like cattle—before shipping them down to plantations farther south. From there visitors are directed along a winding route (winding like the Ohio River) through various multimedia experiences. The film theaters here don't just show films, they barrage you with images and sounds from all directions. One reason for coming here with children is so you have an excuse to participate actively in the **Freedom Seekers** section, where storytelling and role-playing exercises put kids in the shoes of runaway slaves; a warmly lit brick housefront beckons with a cellar door left ajar for secret nighttime visitors to slip in. The **From Slavery to Freedom** section tackles a wider chunk of history, with walk-through life-size dioramas

Slave pen at the Underground Railroad Freedom Center.

exploring New World history from the first arrivals of African slaves (and slavery was here from the get-go), through the Revolutionary War, tortuous constitutional debates, and the rise of abolitionism in the 19th century.

In the **Everyday Freedom Heroes** gallery, interactive kiosks allow visitors to learn the inspiring stories of many individuals, not just African Americans, who fought for social freedom. And once you've passed through all the exhibits, the two final rooms encourage visitors to gather together to discuss what they've just seen, and its implications for the world they live in. Somewhat like the Jewish Museum Berlin **278**, this is by no means a special-interest museum; we are all implicated in this struggle for freedom, and the message is one we can all respond to.

(i) 50 E. Freedom Way ((C) **877/648-4838** or 513/333-7500; www.freedomcenter.org).

✈ ⊨ See Cincinnati Zoo **133**.

WHY THEY'LL THANK YOU: Imagining the courage it took, for the runaways and for their protectors.

Booker T. Washington Birthplace
A Slave Boy, a Free Man
All ages • Hardy, Virginia, USA

IT'S EASY TO IMAGINE that every plantation in the Old South was straight out of *Gone With the Wind*. The tobacco plantation where Booker T. Washington, Jr., was born in 1856, however, followed a different model: With only 207 acres and 10 slaves, owner James Burroughs and his sons

worked in the fields right alongside their slaves. It does seem amazing that a boy born into slavery should become a college president and the country's foremost black leader (in the eyes of whites at least—some blacks chafed at Washington's pragmatic stance on issues like lynching and voting rights). But walking around the Burroughs plantation, it becomes clear how the man Booker T. Washington grew out of this Virginia slave boy.

Although no original buildings are left from Washington's childhood, several **reconstructions** show visitors a typical Piedmont farm of this era: a smokehouse, blacksmith shed, corncrib, horse barn, chicken lot, and the tobacco barn where harvested leaves were hung to dry. Made authentically of hewn logs chinked with clay, these buildings show a hardscrabble farm very different from the King Cotton plantations of the Deep South. The reconstructed kitchen cabin replicates the one where Washington, whose mother was the plantation's cook, was born. Stone outlines in the grass show the actual location of the original kitchen cabin and the "big house"—a mere five rooms—where the owner's family lived (with 14 children, they outnumbered the slaves). Only about 5 acres were actually planted with tobacco, the farm's sole cash crop; other crops and livestock fed and clothed the family, a model of self-sufficiency that underlay Washington's lifelong commitment to making African Americans economically self-reliant. All children on the farm worked (hard work was another of Washington's lifelong ideals) and one of Booker's jobs was to fan flies from the Burroughs's dinner table, where he overheard mealtime conversations that informed his view of the world. His familiarity with the white owners may have made it easier for him as an adult to cultivate white philanthropists to underwrite his projects, notably Tuskegee Institute in Alabama. Young Booker became passionate about education, begging his father to let him attend a local black school, doing extra chores to earn money to go at age 16 to Hampton Institute. Slaves were freed by then, but education was Washington's key to escaping farm drudgery, and he devoted the rest of his life to ensuring education for other African Americans.

A 1.3-mile-long **nature trail** through the adjoining woods shows where slaves foraged, fished, and chased the family's free-ranging hogs. Walking in these cool, lovely woods along a crystalline brook, you can imagine a slave boy slipping away here to dream of making something of himself.

(i) 12130 Booker T. Washington Hwy. (VA 122; (C) **540/721-2094;** www.nps.gov/bowa).

✈ Roanoke, 25 miles.

🛏 $ **Colony House Motor Lodge,** 3560 Franklin Rd., Roanoke ((C) **866/203-5850** or 540/345-0411). $$$ **Hotel Roanoke,** 110 Shenandoah Ave., Roanoke ((C) **800/222-TREE** or 540/985-5900; www.hotel roanoke.com).

WHY THEY'LL THANK YOU: Preaching the gospel of hard work.

Black American History **248**

George Washington Carver's Birthplace
Nature's Laboratory
All ages • Diamond, Missouri, USA

Kᴵᴰˢ ᴼᶠᵀᴱᴺ ᴳᴱᵀ George Washington Carver confused with Booker T. Washington, and not just because they both had "Washington" in their names (though Carver added it later in life): Both were born into slavery, worked hard to get an education, and won fame at Tuskegee Institute in Alabama. But they were two quite different sorts of men, one a savvy political leader, the other a gentle scientific genius. Following the walking trail through the Missouri farm where

George Washington Carver was born, you begin to see how nature inspired him, even as a boy: This farm was a perfect nature laboratory.

George Washington Carver National Monument.

The Carver homestead was not large, only 240 acres, and owner Moses Carver and his wife, Susan, were by all accounts kind to their few slaves. But they were extra close to young George and his brother Jim: When he was an infant, George and his mother had been kidnapped by Civil War bushwhackers, and when the boy was finally returned, half-dead, Mr. and Mrs. Carver adopted orphan George and his brother and raised them as their own. Because George was frail, he was only given light domestic chores, which left him plenty of time to wander outdoors, observing flowers and trees and experimenting to see what made them grow. He soon became known in the area as the "plant doctor," with amazing self-taught botanical skills. The **interpretive trail** at the historic site leads you past a natural spring, a teeming pond, a fertile patch of deciduous forest, a persimmon grove, a stand of walnut trees, and several acres of the sort of tall-grass prairie that once covered much of the Great Plains; signs along the path point out nature details that we're usually too distracted to notice. George Carver noticed them, and his boundless curiosity led him to wonder *why* plants grew as they did—and then to find the answers for himself.

Though the tiny cabin where he was born was blown away by a tornado years ago, a set of low walls outlines its location; farther on the trail you can go inside Moses Carver's home, not much more than a cabin itself, to see how a Missouri farm family lived in the 1860s. George left this farm at age 11 to attend a black school in nearby Neosho. Over the next 19 years, while patiently supporting himself with menial household labor, he eventually earned a master's degree and was hired by Booker T. Washington to teach agricultural chemistry at Tuskegee. Beyond his famous work with peanuts, he made so many scientific discoveries that he became known as the Wizard of Tuskegee. Generations of African-American students have been inspired by him.

(i) Carver Rd. 9 (☎ **417/325-4151;** www.nps.gov/gwca).

✈ Joplin, 15 miles.

🛏 $ **Best Western Oasis Inn,** 3508 S. Range Line Rd., Joplin (☎ **800/780-7234** or 417/781-6776; www.bestwestern.com). $$ **Holiday Inn,** 3615 S. Range Line Rd., Joplin (☎ **800/315-2621** or 417/782-1000; www.holiday-inn.com).

WHY THEY'LL THANK YOU: How a natural genius saw nature.

250

Black American History

Dr. King's Legacy

Ages 6 & up • Atlanta, Georgia, USA

THE CIVIL RIGHTS LEADER Martin Luther King, Jr., is by any measure a great man. In his hometown of Atlanta, Georgia, the 10-block area around Auburn Avenue is one of the city's most-visited sites, encompassing King's boyhood home and the Baptist church where King, his father, and his grandfather were all ministers. While other civil rights sites may illuminate the issues of that tumultuous era better, this is the place where you'll really get a feeling for this complex, gifted man who dared to change history.

To me the real heart of the site is the historic buildings associated with King. Start out at the gracefully landscaped visitor center, where you can book tours of the sites (get here early in the day, at least in summer, because tickets do run out) and bone up on King's life and times with audiovisual programs and exhibits. First off is the **Birth Home of Martin Luther King, Jr.,** 501 Auburn Ave. (*✆* **404/331-3920**), the modest Queen Anne–style house where Martin Luther King, Jr., was born on January 15, 1929, and lived until he was 12. The house has been restored to its appearance when young Martin lived here—even the linoleum is an authentic reproduction, and a good deal of King memorabilia is displayed. His father (Martin Luther King, Sr., obviously) was a Baptist minister and pastor of the **Ebenezer Baptist Church** down the street at 400–407 Auburn Ave. (*✆* **404/688-7263**), a Gothic Revival–style church founded in 1886 and completed in 1922. Years later, from 1960 to 1968—at the height of the civil rights struggle—Martin Luther King, Jr., served as his father's co-pastor here, the two actively using their pulpit to press for social change. The National Park Service

operates it as a living museum, with guided weekday tours, periodic church services, and a monthly choir performance. In nearby **Freedom Plaza** rests Dr. King's white marble crypt, surrounded by a five-tiered reflecting pool.

The district is somewhat dominated by the hulking modern **King Center,** 449 Auburn Ave. (*✆* **404/524-1956;** www.thekingcenter.org), a memorial and educational center directed by King's son. It has a huge library and archives on the civil rights movement, including Dr. King's personal papers, but many visitors are most interested in the exhibition hall, where selected memorabilia of King and the civil rights movement are displayed. You can see his Bible and clerical robe and a handwritten sermon; on a grim note, there's the suit King was wearing when a deranged woman stabbed him in New York City, as well as the key to his room at the Lorraine Motel in Memphis, Tennessee, where he was assassinated (see the **National Civil Rights Museum 251**). The best reason to come here is to settle down in the Screening Room to watch videos of Dr. King's most stirring sermons and speeches, including "I Have a Dream." The man's words still move us.

ⓘ **MLK, JR., National Historic Site,** 449 Auburn Ave. (*✆* **404/331-5190;** www.nps.gov/malu).

✈ 🛏 See Stone Mountain **91**.

WHY THEY'LL THANK YOU: The "I Have a Dream" speech.

Alabama's Civil Rights Trail

Ages 8 & up • Montgomery, Birmingham & Selma, Alabama, USA

WHAT SEEMS LIKE YESTERDAY'S HEADLINES to us grown-ups is in fact the foggy past to our kids. Take, for example, that afternoon in 1955 when a black seamstress named Rosa Parks was arrested for not yielding

her seat to a white man on a Montgomery, Alabama, public bus. A controversial bus boycott (led by a young Rev. Martin Luther King, Jr.) followed, one of the first skirmishes in the civil rights battle of the

1960s. We refer to it so casually, as if everyone should know about this tumultuous era, but it's all new to the kids—and even adults may find they didn't know as much as they thought.

That 1955 street scene is re-created at the **Rosa Parks Library and Museum,** 252 Montgomery St. (℃ **334/241-8615;** http:// montgomery.troy.edu/ museum), with a replica of the bus Parks rode, video images, and a multimedia tableau. Wonderful interactive displays throughout the museum engage children in Parks's inspiring life as an activist. King's role, of course, was pivotal, as you'll learn on the twice-daily guided tours of the neat **Dexter Avenue King Memorial Baptist Church,** 454 Dexter Ave. (℃ **334/263-3970;** www.dexterking memorial.org), where King used his pulpit to press for social change. Even more evocative is the **Dexter Parsonage Museum,** 309 Jackson St. (℃ **334/261- 3270;** www.dakmf.org), a simple white bungalow that's been furnished as it was in the 1950s, when King and his family lived here: You can see the study where he wrote his sermons, the dining room where activists met to plan the boycott, and a front window shattered by a bomb meant to scare King off his campaign. Downtown, the black granite **Civil Rights Memorial,** 400 Washington Ave., designed by Maya Lin, pays tribute to those who fought for racial equality.

You have to credit Alabama for embracing this anguished chapter of its past. Birmingham, 90 miles north of Montgomery, has an entire downtown district memorializing civil rights events: engrossing displays (segregated water fountains, a bombed-out bus, King's jail cell) in the

Statue of Rosa Parks in Alabama.

Birmingham Civil Rights Institute, 520 16th St. N. (℃ **05/ 328-9696;** www. bcri.bham.al.us); the historic **16th St. Baptist Church,** 1530 6th Ave. N. (℃ **205/ 251-9402**), where a 1963 bombing by the Ku Klux Klan killed four adolescent girls; and outdoor **Kelly Ingram Park,** where a paved Freedom Path recounts crucial events with plaques and sculptures. An hour's drive west of Montgomery in Selma, you can see the **Edmund Pettis Bridge,** site of the 1965 "Bloody Sunday" riot, where a voting-rights protest march met brutal resistance from police and local vigilantes, then stop in the **National Voting Rights Museum,** 1012 Water Ave. (℃ **334/418-0800**), which displays artifacts about voter-registration campaigns—just one phase of the not-yet-won war for civil rights in America.

ⓘ www.touralabama.org.

✈ Birmingham, 90 miles to Montgomery.

🛏 $$ **Crowne Plaza-Redmont,** 2101 Fifth Ave. N., Birmingham (℃ **877/536- 2085;** www.crowneplaza.com). $$ **Embassy Suites Hotel Montgomery,** 300 Tallapoosa St., Montgomery (℃ **334/269-5055;** www. embassysuites.com).

WHY THEY'LL THANK YOU: Dr. King had a dream.

National Civil Rights Museum
How Racial Equality Became Reality
Ages 8 & up • Memphis, Tennessee, USA

THANK GOODNESS our children's generation isn't familiar with some of these sights: the segregated lunch counter from which black students in 1960 were evicted; a public bus where in 1955 black people were expected to yield their seats to whites; the burned shell of a Greyhound bus upon which Freedom Riders were attacked in 1961. But the most sobering artifact of all in this comprehensive Memphis, Tennessee, museum is a standard 1960s-era motel room in the attached building, formerly the Lorraine Motel. The Rev. Martin Luther King, Jr., stepped out onto this balcony on the night of April 4, 1968, only to meet the

National Civil Rights Museum.

gunfire of a man named James Earl Ray, lying in wait in a rooming house across the street. This historic motel, rescued in the nick of time from demolition, became the starting point for the National Civil Rights Museum, a tribute to Americans of all races who waged the battle for social justice.

Tracing roughly a century of hard-won progress, the museum begins with the Civil War and ends with that tragic night in 1968 (a new annex was recently opened to develop post-1968 coverage). While the earlier galleries in the chronological story are a bit static, relying mostly on historical photos and documents, the displays become more engrossing as they deal with the so-called **"Jim Crow laws"** that institutionalized racial segregation in the United States: You'll see a chillingly anonymous Ku Klux Klan white robe and pointed hood, and a sign pointing out "white" and "colored" restrooms. By the time you get to the **school integration struggle**—an issue that really hits home with youngsters— more modern media such as video footage and taped oral histories are available to tell the story. Dioramas present landmark civil disobedience acts in Montgomery, Greensboro, Birmingham, and Memphis, with video footage in the background. (Provocatively, all figures in these tableaus are rendered in the same blank white plaster, whether the original actors were black or white.) The scene depicting the 1968 March on Washington conveys the immense crowds of that day with a blizzard of protest placards.

While bits and pieces of this story may be told more powerfully at their own sites, covered elsewhere in this section, this is the one museum that tries to make sense of the whole continuous story, and of that it does a pretty darn good job.

(i) 450 Mulberry St. ((C) **901/521-9699;** www.civilrightsmuseum.org).

✈ Memphis International.

🛏 $$ **Homewood Suites,** 5811 Poplar Ave. ((C) **800/CALL-HOME** or 901/763-0500; www.homewoodsuites.com). $$$ **The Peabody Memphis,** 149 Union Ave. ((C) **800/PEABODY** or 901/529-4000; www.peabodymemphis.com).

WHY THEY'LL THANK YOU: A century of struggle, thoughtfully told.

---

252 **Black American History**

Brown v. Board of Education
School Segregation Stops Here
Ages 8 & up • Topeka, Kansas, USA

FROM THE OUTSIDE, the **Monroe School** in Topeka, Kansas, looks like any other mid-20th-century American public school, a solid two-story building of red brick faced with limestone. It was a perfectly acceptable modern school when it opened in 1926, but there was one catch: Only African-American students could go there—and even if they wanted to attend a school closer to their homes, they couldn't. The legal challenge to this segregated school system went all the way to the Supreme Court, resulting in a landmark 1954 decision that forever changed American public education. If you want the kids to understand what the civil rights movement was all about, here's a great place to start, in a place where racial prejudice affected children their age.

Entering the school building, you won't see classrooms full of desks and dusty chalkboards (declining enrollment shut down Monroe Elementary in 1975). What you will see is a stark sign showing **separate entrances** for blacks and whites. True, there was never such a sign here, because whites didn't come here at all, but the sign is a graphic statement of the "separate but equal" approach to education that prevailed in 1950. A dramatic 25-minute film in the old school auditorium puts the school desegregation fight

into the larger context of race in America; you'll then pass through three galleries of **interactive exhibits**—videos, sound clips, touch screens, pull-out drawers, and light-up buttons—that deconstruct the *Brown v. Board of Ed* case and the importance of education in the struggle for racial equality.

Brown v. Board of Ed wasn't just some local school squabble; 13 Topeka parents, with the support of the National Association for the Advancement of Colored People (NAACP), brought the suit in the summer of 1950 after they tried to enroll their children at various white schools nearer their homes; their class action suit was consolidated with four similar cases from around the country in the final Supreme Court decision. Only three of the children involved went to Monroe, one of them being little Linda Brown, whose father, Oliver, was the first named plaintiff in the case. But the exhibits at Monroe Elementary don't just narrate one incident at one school, they tell the story of a systematic pattern of exclusion at many schools, born out of a racial discrimination woven into the fabric of American society.

The final gallery you'll pass through is the one that feels most like a classroom, the old **kindergarten room,** where visitors are asked to write, discuss, and reflect on what they've learned today. Now's the time to ask the children if the schools they know are truly different from the ones in Linda Brown's day—and why.

(i) 1515 SE Monroe St. (✆ **785/354-4273;** www.nps.gov/brvb).

✈ Kansas City, 70 miles.

🛏 $$ **Capitol Plaza Hotel,** 1717 SW Topeka Blvd. (✆ **785/431-7200;** www. jqh.com). $$ **Ramada Inn Downtown,** 420 E. 6th St. (✆ **800/311-5192** or 785/ 234-5400; www.ramada.com).

WHY THEY'LL THANK YOU: Where you go to school makes a difference.

Little Rock Central High School
Passing the Integration Test
Ages 10 & up • Little Rock, Arkansas, USA

Aᴌᴌ ʀɪɢʜᴛ, ꜱᴏ ᴛʜᴇ 1954 ᴅᴇᴄɪꜱɪᴏɴ in *Brown v. Board of Education* had officially declared school segregation unconstitutional. That didn't mean the struggle was over. The test came 3 years later, in September 1957, when nine African-American students walked into Central High School in Little Rock, Arkansas, only to be assailed by an angry mob. In the end, President Eisenhower had to send in federal troops, as the world watched with bated breath.

The Little Rock story is much grimmer than that of *Brown v. Board of Education* 252, which was mostly waged in the courts; in Little Rock, it was waged by nine courageous teenagers risking physical danger. Standing outside the place, it's easy to see that **Central High,** built in the 1920s, was a showcase high school, an imposing Collegiate Gothic beauty with a turreted roofline and sweeping front staircase. Central had 100 classrooms, a field house, a football stadium, and many other luxuries unheard of at Dunbar High, the black school a few blocks away. On September 2, Arkansas's legislature and governor, openly defying federal desegregation orders, had the Arkansas National Guard turn away nine African-American students who had enrolled at the prestigious all-white high school. Three weeks later, the Nine finally managed to enter the building and start classes, but an incensed crowd of protesters made the scene outside more and more dangerous, and the Little Rock

Little Rock Central High School.

police had to escort the kids out. The next morning, the 101st Airborne arrived from Kentucky to usher the nine students safely inside. As the school year wore on, the troops and TV cameras stopped hovering outside, but opponents of integration kept tempers at a boiling point inside Central—"if parents would just go home and let us alone, we'll be all right," one white student remarked. One of the Nine, tired of continual harassment, quit school and moved to New York City. Another, Ernest Green, graduated in spring, commenting wryly, "It's been an interesting year. I've had a course in human relations firsthand." The crisis still wasn't solved, though; rather than integrate, all Little Rock high schools were closed the entire next school year.

Because Central High is still a working school, visitors get most of the story across the street, in an old Mobil gas station that's now the **Central High Museum and Visitor Center,** full of videos and eyewitness accounts of the crisis. There's a commemorative garden behind the school where the events of that watershed year are honored. But I'd advise planning several weeks ahead to book a **group tour,** available for 10 or more, outside of school term. Knowledgeable tour guides will take you inside the school building to relate where specific incidents happened—where the battle was fought, day after day, by the teenagers themselves. It's a window into a time of agonizing social change.

(i) 2125 W. Daisy L. Gatson Bates Dr. ((C) **501/374-1957;** www.nps.gov/chsc).

✈ Little Rock National.

🛏 $$ **Doubletree Hotel Little Rock,** 424 W. Markham ((C) **501/372-4371;** www.doubletreelr.com). $$$ **The Peabody Little Rock,** 3 Statehouse Plaza ((C) **501/ 906-4000;** www.peabodylittlerock.com).

WHY THEY'LL THANK YOU: And they think their high school sucks?

Bloody Battlegrounds . . . 283
History at Sea . . . 295
World War II & the Cold War . . . 305

The cenotaph at the Alamo.

1066 & All That: The Battle of Hastings

Ages 10 & up • Battle, England

Few historical battles were as pivotal as the Battle of Hastings in 1066, a date engraved in English memory. When the duke of Normandy landed on the Sussex coast that autumn with a crack French fighting force, he was just another raider from across the sea. King Harold of the Saxons hurried south with his own valiant army, confident of repelling the Normans as he had the Danes. But by the end of one fatal day—October 14, 1066—Harold was dead, and William the Invader had become William the Conqueror.

The Battle of Hastings is somewhat of a misnomer—the Normans used the town of Hastings, 101km (63 miles) southeast of London, as their base of operations, but the actual battle occurred 10km (6¼ miles) inland. While legend claims that Harold was killed by an arrow through the eye, and his body dismembered, careful studies of the Bayeux Tapestry **198** suggest his death wasn't quite that dramatic. Nevertheless, the last of the Saxon kings was slain that day, and what you see here today is the ruins of the abbey William ordered built as an act of penance in 1070 (once his conquest was assured), using stone shipped from his lands at Caen in northern France. Medieval parts of the abbey still stand—notably the towered gatehouse at the top of Battle's main street—but very little is left of the Norman parts. The church's altar was supposedly set on the very spot where Harold died; today it's marked by a plaque on the ground, along with a nearby monument to Harold presented by the people of Normandy in 1903.

Behind the **Abbey ruins,** however, you can walk around a stretch of parkland where the battle was fought. Be sure to pick up the free interactive **audio tour,** which re-creates the sounds of the battle as you stand where the Saxon army was positioned, atop Senlac Hill, blocking the road to London. (The ground, unfortunately, was leveled when the abbey was built; you'll have to imagine the original steep slope.) The two armies were equal in number, about 8,000 each, and the Saxon defense was based on a seemingly impregnable wall of shields. The Normans, however, with greater numbers of archers and cavalry, figured out that if they pretended to flee, the Saxons would charge prematurely, leaving gaps in the shield wall, and by nightfall victory was theirs.

Tour the exhibits in the abbey first to get background on the battle; there's also a themed play area.

ⓘ **Battle Abbey,** South end of High St. (ⓒ **01424/773792**). **Battle Tourist Information Centre,** 88 High St. (ⓒ **01424/773721;** www.battle-tourism.co.uk).

🚆 Hastings, 1½-2 hr. from London.

🛏 $$$ **Powder Mills Hotel,** Powder Mills Lane (ⓒ **01424/775511;** www.powdermillshotel.com).

BEST TIME: Mid-Oct when costumed reenactors commemorate the anniversary of the battle.

WHY THEY'LL THANK YOU: A peaceful spot to contemplate a fateful day.

Culloden Battlefield
Bonnie Prince Charlie's Last Stand
Ages 6 & up • Inverness, Scotland

AT CULLODEN BATTLEFIELD the last of Scotland's royal blood, Charles Stuart, aka Bonnie Prince Charlie, and his rebel army were finally crushed on April 16, 1746. Pick a gray and gloomy day to visit this windswept plain where Scotland's dream of regaining the throne died a poignant death.

The visitor center's audiovisual presentation gives a good introduction to the complicated politics leading up to Culloden. In 1603, England and Scotland joined their crowns when James Stuart became king of England, but over the next century, Scotland was treated more and more shabbily by the powers-that-were in London. In 1715 the first Jacobite rebellion (so called because they were trying to restore James Stuart to the joint throne) was led by the son of England's deposed King James II—James Stuart, often called the Old Pretender. His son Charles, the Young Pretender, led a second and more persuasive Jacobite rebellion in 1745. Prince Charlie's dashing personality at first won many supporters, but none of them made good on their promises. His gallant army of 5,000 nevertheless faced down an English force 9,000 strong, led by the brutal duke of Cumberland, and in a mere 40 minutes the battle was lost. Prince Charlie escaped and eventually fled to France. With typical contrariness, the Scots have ever since revered this humiliating defeat for its romantic (and anti-English) associations.

Once you've got the history straight, follow a path from the visitor center around the battlefield, with its several marked sites. The **Field of the English** is a graveyard for English soldiers; a much more affecting sight is the **Graves of the Clans,** where Scottish fighters are interred under a few simple stones that indicate communal burying places for the dead of each clan. (The Jacobites lost 1,200 men, nearly a quarter of their number, while only 300 English died, a mere 3.3% of their ranks.) You can also see the huge **Cumberland Stone,** where "Butcher" Cumberland is said to have stood watching his bloody victory. The great memorial cairn wasn't erected until 1881.

Culloden.

(i) **Culloden Moor,** 10km (6¼ miles) SE of Inverness ((C) **01463/790607;** www.nts.org.uk or www.culloden.org).

🚂 Inverness, 3 hr. from Edinburgh or Glasgow.

Culloden House, A96 5km (3 miles) west of Inverness (© **01463/790461;** www.cullodenhouse.co.uk).

WHY THEY'LL THANK YOU: The valiant last stand of a lost cause.

Lexington & Concord
The Shot Heard 'Round the World

Ages 6 & up • Concord, Lexington & Lincoln, Massachusetts, USA

THE OPENING SALVOS of the American Revolution—the so-called Shot Heard 'Round the World—were fired in the villages of Lexington and Concord, Massachusetts, on April 19, 1775. No need to memorize the date; you'll hear it everywhere when you visit **Minute Man National Historical Park.** After I read my favorite childhood book, *Johnny Tremain,* to my kids, we just had to come here to see where the climactic battle really happened—and they loved it.

To take things in chronological order, begin in Lexington, where two messengers from Boston, Paul Revere and William Dawes, raised the alarm late on the night of April 18. The **visitor center** on the town common—or Battle Green, as they call it—has a diorama of the early-morning skirmish between local militia, known as "Minutemen" for their ability to assemble quickly, and a large force of British troops. The statue on the green depicts Capt. John Parker, who commanded the militia. You can visit the **Hancock-Clarke House,** 36 Hancock St. (© **781/861-0928**), where patriot leaders John Hancock and Samuel Adams were awakened by Revere and Dawes, and **Buckman Tavern,** 1 Bedford St. (© **781/ 862-5598**), on the green, where the Minutemen assembled at dawn. Ordered to disperse, the ragtag (and no doubt sleepy) band of colonists stood their ground—fewer than 100 poorly armed colonists versus some 700 red-coated British soldiers. Nobody knows who

started the shooting, but when it was over, 8 militia members lay dead, including a drummer boy, and 10 were wounded.

Next move on to Concord, where the British proceeded in search of stockpiled arms (which militia members had already moved). Begin at the **North Bridge Visitor Center,** 174 Liberty St., with its diorama and video program, then proceed down Monument Street to the **Minute Man National Historical Park** (© **978/369-6993;** www.nps.gov/mima). A path leads from the parking lot to the one don't-miss sight, **North Bridge,** where a much larger force of Minutemen massed to attack British regulars and set off the war's first full-fledged battle. Narrative plaques and audio presentations along the path describe the onset of the battle; Daniel Chester French's famous Minuteman statue stands nobly poised by the bridge.

Drive east on Lexington Road to the next park section, where you can follow the **Battle Road Trail,** a 5.5-mile interpretive path (wheelchair, stroller, and bicycle accessible) tracing the route of the defeated British troops straggling back toward Boston. (In summer, ask at the visitor centers about ranger-led guided tours along Battle Rd.) At the Lexington end of the park, the **Minute Man Visitor Center** off Route 2A has a fascinating multimedia program about the Revolution and a 40-foot mural illustrating the battle.

North Bridge.

ⓘ **Lexington Visitor Center,** 1875 Massachusetts Ave., Lexington (www. lexingtonchamber.org). **Concord Visitor Center,** 58 Main St., Concord (www. concordchamberofcommerce.org).

✈ Boston, 18 miles.

🛏 See Boston Common ⑥⓪.

WHY THEY'LL THANK YOU: Listen my children, and you shall hear . . .

Bloody Battlegrounds **257**

Fort Ticonderoga
New England's Pivotal Outpost
Ages 6 & up • Ticonderoga, New York, USA

Mɪʟɪᴛᴀʀʏ ʜɪsᴛᴏʀʏ ʙᴜꜰꜰs ᴡɪʟʟ ʙᴇ ɪɴ ʜᴇᴀᴠᴇɴ at this 18th-century fort set on a bluff over-looking Lake Champlain at the eastern edge of New York State's Adirondack Mountains. There was a tug of war over this strategic location during not one but two wars—the French and Indian War and its sequel, the American Revolution—and it was occupied at different times by a shifting cast of French, English, or American troops (along with their various Native American allies). Few sites give a better sense of the turbulence of those 20 or so years when the American nation was forged.

Everybody, it seems, wanted a piece of this lonely little outpost. Built by the French in 1755, Fort Carillon (as it was then named) protected a key strategic

point—the portage connecting Lake Champlain and Lake George. During the French and Indian War, French forces lost the fort to British attackers in 1758, and British general Lord Jeffrey Amherst renamed it Fort Ticonderoga. Sixteen years later, at the outset of the American Revolution, Ethan Allen made a daring raid with his Green Mountain Boys from Vermont, capturing the fort from the British (communications being what they were in those days, they hadn't yet heard that war had broken out at Lexington and Concord, Massachusetts). The British recaptured it from commander Benedict Arnold in early 1777 but set it on fire and fled after the Battle of Saratoga later that year. Tourists began to visit the ruins in the 1790s, and it's been a tourist attraction ever since.

Your **guided tour** of the fort is led by a costumed reenactor, who could be French or British or American or Native American, depending on who's working that day. The **collection** is anything but dry, with nearly 1,000 muskets, bayonets, pistols, and swords on display, as well as a unique collection of uniforms. You'll see everything from Ethan Allen's blunderbuss to the handwritten note an American private left in his backpack to tell his ancestors why he fought in the American Revolution. There are musketry and cannon-firing **demonstrations**, and a fife-and-drum corps plays throughout the day. But what really got through to my kids—and what I most remembered from visiting as a kid myself—was the sense of

how lonely life must have been for the small garrison stationed here, valiantly hanging onto their foothold in the wilderness.

ⓘ On Rte. 74, Lake Champlain (ⓒ **518/585-2821;** www.fort-ticonderoga.org).

✈ Burlington, VT, 56 miles.

🛏 **Lake Champlain Inn,** 428 County Rte. 3, Ticonderoga (ⓒ **518/547-9942;** www.tlcinn.com).

BEST TIME: Fort open mid-May to mid-Oct.

WHY THEY'LL THANK YOU: Gives the concept of "holding the fort" a whole new meaning.

258 **Bloody Battlegrounds**

Valley Forge
The Winter That Saved America
Ages 6 & up • Valley Forge, Pennsylvania, USA

Bᴀᴛᴛʟᴇғɪᴇʟᴅs ᴛᴇʟʟ ᴏɴᴇ ᴋɪɴᴅ ᴏғ ᴡᴀʀ sᴛᴏʀʏ; Valley Forge tells another—a victory not of weapons but of perseverance and will. Here, in the bitter-cold winter of 1777–78, George Washington really earned the nickname Father of His Country. It's the essential sequel to visiting **Independence Square** ⑥, and an easy day trip from Philadelphia, only 30 miles by today's highways, though quite a march away in those pre-automobile days. When the ragtag Continental Army straggled into winter camp 18 miles up the Schuykill River from Philadelphia, they had just lost two major battles, at Brandywine and Germantown. With Philadelphia captured by the British—the Liberty Bell smuggled out of town, the Continental Congress on the run—the battle of American independence was on the verge of being lost. Come to this patch of Pennsylvania farmland to find out how George Washington saved the day.

Arriving at Valley Forge, the Continental Army—some 12,000 hungry, homesick men and boys—found the British had already destroyed the gristmill and sawmill they'd hoped would provide food and shelter. There were 6 inches of snow on the ground, the rivers had iced up, and things looked bleak indeed. Privately, Washington despaired "that unless some great and capital change suddenly takes place . . . this Army must inevitably . . . starve, dissolve, or disperse." Almost 2,000 troops died that winter, and many others deserted. Yet with his almost-mystical leadership quality, Washington somehow kept the army going. He challenged the soldiers to build 12-man log huts, offering cash to those who finished first. Others dug earthworks to defend the camp, hoping to keep the British bottled up in Philly. On the one hand, Washington invigorated the troops' spirits; on the other, he browbeat Congress into sending supplies. On the hard-packed

287

Washington's Valley Forge Headquarters.

parade ground, Washington's training master, Prussian veteran Baron von Steuben, drilled this rabble of farmers and backwoodsmen in military skills. By springtime, the revamped Continental Army had against all odds become a force

to fear, and the tide of the war soon turned.

Walking around the rolling fields today, you can see replicas of the **soldiers' huts** (with costumed interpreters in high season), the grassy mounds of their old defenses, farmhouses the officers used as lodgings, the **parade ground,** and a sprinkling of **memorials.** An excellent 15-minute film at the visitor center explains the encampment in detail; the center also displays Washington's own tent and cases of artifacts—cooking utensils, blankets, chamber pots, bullets. For an extra admission fee, you can tour the **Isaac Potts House,** a fieldstone farmhouse that Washington used as his headquarters. With most historic sites, summer is the best time to visit, but we came here during winter break and it was perfect weather for grasping the true drama of Valley Forge.

ⓘ PA 23 and N. Gulph Rd. (✆ **610/783-1077;** www.nps.gov/vafo).

✈ ⟺ See Philadelphia **62**.

WHY THEY'LL THANK YOU: Feeling the wind whistle through the barracks' ramshackle log walls.

Bloody Battlegrounds **259**

Where Napoleon Met His Waterloo

Ages 8 & up • South of Waterloo, Belgium

SO WHY WAS THE FAMOUS BATTLE called Waterloo when it really took place in Mont-St-Jean, a farm village 20 minutes south of Brussels? The Brussels suburb of Waterloo was where the Duke of Wellington was staying in a coaching inn (now the **Musée Wellington,** chausée de Bruxelles 147) when he sent home his momentous announcement: On June 18, 1815, Napoleon Bonaparte, the upstart French emperor who had harassed the rest of Europe for the past 12 years, was finally vanquished for good.

Approaching the battlefield, you can't help but notice the immense grassy cone rising from the rolling countryside, topped off with a cast-iron lion, a traditional symbol of victory. This **Lion Mound** was created after the battle to provide a view of the hallowed plain, with 226 steps running like a zipper straight up the slope to its summit. Stop at the visitor center before climbing the mound; a sound-and-light narration and a big-screen film shown inside will help the kids picture early-19th-century combat, when brightly uniformed troops marched in straight ranks toward the enemy line, only to be mowed down by bullets, cannon fire, and the slashing swords of swift-galloping cavalrymen. Some 350,000 soldiers marched onto this battlefield that fateful June day; 9,500 of them never left, and another 32,000 were wounded.

Climb the mound to visualize the layout of the battle, with Napoleon's forces, outnumbered two to one, caught in a pincer between Wellington's army and General Blücher's Prussian troops. Down the Brussels–Charleroi road you can spot La Haie-Stainte, a farmhouse that providentially shielded Wellington's center from direct attack; 135 monuments to various heroes and regiments punctuate the plain. Follow the signposted trail from the mound to nearby **Hougoumont Farm,** which describes one crucial phase of the fighting in detail. You also can drive 5km (3 miles) south to the village of Le Vieux Genappe to see **Le Caillou Farm,** chaussée de Bruxelles 66, Napoleon's quarters, where he planned the battle the night before—you'll see his spartan camp bed and the playing cards with which he whiled away his last night as the scourge of Europe.

On July and August weekends, costumed reenactors hold rifle and artillery demonstrations. Beside the visitor center are two other attractions, a rather tired **waxwork museum** and a painted 360-degree **panorama** of the battle, which was evidently quite a sensation in the days before moving pictures (battle sound effects have been added to try to give it more pizazz for today's tourists). I like these reminders that Waterloo has been a tourist site for a long time—generations have come here to contemplate how 1 day changed the course of European history.

(i) Route de Lion (© **02/385-19-12;** www.waterloo1815.be).

✈ Brussels National, 24km (15 miles).

🛏 $$$ **Bristol Stephanie,** av. Louise 91–93, Brussels (© **02/543-33-11;** www.bristol.be). $ **De Boeck's,** rue Veydt 40, Brussels (© **02/537-40-33;** www.hotel-deboecks.be).

WHY THEY'LL THANK YOU: Reaching the top of the Lion Mound.

Gettysburg National Park
Blood & Sorrow in the Civil War
Ages 6 & up • Gettysburg, Pennsylvania, USA

"**A**WESOME" DOESN'T BEGIN TO DO JUSTICE to this vast battleground, where thousands of Union and Confederate soldiers clashed for three sultry July days in 1863. As Abraham Lincoln himself said in his famous 1864 speech here, this land has been consecrated by blood—over 50,000 deaths—and an almost-eerie atmosphere hangs over this tranquil patch of rolling farmland, now peppered with war monuments.

The park visitor center has an excellent light-and-sound presentation with a scale-model map of the battlefield, which is quite helpful—after all, the battle raged over a large patch of country in the course of 4 days, and there's a lot to keep straight. Audiotapes are available for self-guided driving tours around the 250-acre battle site, but we found that this was one place where it paid to invest in a personal guide, who drove us in our station wagon around the battlefield for 2 hours. Gettysburg's guides are gold mines of Civil War information, tailoring the tour to your particular

Copse of Trees and High Water Mark Monument at Gettysburg.

interests; there wasn't a question we lobbed at him that he couldn't handle, whether biographies of the commanders or the physics of cannon fusillades.

We were completely engrossed by **Seminary Ridge,** where the main Confederate forces were camped; we could look down the hillside where the heroes of Pickett's Last Charge plunged to their gallant end. But we were most moved by **Little Round Top,** where a plucky band of Northern soldiers held the high ground

against a furious Confederate onslaught surging up out of the boulder-strewn hollow called Devil's Den. Observation towers near Seminary Ridge give you a great aerial overview, but walking around the landscape is the only way to appreciate how hard-won every inch of ground was.

The **Cyclorama Center,** next to the visitor center, a 360-degree depiction of Pickett's Charge painted in 1883, is just the sort of pre-video-era special effect I love. In the town of Gettysburg itself, we enjoyed the **American Civil War Museum,** 297 Steinwehr Ave. (© **717/334-6245**), which tells the full Civil War history in waxwork dioramas; normally I find wax figures hokey or creepy but this was actually tasteful and informative. The most special part of our visit, though, was seeing the costumed reenactors—many of them amateur Civil War buffs here for the fun of it—socializing around campfires or demonstrating their rifle skills. For a flicker of a moment we traveled through time, feeling the Gettysburg tragedy in our bones.

ⓘ **Visitor Center,** 97 Taneytown Rd. (© **717/334-1124;** www.nps.gov/gett).

✈ Baltimore-Washington International, 60 miles.

🛏 $$$ **Holiday Inn Battlefield,** 516 Baltimore St. (© **888/465-4329** or 717/334-6211; www.ichotelsgroup.com). $$ **Quality Inn,** 380 Steinwehr Ave. (© **800/228-5151** or 717/334-1103; www.gettysburgquality inn.com).

WHY THEY'LL THANK YOU: Brother fought brother on this bloody ground.

Bloody Battlegrounds **261**

Vicksburg: Dixie's Darkest Day

All ages • Vicksburg, Mississippi, USA

Mʏ ꜰᴀᴍɪʟʏ ꜱᴛɪʟʟ ᴡᴀᴛᴄʜᴇꜱ grainy home movies of my childhood trip to Vicksburg, Mississippi. I remember the sweltering Delta heat, abated by lazy breezes off the

Mississippi River; I remember the hilly green landscape; I remember clambering over fat black cannons. I've just realized that this must have planted in me a lifelong

Illinois Monument at Vicksburg.

love of visiting battlefields—vast outdoor spaces where kids can run off steam while adults somberly ponder the nature of war.

In war, topography is destiny. Vicksburg—known as the Gibraltar of the Confederacy—protected a strategic strait along the Mississippi River. The Union needed to gain control of the Mississippi, not only to reclaim this vital shipping route but also to sever the South in two. Union commander Ulysses S. Grant waged a bitter campaign across central Mississippi in the spring of 1863. He headed relentlessly toward Vicksburg, but realized when he neared the city that its hilly landscape made it nearly impossible to assault. The wily general then switched tactics, laying siege to the city instead. His troops starving, reinforcements cut off, Confederate commander John C. Pemberton finally surrendered to Grant on July 3, 1863, after 47 brutal days.

A 16-mile **driving trail** winds through the park, past cannon emplacements, grassy foundations of old forts, and the trenches Grant ordered dug to set mines beneath Confederate redoubts. Every state that fought in the campaign has its own memorial; our favorite was the Illinois monument, a domed neoclassical structure set on a hill up two long rippling flights of steps where we hopped around for a full half-hour.

The first half of the tour follows the Union siege lines. You'll pass the simple white house where the Shirley family huddled fearfully throughout the Union advance; near Grant's headquarters, a circle of bronze tablets details the other battles in Grant's long Mississippi campaign. The USS *Cairo,* a 13-gun ironclad gunboat, is on display, the first ship in history to be sunk by an electronically deployed torpedo. Halfway through the drive, you'll visit the Vicksburg cemetery, containing the graves of 17,000 Union soldiers (the 5,000 Confederate graves are at the Vicksburg City Cemetery). Then you begin to trace the Confederate lines, starting with the grassy site of Fort Hill, on a riverside bluff where gunners could strafe the Union ships down on the river below. Eventually you reach the site where Pemberton surrendered to Grant on July 3—in a grim coincidence, the very same day another arm of the Confederate army lost the Battle of Gettysburg 260.

(i) 3201 Clay St. ((C) **601/636-0583;** www. nps.gov/vick).

✈ Jackson, MS, 40 miles.

🛏 $$ **Annabelle,** 501 Speed St. (✆ **800/ 791-2000** or 601/638-2000; www.annabelle bnb.com). $ **Battlefield Inn,** 4137 I-20

Frontage Rd. (✆ **800/359-9363** or 601/ 638-5811; www.battlefieldinn.org).

WHY THEY'LL THANK YOU: Grant's cunning, the South's downfall.

Bloody Battlegrounds **262**

Remembering the Alamo

Ages 4 & up • San Antonio, Texas, USA

Visiting San Antonio without going to the Alamo is like visiting London and not seeing Big Ben: You can do it, but it would be wrong.

Expect the kids to be let down at first. The Alamo looks downright dinky, set smack in the heart of downtown San Antonio, surrounded by skyscrapers and traffic. But the whole point of the Alamo is that it *was* such a tiny fort, and the valiant Texan volunteers never had a ghost of a chance of escaping the siege— and still they fought, they fought to the death. That's heroism, Texas style.

There were only 188 Texans defending the Alamo in February 1836, facing the 4,000-strong army of General Santa Anna, who was bent on squashing the Texas territory's bid for independence from the new Mexican Republic. The Texans held out doggedly for 13 days, waiting for reinforcements that never arrived, until all the men—every last one of them, including pioneer heroes Davy Crockett and Jim Bowie—were killed in a crushing dawn attack on March 6. But a month later, when Sam Houston was leading another troop of Texans into the battle of San

The Alamo.

Jacinto, he fired them up with the cry, "Remember the Alamo!" With that heroic example to live up to, the Texans fought like demons, and this time they won, becoming the independent Republic of Texas. (It didn't join the U.S. until 1846.)

What you see today isn't much of a fort—in 1836 the fortified compound was a bit larger, its outer walls ringing much of what is today Alamo Plaza (look for foundation stones near the steps down to River Walk). After the defeat at San Jacinto, the retreating Mexican forces pulled down much of the Alamo fort so that the Texans couldn't easily refortify it. Only two original buildings remain. First is the gabled stone **mission church**—now officially a Shrine, so show respect by removing hats and taking no photos— which was built in 1756 for the Mission San Antonio de Valero, founded in 1718 to convert local Native American tribes. By the end of the 18th century, the mission had been secularized and turned over to a

Spanish cavalry unit, which renamed it the Alamo (Spanish for "cottonwood") after their Mexican hometown. Besides the church, you can visit the **Long Barracks,** originally the missionaries' living quarters, or *convento,* and later a barracks for the cavalry troops. A **museum of Texas history,** with in-depth exhibits on the battle, is in the barracks, but the children will be more affected by **artifacts** displayed in the church: things like a Bowie knife, Crockett's buckskin jacket, and one of the antiquated flintlock rifles the Texans used to defend the fort. Several cannons from the battle are set around the courtyard, mute witnesses to that day of incredible valor.

ⓘ 300 Alamo Plaza (✆ **210/225-1391;** www.thealamo.org).

✈ ⇔ See San Antonio River Walk ➏➐.

WHY THEY'LL THANK YOU: Heroes against the odds.

Verdun
World War I's Bloodiest Battleground
Ages 10 & up • Verdun, France

Vᴇʀᴅᴜɴ ɪꜱ Fʀᴀɴᴄᴇ'ꜱ Gᴇᴛᴛʏꜱʙᴜʀɢ; nearly 700,000 soldiers died here, in World War I's longest and bloodiest battle, which lasted from February to December of 1916. You'll need a car to tour the battlefield, but it's a site you'll never forget. Left untouched by development, the Verdun battlefield still wears its battle scars—a bomb-cratered landscape littered with tangled barbed wire, rusty bullets, shards of shrapnel, and even in some cases unexploded shells and grenades (warn the children to step carefully and not to touch anything on the ground). Peering down into a warren of trenches and imagining the doughboys living there day and night under a continual barrage of

shellfire bring home the true horrors of World War I.

Verdun had been a military garrison town since Roman times, and its fortress became a symbol of French toughness in the Franco-Prussian War (1870–71)— which is why the Germans chose to launch a major assault here, for its psychological value. Nearly a million German troops faced 200,000 French defenders in the first attack on February 21, 1916. By summer, all seemed lost, but French military leader Marshall Pétain staunchly declared, "They shall not pass!"—and the Allies held out. When the battle ended on December 18, the Allies had won—but the cost in human lives was staggering, all to gain a few yards of ground.

A 32km (20-mile) signposted **driving tour** follows routes D913 and D112 on the Meuse's right bank. To get an overview of the battle, stop first at the **Mémorial de Verdun,** Fleury Devant Douaumont (✆ **03-29-84-35-34;** closed mid-Dec to Jan), which displays weapons, uniforms, and photographs. You can visit two important fortifications, both huddled largely underground, which fell to the Germans in the summer but were recaptured in the fall by the French. **Fort Vaux** is where French commander Raynal staged such a heroic defense that even the Germans paid tribute to him; the larger **Fort de Douaumont** is where the fiercest German assault, the "hell of Verdun," was unleashed. Stand on the roof of the fort and look out at a vast field of corroded tops of "pillboxes," bunkered gun emplacements. Near Douaumont are the sobering **Ossuaire de Douaumont,** a memorial tower embedded with the unidentifiable bones of those blown to bits, and the equally grim **Trench of Bayonets** (Tranchée des Baïonnettes), a restored concrete trench dedicated to French troops killed by a shell explosion, their bayonets left sticking out of the earth. On the road back to Verdun lies a **French cemetery** of 16,000 graves—this seemingly endless field of crosses is more eloquent than any words.

ⓘ 3.2km (2 miles) east of Verdun off N13 toward Metz (www.verdun-tourisme.com).

🚃 Verdun, 261km (162 miles) from Paris.

🛏 $$$ **Chateau des Monthairons,** Rte. D34, Dieue-sur-Meuse (✆ **03-29-87-78-55;** www.chateaudesmonthairons.fr).

WHY THEY'LL THANK YOU: Trench warfare at its most tragic.

Ypres: The Poppies of World War I

Ages 10 & up • Ieper, Belgium

"IN FLANDERS FIELDS the poppies blow/ Between the crosses, row on row . . ." The most famous poem about World War I was written by Canadian surgeon Maj. John McCrae in anguished response to what he saw at Ypres—or "Bloody Wipers," as the English servicemen called it. Bright red poppies grow wild here— you can still see them blooming every spring around this gentle Belgian hill country, like drops of blood on the ravaged landscape. They get me every time.

Wedged between France and Germany, Belgium always got caught in the crossfire in Europe's wars, but World War I hit it worst. Ypres sat squarely on the battle front that slashed across the face of Europe like a livid dueling scar; though there were only two official battles here, the area was bombarded almost continually for the entire 4 years of the war, from 1914 to 1917. Afterward there was pretty much nothing left of the town—a fact that's hard to believe when you visit it today. Ieper (the Flemish spelling) was rebuilt after the armistice, brick by brick, and though it looks charmingly medieval, look closer and you'll see that those aren't timeworn stones; the gabled guild houses and patrician mansions around the Grote Markt are stage-set perfect.

At the west end of the Grote Markt, in the extravagantly Gothic Lakenhalle, your one essential stop in town is **In Flanders Field** (✆ **057/23-92-00**), a museum designed for emotional effect as much as for conveying information. Each visitor gets an ID card of an ordinary soldier or citizen, which you insert in slots at various kiosks to discover what "you" would have experienced during the war. Toward the end you enter a dark room full of disorienting smoke and horrid noises and acrid smells—just a sample of what the

soldiers endured day after surreal day. After that, driving around the battlefield has a much keener impact. Local companies run minibus tours, or you can drive an 80km (50-mile) route on signposted roads past all the main sights. With the kids, however, it'll be enough to drive out N8 to Canadalaan to **Sanctuary Wood,** a preserved stretch of muddy trenches complete with shell holes and shattered trees. Just imagine a giant network of such trenches snaking over the countryside as far as the eye can see—that was Ypres.

No fewer than 185 military cemeteries surround Ieper—those "crosses, row on row"—and back in town, war memorials are tucked into every spare corner. The most poignant one to me is the **Missing Memorial,** a marble arch inscribed with the names of 54,896 British troops who died here; the adjacent **Australian Memorial** commemorates the 43,000 Aussies who gave their lives. Those numbers just boggle my mind—an entire generation of men wiped out. Every evening at 8pm, traffic is halted here while Ypres firefighters play *The Last Post* on silver bugles. I dare you not to feel a chill.

ⓘ **Toerisme Ieper,** Lakenhalle, Grote Markt (✆ **057/23-92-00;** www.ieper.be).

✈ Brussels National, 113km (70 miles).

🛏 $$$ **Regina,** Grote Markt 45 (✆ **057/ 21-88-88;** www.hotelregina.be).

WHY THEY'LL THANK YOU: Knowing why this was called "the war to end all wars."

Norse Ships Asail: The Bygdøy Peninsula

Ages 4 & up • Oslo, Norway

ON A SUMMER'S DAY, a quick ferry ride south from Oslo is the ideal way to approach the Bygdøy peninsula. After all, Bygdøy is all about boats; why not see it first from the water? For Viking fans like my kids, this is the place to go to savor a bit of Norway's long-standing love affair with the sea.

Begin at the **Vikingskiphuset,** Huk Aveny 35 (✆ **22-13-52-80;** www.khm. uio.no), a long tunnel-like building displaying three ancient vessels excavated from the Oslofjord. These long, low-slung wooden craft were built for Viking funerals, in which a dead hero is shot out to sea on a boat loaded with all the riches needed for the afterlife. The star of the collection is the 9th-century *Oseberg,* 19m (63 ft.) long and richly ornamented in honor of the queen who was buried on it. Standing here gazing upon these ancient timbers is a real century-dissolving moment.

The **Norsk Sjøfartsmuseum** (Norwegian Maritime Museum), Bygdøynesveien 37 (✆ **24-11-41-50**), takes up the story from the Viking era and chronicles the history of Norwegian seafaring up to the present, with exhibits including a replica ship's deck, a section of a passenger steamer, a three-masted schooner dating from 1916, and a polar vessel used by Roald Amundsen in his search for the Northwest Passage. Another polar exploration ship Amundsen sailed, the *Fram,* is at the nearby **Frammuseet,** Bygdøynesveien (✆ **23-28-29-50**).

The next museum focuses on a newer vessel, but to look at it you'd think it was the oldest of all: the *Kon-Tiki,* Bygdøynesveien 36 (✆ **23-08-67-67;** www. kon-tiki.no), a raft made of balsa wood— yes, the same stuff you make cheap toy gliders out of—which was sailed 6,880km (4,275 miles) across the Pacific, from Peru to Polynesia, by the young Norwegian scientist Thor Heyerdahl and five comrades in 1947. Their goal was to prove that prehistoric South Americans could have sailed over to settle Polynesia with their primitive technology. The 14m-long (45-ft.) *Kon-Tiki,* with its large square sail lashed to a mangrove pole, may not be as small as you'd expect, but I personally wouldn't venture across the Pacific for 101 days on this baby, and I can only admire the Viking spirit of those who did. There are also artifacts from later trips Heyerdahl took to Easter Island **167**, and the raft on which he crossed the Atlantic in 1970, an even frailer vessel called the *Ra II*, made of—get this—papyrus paper.

(i) www.visitoslo.com.

✈ Oslo International, 56km (35 miles).

⊨ $$$ **Hotel Bristol,** Kristian IV's Gate 7 ((*C* **22-82-60-00;** www.bristol.no).

$ **Rainbow Hotel Norrøna,** Grensen 19 ((*C* **23-31-80-00;** www.thonhotels.no).

WHY THEY'LL THANK YOU: The dragon boats speak to the Viking in all of us.

History at Sea **266**

The *Golden Hinde*
The Wooden Ship That Sailed around the World
Ages 6 & up • London, England

IN THESE DAYS OF INTERNATIONAL JET TRAVEL and space shuttles and surveillance satellites, it's hard to imagine the courage it took to set off over uncharted oceans on a tiny, frail wooden ship. And yet Sir Francis Drake did just that, in 1577–80, becoming the first British sailor to cruise all the way around the world—and turning overnight into a national hero (not to mention a virtual millionaire).

Visitors are amazed to stumble upon an exact full-scale replica of the *Golden Hinde,* the Tudor galleon in which Sir Francis Drake made his famous circumnavigation, moored at the old dock of St. Mary Overie, right in the middle of London. Drake initially set sail with five ships; 3 years later, after various sea fights and storms and mutinies, he returned with only one, but a fortune in gold, spices, and other valuables (the equivalent of £25 million today. Queen Elizabeth I promptly took half of it, in return knighting Drake and making him an admiral. A few years later, commanding a different ship, Drake helped to vanquish the Spanish Armada, but much of the treasure he captured in that battle shrewdly and conveniently disappeared before the queen got her take—and thus began Drake's eventual slide into disgrace.

Built in 1973, nearly 4 centuries after Drake's original, the replica *Golden Hinde* looks amazingly tiny for such an around-the-world voyage. But this actual ship, its square white sails boldly decorated with red crosses, has proven itself plenty seaworthy, sailing around the world some two dozen times, exploring both oceans and the American coast, logging some 140,000 sea miles. In fact, it's wise to call ahead to make sure the ship is actually in port and not off gallivanting on the seven seas. Visitors can explore the ship's five decks, chat with the costumed actors on board, and, as part of a guided tour, may even be allowed to turn the capstan, raise the anchor, or help load and fire one of the 22 sea cannons. Mind your heads while poking around, though—some of those beams hang pretty darn low, and you've got to be spry to scamper up and down the narrow wooden stairways.

(i) Horseshoe Wharf 6a Clink St. ((*C* **020/7403-0123;** www.goldenhinde.co.uk).

✈ ⊨ See London **55**.

WHY THEY'LL THANK YOU: From cabin boy to captain, there's a sea dog in all of us.

Vasamuseet
The Warship That Rose from the Dead
Ages 6 & up • Stockholm, Sweden

SCANDINAVIANS HAVE ALWAYS BEEN SEAFARERS, SO it makes sense that the number-one tourist attraction in Sweden should be an old boat. But the *Vasa* isn't just any old boat—it's *the oldest* boat in the world, or at any rate the oldest complete ship. And it comes with a story that'll hook the kids in at once.

Imagine thousands of onlookers lining Stockholm Harbor in August 1628 to watch the launching of the royal navy's newest and grandest warship. Under King Gustavus Adolphus, Sweden was locked in a Baltic war with Poland, and the *Vasa* was built to strike fear into the hearts of the enemy, with 64 powerful guns, two gun decks, and some 700 painted and gilded sculptures bristling from its decks, including a spirited figurehead of a lion, the king's personal mascot. But as the ship sailed festively out of its berth, the crowd could only watch in shock as the *Vasa* heeled over and sank before their eyes, right there in the harbor—overbalanced, ironically, by the very weight of those massive guns. Of the 150 seamen on board, up to a third died. Even the *Titanic* didn't sink this fast.

And so for the next 333 years the *Vasa* lay intact at the bottom of Stockholm harbor, its timbers soaking, rigging rotting, waves flaking the paint off its carvings. It lay there, waiting, until an ambitious salvage operation raised it in 1961, bringing the wreck upward in stages and making it watertight while still submerged, to prepare for the pressure of breaking the surface. Swedish TV broadcast live its final triumphant raising—the nation watching intently, much as it did in 1628, only this time on a vast televisual scale.

On board, archaeologists found a trove of **17th-century objects:** carpenters' tools, medical instruments, sailors' pants (in a color known as Lübeck gray), more than 4,000 coins, even a sailor's backgammon board, which are displayed today in this museum on forested Djurgården (Deer Park) island, east of Stockholm's Old Town. The great timbered ship, meticulously restored, is set in its own high-raftered ship hall. You can circle around it but can't climb aboard; a replica of portions of the upper decks in a side gallery shows visitors what the interior looks like. Several other side exhibits fill in the historical details of 17th-century naval warfare and the salvage operation.

The Vasamuseet stands conveniently near Stockholm's other top historical

Skansen.

297

attraction, **Skansen,** Djurgården 49–51
(℡ **08/442-80-00**), a 30-hectare (75-acre)
open-air museum with more than 150
buildings brought here from all over
Sweden, dating mostly from the 18th and
19th centuries.

ⓘ Galärvarvsvägen 14, Djurgården (℡ **08/
5195-4800;** www.vasamuseet.se).

✈ ⊨ See Stockholm: City of Islands ㊾.

WHY THEY'LL THANK YOU: Imagine
being there the day this ship tipped over.

Old Ironsides
The Unsinkable Frigate of 1812
Ages 6 & up • Charlestown, Massachusetts, USA

Oɴʟʏ 25 ʏᴇᴀʀs after the United States ended
its first war against Great Britain, another
broke out, much of it fought at sea. And
this time, America proved once and for all
that it could stand on its own two feet—
thanks in large part to a staunch little warship, fondly known as Old Ironsides.

Old Ironsides.

The **USS *Constitution*** is berthed at
the end of Boston's Freedom Trail in the
Charlestown Navy Yard. A real Bostonian,
it was one of the U.S. Navy's six original
frigates, built in the North End between
1794 and 1797 at the then-staggering
cost of $302,718. Its bolts, spikes, and
other fittings came from the foundry of
Paul Revere, the silversmith and patriot
leader. Whatever magic Revere's workers
put into it, *Constitution* played a key role
as the new nation built its naval and military reputation. In its 18 years of active
service, this hardy warship never lost a
battle. First there were French privateers
and Barbary pirates to drive off. Then the
War of 1812 broke out, drawing the
young nation's fledgling navy into sea
fights against the renowned British fleet.
The *Constitution* participated in no fewer
than 40 engagements and captured 20 of
His Majesty's vessels. As for that nickname, the frigate earned it on August 19,
1812, when shots from HMS *Guerriere*
bounced off its thick oak hull as if it were
iron. Retired from combat in 1815, *Constitution* was slated for demolition when
prominent Boston poet and essayist
Oliver Wendell Holmes published a poem
called "Old Ironsides" that launched a
preservation movement in 1830. It
remained here in the Navy Yard, sailing
infrequently, moored more or less permanently after 1881. To honor its bicenten-
nial in 1997, the frigate was completely

overhauled and sailed under its own power again. Tugs tow *Constitution* into the harbor every Fourth of July for its celebratory "turnaround cruise." Today, active-duty sailors lead tours on deck, wearing 1812-vintage dress uniforms.

Just inland from the ship, the **USS Constitution** Museum (© 617/426-1812; www.ussconstitutionmuseum.org) satisfies kids' longings to play sailor: Participatory exhibits allow visitors to hoist a flag, fire a cannon, and learn more about the ship, via interactive computer displays and more than 3,000 naval artifacts.

ⓘ Off First Ave. (© **617/242-7511;** www. oldironsides.com).

✈ 🛏 See Boston Common **60**.

WHY THEY'LL THANK YOU: If a ship can be heroic, this one is.

---

269 History at Sea

The Ships of Portsmouth
Ages 6 & up • Portsmouth, England

IN THE MIDDLE OF ENGLAND'S SOUTHERN COAST, the great naval base of Portsmouth offers a staggering concentration of historic naval attractions, from a sunken Tudor flagship to Admiral Nelson's warship from the Battle of Trafalgar to a modern submarine.

For one ticket, you can visit four attractions lined up around Portsmouth's historic dockyard. The oldest part of the story is told by the *Mary Rose,* flagship of the fleet of King Henry VIII's wooden men-of-war, which sank in the Solent Channel in 1545 with the king himself watching in horror from shore; after more than 4 centuries on the ocean floor, it was brought back to the surface in 1982. The hull and more than 20,000 items retrieved by divers constitute one of England's major archaeological discoveries. On display is an amazing assemblage of artifacts—an almost-complete set of the ship's doctor's equipment; longbows and arrows, some still in shooting order; carpenters' tools; leather jackets; and some fine lace and silk. It also has a spectacular two-deck reconstruction of a segment of the ship, including the original guns.

The star of the show, though, is the **HMS** *Victory,* Lord Nelson's flagship, a 104-gun, first-rate ship that is the oldest commissioned warship in the world, launched May 7, 1765. It earned its fame on October 21, 1805, in the Battle of Trafalgar, when the English scored a decisive victory over the combined Spanish and French fleets, though the battle cost Nelson his life. Nelson's victory at Trafalgar and Wellington's at Waterloo dealt Napoleon a one-two punch from which he never recovered. Next to the *Victory,* the **Royal Naval Museum** houses relics of Nelson and his associates, as well as ship models, naval ceramics, figureheads, medals, uniforms, weapons, and other memorabilia. The fourth attraction is another warship, the 1860 **HMS** *Warrior.*

Two related Portsmouth attractions are the **Royal Navy Submarine Museum,** Haslar Jetty Road, Gosport (© 023/9252-9217; www.rnsubmus.co. uk), which features tours of the HMS *Alliance* submarine; and the **D-Day Museum,** Clarence Esplanade, Southsea (© 023/9282-7261; www.ddaymuseum. co.uk), devoted to the Normandy landings, which set sail from Portsmouth in 1944. Among its exhibits are a DUKW (popularly called a Duck) amphibious truck, as well as the Overlord Embroidery, which tells the complete story of

HMS *Victory*.

Operation Overlord in an immense appliquéd embroidery.

(i) College Road (© **023/9286-1512;** www. historicdockyard.co.uk).

🚃 Portsmouth, 2½ hr. from London.

🛏 $$ **Royal Beach Hotel,** South Parade, Southsea (© **023/9273-1281;** www.royal beachhotel.co.uk).

WHY THEY'LL THANK YOU: All you ever needed to know about fighting ships through the ages.

History at Sea **270**

O Say, Can You See
The Ships of Baltimore's Inner Harbor
All ages • Baltimore, Maryland, USA

PAST THE SEAWALL, just beyond the huge Domino Sugar sign, you can see cargo ships and active naval vessels docked in Baltimore Harbor, still a working deep-water port. But the **Inner Harbor** is the place where visitors cluster, thanks to redevelopment that loaded the old water-front with the Harborplace shopping mall, the **National Aquarium** , and a host of other tourist venues (a Hard Rock Cafe, an ESPN Zone, you know the drill). The

Inner Harbor development somehow got it right: It's compact but not crowded, and the authentic seaport feeling is kept alive by a collection of vintage seagoing vessels, which our kids clambered around happily for an afternoon. Add a Baltimore Orioles game at Camden Yard, within walking distance, and we had a weekend that made everyone in our family happy as clams.

Our favorite ship was the **USS Constellation,** a triple-masted sloop-of-war launched in 1854. The *Constellation* is the last Civil War–era vessel still afloat, and it was the first ship moored here. My kids eagerly prowled her gun decks, visited the wardrooms, watched a cannon being fired, and learned about the life of a sailor from the costumed staff on board; when it came time for the hourly raising-of-the-colors ceremony, they put on costumes and tugged the flag cords like seasoned salts.

The Harbor's other three ships, packaged as the Baltimore Maritime Museum, are also fascinating, if newer. It doesn't take much time to scoot around the gray iron decks of the Coast Guard Cutter *Taney,* the last floating survivor of the bombing of Pearl Harbor, which also was involved in the battle of Okinawa. Plunging into the underwater bowels of the **submarine USS Torsk** tested my sons' claustrophobia, but it's not every day you get to see inside a ship that torpedoed the last Japanese warships in World War II. The sturdy lightship *Chesapeake*—you can't miss that bright-red hull with CHESAPEAKE in huge white letters—also saw war

duty (it was painted a quiet gray during the war), but spent most of its days as a floating lighthouse riding the rough waters at the mouth of Chesapeake Bay. Past the Aquarium, we also climbed up the Seven-Foot Knoll Lighthouse to see the gigantic **Fresnel light.**

In the War of 1812, this prime harbor was a prize the British navy wanted badly—but star-shaped **Fort McHenry,** East Fort Avenue (📞 **410/962-4290;** www.nps.gov/fomc), across the water, protected Baltimore from British attack in 1814, in the battle Francis Scott Key commemorated in the "Star Spangled Banner." We rode the water taxi over to the fort, where we sprawled on the slopes and tried to picture the battle. We could almost see the rocket's red glare illuminating the Inner Harbor before us.

ⓘ Piers 3 and 5, Inner Harbor (📞 **410/ 396-3453;** www.baltomaritimemuseum.org).

✈ 🛏 See National Aquarium **142**.

WHY THEY'LL THANK YOU: Playing hide-and-seek between decks.

When England Ruled the Seas
The Cutty Sark *& the National Maritime Museum*
Ages 4 & up • Greenwich, England

NEARLY 6KM (3¾ MILES) EAST OF LONDON, at Greenwich Pier, in permanent dry dock lies the last and ultimate word in sail power: the sleek black three-masted *Cutty Sark,* the greatest of the clipper ships that brought home to Britain lucrative cargoes of tea from China and wool from Australia. Young fans of *Master and Commander* will thrill to the sight of her complicated masts and rigging—43 sails and 18km (11 miles) of rigging, dominated by a 46m-high (152-ft.) mainmast—ingeniously designed to catch every

breath of wind on the ocean and convert it to sheer speed.

Launched in Scotland in 1869, and named after the witch in Robert Burns's poem *Tam O'Shanter,* the **Cutty Sark** shattered speed records for its era, with its fastest voyage clocked at a then-unsurpassed 584km (363 miles) in 24 hours. On board the *Cutty Sark,* visitors can see the great ship's wheel on the poop deck, tour the wood-paneled officers' cabins, or peek into the cramped deckhouse cabins and the even-less-luxurious quarters for

The *Cutty Sark*.

the common seamen (nothing democratic about shipboard accommodations). Lower cargo decks now hold a **museum** devoted to clipper lore, as well as a very cool collection of carved figureheads from other ships.

To get a bit more of the story behind the ship, head to Greenwich Park to the **National Maritime Museum,** full of cannons, ship models, relics, and paintings that illustrate the glory that was Britain at sea. Look for some oddities here—everything from the dreaded cat-o'-nine-tails used to flog sailors to naval hero Lord Nelson's coat from the Battle of Trafalgar, with the prominent bullet hole in the left shoulder that killed him.

Frequent ferryboats from either Charing Cross Pier or Tower Pier run every half-hour or so to Greenwich, taking about an hour; the train trip from Waterloo Station is faster, about 15 minutes, but less atmospheric.

Nearby you can also visit the **Royal Observatory** 306 and the **Royal Naval College,** King William Walk (© **020/8269-4747**), designed by Sir Christopher Wren, which contains a magnificent painted hall where Lord Nelson lay in state in 1805 for the adoring public to pay their last respects.

ⓘ **Cutty Sark,** King William Walk © 020/8858-3445; www.cuttysark.org.uk).
National Maritime Museum, Park Row (© 020/8312-6608; www.nmm.ac.uk).

✈ ⇥ See London 55.

WHY THEY'LL THANK YOU: Britannia ruled the waves.

History at Sea **272**

Mystic Seaport
Salty Thrill of a Vintage Shipyard
Ages 6 & up • Mystic, Connecticut, USA

ONCE A DYNAMIC WHALING and shipbuilding center, the town of Mystic, Connecticut, is the perfect place for an open-air village that's all about maritime life. The heart of its collection is an ever-growing cache of some 500 ships, 2 centuries' worth of seagoing vessels, powered by everything from oars and sails to steam paddle wheels and engines. Standing on the Seaport's **re-created waterfront,** we

Mystic Seaport.

gazed out across the wide estuary of the Mystic River and found it just about impossible not to feel the lure of the open sea.

Rather than adhering to one historic period, Mystic Seaport adheres to its nautical theme. Yes, there are the requisite print ship, cooperage, schoolhouse, general store, and tavern, but the 17-acre site also features a ropewalk, a boat shed, a sail loft, a rigging loft, a lifesaving station, even shops for ship carvers and makers of nautical instruments. Staff members working in these shops aren't dressed in costumes and they aren't actors; they are real experts in the crafts they demonstrate, and delighted to share their knowledge with visitors—and somehow this makes the site feel more authentic, not less.

The most important ships in the collection have been designated national landmarks: the three-masted square-rigged whaler *Charles W. Morgan* (1841); the 1866 sloop smack *Emma C. Berry,* a graceful wood-hulled fishing boat; the 1908 paddle-wheeled excursion steamer

Sabino; and the 1921 two-masted fishing schooner *L. A. Dunton.* But the one that my kids found most fascinating to climb aboard was the replica of the impossibly cramped slave trade schooner *Amistad,* which was re-created right here in the Seaport's restoration workshops. Museum buildings on-site display extensive collections of things like scrimshaw and ship models and figureheads. A variety of boat trips are offered; inquire at the desk when you arrive, because once you've wandered around the site for a while, the urge to get out on the water becomes pretty strong. When you exit for the day, ask the gatekeeper to validate your ticket so you can come back the next day for free.

ⓘ 75 Greenmanville Ave. (Rte. 27; ✆ **888/ 9-SEAPORT** or 860/572-5315; www.mystic seaport.org).

✈ ⊨ See Mystic Aquarium 🅭.

WHY THEY'LL THANK YOU: Going down to the sea in ships.

Intrepid Sea-Air-Space Museum
The Great Gray Ghost Ship
Ages 6 & up • New York, New York, USA

YOU DON'T HAVE TO BE a weapon-obsessed boy to be fascinated by this rambling military museum, set on a vast aircraft carrier conveniently moored in New York City. From the wind-whipped landing deck, while your children scamper around stealth bombers, fighter jets, and choppers, you can enjoy wide-open Hudson River views and a Manhattan skyline panorama. But below, on the cavernous hangar deck, is where the real story is told, and the more you browse among its exhibits, the more you feel stirred by respect for America's fighting men and women.

During World War II, the *Intrepid* earned the nickname "The Ghost Ship" because it survived no fewer than seven bombings, five kamikaze raids, and one torpedo hit. After the war, it was reconditioned for use as a NASA recovery vessel and for tracking Soviet subs during the cold war. As the name implies, the *Intrepid* builds upon its multifaceted history to celebrate all branches of the armed forces, with a memorial to New York City police and firefighters thrown in for good measure. While some areas re-create day-to-day life on board a carrier—the dormlike Marine berths, the mess deck—within the battleship-gray steel walls of the hangar deck a wealth of exhibits have been set up, covering all the bases: uniforms, weapons, equipment, vintage aircraft, and memorabilia (Tom Clancy fans in the family will eat up the extensive technical stats provided for each of the aircraft on display). Take time to imagine the courage it took to explore the ocean floor in a

The deck of the *Intrepid*.

vintage bathysphere, or to rocket beyond Earth's atmosphere in the incredibly tiny early space capsule.

Moored across the pier are even more craft to explore: the **nuclear missile submarine** *Growler* and the retired supersonic jet **Concorde,** which you can tour as part of your *Intrepid* admission. For extra fees, you can satisfy the Play-Station generation with a couple of simulation rides and a rock-climbing wall, but for my money the real trip is hooking up with one of the veterans who volunteer to hang around and bend visitors' ears about their wartime experiences.

ⓘ Pier 86 at Hudson River and W. 46th St. (ⓒ 212/245-0072; www.intrepidmuseum. org).

✈ ⊨ See Manhattan **56**.

BEST TIME: UPDATE: The *Intrepid* Sea-Air-Space Museum Complex is closed for renovation until Fall 2008. The *Intrepid* has been moved from Pier 86 to Bayonne, N.J., for refurbishing.

WHY THEY'LL THANK YOU: Reliving battles in the air, on land, and sea.

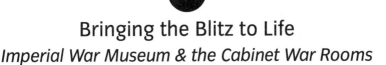

Bringing the Blitz to Life
Imperial War Museum & the Cabinet War Rooms
Ages 8 & up • London, England

FOR THE FIRST SEVERAL YEARS of World War II, with France occupied and the U.S. refusing to declare war, Great Britain fought almost single-handedly against the Axis powers, the lone dogged champion of freedom. It's an incredibly moving story, and nowhere is it told more poignantly than at London's Imperial War Museum and its satellite installation, the Cabinet War Rooms.

Among the equipment displayed at the museum is a Mark V tank, a Battle of Britain Spitfire, and a German one-man sub. In the **Documents Room** you can read the famous "peace in our time" agreement that Prime Minister Neville Chamberlain signed in 1938 to appease Hitler. But what most brings the war alive for children is the exhibit on the **Home Front,** September 1940 to late spring 1941, when the British people's famous pluck was tested to the utmost by food and petrol rationing, conscription of men as well as women, and a staggering influx of refugees and foreign servicemen. Many English children were sent to live away

from their families, in some cases for years. The **Blitz Experience** reconstructs an air-raid shelter and a blitzed street, with evocative sights, a sounds, and smells to capture the sensation of being caught in the bombing. A sobering exhibit on the Holocaust occupies two other floors; espionage and clandestine warfare are the themes of the Secret War Exhibition.

The perfect complement to this history lies across the river, near the government buildings of Whitehall, in the Cabinet War Rooms. This is no reconstruction but the actual secret warren of bombproof rooms abandoned by Prime Minister Winston Churchill and the British government at the end of World War II. Churchill directed Britain's valiant war effort from this underground lair, working here for months at a time. Look for the BBC microphone in his bedroom, from which he broadcast radio speeches that galvanized the British nation. In the **Map Room,** see the pinholes peppering the Atlantic Ocean, each pin representing the location of a convoy of ships. Notice, too, the chamber pots

The Imperial War Museum.

under the beds—there were no flush toilets down here. And don't miss the cramped closet called the **Transatlantic Telephone Room,** where a special scrambler phone allowed Churchill to hold secure phone conversations with President Franklin Roosevelt, convincing the Americans to join the effort and turn the course of the war.

ⓘ **Imperial War Museum,** Lambeth Rd. (✆ **020/7416-5000;** www.iwm.org.uk). **Cabinet War Rooms,** King Charles St. (✆ **020/7930-6961;** www.iwm.org.uk).

✈ ⊨ See London **55**.

WHY THEY'LL THANK YOU: Those who cannot learn from history are doomed to repeat it.

World War II & the Cold War **275**

The Nazi Invasion of England

Ages 6 & up • Jersey & Guernsey, England

PHYSICALLY CLOSER TO FRANCE than to Great Britain, Jersey and Guernsey have been part of the English kingdom ever since William the Conqueror. The only exception was the period from 1940 to 1945, when German soldiers occupied the islands as part of Hitler's Atlantic Wall defenses. Today the Channel Islands are popular vacation spots, with beautiful

beaches and cliff-top walks, but wartime gun emplacements, secret tunnels, and concrete bunkers can still be found around both islands—if you know where to look.

On Jersey, the first place to go is in the island's capital, St. Helier, right on the harborfront. **The Island Fortress Occupation Museum,** 9 Esplanade

(☎ **01534/734306**), has videos and exhibits describing the occupation, with several artifacts from that grim time, including lots of cool motorbikes. Also in St. Helier, the **Maritime Museum** on New North Quay displays the **Occupation Tapestry,** a 24m-long (79-ft.) tapestry embroidered by volunteers from every Jersey parish, recounting the story of the occupation. Probably the most intriguing site, however, is in St. Lawrence parish, the **Jersey War Tunnels,** Meadowbank, Les Charrieres, Malorey (☎ **01534/860808;** www.jerseywartunnels.com), where former Nazi hospital tunnels have been fitted out with videos, digital effects, and dioramas, as well as glass cases full of artifacts. Aboveground, a War Trail has been laid out, taking in remnants of German defenses. The **Channel Island Military Museum,** 5 Mile Rd., St. Ouen (☎ **01534/723136;** open in summer), is also worth a stop. Jersey has several bunkers and gun emplacements on headlands around the island, which can be visited at limited hours. One of the most chilling is the slitted concrete observation tower on Noirmont Point, which almost looks as if it is leering evilly out to sea.

In the center of the island of Guernsey are three fascinating sites. The **German Military Underground Hospital,** La Vassalerie, St Andrews parish, is a labyrinthine complex of concrete tunnels built over 3½ years by compulsory labor (Nazi captives from France, Spain, Morocco, Algeria, Belgium, Holland, Poland, and Russia, often working with their bare hands). All that show aboveground are the entrances and the square holes of escape shafts. The **German Occupation Museum,** Les Houards, Forest (☎ **01481/238205**), has more tunnels, as well as a re-created street showing life in Nazi-occupied Guernsey. Another restored bunker at St. Jacques was once the Germans' **Naval Signals Headquarters.** As on Jersey, guns, casemates, and observation towers dotted around the Guernsey coast have been restored by local enthusiasts; they are open limited hours, usually on weekends.

ⓘ Jersey (www.jersey.com). Guernsey (www.occupied.guernsey.net).

✈ Jersey and Guernsey, served from many U.K. airports.

🛏 $$$ **Apollo Hotel,** St. Saviour's Rd., St. Helier, Jersey (☎ **1534/725441;** www.huggler.com/apollo-hotel-jersey). $$ **Le Friquet Country Hotel,** rue de Friquet, Castel, Guernsey (☎ **1481/256509**).

WHY THEY'LL THANK YOU: Tunnels, bunkers, and towers—a hidden tale of war.

276 World War II & the Cold War

Day of Infamy: Pearl Harbor

Ages 8 & up • Honolulu, Hawaii, USA

TODAY HAWAII IS so synonymous with leis, luaus, and tropical suntans, it's weird to realize that most Americans had barely heard of this South Pacific U.S. possession before December 7, 1941, when the horrifying news came over the radio: Japanese bombers had attacked U.S. ships at Pearl Harbor, Honolulu. Hawaii wasn't even a state, but it was still American soil, which was under attack for the first time since the War of 1812. President Franklin D. Roosevelt called it "a day that will live in infamy," and after years of pretending that World War II wasn't our fight, we realized it was. Pearl Harbor is a site that inspires reflection on war and peace and our place in the global community.

The **USS *Arizona* Memorial** at Pearl Harbor is a truly special monument. Just 6 feet below the surface of the sea, you can see the deck of the 608-foot battleship USS *Arizona,* which sank in a swift 9 minutes, killing 1,177 of its men, more than half the total casualties that tragic day. Oil still oozes up from its engine room to stain the harbor's calm blue water—some say the ship's still weeping for its lost crew. Moored a short distance from shore, the memorial is a stark white rectangle with a scooped-out roof that spans the hull of the ruined ship; on its walkways you can ponder over the ship's bell, dredged up from the wreckage, and a shrine room with the inscribed names of the dead. The gallant flagpole overhead is attached to the mainmast of the sunken ship. You'll ride out to the memorial on Navy launches from the visitor center; go early if you can, because you'll wait 2 to 3 hours at midday. A 20-minute film and exhibits at the center fill in the history for the kids while you're waiting for your assigned ship time.

Two other ships in the harbor tell the rest of the World War II story, so you're not left on a tragic note. Next to the *Arizona,* you can board a World War II submarine, the **USS *Bowfin*** (© **808/ 423-1341;** www.bowfin.org), nicknamed the "Pearl Harbor Avenger" for the way it harried the Japanese throughout the rest of the war. This is a great place to see how submariners lived in their cramped underwater quarters. From the *Bowfin*'s visitor center you can also visit the **USS *Missouri*** (© **800/423-2263;** www. ussmissouri.com), a 58,000-ton battleship that fought at Tokyo, Iwo Jima, and Okinawa. Fittingly, the Japanese surrender was signed on September 2, 1945, on the deck of the *Missouri.* The guided tour, complete with 1940s music played on the shuttles to the ship, is a fascinating look at a massive seagoing vessel.

ⓘ Pearl Harbor (© **808/422-0561;** www. nps.gov/usar).

✈ Honolulu International.

🛏 $ **Hawaiiana Hotel,** 260 Beach Walk (© **800/367-5122** or 808/923-3811; www. hawaiianahotelatwaikiki.com). $$$ **Outrigger Waikiki on the Beach,** 2335 Kalakaua Ave. (© **800/OUTRIGGER** or 808/923-0711; www.outrigger.com).

WHY THEY'LL THANK YOU: Staring through the waves at a watery grave.

World War II & the Cold War   277

The D-Day Beaches of Normandy

Ages 6 & up • Arromanches-les-Bains to Grandcamps-les-Bains, France

EVEN WITHOUT A VETERAN in the family, 21st-century youngsters—who grew up in the shadows of two Gulf Wars—can relate to the Normandy Invasion. The tale has been told in films from *The Longest Day* to *Saving Private Ryan* and *Band of Brothers,* but nothing beats standing where it actually happened.

The Allied invasion of occupied France was swift, sudden, and a complete surprise to Hitler's formidable "Atlantic wall." In June 1944, the greatest armada ever—

soldiers and sailors, warships, landing craft, tugboats, jeeps—assembled along the southern coast of England. At 9:15pm on June 5, the French Resistance got a signal to start dynamiting railways in Normandy; around midnight, Allied planes began bombing the coast; by 1:30am paratroopers dropped onto French soil to cut off roads and isolate Nazi forces. At 6:30am, the Americans began landing on the beaches, code-named Utah and Omaha, followed an hour later by British and Canadian forces at Juno, Gold, and Sword.

I recommend starting in Caen, at the **Caen Memorial,** Esplanade Eisenhower (www.memorial-caen.fr). Perhaps Europe's best museum on World War II, it opened in 2004 to commemorate the 60th anniversary of D-day. In Bayeux, the **Normandy Battle Memorial Museum,** boulevard Fabian Ware (✆ **02-31-51-46-90**), has maps, models, and stirring eyewitness accounts of the battle. But the main thing is to visit the beaches themselves, where the story is told through narrative plaques (many in English), stark monuments, and the occasional war debris intentionally left in place—snarls of barbed wire, crumpled concrete bunkers, and rusted vehicles stranded on the flat sands.

At **Arromanches-les-Bains,** the **Musée du Débarquement,** place de 6-juin (✆ **02-31-22-34-31;** closed Jan), tells the story of the mammoth movable port (nicknamed Winston, after Churchill) that was towed across the Channel and installed to supply successive waves of Allied troops. The remains of this prefab harbor can still be seen. Moving west, **Omaha Beach** has been obscured by tourist development, but the section near

Colleville is still evocative, especially nearly 10,000 marble crosses and Star of David at the **Normandy American Cemetery** (✆ **02-31-51-62-00**). There's also a Canadian cemetery at Reviers, a British one in Bayeux, and a German one at LaCambe, but the American cemetery is by far the largest, for the simple, tragic reason that the heaviest fighting was on Omaha and Utah beaches.

Farther west, see the jagged lime cliffs of **Pointe du Hoc,** where daring American Rangers scaled the cliffs to capture gun emplacements on top (ironically, the guns had already been moved); its clifftop terrain scooped out by bomb craters vividly summons up images of the battle. Farther along the Cotentin Peninsula are **Utah Beach,** where the 4th U.S. Infantry Division landed, and the hamlet of **Ste-Mère-Eglise,** where the 101st Airborne parachuted into enemy territory—look for the statue of a paratrooper dangling on the spire of the village church.

ⓘ **Caen Tourist Board,** place Saint Pierre (✆ **02-31-27-14-14;** www.caen.fr/tourisme).

🚌 🛏 See Bayeux **198**.

WHY THEY'LL THANK YOU: The tide of World War II turned here.

---

278 **World War II & the Cold War**

Jewish Museum Berlin
Ages 8 & up • Berlin, Germany

THE MOST TALKED-ABOUT MUSEUM IN BERLIN, the **Judisches Museum Berlin** occupies one of the most spectacular buildings in the city. Europe's largest Jewish museum, it covers the entire panorama of German-Jewish history, from the arrival of Jewish merchants to trade with Roman legions, through the medieval Ashkenazi period, and on through centuries of assimilation when Judaic customs and rituals preserved an often fragile cultural identity. But what makes its presence in Berlin

especially powerful is the inevitable chapter on the Holocaust, when the Nazi regime systemically exterminated at least 6 million Jews, some 200,000 of them from Germany. Berlin, as Germany's center of commerce and intellectual life, had always had a prominent Jewish population, which was decimated by the Nazi horrors. The opening of this museum marks an important step in laying the ghosts of the Holocaust to rest.

Called "the silver lightning bolt," the museum was designed by architect

d. To some viewers, its
ts a shattered Star of
'on underscored by the
plated facade, and the
..dows haphazardly
..in the outer walls. Inside,
..s have intentionally been designed
..o make the visitor uneasy and disori-
ented, simulating the feeling of those who
were exiled. A vast hollow cuts through
the museum to mark what is gone. When
the exhibits reach the period of the Third
Reich, the hall's walls, ceiling, and floor
begin to close in. Perhaps the most chilling effect of all is in the hollow **Holocaust
Void,** a dark, windowless chamber that
evokes what was lost.

The exhibits concentrate on three
themes: Judaism and Jewish life, the devastating effects of the Holocaust, and the
post–World War II rebuilding of Jewish life
in Germany. But there's one other dramatic
fact the children will appreciate knowing:
that a fair amount of the material on display was resurrected from an older Jewish

museum, which opened in Berlin in
1933—not the best timing, for shortly
thereafter Hitler rose to power, and by
1938 the Gestapo had shut down the
museum, confiscating its collection of
art and Judaica. Only recently, after
reunification, could it be reassembled here
in this striking new site.

At the corner of Lewetzov and Jagow
streets—where a synagogue once stood,
which was destroyed by the Nazis—a
poignant **Jewish War Memorial** commemorates the many Berliners who were
deported, mostly to their deaths, from
1941 until the end of the war in 1945. Its
centerpiece is a life-size sculpture of a
freight car from one of the notorious
"death trains," with victims being dragged
into it.

ⓘ Lindenstrasse 9–14 (✆ **030/259933;**
www.jmberlin.de).

✈ ▭ See Berlin **281**.

WHY THEY'LL THANK YOU: Journeying
through 2,000 years of German-Jewish history.

Dachau Concentration Camp Memorial Site
Ages 12 & up • Dachau, Germany

Only 16KM (10 MILES) FROM MUNICH, what was
once a quiet little artists' community
became, in the course of 12 years, a notorious symbol of Nazi atrocities. It's an
easy side trip from the city in terms of
travel time, but the emotional impact of
visiting Dachau can be shattering. Make
sure your children are old enough to
handle it—and if they are, don't miss the
opportunity to bring them here.

In 1933, shortly after Adolf Hitler
became chancellor of Germany, Heinrich
Himmler and his SS replaced a former
ammunition factory in Dachau with the
first German concentration camp. Its list
of prisoners—identified as enemies of
the Third Reich—eventually included
everyone from communists and Social

Democrats to Jews, homosexuals, gypsies, Jehovah's Witnesses, clergymen,
political opponents, and certain trade
union members. More than 206,000 such
prisoners from 30 countries were imprisoned at Dachau. Some were forced into
slave labor, building roads or manufacturing Nazi armaments. SS doctors conducted grotesque medical experiments
on others. Eventually Dachau became a
laboratory for systematic mass murder:
Starvation, illness, beatings, and torture
killed thousands who were not otherwise
hanged, shot by firing squads, or lethally
injected. Official records admit to at least
30,000 deaths at Dachau between 1933
and 1945, but thousands of others simply
weren't recorded. The SS abandoned the

camp on April 28, 1945; the U.S. Army took charge the following day, liberating some 67,000 prisoners—all on the verge of death.

Entering the camp, you pass through a wrought-iron gate with the iniquitous slogan *Arbeit macht frei* (Work sets you free). In a vast graveled central yard, prisoners lined up for daily roll calls, a long, exhausting, and often humiliating procedure (even the dead had to show up for roll call). In the concrete shower rooms, new arrivals were stripped, disinfected, shaved, and given uniforms; in the bunker prison, punishments and torture were carried out in tiny cells. The main camp road, today lined with graceful poplars, back then was flanked by 32 barracks, each housing 208 prisoners (more in the overcrowded last year of the war). Two barracks have been rebuilt to show visitors the horrible conditions the prisoners endured. A large building that once contained the kitchen and laundry has been converted into a museum, where photographs and documents explicate the rise of the Nazi regime and the persecution of prisoners. Three memorial chapels—Catholic, Protestant, and Jewish––offer condolence at the far end of the road. Outside the camp walls is a brick crematorium, where the dead were reduced to ashes (a gas chamber was built here but never put into service). Words fail to convey the impact of this haunted—and haunting—place.

(i) **KZ-Gedenkstätte Dachau,** Alte-Roemar-Strasse 75 (© **08131/669970;** www.kz-gedenkstaette-dachau.de). Closed Mon.

🚆 Dachau, 16km (10 miles) from Munich.

🚏 See Munich's Marienplatz **47**.

WHY THEY'LL THANK YOU: Some horrors can only be understood by going there.

Hiroshima: The Original Ground Zero

Ages 10 & up • Hiroshima, Japan

THIS MODERN CITY IN SOUTHERN HONSHU, Japan's main island, has one tragic claim to fame: It was the first city ever destroyed by an atomic bomb, on August 6, 1945, at 8:15 in the morning. Kids have been taught about this tragic chapter in world history, but the full impact of it can only be felt here, at the first Ground Zero.

Peace Memorial Park (Heiwa Koen) lies in the center of Hiroshima. Among the memorials you'll see are the **A-Bomb Dome,** the skeletal ruins of the former Industrial Promotion Hall; the **Atomic Bomb Memorial Mound,** which contains the ashes of 70,000 unidentified victims; the **Memorial Cenotaph,** with the names of all of those killed by the bomb; the **Peace Flame,** which will burn until all atomic weapons vanish from the earth; and **Hiroshima National Peace Memorial Hall for the Atomic Bomb Victims,** with its panorama of the bombed city, made of 140,000 tiles (one for every Hiroshiman who had died by the end of 1945). The memorial kids will be most affected by is the **Statue of the A-Bomb Children**—a statue of a girl with outstretched arms, and rising above her a crane, a traditional Japanese symbol of happiness and longevity. Streamers of paper cranes from school kids all over Japan flutter in the breeze around her. The statue is based on a real-life girl who suffered from the effects of radiation after the bombing. Believing that if she could fold 1,000 paper cranes she would become well again, she folded 1,300 cranes—but still died of leukemia.

The main focus of the park is the **Peace Memorial Museum.** Its East Building tells

The A-Bomb Dome at Hiroshima.

of Hiroshima before and after the bomb, and rather than presenting the city as a blameless victim, as was done for years, these exhibits own up to Hiroshima's militaristic past. The museum also documents Hiroshima's current dedication to abolishing nuclear weapons. Be prepared to self-edit your walk-through of the West Building, for many of its images of the bomb's effects are too graphic for young children—photographs of burned and seared skin, charred remains of bodies, and people with open wounds. There's a bronze Buddha that was half-melted in the blast; some granite steps show a dark shadow that suggests someone had been sitting there at the time of the explosion—the shadow is all that remains.

Visiting Peace Memorial Park is a sobering experience, but perhaps a necessary one. What was dropped on Hiroshima is small compared to the bombs of today. The decision whether or not to use them will someday be in the hands of our children—let's make sure they know what chaos they could be unleashing.

ⓘ **Peace Memorial Park,** 1–2 Nakajima-cho, Naku-ku (© **082/241-4004;** www.pcf. city.hiroshima.jp).

🚄 Hiroshima, 5 hr. from Tokyo by bullet train.

🛏 $$ **Hotel Sunroute,** 3–3–1 Ohtemachi, Naka-ku (© **082/249-3600;** www.sunroute. jp). $$$ **Rihga Royal Hiroshima,** 6–78 Motomachi, Naka-ku (© **082/502-1121;** www.rihga.com).

WHY THEY'LL THANK YOU: They may not.

A City Once Divided
The Shadow of the Berlin Wall
Ages 8 & up • Berlin, Germany

History has a way of slipping past; it's startling to realize that most kids today were born after the fall of the Berlin Wall. Those of us who grew up with it may not realize how bizarre this chapter of history seems to a youngster. But visiting Berlin, I still find its shadow cast over the city, and the children listen with mouths agape to the story.

I don't know which part is strangest—the way vanquished Germany's capital, Berlin, was divvied up by the victors at the end of World War II; or how escalating Cold War tensions made the Soviet Union shut off East Germans from the western sectors. In 1948–49, Soviet and American tanks faced off on Frederickstrasse, as the Soviets tried to cut off access to West Berlin; the Allies coordinated airlifts to get supplies to West Berliners, and the Soviets finally eased their blockade. But with some 2.5 million East Germans defecting to the West from 1948 to 1961, the Soviet tightened the border between East and West Germany—and Berlin was its most vulnerable point. Overnight on August 13,

1961, the Soviet abruptly threw a barbed wire barrier around the western sectors, euphemistically named an *"antifaschistischer Schutzwall"* (anti-fascist protection wall). Eventually replaced by a hulking wall of concrete, covered with colorful political graffiti (on the west face only), it stretched east and north from Potsdamer Platz, absorbing one of Berlin's loveliest landmarks, the neoclassical triumphal arch of the **Brandenburger Tor,** Unter den Linden. Today, a Room of Silence in one of the restored arch's guardhouses lets visitors reflect on Germany's recent past.

The final version of the Berlin Wall was two parallel walls with a booby-trapped no man's land between, searchlit at night so armed Soviet guards could shoot escapees. Desperate East Germans did everything they could to get to freedom. Some 5,000 succeeded, but Soviet guards fatally shot at least 192 East German citizens in mid-escape. All this is commemorated at the small **Museum Haus am Checkpoint Charlie,** Friedrichstrasse 44 (✆ **030/2537250**).

A segment of the Berlin Wall.

Then, miraculously, the Soviet Union fell apart—almost overnight, it seemed—and on November 9, 1989, the Wall came tumbling down, with jubilant Germans on both sides cheering on the bulldozers and snatching souvenir chunks of the infamous stone. But lest we forget, the reunified German government reconstructed a 70m (230-ft.) stretch of the wall, the **Berlin Wall Memorial**—two stainless-steel walls embedded with fragments of the original wall. Visitors are free to peer through slits in the wall at the other side of the city, once so achingly out of reach.

(i) Ackerstrasse at Bernauer Strasse (www.wall-berlin.org). **Berlin Tourist Information,** Europa-Center (www.berlin.de).

✈ Berlin-Tagel.

🛏 $$ **Hotel Hackescher Markt,** Grosse Präsidentenstrasse 8 (✆ **030/280030;** www.hackescher-markt.com). $$ **Myers Hotel Berlin,** Betzer Strasse 26 (✆ **030/440140;** www.myershotel.de).

WHY THEY'LL THANK YOU: Daring escapes and tragic shots in the night.

World War II & the Cold War

The Spy Museum: Combat under Cover

Ages 6 & up • Washington, D.C., USA

LEAVING BEHIND ALL OF D.C.'s worthy Mall museums and sneaking up to F Street to see the Spy Museum seemed like a guilty pleasure. But the parents in our group all grew up in an era when Bond movies still seemed credible, and we were hot to see it, however schlocky. The kids trailed along, expecting some sort of Austin Power–ish romp. But what impressed me most was that this smartly packaged attraction is also plenty educational—a little science here, a little history there, lots of geography—we didn't have to feel guilty at all.

The entryway to the museum has a certain clandestine allure, as you pass through a blue-neon-lit tunnel and step into a very secure-looking elevator. We could have stayed forever in the **School for Spies** section, devoted to the tradecraft of espionage—everything from buttonhole cameras and invisible ink to microdots and disguised weapons. Several interactive kiosks let the kids hone their own skills, from detecting the bugging devices in a room to spotting covert activity in a seemingly harmless videoed street scene. The movie connection runs strong here, with a gadget-laden Bond car and a display of disguise techniques developed by Hollywood makeup artists. The kids were visibly getting drawn in.

The next gallery traces **intelligence gathering** through the ages, proving that the modern age has no monopoly on paranoia and secrecy—even leaders such as Moses and George Washington used secret agents, and don't get me started on the spying that went on in Tudor England (that's how Sir Walter Raleigh ended up in the Tower of London). I hadn't before thought of the Underground Railroad as a spy network, but

This shoe with a heel transmitter was used by the KGB during the Cold War.

what else was it, with all its secret codes and furtive activity?

The **World War II** section was especially gripping, partly because so many artifacts still exist (all declassified now, evidently). Hindsight is 20/20, they say, but it was shocking to learn how the U.S. government ignored spy warnings of Japan's imminent attack on Pearl Harbor (reminiscent of the unheeded FBI warnings before 9/11), and how the super-secret technology behind the first atom bomb slipped into the wrong hands. The section on **Bletchley Park,** where British code breakers feverishly worked to break Germany's famed Enigma code, engrossed me so much, the kids literally had to pull me away. Then we turned a corner and the **Cold War** was upon us, the great face-off between the CIA and the KGB that made paranoids of all us

baby boomers. I loved this section, especially the reconstruction of an East Berlin street corner, on top of the CIA's high-tech surveillance tunnel beneath the Soviet Embassy. Classic John LeCarre territory.

Coming out 2 hours later, the kids peppered us with questions: what was the Cold War all about, and who was this Cardinal Richlieu, and was the guy who wrote *Chitty Chitty Bang Bang* really a spy? Forget the PlayStation we were longing to get back to . . .

ⓘ 800 F St. (✆ **202/393-7795;** www. spymuseum.org).

✈ 🛏 See The National Mall ⓺.

WHY THEY'LL THANK YOU: Being Bond for an afternoon.

Chapter 8   For Budding Scientists

Science Museums . . . 317
The History of Flight . . . 328
Inventions & Industry . . . 334
Stargazing . . . 341

Wright Brothers National Memorial.

American Museum of Natural History
Discovering Dinosaurs
All ages • New York, New York, USA

How many children have fallen in love with dinosaurs in the echoing galleries of this world-class New York City museum? And the dinosaurs are only the tip of the iceberg: Over the years, Holden Caulfield brooded over its collection of Northwest Indian totem poles in *The Catcher in the Rye;* in the planetarium, Woody Allen wooed Diane Keaton in the 1979 film *Manhattan;* and curious scientists plonked Darryl Hannah's mermaid into a tank to examine her in the 1984 movie *Splash.* It's one of America's great museums, and invariably engrossing for children.

When you enter the magnificent rotunda at the top of the Central Park West steps—named for Theodore Roosevelt, the outdoors-loving President who

The Hall of African Mammals at the AMNH.

helped found the museum—a rearing skeleton of a mommy dinosaur protecting her baby from a small, fierce predator clues you in that the dazzling interactive fourth-floor dinosaur halls are the perennial star attraction. But our favorite sights are the superb dioramas in the **North American Mammals**—the grizzly bear raking open a freshly caught salmon, majestic elks lifting their massive antlers, wolves loping through eerie nighttime snow—or, on the floor above, the bi-level **African Mammals Hall,** where you can circle around a lumbering herd of perfectly preserved elephants or check out the giraffes browsing by their water hole. In the dimly lit **Ocean Life** room, a gargantuan model of a blue whale swims overhead while dolphins arc through plastic waves. Around the corner, the less-well-visited **North American Forest** dioramas are our family secret—a peaceful part of the museum where you can hunt for blue jays in oak trees and rattlesnakes behind the cactus. Haunting music playing in the **African** and **Asian peoples** sections lull you into studying precisely detailed displays of cultural artifacts: a Chinese bride's ornate sedan chair, a pygmy's blow darts, a re-creation of a Siberian shaman healing rite, a Yoruba ceremonial costume made of red snail shells.

The stunning **Rose Center for Earth and Space,** a 95-foot-high glass cube, includes an interactive exhibit on the nature of the universe, where you can step on a scale that shows your weight on Saturn, see an eerie phosphorescent model of the expanding universe, and touch cosmic debris. There are an IMAX theater, a space show, and always at least a couple of traveling exhibitions (my only quibble with the museum is the substantial extra fees charged for these, on top of an already hefty admission price). But there's enough to do here that you don't need to go for the extras. Wander at will, keeping your eyes open and your imagination at the ready. It's a magical place.

ⓘ Central Park West and 79th St. (📞 **212/769-5100;** www.amnh.org).

✈ 🛏 See Manhattan **56**.

WHY THEY'LL THANK YOU: The dioramas and the dinosaurs.

Science Museums 284

Field Museum: Visiting Sue & Friends
All ages • Chicago, Illinois, USA

THE MINUTE YOU WALK IN HERE and gape up at the world's largest, most complete *Tyrannosaurus rex* **skeleton**—named Sue for the paleontologist who dug it up in 1990 in South Dakota—you know you're in a world-class science museum. This beloved Chicago museum is so jampacked with bones, rocks, stuffed critters, and dioramas, it's no wonder Steven Spielberg made it home turf for his adventure hero Indiana Jones. Members of the video-game generation can learn a lot from a little chill time here, where it's not all about punching buttons and guiding cursors, but about using your eyes and your imagination to enter different habitats.

Animals, even dead ones propped into permanent poses, are always a natural draw for kids—call it the taxidermy version of a zoo—and the Field has some dramatic ones, notably the **lowland gorilla Bushman** (formerly of the Lincoln Park Zoo), and a notorious 19th-century pair of **man-eating lions** from East Africa. But there's another side to natural history, and the Field does an especially good job with the anthropological side of things, in exhibits like the **Pawnee Earth lodge,** the scenes of South Pacific island cultures, or the continent-hopping **African peoples** gallery, which ends up on a slave ship to the Americas (just in case you needed that bit of political history underlined). Best of all in this vein is the downstairs **Egyptian exhibit,** which doesn't just set out artifacts in glass cases but re-creates scenes of day-to-day life in ancient Egypt, from a burial rite to a teeming daily marketplace to a royal barge trip down the Nile (complete with locks). Inspired by the excavated tomb of Unis-ankh in Saqqara, this classic exhibit has been perked up with touch-screens and kid-friendly activities, such as making parchment from real papyrus plants plucked from the gallery's living marsh.

The dinosaur galleries here, while not as extensive as the ones at the American Museum of Natural History **283** in New York, have been incorporated into **Evolving Planet,** a huge new exhibit that's heavy on the interactives, which covers a 4-billion-year continuum of life on Earth (a bold move, opting to support Darwin despite the current culture wars). And then there's **Underground Adventure,** a very popular "total immersion environment" where supersized mechanized replicas of subterranean creatures—earwigs, centipedes, wolf spiders—will terrorize your children for an extra admission fee. The kids will probably beg to try this out, and who can blame them?

ⓘ Roosevelt Rd. and Lake Shore Dr. (📞 **312/922-9410;** www.fieldmuseum.org).

✈ 🛏 See Chicago **57**.

WHY THEY'LL THANK YOU: Taking enough time to let each kid find his or her favorite spot.

285

National Museum of Natural History
Science Central
All ages • Washington, D.C., USA

Wᴴᴇʀᴇᴀs ɪᴛs ʀɪᴠᴀʟs ɪɴ Chicago and New York (see above) hit visitors with a dinosaur skeleton right by the entrance, this
Smithsonian museum in Washington, D.C., plays its hand more casually, starting out with a huge African bush elephant in the Rotunda, where you first enter from the Mall. But that doesn't mean there aren't dinosaurs here—there are, literally tons of them, as well as one of the world's oldest fossils and a 70-million-year-old dinosaur egg. This is in fact the largest natural history museum in the world, with 125 million artifacts and specimens—nearly 90% of the Smithsonian's total holdings! And this being a Smithsonian museum, admission is free, which makes it all the easier to cruise in even if you only have a couple hours to spare. Given all the history stuff you'll probably be seeing in Washington, this place is a breath of fresh (and very kid-friendly) air.

With so much to see, the challenge is to navigate wisely. Here are the exhibits my children enjoyed most: The **Insect Zoo,** where toddlers can crawl through a model of an African termite mound; **Life in the Ancient Seas,** where you can walk around a diorama of a 230-million-year-old coral reef teeming with models of weird primitive fish; and the **Hall of Mammals,** right off the rotunda, where up-to-date lighting and sound make the dioramas of 274 taxidermied mammals completely interactive. Every once in a

while, the hall erupts with animal sounds, all part of the exhibit wizardry that makes this a lifelike experience. Similar interactive techniques have jazzed up the **Hall of Geology, Gems, and Minerals,** on the second floor, which really gives a "big picture" story of earth's evolution. The huge new **Ocean Hall** was still under construction when we visited, but by all accounts it should be a knockout when it's finished. Being regular visitors to New York's natural history museum, my kids are hard to impress when it comes to dinosaur halls, and the one in D.C. is slated for an overhaul; it does have some amazing specimens, though, including a pterosaur with a 40-foot wingspan, and the jaw of a monstrous ancient shark, the *Carcharodon megalodon,* with teeth 5 to 6 inches long.

We also loved the outdoor **butterfly garden,** which is open year-round, with four habitats—wetland, meadow, wood's edge, an urban garden. My city kids really responded to this little slice of nature in the middle of the nation's capital. Sometimes it's the little things that grab them—you just can't predict it.

ⓘ Constitution Ave. between 9th and 12th sts. (ⓒ **202/633-1000;** www.mnh.si.edu).

✈ ⊨ See the National Mall **63**.

WHY THEY'LL THANK YOU: When the lions start to roar in the Hall of Mammals.

Franklin Institute
In the Spirit of Old Ben Himself
Ages 4 & up • Philadelphia, Pennsylvania, USA

LET'S NEVER FORGET that Benjamin Franklin was a scientist as well as a statesman, publisher, and philosopher: The Franklin stove and bifocal glasses were just two contraptions he invented, and of course there's that whole experiment with the kite in the thunderstorm. It warms my heart to visit the Franklin Institute in Philadelphia, which pays homage to the quirkiest of our Founding Fathers. At the core of this museum is the **Franklin National Memorial,** with a 30-ton statue of its namesake and an evocative hands-on gallery on Franklin's inventions and the scientists he inspired. While it looks all stately and neoclassical on the outside, however, this place wouldn't reflect the spirit of Franklin if it didn't have a fascinating clutter of other exhibits that simply encourage kids to putter around.

Hands-on is the watchword at the Franklin Institute; pick up a schedule of the museum staff's frequent **daily demonstrations** so you won't miss the fun stuff. The collection of science- and technology-oriented exhibits ranges from a gigantic walk-through heart to the Train Factory, where you can play engineer for a 350-ton locomotive, to a Van de Graaff generator that'll make your hair stand on end at the Electricity gallery. Kid Science, on the lower level, uses a dramatic animé-like storyline to teach basic science

concepts to children ages 5 to 8. On the third floor, Sir Isaac's Loft demonstrates the principles of Newtonian physics with Rube Goldberg–ian machines, noise-makers, and light shows. The Sports Challenge section was intriguing, looking at the science behind popular sports like surfing and rock climbing, and we couldn't resist the Skybike, which you can ride along a 1-inch cable three stories above the atrium floor. The whole museum is all about curiosity, and it's one of the best embodiments of the scientific method you'll ever play in.

In the warmer months, a great **high-tech playground** sprouts out on the lawn, where young kids can really mess around with science concepts—the step-on organ is a crowd pleaser, as are the maze and the high-wire tandem bicycle. If your kids like this kind of stuff, you'll probably also want to devote some time to the nearby **Please Touch Museum,** 210 N. 21st St. (© **215/963-0667;** www.pleasetouchmuseum.org).

ⓘ Logan Circle, 20th St. and Benjamin Franklin Pkwy. ((© **215/448-1200;** www. fi.edu).

✈ ⊨ See Philadelphia **62**.

WHY THEY'LL THANK YOU: Playing with electricity at Ben Franklin's museum.

Museum of Science and Industry
You Can't Beat the Classics
All ages • Chicago, Illinois, USA

MY SENTIMENTAL FAVORITE among the world's great science museums, Chicago's Museum of Science and Industry was a wonderland to me when I visited it as a kid—and if anything, its appeal has only grown through the years, with a slew of great new exhibits to involve kids in learning. This place has both cool historic things to look at *and* lots of Exploratorium-type activities to play with—the best of both worlds. It doesn't even matter that it's way the other end of Lake Shore Drive from Chicago's other great science museums, the **Field Museum 284** and the **Shedd Aquarium 144**; this place deserves a full day to itself.

There were three iconic exhibits I absolutely had to make my children see, greatest hits from my own childhood: the **U-505,** a German submarine captured in 1944; the full-scale **Coal Mine,** which simulates a trip down into a dark, mysterious mine shaft; and the giant walk-through **model of the human heart.** (Another reason to make a full day of this museum—you want to get there early to beat the long lines for these three crowd favorites.)

The train lovers in my family had to be dragged away from the refurbished **Burlington Pioneer Zephyr train,** where you can climb on board and fiddle with loads of interactive thingies, but there was no rushing past the massive model train layout called **The Great Train Story,** which re-creates a train's journey from Seattle across the Rockies and the Great Plains to Chicago. In the **Transportation Zone,** every 7 minutes a full-size 727 airplane revs up its engines and plays voice recordings to simulate a "flight" from San Francisco to Chicago; nearby we could gape at a real lunar exploration module, a Mercury space capsule, and an Apollo command module. The fantastic collection

of famous **ship models** includes a mock-up of the quarterdeck of a 19th-century tall ship where you can give the wheel a spin. We all giggled with delight at **Out to Lunch,** a gargantuan collection of fast-food giveaway toys (including several I remembered prying out of our car seats). **Toymaker 3000** is a captivating interactive gallery that shows how industrial robots perform simple tasks.

Last but certainly not least, it did my heart good to see my daughter entranced by **Colleen Moore's Fairy Castle,** a storybook miniature palace filled with priceless treasures (check out the chandeliers—they sparkle with real pearls and diamonds). Gee, I felt the same way when I was her age.

ⓘ 57th St. and Lake Shore Dr. (ⓒ **800/468-6674** or 773/684-1414; www.msichicago.org).

✈ ⃞ See Chicago **57**.

WHY THEY'LL THANK YOU: Happily exhausted by 5pm.

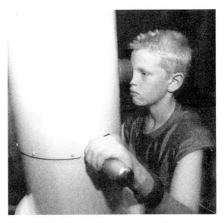

"On the Attack" Interactive Periscope at the Museum of Science and Industry.

The Exploratorium
The Ultimate Hands-On Museum
All ages • San Francisco, California, USA

"THE BEST SCIENCE MUSEUM IN THE WORLD" is what *Scientific American* magazine once called this San Francisco attraction, right by the waterfront parks of the Marina District. Set in a sprawling former airplane hangar, every bit of floor space is taken up with inventive activity stations and displays that just cry out for youngsters to press, jiggle, squeeze, fiddle, poke, and manipulate to their heart's content. I've been there with toddlers and I've been there with teens, and everyone has always been totally absorbed. They don't seem to care that they're also learning scientific concepts, in a way that will really stick.

The Exploratorium staff is constantly engaged in dreaming up new exhibits, so there's no guarantee that the stuff we loved won't have been replaced by

something even cooler by the time you get there. The giant soap-bubble maker is perennially popular, as is the shadow wall, the visual distortion room, and machines that make sand patterns with sound waves. The **Tactile Dome** is an amazing experience for older kids, where they grope their way around in complete darkness, dependent on senses other than sight. Across Marina Boulevard, at the end of the Marina breakwater, you'll find one of the Exploratorium's most intriguing inventions: the **Wave Organ,** a hunk of concrete embedded with listening tubes that lead underwater to translate the ebb and flow of ocean currents into strange gurgles and humming sounds.

There's a handmade quality to many of the displays that I find very appealing—

The Exploratorium.

clearly they've been bolted and knocked together out of plywood, wires, PVC pipes, whatever is on hand, and I can't help but think this encourages kids to become putterers and inventors themselves. As my kids get older, their interests change; the last time we were there, they gravitated to exhibits on principles of light, optics, and perception, whereas in years past they were engrossed in the simple physics concepts demonstrated in the section on matter. Biology and electricity sections on the mezzanine are fascinating too. (There's a **play area** for under-4s, a godsend if you need to entertain a toddler while your older kid works the exhibits.) On our most recent visit, I watched my continually squabbling son and daughter sit for 15 minutes on either side of a mirrored pane of glass, watching their grinning faces blend together as lighting levels were gradually raised and lowered—so much for hating your siblings.

You'll find local youngsters here, not just tourists and bored school groups. It's a noisy, high-raftered, under-lit space and eventually we hit overload and have to bail out. But we never leave because we've run out of things to do.

(i) 3601 Lyon St. (© **415/397-5673;** www. exploratorium.org).

✈ 🛏 See San Francisco Cable Cars **68**.
WHY THEY'LL THANK YOU: Hands-on = brains on.

---

289 Science Museums

Powerhouse Museum
Where Sydney Gets Interactive
All ages • Sydney, Australia

Aᴜꜱᴛʀᴀʟɪᴀ'ꜱ ʟᴀʀɢᴇꜱᴛ ᴍᴜꜱᴇᴜᴍ looks so sleek and interactive, it's surprising to learn that it began more than a century ago, in 1880, as an outgrowth of the 1879 international Garden Palace Exhibition in Sydney. Like the Smithsonian in Washington, D.C., it has a sort of "nation's attic" collection, with some 385,000 objects spanning a number of fields: science, technology, engineering, transport, Australian history, and the decorative arts.

Here are just a few of the coolest things in the 22 permanent exhibitions: a priceless Boult & Watt rotative steam engine; a Catalina flying boat; a steam locomotive; a reconstructed 1930s Art Deco cinema; a re-created 19th-century sheep farmers' rural store; a Russian spacesuit; an 1880s bush-hut kitchen; a 1920s "germ-free" kitchen. What's more, the accompanying text and touch-screens aren't full of geeky technical explanations—they emphasize the role of human curiosity and creativity, hoping to inspire tomorrow's innovators. Kids will probably gravitate to the **hands-on displays** in the computer, science, and technology exhibits, which allow them to learn scientific concepts by conducting their own miniexperiments. Then there are the **media labs,** SoundHouse and VectorLab, where kids can sign up for workshops in digital graphics and music production. The under-8s have their own section, **Kids Interactive Discovery Spaces,** where simpler hands-on activities are set up in primary-colored play areas.

The Powerhouse also owns the historic **Sydney Observatory,** Watson Road, Observatory Hill, The Rocks (© **02/9241 3767;** www.sydneyobservatory.com); light pollution in the metropolitan area has made its stargazing days a thing of the past, but as a museum of astronomy it's still got some cool old telescopes and exhibits, not to mention a 3-D Space Theatre.

ⓘ 500 Harris St., Ultimo (near Darling Harbour; ℃ **02/9217 0111;** www. powerhousemuseum.com).

 See Sydney Harbour Bridge ⑯.

WHY THEY'LL THANK YOU: Each visitor finds his or her own moment of wonder.

The Science & Natural History Museums

All ages • London, England

Hᴇʀᴇ's Lᴏɴᴅᴏɴ's ᴋɴᴏᴄᴋᴏᴜᴛ one-two punch: two world-class science museums, on adjacent sites in South Kensington, and both of them free. It's quite tempting to do them both in 1 day, but be forewarned: Their collections are so huge, and so engrossing, that it may be hard to

London's Natural History Museum.

move your kids on from one to the other.

The **Science Museum** is a place of hands-on galleries, working models, and video displays galore, all tracing the development of science and industry and—especially important for kids—showing their influence on everyday life. Marvelous interactive consoles placed strategically throughout the museum help you plot your visit according to your special interests. You'll see Stephenson's original rocket and the tiny prototype railroad engine; you can also see Whittle's original jet engine and the Apollo 10 space module. The King George III Collection of scientific instruments is the highlight of a gallery on science in the 18th century, an era when a gifted assortment of British scientists, many of them brilliant amateurs, led a Golden Age of scientific discoveries. In a newer wing, exhibits explore such cutting-edge topics as genetics, digital technology, and artificial intelligence—learn how engineers observe sea life with robotic submarines, or how DNA was used to identify living relatives of the Bleadon Man, a 2,000-year-old Iron Age Man.

Science of a more organic nature reigns at the **Natural History Museum.** The Science Museum's exhibits may be more exciting, but I must admit I'm a sucker for the exotic Victorian architecture of the Natural History Museum's main hall. While not quite as amazing as the New York and Washington, D.C., natural history museums, London's is a don't-miss for dinosaur lovers, and there are magnificent specimens of all sorts of living and fossil plants, animals, and minerals. The geological history of our planet is dramatically illustrated in the exhibit "Earth Today and Tomorrow"—it truly puts the Bang in the Big Bang.

ⓘ **Science Museum,** Exhibition Rd. (ⓒ **0870/870-4868;** www.sciencemuseum. org.uk). **Natural History Museum,** Cromwell Rd. (ⓒ **020/7942-5000;** www.nhm.ac.uk).

✈ 🛏 See London **55**.

WHY THEY'LL THANK YOU: Science is their future.

Science Museums

291

Glasgow Science Centre
High-Tech Revolution for the New Millennium
All ages • Glasgow, Scotland, UK

Aᴅᴜʟᴛꜱ ᴍᴀʏ ᴘᴜᴛ Glasgow on their travel itineraries because they want to see the mind-boggling art in the Burrell Collection, but for the kids, it's all about the dynamic Glasgow Science Centre.

You'll spot the Science Centre from a long way off, its gleaming titanium-clad crescent shape reflected in the river. The crescent is punctuated by the slender aerodynamic **Glasgow Tower,** which rotates 360 degrees (the whole thing rotates from the ground up, not just a platform at the top—it's the world's only structure to spin like this); a quick zip upward in an elevator and you have a panoramic view of the city, along with multimedia displays on Glasgow's history and future. The center also has a planetarium and IMAX screen (the only one in Scotland). The exhibits do emphasize Scottish scientists and inventors, specifically Glaswegians, but for good reason: Glasgow boomed during the Industrial Revolution, with great ironworks and steelworks and a huge shipbuilding industry, and engineers and designers were a vital part of all that. This is no stuffy historical display, however: Following the pattern of such successful American museums as the Exploratorium (see **288**) and the Liberty Science Center, the Glasgow Science Centre explains technology in such an entertaining, interactive way that kids are completely drawn in. They'll be able to make their own soundtrack and animation, star in their own digital video, or do a 3-D head scan and then rearrange their facial features. At special shows and workshops, you'll see a glass smashed by sound, "catch" shadows, experience a million volts of indoor lightning, see liquid nitrogen, view the bacteria that lurk on you, and build a lie detector.

ⓘ 50 Pacific Quay (ⓒ **0141/420-5010;** www.gsc.org.uk).

✈ Glasgow, 16km (10 miles) west of the city.

🛏 $$$ **Hilton Glasgow Hotel,** 1 William St. (ⓒ **800/445-8667** in the U.S., or 0141/ 204-5555; www.hilton.co.uk/glasgow).

WHY THEY'LL THANK YOU: Futuristic outside, geeky fun inside.

Cité des Sciences et de l'Industrie

All ages • Paris, France

As PART OF AN AMBITIOUS urban-renewal scheme for northeastern Paris, the French government completely gutted a vacant slaughterhouse, sheathed it with a sleek new facade, surrounded it with a moat, and crowned it with a huge reflective geodesic dome—*voilà!* La Cité des Sciences et de l'Industrie was born. Opened in 1986, to coincide with the most recent flyby of Halley's Comet, La Cité was worth the $642-million price tag, drawing crowds (and not just children) to the long Métro ride out to Parc La Villette's leisurely green expanse. It's popular enough that you should call ahead to reserve timed-entrance tickets, although agreeably whiling away an hour or two in the surrounding park is no problem either.

La Cité may seem overwhelming at first but most families know to head straight for **La Cité des Enfants,** where a couple hundred hands-on activity stations painlessly educate children. Divided into two sections, one for ages 3 to 5 and another for ages 6 to 12, it features incredibly cool stuff like seeing an "X-ray" of your body breathing or racing a skeleton on a bicycle to see which bones and muscles move.

The top three floors of the museum are devoted to the Explora, geared for adults as well as children, laymen and scientists alike: Its displays are organized to relate to four themes—the universe, life, matter, and communication. These well-lit, handsomely mounted exhibits, which are continually updated and replaced, stretch the length of the building, so don't even try to see them all—stroll along and sample what appeals to you (like a recent one titled **Grossology**—what child could pass

La Cité des Sciences et de l'Industrie.

that up?). We appreciated the peculiarly Gallic sense of humor, such as the demonstration of seismographic activity presented as the comic-strip adventures of a jungle explorer. Visitors can also climb aboard the *Argonaut,* a diesel submarine originally built in 1905 that's like something out of Jules Verne's science fiction, a prophetic prototype for the giant nuclear subs of the later 20th century.

It's almost de rigueur for a museum of this sort to have an IMAX-style theater, but the one here, the Géode, is a doozy, occupying that striking 34m (112-ft.)

silver-skinned dome that's the focal point of the complex. There's a planetarium too, and a simulator ride—no feature of such science museums has been left out. You could easily spend a full day here, making that long subway ride more than worth it.

(i) 30 av. Corentine-Cariou, La Villette ((C) **01-40-05-80-00;** www.cite-sciences.fr).

✈ 🛏 See Paris **54**.

WHY THEY'LL THANK YOU: A welcome antidote to the history overload in Paris.

---

293 Science Museums

Deutsches Museum
The Great German Tech Shrine
All ages • Munich, Germany

MY KIDS ARE CONVINCED that Germans are the world's finest scientists and engineers, and I have a sneaking suspicion that that impression was riveted into their brains by visiting the German Museum of Science and Technology. It's a knockout attraction, the world's largest technology museum, set prominently on an island in the middle of the river Isar as it flows through Munich.

I instantly felt at home here, harking back to my childhood days at Chicago's Museum of Science and Industry **287**, but the more I explored, the more I marveled at the historic nature of this collection, with so many one-of-a-kind artifacts and priceless originals. Yes, most of the important **inventions** highlighted here are German-made, but that's because Germans were at the forefront of so many scientific developments in the 19th century. You'll see the first electric dynamo (built by Siemens in 1866), the first automobile (built by Benz in 1886), the first diesel engine (Diesel, 1897), and the laboratory bench at which the atom was first split (Hahn and Strassmann, 1938). I was astonished to see an X-ray machine from

1895 and the first truly powerful refracting telescope, which discovered Neptune in 1846. There's as much history as science here—an 1806 Jacquard loom, championed by Napoleon, that revolutionized the textile industry (thus replacing a cottage industry with factories), or the ciphering machines used in World War II to translate messages into the long-unbroken Enigma code.

Even children too young to appreciate these ground-breaking inventions will enjoy the **hands-on exhibits,** with hundreds of buttons to push, levers to crank, and gears to turn. Lots of knowledgeable staff (excellent English speakers, generally) hang around to answer questions and demonstrate the scientific principles that make steam engines and pumps work.

Don't get hung up on seeing everything; get a museum guide and head for the areas your family is most interested in, whether it be airplanes, bikes, clocks, cars, or computers. We loved the agriculture section's detailed scale models of farms throughout the ages. The electrical power hall is also intriguing, with high-voltage displays that actually produce lightning. My husband, the amateur astronomer, made sure we spent time in the astronomy exhibit—the largest in Europe—complete with a planetarium and a two-domed observatory with a solar telescope. World-class in every way.

(i) Museumsinsel 1 (② **089/21791;** www. deutsches-museum.de).

✈ ⊨ See Munich's Marienplatz **47**.

WHY THEY'LL THANK YOU: From the Gutenberg Bible to the Helios space probe and everything in between.

The History of Flight
294

Kitty Hawk
The Wright Brothers Learn to Fly
Ages 4 & up • Kill Devil Hills, North Carolina, USA

THE NAME KITTY HAWK is forever associated with Orville and Wilbur Wright—it says so right on North Carolina's license plates. That's the place where, on December 17, 1903, this brother-brother team from Dayton, Ohio, achieved the world's first sustained, controlled, heavier-than-air powered flight. (You need all those adjectives to distinguish the Wrights' flight from a mere glider or hot-air balloon flight.) But you could score big trivia points for knowing that the Wrights didn't take off from the town of Kitty Hawk, but from a nearby 90-foot-high dune called **Kill Devil Hill** on the Outer Banks, a bony finger of land that separates the Atlantic Ocean from the inner sounds and estuaries of North Carolina's coast. Ask the

A Glider at the Wright Brothers National Memorial.

kids: If you were flying an experimental aircraft into the teeth of gusting Atlantic winds, would you really want to launch from a place called Kill Devil Hill?

Desperate to get home to Dayton in time for Christmas, Orville and Wilbur did get the Wright Flyer off the ground that windy December day in 1903, keeping it aloft for 59 seconds and flying a distance of 852 feet. Their feat is commemorated at the **Wright Brothers National Memorial,** an imposing 60-foot-high pylon of white North Carolina granite, erected in 1932 on Kill Devil Hill. In fact, the Wrights made four successful flights that day, of increasing lengths; numbered markers on the long slopes show how far they made it each time, until on the fourth go the Wright Flyer crash-landed. The visitor center features a replica of that **Wright Flyer,** plus a glider they flew here in 1902, along with a few exhibits telling the Wright Brothers' story; park rangers lead twice-daily tours, and run afternoon family activities such as kite flying or paper-airplane building. You can explore reconstructions of the hangar Orville and

Wilbur built for their plane and their workshop/living quarters. The main thing, though, is to stand on the big grassy dune and feel the breezes rise off the water; it suddenly becomes clear why the Wright brothers traveled all the way to North Carolina to get their spidery winged craft aloft.

Not far away, at the highest sand dune on the East Coast, 138-foot-high Jockey's Ridge, you can try out those Outer Banks winds yourself by taking a hang-gliding lesson from the world's largest hang-gliding school, **Kitty Hawk Kites,** near the visitor center of Jockey's Ridge State Park (milepost 12 off U.S. 158 Bypass; ✆ **252/441-7132**). Beginning, intermediate, and advanced instruction are provided; for reservations, call ✆ **877/359-8447** or 252/441-4124; or go to www.kittyhawk.com.

ⓘ Milepost 8, U.S. 158 Bypass (✆ **252/441-7430**; www.nps.gov/wrbr).

✈ ⊨ See Roanoake Island **235** or Cape Hatteras National Seashore **445**.

WHY THEY'LL THANK YOU: Feeling the wind beneath their wings.

Dayton Aviation Heritage Park
The Wright Stuff
Ages 6 & up • Dayton, Ohio, USA

When Orville and Wilbur Wright returned home from Kitty Hawk, North Carolina, in December 1903, they weren't national heroes. Sure, they had flown their frail contraption on the strong air currents gusting off the Outer Banks, but they still hadn't invented a practical means of powered flight. That job was still ahead

of them—and Dayton, Ohio, was where they made it happen.

The Dayton Aviation Heritage Park celebrates the next 2 years of the Wright brothers saga. The core of the park is the replica **Wright Brothers Cycle Company,** a pleasant brick corner shop where the Wrights had made bicycles since 1892. (The original shop,

A SPAD XIII at the National Museum of the United States Air Force.

329

and the Wright brothers' Dayton home, were moved to Greenfield Village ㉕). Back in their workshop, the brothers ignored their bicycle business—itself a newfangled technology then—to focus on their fledgling airplanes. The **visitor center** at 30 S. Williams St. occupies a site that was once the brothers' printing business, another sideline that financed the aviation obsession.

East of town, on the grounds of Wright-Patterson Air Force Base, is **Huffman Prairie Flying Field,** 2380 Memorial Rd. (𝄐 **937/425-0008**), an open pasture which the brothers used for test flights. You can see a replica of their hangar, plus a catapult tower they built to launch the pesky Wright Flyer II. The ultimate outcome was the 1905 Wright Flyer III, which could reliably take off, land, turn in midair, and fly as long as it had fuel in the gas tank. The Wright Flyer III can be seen at **Carillon Park,** 1000 Carillon Blvd. (𝄐 **937/ 293-2841;** www.carillonpark.org), a 65-acre open-air history park with 25 exhibit buildings; from April to October, the Wright Brothers Aviation Center here displays the plane, three original Wright Bros. bicycles, and other Wright artifacts.

While you're out at Wright-Patterson Air Force Base, aviation geeks could spend at least half a day at the **National Museum of the United States Air Force,** 1000 Spaatz St. (𝄐 **937/255-3284;** www.wpafb. af.mil/museum), and the neighboring **National Aviation Hall of Fame,** which honors famous flyers.

By a cool coincidence, the famous black poet **Paul Laurence Dunbar** was a schoolmate of Orville's and friend of the Wrights, who published his poetry in their printing shop. You can tour his house at 219 Paul Laurence Dunbar St. (𝄐 **937/224-7061**) on weekends April and September, Wednesday to Sunday from May to August.

ⓘ 22 S. Williams St. (𝄐 **937/225-7705;** www.nps.gov/daav).

✈ Dayton International.

🛏 $$$ **Crowne Plaza,** 33 E. 5th St. (𝄐 **877/2-CROWNE** or 937/224-0080; www.ichotelsgroup.com). $ **Days Inn Wright-Patterson,** 1891 Harshman Rd. (𝄐 **937/236-8083;** www.daysinn.com).

BEST TIME: May–Sept.

WHY THEY'LL THANK YOU: Getting off the ground was just the beginning . . .

National Air and Space Museum
Plane Fantastic
All ages • Washington, D.C., USA

T**HE ONE DO-NOT-MISS STOP** for families visiting our nation's capital, Air and Space is pretty much the star player on the Smithsonian museum team, at least as far as kids are concerned. I still catch my breath when I walk into its sleek entrance hall off the Mall and see all those **historic aircraft** dangling from the ceiling—the Wright brothers' historic 1903 Wright Flyer, Charles Lindbergh's *Spirit of St. Louis,* the *Enola Gay* bomber that devastated Hiroshima, the *Friendship 7* capsule

that took John Glenn into space. Jaded as I am by IMAX movies, I made a point of having my kids sit through the classic *To Fly,* still my favorite of the genre; we spent another afternoon out in Virginia at the satellite location so we could see the space shuttle *Enterprise.* Whether you come here for the history, the science, or just the technothrill of seeing so much heavy metal, Air and Space delivers the goods.

Air and Space holds the largest collection of historic aircraft and spacecraft in the world; only about 10% of what it owns is actually on display, even with the annex out in Virginia. Besides gawking at the famous planes hanging out in the lobby, kids love to walk through the **Skylab orbital workshop**; other galleries highlight the solar system, U.S. manned spaceflights, and aviation during both world wars. You can sneak in some hard science education with **How Things Fly,** an interactive exhibit that demonstrates principles of flight and aerodynamics (the wind and smoke tunnels are especially fun), and get into some heady astrophysics with **Explore the Universe,** which probes theories about how the universe took shape. But this big, noisy, kid-packed museum isn't the sort of place where you want to be serious and thoughtful; besides the IMAX movie we wanted to do all the pumped-up extras like the **flight simulators** and the **space show** at the planetarium—admission to the museum is free, but very few families get away without buying a ticket for one of these add-ons.

The second part of the museum is out near Dulles Airport in Chantilly, Virginia, at 14390 Air and Space Museum Pkwy., where two gigantic hangars—one for aviation artifacts, the other for space artifacts—accompany a 164-foot-tall **observation tower** for watching planes land and take off at Dulles. The **space hangar** is the length of three football fields—it has to be in order to house such huge artifacts as the space shuttle, rocket boosters, spacewalk capsules, and a full-scale prototype of the Mars Pathfinder lander. The scale of this technology is awesome, and you just can't appreciate it unless you stand right next to these babies and crane your neck upward.

ⓘ Independence Ave. SW, between 4th and 7th sts. (✆ **202/633-1000;** www.nasm. si.edu).

✈ 🛏 See the National Mall **63**.

WHY THEY'LL THANK YOU: Historic flying machines soaring in the lobby.

---

297 **The History of Flight**

Kennedy Space Center: 10 . . . 9 . . . 8 . . .

Ages 4 & up • Titusville, Florida, USA

SPACEFLIGHT HAS LOST SO MUCH of its glamour that it can be hard for kids to comprehend how exciting it once was to watch a mighty booster rocket blast off from the launchpad at Cape Canaveral. So pop in a DVD of *The Right Stuff* or *Apollo 13* before your trip to the Space Coast. Make them see how being an astronaut was once the coolest job a kid could aspire to.

You don't have to be a space buff to be awed by the sheer grandeur of the facilities at NASA's primary space-launch facility. Begin your visit at the **Kennedy Space Center Visitor Complex**—though it's a bit theme-park-slick, it does outline the history of space exploration well, and there are real NASA rockets on display, as well as (the coolest thing to me) the actual Mercury Mission Control

Room from the 1960s. Hands-on activities, a daily "Encounter" with an astronaut, and an IMAX theater make this a place where kids will want to hang out. The **Astronaut Hall of Fame,** a separate attraction at the center, pays tribute to the Mercury, Gemini, and Apollo space jockeys, along with even more vintage spacecraft—a Mercury 7 capsule, a Gemini training capsule, and an Apollo 14 command module—and several space-y simulator rides. Plan ahead (call ✆ **321/ 449-4400** for a reservation) to snag a **lunch with an astronaut**—even such greats as John Glenn, Jim Lovell, Walt Cunningham, and Jon McBride have taken their turns in this daily event.

Narrated **bus tours** depart every 10 minutes to explore the sprawling space-center grounds. Stops include the LC-39 Observation Gantry, with a dramatic 360-degree view over launchpads; the International Space Station Center, where scientists and engineers prepare additions to the space station now in orbit; and the Apollo/Saturn V Center, which includes artifacts (a moon rock to touch!), films, interactive exhibits, and the 363-foot-tall Saturn V, the most powerful U.S. rocket ever launched. It's not all Disneyfied, which in my opinion is a plus, but if the kids get restless (especially given the typical Florida heat), you can hop on the next bus and move on.

The real thrill, of course, is to see a **shuttle launch;** call ✆ **321/867-5000** or check www.ksc.nasa.gov for a schedule of upcoming takeoffs (always an iffy thing, depending on weather or equipment problems), then buy tickets at the visitor complex or online at www.ksctickets.com. Or view shuttle launches the way the locals do: from the causeways leading to the islands and on U.S. 1 as it skirts the waterfront in Titusville.

ⓘ NASA Pkwy. (Fla. 405; ✆ **321/449-4444** for info, 321/449-4444 for reservations; www.kennedyspacecenter.com).

✈ Melbourne International, 22 miles. Orlando International, 35 miles.

Riding a space chair at the Kennedy Space Center.

🛏 $$$ **DoubleTree Hotel Cocoa Beach Oceanfront,** 2080 N. Atlantic Ave., Cocoa Beach (✆ **800/552-3224** or 321/783-9222; www.cocoabeachdoubletree.com). $$ **Riverview Hotel,** 103 Flagler Ave., New Smyrna Beach (✆ **800/945-7416** or 386/428-5858; www.riverviewhotel.com).

WHY THEY'LL THANK YOU: Huge rockets up close.

The History of Flight

298

Space Center Houston

The Face of Flight Control

Ages 6 & up • Clear Lake, Texas, USA

Once NASA spacecraft take off from the Kennedy Space Center at Cape Canaveral, during flight they are monitored from the Johnson Space Center in Houston, hence the famous quote from *Apollo 13*—"Houston, we have a problem." Like its Florida sibling, the Houston Space Center has turned its visitor center into an exciting **interactive exhibit hall** that makes the tram tours of the actual facility almost beside the point. In fact, the folks in Houston upstaged their Florida colleagues by bringing in Disney Imagineering to help design its exhibits—but having real access to the NASA goods makes this so much more than a theme-park attraction.

Inside the Space Center, for example, you can take a virtual visit to the hottest project in space, the 16-nation 361-foot-long **International Space Station,** via computer console in a gallery that simulates outer-space weightlessness. The **Feel of Space** gallery explores what life is like for astronauts aboard the space station, with a Mission Briefing Officer showing how everyday tasks like showering and eating are complicated by a microgravity environment. After this entertaining presentation, you're free to enter a training module loaded up with sophisticated computer technology to try your hand at landing a lunar orbiter, retrieving a satellite, or exploring a shuttle system. Artifacts in the **Starship Gallery** include the Mercury Atlas *Faith 7* capsule flown by Gordon Cooper, the Gemini V Spacecraft piloted by Pete Conrad and Gordon Cooper, a Lunar Roving Vehicle Trainer, the Apollo 17 Command Module, the giant Skylab Trainer, and the Apollo-Soyuz Trainer. The **Kids Space Place** is a playgroundlike area where kids can try out for themselves various tasks an astronaut must master. In *Blastoff!* a film audience is treated to the sensation

of liftoff before getting an update on current flight missions by a live NASA information officer. And that's not to mention the largest IMAX in Texas . . .

For a direct experience of NASA you can take the 1½-hour **tram tour** that takes you to, among other places, the **International Space Station Assembly Building** and the **Historic Mission Control Center.** This is still a working facility, so expect the precise tour route to change according to what projects are in high gear at the time; but you do get to see things as they happen, especially interesting if there's a shuttle mission in progress. Look for astronauts in midtraining—someday it could be one of your kids.

ⓘ 1601 NASA Rd. 1 (ⓒ **281/244-2100;** www.spacecenter.org).

✈ George Bush Intercontinental, 37 miles.

🛏 $$$ **Hilton University of Houston,** 4800 Calhoun Rd. (ⓒ **800/hoteluh** or 713/741-2447; www.hilton.com).

WHY THEY'LL THANK YOU: Zero gravity.

---

299 The History of Flight

Kansas Cosmosphere
Chronicles of the Space Race
Ages 6 & up • Hutchinson, Kansas, USA

AS A SPACE RACE BABY, I'm forever intrigued by the image of two world powers pitted head-to-head for outer-space supremacy—Sputnik versus Telstar, Yuri Gagarin versus Alan Shepard, Kennedy versus Khrushchev. I remember watching those first thrilling early-'60s space launches in school on grainy black-and-white TV screens. Considering how the U.S. initially lagged, the fact that American astronauts got to the moon first in 1969 was a national triumph. The U.S. space program has been sadly tarnished since then, and today's kids have no idea how spaceflight once captured the American imagination. A visit to the Kansas

Cosmosphere may be just what they need.

With its futuristic jumbled exterior, bookended by a towering pair of booster rockets, the Kansas Cosmosphere and Space Center makes a bold statement on the flat Kansas landscape. Thanks to an affiliation with the Smithsonian, and the good luck to purchase artifacts at the right moments, the Cosmosphere has some fascinating space souvenirs on display, especially from the former U.S.S.R. (it owns the only **Soviet *Vostock* rocket** in the West). The story of the **Space Race** is told from the beginning, in World War II, when German V-2 rockets were designed by Werner von Braun, whose real agenda was not winning the war but conquering outer space. There's a Cold War spyplane, a T-38 jet used to train astronauts, and the X-1 aircraft in which Chuck Yeager broke the sound barrier. Here too is the actual **Apollo 13 capsule,** a story the kids may know from the Tom Hanks film ("Houston, we have a problem . . ."). Every time I see one of these space capsules I'm shocked anew at what tiny spaces the astronauts were strapped into, all the worse in this life-or-death situation of an unexpected malfunction.

If you're coming up from Wichita, you might stop first at the underfunded but lively **Kansas Aviation Museum,** 3350 George Washington Blvd., Wichita (© **316/ 683-9242;** www.kansasaviationmuseum. org), set inside Wichita's Art Deco former municipal airport building. The aeronautics industry was always big in Kansas, and

over 25 vintage aircraft from local companies are on display, including a 1927 Laird Swallow barnstormer, a World War II B-52, a zippy little private Learjet, and a commercial Boeing 737. Just try to imagine the original runways here, sod covered in buffalo grass, where air shows were first held back in the 1920s. From here to the space shuttle, in less than a century—that's an awesome achievement.

ⓘ 1100 N. Plum St. (© **800/397-0330** or 620/662-2305; www.cosmo.org).

✈ Wichita Mid-Continent, 50 miles.

🛏 $ **Comfort Inn,** 1621 Super Plaza (© **800/424-6423** or 620/663-7822; www. choicehotels.com). $$ **Grand Prairie Hotel,** 1400 N. Lorraine (© **800/362-5018** or 620/669-9311; www.grandprairiehotel.com).

WHY THEY'LL THANK YOU: Where *The Right Stuff* came from.

300

Ironbridge Gorge
When Technology Changed the World
Ages 6 & up • Telford, England

The 19th-century Industrial Revolution, as taught in most schools, can be a dull and dreary subject. Not so here, at this complex of historic museums in the English Midlands, just north of Birmingham. The Ironbridge Gorge Museums vibrantly bring to life how this 19th-century burst of technology changed the world.

The iron-rich Severn Valley was like the Silicon Valley of its time. In 1709 a Quaker ironmaster named Abraham Darby invented a new iron-smelting process, marking the beginning of new transportation and engineering innovations that started the area buzzing. The most impressive feature of the site is the famous **Iron Bridge** across the River Severn, cast in 1779 by Abraham Darby III. An engineering marvel of its time, its great arch drew tourists from all over the world;

the original tollhouse, at the southern end, has exhibits about its history. At the **Museum of the Gorge,** a Gothic-style riverside warehouse from 1834, exhibits detail the history of the Gorge, including a 12m (40-ft.) scale model of the river valley as it was in 1796. In the **Coalbrookdale Museum of Iron** and **Darby Houses** you can tour the first modern ironworks, with its vast water-power system and great blast furnace, and peer into the ironmasters' houses, workers' cottages, chapels, and church. There are even more historic re-creations at the **Blists Hill Open Air Museum,** which presents an entire small Victorian town complete with bank, grocer's shop, chemist, printing shop, bakery, and sweet shop; the back streets are busy with small offices, works, and factories including a working foundry and iron

Ironbridge Gorge Museums.

rolling mill, all explicated by costumed staff. Lots of ancillary industries sprang up around the ironworks, and these sites offer lots of hands-on activities for children: the **Jackfield Tile Museum,** with its wealth of decorative tiles and ceramics; the **Coalport China Museum,** in a restored china factory; and the **Broseley Pipeworks,** a wonderfully preserved example of an ancient local industry, the manufacture of clay tobacco pipes. Of course, abundant natural resources made all this manufacture possible, a fact underscored when you visit the underground **Tar Tunnel,** where natural bitumen oozes freely from the walls.

The site's newest and most high-tech attraction, **Enginuity,** is an interactive museum full of gadgets; kids can pull a locomotive, harness water power to generate electricity, or compete against a robot.

ⓘ **Ironbridge Gorge Museums** (✆ 01952/ 433522 weekdays, 01952/432166 Sat–Sun; www.ironbridge.org.uk).

🚆 Telford, 3 hr. from London.

🛏 $ **Library House,** 11 Severn Bank, Ironbridge (✆ 01952/432299; www.library house.com). $$ **The Valley Hotel,** Ironbridge (✆ 800/528-1234 in the U.S., or 01952/ 432247; www.thevalleyhotel.co.uk).

BEST TIME: Easter to early Nov (some sites closed mid-Nov to Mar).

WHY THEY'LL THANK YOU: It puts the Revolution back into the Industrial Revolution.

---

301 Inventions & Industry

Edison Historic Site
The Light Bulbs Go On
Ages 6 & up • West Orange, New Jersey, USA

"I ALWAYS INVENTED to obtain money to go on inventing," Thomas Edison once said. The romantic notion of a genius tinkering alone at night over a breakthrough invention? That wasn't Edison. Yes, he was a gifted chemist and visionary, but he was also a

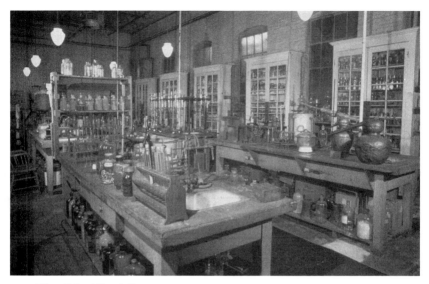

Edison National Historic Site.

shrewd businessman who amassed a fortune. Touring the Edison Laboratories is a fascinating look at one of the most efficient R & D operations in history.

Though Edison's first lab was in Menlo Park, New Jersey, this larger West Orange complex was in operation for over 40 years and accounted for over half of his patents. Notice how closely the ivy-covered red-brick buildings are set together—Edison designed it this way so he wouldn't waste too much time scurrying from chemistry lab to machine shop to drafting room. The kids may be surprised to learn that, of the 1,093 patents credited to Edison—the most any American has ever obtained—many were actually invented by other scientists who worked for him. Walking around the restored lab complex, you can visualize his team of some 200 researchers, hired to refine and improve existing inventions. There were light bulbs before Edison's, but his was more reliable, long-lasting, and easy to manufacture; the telegraph, the phonograph, the stock ticker, the movie camera and projector were all devices that other scientists pursued at the same time, but Edison's versions *worked better.* Another

10,000 workers in the attached factory (not part of the historic site) then mass-produced these inventions for commercial sale—he controlled the entire cycle. Accessories, too—there's a music recording studio you can peek into, where Edison engineers made sure phonograph customers would have something to play on their new machines.

One mile from the lab complex, you can see the fruits of Edison's labors in **Glenmont,** a 29-room red Queen-Anne-style mansion in Llewellyn Park which Edison bought for his second wife, Mina. All the original furnishings are here, reflecting the formal Victorian style of the era, with lots of ornate carved wood, damask wallcoverings, and stained-glass windows; things get comfier upstairs in the family living room, where Edison's children sometimes helped him look up scientific references in shelves full of books. One thing's for sure: This was probably the first house in the neighborhood with a phonograph, let alone the Home Projecting Kinetoscope—the Edison children must have been very in demand for play dates.

(i) Main St. and Lakeside Ave. ((C) **973/736-0551**; www.nps.gov/edis).

✈ Liberty International, Newark, NJ, 15 miles.

🛏 See Manhattan **56**.

WHY THEY'LL THANK YOU: One percent inspiration, 99% perspiration.

302 **Inventions & Industry**

Hoover Dam
Concrete Colossus of the Southwest
Ages 6 & up • Boulder City, Nevada, USA

U.S. 93, WHICH RUNS between Las Vegas, Nevada, and Kingman, Arizona, lays its ribbon of concrete right across one of the great engineering wonders of the world, Hoover Dam. Built between 1931 and 1935, this behemoth Depression-era project redrew the map of America: If it hadn't been for Hoover Dam, Arizona and California would never have had enough electricity and water to sustain their subsequent population boom. And yes, the dam also created the largest artificial lake in the United States, 110-mile-long **Lake Mead.** Driving across Hoover Dam, traffic crawls as motorists gape at the view, with smooth Lake Mead on one hand and a plummeting gorge on the other. But why let the kids be content with a mere view, when you can go inside the belly of the beast?

Going face to face with this much concrete is an awesome experience. Hoover Dam stands 726 feet tall from bedrock to the roadway atop it. At the top, it's 45 feet thick, which is stout enough, but it widens the farther down you go, until at the base it's a whopping 660 feet thick. The dam was named after Herbert Hoover (see **389**), not just because he was president when the bill was signed to build it, but because the Boulder Canyon dam was in many ways his idea—as Secretary of Commerce in the early 1920s, Hoover, a civil engineer himself, first urged the southwestern states to consider such an undertaking.

While much of the Hoover Dam story is told via **historic photographs** in interpretive galleries, the part kids really remember is taking **elevators** 500 feet down into the wall of Black Canyon, then walking down a 250-foot-long tunnel to look at the guts of the power plant, with its eight huge generators. At the end of the tour, don't miss going up to the observation deck to get that **panoramic view** of Lake Mead and the Colorado basin. Functional as it is in many ways, the dam still has a streamlined Art Deco flair—check out the sculptured panels decorating the central two elevator towers rising from the top of the dam, the Nevada one celebrating the dam's benefits—flood control, navigation, irrigation, water supply, and power—the Arizona one paying tribute to Indian tribes that once lived here.

Hoover Dam makes a handy day trip from Las Vegas, 30 miles away, though I'd recommend combining a Hoover Dam visit with a stay on Lake Mead in a **houseboat** (contact **Seven Crown Resorts,** Box 16247, Irvine, CA; (C) **800/752-9669;** www.sevencrown.com). Another fun way to visit the dam is on a **paddle-wheeler cruise** from **Lake Mead Cruises** ((C) **702/293-6180;** www.lakemeadcruises.com).

(i) U.S. 93 ((C) **866/291-TOUR** or 702/294-3517; www.usbr.gov/lc/hooverdam).

✈ 🛏 See Las Vegas **46**.

WHY THEY'LL THANK YOU: Feeling the power of those generators.

The Louisville Slugger Museum
For Big Swingers
Ages 4 & up • Louisville, Kentucky, USA

NO ONE HAS EVER PROPERLY EXPLAINED to me why major-league baseball players still hit with wooden bats instead of aluminum, but they do, and 60% of them buy their wooden bats from this century-old company. You can spot its headquarters as you drive up Main Street in Louisville's historic downtown area—no place else has a 120-foot-tall baseball bat leaning against the outer wall, a replica (made of steel, but painted to look like wood) of Babe Ruth's power-hitting bat.

Inside is a museum of Sluggers used by famous sluggers—everyone from Ty Cobb to Ted Williams to Hank Aaron—as well as several **interactive areas,** such as a batting cage where you can swing replicas of those historic bats, a diorama of a dugout/home plate area with audio-clip commentaries, and a brief film. Little kids can climb all over a 17-ton limestone sculpture of a giant baseball glove. But to me the coolest thing about this attraction is the half-hour walk through the factory itself, a throwback sort of place where sparks fly and machines whine as skilled craftsmen give personalized attention to every handmade product.

The H & B Company also makes baseball mitts, golf clubs, ice hockey sticks, and, since 1978, aluminum bats, but all of these are made somewhere else. The wood bats, though, are still crafted in Louisville, where teenager Bud Hillerich, an apprentice in his family's wood-turning shop (manufacturers of bedposts, bowling pins, and porch balustrades) first shaped a baseball bat on his lathe in 1884 for a local pro player. Although Bud's father resisted this new line for years, eventually the bat business took over. Today H & B—still run by the Hillerich family—produces one-million-plus Sluggers a year.

Walking through the factory, you'll see actual blocks of finely grained white ash being turned on the lathes by hand, the handles and barrels shaped into Louisville Sluggers right before your eyes—down to the final coat of lacquer, carefully applied to give the pale wood that major-league sheen. Warn the kids that the factory floor will be noisy, with wood dust flying around in the air—after all, this is a *factory.* Just be sure you arrive before 3pm, when the production line shuts down. (And there's no work at all done on Sun.) Don't tell the kids, though, about the surprise they'll get at the end of the tour: their own miniature Louisville Slugger to keep as a souvenir.

(i) 800 W. Main St. ((C) **877/7-SLUGGER;** www.sluggermuseum.org/visitorguide.aspx).

✈ Louisville International.

🛏 $$ **Camberley Brown,** 4th St. and W. Broadway ((C) **502/583-1234;** www.thebrown hotel.com). $$$ **Seelbach Hilton,** 500 4th St. ((C) **502/585-3200;** www.seelbachhilton.com).

WHY THEY'LL THANK YOU: Watching the lathes sculpt the wood.

Factories with a Homespun Touch

All ages • Waterbury & Shelburne, Vermont, USA

ONLY AN HOUR'S DRIVE apart in the rural state of Vermont, visitors can tour two small, quirky factories that reveal another side to American entrepreneurship. Cynics may argue that these factory tours are thinly veiled advertising for their products, and of course they're right. But it's hard to resist when the end results are something kids love—namely ice cream and teddy bears.

The bigger and more high-tech factory is in Waterbury—the **Ben & Jerry's Ice Cream Factory.** The classic "hippie capitalists," Ben Cohen and Jerry Greenfield started the company in nearby Burlington in 1978 with $12,000 and a few mail-order lessons in ice-cream making, selling their product out of an old downtown gas station. Their free-spirited approach, along with the exceptional quality of their ice cream, built a successful corporation, with sales rising into the hundreds of millions of dollars.

Even though Ben and Jerry have sold their interest to a huge multinational food concern—a move that raised not a few eyebrows among its grass-roots investors—the company's heart and soul (and manufacturing) remains squarely in Vermont. In summer the Waterbury plant has a festival marketplace feel to it, as crowds mill about good-naturedly, waiting for the 30-minute **factory tours** (first-come, first-served). Browse the small **ice-cream museum,** buy a cone of your favorite flavor at the scoop shop, or visit the "cemetery" where retired flavors are commemorated on mock tombstones. Be aware that ice cream is made only Tuesdays through Fridays; tours are run 7 days a week, but we came on a Monday and felt let down that we couldn't see the heavy machinery in operation. We still got the free samples at the end, though, which made us feel *much better.*

The **Vermont Teddy Bear Factory,** an hour-and-a-half's drive west in Shelburne, is as cutesy as Ben & Jerry's is hippieish, but somehow the sweet spirit of the place works, from the rainbow-colored silo outside to the open-raftered work space within. Visitors walk past various stages of the simple manufacturing process, watching cuddly stuffed bears come into being, and of course, at the end, you're funneled into a shop where it's almost impossible not to purchase a **custom-made bear** (with its own birth certificate and a heart sewn inside). But whereas Build-a-Bear Workshops follow much the same process, this homey factory setup was my kids' first taste of what manufacturing is all about, and for that it was worth it. We added the price of the bear to the tiny tour fee and still felt we'd bought a worthwhile experience—and hey, we got to take our bears home and love them forever.

(i) **Ben & Jerry's,** Rte. 100 ((C) **866/ BJTOURS** or 802/882-1240). **Teddy Bear Factory,** Rte. 7 ((C) **802/985-3001;** www. vermontteddybears.com).

✈ Burlington, 26 miles from Waterbury, 15 miles from Shelburne.

🛏 See Shelburne Museum **224**.

WHY THEY'LL THANK YOU: Lovable teddy bears and free ice cream. What's not to like?

Moving Down the Assembly Line

Ages 4 & up • Eastern Pennsylvania, USA

THERE ARE FACTORY TOURS and there are factory tours. My family spends a lot of time in eastern Pennsylvania—my in-laws live there—and we're always nosing around for something to do with the kids. These three factory tours we found are as different from each other as they could possibly be, from the heavy industrial vibe of Mack Trucks to the slick mass production of Crayola Crayons to the fine hand craftsmanship of the Martin Guitar Company.

When the kids were young and crayons were a major part of their lives, the **Crayola Factory** at 30 Centre Sq. in Easton (© **610/515-8000;** www.crayola.com/factory) was right up their alley. They didn't mind that they weren't actually seeing a factory, just videos of the simple production process and a few mocked-up machines to play with, before running next door to the hands-on creativity games and the giant drawing room. When they got older, they were ready to put on safety glasses and tramp through the **Mack Truck** assembly plant at 7000 Alburtis Rd. in Macungie (© **610/709-3566;** www.macktrucks.com; ages 7 and up only). It's a 1½-mile walk through a noisy, vibrating million-square-foot plant, and the sight of all those huge parts being clapped together into gargantuan heavy-duty trucks was a bit overwhelming. Ever since then, the kids check out every truck they see for the trademark Mack bulldog mounted on the hood.

But the factory tour that meant most to us—and not just because my husband and son both play guitar—was the **Martin Guitar Company** at 10 Sycamore St. in Nazareth (© **610/759-2837;** www.martinguitar.com). Though this hour-long tour takes a bit of planning—it's only offered at 1pm on weekdays—it's worth it. The factory, though modern, includes a replica of the old red-brick building where Martin guitars began to be made back in 1833 (the company is still owned by the fourth generation of Martins). Many famous musicians swear by their Martin guitars, as you'll see in the visitor center, and when you see the art involved in making them, it all makes sense. Each guitar is made over a span of 6 months, with more than a dozen artisans involved in over 300 individual steps. You'll stand right next to these craftsmen as they intently shape, glue, sand, and lacquer each instrument, from the first die-cut body shape to the final adjustment of the tuning pegs; though sophisticated computers and high-tech precision machines are involved, every guitar is also fine-tuned with hand tools, to make not only a thing of beauty but the source of a beautiful, resonant, true sound. You measure, you adjust, you let it sit, you listen to how it sounds, then you work on it some more. A pretty good work ethic for the kids to discover.

ⓘ www.visitpa.com.

✈ Allentown-Bethlehem-Easton International.

🛏 $$ **Fairfield Inn,** 2140 Motel Dr., Bethlehem (© **610/867-8681;** www.fairfieldinn.com). $$ **Holiday Inn Express,** 90 Kunkle Dr., Easton (© **800/315-2621** or 610/923-9495; www.holidayinn.com).

WHY THEY'LL THANK YOU: Watching the craftsmen's hands on the guitars.

Greenwich: Where Time Begins

Ages 8 & up • England

It's ONE OF THOSE CLASSIC PHOTO OPS: Standing astride the **Greenwich Line,** 0° 0′ 0″ longitude, the point from which since 1884 all terrestrial longitudes around the globe are calculated. Tell your children they're standing on the dividing line between the Eastern and Western hemispheres; if they were here at the stroke of midnight, they could have one foot in 2 different days, for by official world decree a new day begins at the Greenwich Line.

The red-brick house on the hill was designed by a then-unknown architect, Sir Christopher Wren (himself a passionate amateur astronomer), who won the commission from Charles II in 1675. The king's motives were quite practical: Improvements in astronomy would lead to better navigation techniques, which would help Britain dominate the seven seas. (And, no surprise, it worked out exactly the way he'd hoped.) Wren's elegant **Octagon Room** was the observatory used by the first Astronomer Royal, John Flamsteed; unfortunately, because it wasn't properly aligned with celestial meridians, it was useless for observation—a fact no one bothered to tell the king—and telescopes were surreptitiously installed in a shed in the garden instead. As the years passed, uniform timekeeping became more and more important, especially to regulate railway schedules. The synchronized clocks of Victorian England eventually became a model for the rest of the world, and just as all distances were calculated from Greenwich, so was Greenwich Time established as the world standard. In this respect at least, England will always remain the center of the world.

Although the **Royal Observatory** is no longer a working observatory—light pollution from the metropolis forced a move in the 1940s—it does have galleries full of historic stargazing and timekeeping instruments (including England's largest refracting telescope, a 28-in. lens, and a rare camera obscura), which children will find of varying interest. But be sure to go out onto the roof, where there is a spectacular panorama of London, especially the nearby skyscrapers of Canary Wharf. Look up to see the red **Time Ball,** which slides down its mast every day at 13.00 hours—the world's first public time-indicating device.

Frequent ferryboats from either Charing Cross Pier or Tower Pier run every half-hour or so to Greenwich, taking about an hour; the train trip from Waterloo Station is faster, about 15 minutes, but less atmospheric.

Telling time in Greenwich.

(i) **The Royal Observatory,** Greenwich Park ((C) **020/8312-6608;** www.nmm.ac.uk).

✈ ⊨ See London ⑤⑤.

WHY THEY'LL THANK YOU: Every time they look at a clock, they'll remember where the day begins and ends.

Stargazing ③⓪⑦

Stargazing on Nantucket

Ages 6 & up • Massachusetts, USA

THOUGH HER FAME HAS SADLY FADED, Nantucket native **Maria Mitchell** (1818–89) was quite possibly the most famous American scientist of the 19th century, man or woman. In October 1847, on the rooftop of her family home, this self-educated 29-year-old trained her telescope on the night sky and became the first person ever to record a sighting of a comet that was invisible to the naked eye, an accomplishment that vaulted her to international honor.

On Nantucket Mitchell is remembered at a complex of science centers. Your first stop should be on the southwest edge of Nantucket Town at Maria's birthplace, the **Mitchell House,** 1 Vestal St. ((C) **508/228-2896**), a modest Quaker home built in 1790. It was turned into a museum soon after Mitchell's death by her former students and colleagues and contains many family artifacts, including her own telescope. Take time to wander through its wildflower and herb gardens. The nearby **Hinchman House Natural Science Museum,** 7 Milk St. ((C) **508/228-0898**), expands Mitchell's passion for observation beyond astronomy; yes, there are exhibits about Nantucket flora and fauna, but there's also a raft of activities, like bird-watching, wildflower walks, and hands-on discovery classes for both children and adults. Dissecting an owl pellet can be fascinating. Over on the harborfront, the Maria Mitchell Association's **aquarium,** 28 Washington St. ((C) **508/228-5387**), is small but very kid-friendly, focusing on the local marine ecology.

It's only fitting that, because of Maria Mitchell, this tiny island has not one but two observatories, and if the night sky is clear, don't pass up the opportunity to stargaze here, far from the light pollution that frustrates astronomers in big cities. Out on a hill south of town, **Loines Observatory,** 59 Milk St. Extension ((C) **508/228-8690**), is open to the public every clear Monday, Wednesday, and Friday night in summer at 9pm (rest of the year Fri 8pm); if there's an interesting sky event, like the close orbit of Mars the summer we visited, the line may be out the door. The **Vestal Street Observatory** in town at 3 Vestal St. ((C) **508/228-9273**), where Maria and her astronomer father swept the skies in the 19th century, is too close to town for nighttime stargazing, but tours every day at 11am show off a good exhibit on the science of astronomy. Don't miss the outdoor scale model of the solar system.

(i) **Maria Mitchell Association,** 4 Vestal St. ((C) **508/228-9198;** www.mmo.org).

✈ Nantucket Airport.

⊨ **Jared Coffin House,** 29 Broad St., Nantucket ((C) **800/248-2405** or 508/228-2400; www.jaredcoffinhouse.com).

BEST TIME: Early June to late Aug.

WHY THEY'LL THANK YOU: A great place to start peering through telescopes.

Griffith Observatory
Planetarium Hollywood
Ages 6 & up • Los Angeles, California, USA

FILM BUFFS INSTANTLY RECOGNIZE this streamlined **Art Deco observatory** in L.A.'s rambling Griffith Park from the climactic scenes of the 1955 James Dean classic film *Rebel Without a Cause*. My kids, however, know it from the climactic scenes of the 1999 Steve Martin–Eddie Murphy comedy *Bowfinger*. But so what if they don't get the *Rebel Without a Cause* reference? Who could fail to dig this white stucco complex with its three bronze domes, slung into the south side of Mount Hollywood with a killer panorama of Los Angeles spread out below? In the daytime, the lawn of the observatory is one of the best places in the city to view the famous Hollywood sign; on warm nights, with the lights twinkling below, the Griffith Observatory's wide terrace is one of the most romantic places in L.A. And if you manage to steer the children inside to do a little stargazing while you're up there at night, you're ahead of the game.

This Hollywood Hills landmark was built in 1935 in the vaguely Mediterranean style studio moguls of that era favored, and underwent a major renovation during 2003–06. A white obelisk in front honors six great astronomers of the past: Hipparchus, Copernicus, Galileo, Kepler, Newton, and Herschel. The large central dome houses a state-of-the-art **planetarium,** where narrated projectors display the stars and planets that are nearly impossible to observe outdoors, what with all the smog and light pollution of the L.A.

metrosprawl. Like most planetariums, it also screens various multimedia shows of varying scientific seriousness. We generally skip the planetarium, however, and head straight into the adjacent **Hall of Science,** which holds exhibits on galaxies, meteorites, and other astronomical subjects—cool objects like a mechanical orrery, a Tesla coil, and scales where you can check your weight on different planets. A Foucault pendulum mesmerized my boys as it methodically swung in the main rotunda, demonstrating the earth's rotation, and detailed 6-foot topographical models of the earth and the moon provide focal points in the side galleries.

The observatory's two flanking domes each house a telescope—in the west one, a triple-beamed **solar telescope** trained on the sun for daytime visitors, in the east one a 12-inch **refracting telescope.** On clear nights visitors can climb to the roof and wait their turn to gaze through it at the moon and planets. This is, after all, an observatory, and although it has never had the astronomical prestige of its California neighbor **Mount Palomar 309,** it does attend to sky matters.

(i) 2800 E. Observatory Rd., Griffith Park (© **323/664-1191;** www.griffithobs.org).

✈ ⊨ See Hooray for Hollywood **355.**

WHY THEY'LL THANK YOU: A chance to study the other Hollywood stars.

Mount Palomar
Where Stars Shine over the Desert
Ages 8 & up • Mount Palomar, California, USA

In July 2005, the world was startled to learn that a 10th planet had been found orbiting our sun (just after my sixth grader got an A for his model of the solar system—a model that's now obsolete). And where was that astonishing observation made? At Mount Palomar, California, where Cal Tech astronomers have been making scientific headlines since 1949.

This mountaintop in San Diego County was purchased in 1934 because light pollution from the fast-growing Los Angeles metropolis had become a problem for Cal Tech's former observatory, atop Mount Wilson in Pasadena. For the new site, Mount Wilson's 100-inch telescope—through which Edwin Hubble had studied distant galaxies to prove the universe is expanding—was to be outdone with a **200-inch reflecting telescope.** A Depression-era American public eagerly tracked the progress of this grandiose plan. At first, no one could build a stable lens that big—until the Corning Glass company made one using its new heat-resistant Pyrex glass. The immense glass blank was carefully shipped cross-country, then was ground and polished for a couple of years. Meanwhile, other parts for the telescope had to be made in shipyards, the only workshops geared to manufacture parts that big (which explains the battleship-gray hue of the scope's housings). After a 5-year hiatus during World War II, the telescope was finally ready to assemble in 1947.

Dedicated in 1948, the Mount Palomar telescope was the world's largest until 1976 (when an even-larger Soviet model debuted). Today, visitors can stand on the gallery surrounding the 200-inch Hale telescope to see the big instrument, but be prepared—the dome is kept at a steady temperature calibrated to nighttime temperatures on this mountain, so you'll need a sweatshirt or jacket even in summer. To get the full scoop, come on a Saturday for an hour-long explanatory **tour** (book a week ahead). **Astronomical photos** and other exhibits are displayed in an outer gallery, but nothing as extensive as the ones at **Griffith Observatory** 308 down in Los Angeles.

My kids were baffled by the back-roads trek it took to get here, until we explained that isolation is *good* for astronomy. They were surprised when they saw the small, simple facility beneath that serene-looking dome in a mountain meadow. But the size of the Hale telescope, and the quiet hum of serious science going on, gradually began to impress them. They no longer felt like tourists—they felt like hardy explorers in pursuit of knowledge.

(i) 35899 Canfield Rd. ((C) **626/395-4033;** www.astro.caltech.edu/palomarnew).

✈ ⊨ See San Diego Zoo **131**.

WHY THEY'LL THANK YOU: Big scope, bigger sky.

310 Stargazing

Mauna Kea
Stargazing at the Top of the World
Ages 13 & up (summit), 10 & up (visitor center) • Mauna Kea, Hawaii, USA

THE SNOWCAPPED SUMMIT OF MAUNA KEA—the world's tallest mountain, if measured from its base on the ocean floor—is the best place on earth for astronomical observation. It's not just the height, it's also its location near the equator, where clear, pollution-free skies give way to pitch-black nights undisturbed by urban light. That's why Mauna Kea is home to no fewer than 13 world-class telescopes, including the **Keck Telescope,** the world's largest. Even with the naked eye, the stargazing from here is fantastic.

Many tours that go to the summit won't take anyone under 16 or any pregnant women, due to the high altitude. If you opt not to go up, it's still cool to view the model of the Keck Telescope down in Waimea, 65-1120 Mamalahoa Hwy. (*©* **808/885-7887;** www.keckobservatory. org). Developed by the University of California and the California Institute of Technology, the Keck is an infrared telescope eight stories high, weighing 150 tons, and with a 33-foot-diameter mirror made of 36 perfectly attuned hexagon mirrors—like a fly's eye—rather than one conventional lens.

You'll need a four-wheel-drive vehicle if you do drive up the mountain. **The Onizuka Visitor Center,** named after a Hawaiian astronaut who died in the *Challenger* explosion, is an hour's drive from Hilo or Waimea; from Highway 190, take the narrow, rutted Saddle Road (Hwy. 200) 28 miles, then turn onto unmarked Summit Road and go another 6¼ miles to the visitor center. At this point you're already 9,000 feet up, so stop for half an hour to acclimate. With younger kids, this may be your endpoint, so time your visit to join the nighttime **stargazing sessions,** 6 to 10pm, which include a lecture, a video, and the chance to peer through 11-inch, 14-inch, and 16-inch telescopes.

It's 6 miles from here to the summit, but it can take 45 minutes to drive this rough, unpaved, winding road, in low gear all the way—a climb of another 4,200 feet—to 13,796-foot-high **Observatory Hill.** Dress warmly and drink lots of liquid; wear dark glasses to avoid snow blindness, and use plenty of sunscreen. At the top, 11 nations, including the U.S., Japan, the U.K., France, and Australia, have set up 13 powerful infrared telescopes to look into deep space. On this bare peak, their bulbous pale domes sprout around a loop of road like alien spacecraft plopped down on the moon. Visitors can't use those telescopes, of course, though you can look at a couple (including the Keck) from galleries. (They won't be active until light, anyway.) If you take a narrow footpath past the observatories, however, there's a cairn of rocks where you can sit and contemplate an incredible 360-degree view across the Pacific. Even if you're socked in by clouds, it's a true top-of-the-world view, with the summits of Mauna Loa and Maui's Haleakala poking through the puffy white cumulus clouds beneath your feet.

(*i*) *©* **808/961-2180;** www.ifa.hawaii.edu/ info/vis.

✈ ⊨ See Hawaii Volcanoes National Park **76**.

WHY THEY'LL THANK YOU: That monster telescope, that killer view.

Polar Nights & Northern Lights

Ages 6 & up • Tromsø, Norway

JUST ABOUT EVERY ATTRACTION IN Tromsø, Norway, bills itself as the "world's northernmost" this or that—the northernmost university, the northernmost cathedral, the northernmost golf course, the northernmost brewery. What else would you expect of a city 400km (250 miles) north of the Arctic Circle? But for sky watchers, Tromsø's extreme location means great opportunities year-round to observe all sorts of unique phenomena, from the comforts of a city so cosmopolitan it's been nicknamed the Paris of the North.

Let's start with the rarest phenomenon: The Northern Lights, or **aurora borealis,** created by stray particles from storms on the sun's surface eddying around that big magnet known as the North Pole. On dark, clear nights from about 6pm to 2am, you can see their energy released in wonderful shimmering curtains of light—in Tromsø, one of the few towns on Earth where the Lights are visible, you can see them even from the city center nightly from October through April. Green is the prevailing color up here, though on good nights the whole spectrum glows. And you do get a lot of nighttime from November 21 to January 21, when the sun never rises above the horizon. Scandinavians put a positive spin on this by calling it **Polar Nights,** and having star-spangled skies 24-7 truly isn't all bad, especially not when the aurora borealis kicks in. Tromsø is blessed with a surprisingly mild climate, even in winter, so you can get outdoors and enjoy those winter skies; several local tour operators take groups out into the countryside to see them at their most spectacular.

This Tromsø photo was taken at 1am in summer.

You can't see the Northern Lights from May through August, though, for the simple reason that the sun is always in the way: May 21 to July 21 is the season of the Midnight Sun. It sounds simple, but if you've ever experienced it, it's truly magical, to feel the world kissed with sunshine around the clock. Summertime in Tromsø also offers whale-watching (✆ **77-62-44-40;** www.arcticvoyager.com) or roaming around the open-air **historic museum,** Kvaløyveien 55 (✆ **77-60-19-10**), and the university's large **Alpine Botanic Garden,** full of rare Arctic flora. If you do come here in summer—which, given school vacations, may well be your time frame—you don't have to miss the Northern Lights entirely: The **Northern Lights**

Theatre, Prostneset (✆ **92-84-27-13**), shows a film of the aurora all summer, and the University Museum of Tromsø has what it calls a **Northern Lights Machine** to simulate the experience.

ⓘ **Tourist information office,** Storgaten 61–63 (✆ **77-61-00-00;** www.destinasjon tromso.no).

✈ Tromsø.

🛏 $$$ **Clarion Hotel Bryggen,** Sjøgata 19–21 (✆ **77-78-11-00;** www.choicehotels. no). $$ **Grand Nordic Hotel Tromsø,** Storgaten 44 (✆ **77-75-37-77;** www.rica.no).

WHY THEY'LL THANK YOU: Continuous sun or stars.

Chapter **9**   Holy Places

Western Wall Plaza in Jerusalem.

312

The Temple Mount
Jerusalem's Rock of Ages
Ages 6 & up • Jerusalem, Israel

I THINK IT'S PRETTY SAFE to call Jerusalem the world's holiest city. Three world religions—Judaism, Islam, and Christianity—have major shrines here, and all three intersect at one spot: Mount Moriah, better known as Temple Mount. To stand on Temple Mount is to see centuries of faith laid literally atop one other.

According to Jewish tradition, this stony plateau is where the patriarch Abraham proved his faith to God by nearly sacrificing his son Isaac. Around 1800 B.C. King David of Judah bought this land, but it fell to his son, Solomon, to erect the first great Jewish temple in 957 B.C. And then, as so often in Judaic history, politics intervened: Nebuchadnezzar invaded and destroyed the First Temple in 586 B.C. Jews returning from Babylonian captivity in 515 B.C. built a modest Second Temple; ambitious King Herod in 34 B.C. built it into the greatest religious complex in the eastern Roman Empire. And again, it was destroyed, this time by the Romans in A.D. 70.

At Temple Mount's foot today is the holiest of Jewish sites, a surviving fragment of Herod's wall known as the **Western Wall** (Ha-Kotel Ha-Ma'aravi) or the "Wailing Wall" because for centuries Jews crowded into a narrow alley here to mourn the loss of their temple. The prayer section of the Western Wall is an unforgettable sight, the unmortared cracks of its chalky, yellow-white stone stuffed with prayers scrawled on bits of paper; Orthodox Jews stand alongside, chanting and swaying. Visitors are welcome to pray silently; men must wear hats, and women have to stand in a separate section.

After the Muslim conquest of A.D. 638, Temple Mount was rebuilt—this time with Islamic holy places. (Except during the Crusades, of course, when it was converted to a Christian site by the Knights Templar). Called **Haram es-Sharif,** the Noble Sanctuary, it contains two major sites: **Al-Aqsa Mosque,** the third-holiest Muslim place of prayer after Mecca and Medina, and the **Dome of the Rock.** Completed in A.D. 720, Al-Aqsa is one of the world's most beautiful mosques, a large serene open hall hung with chandeliers and covered with oriental rugs. (Non-Muslims can visit, outside of prayer services, but must dress modestly and remove their shoes.) Up a broad flight of ceremonial stairs is the dazzling **Dome of the Rock,** with its splendid facade of Persian blue tiles erected in the mid–16th century by Sultan Suleiman the Magnificent and re-covered with gold by Jordan's King Hussein in 1994. This beautiful octagonal Muslim shrine, founded in A.D. 691, has a circle of striped arches and marble columns centered around one huge rock—according to Islam, the rock from which the Prophet Muhammad ascended to view Paradise. Look on the surface of the rock for Mohammed's footprints, and in a nearby latticework cabinet for a few strands of his hair. According to Judaism, of course, it's the rock of Abraham and Isaac. From Abraham to Solomon to Herod to Suleiman to the Crusaders to King Hussein—that's a pretty amazing heritage for any one piece of real estate.

(i) **Tourist information center,** Jaffa gate, Omar Katab square in the Old City (✆ **02/ 6280403;** www.tourism.gov.il/TourismEng).

349

Dome of the Rock & Al-Aqsa Mosque.

✈ Jerusalem.

🛏 $$$ **Jerusalem Sheraton Plaza,** 47 King George St. (© **800/325-3535** or 02/ 629-8666; www.sheraton.com). $$ **King**

Solomon Hotel, 32 King David St. (© **02/ 569-5555**).

WHY THEY'LL THANK YOU: Seeing the massed humanity at the Western Wall.

The Church of the Holy Sepulcher

Ages 6 & up • Jerusalem, Israel

SULEIMAN THE MAGNIFICENT SPARED NO COST in building the **Dome of the Rock** 312, with one goal in mind: To outshine Jerusalem's great Christian shrine, the Church of the Holy Sepulcher at Golgotha.

Looking at the place today, it's hard to imagine why. Suleiman's Dome is glorious, and the Church of the Holy Sepulchre looks distinctly frumpy. Its history has been full of ups and downs. One of Christianity's oldest churches, it was founded on the site of an old Roman temple, built in the 4th century by Constantine, the first Christian emperor of Rome. His mother, on a pilgrimage to the Holy Land, had discovered the tomb of Jesus Christ

(subsequent excavations nearby also turned up the Cross Jesus was crucified on), and whether or not it was authentic, Constantine and his mother, bent on glorifying the new faith, raised a fine church for it. Emperor Justinian added to its glories 200 years later. But then came years of fire, earthquake, and ransacking; the True Cross was carted away by the Persians, and the church was more or less razed, though its holy shrines were saved. The facade you see today dates from the 12th century, when the Crusaders had conquered Jerusalem and reclaimed its churches. The children may be a bit disappointed; while the sandy-colored

Romanesque exterior is attractive enough, it certainly doesn't have the harmony of the great Gothic cathedrals. Even though this building is "new" for this site, it's crumbling and worn compared to what you may have seen in Europe.

But beauty is almost beside the point, for this is a site so holy that six Christian factions claim it: Roman Catholic, Armenian Orthodox, Greek Orthodox, Egyptian Coptic, Ethiopian, and Syrian Orthodox. Walk around comparing the various chapels, each vying for supremacy. Three incredibly **holy relics** are encompassed in this one cluttered church: the rocky outcropping of **Mount Calvary**, traditionally the site where Jesus was crucified (the huge crucifix in this chapel is particularly gruesome); the **Stone of Unction,** believed to be the same marble slab where Christ's broken corpse was prepared for burial; and, underground, a primitive stone cave traditionally accepted as the **tomb** where Jesus was buried for 3 days, before miraculously rising from the dead. Lines to go down to the sepulcher can be long, but if you've come this far, don't let that deter you. The rough, hollowed-out gray stone cave is almost a relief after all the sacred decoration upstairs, as if you've peeled off encrusted layers to see the essence of Christ's life. Through centuries of political

Church of the Holy Sepulchre.

turmoil, the faithful always clung to this shrine. It *means something*.

(i) For general information on Jerusalem, including airport and lodging, see The Temple Mount **312**.

WHY THEY'LL THANK YOU: The crucifix in the Cavalry chapel, crown of thorns and all.

Church of the Nativity
Bethlehem's Original Crèche
Ages 8 & up • Bethlehem, Israel

FOR MORE THAN 17 CENTURIES, Christian pilgrims have flocked to the city of Bethlehem to see the birthplace of Jesus Christ. Though it's only 8km (5 miles) south of Jerusalem, Bethlehem is in the West Bank, that political tinderbox torn between Israel and Palestine, so I'd opt for a guided day trip from Jerusalem. Let a tour guide

sort out the hassles so you can focus on sorting out Jesus' humble birth from the chaos of busy, modern Bethlehem.

Join the faithful crowds at Manger Square, site of the ancient **Church of the Nativity.** Built in A.D. 326 by the Roman emperor Constantine, rebuilt 200 years later by Emperor Justinian, it was rebuilt again by 12th-century Crusaders (blame them for its fortresslike facade). Point out to the kids the different priests walking about, all protecting their sects' claim to this sacred site—Franciscan priests in brown robes, Armenians in purple and cream-colored robes, and bearded Greeks in black robes with long hair tied into a bun. After being fought over for centuries, it's no surprise the church looks clunky and dilapidated. The stately Corinthian pillars that line the basilica's naves bear faded paintings of apostles, bishops, saints, and kings; gilded lamps hang from the oak ceiling, and trapdoors in the stone-and-wood floor give mere glimpses of old Byzantine mosaic glories beneath.

On either side of the ornate gold-and-silver main altar, narrow staircases lead down to a marble grotto, draped in tapestries. Ancient tradition claims Mary gave birth to Jesus in this shallow cave, as was the custom of those times; altars mark nearby spots where the manger stood and where the Magi bowed to the baby Jesus. Historically accurate or not, after centuries of adoration this hushed grotto is full of spiritual aura. For a more authentic-looking relic, go to the grand

Franciscan church just north of the Church of the Nativity; a stair from the back of its nave leads to an underground maze of rock-hewn rooms and chambers that supposedly includes the stable where Joseph and Mary stayed the night of Jesus' birth.

Your group may also take a 2-hour walk to the **Shepherds' Fields,** where tradition says angels proclaimed Jesus' birth to simple shepherds. There are two competing Shepherds' Fields, one Roman Catholic and the other Greek Orthodox—whichever you visit, you'll see real shepherds still tending their flocks on this rocky landscape. And that makes the story come real.

GUIDED TOURS: Egged Tours (✆ 02/530-4422). **United Tours** (✆ 02/625-2187). **Alternative Tours** (✆ 052/864-205 or 02/628-3282; raed@jrshotel.com).

✈ ⊨ See The Temple Mount ❸❶❷.

Heartland Christian Biblical Tours (✆ 02/940-0422).

WHY THEY'LL THANK YOU: Away in a manger.

The Vatican: Michelangelo's Masterpiece
Ages 6 & up • Rome, Italy

WHETHER OR NOT you're a practicing Catholic, the Vatican—the world's second-smallest sovereign independent state—is a must-see when you're in Rome, if only for its enormous art collection. In truth, it has more art than most children (or most adults) can appreciate, so keep your focus narrow: Tell the kids you're here to see the work of one great artist, Michelangelo. Everything else is icing on the cake.

You enter Vatican City through grand colonnaded **St. Peter's Square,** where the Pope himself appears on a balcony at noon every Sunday (except mid-July to

mid-Sept) to bless the gathered multitudes. Straight ahead is the massive facade of **St. Peter's Basilica,** Piazza San Pietro (✆ **06-69881662**), topped by a majestic dome designed by Michelangelo. (**Note:** The basilica has a strict dress code: no shorts, no skirts above the knee, no bare shoulders and arms.) St. Peter was allegedly buried here in A.D. 64; this is the second basilica on the site, mostly completed in the 1500s and 1600s. Don't be surprised if the riot of gilt, marble, and mosaic inside overwhelms you all—that's what it was designed to do. Steer the kids

The Vatican.

into the first nave on the right to see (sadly, behind reinforced glass) a young Michelangelo's exquisite sculpture of the **Pietà,** with a tender Virgin Mary cradling the crucified body of her son Jesus. Pass through the grottoes, getting a peek at St. Peter's tomb, then wait in line to climb to the dome (separate ticket). You can walk up all 491 steps or take an elevator and walk only 320 steps (only!); at the top you'll have an astounding view over the rooftops of Rome.

Next you visit the **Vatican Museums** (yet another ticket line), housed in a section of the papal palaces, a labyrinthine series of lavish apartments and galleries. This collection of treasures from antiquity and the Renaissance is so big that visitors are given a choice of four partial tours—all of them ending in the **Sistine Chapel.** Among much else, you may choose to see the **Borgia Apartments,** with their frescoes of biblical scenes, or the **Raphael Rooms,** decorated by Raphael and his workshop for Pope Julius II (the

highlight is the second room's scene of the Greek philosophers, who are actually portraits of great Renaissance artists). Eventually you'll reach the **Sistine Chapel,** Michelangelo's command performance for Pope Julius II. It took the artist 4 taxing years in his 30s to complete the nine panels on the ceiling, whose themes are taken from the pages of Genesis. The most famous are Adam and Eve being expelled from the Garden of Eden and the Creation of Man—bring binoculars so the kids can see the details, especially God's outstretched finger giving the divine spark of life to Adam. On the altar wall is a late Michelangelo painting, the *Last Judgment,* wherein some of the doomed sinners resemble Michelangelo's enemies. Hey, even great artists can be petty.

ⓘ ✆ **06-69883333;** www.vatican.va.

✈ ⇌ See Rome **53**.

WHY THEY'LL THANK YOU: Michelangelo's genius.

316

Notre-Dame de Paris
Flying Buttresses & Gothic Gargoyles
Ages 6 & up • Paris, France

CHANCES ARE the children only know Paris's Notre-Dame cathedral from *The Hunchback of Notre Dame*—and I mean the animated Disney movie, not the classic horror film (let alone the Victor Hugo novel upon which they were based). Still, that'll get them interested, and once they see it in person, this magnificent Gothic cathedral will win them over.

In the heart of old Paris, **Notre-Dame** crowns the island in the middle of the Seine (Ile de la Cité) where the city first grew. It was the focal point of medieval Paris. Start out across the Seine, on the Left Bank quay, where you can view it as a glorious whole, bristling with gargoyles and flying buttresses. Then cross the bridge and stand in the front courtyard to gaze upon the trio of **13th-century sculpted portals.** Notre Dame means Our Lady, and the church is dedicated to the Virgin Mary, who is celebrated in the left- and right-hand portals (the theme of the central one is the Last Judgment and Christ's Resurrection). Go inside and turn around to admire the **rose window** over the central portal, a marvel in stained glass showcasing a statue of the Virgin and Child. There are two other beautiful round windows inside; the north rose window in the transept, from the mid–13th century, is particularly spectacular.

A perfect place for an architecture lesson, Notre-Dame is a classic example of **Gothic style** with slender, graceful columns soaring to a high cross-vaulted ceiling. Its floor plan resembles a huge cross, with the altar at the intersection; numerous small chapels devoted to various saints are tucked around the outer edges. Like most medieval cathedrals, it was decorated with images that educated a largely illiterate congregation—for example, the Biblical scenes carved on the elaborate stone screen separating the choir from the long nave. To visit the **gargoyles** where Quasimodo lurked, you can scale steps leading to the twin square towers, 68m (223 ft.) high. Once here, you can inspect those devils (some sticking out their tongues), hobgoblins, and birds of prey.

For a study in contrasts, take a short walk to the nearby royal chapel of **Ste-Chapelle,** tucked away in the Palais de Justice, 4 bd. du Palais (© **01-53-73-78-50;** www.monum.fr). Between them, they illustrate the class divide of the Middle Ages: Ste-Chapelle is as intimate and aristocratic as Notre-Dame is monumental and all-encompassing. Save it for a sunny day so you can see its stained-glass windows at their most brilliant—with reds so red that Parisians often use the phrase "wine the color of Ste-Chapelle's windows." Delicate

Notre-Dame.

as lace, Ste-Chapelle's 15 windows take up most of its walls, depicting Bible scenes.

ⓘ 6 place du parvis Notre-Dame (✆ **01-42-34-56-10;** www.paris.org/Monuments/NDame).

✈ 🚆 See Paris **54**.

WHY THEY'LL THANK YOU: Rose windows for beauty, gargoyles for the beast.

Mont-St-Michel
The Fortress Abbey of Normandy
Ages 6 & up • Mont-St-Michel, France

Sᴇᴛ ᴜᴘᴏɴ ᴀ ᴍᴀꜱꜱɪᴠᴇ ʀᴏᴄᴋ just off the Normandy coast, the great Gothic abbey church of Mont-St-Michel is often called the Marvel of the West. Approaching across the coastal flatlands, I get chills when I see its Gothic splendor triumphantly piercing the sky, usually cloaked in dramatic fog. Legend claims it is protected by the archangel Michael, but the abbey is guarded by earthly elements as well—powerful tides churn around the tiny island, and massive rampart walls circle the abbey itself. Think of the engineering required to build on this sheer outcrop—it's a marvel it has stood this long, yet it does, a magnificent pile rising to a spire with a gilded statue of St. Michael.

In the Middle Ages, this was a popular pilgrimage site, founded in the 8th century by St. Aubert, the bishop of Avranches, upon the divine orders of St. Michael (the bishop procrastinated at first, but he came around once the angel burned a hole in his skull, so the story goes). Nowadays the island is connected to shore by a causeway, but medieval pilgrims could get here only at low tide, walking across treacherous tidal sands. (The kids eyed that causeway with respect, wondering if the next high tide would wash over it and strand us on the island.) In the 10th century the oratory was upgraded to a Benedictine monastery, and the monks continued to

build and renovate over the next 6 centuries, as various parts burned down or toppled over. Bristling with spires as it climbs the steep slopes, the abbey looks more like a fortress than a holy retreat—a fact that served it well in the Hundred Years' War (1337–1453), when it almost miraculously resisted capture by the English. The rampant walls also made it easy to convert to a prison, after the monks were disbanded, in the days of the French Revolution. It's been a national monument since the late 19th century, and recently some new monks have settled in as well.

Warn the kids that there'll be a lot of climbing: It's a steep walk to the abbey up Grande Rue, lined with half-timbered 15th- and 16th-century houses, and inside the abbey walls are more staircases. Secreted within the abbey are some lovely Gothic interiors, most notably the **Salle des Chevaliers (Hall of the Knights)** and graceful **cloisters** with pink granite columns. Crowning the summit is the splendid abbey church, begun in the 11th century—note the round Romanesque arches in the nave and transept, whereas the pointy arches of Flamboyant Gothic were in fashion when the choir was rebuilt in the 15th century. In the summer you can even visit the church at night—not a bad idea if you want to avoid those modern pilgrim hordes on day-tripping coach tours.

ⓘ **Mont-St-Michel** (ℂ 02-33-89-80-00). **Office de Tourisme,** Corps de Garde des Bourgeois (ℂ 02-33-60-14-30; www. baie-mont-saint-michel.fr).

🚄 Rennes, 2½ hr. from Paris.

🛏 $$ **Les Terrasses Poulard,** Grande Rue (ℂ 02-33-60-14-09; www.mere-poulard.fr).

WHY THEY'LL THANK YOU: Built by faith, against all logic.

Canterbury Cathedral: Holy Survivor

All ages • Canterbury, England

FOUR THINGS MAKE THIS CATHEDRAL a must-see destination: its Gothic architecture; its status as the Church of England's mother church; its starring role in the English language's first masterpiece, *The Canterbury Tales;* and the treacherous murder of Thomas à Becket in 1170. The first three factors may not grab your kids, but the fourth will.

Canterbury is one of those places where layers of history pile atop each other. Britain's earliest settlements flourished in this southeast corner, the closest area to the European continent, and there was a town here well before the birth of Christ. When the Romans came to Britain, this became a major center, Durovernum Cantiacorum. When Pope Gregory I sent St. Augustine to Britain to convert the pagan Saxons to Christianity, Augustine built his abbey here. But what really established Canterbury as England's religious capital was the murder of **Thomas à Becket,** archbishop of Canterbury, who was killed on December 29, 1170, by four knights who thought King Henry II wanted him out of the way. Henry denied he ever issued such orders, and even if he did, the scheme backfired—Becket's tomb immediately became a shrine, visited by faithful worshipers from all over, and the murder victim was named a Catholic saint.

Four years after the murder, a mysterious fire leveled the monastic church. It was replaced by the magnificent early **Gothic choir** section, England's first major example of that architectural style. Like most medieval cathedrals, Canterbury

was a work in progress that spanned centuries; the nave, the long main body of the church, wasn't completed until the 1300s. By 1388, when Geoffrey Chaucer portrayed a motley crew of pilgrims in his ***Canterbury Tales,*** this was England's major tourist destination. The cathedral has several noteworthy **medieval tombs,** including those of King Henry IV and the renowned warrior Edward the Black Prince (loaded down with armor and weapons).

Canterbury Cathedral.

When Henry VIII decided to split England from the Roman Catholic church, in 1538 he had Becket's shrine destroyed and its treasures carted off to line his own coffers. As a result, the interior looks remarkably restrained and pure, with pale stone surfaces, pointed arches, soaring spires, high ceilings, subtle gargoyles, and exterior supporting arches (called flying buttresses). One thing Henry left was the lovely stained-glass windows. In 1941, when Nazi Germany began bombing Great Britain, Canterbury's officials removed the precious glass for safekeeping. During a German air raid in 1942, the replacement windows were blown to bits. The originals were safely put back after the war and you can see them here today.

Elsewhere in Canterbury, you can walk along what remains of the medieval **city walls,** explore quaint medieval-relic streets like **Mercery Lane,** and perhaps visit the **Museum of Canterbury** on Stour Street or the excavated **Canterbury Roman Museum** on Butchery Lane.

(i) 11 The Precincts (© **01227/762862;** www.canterbury-cathedral.org).

Canterbury, 1½ hr. from London.

$$ **The Swallow Chaucer Hotel,** 63 Ivy Lane (© **01227/464-427;** www.swallow-hotels.com).

WHY THEY'LL THANK YOU: A real-life crime scene, in dramatic Gothic surroundings.

319

Clonmacnois
Mystical Ruin of the Irish Monks
All ages • Shannonbridge, Ireland

RESTING SILENTLY on the east bank of the Shannon, Clonmacnois is one of Ireland's most profound ancient sites. You'll have to follow a twisting series of country roads to get to this remote, peaceful place, and when the kids see it's just a bunch of ruins, they may wonder at first why you bothered—until they've wandered around and let the gray stones work their mystical spell.

Standing here today, it's amazing to imagine this as one of Europe's great centers of learning and culture. But back in the Dark Ages, monasteries were vital repositories of knowledge, and ancient Ireland revered its monks. **St. Ciaran** founded a monastic community here in A.D. 548 because it was where the road between Dublin and Galway crossed the Shannon

River (its modern equivalent, the N6 highway, passes a few miles north), and Clonmacnois flourished for the next 1,000 years under the patronage of numerous Irish kings. The last high king, Rory O'Conor, was buried here in 1198. In the course of time, however, Clonmacnois was raided repeatedly, first by native chiefs, then by Danish Vikings, then by Anglo-Norman invaders, until it was finally abandoned in 1552 when the monasteries had lost their power. The exhibits in the visitor center tell the story well, so don't rush past them. When you come outdoors from the visitor center, all that you'll see are the foundations of a cathedral, a castle, and eight churches; a few wall fragments and arched

Clonmacnois.

doorways still rise, as well as two round towers you can peek into. Wander about and let the great monastery take shape in your mind's eye. Conjure up for yourselves those old robed monks, pacing meditatively from church to church. My children were particularly fascinated by the three high crosses, their intricate surface sculptures worn down by the elements but still telling their runic stories. More than 200 monumental slabs are laid out in a vast graveyard; plaques mark several important figures buried here. Beyond low stone walls, the ground slopes down to the gentle, marshy banks of the river. Cows graze placidly in an adjacent meadow, and even on an overcast day the grass glows a vivid emerald-green. It's magical.

(i) R357, 6km (3¾ miles north of Shannonbridge (© **090/967-4195**).

✈ Shannon, 113km (70 miles).

🛏 $ **Brosna Lodge Hotel,** Main St., Banagher (© **0509/51350;** www.brosna lodge.com). $$$ **Wineport Lodge,** Glasson, Athlone (© **090/643-9010;** www.wineport.ie).

WHY THEY'LL THANK YOU: A holy place for contemplation.

320

The Sacred Isle of Iona

Ages 6 & up • Iona, the Hebrides, Scotland

REMOTE, TREELESS IONA, just off the southwestern coast of Mull in Scotland's Hebrides islands, has been a place of spiritual pilgrimage for centuries. The first Christian settlement in Scotland was founded here, its monks becoming the stalwart guardians of ancient learning throughout the Dark Ages. Some 1,000 visitors a week step off the ferry in summer, and yet somehow the island's atmosphere remains tranquil. It helps that most visitors are contemplative sorts, interested in the other-worldly values of a Benedictine abbey and relics of old saints.

You arrive by passenger ferry from the Isle of Mull, itself a 45-minute ferry trip from Oban (**Caledonian MacBrayne ferries;** © **01688/302017**), leaving your car behind and trusting to your own two feet to get around—not too hard, since the island is only 5.6km (3½ miles) long by 1.6km (1 mile wide). Walk off among the sheep and cows that wander freely everywhere; climb to the top of **Dun-I,** a small gray mountain, to contemplate the ocean and the landscape around you.

St. Columba arrived in A.D. 563 with a dozen companions, using this as their base for converting Scotland to Christianity. Nothing remains of the original monastery, which Norse invaders destroyed. The present-day abbey site encompasses the **ruins** of a Norman-era nunnery, the 11th-century **St. Oran's Chapel,** and square-towered **Iona Cathedral,** with its Norman arches and short round pillars. Built in spurts, the church is a jumble of styles from the 12th to the 16th centuries—but really, architectural splendor is beside the point. It's simply an incredibly holy place.

The monks of Iona played one other role: maintaining the eternal resting place of the kings of Scotland (its remoteness was an advantage; rival chieftains could not get here to desecrate their remains). Tradition claims that **St. Oran's Cemetery** holds the mossy graves of 48 Scottish kings, including Macbeth and his rival Duncan, along with assorted Irish, Norwegian, and French kings and church dignitaries.

Owned by the dukes of Argyll since 1695, Iona was recently sold to Sir Hugh Fraser, who ensured that National Trust money would be turned over to the trustees of the abbey, the **Iona Community.** This ecumenical religious group lives communally on the grounds, and interested visitors are welcome to join them for a night or two. If the spirit of this place gets to you, a stay with the Community could be a very special experience.

(i) (✆) **01681/700404.**

🚂 Oban, 3 hr. from Glasgow.

🛏 **Argyll Hotel** (✆ **01681/700334;** www.argylhoteliona.co.uk).

WHY THEY'LL THANK YOU: A chance to get in touch with their spiritual side.

Cologne Cathedral
Cathedral of the Three Kings
Ages 4 & up • Cologne, Germany

"We Three Kings" is our family's favorite Christmas hymn, so we looked forward to visiting Cologne Cathedral, where a precious chest houses the mortal remains (supposedly) of the Magi. We weren't prepared, though, for the magnificence of this Gothic church. In a city heavily damaged by Allied bombing in WWII, the cathedral miraculously survived—partly because its soaring towers made a handy landmark for bomber crews, but also because in the end they could not bring themselves to destroy such an architectural marvel.

Cologne ("Köln" in German) means "colony," and this was a Roman town starting in 38 B.C. A temple was built on this site as soon as Emperor Constantine permitted open Christian worship. In 1164, Holy Roman Emperor Frederick Barbarossa acquired the holy bones of the Magi and put their shrine in Cologne, where it became a popular pilgrimage site. In 1248, work began on a suitably grand church for the relics, designed in High Gothic style. In the stop-and-go manner of medieval cathedral building, its chancel, south tower, and north-side aisles were completed by 1560, then, as the Reformation disrupted Europe, work halted for nearly 3 centuries. But in 1823, the Prussian court, inspired by the Romantic movement's veneration of all things medieval, revived the project, digging up the original plans to ensure it was completed in authentic Gothic style.

Outside, stand back from the south transept for a sweeping overall view of the huge cathedral. Note that there are no important horizontal lines—everything is vertical. The west side (front) is dominated by two towering spires, making this the tallest Gothic structure in the world. Entering the church, your eye is inevitably drawn upward—to God, its designers intended—by the nave's soaring arches. The medieval/Victorian mix is exemplified by the glowing windows high in the side walls: 16th-century stained glass on the north, 19th-century Bavarian glass on the south. Behind the high altar, in the chancel, is **The Shrine of the Three Magi,** shaped like a minicathedral of gold and silver. In its highsecurity trappings, you can't see much of the elaborate sculpted figures covering its surface, but the effect is still awesome. Admire the richly carved oak choir stalls, dating from 1310. Among the out-lying chapels, the Chapel of the Cross, beneath the organ loft, shelters a painted wooden crucifix that is the oldest full-size cross in northern Europe; in Our Lady's Chapel, a famous 15th-century triptych over the altar opens up to a beautiful painting of the Three Kings worshiping the infant Jesus in the manger. Cue it: "We three kings of Orient are . . ."

(i) Dompropstei Margarethenkloster 5 (✆ **0221/92584731;** www.koelnerdom.de).

✈ Köln/Bonn 23km (14 miles).

🛏 $$ **Hopper Hotel et cetera,** Brüsseler-strasse 26 (✆ **0221/924400;** www.hopper.de).

WHY THEY'LL THANK YOU: A cathedral beautiful enough to survive a world war.

Catedral de León (Santa María de Regla)
Inside a Stained-Glass Kaleidoscope
Ages 4 & up • León, Spain

IN THE CHURCH-BUILDING SWEEPSTAKES of the Middle Ages, every Gothic cathedral vied to distinguish itself with some superlative trait. Milan Cathedral was the biggest, Chartres had the most inspiring stained-glass pictures, Palma de Majorca had the largest rose window, and so on. But León—at the time the leading city of Christian Spain—set the record for the highest proportion of window space. Its **stained-glass windows** occupy 1,672 sq. m (18,000 sq. ft.), or almost all the space where you'd expect the walls to be; they soar 34m (112 ft.) to the vaulted ceiling, framed by the slenderest of columns. It's a wondrous feat of engineering—but all your kids will notice is that the interior glows with color, like no place else on earth.

The cathedral's 13th-century archi-tects, Juan Pérez and Maestro Enrique, were, in effect, precursors of Mies van der Rohe, with one hitch—they didn't have steel girders to support their glass walls. And while it has stood for 7 cen-turies, the cathedral contains some 125 original stained-glass windows, plus 57 oculi, and their weight strains the walls.

The job of supporting the roof (its delicate vaulting was added in the Renaissance) was taken over by flying buttresses on the exterior; the walls have all they can do just to hold the glass.

An air of dignified calm pervades the cathedral's cloisters, full of faded frescoes and Romanesque and Gothic tombs; a short walk northwest of the cathedral you can visit a splendidly decorated Romanesque church, **Pantéon y Museos de San Isidoro,** Plaza San Isidoro 4 (✆ **98-787-6161**), which contains the tombs of 23 Leónese kings. Surrounding the two churches, León's historic quarter is also worth exploring, since you're already here. But the reason to come is those glorious windows; everything else in town literally pales in comparison.

(i) Plaza de Regla (✆ **98-787-5770**)

🚆 León's Estación del Norte, 4–5 hr. from Madrid.

🛏 $$$ **Hotel Alfonso V,** Padre Isla 1 (✆ **98-722-0900;** www.iova-sa.com).

WHY THEY'LL THANK YOU: Like being inside a kaleidoscope.

Gaudí Days in Barcelona

Ages 4 & up • Barcelona, Spain

TRAVELING AROUND EUROPE, it's easy for kids to get Gothicked-out, bopping from palace to cathedral to fortress—enough! Yes, there is a Gothic **cathedral** in Barcelona, quite a lovely one, begun at the end of the 13th century and mostly completed by the mid–15th century, with an especially charming cloister surrounding a garden of magnolias, medlars, and palm trees. Look for it at Plaça de la Seu s/n (© **93-315-1554**). But the church that children most remember from Barcelona is the exuberantly unGothic **La Sagrada Família,** the crowning achievement of the great 20th-century architect Antoni Gaudí.

You don't need to be an art historian to see that La Sagrada Família—the Church of the Holy Family—is a bizarre wonder. Begun in 1882 and incomplete at the architect's death in 1926, this languid, amorphous structure embodies the essence of Gaudí's signature style: *modernismo,* a romantic, voluptuous Catalonian offshoot of Art Nouveau that flourished from about 1890 to 1910. Modernismo emulated forms found in nature; symmetry was out, handcrafted decoration was in. Gaudí loved drooping masses, melting horizontal lines, and giddy spirals. This cathedral erupts skyward with clusters of honeycombed spires, looking more like encrusted stalagmites than like traditional Gothic towers; its arches are neither pointed Gothic nor rounded Romanesque, but tapering curves with a certain *Star Trek*–ish flair. (Gaudí's versions of flying buttresses are more Space Age struts.) Sculpted figures seem to grow organically out of its portals and arches, with variegated color lent by several different types of stone. La Sagrada Família's **rose windows** really do look like roses, its fluted columns like flower stalks, rising to a vaulted ceiling pattern that made us think of a field spangled with daisies.

Two facades have been finished, with the central nave, still under construction, standing open to the sky. Bitten by the Gaudí bug, our family trooped around Barcelona looking for more modernismo, and enjoyed the wavy balconies of **Casa Batlló,** Passeig de Gràcia 43 (© **93-488-0666**), and the sculpted vegetable and fruit shapes bedecking the apartment complex **La Pedrera,** Passeig de Gràcia 92 (© **93-484-59-80,** 93-484-5900, or 93-484-5995), with its phantasmagoric chimneys. The Espai Gaudí (Gaudi Space) in the attic has an intriguing multimedia display of the controversial artist's work.

ⓘ **Carrer de Sardenya** or Carrer de la Marina (© **93-207-3031;** www.sagrada familia.org).

✈ Barcelona.

🛏 $$ **Duques de Bergara,** Bergara 11 (© **93-301-5151;** www.hoteles-catalonia. com). $$$ **Hotel Hesperia Sarriá,** Los Vergós 20 (© **93-204-5551;** www.hesperia-sarria. com).

WHY THEY'LL THANK YOU: Gaudí designed the kinds of buildings children draw themselves.

Where Constantinople Meets Istanbul
Mosques, Mosaics & Minarets
All ages • Sultanahmet, Istanbul, Turkey

ISTANBUL, FORMERLY CONSTANTINOPLE, is a city with a foot in both Europe and Asia, and its religious heritage is equal parts Islam and Christianity (even its Christian history is half Roman Catholic, half Greek Orthodox). The kids may not always be able to keep all these elements straight, but one thing they'll remember about the Turkish capital: the exquisite mosaics and domes of its great houses of worship.

The masterpiece is **Ayasofya,** which for almost a thousand years was the largest Christian church in the world (the Statue of Liberty's torch would barely graze the top). Built by the Emperor Justinian in A.D. 537, it became the majestic symbol of Byzantine power. Its history has been turbulent; for one thing, in this earthquake-prone region, clunky flying buttresses had to be added to support its red-tinted outer walls. In 1204 the Crusaders stripped the church of its relics, a sacrilege that caused the Greek Orthodox church to split from the Roman Catholic church. Then in 1453 Mehmet II took over the city (look for his stone cannonballs along the path in the inner courtyard), and his first official act was to declare the great church a mosque. Frescoes and mosaics were covered up, since Islam forbids the representation of figures; slim pointed minarets were erected; the altar was shifted to accommodate a *mihrab* (a niche pointing toward Mecca); and an ablution fountain was plunked down in the courtyard. In 1935, when Atatürk converted it to a museum, its hidden mosaics and icons were restored.

If you've never seen a **Byzantine church** before, this one will astound you, with some 1.6 hectares (4 acres) of mosaics covering the interior. The glistening narthex, or inner vestibule, is just the prelude; the 15-story-high main dome is crowned with 40 windows to filter light onto its dazzling gold mosaics. Point out to the kids that, per Islamic tradition, many mosaics have calligraphy or abstract motifs; go up in the southern gallery to find the really old ones with pictures.

When Sultan Ahmet I built his namesake mosque in 1609, the beauty of Ayasofya so galled him, he set out to surpass it. The result is the **Blue Mosque,** a grand bubble of masonry that's a defining feature of Istanbul's skyline, with its cluster of domes and minidomes and its six gold minarets (the mosque in Mecca had to add a seventh minaret to top it). You enter through a door off the Hippodrome (remove your shoes!), beneath a symbolic chain that required even the sultan to bow his head when he arrived on horseback. The kids will be awed by the girth of the enormous "elephant foot" pillars supporting the series of domes overhead. As the sun pours in through 260 windows, the lofty space swirls with colors from the exquisite decorative tiles—mostly blues and greens, of course, hence the name. Ah, but does it surpass Ayasofya, as Ahmet hoped? There's your dinner-table discussion tonight.

ⓘ **Ayasofya Museum** (✆ **0212/522-1750**).

✈ Atatürk Internatioal, Istanbul.

🛏 $$$ **Çiragan Palace Hotel Kempinski Istanbul,** Çiragan Cad. 84 (✆ **800/426-3135** in the U.S., 0212/258-3377 in Istanbul, www.ciraganpalace.com). $$ **Mavi Ev (Blue House),** Dalbasti Sok. 14 (✆ **0212/638-9010;** www.bluehouse.com.tr).

WHY THEY'LL THANK YOU: Imagine how many tiles it took to line those domes.

325

The Painted Churches of Moldavia

Ages 4 & up • West of Suceava, Romania

WHEN MOST OF THE CONGREGATION IS ILLITERATE, how does a church teach Biblical lore? In medieval northern Europe, they depicted the stories in grand Gothic windows of stained glass; in Greece and other Orthodox countries, intricate mosaics were the medium. But only in northern Romania, in a kingdom once known as Moldavia, were churches—even simple country churches—painted inside and out with vivid, dramatic narrative murals, in the iconic Byzantine style common in Eastern Rite churches. Only about a dozen of these painted churches remain today, and often they are too poor to properly restore and preserve these treasures. The sooner you get here the better.

While Moldavia struggled against the Ottoman invaders sweeping northward from Constantinople (today's Istanbul)

toward Vienna, from 1522 to 1547 a handful of artists moved around this mountainous countryside painting frescoes on church after church, all in the distinctive architecture of the region—with round towers and apses, octagonal steeples set on a star-shaped base, and wide-eaved roofs like brimmed hats clapped on top. These itinerant artists used simple paints, plus household ingredients like charcoal, egg, vinegar, and honey to preserve the color, which evidently worked—they have withstood the rugged Carpathian climate for over 450 years. No doubt it helped that they were in small out-of-the-way towns, near the Ukrainian border, situated only a few miles from one another along narrow roads and mountain passes.

If you can only see one, make it **Voroneț,** with its amazing Last Judgment

A painted church in Moldavia.

on one large west wall. I'm also partial to **Humor** because of all the daring political references its artist slipped in—look for turbaned Turkish enemies in many of his murals. Green is the dominant color at charming little **Arbore,** which has a detailed painting of the story of Genesis. **Sucevita** is not just one church but an entire fortified monastery compound, with thousands of pictures—notice the one blank wall, which was left unfinished, the story goes, when the painter fell off his scaffolding to his death. **Moldovița** has a particularly panoramic depiction of the

Siege of Constantinople, a major event for the Greek Orthodox Church. All five can be visited in a few hours, on a loop of back roads west of Suceava.

✈ Suceava, 24–32km (15–20 miles).

🛏 $$ **Balada Hotel,** Str. Mitropoliei 3, Suceava (✆ 230/522146; www.balada.ro). $$$ **Best Western Hotel Bucovina,** 4 Bucovina Ave., Gura Humorului (✆ 230/32115; www.bestwestern.com).

WHY THEY'LL THANK YOU: Literally, storybook churches.

St. Basil's Cathedral
Ivan the Terrible's Moscow Fantasy
Ages 6 & up • Moscow, Russia

On THE NIGHTLY NEWS, whenever reporters broadcast stories from Moscow, this is where they stand: on **Red Square,** the city's central plaza, with St. Basil's Cathedral in the background, a gaudy riot of exotic bulbous domes and towers. Along with the solid red-brick wall of the Kremlin and the gray cobblestones of Red Square, on TV it looks like a psychedelic stage set. Who would ever build such a crazy candy-colored building? But that's just what makes it appealing to children.

St. Basil's is essentially a union of nine different Byzantine churches, topped with nine distinct roofs (count them), arranged in an eight-pointed star, an important symbol in medieval Christian iconography. This "tented" style of architecture was typically Russian; note that the eight smaller domes are onion-shaped, a common silhouette in Orthodox churches, clustered around one central unifying spire of a more European design. It's like a visual reminder that Russia is as much Asian as it is European. Yet even the onion domes have subtle differences in design, accentuated by their contrasting

bold color schemes. Bring a sketch pad with you and let the kids have a go at drawing the domes.

St. Basil's—in Russian, Khram Vasiliya Blazhennogo—was originally built under Ivan the Terrible to honor Russia's victory over Mongol Tatars in 1555. Moscow already had several beautiful cathedrals in **The Kremlin** 209 across the Square, but Ivan wanted to surpass them: Legend says he had the architect's eyes poked out afterward to keep him from ever again making anything to rival Moscow's "stone flower." Inside, the cathedral has a much more dour character than you'd expect. Ivan's idea was to make a separate chapel for each saint upon whose feast day he had won a battle, so instead of one main nave, like the Gothic cathedrals of western Europe, St. Basil's houses several dim and chilly sanctuaries, which you can only reach via narrow, winding passages and treacherously worn stairs. There aren't a lot of brochures or plaques around to help you sort it out, though stalls do sell icons and souvenirs. Surrender to its irrational charm and wander around, soaking up the dank medieval atmosphere. From the upper-floor windows you get a close-up of those fantastic pilasters and a broad view of the Moscow River.

(i) ℂ **095/298-3304.**

✈ 🛏 See The Kremlin **209**.

WHY THEY'LL THANK YOU: Outlining the domes, then coloring them in.

The Golden Temple
Ages 8 & up • Amritsar, Punjab, India

IN THE NORTHERN PUNJABI CITY OF AMRITSAR rests India's most dazzling sacred site, the Golden Temple, begun in 1574 but constantly embellished and adorned over the years since. It's not only an architectural landmark, it's the holiest of holies for the Sikh religion, a faith that actively preaches unity and equality among all religions. All visitors are welcome to share the temple experience. Before entering you must leave your shoes at the entrance, cover your head (bandanas are provided), wash your feet in the shallow pool by the doorway—and prepare for a very moving sight.

It's not just that the temple is spectacular, although it is that. The heart of the complex, the **Hari Mandir** (Divine Temple) is a gold-plated building with copper cupolas and jewel-encrusted marble walls that almost seems to float serenely in the surrounding pool of water. (Some 100 kilograms of gold were used to coat its inverted lotus-shaped dome.) But the complex is laid out so that the process of getting there is a ritual in itself—a clockwise walk around the sacred pool, past several smaller shrines, through a magnificent silver gate and over the long **Guru's Bridge**—meant to symbolize the soul's journey after death. Then once you're in the Hari Mandir, you take in a trancelike scene of worship, usually being broadcast live to Sikhs around India. Scriptures are chanted from a Holy Book, a ceremonial whisk is flicked over its pages, musical instruments play, and lines of devotees (you can recognize male Sikhs by their turbans, beards, and steel

wrist bangles) circulate clockwise, touching their heads in a trancelike rhythm to the temple floor and walls. In another hall, the **Guru-ka-Langar,** around 35,000 worshipers are fed every day by temple volunteers; anyone and everyone is accepted at the table, in the egalitarian spirit of Sikhism.

The majority of India's Sikhs live in the Punjab. For more background on this faith, you can stop in the **Central Sikh Museum** at the main entrance, but be forewarned: It includes some graphic portraits of gurus being tortured and executed in terrifying ways.

The best time to visit is in the evening for the **Palki Sahib,** or Night Ceremony, when the Holy Book is carried on a palanquin from the Hari Mandir to the sanctum where it rests overnight. Men line up and shift the palanquin forward from shoulder to shoulder, as if moving it along a human conveyor belt. Joining in the common task, every individual seems merged in one collective motion, the many becoming one. We can all learn from this.

(i) ℂ **0183/255-3954.**

✈ Amritsar.

🛏 $ **Mrs. Bhandari's Guesthouse,** No. 10, Cantonment (ℂ **0183/222-8509;** bgha@glide.net.in). $$ **Ritz Plaza Hotel,** 45 Mall Rd. (ℂ **0183/222-6606;** ritz@del3.vsnl.net.in).

WHY THEY'LL THANK YOU: Getting caught up in the spirit.

The Cave Temples of Ajanta & Ellora

Ages 10 & up • Near Augangabad, India

IT'S QUITE A PROPOSITION, getting to the ancient cave temples of Ellora and Ajanta, in far-flung Maharashtra, India, about 388km (241 miles) east of Mumbai. What really makes it worth the trip is not the beauty of these two worship sites—though they certain are beautiful—it's the fact that they were built at all, chiseled patiently out of the hillsides, chip by chip, using nothing but hand-held tools. The faith that inspired such an undertaking must have been powerful indeed—and it still seems to animate the stone with spiritual grace.

Ajanta is by far the older of the two complexes, begun in the 2nd century B.C. and carved out over the next 700 years by Buddhist monks. Rediscovered by a British soldier in 1819, this horseshoe of 29 caves is packed with **sculptures** and **colorful murals** of astonishing detail, telling the story of Buddhism. Some caves are chaityas, or shrines, and others are viharas, or monasteries; the pictures were meant to inspire spiritual contemplation on the life and teachings of Buddha. As you walk through with the kids, don't linger too long in any one cave: Simply imagine the long-ago monks tending to their devotions. The most brilliantly painted is **Cave 17,** where maidens float overhead, accompanied by celestial musicians, lotus petals, and scrollwork. The great mandala, or sacred meditative design, on the ceiling of **Cave 2** is also awesome.

The 34 Ellora caves are much newer—if you can imagine thinking of the 4th to 11th centuries A.D. as recent times. Located on a major trade route, Ellora was never "lost" as Ajanta was; parts were used for worship as recently as the 19th century. What I find fascinating about Ellora is that it isn't strictly Buddhist, but a combination of 12 Buddhist, 17 Hindu, and 5 Jain temples, where you can compare the symbols and stories of the three religions. All the entrances face west, so try to visit in the afternoon, when the sunlight pours in. Be sure to see the huge **Buddha** of Cave 10 and the monks' **rock beds** in Cave 12. The showpiece of Ellora is Cave 16, the **Kailashanath Temple,** the world's largest monolithic structure. It took 800 artisans 150 years to whittle one massive piece of rock into this Hindu shrine, designed to resemble Mount Kailash, the mythical home of Shiva in the Himalayas. In general the sculpture at Ellora isn't as fine as Ajanta's, and it doesn't have those vibrant paintings; but as a feat of architecture it's incredible—many of these temples are two or three stories high and so intricate that you'll need to remind yourselves that they were cut out of the mountainside, not built as freestanding structures.

(i) **Maharashtra Tourism Development,** Holiday Resort, Station Road, Aurangabad ((C) **0240 2331513;** www.maharashtra tourism.gov.in).

✈ Aurangabad, 107km (66 miles) to Ajanta, 26km (16 miles) to Ellora.

🛏 $$ **The Ambassador Ajanta,** Jalna Rd., Aurangabad ((C) **0240/248-5211;** www. ambassadorindia.com). $$ **Quality Inn The Meadows,** Gat nos. 135 and 136, Village Mitmita, Aurangabad ((C) **0240/267-7412;** meadows@gnbom.global.net.in).

WHY THEY'LL THANK YOU: Imagine the monks carving away.

Nikko

Buddhist Serenity in the Mountains of Japan

All ages • Nikko City, Japan

YOU MIGHT WANT TO COME HERE to see one of Japan's great mountain Buddhist retreats. Or you might want to pay homage to Tokugawa Ieyasu, the model for James Clavell's novel *Shogun*. But if you want the kids to enjoy this expedition from Tokyo, tell them you're on safari, looking for **animal images** in this magnificent 17th-century Japanese shrine.

On the edge of town, walk onto the vermilion-painted **Sacred Bridge (Shinkyo),** built in 1636; in the past, only shoguns and their emissaries were allowed to cross it. Up the stone steps is the 8th century **Rinnoji** Temple, housing the "gods of Nikko," three 8.4m-high (28-ft.) gold-plated wooden images of Buddha. Today the gods are taking prayers for world peace. Through a grove of ancient Japanese cedars, you come to the showpiece of Nikko, **Toshogu Shrine,** built in the 1630s by Tokugawa's grandson. No expense was too great in creating the monument: Some 15,000 craftspeople were brought from all over Japan, and after 2 years' work, they completed a cluster of buildings more elaborate than any other Japanese temple or shrine, gilded with a dazzling 2.4 million sheets of gold leaf. Go up the stairs through a huge stone torii gateway; on your left is a five-story pagoda. (Pagodas are normally found at Buddhist temples, not Shinto shrines, but the two mingle happily here.) Up more stairs to your first animal image: the **Sacred Stable,** which houses a sacred white horse (horses have long been

held sacred to Shinto gods). Above the stable door is my personal favorite carving at Nikko—three monkeys enacting "see no evil, hear no evil, speak no evil"; they're the guardians of the sacred horse. Across from the stable is **Kami-Jinko,** with a famous painting of two elephants—pretty accurate, considering that the artist had read about elephants but never actually seen one. Up the next flight of stairs, to the left is **Yakushido,** known for its dragon painting on the ceiling. Tell the kids to clap their hands under it; the resulting echo sounds like a dragon's roar. The shrine's most stunning feature is **Yomeimon Gate,** often called the Twilight Gate because it could take you all day (until twilight) to see everything on it. Painted in red, blue, and green and decorated with gilt and lacquerwork, this gate has about 400 carvings of flowers, dragons, birds, and other animals. To the right of the main hall, look for the beloved carving of a sleeping cat above the entrance to **Tokugawa Ieyasu's mausoleum.** Beyond that, stone steps lead past cedars to Tokugawa's strikingly simple tomb.

Directly to the west of Toshogu Shrine is Futarasan Shrine (1617), where the kids should look for the **ghost lantern,** enclosed in a small wooden structure. According to legend, it used to come alive at night and sweep around Nikko in the form of a ghost, scaring one guard so much that he struck it with his sword 70 times— you can still see the marks on the lamp's rim. Spooky.

See no evil, hear no evil, speak no evil.

(i) **Nikko Information Center** (© **0288/ 54-2496**).

🚄 Nikko, 2 hr. from Tokyo.

🛏 $ **Annex Turtle Hotori-An,** 8–28 Takumi-cho (© **0288/53-3663;** www.turtle-nikko.com).

WHY THEY'LL THANK YOU: The monkeys.

Angkor Wat: Glory in the Jungle

Ages 8 & up • North of Siem Reap, Cambodia

WHEN FRENCH NATURALIST HENRI MOUHOT, hacking his way through the Cambodian jungle in 1861, first stumbled upon the ruins of the ancient city of Angkor Wat, I wonder what he thought. Lying before him, shrouded in roots and vines, was the largest religious monument ever constructed, a mysterious collection of hulking laterite and sandstone blocks. When it was cleared, the temple complex—capital of the Khmer kingdom from 802 until 1295—proved to cover 98 sq. km (38 sq. miles). Today it's Cambodia's chief tourism attraction, and definitely one of the great marvels of the world.

You'll probably need more than 1 day to visit Angkor Wat, to let the magic of its timeless stones begin to work their spell. This is one place where it's worthwhile to hire a guide, to illuminate this welter of crumbling stones, carvings, and columns with background information on Buddhism, Hinduism, and Khmer history. Besides, a guide will help you catch the priceless photo ops, such as a temple's perfect reflection in a pool at sunset.

Angkor Wat.

The resplendent **main temple,** also called Angkor Wat, is only the beginning, though its four-spired profile is the one you'll recognize (it has virtually become the symbol of Cambodia). Dating from the 12th century, it stands 213m (669 ft.) high from its base to the tip of its highest lotus-shaped tower. The whole Angkor complex is full of storytelling bas-reliefs, which will intrigue the kids, but on the first level is one of the most famous, narrating a Hindu legend in which various gods stir the oceans to extract the elixir of immortality. Scholars have worked out that this sandstone temple's symmetry mirrors the timeline of the Hindu ages, like a map or calendar of the universe. (See why you'll need a guide?) Approaching from the main road over a *baray,* or reservoir, you climb up three levels to the inner sanctum; the steps can be tricky, but you'll soon be high up for an inspiring view.

The name Angkor Thom means "great city" in Khmer, and this other sprawling temple complex is dotted with many temples—don't miss the **bas-reliefs** on the Terrace of the Leper King and the Terrace of Elephants. The central temple, the

Bayon, is the most fantastic. Though this is a Buddhist temple, built slightly after Angkor Wat in 1190, it also alludes to Hindu cosmology. Gaze upon its four huge stone faces, each aligned with a compass point (the same is true of each of its 51 small towers)—the expression on the face, possibly the image of the king who built the temple, is as enigmatic as that of the *Mona Lisa.*

To get an idea of what this site looked like when Mouhot found it, visit the **Ta Prohm temple,** which has been left entangled in the jungle foliage, the roots of fig, banyan, and kapok trees cleaving its massive stones and growing over the top of temple ramparts.

ⓘ **Siem Reap Tourism Office** (✆ 012/630 066; www.mot.gov.kh).

✈ Siem Reap.

🛏 $ **La Noria,** off Rte. 6 northeast of Siem Reap (✆ 063/964-242). $$$ **Sofitel Royal Angkor,** Vithei Charles de Gaulle (✆ 063/964-6000; www.accor.com).

WHY THEY'LL THANK YOU: A great secret hidden in the jungle.

Borobudur: A Buddhist Climb to Paradise

Ages 6 & up • South of Magelang, Central Java, Indonesia

SET ON A SMOOTH GREEN PLAIN on the garden-like Indonesian island of Java, Borobudur is not only the largest Buddhist monument in the world, but also quite simply one of the most stunning architectural creations you'll ever see. Some two million blocks of lava rock completed the original pyramid-like design, though some have been lost over the centuries. Seen from the ground, it looks like a mountain, bristling with odd little spires; seen from above, it looks like an open lotus blossom, the sacred expression of Buddhism. Any kid who's ever played with Legos will get the compulsive beauty of its symmetry.

But the true brilliance of Borobudur can only be understood if you walk around it. Like the labyrinths in medieval Christian cathedrals, the **walkways** around each level of this stepped pyramid are an exercise in meditation; you'll see saffron-robed Buddhist priests pacing along, chanting as they wind around the 3km-long (1¾-mile) route to the top. The first six levels (plus another underground to stabilize the pyramid) are rectangular in shape, decorated with sculpted bas-relief panels, 1,460 in all. Seen in order, the panels are more or less a spiritual textbook, depicting the life and lessons of Buddha. Each ascending level represents a higher stage of man's spiritual journey. The top three levels, however, are circular terraces with no ornamentation, for Buddhism considers plainness and simplicity more virtuous than decoration. Instead of carved panels, these upper levels hold a regimented series of beehivelike stone **stupas,** their bricks set in perforated checkerboard patterns, almost as if to let in air for the **stone Buddhas** tucked inside. Each inscrutable Buddha sits cross-legged, making a hand gesture that signifies one of five spiritual attainments. At the top, one large central stupa crowns the pyramid, empty inside—scholars debate whether it once contained a bigger Buddha, or whether its emptiness symbolizes the blessed state of nirvana.

One of the many mysteries of Borobudur is why it was abandoned. When Sir Thomas Stanford Raffles discovered it in 1814, Borobudur was buried under layers of ash from nearby Mount Merapi.

Perhaps it was buried Pompeii-style; or maybe a series of eruptions brought famine to the region, causing the population to move away. Either way, Borobudur lay forgotten for centuries. It's now a UNESCO World Heritage Site, and perhaps Java's most admired tourist destination. Antiquities officials, worried that tourist footprints are wearing down the ancient stone, are pressing to have the terraced walkways closed to visitors. Go now before you lose your chance.

ⓘ www.central-java-tourism.com or www. borobudurpark.com

✈ Yogvakarta, 40km (25 miles).

🛏 $$ **Manohara Hotel,** Borobudur Archaeological Park, Magelang (✆ **361/ 731520;** www.baliwww.com). $$$ **Sheraton Mustika,** JL Laksda Adisucipto, Yogyakarta (✆ **274/488588;** www.sheraton.com).

WHY THEY'LL THANK YOU: Walking the circuit, reading the walls.

Chapter **10** A Dose of Culture

Masterpieces of Art . . . 372
Music . . . 382
Theater & the Movies . . . 391

Discovering the Louvre.

The Uffizi Gallery
Pearl of the Italian Renaissance
Ages 6 & up • Florence, Italy

LET'S FACE IT: Renaissance art can be a hard sell to kids. But my husband and I didn't want to miss the Uffizi Gallery, unquestionably one of the world's great museums, a treasure-trove of—you guessed it—Italian Renaissance art. (What else would you expect inside a former Medici palace in Florence?) Fortunately, we found a strategy that clicked: We made our visit to the Uffizi into a treasure hunt.

Here's how it worked: In the earlier rooms, you'll see painting after painting of the classic Madonna and Child pose, each artist giving his own distinctive take. We asked our youngsters to study them all (kids like looking at pictures of kids anyway) to see how through the ages the babies began to look more realistic. We also pointed out the flat, stylized backgrounds of the earlier paintings so that

they could see how the scenes became deeper and more natural as painters developed the art of perspective.

A new theme starts in rooms 10 to 14, the **Botticelli rooms**—the highlight of the Uffizi for most visitors, me included. In the mid-1400s, classical mythology had become a popular subject, and so we looked for pictures of Venus, the goddess of beauty—which pointed us straight to the Uffizi's ultimate masterpiece, Botticelli's *Birth of Venus*. (Consider whether or not you want to tell them its nickname, "Venus on the Half Shell," because once you tell them they won't ever think of it as anything else.) We found ourselves even more engrossed by Botticelli's *Allegory of Spring,* or *Primavera,* which depicts Venus in a citrus grove with Cupid hovering suggestively over her head. Before leaving the

Outside the Uffizi Gallery.

room, look for Botticelli's *Adoration of the Magi*, in which many figures are Medici portraits (the man in the yellow robe at the far right is Botticelli); compare it to Leonardo da Vinci's unfinished *Adoration* in room 15. To carry on the Venus theme, check out the Greek statue *Venus of the Medici* in beautiful room 18 with its dome of pearl shells, and a couple of voluptuous Titian Venuses in room 28.

In rooms 23 to 25, get the kids to notice how art began to embrace storytelling by looking for episodes in the life of Jesus—Correggio's *Rest on the Flight to Egypt;* Andrea Mantegna's *Epiphany, Circumcision,* and *Ascension;* and, in room 25, Michelangelo's magnificent *Holy Family.*

Speaking of Michelangelo, it's too bad you have to pay another admission fee (and wait in line) to enter the **Galleria dell'Accademia,** Via Ricasoll 60 (*©* **055-2388609**), where the only thing the kids will want to see is Michelangelo's colossal statue of **David.** We cut our losses,

looked instead at the inferior copy outdoors in the Piazza della Signoria, and then headed out to **St. Mark's Museum,** Museo di San Marco; Piazza San Marco 1 (*©* **055-294883**). Originally a Dominican convent, its bleak, bare cells are decorated with frescoes by the mystical **Fra Angelico,** one of Europe's greatest 15th-century painters. You've been telling the kids for years not to write on the walls, but oh, if they could create scenes like these, you'd let them paint their hearts out.

(i) Piazzale degli Uffizi 6 (*©* **055-23885;** www.uffizi.firenze.it).

🚂 Florence, 2–3 hr. from Rome.

🛏 $$$ **Grand Hotel Villa Medici,** Via il Prato 42 (*©* **055-2381331;** www.villamedici hotel.com). $ **Hotel Casci,** Via Cavour 13 (*©* **055-211686;** www.hotelcasci.com).

WHY THEY'LL THANK YOU: The Botticelli Venuses.

---

333 Masterpieces of Art

The Last Supper
On the da Vinci Trail in Milan
Ages 8 & up • Milan, Italy

THOUGH BORN IN FLORENCE, Leonardo da Vinci spent many years in Milan (1482–99 and 1506–13), under the patronage of the dukes of Milan. The finicky artist produced endless studies and sketches for projects he never finished; one he did complete, however, was a mural that Duke Ludovico commissioned for the convent of Santa Marie delle Grazie church. It just may be the master's greatest painting—but its condition is endangered. Get your kids here now, because it may not exist when they've grown up.

Set above a doorway in what was once a dining hall, **The Last Supper** (*Il Cenacolo Vinciano*) is a huge artwork—8.5m wide and 4.6m tall (28×15 ft.)—depicting

one of the most famous meals of all time: Christ's last Passover Seder in Jerusalem, shortly before his arrest. There's nothing static about this scene: Jesus, hands outspread (as if to display his future wounds) has just announced that one of his followers will betray him, and the disciples all lean away, aghast, each in his own manner protesting his fidelity. Ask the kids to pick out Judas—he's the one with his face in shadow, already clutching the bag of money he was paid to betray Jesus. Christ's sorrowful figure is isolated, the curved pediment of a doorway over his head suggesting a halo; light streams in from the windows behind him, while darkness looms behind the disciples. It's a masterpiece of composition, both technical and dramatic, and no matter how often it's parodied (Mel Brooks, Monty Python, and George Carlin have all had a go at it), the original still takes your breath away.

The kids may be shocked to see how fragile the mural looks, but to me that adds human dimension to da Vinci's artistic achievement. The painting began to disintegrate almost as soon as Leonardo finished it, for he had experimented with risky new paints and application techniques. But it is so clearly a work of genius that over the centuries artists and restorers felt drawn to save it, repainting it in the 1700s, the 1800s, and again quite recently. It's been said that all that's left of the original *Last Supper* is a "few isolated streaks of fading color"—everything else was layered on by later hands. So what are we looking at here, and why? If you

can get your kids to discuss this paradox, you'll really expand their minds.

Only 25 viewers are admitted at a time (be prepared to wait in line), and you must pass through antipollutant chambers before you get your allotted 15 minutes in front of the painting. A lot to go through, but *The Last Supper* is worth it.

(i) Piazza Santa Maria delle Grazie (off Corso Magenta; ☎ **02-4987588**). Reservations required; closed Mon.

✈ Milan's Aeroporto di Linate (internal European flights). Aeroporto Malpensa (transatlantic flights).

🛏 $$ **Antica Locanda Leonardo,** Corso Magenta 78 (☎ **02-463317;** www.leoloc. com). $$$ **Four Seasons Hotel Milano,** Via Gesù 8 (☎ **02-77088;** www.fourseasons.com).

WHY THEY'LL THANK YOU: The da Vinci mystique hovers here.

Paris for Art Lovers
Ages 10 & up • Paris, France

THE MUSÉE DU LOUVRE just may be the world's most impressive art museum—to go to Paris and *not* visit it would almost be absurd. Yet the collection is so staggeringly huge, you simply can't see everything. And if your adult mind soon starts to whirl, just imagine how children feel.

Don't miss the Louvre, but be smart about it: Avoid the long line at the glass pyramid entrance by using the automatic ticket machines, or order tickets in advance by credit card (☎ **08-92-68-46-94**). Skip the 90-minute guided tours; they're pitched over kids' heads, and they make every room they enter instantly crowded. Once you're through the doors, simply pick up a museum map and plan your own visit to loop past the Big Three Masterpieces: da Vinci's *La Giaconda* (better known as the **Mona Lisa**), the armless classical sculpture **Venus de Milo,** and the ancient

headless statue **Winged Victory.** Everybody else is trying to see them too, so expect to be jostled; the *Mona Lisa* in particular is a letdown, a small, dark painting you can't get close to. Once you've seen it, hunt for other da Vincis in the surrounding galleries, then cut over to the superb **ancient Egypt collection,** which the Louvre has been amassing since Napoléon occupied Egypt in 1798. Then spend 40 minutes or so wandering around the **Richelieu Wing,** which houses northern European and French art; my favorite bit here is the grand salons of Napoléon III.

Now you've done it, you've visited the Louvre—the children can say they saw the *Mona Lisa* in person. And having successfully avoided an art overdose, you've got a shot at steering them into three other Paris art museums they'll enjoy more. Across the Seine, the **Musée d'Orsay,**

1 rue de Bellechasse (☎ **01-40-49-48-14;** www.musee-orsay.fr), set in a transformed neoclassical train station, focuses on 1848–1914, which means it has lots of impressionists, pointillists, and realists—painters such as Van Gogh, Manet, Monet, Degas, and Renoir. Masterpieces include Renoir's *Moulin de la Galette,* Van Gogh's *Starry Night,* James McNeill Whistler's *Arrangement in Gray and Black: Portrait of the Painter's Mother,* and Manet's *Déjeuner sur l'herbe,* with its shocking-for-its-time nude woman picnicking.

The **Musée National Auguste Rodin,** Hôtel Biron, 77 rue de Varenne (☎ **01-44-18-61-10;** www.musee-rodin.fr), is set in the great 19th-century sculptor's own mansion, with splendid rose gardens. Stand next to *The Thinker*

Venus de Milo.

and you'll understand how marble comes to life in the hands of a genius.

Musée Picasso, Hôtel Salé, 5 rue de Thorigny (☎ **01-42-71-25-21;** www.paris.org/Musees/Picasso), displays the world's greatest Picasso collection, including his fabled gaunt blue figures and harlequins, a career-spanning range of the Spanish artist's paintings and sculptures in a lovely restored mansion. It was my kids' favorite art museum in all of France—we were glad we saved it for last.

ⓘ **Musée du Louvre,** 34–36 quai du Louvre, 1er (☎ **01-40-20-53-17;** www.louvre.fr).

✈ ⊨ See Paris ㊴.

WHY THEY'LL THANK YOU: The *Mona Lisa, Whistler's Mother,* and *The Thinker*—a trifecta of Great Art.

Museo del Prado
Where Three Old Masters Reign in Spain
Ages 6 & up • Madrid, Spain

WITH MORE THAN 7,000 PAINTINGS, **the Prado** is one of the most important repositories of art in the world, based on a royal collection fattened over the years by the wealth of the Habsburgs and the Bourbons. Don't make the kids see everything; on your first visit, concentrate on the three great Spanish masters—Velázquez, Goya, and El Greco, who can be appreciated here as nowhere else.

One picture they must see: *Las Meninas* by **Diego Velázquez** (1599–1660). The figure of a small Spanish infanta in her splendid satin gown is the focal point, her self-possessed gaze as quixotic as the Mona Lisa's. Two figures in the painting

look directly at the viewer: the princess and that dark-clothed figure behind her painting the royal family, a self-portrait of Velázquez. The faces of the queen and king are merely reflected in a mirror on a back wall. Then there's that departing figure on the stairs in the back—Velázquez's virtuoso technique is one thing, but this painting is so dramatically composed, we could barely drag ourselves away.

We love the work of his older contemporary **El Greco** (ca. 1541–1614), a Crete-born artist who lived much of his life in Toledo. His huge canvases look astonishingly modern, with their impressionistic lights and shadows. The Prado displays several of his rapturous saints, Madonnas, and Holy Families, even a ghostly John the Baptist.

It's also fascinating to see the work of **Francisco de Goya** (1746–1828)—note the contrast between his portraits of Charles IV and his family (so unflattering, you wonder why they continued their patronage) and politically charged paintings like the *Third of May* (1808) and sketches depicting the decay of 18th-century Spain. One pair of canvases, *The Clothed Maja* and *The Naked Maja,* make a brilliant contrast—almost identical portraits, except that in one the woman is clothed and in the other she's nude.

My teenagers also got into Hieronymus Bosch's *The Garden of Earthly Delights, The Seven Deadly Sins,* and his triptych *The Hay Wagon,* along with the ghoulish *The Triumph of Death* by Pieter Breughel

the Elder. But we only had 1 day, and we needed to scoot over to the **Museo Nacional Centro de Arte Reina Sofía,** Santa Isabel 52 (✆ **91-467-5062** or 91-468-3002; www.museoreinasofia.es), the Prado's modern-art sequel, where Pablo Picasso's antiwar masterpiece *Guernica* is the star, alongside works by Juan Gris, Joan Miro, and Salvador Dalí.

ⓘ Paseo del Prado (✆ **91-330-2800;** www.museoprado.es).

✈ Madrid, 14km (8⅔ miles).

🛏 $ **Hotel Best Western Cortezo,** Doctor Cortezo 3 (✆ **91-369-0101;** www.hotel cortezo.com). $$$ **Hotel Preciados,** Preciados 37 (✆ **91-454-4400;** www.preciados hotel.com).

WHY THEY'LL THANK YOU: That enigmatic, unforgettable infanta.

Amsterdam's Museumplein Masterpieces
Dutch Masters & Then Some
Ages 6 & up • Amsterdam, The Netherlands

MAYBE IT HAS SOMETHING to do with the austere northern slant of light, but from Rembrandt van Rijn to Vincent van Gogh, there's a tradition of Dutch painting that other nations can only envy. Realistic scenes of middle-class domestic life, moody polder landscapes with cloud-scudding skies, arresting portraits of shrewd burgers—it's the sort of art that looks you straight in the face and holds a conversation, and I personally love it. Now I had to turn my kids on to it, too.

The **Golden Age** of Dutch painting came in the 17th century, the high point of Holland's international power and wealth, and naturally the **Rijksmuseum,** Holland's national museum, has a rich collection of those Dutch masters. My favorites are the **Vermeers,** those almost photographic household scenes, bathed in natural light. Compared to his delicately frozen

moments, the robust paintings of Jan Steen and Frans Hals look downright jolly. Crowds flock around Rembrandt's immense *Nightwatch,* a dramatically lit group portrait of a cadre of militiamen checking their weapons before going out on patrol. Even more than *Nightwatch,* our favorite Rembrandt group portrait was the iconic *The Sampling Officials,* a cluster of guildsmen in almost identical black suits, square white collars, and brimmed black hats. Rembrandt painted each man staring outward with an arresting gaze that cuts through the centuries like a knife.

We felt a bit let down by the **Museum Het Rembrandthuis** (Rembrandt House Museum), Jodenbreestraat 4–6 (✆ **020/ 520-0400;** www.rembrandthuis.nl). It was interesting to see inside a 17th-century house, but there weren't many personal possessions—and Rembrandt himself, so good at revealing the personalities of others in his paintings, remained tantalizingly mysterious, like one of his shadowy self-portraits.

The raw emotion of Vincent van Gogh's painting flares like a comet at the **van Gogh Museum,** a short walk down Museumplein from the Rijksmuseum. Few painters deserve a solo museum more than van Gogh, whose saturated colors and bold sinuous outlines make neighboring canvases look pallid. More than 200 van Gogh paintings are hung here—landscapes, portraits, still lifes—and as we moved through the galleries, arranged in chronological order, we got an eerie sense of the

meteoric development in this artist's brief career (1880–90). From the early, brooding *Potato Eaters* to the vivid late *Sunflowers,* the evolution was startling enough to bowl over the kids. Mission accomplished.

(i) **Rijksmuseum,** Jan Luikenstraat 1 (© **020/647-700;** www.rijksmuseum.nl). **van Gogh Museum,** Paulus Potterstraat 7 (© **020/ 570-5200;** www.vangoghmuseum.nl).

✈ 🛏 See The Canals of Amsterdam **51**.

WHY THEY'LL THANK YOU: From Vermeer's Delft kitchen to van Gogh's Arles bedroom.

---

337 Masterpieces of Art

The Hermitage
Art Treasures of the Czars
Ages 8 & up • St. Petersburg, Russia

ONE THING YOU HAVE TO SAY about the Russian czars—they collected some great art over the centuries, especially Catherine II and her grandson Nicholas I. Determined to prove that they were enlightened European monarchs, they spent their imperial fortunes recklessly on paintings and statues, as well as coins, antiquities, and jewelry. And then, of course, in 1917 the Russian revolution came along, and the czars were history. Except for their art—the savvy Bolsheviks hung onto that all right.

The ghosts of that czarist era still linger in St. Petersburg, nowhere more so than at elegant **Palace Square** (Dvortsovaya Ploshchad). Standing under the Alexander Column—a 600-ton monolith topped by a cross-carrying angel—imagine all that this asymmetrical plaza has seen, from royal coaches pulling up to the baroque **Winter Palace** on one side, to Communist solidarity marches in front of the long curved General Staff Building. Through the grand courtyard of the Winter Palace today, you enter the State Hermitage Museum, where, in the

absence of the czars, the art has finally taken over. In these extravagantly decorated salons, with their marble columns and parquet floors and dazzling chandeliers, it seems as if every inch of the red walls is covered with artworks in fussy gold frames. And yet, believe it or not, this is only a fraction of the collection.

The Hermitage has an incredible catalog of **Renaissance Italian art,** including two rare da Vinci Madonnas, and loads of **Dutch and Flemish masters** (look for Rembrandt's *Return of the Prodigal Son* and *Old Man in Red*). Among its **Spanish masterpieces** are one of my favorite El Grecos, *The Apostles Peter and Paul,* and Velázquez's arresting portrait of Count Olivares. The Hermitage has so many French artworks—more than any museum outside of France—that my personal favorites, the **French impressionists** and two rooms of early **Picasso,** have been crowded up to plainer rooms on the third floor, which can be stuffy and crowded in summer. Crowds are thinner in the **Antiquities halls** on the ground floor, which displays relics from the Greeks, Romans, and Egyptians.

Many visitors are so busy squinting at the pictures, they forget to look around them—and that's missing the point of this great Fabergé egg of a museum. The czars longed so desperately to impress the world with how cultured they were, they probably overdid it. But after the Revolution, did anyone ever again build a place as beautiful as this?

(i) 1 Palace Sq. (📞 **812/110-9079;** www.hermitagemuseum.org). Closed Sun–Mon.

✈ Pulkovo-2 International Airport 16km (10 miles).

🛏 $$$ **Corinthia Nevsky Palace,** 57 Nevsky Prospekt (📞 **812/380-2001;** www.corinthia.ru). $$ **Pulford Apartments,** 6 Moika Embankment (📞 **812/325-6277;** www.pulford.com).

WHY THEY'LL THANK YOU: Remembering to look up at the ceilings.

Masterpieces of Art

338

The Metropolitan Museum of Art
Manhattan's Treasure Trove
All ages • New York, New York, USA

THE ECHOING MARBLE-CLAD Great Hall tells you as you enter that this is a Serious Art Museum. But don't let that put you off—New York City's number-one tourist attraction can be a lot of fun for children, even toddlers. Make a beeline for the areas kids really love: **Arms & Armor** (first floor), the extensive **Egyptian rooms** (also on the first floor—don't miss the glorious mummies), **musical instruments** (second floor, off the American Wing's courtyard), the **Costume Institute** (ground floor—rotating installations will often be of interest to kids), and the **European and American furniture rooms** (all over the place—any kid who's read *From the Mixed-Up Files of Mrs. Basil E. Frankweiler,* about a brother and sister who hide out for weeks in the Met, will adore these). On the first floor of the American Wing, a side gallery displays vintage baseball cards, and a whole gallery of grandfather clocks ticks away on the second floor. Older kids who are beginning to appreciate art may go for the **impressionist gallery** (second floor), full of Monets and Van Goghs they'll instantly recognize, or the **Lehman Pavilion,** set up like the town house of a wealthy collector—it's art in small enough doses that it doesn't overwhelm.

Our favorite corner, hands down, is the **courtyard of the American Wing,** a light-filled open space with plantings, benches, and statues kids can actually relate to (a mountain lion and her cubs, a pensive Indian brave). Back in the corner is an entire Frank Lloyd room, all dark wood and low-slung right angles, that our family could move into at a moment's notice. Bring lots of small change for kids to throw into the American Wing reflecting pool and in the pool in front of the Egyptian Wing's serene **Temple of Dendur.** In the Japanese galleries, find the room overlooking the Temple of Dendur; off the musical instruments gallery, find the balcony overlooking the mounted knights in armor. Get the idea? Wander around this immense museum, keep your eyes open, and be willing to walk away from anything that doesn't interest your children.

The huge museum gift shop has a lot of good stuff for kids, and there are plenty of free children's programs.

(i) Fifth Ave. and 82nd St. (📞 **212/535-7710;** www.metmuseum.org).

✈ 🛏 See Manhattan **56**.

WHY THEY'LL THANK YOU: Great art is great art.

339

The Art Institute of Chicago
Hitting Art's Highlights in the Loop
Ages 4 & up • Chicago, Illinois, USA

MY KIDS ARE GREAT FANS of the movie *Ferris Bueller's Day Off,* the greatest Chicago travelogue ever made, in my opinion. What Ferris (Matthew Broderick) and his two pals do in Chicago while playing hooky from their nice North Shore high school is our dream itinerary for a day in the Windy City: a Cubs game, a parade—and a stroll through the Art Institute of Chicago. If it was fun enough for Ferris, my kids figured, it would be fun enough for them.

Of course we were compelled to begin, like Ferris, with the immense pointillist canvas by George Seurat, ***Sunday Afternoon on the Island of La Grande Jatte.*** Like every other visitor there, we alternated standing up close to see the individual dots, then standing way back until the dots blur into a busy panorama of springtime in the park. But like the Seurat painting, The Art Institute has so many individual pieces of art, you can lose the big picture. The trick is to steer them to see the things they'd love before they hit Museum Overdose. After *La Grande Jatte,* we wandered dreamily through the rest of the **impressionists,** a collection so rich in Renoirs and Monets that we almost felt a sugar high; we hunted down the Van Gogh self-portrait and then Picasso's blue-period *The Old Guitarist* and felt very satisfied.

Going from the hazy impressionists to sharply detailed 20th-century American paintings was a bracing contrast. We homed in on two masterpieces: the iconic **American Gothic** by Grant Wood, which they've seen spoofed so often, and Edward Hopper's evocative late-night diner scene **Nighthawks.** Then off we went to my favorite nook in the museum: the reconstructed turn-of-the-century **Chicago Stock Exchange trading room,** a dazzling Louis Sullivan showpiece with art-glass insets and stenciled decorations and molded plaster capitals—a perfect expression of Gilded Age tycoonery.

From there, we zigzagged back to the **Thorne Miniature Rooms,** filled with tiny reproductions of furnished interiors from European and American history (heaven for my dollhouse-loving daughter) and then rewarded the boys for their patience with a browse through the great hall of **European arms and armor,** where more than 1,500 objects range from horse armor to maces to poleaxes.

We missed the world-famous collection of glass paperweights; we missed the splendid Japanese wood block prints—who cared? We didn't even worry about plotting a logical course through the museum, since scuttling back and forth allowed us to pass Marc Chagall's jewel-toned **stained-glass windows** more than once, always a good thing.

(i) 111 S. Michigan Ave. ((C) **312/443-3600;** www.artic.edu).

✈ ⊨ See Chicago **57**.

WHY THEY'LL THANK YOU: Connecting the dots.

Huntington Library
Pasadena's Great Portrait Gallery
Ages 6 & up • San Marino, California, USA

THE WORD "LIBRARY" in the name may make the kids wince—why visit a musty old library on vacation? Well, even if they wanted to, they couldn't flip through the rare items in Henry E. Huntington's book collection. What they can see, though, is his terrific **art collection** in a stately Italianate mansion on a 207-acre hilltop estate.

As a girl, I was captivated by one pair of paintings here: Thomas Gainsborough's ***The Blue Boy*** and Thomas Lawrence's ***Pinkie,*** a long-haired boy in blue satin and a slim, dark-haired girl in a filmy white gown and pink bonnet, warily eyeing each other from facing walls of a wood-paneled salon. These life-size paintings capture the moodiness of adolescence so perfectly, you almost expect the kids to step out of those frames and start dissing each other. Blue Boy—aka Jonathan Buttall, son of a wealthy hardware merchant—peers guardedly at us, left hand cockily set on his hip. My sons thought his lace-collared outfit was "kinda sissy"; I explained that it wasn't the style of his time, but an homage to Flemish painter Anthony Van Dyck. Pinkie—in real life Sarah Barrett Moulton, an aunt to the Victorian poet Elizabeth Barrett Browning—stands poised on tiptoe, the satin ribbons of her askew bonnet fluttering, one hand raised defensively. Stormy skies boil behind both subjects, mirroring their defiant teenage expressions. *Pinkie* was painted 25 years after *Blue Boy,* and there was no specific connection between the two—until Henry Huntington bought them both and set them here, a sort of blind date for eternity.

It's always interesting to see great art in a private home setting (if nothing else, it's less intimidating for children than a big formal Art Museum), but it's particularly apt for 18th-century English portraits, which were originally commissioned by aristocrats to decorate their own country manors. The Huntington's main gallery presents the best assemblage anywhere of **full-figure English portraits,** with work by Romney and Reynolds as well as Gainsborough and Lawrence—the Fab Four of late-18th-century portraiture. And the Huntington adds the final touch by serving daily **high tea** (or at any rate

The Blue Boy, a modern interpretation.

what Americans think of as high tea, with pastries and finger sandwiches) in a tea-room overlooking a fabulous rose garden (call ✆ **626/683-8131** for reservations, at least 2 weeks in advance). For locals, the **botanical gardens** are the Huntington's main draw—an exotic cactus garden, a lush jungle garden, soothing lily ponds, and a Japanese garden with open-air house, koi-filled stream, and Zen garden.

The gardens are lovely indeed, but *Blue Boy* and *Pinkie* are what make us return.

ⓘ 1151 Oxford Rd. (✆ **626/405-2100;** www.huntington.org).

✈ ⏍ See Hooray for Hollywood **355**.

WHY THEY'LL THANK YOU: Blue Boy and Pinkie, sitting in a tree . . .

---

341 Masterpieces of Art

The Menil Collection
Getting Surreal down in Houston
Ages 8 & up • Houston, Texas, USA

ONE OF THE WORLD'S GREAT private art collections is tucked away in a residential neighborhood in Houston, Texas; coming here is almost like sharing a secret with your children. Kids tend to feel at home at the Menil Collection, because it's not huge and overwhelming. They can cut straight to the chase and see weird old stuff and weird new stuff, and maybe even dream about making such art themselves.

When Jean and Dominique de Menil fled occupied France during World War II, they settled in Houston and spent the next 4 decades not only buying but commissioning new works of art. They began with a passion for **20th-century modern** works, but then they discovered the **tribal art** that had inspired cubism and surrealism, and from there they drifted into **Middle Eastern antiquities** and then **Byzantine and medieval art.** As collectors, the de Menils followed their own innate taste, and when it's all displayed together, you're suddenly struck by family resemblances—for example, between a Cycladic stone figurine from Greece, primitive African wood-carved masks, and the stylized figures of Picasso and Matisse. There's very little representational art at all here, and very little text

to read alongside the works. You don't need a degree in art history to appreciate what you see before you: The old pieces are simply wondrous artifacts from anonymous craftsmen, while the new art—from the droll whimsy of **Magritte** and **Dalí** and **Warhol** to the splatters of **Jackson Pollock**—tends to be full of personality that speaks for itself.

When it came time to install the art in its own museum, Mrs. De Menil instructed Italian architect Renzo Piano to build something self-effacing, low-slung, and discreet, looking small on the outside but feeling large on the inside. Ingenious ceiling louvers adjust the Texas sunshine to illuminate the artworks in natural light. Around the main gallery building, a number of bold, clean-lined abstract sculptures are set on serene green lawns. Surrounding the lawns are three other sites to pop into: the **Byzantine Fresco Chapel,** with two glittering 13th-century frescoes, the only such works in the Western Hemisphere; a beautifully lit gallery of the modern paintings and sculptures of **Cy Twombly;** and the most powerful of all, the **Rothko Chapel,** with 14 brooding abstract paintings that the de Menils commissioned from Mark Rothko just before his death. A couple of blocks away, there's also an installation of neon art by Don Flavin at **Richmond Hall.**

(i) 1515 Sul Rose St. (© **713/525-9400;** www.menil.org). Closed Mon–Tues.

✈ ⊨ See Space Center Houston ❷❾❽.

WHY THEY'LL THANK YOU: Blowing the dust off of fine art.

Music 342

Salzburg: Mozart's Hometown
Ages 6 & up • Austria

HERE'S A DIRTY LITTLE SECRET: Wolfgang Amadeus Mozart didn't even like Salzburg—he couldn't wait to leave his provincial hometown and get to Vienna, where the real action was. Salzburg audiences didn't appreciate him, he complained. Well, the rest of the world didn't either; he died a pauper at age 35, buried (in Vienna) in an unmarked grave. But today Salzburg appreciates him all right—Mozart is Salzburg's main tourism draw, with a huge Mozart festival every summer, a Mozart Week in January, and frequent concerts at the town's premier concert hall, the (you guessed it) Mozar-teum. Better late than never, I guess.

A statue of Mozart was erected in 1842 in the center of town, in a cafe-lined plaza renamed, naturally, Mozartplatz, a charming place to feel the pulse of what is still a bourgeois provincial town, like a time warp of mustard-colored baroque architecture. Head through the narrow shop-lined streets of the historic district to the composer's birthplace, the **Mozart Geburthaus,** where the Mozart family lived until he was 17. As a child prodigy propelled by an ambitious father, he was constantly on tour, but when he came home it was to this cramped apartment; his boyhood violin, his concert violin, and his viola, fortepiano, and clavichord are on display. As a child, Mozart often trooped from these drab quarters to perform at the **Residenz,** Residenzplatz 1 (© **0662/80422690**), the grand baroque palace of the prince-archbishop of Salzburg; a tour

of its lavish staterooms is quite a contrast to the Mozart digs. In 1773 the family moved across the river to the roomier **Mozart Wohnhaus,** which was badly bombed in World War II. Rebuilt as a Mozart museum in 1996, it has comprehensive exhibits on his poignant life and glorious music.

Should you take the kids to the Mozart Festival? Only if they adore classical music, because it's an expensive crush of high-profile music lovers that snares every hotel room in town. (Try your luck with the **Salzburg Festival box office,** Hofstall-gasse 1, A-5020 Salzburg; © **0662/8045;** www.salzburgfestival.at.) You can hear Mozart's music in more relaxed circumstances around town all year, not to mention seeing kid-friendly shows at the **Salzburger Marionetten Theater,** Schwarzstrasse 24 (© **0662/8724040;** www.marionetten.at).

(i) **Mozart Birthplace,** Getreidegasse 9 (© **0662/844313**). **Mozart Residence,** Makartplatz 8 (© **0662/844313**).

✈ Salzburg-Mozart Regional.

⊨ $ **Altstadthotel Wolf-Dietrich,** Wolf-Dietrich-Strasse 7 (© **0662/871275;** www. salzburg-hotel.at). $$ **Hotel Mozart,** Franz-Josef-Strasse 27 (© **0662/872274;** www. hotel-mozart.at).

WHY THEY'LL THANK YOU: Realizing that Mozart wrote *Twinkle, Twinkle, Little Star*—among other tunes.

343 Music

The Paris Opera
Where the Phantom Lurked
Ages 8 & up • Paris, France

WHETHER THE ANDREW LLOYD WEBBER musical or the scarifying Lon Chaney silent movie is their reference point, most kids have heard of the Phantom of the Opera. Perhaps they'll be disappointed to learn such a tragic fellow never existed, but was merely a literary creation from a 1910 novel by Gaston Leroux. However, the building he haunted absolutely does exist, and a **guided tour** lives up to all weird and wonderful expectations.

Officially called the Opéra de Paris Garnier, it was designed by 19th-century architect Charles Garnier for Emperor Napoleon III. Napoleon III's reign was known as the Second Empire and prized a highly decorated aesthetic style, as if the reinstated monarchy was determined to outdo the old regime's Sun King opulence—to out-Versailles Versailles **367**.

There is no better example of Second Empire luxury than the **Paris Opera.** Topped by a green copper dome and heavily ornamented pediment, the facade is a crazy excess of rose marble columns, friezes, massed sculptures, and gilded statues. Things only get more lavish once you venture inside the lobby, with an immense marble grand staircase and a grand foyer with tons of chandeliers and Venetian mosaics all over the ceiling. Inside the actual auditorium, everything is upholstered in red velvet, with plaster cherubs capering over walls and ceilings and gold-leaf accents glinting on every possible surface. The luminous ceiling painting by Marc Chagall is stunning, though not precisely fitting the period. But oh, that **chandelier,** just as in the musical's climactic scene—six tons of

The Paris Opera.

sparkling crystal suspended over the orchestra seats. The term *pièce de résistance* was coined to describe just this sort of showstopping beauty.

Although workers started building the Opera in 1862, work halted for some time when an underground lake—again, just as in the Phantom story—was discovered beneath the site. (It's still there.) Finally competed in 1875, the grandiose Opera became Paris's premier opera house. But your kids don't have to worry—you can't drag them to watch an opera, chiefly

because the modern Opéra de Paris Bastille opened in 1989, relegating the Opéra Garnier to host mainly ballet. Wonder what the Phantom would think of that?

(i) **Place de l'Opera** (✆ **01-40-01-22-63** or 01-40-01-19-70 for tours).

✈ ⊨ See Paris **54**.

WHY THEY'LL THANK YOU: A theater so grand, it deserves a phantom.

Music **344**

Doolin
The Haunting Keen of Irish Folk Music
Ages 8 & up • Doolin, County Clare, Ireland

SO YOU'RE HERE IN County Clare, Ireland, and you've seen the spectacular Cliffs of Moher **7** and the Burren **80**. What do you do at night? Head to the secluded fishing village of Doolin, where you'll get a taste of another side of Irish life—the **traditional music** of fiddle and flute, harp and bodhran drum, performed live in atmospheric pubs strung along one steep village street.

True, **pubs**—short for "public houses," which have a license to sell alcoholic beverages—are more or less bars; but in Ireland they are also community gathering places, so don't hesitate to take kids there for an evening, especially not when music, rather than drinking, is the pub's chief attraction. Simple bar food is served, sawdust litters the floor, and seating is often on hard benches (some nights it's standing room only). Don't worry if you can't get a good view of the musicians; you'll hear them all right. Traditional music, usually referred to simply as **"trad,"** is a vital part of contemporary Irish culture, not relegated to secondary folk-music status, and it often shades into acoustic rock, with many musicians writing their own trad-style songs as well as performing the folk classics. Listen to a

couple of albums by the Chieftains or Cherish the Ladies or the Clancy Brothers before you go so the kids will recognize beloved tunes like "Carrickfergus" and "Foggy Dew" and "Raglan Road" when they break out—everyone else in the pub is sure to clap in recognition when they hear the first strains.

The best-known place in town is **Gus O'Connor's,** Fisher Street (✆ **065/707-4168**), situated in a row of thatched fishermen's cottages near the pier; it's been around since 1832, so expect those rafters to be weathered with years of smoke. But it's popular with tourists and often crowded. Up on Lisdoonvarna Road, at **McGann's** (✆ **065/707-4133**) or **McDermott's** (✆ **065/707-4133**), the music is just as good and the audience more local. Besides the advertised performers, these pubs are magnets for musicians from all over the world, who are quite likely to join in an impromptu jam.

(i) www.doolin-tourism.com.

✈ ⊨ See the Cliffs of Moher **7**.

WHY THEY'LL THANK YOU: Skirling fiddles, thumping bodhrans, heart-piercing tin whistles—no music lover can resist.

Liverpool Beatles Tour
Ages 8 & up • England

IT WAS MORE THAN 20 YEARS AGO today—1962, as a matter of fact—that a quartet of hungry young musicians from this grimy port city rocketed to the top of the pop charts, not only in the U.K. but around the world. Their sound was so fresh, so original, and so exciting, that in some respects music would never again be the same. If your kids aren't already Beatlemaniacs, a visit to their birthplace should change things.

Liverpool, grimy no more, has had a serious face-lift since the 1960s; the spruced-up waterfront around Albert Dock now has boutiques in converted warehouses, a branch of the Tate art museum, and of course the slick **The Beatles Story,** Britannia Pavilion, Albert Dock (✆ **01517/091963;** www.beatles story.com), an audiovisual "experience" housing Beatles memorabilia, including a yellow submarine with live fish swimming past the portholes. Cheesy it may be, but my kids loved it. But for a deeper insight, contact the **National Trust** (✆ **0870 900 0256;** www.nationaltrust.org.uk) to book tours of Paul McCartney's and John Lennon's boyhood homes, meticulously restored to their 1950s appearance. Here you'll see the lumpy brown sofa where Paul and John scribbled their first songs, and John's tiny bedroom with its Elvis Presley and Brigitte Bardot posters on the walls. You'll get the point that musical genius raised these two from humble roots indeed.

You can also stop by the **Cavern Club,** downtown at 8–10 Mathew St. (✆ **01512/ 369091;** www.cavern-liverpool.co.uk), a replica of the venue where the Beatles were virtually the house band, playing 292 gigs between 1961 and 1963; it was here that their future manager, Brian Epstein, first heard them on November 9, 1961. The Cavern hands out maps for a walking tour of pertinent Beatle sites in the city center and operates a 2-hour Magical Mystery bus

tour, which takes in Beatles-related sites such as the bustling Penny Lane intersection, and the Salvation Army children's home Strawberry Fields.

There's a **Beatles** shop at 31 Mathew St., and the Beatles-themed **Hard Day's Night** hotel is around the corner on North John Street. And even though the song "Ferry Cross the Mersey" was by fellow Liverpudlians Gerry & the Pacemakers, not the Beatles, kids will enjoy taking a boat from Pier Head to Woodside for a sweeping view of the port. Contact **Mersey Ferries** (✆ **01516/301030;** www.merseyferries.co.uk).

The Cavern Wall of Fame in Liverpool.

A DOSE OF CULTURE

(i) **Liverpool Tourist Information Centre,** Maritime Museum, Albert Dock (© **01517/ 088854;** www.visitliverpool.com).

🚆 Liverpool, 3 hr. from London, 45 min. from Manchester.

🛏 $$ **The Feathers Hotel,** 117–125 Mt. Pleasant (© **01517/099655;** www.feathers. uk.com).

WHY THEY'LL THANK YOU: The Fab Four forever.

Music 346

Graceland: Memphis Music Mecca

Ages 6 & up • Memphis, Tennessee, USA

To MANY MUSIC FANS, Memphis, Tennessee, means one thing: the world's greatest Elvis shrine, Graceland. But chances are your kids know more about tacky Elvis impersonators than they do about the King himself. So when you come to Memphis, show them the whole story—the amazing music heritage that first drew the shy teenager from Tupelo, Mississippi, to this Tennessee river city.

Sun Records Studio.

Begin on **Beale Street,** the nerve center of the South's most vital post–Civil War black community. W. C. Handy brought the blues sound up Highway 61 🖅 from Mississippi at the turn of the century and it caught fire in the clubs of Beale Street; later such legends as B. B. King, Muddy Waters, and Howlin' Wolf added their voices. Stroll along the street, read the historic markers, and check out who's playing at the nightclubs between Second and Fourth streets. Visit the **W. C. Handy House Museum,** 352 Beale St. (© **901/ 527-3427**), and the Smithsonian's **Rock 'n' Soul Museum,** 191 Beale St. (© **901/ 205-2533**), with photos, recordings, and artifacts from a satin Elvis Presley suit to Ike Turner's piano.

In 1950, in a tiny brick corner storefront, recording engineer Sam Phillips opened **Sun Records Studio,** 706 Union Ave. (© **901/521-0664;** www.sunstudio. com), where then-unknowns Carl Perkins, Roy Orbison, Jerry Lee Lewis, Johnny Cash, and Elvis Presley took the blues sound, mixed it with country and bluegrass, and came up with a new sound: rock 'n' roll. You can tour Sun Studio's surprisingly Spartan setup; records are still made here by current artists like U2 and Bonnie Raitt.

Yet another sound was born in Memphis in 1959, when Stax Records began recording such soul-music greats as Isaac Hayes, Otis Redding, and Wilson Pickett. The **Stax Museum of American Soul Music,** 926

E. McLemore Ave. (✆ **901/942-SOUL**), has such evocative exhibits as a re-created gospel church and the dance floor from the TV show *Soul Train.*

Now that you've placed Elvis in music history, head out Elvis Presley Boulevard to **Graceland,** the colonial-style mansion Elvis bought in the late 1950s for the then-huge price of $100,000. As the King's fame grew, 14-acre Graceland became his refuge, and eventually his retreat from reality. Touring the mansion, you'll get a glimpse of the lavish lifestyle the poor Delta boy chose once he hit the big time: carpeted wall-to-wall in white, with gold accents and satin drapes everywhere. Walls covered with gold record plaques, mannequin after mannequin sporting Elvis's stage outfits—it's an

assault on the senses. Don't miss the flower-laden memorial garden where Elvis is buried alongside his parents. It completes the whole arc of Elvis's career, from raw young rockabilly to hip-swiveling teen heartthrob to sequin-jumpsuited megastar. As you drive away, play a mix-tape of Elvis hits from *That's All Right Now Mama* and *All Shook Up* to *Love Me Tender* and *Suspicious Minds.* Now the kids *know* who Elvis is.

ⓘ 3734 Elvis Presley Blvd. (✆ **800/238-2000** or 901/332-3322; www.elvis.com).

✈ ⊨ See the National Civil Rights Museum **251**.

WHY THEY'LL THANK YOU: Elvis never left *this* building.

---

347 **Music**

Highway 61 Revisited—Again

Ages 8 & up • Memphis, Tennessee, to Leland, Mississippi, USA

WHEN BOB DYLAN NAMED his 1965 album *Highway 61 Revisited,* his folkie fans said, "Where?" But what Dylan was doing was acknowledging his debt to Delta blues: U.S. 61 is the two-lane road that took legendary bluesmen north from the cotton plantations of the Mississippi Delta. Drive down this highway—which begins as 3rd Street in Memphis—and you'll pass through a flat landscape of fertile fields, endless railroad tracks, and run-down shacks. Load up some appropriate CDs for the drive—maybe Eric Clapton's *Me and Mr. Johnson*—and surrender yourself to the heart of the Deep South. You don't have to be a blues maven to appreciate it, but it just may turn you into one.

Where Highway 61 meets Highway 49, in Clarksdale, Mississippi, a guitar statue marks **The Crossroads,** the spot where, legend has it, 1930s bluesman Robert

Johnson sold his soul to the devil in exchange for the gift of playing genius guitar. The so-called Father of the Blues, W. C. Handy, was playing ragtime in Clarksdale in 1903 when he first heard this heady local mix of African-American gospel and cotton-field work songs. Clarksdale was a regional railroad hub, and at the station, Handy wrote, itinerant musicians "would pour out their hearts in song while the audience ate fish and bread, chewed sugar cane, dipped snuff while waiting for trains to carry them on down the line." How fitting, then, that the **Delta Blues Museum,** 1 Blues Alley (✆ **662/672-6820;** www.deltablues museum.org), is based in the old depot. Here you can see B.B. King's guitar Lucille, as well as a case of the sort of improvised instruments that early blues musicians used: juice harps, bottleneck

Muddy Waters's log cabin.

slides, and harmonicas. Artifacts from Mississippi musicians such as Son House, Sonny Boy Williamson, Sam Cooke, Ike Turner, and Albert King are displayed, and in the center of the museum is the reconstructed log cabin where cotton sharecropper Muddy Waters was living when musicologist Alan Lomax discovered him.

Drive by local blues radio station **WROX,** which broadcasts from a bright yellow building near The Crossroads, at 419 State St., and the **Riverside Hotel,** 615 Sunflower Ave. (© **662/624-9163**), once a blacks-only hospital where blues singer Bessie Smith died after a car crash in 1937. After it was converted to a hotel, Sonny Boy Williamson, Ike Turner, and Robert Nighthawk stayed here. Another good stop is **Cathead Delta Blues & Folk Art,** 252 Delta Ave. (© **662/624-5992;**

www.cathead.biz), where you can buy just about any blues CD or DVD.

If you continue south on Highway 61 for another 65 miles, stop in the small town of Leland at the **Highway 61 Blues Museum,** 400 N. Broad St. (© **662/686-7646**). Though it's only one large L-shaped room, there are enough photos, instruments, farm implements, and other artifacts to make it worth seeing. It ain't big and it ain't glitzy—but then, neither is the blues, man.

ⓘ www.visitmississippi.org.

✈ Memphis International.

🛏 $ **Comfort Inn,** 818 S. State St., Clarksdale, MS (© **662/627-5155;** www.choicehotels.com).

WHY THEY'LL THANK YOU: Authentic heart of authentic music.

The Nashville Music Scene
Country Music's Capital
Ages 8 & up • Nashville, Tennessee, USA

NASHVILLE: The very name is synonymous with music, specifically the brand of country music played on the Grand Ole Opry radio show, broadcast from here since 1927. To perform on the Grand Ole Opry is to officially "make it" in country music, and thus it's a town buzzing with music-biz execs, state-of-the-art studios, and happening clubs, with a surprising amount of jazz and rock going down as well. I love Nashville, and even though I'm no country-music aficionado, it only takes a couple hours here to get hooked on its twangy energy.

A music pilgrimage to Nashville centers on three areas: downtown near Ryman auditorium, the original home of the Opry; in the West End along 16th Avenue, known as Music Row, where you can often spot music stars going in and out of the studios; and east of town at the vast Opryland complex where the Opry relocated in 1974. Out at Opryland, the current **Grand Ole Opry House,** 2802 Opryland Dr. (© **615/889-6611;** www.opry.com), produces three live TV shows a week, April to December—order your tickets well in advance. Exhibits at the **Grand Ole Opry Museum** next door at 2804 Opryland Dr. celebrate Opry stars past and present. For a more rounded idea of country music, though, head downtown for the **Country Music Hall of Fame and Museum,** 222 5th Ave. (© **800/852-6437** or 615/416-2001; www.countrymusichalloffame.com). From sequin-spangled costumes to historic guitars to over-the-top custom cars (a crucial status symbol in country music culture), it's an impressive roundup

of artifacts, and the kids really get into the video and audio clips, interactive jukeboxes, and touch-screen computer kiosks, exploring the differences between intertwined musical genres—bluegrass, cowboy music, rockabilly, Cajun, honky-tonk, country swing. Once you're grounded in the music, walk 2 blocks to the **Ryman Auditorium,** 116 5th Ave. (© **615/254-1445;** www.ryman.com), aka The Mother Church of Country Music (built as a church in 1892, it still has stained-glass windows). Dowdy as it looks outside, inside it's a finely restored arena-like theater with top acoustics. By day, it offers memorabilia exhibits, a backstage dressing room tour, and a booth where you can record your own live CD; by night, it has a full roster of live concerts. Then take in an early-evening show at the **Bluebird Café,** 4104 Hillsboro Rd. (© **615/383-1461;** www.bluebird cafe.com), to hear today's up-and-coming singer-songwriters.

ⓘ **Nashville Visitor Information Center,** Gaylord Entertainment Center, 501 Broadway (© **615/259-4747;** www.nashvillecvb.com).

✈ Nashville International, 8 miles.

🛏 $$ **Courtyard Marriott Nashville Vanderbilt/West End,** 1901 West End Ave. (© **800/245-1959** or 615/327-9900; www.marriott.com). $$-$$$ **Opryland Hotel,** 2800 Opryland Dr. (© **615/883-2211;** www.gaylordhotels.com).

WHY THEY'LL THANK YOU: When their boots start a-tapping.

Rock 'n' Roll Hall of Fame: Cleveland Rocks

Ages 6 & up • Ohio, USA

WHY CLEVELAND? Why not? This is the town where DJ Alan Freed first coined the term *rock 'n' roll,* where Chuck Berry played his first public gig; it's the hometown of musicians from Phil Ochs to Chrissie Hynde to Trent Reznor. And what's more, it's within a day's drive of 50% of the U.S. population, so this high-profile shrine can be visited by as many music lovers as possible.

Designed by I. M. Pei, the museum building is an all-shook-up mass of porcelain-tiled geometric shapes, piled up like a guitar and amps in the back of a roadie's van, with a glass pyramid jutting out from one side over Lake Erie. Inside is a cool collection of **pop-culture memorabilia** to browse through. Even if you and the kids don't listen to the same artists, there's plenty here for everyone to groove on. Exhibits display programs, posters, photos, instruments (from Junior Walker's lovingly shined saxophone to a smashed guitar from Paul Simonton of the Clash), and stage costumes (James Brown's red rhinestone-studded tuxedo coat, Neil Young's fringed leather jacket). But what really grabs kids are the artifacts from rock stars' childhoods—things like Jimi Hendrix's baby picture, Jim Morrison's Cub Scout uniform, John Lennon's report card, Joe Walsh's high-school football jersey. Not to ignore current chart toppers, on the plaza level a rotating exhibit features today's artists, from Destiny's Child to Rage Against the Machine. For those of us who actually remember the

1950s, the **Rave On exhibit** displays mementos from rock 'n' rollers like Eddie Cochran, Buddy Holly, and the Everly Brothers on a curved wall evoking a chrome-and-neon diner.

Still, rock 'n' roll isn't about artifacts, it's about performance, which is why it's stirring to watch the filmed Hendrix performance in the **Jimi Hendrix Surround Sound Theater.** Up in the **Hall of Fame,** a video collage of all the 200-plus inductees is mesmerizing. The Hall of Fame includes mostly musicians (eligible 25 years after their first record release), as well as a few producers, DJs, and journalists. Though displays near the entrance focus on the most recent class of inductees, huge "virtual jukebox" stations let you access just about any song recorded by any Hall of Famer; their autographs are etched in glass on a great wall projecting over the lake. As with all such ventures, the list of who's in and who's not is controversial, but then that makes for great dinner-table arguments.

(i) 1 Key Plaza ((C) **888/764-ROCK** or 216/781-7625; www.rockhall.com).

✈ Cleveland International, 10 miles.

🛏 $$ **Cleveland Marriott Downtown,** 127 Public Sq. ((C) **800/228-9290** or 216/696-9200; www.marriott.com). $$ **Holiday Inn-City Center Lakeside,** 1111 Lakeside Ave. ((C) **888/425-3835** or 216/241-5100; www.ichotelsgroup.com).

WHY THEY'LL THANK YOU: It's only rock 'n' roll, but they'll like it.

Rock and Roll Hall of Fame.

Experience Music Project (EMP)

Ages 6 & up • Seattle, Washington, USA

Gliding on the monorail from downtown Seattle to the Space Needle, Seattle's flying-saucer-ish landmark from the 1962 World's Fair, you'll roll right past an angular multicolored jumble of architecture—Frank Gehry's controversial home for the Experience Music Project. While our local friends complained that the Experience Music Project was too pricey for what it is, I beg to disagree. Pricey it is, but we spent hours at the EMP, loving every minute of it, and if your kids are at all into rock music they will too.

The brainchild of Microsoft founder Paul Allen, this museum was originally intended as a tribute to Seattle native son Jimi Hendrix, and the **Hendrix gallery** is wonderfully comprehensive, from mementos of his childhood to stage costumes to a mixing board he used. But the collection grew to encompass a great deal more, from the early Northwest rock scene (bands like the Ventures, the Fleetwoods, and the Kingsmen, notorious for "Louie, Louie") all the way to Nirvana, Pearl Jam, Soundgarden, and the incredibly fertile grunge scene of the 1990s. Special exhibits feature current trends in music, and the dramatically lit specimens in the guitar gallery show the whole family tree of today's electric guitars. The exhibits are somewhat text-heavy, although videos play everywhere, giving some kids their first taste of the magic of great performers of the past (the Bob Dylan exhibit we saw was especially good at setting the 1960s folk-music context out of which Dylan grew). Eventually, of course, it's not enough just to hear music, you want to make some of your own, and as you'd expect from a high-tech guru's pet project, there are extensive **sound labs** where you can try your hand at different instruments and studio production techniques. It seems like someone's always hogging the console you want, unfortunately, but patience is rewarded.

Connected to the EMP, the somewhat smaller **Science Fiction Museum** is offered as a possible add-on. While we were disappointed in it, hard-core sci-fi fans may feel differently.

ⓘ 325 Fifth Ave. N (📞 **877/EMPLIVE** or 206/EMPLIVE; www.emplive.com).

✈ Seattle-Tacoma International, 14 miles.

🛏 $$ **Comfort Suites Downtown/Seattle Center,** 601 Roy St. (📞 **800/517-4000** or 206/282-2600; www.comfortsuites.com). $$$ **Westin Seattle,** 1900 Fifth Ave. (📞 **800/WESTIN-1** or 206/728-1000; www.westin.com/seattle).

WHY THEY'LL THANK YOU: Learning the real lyrics to "Louie, Louie."

The Ancient Theatre of Epidaurus
Greek Drama under the Stars

All ages • Peloponnese, Greece

Whereas many ancient sites were pillaged for building blocks, the Theatre of Epidaurus is just far enough off the beaten track that it was left more or less alone—it's the best-preserved of all ancient Greek theaters, where simply robed actors first brought heroic dramas to life. Even when it was new, it was known for its miraculous acoustics: Though it is an open-air amphitheater that seats 14,000, a whisper can be heard all the way from the stage to the top rows of seats. Every ham in the family will want to run down and give it a try.

The theater is only the most famous part of the **Sanctuary of Asklepios,** an important healing center attached to a cult worshiping Asklepios, the healer god and son of Apollo. Along with lodgings for patients and other guests, it had bathhouses, a gymnasium, and several temples and shrines; little is left but foundation stones, which you can walk around, imagining the bustling site in its prime. As the Sanctuary grew in wealth and fame it added attractions such as a stadium, where games were held every 4 years (much like Olympia 462), and poetry and music performances. In the 4th century the celebrated architect Polykeitos was hired to design a full-scale theater, and what a triumph it was. The audience area, or *theaton* (meaning "seeing place"), originally had 34 rows of seats; 21 upper rows were added in the 2nd century B.C., under the Romans. The stage area—the "orchestra"—is a full circle, which is rare (the Romans changed most theaters' orchestras to the semicircle they preferred). The low building behind it, the *skene,* was where actors kept costume changes and props; its roof was sometimes used as a second stage level. Nowadays the *skene* has tumbled down, revealing a glorious valley view that makes a stunning backdrop for performances. Every summer ancient Greek tragedies and comedies (usually in modern Greek translations) are performed here on weekend nights. The theater's stark grandeur is a brilliant venue for the stripped-down theatrics of Aeschylus and Sophocles. Packages that include bus service are available in Athens from the **Greek National Tourism Organization** (📞 210/327-1300); the **Hellenic Festival Office,** 39 Panepistimiou (📞 210/322-1459); and the **Rex Theater** box office, Panepistimiou (📞 210/330-1881). You can sometimes get tickets at the theater itself just before a performance.

One word of warning: A nearby town is called Ancient Epidaurus, and just to add to the confusion, it also has a small ancient amphitheater. Be careful which signs you follow!

ⓘ Lygourio (📞 27530/22-009).

✈ Athens, 177km (110 miles).

🛏 $$ **Hotel Agamemnon,** 3 Akti Miaouli, Nafplion (📞 27520/28-021).

WHY THEY'LL THANK YOU: Whispering on that stage.

Shakespeare's Globe Theatre

Ages 10 & up • London, England

Iᴛ ᴡᴀѕ ᴘʀᴏʙᴀʙʟʏ the most important public theater ever built, the place where such masterpieces as *Julius Caesar, Hamlet, Othello,* and *King Lear* premiered, all written by the resident playwright, William Shakespeare. While a visit to Stratford-upon-Avon 353 is useful for filling in the sketchy details of Shakespeare's life, Shakespeare is remembered today for what he achieved while living in London, and the Globe Theater really brings this to life.

This circular half-timbered open-air theater is a meticulous reconstruction of the original Globe Theatre, built in 1599 as a playhouse for Shakespeare's theatrical troupe, the King's Men, and located on the Thames's disreputable south bank along with the rest of London's theaters. (The original Globe was torn down in 1644, during the Reformation, when all theaters were closed.) The late American filmmaker Sam Wanamaker worked for some 20 years to raise funds to re-create the theater as it existed in Elizabethan times, thatched roof and all. He was able to acquire a site only 200 yards from the original, near where another Elizabethan theater, The Rose, had already been excavated. The Globe you'll see today re-creates the typical floor plan of the period, based on the designs of Roman amphitheaters (remember, the Romans once occupied Britain, and the remains of a Roman amphitheater can still be seen up in Chester **197**). A raised two-level stage thrusts out in the audience, triple-decked galleries seat wealthier patrons, and the ground floor area right in front of the stage is where the so-called "groundlings" stand. If it rains, everyone in the galleries stay nice and dry, but the groundlings had better wear hoods or hats.

Part of Wanamaker's vision was to make this an operating theater, and some half-dozen **plays** (most but not all by Shakespeare) are produced here May through September. Scenery is minimal, costumes elaborate; all music is live and the actors wear no mikes. If you can't take in a play, you can still visit the attached **exhibit** (a tour of the theater is included if there's no play in progress), which many children will enjoy more than a performance. The exhibits include live demonstrations of sword fighting and costumes, musical instruments, and

The Globe Theatre.

printing presses, as well as touch-screen terminals explaining how the Elizabethans pulled off such special effects as Lear's thunder, Lady Macbeth's bloody hands, and Puck's flying.

ⓘ 21 New Globe Walk (✆ **020/7902-1400;** www.shakespeares-globe.org).

✈ 🚉 See London **55**.

WHY THEY'LL THANK YOU: The play's the thing.

---

353 **Theater & the Movies**

Stratford-upon-Avon
Birthplace of the Bard
All ages • England

THIS CHARMING WARWICKSHIRE MARKET TOWN on the banks of the river Avon has one claim to fame, but it's a biggie: William Shakespeare was born here, grew up here, and

retired here. From Victorian times on, Shakespeare worshipers made sure that many of Stratford's Tudor/Jacobean buildings were preserved. What you see today

Shakespeare's birthplace.

gives you a pretty good idea of an Elizabethan-era provincial town.

Stratford feeds upon Shakespeare's legend, and thousands of tourists flood through each year (summers are especially crowded). Along with souvenir shops and Shakespeare-themed eateries, there are several historical sights in town, all charging brisk admission fees. The one exception is **Holy Trinity Church,** where Shakespeare was baptized and buried; admission is free, and there's only a small charge to visit his tomb (alongside those of his wife, Anne Hathaway, and daughter Susanna). The Shakespeare Trust sells a five-in-one ticket to five main sights: **Shakespeare's Birthplace** on Henley Street, in the center of town, a modest half-timbered home, suitable for a middle-class craftsman's family (Shakespeare's father was a glove maker); **New Place/ Nash's House** on Chapel Street, the 16th-century home of Shakespeare's granddaughter, adjoining the garden of the torn-down house where Shakespeare moved in 1610; **Hall's Croft** in Old Town, near Trinity Church, a fine Tudor town house where Shakespeare's daughter Susanna lived with her physician husband; **Anne Hathaway's Cottage,** the thatched farmstead where

Shakespeare's wife grew up, a mile's walk outside of town in Shottery; and **Mary Arden's House,** a farmhouse even farther out of town (in Wilmcote) that pretends to be, but isn't, the girlhood home of Shakespeare's mother. If you only have time for one, Shakespeare's Birthplace is the most impressive, and exhibits in the attached **Shakespeare Centre** tell the story of the Bard's life in vivid detail.

These days, a Stratford boy wouldn't need to leave town to have a major theater career, since the prestigious **Royal Shakespeare Company** (launched in 1960, out of the seeds of a company started in 1875) built a sprawling brick complex of performance spaces on the banks of the Avon. The RSC presents five plays a season, which lasts April to October. For tickets, call the box office at ✆ **0870/6091110.** Guided backstage tours are conducted a couple times a day; call ✆ **01789/403403** for schedules.

ⓘ **Shakespeare Centre** (✆ **01789/204016;** www.shakespeare.org.uk).

🚆 Stratford-upon-Avon, 2 hr. from London.

🛏 $$ **Alveston Manor,** Clopton Bridge, off B4066 (✆ **800/225-5843** in the U.S.

and Canada, or 0870/400-8181; www. macdonaldhotels.co.uk). $ **Victoria Spa Lodge,** Bishopton Lane (✆ **01789/267985;** www.stratford-upon-avon.co.uk/victoriaspa. htm).

WHY THEY'LL THANK YOU: It turns Shakespeare from a literary god into a human being.

American Museum of the Moving Image
New York on Film
Ages 6 & up • Astoria, Queens, New York, USA

Dᴏɴ'ᴛ ᴛᴇʟʟ Hᴏʟʟʏᴡᴏᴏᴅ, but New York City is really the home of the American movie industry—it's where Thomas Edison screened his first moving pictures and the early talkies were all shot, many of them in Paramount's 13-building studio complex in Astoria, Queens, just a hop, skip, and a jump over the 59th Street Bridge from Manhattan. And if you're not convinced, you will be after visiting the American Museum of the Moving Image, an in-depth museum for TV and movie fans housed in one of those Astoria studio buildings.

Many of the historic artifacts on display—a 1910 wooden Pathé camera, a 1959 Philco TV set—will mean little or nothing to youngsters, but the extensive **costume gallery** should grab them, with items like Robin Williams's padded housedress from *Mrs. Doubtfire*. Famous props exhibited range from Charlton Heston's chariot from the classic film *Ben Hur* to a Yoda puppet constructed for the 1980 film *The Empire Strikes Back*. The Monk's Coffee Shop set from *Seinfeld* is re-created here, and there's a fun display of tie-in toys and lunchboxes promoting TV shows from *Howdy Doody* to *The Simpsons*.

What really fascinates kids, however, are the hands-on exhibits demonstrating the moviemaking process. While it may

be demonstrated with more flash at Universal Studios (see **355**), here the kids get more involved in the process and really learn how it's done. At interactive workstations you can fiddle with sound effects, dub in new dialogue, call up different soundtracks, and even add your face (a la Woody Allen's *Zelig*) to classic movie scenes. Sit in front of a camera and make a series of wacky expressions and, presto! They're reproduced in your own flipbook, which you can take home. At the digital animation stands, you can move cardboard cutouts around to create your own animated short. The makeup exhibition, too, has more than enough ghoulish masks to satisfy young horror movie fans, with staffers on hand to demonstrate how they were made.

While in New York, media mavens should also take in the **Museum of Television and Radio** in Manhattan, 25 E. 52nd St. at 5th Avenue (✆ **212/621-6600;** www.mtr.org.

ⓘ 35th Ave. and 36th St. (✆ **718/784-0077;** www.ammi.org).

✈ ⊨ See Manhattan **56**.

WHY THEY'LL THANK YOU: Taking part in the magic of moviemaking.

Hooray for Hollywood: Movie Mecca

Ages 8 & up • Hollywood, California, USA

THE NAME HOLLYWOOD may be synonymous with moviemaking, but many tourists are disappointed by how shabby the town itself is. I relish its seedy, down-at-heels aura, but my kids were not impressed—until they got an eyeful of **Grauman's Chinese Theatre,** 6925 Hollywood Blvd. (☎ **323/464-MANN**), still one of the world's great movie palaces, with over-the-top Chinese embellishments and an entry court where stars like Elizabeth Taylor have set their signatures and hand- and footprints in cement. So what if the kids didn't recognize most of the names? Nearby is the recently built **Kodak Theatre,** 6834 Hollywood Blvd., where they give out the Oscars every year; we also marveled at the refurbished **Egyptian Theatre,** 6712 Hollywood Blvd., and the Art Deco **Pantages Theatre,** 6233 Hollywood Blvd., for a *Sunset Boulevard* taste of 1920s glamour. Stars who couldn't get a spot at Grauman's were honored with bronze medallions in the pavement along the **Hollywood Walk of Fame,** Hollywood Boulevard between Gower Street and La Brea Avenue; and Vine Street, between Yucca Street and Sunset Boulevard (☎ **323/469-8311;** www.hollywoodchamber.net). John Lennon, Elvis Presley, and Eddie Murphy, those were medallions worth a snapshot or two.

But why settle for sidewalk plaques when you can see films really being made? A quick prefab version is the hour-long tram tour at **Universal Studios Hollywood,** Hollywood Freeway, Universal Center Drive or Lankershim Boulevard exits, Universal City (☎ **818/662-3801;** www.universalstudioshollywood.com), but these days thrill rides are more Universal's raison d'être. We'd rather walk around the wardrobe and prop departments, backlots, and active sets of a real working studio. These walking tours run Monday through Friday and last 2 hours or more; advance reservations are essential. Here are your options: **Paramount Pictures,** 5555 Melrose Ave. (☎ 323/956-1777); **Warner Brothers Studios,** WB Studio Gate 3, 4301 W. Olive Ave., Burbank (☎ 818/972-TOUR; www.wbstudiotour.com; ages 9 and up); **Sony Pictures,** 10202 W. Washington Blvd., Culver City (☎ 323/520-TOUR; www.sonypicturesstudios.com; ages 13 and up); and **NBC Studios,** 3000 W. Alameda Ave., Burbank (☎ 818/840-3537; www.studioaudiences.com).

Or you can get free tickets to join the studio audience for a sitcom or talk show taping (however, many shows don't admit children under the age of 10 or even 18). For these, contact well in advance: **Audiences Unlimited, Inc.** (☎ 818/753-3470; www.tvtickets.com); **TVTIX.COM** (☎ 323/653-4105; www.tvtix.com); **CBS Television City,** 7800 Beverly Blvd. (☎ 323/575-2458); **NBC Studios,** 3000 W. Alameda Ave., Burbank (☎ 18/840-3537); **Paramount Studios** (☎ 323/956-1777); or **Universal Studios** (☎ 800/UNIVERSAL; www.universalstudios.com).

ⓘ **Hollywood Visitor Information Center,** 6801 Hollywood Blvd. (☎ **323/467-6412;** www.lacvb.com).

✈ Los Angeles International.

🛏 $$ **Beverly Garland's Holiday Inn,** 4222 Vineland Ave., North Hollywood (☎ **800/BEVERLY** or 818/980-8000; www.beverlygarland.com). $$ **Roosevelt Hotel, Hollywood,** 7000 Hollywood Blvd. (☎ **800/950-7667** or 323/466-7000; www.hollywoodroosevelt.com).

WHY THEY'LL THANK YOU: Seeing stars.

Ghibli Museum: The Genius of Animation

All ages • Tokyo, Japan

ANIMÉ ADDICTS—you know who you are—just may find this idiosyncratic museum the highlight of their trip to Japan. It's not so much that it pays homage to the animated films of **Hayao Miyazaki,** it's that Miyazaki himself was so involved in developing this museum that his wondrous sensibility is written all over it.

Miyazaki and his fellow animator Isao Takahata are the talents behind **Studio Ghibli.** Miyazaki—the genius behind such classics as *Princess Mononoke, Spirited Away,* and *Howl's Moving Castle*—makes optimistic films with children in mind, because, he has said, he wants them to develop a positive view of the world. His heroines are usually plucky girls, with mysterious animals and otherworldly creatures drifting in and out of their lives almost at random. The animation is so detailed and lifelike, the stories told with such lyrical emotion, that they are truly spellbinding.

It does take a bit of effort to visit the Ghibli Museum. **Tickets** must be bought in advance, up to 3 months ahead, either through the museum's website, through Japan Tourist Bureau offices in Japan or abroad, or at Lawson convenience stores in Japan. When you buy your tickets, you commit to a specific date and time. The museum is not conveniently located, set on the outskirts of Tokyo (a 30-min. train ride from Shinjuku station, followed by a 5-min. bus ride or 15-min. walk along a river). But once you're there, you enter a whimsical flight of imagination.

Even from the outside, the dreamlike quality of Miyazaki's animation is expressed in the rounded stucco buildings, softened by flowers and foliage. Inside, the floor plan is delightfully random, with catwalks and spiral staircases shooting off in all directions, and many of the exhibits are waist-high, speaking directly to children. A ground floor exhibit explains how animation works, using strobe lights and spinning plaster figures from Ghibli films; on the second floor, reproductions of animators' studios demonstrate the filmmaking process, from storyboard to cel painting—you can almost feel the creative energies at work, with a flurry of sketches tacked up over the artist's desk and books piled everywhere. Children can scamper on top of a **giant stuffed kitten bus** like the one from *Totoro* (my children have longed to climb onto that bus ever since they first saw that movie), or scurry up a spiral staircase to the rooftop garden with a metal sculpture of the giant robot from *Laputa: The Castle in the Sky.* A fancifully painted theater shows animated shorts made exclusively for the museum. ***Note:*** The text accompanying displays is only in Japanese, so hang onto the English-language guide you're handed when you enter.

ⓘ 1–1–83 Shimorenjaku, Mitaka City (ⓒ **0442/40-2233;** www.ghibli-museum.jp).

✈ ⊨ See Tokyo ❺❾.

WHY THEY'LL THANK YOU: The kitten bus.

Chapter 11 Historic Homes

Castles & Mansions . . . 399
Famous Homesteads . . . 416
U.S. Presidents . . . 427

Andrew Jackson's Hermitage.

Hadrian's Villa

A Roman Emperor's Fantasy Hideaway

Ages 6 & up • Tivoli, Italy

IN THE 2ND CENTURY A.D., globe-trotting Roman emperor Hadrian retired to one of the greatest estates ever built, in the resort town of Tibur (now Tivoli) about 28km (17 miles) east of Rome. Somewhat like that other compulsive collector William Randolph Hearst (see Hearst Castle 372), Hadrian had filled acre after acre with examples of the **architectural wonders** he'd encountered on his travels. A patron of the arts, a lover of beauty, and even something of an architect, Hadrian was creating much more than a villa: It was his own Xanadu, a self-contained world for his huge royal entourage and the hundreds of servants and guards they required to protect, feed, and bathe them, and satisfy their libidos.

Born in Spain, Hadrian was named emperor of Rome by his predecessor, Trajan, but even while in Rome, Hadrian preferred to retreat outside the city, accompanied by trusted cronies. Tivoli was ideal because its marble quarries could provide tons of travertine for columns, statues, and terraces, as well as water sources to feed the ornamental pools, fountains, canals, and baths artfully laid out around the grounds. Built for pleasure, the villa was a marvel of landscape design, with cunning perspectives and garden panoramas. Hadrian filled the palaces and temples with sculptures,

some of which now rest in the museums of Rome.

In later centuries, barbarians, popes, and cardinals, as well as anyone who needed a slab of marble, carted off much that made the villa so spectacular. Still, enough remains for us to piece together the story. (For a glimpse of what the villa used to be, see the plastic reconstruction at the entrance.) The most outstanding remnant is the **Canopus,** a re-creation of the Egyptian town of Canope and its famous Temple of the Serapis. In the main residential palace, the rectangular ruins of **Piazza d'Oro** (The Golden Court) are surrounded by a double portico, and the **Sala dei pilastri dorici** (Doric Pillared Hall) still has pilasters with Doric bases and capitals holding up a Doric architrave. The ruins of the **Baths** reveal rectangular rooms with concave walls. Only the north wall remains of the **Pecile,** or Poikile, which Hadrian discovered in Athens and had reproduced here. Don't miss the **Teatro Marittimo,** the ruins of a circular maritime theater with a central building ringed by a canal spanned by small swing bridges. It'll take time to wander these vast grounds, but that's the point.

(i) Via di Villa Adriana (© **0774-530203**).

✈ ⊨ See Rome 53.

WHY THEY'LL THANK YOU: Emperor or frustrated architect? You decide.

Elsinore: Prince Hamlet's Come Home

Ages 8 & up • Kronborg, Denmark

SCHOLARS SAY THERE really was a Prince Hamlet of Denmark, and there really is a royal palace in Elsinore (Helsingør in Danish)—the trouble is, that particular Hamlet lived a long time before this palace was built in 1574. Yes, the palace existed when Shakespeare wrote his great tragedy *Hamlet*, but he certainly never visited it. In typical Shakespeare fashion, he made the whole thing up. All the same, when you walk around the corridors of **Kronborg Castle,** full of secret passages and casemates, the brooding spirit of the Danish prince is undeniably present. No wonder so many famous productions of *Hamlet* have been performed here—the castle is a born stage set. Once the kids have visited Elsinore, Shakespeare's greatest tragedy will be so much more to them than just words on a page.

Here, for example, looking out over the Øserund waters, above the battlements is a **waterfront platform,** backed by massive bronze guns—exactly the spot where Hamlet would have seen the ghost of his father. Inside, the **Ballroom** (the largest hall in northern Europe) could have hosted the court banquet where Hamlet staged a cunning little play to "catch the conscience of the king"; down the corridor the **Councillor's Hall** is hung with seven rare tapestries, portraits of Danish kings, any of which snooping Polonius could have been hiding behind when Hamlet mistakenly ran him through with his sword.

A 50-minute train ride north from Copenhagen, the town of **Helsingør** has its own quiet medieval charm, with a handful of 15th-century churches worth a look. Kronborg Castle is less than a kilometer (about half a mile) from the train station, a steeply gabled sandstone pile set on a jutting peninsula guarding the strategic strait between Denmark and its rival Sweden. Cross the moat on a wooden bridge and circle around to the main courtyard, from which you can visit the **royal apartments** (the Danish Maritime Museum also occupies some of the castle). Not much of its former splendor remains, but the spare rooms only add to Elsinore's bleak, austere personality. It doesn't matter if Shakespeare ever saw this place—Kronborg Castle *is* Hamlet's Elsinore, from the tip of its dreaming spires to the bottom of its dank moat.

(i) ✆ **49-21-30-78;** www.kronborgcastle.com

✈ Copenhagen's Kastrup Airport, 53km (33 miles).

🛏 $ **Hotel Ansgar,** Colbjørnsensgade 18–20 (✆ **33-13-19-13;** www.ibsenshotel.dk). $$$ **Sofitel Copenhagen,** Bernstorffsgade 4 (✆ **800/221-4542** in U.S., or 33-14-92-62; www.sofitel.com).

WHY THEY'LL THANK YOU: Finding the statue of Holger Dansk in the basement.

Elsinore Castle.

359

Going Batty at Count Dracula's Castle

Ages 6 & up • Bran, Romania

HIS NAME WAS VLAD TEPES—Vlad the Impaler—but this Romanian prince (1431–76) often signed his name "Dracul," or the Devil, no doubt to unnerve his enemies. Bram Stoker's 1897 novel *Dracula* wasn't really based on Vlad Tepes: No matter how vicious Vlad was, no one ever accused him of being a vampire. Still, the creepy association clings to this castle in the heart of the Carpathian Mountains. This Gothic stronghold on a rocky outcrop in the Romanian village of Bran is full of secret passageways, hidden courtyards, overhanging balconies, and steep stone staircases where—you never know—a vampire just might lurk after all.

Bran Castle is a stop on every package tour of Romania, and a cluster of souvenir stands in the village below push the Dracula connection a bit too hard. Historians are quite clear on one point: Vlad Tepes never owned Bran Castle. His grandfather was born here, and Vlad hid out here in 1462 while fleeing the Turks, but only briefly. In those turbulent years, the ruthless warrior Vlad—a Wallachian king, not a Transylvanian count—was one of the Hungarian empire's best hopes for driving out the hated Turk invaders; he was a national hero, not a reviled bloodsucker. (All right, Vlad liked to behead mice, was fond of bats, and tortured his prisoners by impaling them on a spear, but nobody's perfect.)

This fortress was a defensive stronghold, not a royal residence, as you can see from its thick double walls and impregnable-looking gate tower. Guarding the strategic pass between Wallachia and Transylvania, it was fortified specifically to protect the trading city of Brasov, 28km (17 miles) northeast, from the Turks. The castle itself, mostly built in the late 14th century, with its white-plastered stone

Dracula's Castle.

buildings, four fairy-tale turrets, and jaunty red tile roofs looks more *Heidi* than *Dracula*, but be wary—that fountain in the half-timbered inner courtyard leads to an underground labyrinth of secret passages, perfect for clandestine escapes.

Inside, the furnishings reflect another, more recent, resident: the enormously popular Queen Marie of Romania, who made it her summer home from 1920 to 1938. Some of her vast art collection is displayed in the castle's clean and cozy-looking interiors. The most arresting object in the castle to me is the elaborately carved 18th-century

bedstead in her bedroom, its wood stained almost black over the centuries— a bed you can almost imagine Count Dracula occupying.

ⓘ **Bran Castle,** 498 Traian Mosoiu St. (℃ **068/238332;** www.romaniatourism. com/dracula.html).

✈ Otopeni, Bucharest 140km (87 miles).

🛏 $$$ **Hotel Aro,** 27 Eroilor, Brasov (℃ **268/142840).** $$ **Hotel Capitol,** 19 Eroilor, Brasov (℃ **268/418920).**

WHY THEY'LL THANK YOU: Dracula or Vlad the Impaler, he was still one scary dude.

Castles & Mansions **360**

The Tower of London
England's Real-Life Chamber of Horrors
All ages • London, England

THIS ANCIENT FORTRESS just may be the most haunted spot in England. Headless bodies, bodiless heads, phantom soldiers, icy blasts, clanking chains—you name them, the Tower's got them. Every stone of the Tower tells a story, and it's usually a gory one.

This sprawling fortified compound is like its own small city, with a walled moat outside and a spacious grassy keep inside. At the center is the oldest part, the **White Tower,** built by William the Conqueror in 1078 to keep London's native Saxon population in check. For centuries it was a royal residence—one section, fronting on the river, re-creates the era of Edward I, with guides in period costumes and reproduction furnishings including Edward's throne. When James I took over from Elizabeth I in 1608, however, the royal family moved out— understandably, for over the years the Tower had come to be the realm's most important prison. On the walls of the **Beauchamp Tower,** you can still read the last messages scratched by despairing prisoners. According to murky legend,

two little princes (the sons and heirs of Edward IV) were murdered by henchmen of Richard III in the so-called **Bloody Tower**—at least, that's the way Shakespeare told it, although some historians differ. In the lower part of the **Bell Tower** you can tour a whitewashed prison cell where it is believed Sir Thomas More lived for the last 14 months of his life. Sir Walter Raleigh spent a whopping 13 years here when he was out of favor with Elizabeth I. Many of these prisoners arrived by boat through the spiked iron portcullis of **Traitor's Gate,** and were publicly executed in the central courtyard on **Tower Green** (an eerie plaque there commemorates the execution of not one but two of King Henry VIII's wives, Anne Boleyn and Catharine Howard, as well as the so-called Nine-Day Queen, Lady Jane Grey).

As a fortress, the Tower also made a great place to store weapons and treasures. The White Tower today holds the **Armouries,** with an impressive display of weaponry and armor. In the **Jewel House,** you'll find the tower's greatest attraction, the **Crown Jewels,** some of

The Tower of London.

the world's most precious stones set into robes, swords, scepters, and crowns. The Imperial State Crown is the most famous crown on earth; made for Victoria in 1837, it's worn today by Queen Elizabeth when she opens Parliament, and it includes the Black Prince's Ruby, worn by Henry V at Agincourt. Prepare to stand in long lines to catch a glimpse of the jewels as you scroll by on moving sidewalks, but the wait is worth it.

One-hour guided **tours** of the entire compound are given every half-hour by the Yeoman Warders (also known as "beefeaters") in their distinctive red-and-gold uniforms. And oh, yes—don't forget to look for the ravens, six huge, glossy black birds (plus two spares), all registered as official Tower residents. According to legend, the Tower of London will stand as long as the ravens remain—so just to be safe, one wing of each raven is clipped.

ⓘ Tower Hill (✆ **0870/756-6060;** www. tower-of-london.org.uk).

✈ 🛏 See London **55**.

WHY THEY'LL THANK YOU: It's bloody historic.

Hampton Court Palace
Henry VIII's Playground
All ages • Hampton Court, England

THE 16TH-CENTURY PALACE of Cardinal Wolsey serves as a useful lesson: Don't try to outdo your boss, particularly if he happens to be Henry VIII. The rich cardinal did just that, and he lost his fortune, power, and prestige, finally giving his lavish palace to the Tudor monarch. Once Henry took over, of course, he even outdid Wolsey in embellishing this fine red-brick palace, making it the ultimate weekend house of its time.

Hampton Court, 21km (13 miles) west of London, is a great day trip from the city; you can easily get here by car, train, or, best of all, excursion boat. Although the palace enjoyed prestige and pomp in Elizabethan days, it owes much of its present look to the great architect Sir Christopher Wren, who at the behest of the monarchs William and Mary designed the Northern or **Lion Gates,** intended to be the main entrance to the new parts of the palace.

You can parade through the apartments, filled with period porcelain, furniture, paintings, and tapestries. The **King's Dressing Room** is graced with some of the best art, mainly paintings by old masters on loan from Queen Elizabeth II. Tudor additions included the **Anne Boleyn gateway,** with its 16th-century astronomical clock that tells the high-water mark at London Bridge, and one of Henry's major contributions, the aptly named **Great**

Hall, with its hammer-beam ceiling. Be sure to inspect the **royal chapel** (Wolsey wouldn't recognize it). Hampton Court had quite a retinue to feed, as you can see from the **Great Kitchen.**

Other amenities added by Henry were the **Tiltyard** (where jousting competitions were held) and a **tennis court.** What most children remember best, however, is getting lost in the serpentine **shrubbery maze** in the garden (another Wren design), which was a popular source of courtiers' entertainment in those pre-Xbox days. The **formal gardens** here are justly famous, demonstrating examples of garden methods and designs from several important periods of history. If you don't want to pay to enter the palace itself, you can still roam the delightful gardens for free (except for the Privy Garden).

ⓘ North bank of the Thames (ⓒ **0870/ 752-7777;** www.hrp.org.uk).

✈ ➡ See London **55**.

WHY THEY'LL THANK YOU: The amazing maze.

Warwick Castle
A Noble's Medieval Masterpiece
All ages • Warwick, England

Pᴇʀᴄʜᴇᴅ ᴏɴ ᴀ ʀᴏᴄᴋʏ ᴄʟɪꜰꜰ above the River Avon, this magnificent 14th-century fortress, the finest medieval castle in England, is surrounded by gardens, lawns, and woodland where peacocks roam freely.

Ethelfleda, daughter of Alfred the Great, built the first significant fortifications here in 914. Two years after the Norman Conquest, William the Conqueror was on the scene, ordering the construction of a motte-and-bailey castle, and his son created the title Earl of Warwick to give to his Norman cronies, the

Beaumont/Beauchamp family. Simon de Montfort thoroughly sacked it in the Barons' War of 1264; all that's left of the Norman castle is a steep mound in the garden. The Beauchamps' 14th-century reconstruction is pretty much what you see today, a mass of thick white crenellated curtain walls punctuated with formidable towers, their slit windows designed for archers to shoot arrows at besiegers. The earls of Warwick were enormously powerful back then; Richard Neville, earl during the Wars of the Roses, was called "the Kingmaker."

Warwick Castle.

When the castle was granted to Sir Fulke Greville by James I in 1604, he spent £20,000 (a huge sum in those days) converting the existing castle buildings into a luxurious mansion. The staterooms and Great Hall house fine collections of paintings and furniture, but kids will probably be more interested in the arms and armor (one of the finest collections anywhere), not to mention the dungeon, torture chamber, ghost tower, clock tower, and Guy's tower.

The Tussaud company now owns the castle, and the private apartments of Lord Brooke and his family have been opened to visitors as a carefully reconstructed Royal Weekend House Party of 1898. You'll see **wax portraits** of important figures of the time, including a young Winston Churchill; in the Kenilworth bedroom, a likeness of the Prince of Wales, later King Edward VII, reads a letter; the duchess of Marlborough prepares for her bath in the red bedroom. Among the most lifelike of the figures is a uniformed maid bending over to test the temperature of the water running into a bathtub. Purists may shudder, but I'm in favor of anything that helps children get a picture of how the aristocracy actually lived.

(i) (C) **0870/442-2000;** www.warwick-castle.co.uk.

🚃 Warwick, via Stratford-upon-Avon, 2½ hr. from London.

🛏 **Hilton Warwick,** Warwick Bypass, A429 Stratford Rd. ((C) **800/445-8667** in U.S., or 01926/499555; www.warwick.hilton.com).

WHY THEY'LL THANK YOU: A textbook castle, just like kids draw them.

Scotland's Royal Castles
Where Mary Queen of Scots Slept
Ages 4 & up • Edinburgh, Linlithgow & Stirling, Scotland

A CLUSTER OF SCOTTISH CASTLES, all of them either in or near Edinburgh, traces the life of one of history's most tragic figures—Mary Queen of Scots. Don't expect richly furnished apartments like the royal homes in England or France; Scotland's kings lost their crown a long time ago, and the shabby fate of their great palaces is a tale in itself.

Start in Edinburgh, Scotland's capital, where two palaces stand at either end of the **Royal Mile,** a grand street lined with ancient churches, shops, and houses. At its upper end, dour **Edinburgh Castle** (✆ **0131/225-9846**) perches on a rocky summit. Founded in the 11th century by Malcolm III, this seat of Scottish kings was demoted to a mere military garrison for the past couple of centuries. A set of State Apartments has been fitted out for visitors, however, and in Queen Mary's Bedroom, you'll see where Mary Queen of Scots gave birth to her son, James VI of Scotland (later James I of England). Don't miss the Crown Chamber, housing the Honours of Scotland (Scotland's Crown Jewels, but hardly in the same class as England's).

Meander the length of the Royal Mile to the **Palace of Holyroodhouse** (✆ **0131/5567371**), which looks much more royal—no surprise, since most of it was built in the 1660s by the English king Charles II after Scotland and England were united. (It's still a royal residence, and if the Queen's in town you can't go in.) In a surviving old wing, Mary Queen of Scots once lived in King James Tower; her husband, Lord Darnley, had his own rooms on the floor below. Here in 1566 a jealous Darnley and his accomplices stabbed Queen Mary's Italian secretary, David Rizzio, 56 times before her eyes.

Eighteen miles west of Edinburgh is **Linlithgow Castle,** on A706 in Linlithgow (✆ **01506/842896**), where Mary Queen of Scots was born in 1542—6 days before her father, James V, died, making her Queen of Scotland. Beloved by the Stuart kings, who built it in stages from 1425 to 1624 (the last of them, Bonnie Prince Charlie, stayed here in 1745), it met its doom in 1746 when English troops under the Duke of Cumberland camped here, leaving it in flames as they departed—heading north to defeat Charlie at **Culloden 255.** It's one of the country's most affecting ruins, its pink-ocher buttressed walls soaring to the open sky. From the scale of the rooms you can guess how grand they were once.

Another day trip from Edinburgh (37 miles northwest), **Stirling Castle,** Stirling (✆ **01786/450000**), looms high on a basalt rock over the river Forth, a strategic position between the Highlands and Lowlands. Within those forbidding walls are some handsome 15th- and 16th-century residences, only now being restored to their former glory. James V died while building its lavish main palace to impress his new French wife; their daughter, the new Queen Mary, spent the innocent first 4 years of her star-crossed life here.

ⓘ **Edinburgh and Scotland Information Centre,** 3 Princes St., Edinburgh (✆ **0845 22 55 121;** www.edinburgh.org).

✈ Edinburgh.

🛏 $$$ **Carlton Highland Hotel,** 19 North Bridge, Edinburgh (✆ **0131/472-3000;** www.paramount-hotels.co.uk). $ **Thrums Private Hotel,** 14–15 Minto St., Edinburgh (✆ **0131/667-5545;** www.thrumshotel.com).

WHY THEY'LL THANK YOU: Poignant castles for a poignant queen.

The Alhambra
Spanish Castle with a Moorish Heart
Ages 6 & up • Granada, Spain

WHEN YOU FIRST SEE the celebrated Calat Alhambra (Red Castle), you may be surprised by its somber exterior, looming on a rocky outcropping above the city of **Granada.** Deep in southern Andalusia, Granada is where Spain's Muslim past is most evident, nowhere more so than at the Alhambra—but you have to cross the threshold to discover the true delights of this Moorish palace.

It was originally built for defensive purposes, that's true, and a portion of the Alcazaba, the original rugged 9th-century fort, still exists inside. But the castle's Moorish occupants gradually transformed it into a lavish pleasure palace for the

The Alhambra.

Nasrid princes and their harems. The heart of the old Nasrid palace is the arcaded **Patio de los Leonares** (Court of the Lions), with its immense fountain resting on 12 marble lions—representing the hours of the day, the months of the year, and the signs of the zodiac. Every room around this courtyard tells a story: The **Sala de los Abencerrajes,** with its richly adorned honeycombed ceiling, is where the last emir, Boabdil, staged a banquet for his most powerful rivals, only to have his guards massacre them in mid-dinner. Check out the exquisite ceiling paintings on leather in the **Sala de los Reyes** (Hall of Kings), a great banqueting hall where, legend has it, one sultan beheaded 36 Moorish princes here because he suspected one had seduced his favorite wife. The **Hall of the Mexuar** was once the sultan's main council chamber; Spanish rulers converted it into a Catholic chapel in the 1600s.

To me, this conjunction of Muslim and Spanish culture is the most intriguing thing about the Alhambra. After the Reconquest, in 1526 the Holy Roman Emperor, Charles V, had a new Renaissance palace plunked down in the middle of this Moorish stronghold (apparently the Nasrid palace wasn't grand enough for his royal presence). My favorite part of it is the magnificent circular **two-story courtyard** that is open to the sky.

But there's more outside the Alhambra's walls: **The Generalife,** the sultans' summer retreat, where they used to spend their summers locked away with their harems. As a vacation spot, it's full of beautiful courtyards and gardens; look for the **Escalera del Agua** (Water Staircase); an enclosed Asian garden, **Patio de la Acequía,** with water jets arching over its long central pool; and **Patio de la Sultana,** the secret rendezvous point for Zoraxda, wife of Sultan Abu Hasan, and her lover.

The government limits the number of people who can enter the Alhambra. Go as early as possible, but even if you arrive at 10am you may not be admitted until an afternoon time slot. You can book in advance through any branch of **BBVA** (Banca Bilbao & Vizcaya; *C* **90-222-44-60;** www.alhambratickets.com). Come here at night, when floodlights bathe the exotic

gardens and palaces—it's a sight you'll never forget.

(i) Palacio de Carlos V (*C* 95-822-0912).

✈ Granada.

🛏 $$ **Hotel Palacio Santa Inés,** Cuesta de Santa Inés 9 (*C* **95-822-23-62;** www.palaciosantaines.com). $$$ **Parador de Granada,** at the Alhambra (*C* **95-822-1440;** www.parador.es).

WHY THEY'LL THANK YOU: A glimpse inside the harem.

Castles & Mansions 365

The Forbidden City
The Chinese Emperor's Little Hideaway
Ages 8 & up • Bêijīng, China

Tʜᴇ ᴍᴏsᴛ sᴘᴇᴄᴛᴀᴄᴜʟᴀʀ ᴘᴀʟᴀᴄᴇ in China, **Gù Gōng** (to give it its Chinese name), is truly something to see, an immense layout of red-walled buildings topped with glazed vermilion tile and ringed by a vast moat. It was home to 24 emperors over half a millennium, from 1420 to 1923. Although many parts may be closed when you visit, thanks to a massive renovation lasting through 2020 (!), there's more than enough left to explore. It isn't any one structure you've come to see, it's the scale and harmony of the whole, an

irrefutable statement of Chinese imperial might.

An army of workers began construction in 1406, taking only 14 years to complete the complex. Given various ransackings and fires, though, most of what we see today was built in the Qīng dynasty (1626–1912) rather than the earlier Ming era. Point out to the kids the blue and green tiles trimming several of the up-curled roofs—the Qīngs were Manchus, and it's said this color reminded them of their native grasslands.

The Forbidden City.

You enter through the **Meridian Gate,** but before you go farther, check out the largest gate, the **Gate of Heavenly Peace,** where Mao Tse Tung made his dramatic announcement founding the People's Republic in October 1949. You can't miss it—it's the gate with the giant portrait of Mao hanging above the central door, flanked by sonorous inscriptions. The **Gate of Supreme Harmony** leads into the perfectly symmetrical outer court, with its three grand ceremonial halls, where the emperor conducted official business. Just as Islamic temples always face toward Mecca, in the Imperial City most major halls open to the south, the direction associated with imperial rule.

It's the **inner court**—the emperor's private residence—that makes this truly the Forbidden City, for only the imperial family (which included concubines and as many as 1,500 eunuchs) were allowed here. Three palaces, mirroring the three halls in the outer court, are set in the inner court, and at its rear is a marvelous garden of ancient conifers, rockeries, and pavilions, an oasis largely unchanged since the Míng era.

If you really want the kids to get the point of the Forbidden City, though, go beyond the central axis, where all the tourists mass; explore the quieter maze of pavilions, gardens, courtyards, and theaters on the eastern side. (You have to giggle at the useless over-shoe slippers you're required to buy along with this section's extra admission fee.) The **Hall of Clocks** (Zhōngbiǎo Guǎn) is worth tracking down, as is the Zhēnfēi Jǐng (**Well of the Pearl Concubine**), a narrow hole covered by a large circle of stone. Here, a 25-year-old favorite was stuffed down the well as the imperial family fled the aftermath of the Boxer Rebellion; she'd dared to suggest that the emperor stay to face the mobs, since he'd supported the Boxers in the first place. Defying the emperor? *Not* a good idea.

ⓘ North side of Tiān'ān Mén Square, across Cháng'ān Dàjiē (℃ **010/6513-2255,** ext. 615).

✈ 🛏 See The Great Wall of China **210**.

WHY THEY'LL THANK YOU: Discovering a forbidden world.

Fontainebleau: Refuge of Kings

Ages 8 & up • Fontainebleau, France

IF VERSAILLES **367** is all about formal gardens and gilt-encrusted furnishings, the other royal residence within day-trip distance from the capital, Fontainebleau, is all about its ancient forests and grand Renaissance paintings. It has a more impressive history, having been built a century earlier by François I, and remained in use later. Less crowded, and therefore more peaceful, than Versailles, Fontainebleau may appeal to your children even more than its over-the-top cousin.

François I, like Louis XIV after him, sent to Italy for artists to decorate his royal digs. What came to be called the School of Fontainebleau arose, led by the painters Rosso, Fiorentino, and Primaticcio. Their handiwork adorns one of the most outstanding rooms at Fontainebleau: the **Gallery of François I,** where stucco-framed panels on every hand depict such scenes as Jupiter abducting Europa, the Nymph of Fontainebleau (with a lecherous dog peering through the reeds), and the king holding a pomegranate, a symbol of unity.

As you go through the palace, have the kids hunt for the oft-repeated figure of a salamander, symbol of the Chevalier King,

François I. In the **Ballroom,** peer at the splendid decorations to find the interlaced monograms H & D, which stand for François's successor, Henri II, and the woman he loved, Diane de Poitiers. Reminders of Napoléon include his throne room, the room where he abdicated (the abdication document displayed is a copy), his offices, his bedroom (look for his symbol, a bee), and his bathroom.

French kings originally came to Fontainebleau because it offered great hunting, and the surrounding forest is still verdant and inviting—Parisians flock here not only to visit the château but for horseback riding, picnicking, and hiking. Stand on the back terrace and imagine a misty 17th-century morning, with huntsman's horns trumpeting and hounds baying as the king and his boon companions set off into the dusky woods for a day's hunt. Then set off on foot along hiking trails made by French kings through the forest—that's when history comes alive.

(i) Place du Général-de-Gaulle, Avon (📞 01-60-71-50-70).

✈ See Paris **54**.

🛏 $$$ **Hotel Napoleon,** 9 rue Grande (📞 01-60-39-50-50).

WHY THEY'LL THANK YOU: Even Napoléon needed a place to chill out.

Castles & Mansions **367**

Versailles: Palace of the Sun King
Ages 8 & up • Versailles, France

WHEN YOUR NICKNAME is the Sun King, you need a resplendent palace to live up to your image, and Louis XIV of France sought just that in 1661 when he undertook renovations on his father's hunting lodge at Versailles. It took 50 years, but the end result was a royal residence so fabulous that its very name has become synonymous with luxury living. Yes, it's good to be the king.

Under Louis XIV and his equally extravagant great-grandson Louis XV, Versailles typically hosted some 3,000 courtiers and their retinues at a time. Given the constant entertainment and lavish banquets, few turned down the chance to join the glittering throng—to gossip, dance, plot, and flirt away while the peasants on their estates sowed the seeds of the Revolution. It all caught up with the next monarchs, well-intentioned but weak Louis XVI and his frivolous queen, Marie Antoinette, who were eating cake at Versailles on October 6, 1789, when they learned that citizen mobs were converging on the palace. Versailles became a museum under Louis-Philippe (1830–48) and has remained so ever since.

Visitors can tour the **State Apartments,** loaded with ornate furniture, paintings, tapestries, vases, chandeliers, and sculpture; it seems as if every inch on every wall has been gilded or plastered in some baroque design. The most dazzling room—a long arcade called the **Hall of Mirrors,** with windows along one wall and 357 beveled mirrors along the other—is where the **Treaty of Versailles,** officially ending World War I, was signed in 1919. In the **Queen's Apartments,** Marie Antoinette played the harpsichord for guests; in the **Clock Room,** 7-year-old Mozart performed for the court; and the gold-and-white **Royal Chapel** is where Louis XVI married Marie Antoinette in 1770. You won't visit all 700 rooms in the palace, but you'll glimpse a *Dangerous Liaisons*–type lifestyle of wealth, power, and decadence.

The **Gardens of Versailles** are the ultimate in French formal garden design, with geometrical flower beds, terraces, pools, topiary, statuary, lakes, and canals. The kids will enjoy these vast gardens even more if you time your visit to coincide with the summer spectacles—weekend daytime programs where classical music is piped in and all 50 fountains are turned on full blast, or nighttime shows of illuminated fountains, fireworks, and costumed actors portraying Louis XVI and his court. Call ✆ **01-30-83-78-88** for information.

A walk across the park will take you to two outlying residences: the pink-and-white-marble **Grand Trianon,** still used today as a VIP lodging, and the **Petit**

Trianon, where Louis XV held trysts with Mme du Barry. The **Queen's Hamlet,** nearby, is a rustic set of half-timbered buildings where Marie Antoinette and her chums dressed like shepherdesses and lived "humbly."

ⓘ ✆ **01-30-83-78-00;** www.chateau versailles.fr.

✈ 🚃 See Paris **54**.

WHY THEY'LL THANK YOU: Conspicuous consumption to the max.

368 · Castles & Mansions

Topkapi Palace
Relaxing with the Sultans in Istanbul
Ages 8 & up • Istanbul, Turkey

NOTHING SAYS "LAP OF LUXURY" like magnificent Topkapi Palace, built in the 1450s by Mehmet the Conqueror on Istanbul's best real estate, at the tip of a peninsula commanding the Bosporus Strait. For almost 400 years, Ottoman sultans reigned here over their legendary empire. It's an exotic marvel of brilliant-colored ceramic tiles, inlaid ivory, and ornate friezes and mosaics—but it's the elements of cruelty, lust, and political intrigue that will fascinate the kids.

As you enter through the **Gate of Augustus** (aka the Bab-i Hümayün Gate), look up to see where the decapitated heads of uncooperative officials or rebels were displayed as a public warning. The first courtyard, the **Court of the Janissaries,** is a shady public garden; just inside is the Istanbul Archaeology Museum (a bore for most kids). Only the sultan could pass through the **Gate Of Salutation,** flanked by two octagonal prison towers; after beheadings, the executioner washed the blood off his hands in the fountain to the right.

In the second courtyard, you'll see the enormous **Palace Kitchens,** where more

than 1,000 servants worked day and night to serve 5,000 residents (the palace's amazing porcelain collection is on display here now), and the **Imperial Armory,** featuring the swords of Mehmet the Conqueror and Süleyman the Magnificent. The sultan's private quarters began past the **Gate of Felicity** (decapitated heads were impaled above this gate as well). Within that gate, the **Palace Clothing Exhibition** shows off the sultan's absurdly baggy costumes of silk, brocade, and gold-threaded fabrics, while the Treasury displays the awesome spoils of 400 years of Ottoman rule. In room no. 1, check out the priceless **ceremonial thrones;** room no. 4 holds the Treasury's pièce de résistance, the famous **Topkapi Dagger,** as well as the 86-carat **Kaşikḍi Diamond.** At the far corner of the third courtyard is the always-crowded **Holy Relic Section.** It contains the first copy of the Koran, personal belongings of the Prophet Mohammed, and even the staff of Moses.

You'll need a separate admission ticket for a half-hour tour of the **Harem** (buy them near the Carriage Gate in the second courtyard). It may sound sexy and lurid—the word *harem* is Arabic for "forbidden"—but these living quarters were really a deluxe prison. There are three main sections: the cell-like quarters of the Black Eunuchs, the Harem's guards; the claustrophobic inner courtyard where up to 800 concubines lived in cramped cubicles; and, in stark contrast, the lavish seaview apartments reserved for the sultan, his mother, favorite concubines, and heirs to the throne. And, oh yeah, don't miss the **Golden Cage,** where brothers of the sultan were kept under house arrest so they wouldn't take over the throne. Those sultans, they took no chances.

ⓘ At the end of Babuhümayun Cad., Sultanahmet (ⓒ **0212/512-0480**).

✈ 🛏 Hagia Sophia & the Blue Mosque **324**.

WHY THEY'LL THANK YOU: The sultan's rap-star wardrobe.

Castles & Mansions

369

Mad King Ludwig's Castle: Neuschwanstein
Ages 6 & up • Hohenschwangau, Germany

Approaching the castle of Neuschwanstein, children get a shock of déjà vu—where have they seen this before? Disneyland, of course—Walt Disney had this Bavarian fantasy castle in mind when he designed the Cinderella castle in 1955. It's madly popular (be prepared to wait in line for hours in summer) but the kids will remember it always, not just for its fairy-tale facade, but also for the tragic life story behind it.

Ludwig II was a handsome 18-year-old when he became king of Bavaria. A loner who never married, as time passed Ludwig became more and more enmeshed in his own extravagant fantasies—closeting himself away with an indulgent entourage; mounting full-fledged productions of operas by his favorite composer, Richard Wagner, with himself as the only audience; and last but not least, building three lavish castles: Herrenchiemsee, Linderhof, and Neuschwanstein, this ethereally pale, multiturreted medieval folly on a crag high above the little town of Hohenswangau. Finally, Ludwig's extravagance and bizarre behavior drove his advisors to have him declared insane in 1886 at age 41. Three days later, he was found drowned in a lake on the outskirts of Munich—whether murder or suicide, we may never know. When Ludwig died, construction on Neuschwanstein—which had been puttering on for 17 years—stopped abruptly, and there's an eerie sense of abandonment about it today. Ludwig lived here for a total of only about 6 months.

Neuschwanstein is literally a storybook castle, with wall paintings everywhere depicting scenes from Nordic legends—Tannhäuser in his gold-and-silver silk-lined study, Tristan and Isolde in his elaborately carved bedroom, Parsifal in the grand fourth-floor Singer's Hall. In the throne room, kids are entranced by a Byzantine-style floor mosaic showing the animals of the world—but also notice a hauntingly empty space where Ludwig's throne was to have been.

The same parking lot serves both this and Hohenschwangau Castle, built by Ludwig's father, Maximilian I; be prepared for a steep half-mile walk up to Neuschwanstein—that mountaintop site was not chosen for its convenience. You'll visit the castle on a 35-minute guided tour (offered in English), which plays up the dramatic ironies of Ludwig's memorable life. Afterward, hike up to the **Marienbrücke** (the trail is signposted), for a splendid view of Mad King Ludwig's fantasy castle.

(i) Neuschwansteinstrasse 20 ((C) 08362/93988-0; www.neuschwanstein.de).

✈ Munich 116km (72 miles).

🛏 $$ **Hotel Lisl and Jägerhaus,** Neuschwansteinstrasse ((C) 08362/8870;

www.neuschwanstein-hotels.de). $$ **Hotel Müller Hohenschwangau,** Alpseestrasse ((C) **08362/81990;** www.hotel-mueller.de).

WHY THEY'LL THANK YOU: More beautiful than the Disney rip-off—and a better back story.

370

Newport's Mansions
The Gilded Age Elite's Summer "Cottages"
Ages 7 & up • Newport, Rhode Island, USA

DRIVING AROUND NEWPORT, RHODE ISLAND, you can't help but gawp at the turn-of-the-century mansions—Italianate *palazzi,* Tudor-style manors, faux French châteaux, all set in elegant formal landscaping, with imposing gates or walls to keep out the hoi polloi (for example, *you*). It's incredible to imagine the sort of wealth that built these homes, even more incredible to realize that these were just these families' summer houses (offhandedly referred to as mere "cottages").

While many of these houses are still private property, nine are open to the public for guided tours, popular with tourists year-round (though not all are open daily in winter). Don't cram too many into 1 day—the sheer opulence of these interiors can soon bring on sensory overload. The most popular is **The Breakers,** Ochre Point Avenue ((C) **401/847-1000**), a 70-room 1895 mansion designed for Commodore Vanderbilt by Richard Morris Hunt. Patterned after Renaissance Florentine *palazzi,* it has a stunning great hall, an ornate 50-foot cube sheathed in marble. The Breakers even has bathrooms (very high-tech for the time) where both fresh and salt water come out of the taps. Stanford White modeled **Rosecliff,** Bellevue Avenue ((C) **401/847-1000**), after the Grand Trianon at Versailles **367**. Built in 1902 for an heiress of the Comstock Lode mining fortune, it has only 40 rooms (how sad), but it also has Newport's largest ballroom and a heart-shaped grand staircase. **Beechwood,** 580 Bellevue Ave. ((C) **401/846-3772**), was built for the famous Mrs. Astor, who personally maintained a list of who counted and who didn't in New York and Newport society. Kids will especially like this house because actors in period dress are on hand to tell anecdotes about late Victorian high society.

The Breakers in Newport.

Two other Bellevue Avenue houses belonged to the same woman—named Alva Vanderbilt when she was mistress of **Marble House,** 596 Bellevue Ave. (*©* **401/ 847-1000**), so called because it shows off just about every type of marble there is. Its ballroom is literally dazzling, with three kinds of gold encrusting its walls. Alva divorced her Vanderbilt husband and promptly married his best friend, who was a Belmont and lived down the street at **Belcourt Castle,** 657 Belleview Ave. (*©* **401/846-0669**). My daughter couldn't get over the luxurious stables. The Breakers may have had bathrooms, but Belcourt Castle had electricity, designed by Thomas Edison, no less. Tell the kids to look for the 14 secret doors.

(*i*) **Preservation Society of Newport,** 424 Bellevue Ave. (*©* **401/847-1000;** www. newportmansions.org).

✈ Providence, 28 miles.

🛏 $$$ **Hyatt Regency Newport,** 1 Goat Island (*©* **800/233-1234** or 401/851-1234; www.hyatt.com). $$ **Mill Street Inn,** 75 Mill St. (*©* **800/392-1316** or 401/849-9500; www.millstreetinn.com).

BEST TIME: Dec, when the houses are decorated for the holidays.

WHY THEY'LL THANK YOU: Imagine sliding down these banisters.

Castles & Mansions **371**

The Biltmore Estate
The Vanderbilts' Mountain Cabin
Ages 6 & up • Asheville, North Carolina, USA

If THE GILDED AGE MANSIONS in Newport, Rhode Island **370**, were "cottages," what would you call this French Renaissance–style château that George Washington Vanderbilt built in 1895? With 250 rooms, it's the largest private residence in the United States (although open to the public for years, it's still owned by Vanderbilt descendants), covering no less than 4 acres under one sharp-peaked slate roof. It's imposing all right, yet surprisingly airy and light, a gracefully proportioned expanse of warm pale stone. Grand as it is, Biltmore somehow felt like a place I could live.

G. W. Vanderbilt journeyed through Europe and Asia buying up paintings, porcelains, bronzes, carpets, and other antiques. As a result Biltmore is like a miniseminar in the history of decorative arts, with each successive room a fresh surprise. He picked up, for example, exquisite pieces of 18th-century furniture by Chippendale and Sheraton, and he also became a patron of late-19th-century artists, acquiring canvases by Renoir, Sargent, and Whistler when they were still alive to reap the profits. The oak-paneled billiards room looks like an exclusive men's club; the tapestry-hung dining hall has a baronial stone fireplace and 70-foot-high ceilings. Each guest bedroom has a strikingly different decor, inspired by a particular work of art. There are 65 fireplaces, a 23,000-volume library, an indoor pool, a bowling alley, a glass-roofed winter garden full of lush palms and ferns. On and on and on.

If the Biltmore house is rivaled by anything in Asheville, it's by its own **gardens,** a breathtaking layout by Frederick Law Olmstead (the designer of New York's Central Park). French-style formal plots with statuary and pools counterbalance naturalistic English-style areas (the Spring Glade is particularly charming). Capitalizing on the mountain climate, Olmstead went azalea-crazy, planting more than 200 varieties, which are at their most spectacular in late April and May. After exploring that immense house, let the kids romp through the gardens to let off steam.

ⓘ 1 Approach Rd. (U.S. 25; ✆ **800/624-1575** or 828/225-1333; www.biltmore.com).

✈ Asheville.

🛏 $$$ **Grove Park Inn Resort,** 290 Macon Ave. (✆ **800/438-5800** or 828/252-2711; www.groveparkinn.com). $$ **Richmond Hill Inn,** 87 Richmond Hill Dr. (✆ **828/252-7313;** www.richmondhillinn.com).

WHY THEY'LL THANK YOU: It's what you would build if you had the money.

---

372 Castles & Mansions

Hearst Castle
California Palace in the Sky
Ages 8 & up • San Simeon, California, USA

IT'S NOT ENTIRELY TRUE that the hilltop California estate of publishing magnate William Randolph Hearst is a 20th-century replica of an Old World manor. True, it was built from 1919 to 1947, but the bits and pieces are nearly all authentic—400-year-old Spanish and Italian ceilings, 500-year-old mantels, 16th-century Florentine bedsteads, Renaissance paintings, Flemish tapestries, and innumerable other European treasures, which Hearst compulsively acquired for years.

Each week, railroad cars carrying fragments of Roman temples, carved doors from Italian monasteries, hastily rolled canvases by the old masters, ancient Persian rugs, and antique French furniture arrived—5 tons at a time—in San Simeon. Orson Welles's 1941 masterpiece *Citizen Kane,* a thinly disguised fictional biography of Hearst, has an unforgettable shot of priceless antiques warehoused in dusty piles, stretching as far as the eye can see. Only a fraction of what Hearst bought was ever installed in the estate.

Despite this patchwork approach, this sprawling Mediterranean Revival–style compound has a unified look, no doubt because one architect (and a woman at that, Julia Morgan) directed its entire

28-year creation. The main house, **Casa Grande,** alone has more than 100 rooms of baronial splendor. My kids lusted after the red-velvet-padded private movie theater where Hearst (also a movie mogul) screened first-run films. They longed to jump into the fabulous swimming pools—a Roman-inspired indoor

Hearst Castle.

pool with intricate mosaics, and the breathtaking outdoor Greco-Roman Neptune pool, flanked by marble colonnades that frame the distant sea.

Book your **guided tour** in advance if possible—there's not much else around this stretch of California coast, so Hearst Castle doesn't cater to drop-in business (everybody staying at our motel had either been there that day or was going tomorrow). You'll park down at the visitor center and take a bus uphill to the compound. Four different daytime tours visit various parts of the estate, with very little overlap; they last about 2 hours. Tour 1 covered all the essentials my kids wanted, but I regretted not seeing Hearst's private library and Gothic bedroom, which were on Tour 2. Too bad the **evening tours**

were full when we booked—for those, costumed docents portray Hearst's celebrity house party guests. Thanks to Hearst's mistress, actress Marion Davies, the estate was a playground for the Hollywood crowd.

ⓘ U.S. 1 (✆ **805/927-2020** or 800/444-4445 for tour reservations; www.hearst castle.org).

✈ Monterey Peninsula, 94 miles.

🛏 $$ **Best Western Cavalier Oceanfront Resort,** 9415 Hearst Dr. (Calif. 1; ✆ **800/826-8168** or 805/927-4688; www.cavalierresort.com).

WHY THEY'LL THANK YOU: Versailles-scale opulence for an American Sun King.

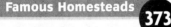

Famous Homesteads 373

The *Little Women* House
Ages 6 & up • Concord, Massachusetts, USA

EVEN GIRLS WHO HAVEN'T READ Louisa May Alcott's 1868 classic novel *Little Women* know the story from its many film versions and the Broadway musical. The story of its author, Louisa May Alcott—Jo in the novel—is even more powerful when you consider that she was one of the first women to earn a living as a writer. My daughter and I were thrilled to feel her presence hovering in every room of **Orchard House.**

The Alcott family lived from 1858 to 1877 in this saltbox-style frame house. Not only was *Little Women* set here, but it also was written here by the adult Louisa, at a shelf desk her father built between two windows in her bedroom. Although Louisa was 26 when they moved into Orchard House, she modeled the March's family's house on it. Other family members were the models for the characters in *Little Women:* Anna ("Meg"), the eldest, an amateur actress;

Elizabeth ("Beth"), a gifted musician who died before the family moved to this house; and May ("Amy"), a talented artist who went to study in Europe on Louisa's profits from *Little Women.* Their mother, the social activist Abigail May Alcott, frequently assumed the role of family breadwinner—her father, Louisa wrote in her journal, had "no gift for money making." Louisa herself, who never married, also helped support the family when she began to publish her short stories at age 22.

Visitors are guided through the modestly furnished house, which features many authentic heirlooms—the family china is laid out on the dining room table, props and costumes await their amateur theatricals, half-finished needleworks lie on side tables, and some of May's drawings are still scribbled on her bedroom walls. Anna's wedding was held in the parlor here, just as Meg's was, and all the sisters took turns cooking in the spartan kitchen.

Also in Concord is **The Wayside,** 455 Lexington Rd. (© **978/369-6975,** closed Nov–Apr), the Alcotts' prior home (the girls called it "the yellow house") where Nathaniel Hawthorne later lived, from 1852 until his death in 1864.

(i) 399 Lexington Rd. (© **978/369-4118;** www.louisamayalcott.org).

✈ Boston, 18 miles.

🛏 See Boston Common **60**.

WHY THEY'LL THANK YOU: Meg, Jo, Beth, and Amy live on here.

Robert Louis Stevenson's Treasured Island

Ages 6 & up • Saranac Lake, New York, USA

Look at the houses around Saranac Lake and you'll notice many share one architectural peculiarity—sleeping porches on the second story. That's because 19th-century Saranac Lake centered on a famous sanitarium, the Trudeau Clinic, where patients with tuberculosis came to be cured in the cool, dry Adirondack forest air. Modern medicine has nearly wiped out tuberculosis, and no one comes to Saranac anymore for "the cure." But on the edge of town there is one relic of those days—the cottage where one of Dr. Edward Trudeau's most famous patients, the writer Robert Louis Stevenson, fought for his life.

The **Stevenson cottage** isn't well advertised; its hours are limited, and you'll have to ring the doorbell hoping the caretaker/curator will come out and let you in. But for Stevenson fans like my kids, that made the experience all the more special. This quiet white frame cottage is absolutely crammed to the gills with Stevenson **memorabilia,** and the curator (who grew up here—his grandparents were caretakers before him) knows just about everything that's worth knowing about the author of such classics as *Treasure Island, Kidnapped,* and *Dr. Jekyll and Mr. Hyde.* While there are other Stevenson museums around the world, each with its own cache of

manuscripts, letters, and clippings, this was the first (founded in 1915) and it's the one most evocative of the great writer's life.

The threadbare Victorian furniture here is all original, and dusty glass cases display such treasures as a lock of his hair, his velvet smoking jacket (a sprig of heather in its buttonhole), the old-fashioned ice skates he wore to skate on the local pond, even burn marks in the mantelpiece from his cigarettes. I fell in love with this place myself as a child and was astounded to find, 40 years later, that it was exactly the same. And having read so many Stevenson books to my kids, I was thrilled to see them fall under its delicate, musty spell, too.

(i) 11 Stevenson Lane (© **518/891-1462;** www.adirondacks.com/robertlstevenson. html)

✈ Saranac Lake.

🛏 $$ **Hotel Saranac,** 101 Main St., Saranac Lake (© **800/937-0211** or 518/891-2200; www.hotelsaranac.com).

BEST TIME: Open July to mid-Sept; rest of year, call curator for appointment.

WHY THEY'LL THANK YOU: The legend of a great storyteller burns bravely on.

Huck Finn Meets Uncle Tom

Ages 6 & up • Hartford, Connecticut, USA

TOM SAWYER, Huckleberry Finn, The Connecticut Yankee in King Arthur's Court: Mark Twain's books are some of the few that make kids laugh out loud when they read them in school. His image is instantly recognizable even today—a white-suited man with wild white hair, an even wilder white moustache, and eyes glinting with sarcastic humor. Twain was in some ways a perpetual kid himself, which is why even young visitors get into the spirit of his house.

Mark Twain was already a successful author in 1874 when he built this 19-room mansion in "Picturesque Gothic" style, with a profusion of steeply peaked gables and patterned painted-brick walls. Inside there's lots of elaborate woodworking and stenciled wallpapers, very Victorian and yet somehow expressive of Twain's own restless, wide-ranging mind. On the hour-long guided tour, you get a sense of his enthusiasm for newfangled gadgets— *Life on the Mississippi* is said to be the first novel written on a typewriter—and we were surprised to see such modern touches as flush toilets and the primitive telephone installed in the entrance hall. On the top floor we visited his main workroom, a large space dominated by a billiard table. The chief impression I got from the tour was of Twain's mercurial nature—his egotism and insecurity, his irascible temper, an imperfectly stifled romantic streak, and his emotional attachments to his children. All in all, a complex and fascinating man.

It's no coincidence that one of Twain's next-door neighbors was another famous writer—**Harriet Beecher Stowe,** whose

Mark Twain's Hartford home.

418

sensationally melodramatic 1852 antislavery novel, *Uncle Tom's Cabin,* was one of the 19th century's biggest bestsellers. (Abraham Lincoln himself believed the book responsible for touching off the Civil War.) This hilltop parcel of land was Nook Farm, an enclave for arty progressive types, so both Twain and Stowe fit right in. Throughout the tour of Stowe's modestly furnished small house, however, I kept wondering how this dowdy theologian's wife (her father and brothers were also clergymen) got along with her outrageous cigar-chomping neighbor. We would never have made a trip solely to visit Harriet Beecher Stowe's house, but the contrast with Twain's was pure serendipity.

(i) **Twain House,** 351 Farmington Ave. (© **860/247-0998;** www.marktwainhouse. org). **Stowe house,** 77 Forest St. (© **860/ 522-9258;** www.harrietbeecherstowe center.org).

✈ Bradley International, 12 miles.

🛏 $$$ **Hilton Hartford Hotel,** 315 Trumbull St. (© **800/445-8667** or 860/728-5151; www.hartford.hilton.com).

WHY THEY'LL THANK YOU: Twain's irrepressible spirit, embodied in bricks and mortar.

The Mark Twain Home
Tom Sawyer's Stomping Grounds
Ages 6 & up • Hannibal, Missouri, USA

WHEN YOU ROLL INTO this laid-back river town, about 130 miles up the scenic Mississippi river road from St. Louis, you may get a nagging feeling that you've been here before. Well, you have—if you've read *The Adventures of Tom Sawyer.* Every scene in that book was based on affectionate memories of the town where a boy named Sam Clemens grew up, long before he became Mark Twain. Sometimes Hannibal leans on the association a bit too much—every third restaurant or shop seems to be named after a Tom Sawyer character—but the historic heart of town really does have a remarkable connection to this beloved American writer.

Eight properties around town, packaged under the name The Mark Twain Museum, have rock-solid associations with Sam Clemens. The main one is the small white frame house at 208 Hill St. where the Clemens family lived from 1844 to 1853; the parlor, the dining room, the kitchen, and the three upstairs bedrooms

are all furnished in the period. You can almost imagine Sam climbing out the window of the back bedroom he shared with his brother Henry, sneaking off to nighttime escapades. Across the street is the much more prosperous house of the Hawkins family, whose daughter Laura—Twain's lifelong friend—was the model for Becky Thatcher. The law office of Sam's father, John Clemens, has been moved to the same street; its tiny front courtroom was the setting for Muff Potter's trial in *Tom Sawyer.* After a shift in the family fortunes, the Clemenses moved to cramped quarters above the old-fashioned pharmacy run by Dr. Orville Grant, over on Main Street. The last stop on this historic trail may not be authentic, but it could be the kids' favorite: the **Museum Gallery,** set in an old department store on Main Street, where interactive displays on *Tom Sawyer* allow children to whitewash a fence, hide in a spooky graveyard, and get lost in a cave, just like Tom and Huck and Becky did.

Of all the peripheral attractions in town, the one that has the most true Tom-'n'-Huck flavor is the **Mark Twain Cave,** a mile south of town on U.S. 79. Whether or not Sam Clemens actually got lost during a school picnic in either of these two caves, it's easy to imagine him making mischief down here, and the guides on the 1-hour tour are sure to work in references to the book.

Sleepy as Hannibal seems most of the year, it crackles to life during the **National Tom Sawyer Days,** the long weekend around July 4. All sorts of Twain-themed activities are held outdoors, from fence painting to frog jumping, and it's just generally the sort of whoop-de-do that Sam Clemens—or Tom Sawyer—would have loved.

ⓘ 208 Hill St. (✆ **573/221-7975;** www.marktwainmuseum.org).

✈ Lambert–St. Louis International, 125 miles.

🛏 $ **Hannibal Travelodge,** 500 Mark Twain Ave. (✆ **800/578-7878** or 573/222-4100; www.hannibaltravelodge.com). $$ **Hotel Clemens,** 401 Third St. (✆ **573/248-1150;** www.hotelclemens.us).

WHY THEY'LL THANK YOU: Channeling an idyllic small-town childhood.

Famous Homesteads **377**

Laura Ingalls Wilder's Homes
Little Houses on the Prairie
Ages 4 & up • Multiple sites, USA

LAURA INGALLS WILDER'S books about her frontier childhood are such an indelible part of the American girl zeitgeist that just about every little girl I know has had a "Little House" phase, even if she didn't get through the entire series. Because the Ingalls family was always on the move, each book recalls a different childhood home of Laura's; today each of those towns tries to claim its own piece of the Little House tourism market. What's a Little House fan to do?

If you're really ambitious, you could probably make a pilgrimage to all the Little House sites in a week or so. The upper Mississippi river town of Pepin, Wisconsin, was Laura's birthplace, where a replica log cabin 7 miles north of town re-creates the environment of what she later called the *Little House in the Big Woods.* Another reconstructed log cabin down in southeastern Kansas, just southwest of Independence, Kansas, claims to be the *Little House on the Prairie,* Wilder's second book. The Ingallses then hauled back north to Walnut Grove, Minnesota, to the home depicted in *On the Banks of Plum Creek;* today the site is merely a well-marked depression in the grassland outside of town, but back in town a cluster of typical late-19th-century buildings—depot, school chapel, a striking onion-domed house—has been fashioned into the thoroughly satisfying **Laura Ingalls Wilder Museum.** This museum snapped up several mementos from the popular 1970s TV series, which supplement the few real pioneer items on display; it does have a quilt Wilder sewed, her family Bible, and lots of letters and photos. The collection of 250 antique dolls has nothing to do with the Little House books, but girls will eat it up. A little over 100 miles west on U.S. 14 was the Ingallses' fourth frontier home, in DeSmet, South Dakota. You can take a walking tour of several period buildings here, including a one-room wood schoolhouse like the one where Laura had her first teaching job.

The only true Little House you can visit is another long drive south in Mansfield, Missouri—the lovely white farmhouse in the Ozark hills where the adult Wilder and her husband moved in 1894. Here at **Rocky Ridge Farm,** Wilder in 1932 sat down to write her memoirs of frontier life; you can see her study, the lap desk upon which she wrote, and several cherished family mementos she had kept, including Pa Ingalls's old fiddle. Somehow I feel closest to little Laura here, where the grown-up Laura plunged back into her memories to create her timeless stories.

(i) **Laura Ingalls Wilder Museum,** 330 8th St., Walnut Grove, MN ((C) **800/528-7280;** www.walnutgrove.org). **Rocky Ridge Farm,** 3068 Highway A, Mansfield, MO ((C) **417/ 924-3626;** www.lauraingallswilderhome. com).

✈ Minnesota/St. Paul International (for Pepin, Walnut Grove, DeSmet). Kansas City International (for Independence, Mansfield).

🛏 $$ **Oasis Inn,** 2550 N. Glenstone, Springfield, MO ((C) **417/866-5253**).

WHY THEY'LL THANK YOU: Imagine covering the distances between these homes in a covered wagon, with no superhighways.

Famous Homesteads

378

Anne of Green Gables Country

Ages 8 & up • Cavendish, Prince Edward Island, Canada

SOMETIMES I WONDER what Prince Edward Island would have done to attract tourism if Lucy Maud Montgomery hadn't written the *Anne of Green Gables* books. Lush and bucolic, blessed with red-sand beaches on the relatively warm Gulf of St. Lawrence, PEI can be enchanting—but you wouldn't necessarily know that without having been drawn here by this wholesome, century-old book series about a red-haired orphan girl.

Start out in Charlottetown with *Anne of Green Gables—The Musical,* which plays every summer at the downtown arts center at 145 Richmond St. ((C) **800/ 565-0278** or 902/566-12670). Chirpy and well performed, it's a quick refresher course in the book's plot and main characters.

Then head for the center part of the island's north coast, where the town of Cavendish is Green Gables Central. Bypass the tourist traps and head to **Green Gables,** a solid white mid-19th-century farmhouse with green shutters (and, naturally, green gable points) that belonged to Montgomery's cousins. In her imagination this tidy farm with its precise white rail fences became the Cuthbert farmstead, where spunky orphan Anne Shirley arrives from Nova Scotia to live with dour Matthew and Marilla Cuthbert. Parks Canada owns the site and has meticulously furnished the rooms according to descriptions in the books. Getting outdoors is essential for falling under the Anne of Green Gables spell, and walking trails from the house lead to settings from the novel such as **Lover's Lane** and the **Haunted Woods.** Although Montgomery spent most of her adult life with her clergyman husband in Ontario, she remained so attached to her native PEI landscape that she asked to be buried in the nearby Cavendish Cemetery.

Amid a stretch of tacky amusement parks and motels, **Avonlea,** Route 6 ((C) **902/963-3050;** www.avonleavillage. com), has a bit more class than its neighbors: Among the faux vintage buildings of its "village center" (Avonlea being Montgomery's fictional name for Cavendish) are a few real historic structures imported from elsewhere in the region, including a schoolhouse in which Montgomery once taught and a church she attended. The costumed staff moves along various kinds of jollity, including hayrides, games, cow milking, and oyster shucking. Commercial, yes, and a little hokey, but younger children especially will find it engaging.

To connect with the rural vibe, head for nearby **Prince Edward Island National Park,** a lovely swath of sand beaches, placid inlets, vast salt marshes, and wind-sculpted dunes topped with marram grass. Pastoral peace and quiet—that's the gift of Anne of Green Gables.

(i) 2 Palmers Lane (℃ **902/963-7874;** www.pc.gc.ca).

✈ Charlottetown, PEI, 40km (25 miles).

🛏 $$ **Red Road Country Inn,** Rte. 6, Clinton (℃ **800/249-1344**). $$$ **Shaw's**

Green Gables.

Hotel, Rte. 15, Brackley Beach (℃ **902/ 672-2022;** www.shawshotel.ca).

WHY THEY'LL THANK YOU: Getting hooked on the books.

Famous Homesteads **379**

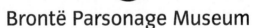

Brontë Parsonage Museum

Ages 8 & up • Haworth, England

THE MOST-VISITED LITERARY SHRINE in England after Shakespeare's hometown of Stratford-upon-Avon, this modest parsonage amid the bleak Yorkshire dales was home to not one but three gifted novelists—Charlotte, Emily, and Anne Brontë. Whether your favorite Brontë heroine is mousy governess Jane Eyre or passionate Catherine Earnshaw of *Wuthering Heights,* the spell of this remote, obscure Yorkshire home is captivating.

The village of **Haworth,** though overrun in summer by Brontë worshipers, still seems to hang precariously onto the edge of the Yorkshire moors. Try to screen out the crowds as you walk its steep, cobbled main street, where you can visit a pub called the Black Bull, which was frequented by the writers' dissolute artist brother, Branwell. Stop by the very post office where in 1847 the sisters

mailed their manuscripts hopefully to London publishers.

At the top of the village on Church Street stands the square, stone-sided Georgian **parsonage** where the Brontë family lived, granted for life to Patrick Brontë, curate of the local Church of St. Michaels. The Brontë children knew tragedy early—their mother and two sisters died when they were young—and though the shy, odd Brontë sisters ventured away for school or teaching jobs, they always fled back to this haven. The sparely furnished house has been preserved complete with personal treasures, pictures, books, original manuscripts, a huge collection of family letters, and the authentic family furniture (some bought with proceeds from Charlotte's literary success). Look at the dining room, where the sisters sat side by side writing their novels at the dining table, and the nursery, where they scribbled on the wall in their tiny, spidery handwriting. The walled garden has been laid out to resemble the one cultivated by the Brontës. Note that the museum tends to be extremely crowded in July and August, and is closed in January.

Charlotte and Emily are buried in Haworth in the family vault under the Church of St. Michael (the one standing here today is not the original church, which was torn down and rebuilt in 1879).

Be sure to allow time to walk out onto the nearby moors, where the spirit of *Wuthering Heights* still sighs in the wind.

ⓘ ☏ **01535/642323;** www.bronte.org.uk.

🚆 Keighley, 3 hr. from London.

🛏 $$ **Old White Lion Hotel,** 6–10 West Lane (☏ **01535/642313;** www.oldwhitelionhotel.com).

WHY THEY'LL THANK YOU: Proof that genius can flourish anywhere.

Famous Homesteads

380

Beatrix Potter Country

All ages • The Lake District, England

Though she was born down in Suffolk, Beatrix Potter—author and illustrator of beloved children's stories like *The Tale of Peter Rabbit*—fell in love with England's stunning Lake District as a teenager when her family summered here, and as soon as she won literary fame she bought a farm near Lake Windermere and spent most of the rest of her life here. It's one of the U.K.'s most evocative (and popular) literary pilgrimages, for adults as well as children.

The logical place to begin is in the Victorian lakeside tourist town Bowness-on-Windermere, at the blatantly commercial **World of Beatrix Potter,** The Old Laundry (☏ **01539/488444;** www.hop-skip-jump.com), a 3-D "experience" where children can cavort around replica figures of Tom Kitten, Jemima Puddleduck, Benjamin Bunny, and other classic Potter animal characters. It does a good job, though, of telling how this nature-loving Londoner happened to turn her detailed drawings into pocket-size children's books, and went on to become a successful Cumbrian farmer and conservationist.

To reach Potter's home, either drive west around the lake or, better yet, follow an 11km (6.8-mile) walking route (get details from the World of Beatrix Potter).

The car ferry across Lake Windermere gives you an excuse for taking in glorious water views of the District's dramatic mountain peaks. Proceed to Sawrey, at the southeast end of Esthwaite Water, to visit **Hill Top,** the 17th-century gray stone farmhouse where Potter lived when she wrote some of her most famous stories. Due to the site's enormous popularity, visitors are issued timed-entry tickets (book ahead if you can); there's an atmospheric pub next door where you can have refreshments while you wait your turn. The deep-windowed, wainscoted interiors appeared in many of her illustrations (such as my favorites from *The Roly-Poly Pudding*) and the splendid cottage garden looks endearingly familiar—you almost expect Mrs. Tiggy-Winkle or the Flopsy Bunnies to pop out of the shrubbery at any moment.

Your next stop is in Hawkshead, at the **Beatrix Potter Gallery,** Main Street (☏ **015394/36355**), where a rotating selection of Potter's original drawings is displayed in the office once used by her lawyer husband, William Heelis, whom she married at age 47 (you may recognize the office as Tabitha Twitchit's shop in *The Pie and the Patty Pan*). There's a shuttle bus back to Bowness from Hawkshead.

(i) **Beatrix Potter Home,** Hill Top, Near Sawrey (✆ **015394/36269;** www.national trust.org.uk).

🚂 Windermere, 3¾ hr. from London.

🛏 $$ **Lindeth Howe,** Longtail Hill, Storrs Park, Bowness-on-Windermere (✆ **01539/ 445759;** www.lindeth-howe.co.uk). $$$ **Rothay Manor,** Rothay Bridge, Ambleside (✆ **01539/433605;** www.rothaymanor.co.uk).

WHY THEY'LL THANK YOU: Childhood images coming vividly to life.

Famous Homesteads **381**

Hans Christian Andersen House
Denmark's Storyteller Supreme
All ages • Odense, Denmark

THOUGH THE CHILDREN may not recognize the name Hans Christian Andersen, they know his stories all right: *The Emperor's New Clothes, The Princess and the Pea, The Ugly Duckling,* or *The Little Mermaid* (yes, the story existed before Disney), immortalized in the famous statue in Copenhagen harbor. Like most gifted writers for children, Andersen tapped into the terrors and humiliations and stubborn yearnings of his own childhood. How better to understand those stories than to get a picture of the boy Andersen was?

Begin at the **Hans Christian Andersen Museum,** a major museum documenting Andersen's life, times, and works. Films, touch-screens, and listening posts bring the writer into focus; a tall, clumsy, ugly man who, beneath his sophisticated manners, remained at heart a poor kid with a chip on his shoulder. You can see a re-creation of the study where he wrote, the bed where he died, and such memorabilia as a lock of his hair, his trademark walking stick, a top hat, a battered portmanteau, and letters to his dear friends the Swedish opera singer Jenny Lind and fellow writer Charles Dickens. Next door is his **birthplace,** a tiny yellow house on a corner where five poor families lived, including Andersen's grandparents and parents, at his birth in 1805.

Andersen's father was a shoemaker, his mother a drunken washerwoman, and Andersen himself grew up a shy, somewhat dorky kid, susceptible to the folk tales and superstitions he heard around him. A few blocks away, the **H.C. Andersens Barndomshjem** (Childhood Home), Munkeøllestraede 3, is the humble half-timbered house where he lived from age 2 until 14—when, dazzled by a traveling theater troupe, young Hans ran off to Copenhagen to become an actor.

The Hans Christian Theatre performs *The Emperor's New Clothes.*

The city of Odense has created a **walking tour** around the downtown area that passes several historic buildings Andersen would have known. Look for granite squares in the sidewalk, decorated with a cheery sun face of Andersen's own design. Try your best to take in the Andersen **plays** performed mid-July to mid-August at 4pm outdoors in **Funen Village,** Sejerskovvej 20 (© **66-14-88-14;** closed Mon), the open-air cultural museum with reassembled historic buildings from around the island. It's a site worth visiting even if you don't attend a play, a good place to recapture the 19th-century lifestyle of Andersen's time. Even though the plays are in Danish, it'll be easy for the kids to follow the visuals—these simple, timeless stories speak a universal language.

ⓘ Bangs Boder 29 (© **66-14-88-14;** www.odense.dk).

🚆 Odense, 3 hr. from Copenhagen.

🛏 $$ **Clarion Hotel Plaza Odense,** Østre Stationsvej 24 (© **877/424-6423** in the U.S., or 66-11-77-45; www.hotel-plaza.dk). $$$ **Radisson SAS H.C. Andersen Hotel,** Claus Bergs Gade 7 (© **800/333-3333** in the U.S., or 66-14-78-00; www.odense.radissonsas.com).

WHY THEY'LL THANK YOU: Discovering the ugly duckling behind the famous writer.

---

382 **Famous Homesteads**

The Anne Frank House
Life in the Secret Annex
Ages 8 & up • Amsterdam, The Netherlands

TEENS AND PRETEENS in particular connect with the spirit of Anne Frank, not because she was anything special, but precisely because she wasn't. She was a mixed-up kid like themselves—only she happened to be a mixed-up kid fleeing the Nazi terror, living pent up for more than 2 years in a secret set of rooms in Amsterdam with seven other people. We know about her only because she poured out her heart in a startlingly frank diary, which now every school kid eventually reads. In summer you may have to queue for an hour or more to get in, but nobody should miss seeing this house, where Anne Frank waited out the darkest days of World War II. Even if they haven't yet read the book, this is the place where kids really get the tragedy of the Holocaust.

The hiding place Anne's father, Otto Frank, prepared for his family and friends was a back section of a house, consisting of four rooms and a tiny damp attic, connected to his office and warehouse. It's a typical Amsterdam canal house, with very steep interior stairs; the entrance to it from the office was hidden by a movable bookcase. Their existence protected by four trusted employees, they remained safe until close to the end of the war—after the landings at Normandy Beach **277** spelled hope for the war to end—when suddenly, tragically, the secret annex was raided by Nazi forces. All eight of the *onderduikers* (divers or hiders) were deported to concentration camps. Anne herself died, with her sister Margot, at Bergen-Belsen; only Otto survived to see the Secret Annex again.

The rooms of the hiding place look surprisingly bare, for all the furniture was confiscated after the arrest; at one time it was refurnished to replicate its appearance from July 1942 to August 1944, but today it is stark and empty and utterly moving. Among the few things left in place are photos Anne pinned up of her favorite actress, Deanna Durbin, and the young English princesses Elizabeth and Margaret, along with a map upon which Otto Frank hopefully charted the progress of the war. The canal side of the house, where the helpers worked, has been restored to its authentic appearance, based on references in Anne's diary. **Personal items** belonging to each of the eight fugitives have been put on display in the building next door, along with the **original manuscript** of Anne's diary, which helper Miep Gies found scattered on the annex floor after the Franks were dragged away. The red-and-white autograph album in which Anne began her diary lies in a glass case, looking so innocent and childish—it makes her tragedy especially poignant.

ⓘ Prinsengracht 263 (✆ **020/556-7105;** www.annefrank.nl).

✈ ⊨ See The Canals of Amsterdam **51**.

WHY THEY'LL THANK YOU: An ordinary teenager, living in extraordinary times.

Famous Homesteads **383**

Verona: Romeo & Juliet's Hometown
Ages 6 & up • Italy

THE MOST FAMOUS LOVE STORY in the English language, Shakespeare's *Romeo and Juliet* was set in Verona, Italy, and though the Bard never set foot here—he "borrowed" the story ready-made from a 1562 version by one Arthur Brooke—Verona is quite happy to trade on the association. Whether Romeo or Juliet ever existed, Veronese entrepreneurs have dreamed up Capulet and Montague sites to snare tourists—which made a useful hook to entice our children on a day trip from Venice to this lovely northern Italian city. Authentic or not, anything that makes them think about Shakespeare is okay by me.

The so-called **Juliet's House,** Via Cappello 23 (✆ **045-8034303**), has no proven connection to any family named Capulet (locals claim that in the 19th century it was a bordello), but this small, sparely furnished home, with its stone balcony and tidy courtyard, fits the image—you can just imagine Romeo saying, "But, soft! What light through yonder window breaks?" The right breast on a bronze statue of Juliet is brightly polished from visitors giving it a traditional good-luck rub, and a blizzard of hopeful love letters are posted outside. A few blocks away, **Romeo's House,** Casa di Romeo, Via Arche Scaligeri 2 at least may have been home to the Montecchi family, the model for Shakespeare's Montagues; it's now an atmospheric restaurant, the **Osteria dal Duca** (✆ **045-594474**).

The nearby **Piazza delle Erbe,** once a Roman-era forum and today a lively open-air food market, is where I imagine Romeo, Mercutio, and Tybalt having their fatal street brawl. The kids decided the Roman statue in the center, called *The Virgin of Verona,* was Juliet—who was I to argue? As for the play's church scenes, we envisioned them set in **Basilica San Zeno Maggiore,** Piazza San Zeno (✆ **045-8006120**), a near-perfect Romanesque church and campanile built between the 9th and 12th centuries west of the river Adige. Coming back along the riverbank, we pictured **Castelvecchio,** Corso Castelvecchio 2 (✆ **045-594734**), built in the 14th century for the ruling Della Scalla family, as the home of the play's Prince Escalus, its crenellated battlements like a perfect Lego castle. We stopped at the wonderfully intact **Roman arena,** dating from the 1st century A.D., then swung south to a Franciscan monastery that claims to hold **Juliet's Tomb,** Via del Pontiere 5 (✆ **045-8000361**).

If you're here in July and August, get tickets for the Shakespearean festival—nothing beats seeing *Romeo and Juliet* or *Two Gentlemen of Verona* in this setting.

ⓘ **Tourist office,** Via degli Alpini, 9 (📞 **045-8068680;** www.tourism.verona.it).

🚆 Verona, 2 hr. from Venice.

🛏 $$ **Colomba d'Oro,** Via C. Cattaneo 10 (📞 **045-595300;** www.colombahotel.com). $$$ **Hotel Gabbia d'Oro,** Corso Porta Borsari 4A (📞 **045-8003060;** www.hotelgabbiadoro.it).

WHY THEY'LL THANK YOU: "In fair Verona, where we lay our scene . . ."

384

Mount Vernon
George Washington's Home
Ages 6 & up • Mount Vernon, Virginia, USA

Sᴛᴀɴᴅɪɴɢ ᴍᴀᴊᴇꜱᴛɪᴄᴀʟʟʏ ᴀᴛᴏᴘ a lawn sloping down to the Potomac River, the white-columned colonial home of George and Martha Washington has been one of America's most-visited shrines since it was opened to the public in 1860. A quick 15-mile drive from Washington, D.C., Mount Vernon is an obvious day trip from the capital, aswarm with tourists every spring and summer. But don't let that deter you: Mount Vernon reveals the man George Washington would have been if all that Father of His Country stuff hadn't got in the way. The remote, mysterious First President becomes human here.

George Washington wasn't even supposed to get this estate; he inherited it in 1752 when his older half-brother, Lawrence, died. George, a surveyor by trade, vigorously set out to become the leading scientific farmer in America. But life has a way of interrupting our plans; when the American fight for independence needed a general, Washington, a military hero from the French and Indian War, accepted the commission. After the Revolutionary War, he retired to Mount Vernon—but again, duty called, and he went to preside over the Constitutional Convention, then reluctantly agreed to become President (some folks wanted to make him king, but he put his foot

down). He finally returned in 1797, only to die in 1799; his burial vault is on the grounds. At last he could stay at Mount Vernon.

About a third of the **furnishings** actually belonged to the Washingtons—Martha's tea service, her granddaughter's harpsichord, the globe in George's study, a key to the Paris Bastille (a gift from the Marquis de Lafayette). It's clearly the home of a country gentleman, prosperous but not ostentatious; note motifs of farm tools and grapevines in the big dining room's plaster moldings. You can also visit the kitchen, smokehouse, stables, heirloom gardens, slave quarters, and gristmill; down by the river, kids love the 4-acre exhibit demonstrating Washington's innovative farming methods.

You'd swear the main house was built of stone, but look closely—it's beveled pine, artfully painted. One thing that is no fake is the sweeping **Potomac view** from the long front porch—I can just imagine Washington standing here to relish that vista. As a farmer and surveyor, Washington knew America's greatest asset was its land. When Jefferson and Adams tussled over whether to ally the U.S. with England or with France, Washington declared that this bountiful country could stand on its own. I like to think the view from Mount Vernon was in his mind when he said that.

(i) End of George Washington Memorial Pkwy. (✆ **703/780-2000;** www.mount vernon.org).

✈ 🚇 See Washington, D.C. ⓺.

WHY THEY'LL THANK YOU: They wanted him to be king, he wanted to be a farmer.

U.S. Presidents **385**

Jefferson's Monticello
The House That Tom Built
Ages 6 & up • Charlottesville, Virginia, USA

THE LOCALS STILL CALL IT "Mr. Jefferson's country," and for good reason: Charlottesville, Virginia, is home not only to Thomas Jefferson's famous estate, Monticello, but also to the University of Virginia, which he founded. Jefferson wasn't just a politician, he was a Renaissance man—statesman, agricultural reformer, philosopher, inventor, and, last but not least, architect, with Monticello his crowning architectural achievement.

As befit the author of the Declaration of Independence, Jefferson was fiercely anti-British; when he began to design this home in 1769, he rejected the popular Georgian style—derived from British architecture—and went for the 16th-century Italian style of Andrea Palladio. After living in France as the U.S. ambassador, he added features he'd admired in Parisian mansions. The kids will instantly recognize its exterior from the back of the U.S. nickel. But what the nickel doesn't show is the perfection of its hilltop setting (in an era when most plantation homes were set beside rivers) and the gardens and many outbuildings of this self-sufficient plantation. Every brick and nail of the house's materials was made in workshops on-site, by Jefferson's slaves and free artisans. Half-hour **guided tours** depart from the visitor center, halfway up the mountain; get

there early or expect a long wait. Note the many octagonal rooms (one of Jefferson's favorite shapes), and all the cunning devices Jefferson designed, like his convertible alcove bed. The library once held 6,000 volumes, which upon Jefferson's death were donated to the nation to become the core of the Library of Congress. Look for the dining room chair with TJ carved into its armrest— the last chair in which Jefferson sat before his death on July 4, 1826, exactly 50 years after signing the Declaration of Independence.

After Monticello, the neighboring estate of fifth President James Monroe, **Ash Lawn–Highland,** County Road 795 (✆ **434/293-9539;** www.ashlawn highland.org), is a letdown. Instead, we drove 25 miles north of Charlottesville to **Montpelier,** 11407 Constitution Hwy., Montpelier Station (✆ **540/672-2728**), the much grander estate of fourth President James Madison; his First Lady, Dolly, is one of those historical figures kids instinctively admire. Jefferson helped Madison expand this red-brick Georgian house, which has been furnished as it was in the 1820s.

(i) Off VA 53 (✆ **434/984-9822;** www. monticello.org).

✈ Charlottesville-Albemarle.

🛏 $ **Econo Lodge University,** 400 Emmet St. (℅ **8900/55-ECONO** or 434/ 296-2104). $$ **Omni Charlottesville Hotel,**

235 W. Main St. (℅ **800/THE-OMNI** or 434/971-5500; www.omnihotels.com).

WHY THEY'LL THANK YOU: Jefferson's clever little inventions.

U.S. Presidents

386

The Hermitage
Andrew Jackson's Frontier White House
Ages 6 & up • Nashville, Tennessee, USA

HIS FACE STARES OUT AT US FROM THE $20 BILL, a restless-looking man with a mane of wild hair and a high cravat. Who was Andrew Jackson, and why should we visit his home in Nashville? Well, at this deceptively gracious antebellum plantation, we really connected with the ornery spirit of our first frontier President, the original Democrat, a passionate "man of the people" who loved a good brawl. I love to hear how Jackson upset the Washington elite on his inauguration day in 1829 by opening the White House to the general public (a drunken mob nearly wrecked the place). Here's a president kids can relate to.

Before Jackson, all our Presidents were Virginia and Massachusetts lawyers and gentleman farmers—what a breath of fresh air when this brash Westerner blazed into office, trouncing the incumbent John Quincy Adams. Born in a log cabin in backwoods South Carolina, the orphaned child of Irish immigrants, Jackson pieced together enough education to become a Tennessee lawyer and circuit judge, but he really made his name as General Jackson, hero of the War of 1812 and the Indian Wars, earning the nickname Old Hickory for his toughness. At first the wide verandas and thick white columns of the Hermitage look too

dignified for a wild man like Jackson, but then we learned that the neoclassical portico was a later addition; the core is a square, plain eight-room brick house, which replaced a log farmhouse only after Jackson had a war-hero image to burnish. As the costumed interpreters explain, the ornate 1830s Empire decor you see today—tufted velvet upholstery, patterned wallpaper, and gilt-trimmed furniture—dates from Jackson's presidency; in earlier days his personal finances were too tight for such opulence (maybe that's why as President he frugally cut spending and erased the national debt). This was definitely a working cotton farm, and in addition to the main house you'll visit the kitchen (a separate building, as was customary then), smokehouse, garden, springhouse (a storage shed built over a cooling spring), the remains of the farm's first log house, and Jackson's tomb—set in a grove of, naturally, old hickory trees.

ⓘ Old Hickory Blvd. (℅ **615/889-2941;** www.thehermitage.com).

✈ 🛏 See The Nashville Music Scene **348**.

WHY THEY'LL THANK YOU: Seeing Old Hickory's well-used sword.

429

387

The Lincoln Trail
From a Log Cabin to the White House
All ages • Multiple sites, USA

EVEN BEFORE HIS ASSASSINATION, Abraham Lincoln was a revered President, the hero who steered America through the Civil War. Long before the modern mania for historical preservation, sites associated with Lincoln were turned into memorials. For kids, however, it's important to peel away the layers of myth to find the flesh-and-blood Lincoln. Drive the Lincoln Trail through Kentucky, Indiana, and Illinois and you'll find the backwoods boy behind the great President.

There's something bizarre about the first stop, in Hodgenville, Kentucky, the **Abraham Lincoln Birthplace National Historic Site,** where a huge neoclassical memorial encloses a tiny log cabin,

reportedly the one where Lincoln was born on February 12, 1809. You'll get a better sense of Lincoln's humble origins 7 miles north of town on Highway 31E at **Lincoln's Boyhood Home,** where he spent ages 2 to 7; though the log cabin here is a reconstruction, its rough log walls and split-rail fences truly evoke a hardscrabble Kentucky childhood.

Cross the Ohio River, taking I-65 north and then I-64 west, a 135-mile drive to Lincoln City, Indiana. The Lincoln family cleared 20 acres here in 1816, when Abe was 7, and farmed the land for 14 years as he grew to manhood. If the boy Abe Lincoln comes to life anywhere on the trail, it's at the **Lincoln Boyhood**

Lincoln's boyhood home.

National Memorial: A symbolic bronze hearth and foundations mark the actual site of the Lincoln cabin; a living history farm (open late April to Oct) re-creates early-19th-century farm life; and you can walk a trail to the grave of Nancy Hanks Lincoln, whose death so grieved her 9-year-old son. The Memorial itself is a bit pompous, but the rooms inside strike a note of pioneer simplicity.

The next leg of your drive is about 250 miles, up to Springfield, Illinois, where the adult Lincoln really began to make his mark. The **Abraham Lincoln Presidential Library** is the snazzy centerpiece to Springfield's Lincoln worship, with loads of important artifacts (including a hand-written copy of the Gettysburg address), dioramas of his log cabin, parts of the White House, and the Ford's Theater box where he was shot. In town, you can visit the **Lincoln Home,** 426 S. 7th St., and a 4-block historic area around it, as well as his old **law office,** 209 S. 6th St., and the stately **Lincoln's Tomb.** But also squeeze in a 20-mile side trip northwest on Route 97 to the restored prairie village of **New Salem,** where from 1831 to 1837 young lawyer Abraham boarded at the Rutledge Tavern and fell in love with the innkeeper's daughter Ann, who died at 21. Some say Abe never got over her—ah, there's the human side of Lincoln again.

(i) **Abraham Lincoln Birthplace National Historic Site,** 2995 Lincoln Farm Rd., Hodgenville KY (© **502/358-3874;** www.nps.gov/abli). **Lincoln Boyhood National Memorial,** Rte. 162, Lincoln City, IN (© **812/937-4541;** www.nps.gov/libo). **Abraham Lincoln Presidential Library,** 212 N. 6th St., Springfield, IL (© **217/558-8848;** www.alplm.org).

✈ Standiford Field, Louisville, KY, 45 miles from Hodgenville. Capital Airport, Springfield, IL.

⊨ $ **Baymont Inn,** 20857 N. U.S. 231, Dale, IN (© **800/301-0200** or 812/937-7000; www.baymontdalein.com). $$ **Mansion View Inn,** 529 S. 4th St., Springfield, IL (© **800/252-1083** or 217/544-7411; www.mansionview.com). $$$ **Seelbach Hilton,** 500 4th St., Louisville, KY (© **502/585-3200;** www.seelbachhilton.com).

WHY THEY'LL THANK YOU: Seeing the modest beginnings of an American icon.

---

388 U.S. Presidents

Calvin Coolidge State Historic Site

Ages 8 & up • Plymouth, Vermont, USA

POSTERITY MAY REMEMBER him as Silent Cal, the famously taciturn American President (when told Coolidge had died, literary wit Dorothy Parker is said to have responded, "How can they tell?"), but Calvin Coolidge's common sense and strong work ethic made him a popular president, a beacon of solid values in the midst of the Roaring Twenties.

In many ways Coolidge was the classic stoic Vermonter, and the **Plymouth Notch Historic District** is more than just his birthplace—it's an entire mountain village that expresses the soul of rural New England. Visiting Plymouth Notch gives you a strong sense of a man shaped by harsh weather, unrelieved isolation, and a strong sense of community and family—a rock-ribbed Republican in the finest sense.

Situated in a high upland valley, the historic district consists of a group of about a dozen unspoiled buildings open to the public—barns, farmhouses, the community church, a farm shop, a general store—and a number of other private residences that may be observed from the outside only. The **Plymouth Cheese Factory** (© **802/672-3650**) up the hill was founded in the late 1800s as a farmer's cooperative by President Coolidge's father, and later revived by the President's son. Coolidge's **birthplace** is here, as well as the larger homestead where the family moved when he was 4. The homestead is still furnished exactly as it was in August 1923 when the vacationing Coolidge—then the Vice President—was awakened and informed that President Warren G. Harding had died. His own father, a notary public, administered the presidential oath of office in the sitting room by the light of a kerosene lamp.

Although Coolidge left the village to move to Massachusetts (where he went to college, practiced law, served in the legislature, and eventually became governor), he returned home to Plymouth Notch whenever he could. During his 5½ years in the White House, he turned the large room over the general store into his "summer White House." Upon leaving office, Coolidge retired to Plymouth Notch, saying, "We draw our Presidents from the people . . . I came from them. I wish to be one of them again."

Coolidge is buried in the cemetery across the road, alongside seven generations of Coolidges. He remains the only president to have been born on Independence Day, and every July 4th, a wreath is laid at his simple grave in a quiet ceremony.

ⓘ Rte. 100A (☎ **802/672-3773;** www.dhca. state.vt.us/HistoricSites/html/coolidge.html).

✈ Burlington, 95 miles.

🛏 **Cortina Inn & Resort,** Rte. 4, Killington (☎ **800/451-6108** or 802/773-3333; www.cortinainn.com).

BEST TIME: Open late May to mid-Oct.

WHY THEY'LL THANK YOU: Meet a President who truly embodied family values.

U.S. Presidents 389

Herbert Hoover Homestead
A Quaker President's Roots
Ages 6 & up • West Branch, Iowa, USA

"I CARRY THE BRAND OF IOWA," Herbert Hoover claimed, pointing to a scar on his foot he'd received as a 5-year-old, stepping on a hot chip of metal at his father's blacksmith shop in West Branch, Iowa. The first President born west of the Mississippi, the immensely popular Hoover won a landslide victory in 1928—only to have the stock market crash and Great Depression, for which he was unfairly blamed, ruin his chances of reelection. That's why visiting the Herbert Hoover National Historic Site, 10 miles east of Iowa City, is such a marvelous surprise: It resurrects the reputation of this underrated leader, our only Quaker President and a great humanitarian.

For younger children, the **historic buildings** of Hoover's early life are the main attraction. There are his birthplace, a small two-room white cottage surrounded by a white picket fence; a blacksmith shop just like his father's; the bare and simple Quaker meetinghouse the Hoover family attended; and the one-room schoolhouse where Herbert had his first lessons. In this sleepy Iowa town, it's easy to picture the boy sledding, fishing, splashing around a muddy swimming hole, hunting pigeons and prairie chickens, and shining up agate pebbles found along the railroad tracks. But there was tragedy in his life, too: his father died of pneumonia when Herbert was 6, his mother of typhoid when he was 8, and the three Hoover siblings were split up to live with various relatives. At age 11, Herbert went

to Oregon to live with an uncle and never lived again in Iowa, but he always felt his roots were here.

Older kids should be engrossed by the **museum** at the Hoover Library, one of the best of this kind, where dioramas and colorful displays tell the up-and-down story of Hoover's career. At a young age Hoover became one of the world's most sought-after mining engineers, working in exotic locales such as Australia, China, and Burma; in World War I he won widespread acclaim for leading emergency relief efforts in Europe, especially Belgium. Thanks to deep-seated Quaker ethics instilled during his childhood, Hoover believed strongly in hard work and the value of caring for the less fortunate, especially war orphans. There's an excellent gallery on the 1920s, a dizzying

period of social transition—the rise of the telephone, radio, air travel, and automobiles, not to mention the turmoil of Prohibition, all of which fell into Hoover's domain as a vigorous Secretary of Commerce. The sorrows of the Depression, the smear campaign waged against Hoover by Democrats, his invaluable role as counselor to Harry S. Truman—it's all told here. By the time you go to the hillside above town to see the flat, simple white gravestones of Herbert and Lou Hoover, you'll be moved more than you ever expected.

ⓘ 210 Parkside Dr. (ⓒ **319/643-5301;** www.hoover.archives.gov).

✈ 🚌 See The Amana Colonies **238**.

WHY THEY'LL THANK YOU: Born in the 19th century, he led America into the 20th.

Franklin & Eleanor Roosevelt's Homes
How America's First Power Couple Summered
Ages 8 & up • Hyde Park, New York, USA

FRANKLIN DELANO ROOSEVELT and his cousin Eleanor, who later became his wife, grew up in New York's Hudson River Valley, where wealthy families like the Vanderbilts had colossal summer homes, so it was natural they'd have a home there even after they became President and First Lady. In fact, they had not one home but three, for both Franklin and Eleanor both had separate getaway cottages on the estate, where they could escape the pressures of political life. To visit these three homes in 1 afternoon is to get a powerful sense of this great American couple.

Franklin Roosevelt's lifelong home, **Springwood,** was a modest farmhouse when FDR's father built it. Franklin expanded it in an eclectic Dutch colonial style, giving it an imposing red-brick porticoed facade—my kids would call it a

mansion, but it isn't by any means as grand as the great river estates nearby. Nevertheless, FDR entertained Winston Churchill, King George VI and Queen Elizabeth of England, and many other dignitaries here. He also designed his own presidential library, the nation's first, while still in his second term. Of all the presidential libraries this is the one that feels warmed by a chief executive's presence—you see his cluttered White House desk, left as it was the last day of his presidency, and his beloved 1936 Ford Phaeton with the hand controls that enabled him to drive all over the estate. FDR and Eleanor are buried in the rose garden on the grounds.

A wooded trail leads from Springwood to the pair of private retreats. Simple, rustic **Val-Kill Cottage** was Eleanor's haven, especially after FDR's death in

1945. This flagstone cottage was in fact the only home she ever owned herself. Shy, awkward Eleanor rose to become one of the most influential women of her time, making her mark on civil rights legislation and international humanitarian issues (as a U.N. delegate, she chaired the committee that drafted the U.N. Human Rights Universal Declaration), and she met with many world leaders here at homey Val-Kill. The grounds were also the headquarters of Val-Kill Industries, which Eleanor and several other women established to teach trades to rural workers and produce colonial revival furniture and crafts.

FDR built his hilltop retreat, **Top Cottage,** in the 1930s, while his work as President included battling the Great Depression. FDR was at his most relaxed here, even allowing himself to be photographed in his wheelchair. Though

A chair at the FDR National Historic Site.

the cottage is unfurnished today, you can go out onto the porch and appreciate his cherished views of the Catskill and Shawangunk Mountains. Imagine what it was like in 1939, when FDR hosted Churchill and the king and queen of England to a hot dog dinner on the porch.

(i) **FDR,** 4079 Albany Post Rd., off Rte. 9 (©) **800/FDR-VISIT** or 845/229-8114; www. nps.gov/hofr or www.fdrlibrary.marist.edu). **Eleanor Roosevelt,** Rte. 9G (©) **845/229-9115;** www.nps.gov/elro).

🚆 Poughkeepsie, 8 miles.

🛏 $$ **Journey Inn,** 1 Sherwood Place, Hyde Park (©) **845/229-8972;** www. journeyinn.com).

WHY THEY'LL THANK YOU: Two American history icons become human here.

Harry S. Truman's Home
The Buck Stopped Here
Ages 6 & up • Independence, Missouri, USA

Wʜᴇɴ Fʀᴀɴᴋʟɪɴ Rᴏᴏsᴇᴠᴇʟᴛ died in 1945 in his fifth term—with a world war raging and the Depression a recent memory—his little-known Vice President, Harry S. Truman, who'd only been in the job 10 weeks, was suddenly thrust into the presidency. The plain-spoken values of Independence, Missouri, were what Harry Truman brought with him to the White House, and they served him well. "If you can't stand the heat, get out of the kitchen" was one of his mottoes; another,

printed on a sign on his Oval Office desk, was "ᴛʜᴇ ʙᴜᴄᴋ sᴛᴏᴘs ʜᴇʀᴇ." (This from a man who'd had to make the decision to drop an atomic bomb on Japan.) What a breath of fresh air.

You can see that desk sign, along with a host of other Truman memorabilia, at the **Harry S. Truman Library** in Independence, a 20-minute drive east of downtown Kansas City. (Sometimes there's a period after the S and sometimes there isn't—he had no middle name, only an initial.) This library, one of the first presidential libraries, was Truman's personal passion in his retirement years; he's even buried in the courtyard. The museum is chock-full of ceremonial gifts given to the Trumans by various world leaders—I like to imagine that the Trumans decided to build a museum because they couldn't figure out what else to do with all this fancy stuff—but there are also mementos of Truman the man: his doughboy uniform from World War I, the natty walking canes and straw hats that were his trademarks, the upright piano Bess played at White House parties, the safety plug that was pulled to detonate the Nagasaki bomb. Hand drawings of Truman sent by his admirers express the genuine affection he inspired.

The place that really conveys Truman's common-man qualities, though, is the Truman home up the street from the library. Both Harry and his wife, Bess, were small-town folks, and their summer White House was simply Bess's family home, a gabled white Victorian with a scrollwork corner porch.

Get tickets early in the day, because they do sell out—the house can only be seen on a guided tour, and tours are limited to eight people because the rooms are fairly small. Inside the house, virtually untouched since Bess Truman died, you'll see the red kitchen table where Harry and Bess ate breakfast, the book-lined study that was Truman's favorite retreat, and the wide back porch where they played cards and ate meals during hot Missouri summers. Then stroll around the quiet neighborhood, as Truman did on his daily morning walks. You'll see the heart of America as Truman saw it—and as he lived it.

ⓘ **Harry S. Truman Home,** 219 N. Delaware St. (✆ **816/254-9929;** www.nps.gov/hstr). **Truman Presidential Library,** U.S. 24 and Delaware St. (✆ **816/833-1225;** www.trumanlibrary.org).

✈ Kansas City International, 40 miles.

🛏 $$ **Embassy Suites,** 220 W. 43rd St., Kansas City (✆ **800/EMBASSY** or 816/756-1720; www.embassysuites.com). $$$ **Westin Crown Center,** One Pershing Rd., Kansas City (✆ **800/WESTIN-1** or 816/474-4400; www.westin.com/crown center).

WHY THEY'LL THANK YOU: Truman, a true man of the people.

LBJ's Texas Homestead
A Slice of Hill Country History
Ages 6 & up • Johnson City, Texas, USA

I LOVE PRESIDENTIAL BIRTHPLACES, the more modest the better—nothing demonstrates the American Dream better than the fact that a child from humble beginnings can one day become President. The Johnson family were typical Texas ranchers until one of them, Lyndon Baines Johnson, became 36th President of the United States in November 1963, upon the assassination of John F. Kennedy. The LBJ ranch shows you the heart of this pivotal 1960s President.

LBJ country is within day-trip range of Austin, in the Texas hill country, perhaps the state's prettiest region—a rolling landscape of lakes and rivers, surprising to outsiders who imagine Texas is all flat, arid rangeland. In the main park in Stonewall, Texas, you can tour a reconstruction of the humble board-and-batten farmhouse that was Lyndon Johnson's **birthplace** on August 27, 1908. With its wide railed porch and open hallway (designed to cool off the house in those pre–air-conditioning days), it's furnished authentically for the early 1900s, down to the wood stove and water pump. You can also visit the one-room district **schoolhouse** where Miss Kate Deadrich, the schoolteacher, taught 4-year-old Lyndon alongside his Johnson cousins; 53 years later, Miss Kate stood here to watch her former pupil sign the Elementary and Secondary Education Act, one of the most important measures of his presidency.

When Lyndon was 5, his family moved to Johnson City, named for LBJ's first cousin once removed, James Polk Johnson. From a visitor center on Ladybird Lane, you can walk to his simple white frame Victorian **boyhood home** on 9th Street, now restored with mid-1920s furnishings. A mile-long nature trail from the visitor center also takes you to the **Johnson Settlement,** its rough log buildings showing how Johnson's ancestors lived and raised longhorn cattle in the 1860s.

Back in Stonewall, ranger-led bus tours also visit the sprawling limestone-and-wood ranch house Senator Johnson bought from his aunt and uncle in 1951. Overlooking the Pedernales River, it was the centerpiece of a working ranch (still in operation); it was dubbed the **Texas White House** in the 1960s when LBJ and his wife, Lady Bird Johnson, came here to escape Washington protocol. World leaders often gathered in lawn chairs under the spreading live oak in the front yard. The Johnsons retired to the ranch in 1969, where 4 years later Johnson died of a heart attack; his **gravesite** is nearby, in the Johnson family cemetery. Also part of the park, at the **Sauer-Beckmann Living History Farm,** costumed interpreters in historic buildings bring to life the Texas-German farm culture into which Johnson was born.

ⓘ 14 miles west off U.S. 290 (ℭ **830/868-7128** or 830/644-2252; www.nps.gov/lyjo).

✈ Austin-Bergstrom International, 60 miles.

🛏 $$$ **Hilton Austin Airport,** 9515 New Airport Dr., Austin (ℭ **800/445-8667** or 512/385-6767; www.hilton.com). $$$ **Rose Hill Manor,** 2614 Upper Albert Rd., Stonewall (ℭ **877/ROSEHILL** or 830/644-2247; www.rose-hill.com).

WHY THEY'LL THANK YOU: The entire cycle of a President's life in one countryside.

The one-room schoolhouse Lyndon B. Johnson attended.

Hiking & Backpacking . . . 438
Cycling . . . 454
In the Saddle . . . 461

Hiking in Bryce Canyon.

Yosemite: Rock-Climbing Heaven

AGES 8 & UP • YOSEMITE, CALIFORNIA, USA

MOST FOLKS VISITING Yosemite National Park don't seem to realize that there's more to it than Yosemite Valley, where crowds of cars and RVs inch along the roads while their passengers stare at the 3,000-foot-high glacier-carved granite walls and the waterfalls that drop down them. Yes, you should drive past the awesome 7,549-foot-high sheer rock face called El Capitan; you should pull off the road to take the easy half-mile trails to view Bridalveil Fall or Lower Yosemite Falls. But don't stop there—go up into the high country, where you can explore wilderness without the crowds.

The eastern half of 39-mile-long **Tioga Road** is open only in summer and fall, and the developed area around **Tuolumne Meadows** is much less crowded than Yosemite Valley; there's even a grove of sequoias, where you can enjoy the gigantic trees in much greater peace than you'll have at larger Mariposa Grove, near the park's south entrance. Coming from the west, Tioga Road rises up through towering pines and then breaks out on solid granite highlands dramatically furrowed by glaciers. Around Olmsted Point, the views become really dramatic—look at a cliff jutting up in the distance, and you'll realize that the ants scaling it are actually rock climbers. Yosemite is the most popular rock-climbing destination in the United States, thanks largely to the **Yosemite Mountaineering School** (📞 209/372-8344; www.yosemitemountaineering.com). The climbing school runs beginner classes daily out of its base in popular Curry Village, but in summer you can also take classes at Tuolumne Meadows. Kids

as young as 14 are accepted, and the instructors will soon have your teenagers inching up the granite walls to heights of 60 feet.

Even children who are too young to scale a sheer rock face can get a little climbing experience in Yosemite's high country. From Tuolumne Meadows Lodge, a 4.2-mile trail leads to the top of **Lembert Dome** (take a shuttle bus back to the lodge from the trail's other end). Another option is off of Glacier Point Road, south of the Yosemite Valley loop. You'll want to drive this road anyway to get to that great Glacier Point overlook, the top of a 3,200-foot vertical cliff. But stop partway along Glacier Point Road at mile 13.2, where a trail head leads 2.2 miles round-trip to **Sentinel Dome,** one of many granite domes in the park whose rounded shapes were formed by glaciers moving over them. It's 8,122 feet high, the second-highest viewpoint into the valley. **Taft Point** is the same distance the other way from the trail head; it has weird and scary cracks as well as cliff-overhang views. The hike itself isn't threatening, but hold hands near the end.

ⓘ Entrances on CA 41, CA 120, and CA 140 (📞 **209/372-0200;** www.nps.gov/yose).

✈ Fresno-Yosemite International, 90 miles.

🛏 $$$ **The Ahwanee,** Yosemite Valley (📞 **559/252-4848**). $ **Tuolumne Meadows Campground** (📞 **800/436-7275,** http://reservations.nps.gov).

WHY THEY'LL THANK YOU: Being on those peaks, not just looking at them.

Joshua Tree
Praying Trees in the California Desert
Ages 4 & up • Twentynine Palms, California, USA

IN THE WINTER, when it gets too cold in Yosemite, the rock climbers of California flock to this bizarre desert landscape near Palm Springs. If you think a desert is just one big sandbox, Joshua Tree's extremes will soon set you straight—part mountainous Mojave Desert, part cactus-studded Colorado Desert lowlands, this national park is a mixture of lush fan palm oases and trackless sand dunes. Come spring, the arid landscape puts on a surprising **wildflower display,** including pale yellow blooms on the twisted yucca for which the park is named. **Rock climbing** is a brilliant way to engage with the tortured rockscape of this fragile ecosystem.

Eight million years ago, this landscape was rolling grasslands where horses, camels, and mastodons grazed, preyed upon by saber-tooth cats and wild dogs. But then came years of climate change, volcanic eruption, savage floods, and shifting tectonic plates, and the land was wrenched into jagged cliffs, boulders, and tilting rock piles—sensational opportunities for climbers. The first climbing routes were laid out in the 1950s, and the sport really took off in the 1960s. Today Joshua Tree offers some 4,000 climbing routes, ranging from the easiest of bouldering to truly difficult climbs. November through May is the prime season. Beginners can learn the ropes, so to speak, at the **Joshua Tree Rock Climbing School** (✆ **800/ 890-4745;** www.rockclimbingschool.com). Bring loads of water with you—there are few places to buy it, and you can get dehydrated quickly in the desert.

If climbing's your focus, stay in the northwest part of the park, where

Rocks like melted candle wax in Joshua Tree National Park.

popular features include **Jumbo Rocks,** with its array of rock formations, Joshua tree forest, and yucca-dotted desert; **Wonderland of Rocks,** 12 square miles of massive jumbled granite; and mile-high **Keys View,** on the crest of the Little San Bernardino mountains. Climbers congregate in the Cap Rock area; even if you're not planning to climb, you can follow the short paved **Cap Rock Nature Trail** and test your footing on the rocks.

One thing I especially like about Joshua Tree is its many kid-friendly nature trails. From Jumbo Rocks, a 1½-mile trail leads to **Skull Rock,** one of many rocks in the area that eerily resemble humans, dinosaurs, or monsters—children get a kick out of spotting these. Near Hidden Valley, the **Barker Dam** trail visits a small lake tucked deep in the Wonderland of Rocks; kids can

scramble atop the old dam and hunt for Native American petroglyphs on the base of cliffs. Down Pinto Basin Road, the **Cholla Cactus Garden** trail leads you through dense clusters of the fluffy-looking "teddy bear cactus" with its deceptively barbed needles—look but don't touch!

(i) **Oasis Visitor Center** (📞 **760/367-5500;** www.nps.gov/jotr or www.joshuatree.org).

✈ Palm Springs, 40 miles.

🛏 $$ **Holiday Inn Express Hotel and Suites,** 71809 Twentynine Palms Hwy. (📞 **760/361-4009**). $$$ **29 Palms Inn,** 73950 Inn Ave. (📞 **760/367-3505;** www. 29palmsinn.com).

WHY THEY'LL THANK YOU: Scaling rocks like a lizard in the desert sun.

Hiking & Backpacking **395**

Climbing Ben Nevis
The Crown of the Highlands
Ages 10 & up • Near Fort William, Scotland

IN THE MIDDLE OF THE SCOTTISH HIGHLANDS, **Ben Nevis,** at 1,342m (4,403 ft.), is the tallest mountain in Britain. Even if you've tackled higher peaks, don't sell Ben Nevis short: The 16km (10 mile) climb is a difficult 8 hours to the summit even along the most popular route, a pony track. The final 300m (984 ft.) is really steep terrain, but having gone this far, few can resist the challenge of going all the way. The trail is much rougher but more scenic if you come up out of lovely Glen Nevis, with its clear rivers and cascading waterfalls, soft meadows and moorlands. The summit is flat and covered with loose stones, sloping off gently to the south, but a series of jagged rock precipices plunge down the northeast side, a challenge suitable for only the most expert rock climbers. Before going, check in with the staff at the **Fort William tourist office,** 6km (3¾ miles) northwest

of the mountain; they can give you advice as well as maps, and they'll pinpoint the best starting places. Note that the unpredictable Scottish weather adds to the challenge: Dress in layers and bring along a waterproof jacket (stout-soled shoes are essential). The mean monthly temperature of Ben Nevis falls below freezing; snow has been reported at all times of year, even during the hottest months of July and August. Howling winds are frequent.

Hikers head up expecting a panoramic view, but that same fickle weather means they're often disappointed—be prepared to appreciate the beauty of whatever you see up there, even if it's a dramatic cloak of swirling mist. If you're so lucky as to have clear weather, you can see the Irish foothills some 193km (120 miles) to the southwest, the Hebridean Isle of Rhum 148km (92 miles) to the west, the Glencoe peaks directly south, and the Cairngorm peaks to the east. If some members of your party vote against climbing, they can still get a pretty darn stunning view by taking the cable car to a panoramic viewing area about halfway up.

(i) **Fort William Tourist information Centre,** Cameron Square, Fort William ((C) **01397/703781**).

Fort William, 4 hr. from Glasgow.

$$ **Alexandra Milton Hotel,** The Parade, Fort William ((C) **01397/702241;** www.strathmorehotels.com).

WHY THEY'LL THANK YOU: An eagle's-eye view of the wild and wooly Highlands.

Mount Kilimanjaro
Africa's Great White Mountain
Ages 12 & up • Kilimanjaro National Park, Tanzania

IT'S AN UNFORGETTABLE SIGHT—the snowy plateau of Mount Kilimanjaro, rising above the Tanzanian plains, just south of Kenya. Named Oldoinyo Oibor, or "white mountain," by the Masai tribesmen and Kilima Njaro, "shining mountain," in Swahili, it's Africa's highest mountain and one of the world's largest free-standing peaks, a triple volcano thrusting out of equatorial jungle and moorland. As world-class peaks go, it's a relatively easy climb—the lower slopes are downright gentle—but you don't need to go all the way to the summit to get the Henmingway-esque thrill of exploring Kilimanjaro.

To ascend the mountain is to pass through radically different climate zones. Kilimanjaro National Park encompasses shouldering moorlands and the barren snowy summits, and the base of the mountain is surrounded by the lush, steamy Kilimanjaro Forest Reserve. Enter at the **Marangu Park Gate**—you should already have obtained park permits and hut reservations (available through a licensed tour operator or local hotels in Moshi), but at the park gate you'll hire a guide, and possibly a porter (you won't be allowed on the mountain without a guide). Park fees are substantial, but they include hut accommodation on the

mountain; guides and porters ask ridiculously low wages, hoping for generous tips on top. If you book with a tour operator (which I recommend), most of this, along with a cook to prepare all meals en route, will be included in your package.

It takes 5 to 7 days round-trip to reach the summit, staying in mountain huts all the way. With kids, though, you may be content to abbreviate this trek, going only partway up the well-traveled **Marangu Trail.** You'll spend your first night on the mountain in the wooden A-frame huts at Mandara, a 3- to 4-hour 12km (7½-mile) walk from the gate through misty, mossy rainforest. On your second day, hike across grassland to the gardenlike Maundi Crater; scramble up to the rim for panoramic views of the barren highlands towering above you. If you're not gung-ho mountaineers, head back down from here, or go on to Hotombo Hut that night and Kibo Hut the third night before turning around. Above 4,000m (13,000 ft.), the mountain suddenly becomes steeper and more barren, with rocky scree underfoot—it's not a technical climb, but it's a strenuous steep hike.

(i) www.tanzania-web.com.

✈ Kilimanjaro International, 56km (35 miles).

441

LODGING & TOUR OPERATORS: Kilimanjaro specialists include **Destination Africa Tours** www.climbingkilimanjaro.com); **Roy Safaris,** Arusha ((℃ **27/2502115;** www. roysafaris.com); and **Tanzania Serengeti**

Adventure, Arusha ((℃ **27/2544609;** www.habari.co.tz/tsa).

WHY THEY'LL THANK YOU: Towering above Africa.

Hiking & Backpacking · 397

Mount Fuji: Scaling the Symbol of Japan

Ages 8 & up • Fuji-Hakone-Izu National Park, Japan

THE JAPANESE CALL IT "FUJI-SAN," as if it were a dear old friend. It's not only the tallest mountain in Japan—an almost perfect cone 3,776m (12,388 ft.) high, its majestic peak usually swathed in clouds—it symbolizes the very spirit of their country. Today, about 600,000 people climb Fuji-san every year, mostly on July and August weekends. It's not like climbing Everest, a challenge for the expert mountaineer; you'll see everyone from grandmothers to children wending their way up those level slopes. It's the quintessential Japanese experience.

You don't need climbing experience to ascend Mount Fuji, just stamina and a good pair of walking shoes. Six well-established trails lead to the summit; another six lead back down. Each is divided into 10 stages, with the actual climb beginning around the fifth stage. From Tokyo, **Kawaguchiko Trail** is the least steep and easiest to get to. Take a shortcut directly to Kawaguchiko's Fifth Stage by **bus** from Shinjuku Station (be sure to book in advance); the trip takes about 2½ hours. From this starting point it's about a 6-hour climb to the summit, with another 3 hours to make the descent; at the top, a 1-hour hiking trail circles the crater.

The highlight of the classic Fuji climb is to watch the sunrise from the peak, which in summer means being there by 4:30am. There are three ways to accomplish this: Take a morning bus, start climbing in early afternoon, spend the night near the summit in a mountain hut, and get up in time to arrive at the peak at sunrise; or

alternatively, take in the sunrise from your hut—that still counts, honest!—and then climb to the top. Then there are the night climbers, who get off the bus at the Fifth Stage late in the evening and climb through the night using flashlights, timing it to hit the summit at sunrise. The mountain huts have futons for as many as 500 hikers each and serve simple Japanese meals (dried fish, rice, soup) if you aren't carrying your own grub; they're open July to August only and you must book early.

It may be disconcerting to get off the bus at the Fifth Stage and see a crush of souvenir shops, blaring loudspeakers, and tour bus hordes—hardly the atmosphere for a purifying ritual. But don't worry, most of those tourists aren't here for the climb. You'll soon find yourself on a steep rocky

Mount Fuji.

path, surrounded only by scrub brush and a few intent hikers below and above you. Settle into your stride, and after a couple hours you'll find yourself above the roily clouds—as if you are on an island, barren and rocky, in the middle of an ocean. Ah, there's your spiritual high.

ⓘ **Yumoto Tourist Office** (℗ **0460/5-8911**).

✈ Narita International, 48km (30 miles).

🛏 To book a hut, call the **Japanese Inn Union of Mount Fuji** (℗ **0555/22-1944**).

BEST TIME: Mid-July to Aug 31.

WHY THEY'LL THANK YOU: As the old Japanese saying goes, "Everyone should climb Mount Fuji once (only a fool would climb it twice)."

Walking the Appalachian Trail

Ages 8 & up • White Mountains, New Hampshire, USA

FOR THE ULTIMATE FAMILY BONDING adventure, nothing quite equals a hike along the Appalachian Trail. No, I'm not suggesting you do the whole rugged 2,100 miles of the Trail, which runs from Maine to Georgia. But you can conquer a segment of it, and one I'd recommend runs 56 miles through the White Mountain National Forest, where the nonprofit **Appalachian Mountain Club (AMC)** runs a unique network of eight huts, each a day's walk apart. Providing food and bedding, they let you travel light, reduced to backpacking essentials: some warm clothes, foul-weather gear, water, snacks. You'll be amid some of the most spectacular scenery in the East—no trash, trailers, or loud music (the curse of overcrowded national park campgrounds), just room for kids to explore the world with new friends, kicking dust, balancing on fallen trees, and learning that when it rains you can't always change the channel.

My personal favorite family hike is a 3-day excursion up **Mount Lafayette.** Begin on the Franconia Notch Parkway (Rte. 93), about 7½ miles north of Lincoln, New Hampshire, where you'll find the signpost for the Old Bridle Path trail head. It's a sometimes-steep 2.9-mile hike from the road to the Greenleaf Hut, just above timberline at 4,200 feet, a warm, friendly

place on Lafayette's west slope. When we last visited, the cook banged a pot with a heavy metal spoon at 6pm sharp, and we joined about 25 others—a lively mingling of singles, couples, and families—at long wooden tables for a very honest chicken-and-vegetable stew, with homemade bread and a mysterious pudding. After dinner, we sat on a rocky ledge and watched the evening mist flow through the valley below.

Next morning is your main hiking day: Climb 1.1 miles to the rocky, often windswept summit of Mount Lafayette. The payoff, on clear days, is the 1.7-mile

Greenleaf Hut in the White Mountains.

(1-hr.) walk from Lafayette along a narrow ridge, with the whole Franconia range stretched below you, to Little Haystack. Retrace your steps to the Greenleaf Hut for your second night. On the morning of the third day, return to your car, an easy 2-hour downhill hike.

Other AMC huts that are popular with families are at **Zealand Falls,** a 2.8-mile walk to a choice four-season spot near waterfalls, perfect for moose spotting; and the even more accessible **Lonesome** Lake Hut, a painless 1.7-mile hike to a lake. Guided hut-to-hut trips can also be arranged.

ⓘ ✆ **603/528-8721;** www.fs.fed.us/r9/forests/white_mountain.

✈ Logan Airport, Boston, MA.

🚌 Contact **Appalachian Mountain Club** (✆ **603/466-2727;** www.outdoors.org).

WHY THEY'LL THANK YOU: The joy of reaching the summit—together.

Hiking & Backpacking **399**

The Great Smoky Mountains
Backpacking in the Misty Forest
Ages 4 & up • Near Gatlinburg, Tennessee, USA

WILDERNESS IS ALL TOO RARE in the Eastern United States, so it's a blessing to find a huge protected swath of it—let alone a huge swath as gorgeous as Great Smoky Mountains National Park. Roughly 60 miles by 20 miles, Great Smoky is a thickly forested sweep of the southern Appalachians—the oldest mountains in the world—where you can hike through dense old-growth forest groves, past brightly flowering rhododendron, wildflower meadows, crystalline waterfalls, and chattering mountain streams. During all seasons, seeing the mist trailing poetically in the folds of the mountains, you'll suddenly get it—oh, so *that's* why they're called the Smokies.

Some 10 million people visit this park every year, 70% of them doing no more than driving **Newfound Gap Road,** a scenic 32-mile route that snakes across the back of the mountains from Cherokee, North Carolina, to Gatlinburg, Tennessee. Most of those who do get out of their cars take the same few short trail hikes, mostly to gape at waterfalls.

So it doesn't take much to escape the crowds and have the wilderness to yourselves. There's an astonishing variety of trees for kids to identify here (bring field guides), ranging from the lower elevations' hickories, yellow poplars, dogwood, and shaggy ancient hemlocks, to the midlevel beech and yellow birch forests, to the evergreens of the higher slopes, chiefly Fraser firs and red spruce. Come here in early October, of course, and the forests of Great Smoky blaze with fall color.

Hiking in the Smokies.

If your family has never tried backpacking, Great Smoky is an ideal place to start. There are about **100 backcountry campsites,** many of them quite close to each other, so you can plan short hikes from one to the next. The park's trails include many loops, so you can plan a trip that returns to your car without covering the same trail twice. It's rarely cold at night in summer (and even in the fall), and although climbing a mountain with a backpack on a hot summer day is sweaty work, you can usually stop and dunk yourself in a creek to cool off. In any season, expect rain and mist—that's what makes the Smokies smoky. Contact the **Great Smoky Mountains Association,** 115 Park Headquarters Rd., Gatlinburg,

TN 37738 (**℃ 865/436-0120;** www.smokiesstore.org), for trail maps to plan your route. Also check out the **Smoky Mountain Field School** (**℃ 865/974-0150;** www.outreach.utk.edu/smoky) for naturalist-led outdoor expeditions on summer weekends specifically designed for families.

ⓘ **Sugarlands Visitor Center,** U.S. 441 (**℃ 865/436-1291;** www.nps.gov/grsm).

✈ McGhee Tyson in Knoxville, 48 miles.

🛏 For permits and campsite reservations, call the park's **backcountry office** (**℃ 865/436-1231**).

WHY THEY'LL THANK YOU: A sleepover in the woods.

---

400 Hiking & Backpacking

Getting Past the Crowds in Yellowstone

All ages • Entrances at Gardiner & West Yellowstone Montana & Jackson & Cody Wyoming, USA

YELLOWSTONE NATIONAL PARK is one of the country's best places for families to go backpacking. Some beautiful campsites are just a couple miles off the road, and it only takes a walk of 20 minutes or so before you feel gloriously alone with the bison, elk, and other wildlife.

Every visitor to Yellowstone wants to see the park's signature attraction, the Old Faithful geyser, which erupts about every 90 minutes. You can drive to Old Faithful on the Lower Loop Road from the park's west entrance and join the crowds of tourists sitting on benches waiting for this baby to blow. Another popular drive-up sight is the limestone terraces of **Mammoth Hot Springs,** near the north entrance, where masses of bacteria and algae in the thermal water turn the rocks orange, pink, yellow, green, and brown. But these two sights only scratch the surface of Yellowstone's geothermal features. You'll have the geysers practically

to yourself if you head for the **Shoshone Geyser Basin,** which begins a mile west of Shoshone Lake (find a trail head for Delacey Creek Trail on the road 8 miles east of Old Faithful; it leads 3 miles to Shoshone Lake). The North Shoshone Trail passes 26 campsites as it winds through a lodgepole-pine forest. The **Bechler Meadows Trail** in the park's southwest corner is rich in waterfalls, cascades, and thermal areas. If its wildlife you're after, try the **Sportsman Lake Trail,** which passes through sagebrush plateaus full of elk and a meadow popular with moose.

Some great family trails for day hikes include these: at Mammoth, the 5-mile **Beaver Ponds Loop** from the hot springs at Liberty Cap (go in the evening or early morning to see the beavers); the 6-mile round-trip hike up **Mount Washburn,** an alpine trail leading to a 10,243-foot-high view over much of Yellowstone (watch for bighorn sheep); and the **Clear Lake trail** from the Wapiti Trailhead, which wanders through beautiful rolling meadows to a strange body of water fed by hot springs.

The backcountry season here is short—mid-June through the end of August, when the snow has finally melted off and streams drop to fordable levels. Contact the **Yellowstone Backcountry Office** (✆ **307/344-2160**); their *Backcountry Trip Planner* details the process for getting permits and includes a map pinpointing all campsites. In peak season, it's wise to make a reservation in advance.

ⓘ ✆ **307/344-7381;** www.nps.gov/yell

✈ West Yellowstone Airport, 2 miles. Yellowstone Regional Airport, Cody, WY, 52 miles.

🛏 $ **Madison Hotel,** 139 Yellowstone Ave., West Yellowstone (✆ **800/838-7745** or 406/646-7745). $$ **Mammoth Hot Springs Hotel** (✆ **307/344-7311;** www. travelyellowstone.com).

Yellowstone National Park.

WHY THEY'LL THANK YOU: Learning to tell an elk from a moose.

Bryce Canyon National Park
Doing the Hoodoo Voodoo
Ages 4 & up • Bryce Canyon, Utah, USA

EVEN PRESCHOOLERS enjoy Bryce Canyon National Park: They may be too young to absorb overwhelming panoramas like the Grand Canyon, but they completely get the point of Bryce's cliffs of weird colored stone and the crazy stone pillars known as hoodoos.

Most park visitors stick to driving the 18-mile-long park road north-to-south, tracing the course of the Pink Cliffs, but don't be content to merely drive by: Hop out and start walking. At the northern end, **Bryce Amphitheater** makes an impressive dent in the cliff, with four stunning overlooks—Sunset Point, Sunrise Point, Inspiration Point, and Bryce Point, where you can look down into the

amphitheater's hundreds of pink, red, orange, and brown hoodoos. The 5-mile **Rim Trail** connects the four overlooks, with a paved half-mile between Sunset and Sunrise points that's stroller accessible. It's a great after-dinner walk in summer, when you can watch the changing evening light on the rosy rocks below.

Even getting down into the canyon is totally doable for kids; there's a 3-mile loop combining the Navajo Loop (trail head at Sunset Point) with the Queen's Garden Trail (trail head at Sunrise Point). Along the **Navajo Loop,** with its dramatic series of graveled switchbacks, you'll pass Thor's Hammer (hard to imagine why it hasn't fallen), and ponder the towering

Bryce Canyon National Park.

skyscrapers of Wall Street. Turning onto the **Queen's Garden Trail,** you'll see some of the park's most fanciful formations, including majestic Queen Victoria, for whom the trail is named, plus the Queen's Castle and Gulliver's Castle. Farther south along the park drive, a short

loop trail from Rainbow Point, the park's highest point, leads to an 1,800-year-old bristlecone pine, believed to be the oldest living thing at Bryce Canyon.

If your kids are good hikers, when you return to the park's north end you may want to try the little-used 8-mile-long **Fairyland Loop Trail,** which descends 900 feet into a small canyon full of strange rock shapes. You'll meet a challenging ascent back to the top of the canyon to Sunrise Point, where you pick up a continuation of the Rim Trail, through a fragrant forest of pinyon and juniper back to Fairyland. Although really, in the end, all of Bryce Canyon is Fairyland.

ⓘ Route 63 south of Route 12 (✆ **435/ 834-5322;** www.nps.gov/brca).

✈ Cedar City, 87 miles.

🛏 $$ **Bryce Canyon Lodge,** Bryce Canyon rim (✆ **435/834-5361;** www.bryce canyonlodge.com). $ **North Campground,** across from visitor center (✆ **877/444-6777**).

WHY THEY'LL THANK YOU: Walking from one hoodoo to the next, they'll never notice how far they're hiking.

Dune Walking in the Sahara

Ages 6 & up • Ksar Ghilane, Tunisia

SOME 4.5 MILLION EUROPEANS, mostly French, vacation each year in Tunisia, offering their oiled bodies to the sun on the powdery white sands of Djerba. This sybaritic North African island has some of the most spectacular beaches in the world—but it's a pity that few tourists bother to travel on to the fantastic desert landscapes to the south. They're missing the thrill of setting foot on the waving dunes of the Sahara, crossing the shifting sands to an abandoned fort. And for kids, there's even a movie tie-in: exploring a town where *Star Wars Episode IV* was filmed.

Granted, it's a long, thankless drive—3½ hours from Djerba to **Ksar Ghilane,** an oasis at the very edge of the Grand Erg Oriental, one of the Sahara's two great sand seas, and it's best to hire a driver so you don't lose your way on these deceptive desert tracks. But when you arrive, the kids will immediately get the concept of an oasis: Rising up out of the desert, a hot spring here feeds a swimming hole and a greenness of tamarisk trees. As befits the desert, you'll stay in **tents,** although quite luxurious tents, air-conditioned and with private bathroom—it certainly beats a

Luxury tents in Ksar Ghilane.

Motel 6. The highlight of your stay in the oasis is a 2km (1.2-mile) walk through the shifting dunes, as smooth and clean as a toddler's cheek, following a trail of camel turds to an **abandoned fort** worthy of Lawrence of Arabia. Kids will understand the importance of turbans here, which they'll need to wear against the blowing sands. (If they're young, you can arrange for an all-terrain vehicle to meet you and drive you back; doing the trek on a camel is a more exotic option.)

Tour packages often combine the Ksar Ghilane expedition with a trip around the amazing **Ksour district** to the east. "Ksour" is the plural for "ksar," a traditional mud-and-stone structure built by the ancient Berber people—communal granaries, where every family in a village had its own chamber for storing grain. In later times, the villages adapted these granaries, turning them into forts against foreign invaders. Most of these ksour are crumbling and abandoned, haunting relics left in the desert when their inhabitants moved to modern towns with electricity and water mains. You can visit

several ksours in the course of a day's desert drive: The best preserved is **Ksar Ouled Soltane,** four stories high; **Guermessa** is another spectacular Berber site, virtually undiscovered by tourists.

For your ksours circuit, do as the tour operators do and base yourselves in the modern town of **Tataouine,** which has the best travel amenities. (It's no coincidence that the name was borrowed by George Lucas for an entire planet in *Star Wars,* for the nearby village of **Ksar Haddada** will be instantly familiar to the kids as the setting for Luke Skywalker's hometown in the original *Star Wars* movie.)

ⓘ TunisUSA (ⓒ **800/474-5500;** www.tunisUSA.com).

✈ Djerba, 3½ hr.

🛏 $$ **Pansea Ksar Ghilane,** Ksar Ghilane (ⓒ **2165/900521;** www.pansea. com). $ **Sangho,** 3km (1¾ miles) west of Tataouine (ⓒ **33/42-97-14-00;** www. sangho.fr/tunisie/sejours/3).

WHY THEY'LL THANK YOU: Strolling through the vast golden Sahara.

Landmannalaugar: World of Fire & Ice
Ages 8 & up • Iceland

TRAVELING AROUND the central highlands of Iceland is a trip to a world that is still being created—a world of shapes and colors most kids have only seen in dreams. The earth steams and bubbles; conical volcanoes rise like islands in a sea of black sand. Twisted lava, cracked and cooled in a thousand grotesque shapes, seems to have eyes that follow you wherever you go. It's a landscape so lunar, NASA astronauts trained here in preparation for landing on the moon. And of the many awesome spots in Iceland's unearthly interior, none is more spectacular than the geothermal hotbed of Landmannalaugar.

One-day bus trips come out from Reykjavik in summer to the hot springs at Landmannalaugar, quickie excursions that leave time for nothing but a look around and a brief dip in the bathtub-warm natural thermal pools, sunk into a boggy lowland. (Bring bathing suits, but you'll find Americans are the only ones who bother to wear them.) Yet one look at the nearby mountains, undulating like folds of silk and tinted with rare mineral colors—blues, yellows, bright reds, even shocking pink—will make the kids itch for more time to explore them. So spend a night or two at one of the mountain huts here, run by the **Iceland Touring Association,** Ferdafélag Islands (✆ **568 2533;** www.nat.is/

fjallaskalareng/skalar_fi_eng.htm) to give yourselves time to hike into those bewitching mountains along the marked trails of the surrounding Fjallabak Nature Reserve. The huts are usually booked up in July and August, so reserve in advance, or arrange to sleep in a tent. Horseback riding is also available from a stable at the site.

If you're ambitious, the premier walk in Iceland is the 3- to 4-day hike from Landmannalaugar to Thórsmörk, through a stark terrain of snow, ice, and rock, sleeping in a series of mountain huts along the way. Any decently fit person 12 years old or older should be able to backpack for the full route, either independently or in a group led by a guide. At the far end of the hike, **Thórsmörk** is another designated nature reserve, a somewhat softer landscape with woods and grass nestling among mountains and glaciers. If you make it all the way to Thórsmörk, you can take a bus back to Reykjavik.

ⓘ **Icelandic Tourist Board** (✆ **212/885-9700** in the U.S.; www.visiticeland.com).

✈ Reykjavík, 4½ hr.

🛏 Ferdafélag Islands (✆ **354/568 2533;** www.fi.is).

WHY THEY'LL THANK YOU: Like walking on the moon.

Traipsing through the English Cotswolds
Ages 4 & up (Ramble), 10 & up (Cotswold Way) • England

KNOWN FOR ITS PICTURESQUE villages of golden-stone cottages, England's charming Cotswolds hills are popular with motorists keen on gardens and antiques.

But the best way to explore this rolling countryside is on foot, following a meandering 167km (104-mile) path called the **Cotswold Way** (www.nationaltrail.co.uk)

that cuts across farms, streams, cottage backyards, and swaths of forest. The payoff is spectacular panoramas and a time-warp sense of being back in medieval England.

The path stretches from Chipping Campden, at the northern edge of the Cotswolds, to Bath, and is easy to follow thanks to bright yellow signs at every intersection. The southbound route (Chipping Campden to Bath) involves slightly less uphill climbing and is less well traveled, so you won't find yourself in pedestrian "traffic jams." Regardless of the direction you follow, it's a significant undertaking to do the whole route: Tourist officials in Chipping Campden report that most participants take between 7 and 8 days to walk the entire path, often emerging blistered, sunburned, rain-drenched, and exhausted. (Of course, with kids you may opt to do only a section of the route.) Bring a raincoat and sturdy shoes.

Most of the route avoids traffic arteries completely, guiding you through **forests and fields** and along rocky escarpments where views sweep out over medieval wool villages. At least a dozen **historic towns** en route can be visited via short detours. Every tourist office in the Cotswolds carries the Ordnance Maps and specialized walking tour guides you'll need to locate the Cotswold Way, and local souvenir shops eagerly provide

mementos like Cotswold Way T-shirts and an official-looking certificate announcing the direction you've walked the path.

For less intrepid hikers, another option is the **Great Cotswold Ramble,** a 4km (2½-mile) mostly paved walk from the car park in Upper Slaughter to the village green at Bourton-on-the-Water, along the course of the River Eye. (Once you're at Bourton, you'll find several kid-friendly attractions—a motor museum, model railway exhibit, model village, and birds-only zoo called **Birdland.**) Follow signs for the Warden's Way; from Lower Slaughter on south, the Warden's Way follows the route of the Fosse Way, an ancient Roman footpath.

ⓘ **The Ramblers' Association,** Camelford House, 87–90 Albert Embankment, London, SE1 7TW (☎ **020/7339-8500;** www. ramblers.org.uk). **Cotswold Voluntary Wardens Service,** Shire Hall, Gloucester (☎ **01451/862000**).

🚇 Moreton-in-Marsh, 2 hr. from London. Cheltenham, 2¼ hr. from London.

🛏 $$$ **Calcot Manor,** Calcot, 6km (3¾ miles) west of Tetbury (☎ **800/987-7433** in the U.S., or 01666/890391; www.calcotmanor.co.uk). $$ **Chester House Hotel,** Victoria St., Bourton-on-the-Water (☎ **01451/820286**).

WHY THEY'LL THANK YOU: Getting inside the postcard views.

Snowdonia National Park
Rambling the Rugged Welsh Mountains
All ages • North Wales

MOUNTAIN PEAKS AND STEEP WOODED SLOPES, spectacular estuaries and rugged cliffs brooding over secluded coves, valleys with tiny towns looking as if they were carved out of granite—all these join to

make up Snowdonia National Park, which sprawls across much of north Wales.

The park takes its name from **Snowdon,** at 1,085m (3,560 ft.) the highest peak in Wales and England; Sir Edmund Hilary trained here before he climbed

Mt. Everest. Many visitors to the park set themselves the task of climbing Snowdon, which takes about 5 hours up and back. The view from the top is spectacular, but it's also possible to get to that spectacular view by taking the **cog railway** to the summit (see **32**). And since the park also encloses lakes, moorlands, river rapids, sprawling estuaries, farms, and charming towns, many families find it more rewarding to enjoy the park by hiking, cycling, and pony trekking. Along its trails you may encounter wild ponies and free-ranging sheep, who don't seem surprised at all to meet hikers. The walking surface is a funny combination of springy turf and gravelly scree, so watch your footing.

Set in the lush Gwydyr Forest along a tumbling river, **Betws-y-Coed** (pronounced Bet-us-ee-Coyd) is almost unbearably picturesque, with eight bridges spanning the river along the short main street. One of the most popular walks here is a steep 4km (2.5-mile) route starting in town from behind St. Mary's church and going up to a small mountain lake, Llyn Elsi, passing en route the breathtaking Swallow Falls, a series of waterfalls robed in swirling mist.

Dolgellau is another good base; a couple of interesting short walks here are the 3km (1¾-mile) Torrent Walk along a dramatic ravine, or the 6.4km (4-mile) Precipice Walk around the flanks of Moel Cynwch. The **Mawddach Valley Nature Reserve,** 3km (1¾ miles) west of town, is a superb place for bird-watching and has a couple of short trails; here you can also pick up the last 12km (7.5 miles) of the Mawddach Trail along the spreading waters and wetlands of the Mawddach river's estuary, walking over a high railway bridge and ending up at the coast in Barmouth. North of Dolgellau, **Coed Y Brenin Forest Park** (✆ 01341-422289) has miles of cycling trails, including some designed for families.

ⓘ **Snowdonia** (✆ **01766/770274;** www. eryri-npa.co.uk). **Betws-y-Coed Tourist Office,** Holyhead Rd. (✆ **01690/710426**).

🚆 Betws-y-Coed, 3½ hr. from London.

🛏 **Ty Gwyn,** along the A5, Betws-y-Coed (✆ **01690/710383**).

WHY THEY'LL THANK YOU: The ponies, birds, and sheep en route.

Snowdonia National Park.

Grindelwald
Glacier Hiking through the Swiss Alps
Ages 8 & up • Switzerland

IT'S ONE THING TO HIKE through a valley sculpted by long-ago glaciers, quite another to hike where the glaciers are still carving their way between peaks, a colossal river of slow-moving ancient ice. But that's just what you'll see in the Swiss Alps at Grindelwald, a popular winter and summer resort town surrounded by chalet-studded hamlets, sparkling streams, and alpine meadows. Even relatively short and easy hikes from Grindelwald will get you and the kids up on those mighty glaciers.

A guided 1-day hiking tour organized by the **Bergsteigerzentrum** (✆ **033/853-52-00**) begins with a scenic mountain train ride from Grindelwald to Eigergletscher (*gletscher* is the German word for "glacier"). A local mountain guide leads you to Bergsteigerzentrum Grindelwald's husky-breeding center (always a hit with kids), then along the foot of the north wall of Mount Eiger. You'll end up in Alpiglen for lunch and then take a train back to Grindelwald.

Another hike, which takes only half a day, goes from Grindelwald along the Milchbach, a river so named because melting glacial ice runs off in a stream that's milk-colored from all the gravel sediment it's carrying. It's an hour's easy climb from Grindelwald to the base of the Upper Grindelwald Glacier; another 45 minutes' walk goes up 850 steps above the Milchbach to the nose of the glacier, where the kids may want to visit the **Blue Ice Grotto,** a chamber carved out of ice. There are some dramatic walking trails from here, leading right along the edge of the glacier. Catch a postal bus back down from the grotto to Grindelwald.

Hikes can only go so far, though; cap off your glacier touring with a trip on the rack-and-pinion railway to Kleine Scheidegg, where you switch to the **Jungfraubahn,** the highest rack railway in Europe. This train climbs up 9.6km (6 miles), mostly

through a tunnel carved in the mountain (at the Eismeer stop, view the sea of ice from windows in the rock), to the Jungfraujoch terminus. Take a few minutes to adjust to the altitude, then board the elevator behind the post office up to the **Eispalast** (Ice Palace), which makes the Blue Ice Grotto look distinctly second-rate: This series of chambers was carved 20m (65 ft.) below the glacier's surface, with everything inside sculpted out of ice, including full-size replicas of vintage cars and likenesses of local chaplains.

ⓘ **Tourist office,** at the Sportszentrum on Hauptstrasse (✆ **033/854-12-12;** www.grindelwald.com).

🚈 Interlaken, 2 hr. from Zurich, 40 minutes from Bern.

🛏 $$$ **Grand Hotel Regina,** Grindelwald (✆ **800/223-6800** or 033/854-86-00; www.grandregina.ch). $$ **Romantik Hotel Schweizerhof,** Grindelwald (✆ **033/853-22-02;** www.hotelschweizerhof.com).

WHY THEY'LL THANK YOU: Seeing just how massive this river of ice truly is.

Jungfraubahn.

Wunderhiking in the Black Forest

Ages 6 & up • Triberg, Germany

ONE OF THE RICHEST TIMBERLANDS in the world lies in southwestern Germany, where the mountains are thickly planted with conifers, their arrow-straight trunks so close together that sunlight barely penetrates to the woodland floor. This is the famous Black Forest, home of traditional woodcarving, cuckoo clocks, and dense chocolate cake, and its fairy-tale atmosphere is irresistible. You can sample its beauty by driving the 144km (89-mile) scenic **Schwarzwald Hochstrasse** (Black Forest High Rd., Rte. B500) north–south from the fashionable 19th-century spa of Baden-Baden to Waldshut on the Rhine. But hiking is the best way to explore its forested heart. On a village-to-village walk, you pass through sunny panoramic pastures and deep, fragrant pine woods, where you almost expect Bambi and Thumper to spring out of the next glade.

Clearly marked signs guide you across this easy trail, which starts at Triberg, traditionally the birthplace of the cuckoo clock. A series of hotels, beginning with the **Parkhotel Wehrle** (see below), have coordinated to map out a route and convey your luggage for you, so you can hike with only a small rucksack. You can hike from 1 or 2 to 10 days, even more if you have the time. Distances between hotels range from 20 to 27km (12–17 miles), and restaurants and farmhouses offer food and refreshment en route.

If you only want a day hike, climb up to the highest waterfall in Germany, **Wasserfelle Gutach,** just outside of Triberg. This lovely cascade drops some 160m (525 ft.), spilling downhill in seven misty and poetically evocative stages. They're only accessible on foot, and only from April through November. Park your car in designated lots in the town center, near the Gutach Bridge, then follow a signposted trail that, round-trip, requires about an hour of moderately difficult hill climbing. Even if you don't make it to the top, there are some very satisfying waterfall vistas partway up.

Triberg can be crowded and touristy, another good reason to get out and hike instead of wandering around town. Being in cuckoo-clock country, however, it may be hard to resist three Triberg-area attractions that promote this trade as well as related crafts like woodcarving and music boxes: the **Schwarzwald-Museum of Triberg,** Wallfahrtstrasse 4 (*C* **07722/ 4434**); the world's largest cuckoo clock at the shop **Haus der 1000 Uhren** (House of 1,000 Clocks), up the B33 on the road to Hornberg at An der Bundesstrasse 33 (*C* **07722/96300;** www.hausder1000 uhren.de; open Easter to Oct); and the **Deutsches Uhrenmuseum** (German Clock Museum), 10 miles south on B500 at Gerwigstrasse 11, Furtwangen (*C* **07723/920117**).

ⓘ **Tourist information,** Hauptstrasse 57 (*C* **07722/9530;** www.triberg.de).

🚌 Triberg, 4½ hr. from Munich, 3 hr. from Frankfurt.

🛏 $$$ **Romantik Parkhotel Wehrle,** Gartenstrasse 24 (*C* **07722/86020;** www.parkhotel-wehrle.de).

WHY THEY'LL THANK YOU: Hearing a cuckoo in the woods.

Bicycling on Nantucket

All ages • Nantucket, Massachusetts, USA

BRINGING A CAR TO NANTUCKET, the tiny Massachusetts island 30 miles off Cape Cod, can be an incredible hassle in summer—there are only six pokey car ferries per day from Hyannis, and they book up months in advance. Day visitors generally choose to come on foot (which frees you to opt for a high-speed ferry), but then they don't explore any further than tourist-mobbed Nantucket Town. Your solution? Rent bikes. Flat, sandy Nantucket is heaven for beginning bicyclists, with paved paths leading all over. Bring helmets with you (they're required for children under 12) or rent them along with bikes in Nantucket Town at shops right by the wharf. Nothing could be easier, or more fun.

Here's the lay of the land: Three major bike routes radiate out from Nantucket Town, one heading west to Madaket, 6¼ miles, one south to Surfside 3½ miles, and the longest one a 17-mile loop out to Siasconset Beach ('Sconset to locals) and Sankaty Head lighthouse. It's classic beachy terrain, with few trees, wide skies, and swaths of tall dune grass on both sides. The pedaling is easy, and the island's small scale makes you feel you're really getting somewhere, especially when you hit the bluffs and get that Atlantic panorama. Picnic benches and water fountains are conveniently provided at strategic points along all the paths, which you'll appreciate if you're towing really young ones in a bike trailer.

Madaket is picturesque, especially at sunset, but has strong surf; with kids, you're better off turning right on Eel Point Road and swimming at gentler Dionis Beach. Popular **Surfside** beach is your best bet with young children, not only because the ride is shorter but because there's a snack bar. My favorite, though, is the ride to **'Sconset**, even though it is the

most demanding, longer and with a few hills. 'Sconset is rarely, if ever, crowded, perhaps because of the water's strong sideways tow. Lifeguards are usually on duty, but the closest facilities (restrooms, grocery store, and cafe) are back in the center of the village, which is lovely and worth a stop anyway. From 'Sconset, head north along the coastal path on Polpis Road, stopping off to snap Nantucket photos in front of the classic lighthouse at Sankaty Head. If you've planned ahead, though, you've booked an unforgettable naturalist-led tour (offered June–Oct) of the barrier beaches with the **Coskata-Coatue Wildlife Refuge** (✆ **508/228-6799**; reservation required); detour up Wauwinet Road to the Wauwinet Inn to meet the tour. By the time you pedal back into Nantucket Town and get back on the ferry, you'll have spent a day in the sun you won't soon forget.

ⓘ **Nantucket Visitor Services,** 25 Federal St. (✆ **508/228-0925**; www.nantucket-ma.gov).

✈ ⇒ See Stargazing on Nantucket **307**.

WHY THEY'LL THANK YOU: A first taste of bike touring that'll leave them wanting more.

Some of Nantucket's bicycle paths run along the water.

New River Gorge
Mountain Biking the Canyon
Ages 8 & up • Fayetteville, West Virginia, USA

WHILE MANY VISITORS come to West Virginia's New River Gorge to shoot the white-water rapids or to climb the hard sandstone cliffs, I much prefer to enjoy this national parkland on the seat of a mountain bike. There are 20 miles of shady mountain bike trails laid out, none too strenuous for competent younger riders, and as you pedal along you'll discover the region's coal-mining history. From 1873 through the 1930s, this southern West Virginia area wasn't the idyllic wilderness you see today—it was King Coal country, laced with railroads and pocked with mining operations. My ancestors worked in the West Virginia coal fields, so I feel a personal connection to this steep-sided river gorge, where vestiges of the industrial past lie half-hidden beneath beautiful new-growth forests.

The easiest trail is the 3-mile **Thurmond to Minden trail,** a flat pedal along an abandoned branch line of the C & O Railroad. You'll rattle across five trestle bridges and can stop at several scenic overlooks with panoramas of the New River and Thurmond Depot. The Thurmond Depot visitor center is well worth a look, with historic furnishings showing its railroading past. Another short route, although more demanding, is the rugged 3.5-mile **Stone Cliff trail,** which climbs up to an abandoned homestead. The 6-mile **Cunard-Kaymoor Trail** visits an abandoned coal mine site, while the bumpy-though-level 6-mile **Brooklyn to Southside Junction trail** winds along another former rail bed, past a handful of old coke ovens and derelict mining towns, so close to the river that you may hear the screams of rafters hitting the Surprise rapids. (Trail distances are all one-way; you can pick up detailed trail instructions at any of the recreation area's four visitor centers.) You're never far from the river on any of these trails—the entire park is a long narrow swath of green snaking along 53 miles of the river's twisting course.

Long after the last coal mines had shut down, travel through the area was radically simplified with the building of the **New River Gorge Bridge** in 1977. The world's second-longest single-arch bridge, it crosses the river just north of Fayetteville along U.S. 19, carrying traffic 876 feet above the river. Views from the bridge are breathtaking any time of year, but come here on **Bridge Day**—the third Saturday every October—and you'll witness a carnival atmosphere as hundreds of base jumpers take their turns plunging into the gorge, against a spectacular backdrop of fall color.

ⓘ Off U.S. 19 (✆ **304/574-2115;** www. nps.gov/neri).

✈ Beckley, WV, 20 miles.

🛏 $$ **Country Inn & Suites,** 2120 Harper Rd., Beckley (✆ **800/456-4000** or 304/252-5100; www.countryinns.com).

WHY THEY'LL THANK YOU: Seeing how quickly nature reclaims land.

Cycling **410**

Mackinac Island: Not a Car in Sight

All ages • Straits of Mackinac, Michigan, USA

YOU PRONOUNCE IT "MACK-I-NAW," like the raincoat (the mainland town where the ferries operate from is spelled Mackinaw City, just so out-of-towners get it straight). Cropping out of the Straits of Mackinac, which separate the Upper and Lower peninsulas of Michigan at their closest point, this summer resort island is a Victorian period piece of white frame houses and trim gardens. The only way to reach it is by private plane or ferry; and since you can't bring a car you have three options for getting around the island: on foot, by horse-drawn carriage, and on a bike. Pedaling happily along the limestone cliffs overlooking the straits, you may wonder why the automobile was ever invented.

A complete circuit of the island on traffic-free **Lake Shore Road** only takes 8 miles, doable even with fairly young riders (rental bikes in town also offer child seats and trailers if that's a better option for you). You'll have to stop along the way, of course, to drink in the views—don't miss Arch Rock on the east coast, a boulder pierced with a gaping 30- by 40-foot hole gouged by waves and glaciers, or Sunset Rock on the west bluff above town. Most of the island is covered by **Mackinac Island State Park** (© 906/847-3328), with 70 miles of paved roads and trails where cyclists can explore the cedar- and birch-forested interior. Above the town, you can also cycle up to **Fort Mackinac** (© 906/436-4100; www.mackinacparks. com), built by British soldiers during the American Revolution to defend the link

between Lakes Michigan and Huron, vital to the lucrative fur trade. Fourteen buildings, mostly from the 1880s, are still intact, and costumed interpreters do military reenactments; shoot off rifles and cannons; lead children's games; and perform bugle, fife-and-drum, and bagpipe music. The cliff-top site was chosen specifically for sentries to watch over the lakes, so you can just imagine how fantastic the views are.

Of course, if you'd rather take in the scenery from a rocking chair, you can always plunk yourself down on the white colonnaded veranda—the world's longest front porch—of the landmark **Grand Hotel** (© 906/847-3331), built in 1887. Even if you're not staying here, you can tour the historic hotel. In the center of town, a few neat low white buildings recall the days of the early-18th-century fur traders, along with a bark chapel built by the original Huron natives.

ⓘ **Mackinac Island Chamber of Commerce** (© 800/454-5227; www.mackinac island.org).

✈ Mackinaw City, 12 miles from ferry docks.

🛏 $$$ **Grand Hotel,** West Bluff Rd. (© 800/33-GRAND; www.grandhotel.com). $$ **Mission Point,** Lake Shore Rd. (© 800/ 833-7711 (reservations only) or 906/847-3312; www.missionpoint.com).

WHY THEY'LL THANK YOU: Overtaking a carriage, your bikes will be the fastest things on the road.

Montréal: Riding Les Pistes Cyclables
Ages 8 & up • Montréal, Québec, Canada

LONG COUNTRY BIKE RIDES attract the Lance Armstrongs among us, but younger riders quickly get bored—they need something to look at as they cycle. Well, they won't get bored bicycling around Montréal—according to *Bicycling Magazine*, it's the number-one bicycling city in North America, with 349km (217 miles) of urban bike paths, or as they say in French-speaking Montréal, *pistes cyclables*.

One of the city's main tourist magnets, the restored harborfront **Vieux-Port** area, has bike paths running along its 2km (1¼-mile) promenade—the kids may beg you to rent one of those four-wheeled Q-cycles they'll see trundling along, a welcome option for families with toddlers. At the eastern end of the port, park your bikes to visit the 1922 clock tower, Le Tour de l'Horloge, with 192 steps climbing past exposed clockwork gears to three observation decks.

Perhaps the city's most popular bike route is the flat 11km (6¾-mile) path to Lac St-Louis along the spruced-up **Lachine Canal,** which begins just west of the Vieux-Port. Stop en route at the open-air **Atwater Market,** 3025 St-Ambroise to pick up freshly baked bread, gourmet cheese, and fruit for a picnic along the canal. Montréal is named after the towering hill in the middle of **Parc Mont-Royal**—start from the top and you'll coast 4km (2½ miles) downhill through woods and grassy expanses. A more ambitious route goes west 16km (10 miles) from the **St-Lambert Lock** to the suburb of Côte Ste-Catherine.

Montréal taxis have bike racks, and the superclean and efficient Métro system will let you take bikes on its subway trains (enter the last car); so it's easy to zip out from downtown to various start points. Take your bikes on the Métro west to Angrigon station to pedal around the 6.4km (4-mile) bike circuit in **Angrigon Park.** Go east to Pie-IX station to ride around the lushly landscaped **Botanic Garden** before you visit the **Biodôme de Montréal,** 4777 av. Pierre-de-Coubertin. The Biodôme is a one-of-a-kind attraction that kids love for its weirdness: four distinct ecosystems—a Laurentian mountain forest, the St. Lawrence marine system, a tropical rainforest, and a polar environment—re-created in almost obsessive detail in one vast structure, which was originally built for the 1976 Olympics as—fittingly enough—a velodrome for bike races.

To rent bikes, check out **CaRoule** in the Vieux-Port, 27 rue de la Commune est (✆ **514/866-0633**), or **Vélo Montréal** near the Botanic Garden, 3880 rue Rachel est (✆ **514/2599-7272;** www.velo montreal.com). At 1251 Rachel St., the headquarters of **Vélo Québec** has a cycling boutique and the **Bicicletta Café,** modeled after Italian bicyclists' cafes.

ⓘ **Vélo Québec,** 1251 Rachel St. (✆ **514/521-8356;** www.velo.qc.ca).

✈ ⊨ See Montréal ㉒.

WHY THEY'LL THANK YOU: Like your own Tour de France.

Cycling the Rim Road: Crater Lake

Ages 8 & up • Crater Lake, Oregon, USA

THE STORY BEGINS with a volcanic explosion so fearsome—scientists estimate it was 42 times as powerful as Mount St. Helens—that it left behind a phenomenally deep crater, which in time filled with water to become America's deepest lake. But this version of events doesn't prepare you for the sight of Crater Lake, for the intense sapphire blue of its cold spring-fed waters reflecting the sheer forested cliffs that encircle it. It's simply breathtaking, a panorama of supreme serenity that belies its violent origins. It takes about 2 hours to drive around Crater Lake—which, unfortunately, is all most park visitors do, rolling along the asphalt, narcotized by the pretty scenery. Trade in those four wheels for two, though, and you'll really feel the transforming power of this volcanic landscape.

The 33-mile **Rim Drive,** open only in summer, has 30 overlooks where you can gaze at these pristine waters cupped in their rocky chalice. Travel clockwise, wear bright clothing so motorists can spot you, and if possible sleep in the park the night before so you can hit the narrow road early before the traffic gets heavy (as it inevitably will). The Rim Drive may look like an easy pedal, but don't underestimate it—it can be demanding, especially on the east side of the lake, where there are more hills (hills you'd scarcely notice if you were just driving). On the other hand, the east side of the lake has more panoramic views, providing good excuses to catch your breath. The **Cloudcap Overlook** is 2,000 feet high, with vistas that stretch as

far as Mount Shasta. Another cool turnoff overlooks the **Phantom Ship,** a jagged basalt formation jutting up out of the lake.

An alternative ride goes from the Rim Village visitor center north to the **Cleetwood Cove Trailhead** and back, 21 miles total, on the flatter west rim. Cleetwood Cove is the sole trail that goes down to the lake's edge; it may only be 2.2 miles round-trip, but the way back is strenuous, like climbing 65 flights of stairs. My advice: Save your strength for the cycling.

No matter which of the park's entrances you come in, you'll drive a few miles to get to the Rim Drive, where you can park your car and get the bikes off your rack. If you've got more than one driver in your party, consider taking turns driving the car to meet the cyclists at each overlook—it'll give the kids the option of pooping out if necessary. (Blame it on the high altitude.) There are no bike rentals in the park, but you can rent them at **Diamond Lake Resort,** 5 miles from the park's north entrance on State Road 138.

ⓘ Along OR 62 (ⓒ **541/594-3000;** www.nps.gov/crla).

✈ Rogue Valley International, Medford, OR, 71 miles.

🛏 $$$ **Crater Lake Lodge,** Rim Rd. (ⓒ **541/830-8700;** www.craterlakelodges.com). $ **Mazama Village Campground,** in the park off OR 62, no reservations.

BEST TIME: Late June to Sept.

WHY THEY'LL THANK YOU: Discovering how rugged this pretty place really is.

413 Cycling

Circling Arran Island on a Bike

Ages 10 & up • Isle of Arran, Scotland

AT THE MOUTH OF THE FIRTH OF CLYDE, the Isle of Arran is often described as "Scotland in miniature" because of its varied scenery. The coast road circles the island in a 97km (60-mile) circuit, which could be done in 1 day if you're ambitious. Break up a 2-day ride with a stay overnight on the west coast. Several intriguing stops en route (many associated with the 14th-century hero Robert the Bruce) will keep kids distracted enough to forget their aching calves.

The ferry docks at Brodick, where you can pick up a picnic lunch in the shops, then rent a bicycle at **Mr. Bilsland** (✆ **01770/302-272**) or **Brodick Cycles** (✆ **01770/302-460**). Heading clockwise around the island (go south from Brodick), you'll come to **Lamlash,** a beachy sea resort, then **King's Cross Point,** where Robert the Bruce is said to have sailed for the mainland after hiding out on Arran for months. The road climbs to **Dippin Head,** and the southern curve of the island's coast is high over the sea with great views of tiny islands and the Ailsa Crag lighthouse. The road goes downhill toward **Sliddery,** where an overgrown mound marks the site of an old Norse keep. At **Tormore,** north of Blackwaterfoot, you can detour a mile inland to visit some standing stones. **Drumadoon Point** on the west coast has basalt columns and the remains of an old fort, and **King's Hill** has caves where Robert the Bruce hid out from his enemies for months.

At the northern end of the island, the scenery turns ever more romantic and Highlands-like, with rugged mountains towering over narrow green glens. Castle ruins at **Lochranza** were reputedly the hunting seat of Robert the Bruce. Back on the east cost, you'll pass dramatic **Glen Sannox** and the **Fallen Rocks,** huge sandstone boulders that have tumbled off the cliffs. On your right looms the island's highest mountain, **Goat Fell** ("mountain of the winds") with its 874m-high (2,867 ft.) conical peak. At its foot are Arran's two major sights—the **Isle of Arran Heritage Museum,** a series of restored buildings tracing life on Arran from prehistoric times to the present, and the red sandstone **Brodick Castle,** ancestral home of the dukes of Hamilton. The castle has fine furnishings inside, but the real attraction is its gardens, which feature plants from such far-flung habitats as Tasmania, Chile, and the Himalayas. The rhododendrons are amazing. Cycle back into Brodick, where you can return your bike and catch the ferry back to Ardrossan.

ⓘ **Arran Island Tourist Office,** The Pier, Brodick (✆ **01770/302-140;** www.ayrshire-arran.com).

🚌 Ardrossan Harbour, 1 hr. from Glasgow, 30-min. ferry to island.

🛏 $$$ **Auchrannie Country House Hotel,** Auchrannie Rd., Brodick (✆ **01770/302-234;** www.auchrannie.co.uk). $$ **Kinloch Hotel,** Blackwaterfoot (✆ **01770/860444;** www.bw-kinlochhotel.co.uk).

WHY THEY'LL THANK YOU: Sparkling sea on your left, stunning scenery on your right.

Arran Island.

Holland's Haarlem: Traversing the Polders

Ages 8 & up • The Netherlands

ONE THING EVERY SCHOOL KID learns about the Netherlands: It's the land of dikes, those walls against the sea that the thrifty Dutch built to turn their flood-prone coastal lowlands into arable farmland. Miles and miles of reclaimed polder land stretch along the North Sea coast west of Amsterdam—no rolling hills, no dramatic seaside cliffs, just a low steady horizon and roads laid straight as arrows. What could be better for bicycling?

Our favorite day trip out of Amsterdam is to head for Haarlem. It's a lovely town with a sedate 17th-century charm, but few sights that will interest kids. We come here for the surrounding countryside, which lives up to all the images of the Dutch landscape painters: neat patchwork farmlands with the occasional windmill, and broody gray clouds scudding against a vast scrim of silvery skies.

Rent bikes in Haarlem at **Rijwielshop Haarlem,** Stationsplein 7 (☎ **023/531-7066**), or **Bike Planet,** Gierstraat 55–57 (☎ **023/534-15020**), and you can be out of town in no time. The beach resort of **Zandvoort** is 7km (4⅓ miles) directly west of Haarlem, an easy cycle through woods, polders, and sand dunes to a seemingly endless stretch of smooth sand lined with seasonal cafes. Or branch off to the **Zuid-Kennermerland National Park,** just north of Zandvoort, a dune-edged nature reserve where you can breathe the salt tang of the North Sea

air. South of Haarlem is another popular cycle, along N206 or N208, where from late January through May masses of vibrantly colored tulips fill the fields. This so-called **Bollenstreek Route** runs 60km (37 miles) all the way to Leiden, though you only need ride as far as you want.

So where are the dikes? Steam pumps did the job when the Haarlem area was reclaimed in the mid–19th century; if the kids are keen to see dikes, drive 62km (39 miles) north of Amsterdam on A7/E22 to the 30km-long (19-mile) **Afsluitdijk** (Enclosing Dike). Completed in 1932, this huge dike finally sealed off the encroaching North Sea, transforming the saltwater Zuiderzee into the freshwater IJsselmeer (and turning several fishing villages into farm towns). Haul out your bikes again, because a bike path runs along the highway as it follows the top of the dike. Expect it to be windy while you're out on this ribbon of highway, with nothing but sea on either side. Halfway across, you can turn around at the monument (with a cafe) that commemorates the workers who built this massive wall against the sea, mostly by backbreaking manual labor.

ⓘ **Tourist office,** Stationsplein 1 (☎ **0900/616-1600;** www.vvvzk.nl).

✈ ☒ See Amsterdam **51**.

WHY THEY'LL THANK YOU: Tulips, dikes, windmills, the whole package.

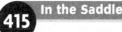

Rocky Mountain National Park
Trail Riding on the Roof of the World
Ages 6 & up • Near Estes Park, Colorado, USA

CHANCES ARE you've never been as close to the sky as you'll be at Rocky Mountain National Park, most of which is at least 8,000 feet high. Up here, the air is so thin and cool you'll feel giddy, the sun's UV rays so intense that sunblock and sunglasses are a must. It's a land of ponderosa pine, gnarled alpine tundra, heathery slopes, bare granite, dizzying views, and so many elk they'll browse right up to your campground. The Continental Divide slices across the middle of this compact park—you can drive over it on Trail Ridge Road, 48 miles of truly spectacular mountaintop views, much of it above the timberline. But to plunge fully into this wilderness, swing into a Western saddle and take a ride on horseback.

While many national parks offer only a standard 1-hour circle ride, at Rocky Mountain you can take guided trail rides from 2 to 8 hours, or even book overnight pack trips. Children as young as 6 can have a horse to themselves, while younger children ride with a parent.

There are two stables inside the park, both run by **Hi Country Stables** (www. colorado-horses.com/hicountrystables): One is at Moraine Park (𝄞 **970/586-2327**), the other is on Sprague Lake (𝄞 **970/586-3244**), near the Glacier Basin Campground on Bear Lake Road. Both of these are on the eastern side of the park, in relatively level valleys plowed out by glaciers, but an ample network of worn dirt trails winds deeper into the countryside past steep, craggy mountainsides and small, round reflecting lakes.

On the west side of the park, just outside park boundaries in the Grand Lake area, **Winding River Resorts** (𝄞 **970/627-3215**) offers 1- and 2-hour trail rides, plus pony rides for younger riders. And on both sides of the park, **Sombrero Ranch Stables,** opposite Lake Estes Dam on U.S. 34 (𝄞 **970/586-4577,** or 970/627-3514 in the Grand Lake area; www.sombrero.com), not only offers trail rides but schedules a 2-hour early-morning expedition that includes a full breakfast.

Rocky Mountain National Park.

(i) U.S. 34 or U.S. 36 (✆ **970/586-1206;** www.nps.gov/romo).

✈ Denver International, 65 miles.

🛏 $$$ **Glacier Lodge,** 2166 CO 66, south of park entrance (✆ **800/523-3920** or 970/586-4401; www.glacierlodge.com). $

Moraine Park Campground, Rocky Mt. National Park (✆ **800/365-CAMP;** http://reservations.nps.gov).

BEST TIME: Mid-May to Mid-Sept.

WHY THEY'LL THANK YOU: The clip-clop of hooves echoing off the top of the world.

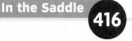

In the Saddle   416

The Grand Canyon
The Mules Know the Way
Ages 7 & up • Arizona, USA

WHILE IT'S AWESOME indeed to stand on the rim of the Grand Canyon and drink in its resplendent panoramas, something about that monumental chasm makes me long to just *dive in.* Any number of hiking trails lead down into this great natural wonder, raft trips ply its waters, and helicopters buzz overhead (see ④⑧⓪)—but surely the most memorable way to explore the Grand Canyon is to pick your way down the steep, narrow trails on the back of an ornery mule. Let the trail-wise mules find their footing on the stony paths while you gaze around you, drinking in the unfolding vistas of this vast network of canyons.

The best options for kids depart from the North Rim and are offered by **Canyon Trail Rides** (✆ **928/638-9875;** www.canyonrides.com). Children as young as 7 can try out the mules on a 1-hour scenic ride along the rim; at 10 years and up, they can do half-day trips, either a longer rim route or one that heads 2,300 feet down the North Kaibab Trail, along a dramatic series of switchbacks through thick forest to the Supai Tunnel. If the kids are 12, they can take a full day trip, going 4,300 feet down and back up the North Kaibab Trail through a terrain of bright red rocks to Roaring Springs (aptly named— you'll hear it well before you reach it).

From the South Rim, the shortest possible excursion is a 12-mile day trip to Plateau Point, an overlook of the Colorado

River rushing 1,300 feet below. The real classics, though, are 1- or 2-night packages that go to the bottom of the canyon and include sleeping arrangements and simple meals at **Phantom Ranch,** the only lodging available below the rim of the Grand Canyon. Don't expect luxury— it's all bunk-bedded cabins and dorms, connected by dirt footpaths and shaded by cottonwood trees, set half a mile north of the Colorado River. All the same, it's more than you might have expected to find down here. These Phantom Ranch trips are so popular, they fill up as soon as reservations are accepted, 23 months in advance (call ✆ **888/297-2757** for reservations). For possible openings the next day, call the Bright Angel Transportation Desk at ✆ **928/638-2631,** ext. 6015. There's no age restriction per se, but riders must be at least 4 feet 7 inches tall; pregnant women are not allowed.

(i) ✆ **800/638-7888;** www.nps.gov/grca.

✈ Grand Canyon National Park Airport, Tusayan, AZ.

🛏 $$$ **El Tovar Hotel,** South Rim (✆ **928/638-2631**). $$ **Grand Canyon Lodge,** North Rim (✆ **928/638-2611**). Reservations for either: ✆ **888/297-2757.**

WHY THEY'LL THANK YOU: Discovering what's in that hole in the ground.

Doing the Dude Ranch Thing

Ages 6 & up • Around Jackson, Wyoming, USA

As a HORSE-MAD GIRL OF 7, I was sick with jealousy when my parents went off to Wyoming for a week at a dude ranch. Don't do this to your children! Dude ranches—or, excuse me, *guest ranches* is the preferred term now—have figured out how to court families, and it's a huge bit of their business. The standard 1-week package may cost $1,200 to $1,800 per person (with discounts for children), but that covers everything—family-style meals, cozy log cabins to sleep in, and all ranch activities, such as horseback riding, fly-fishing, hiking, float trips, nature hikes, paintball, roping lessons, square dances, maybe even big-game hunting—yee-*haw!*

To me, the quintessential ranch experience is in western Wyoming, with constant views of the snow-dusted Grand Teton range and trail rides through sagebrush flats, green foothill meadows, and rocky timberline terrain. A handful of ranches close to Jackson Hole abut national parkland—not just Grand Teton National Park, but the vast Bridger-Teton and Targhee National Forests—which provides a broad choice of trails, not to mention swift sparkling rivers for those float trips and fly-fishing outings.

The **Triangle X Ranch** in Moose (✆ **307/733-2183;** www.trianglex.com) is actually on national parkland, and it's the most stripped-down experience of the lot. At the other end of the spectrum, the **Red Rock Ranch** in Kelly (✆ **307/733-6288;** www.theredrockranch.com) serves up fairly gourmet dinners and even has a heated swimming pool; the **R Lazy S Ranch** in Teton Village (✆ **307/733-2655;** www.rlazys.com) has a swimming hole, though not a pool. Things are a little more

laid-back at **Heart Six Ranch** in Moran (✆ **888/543-2477** or 307/543-2477; www.heartsix.com) and at the **Gros Ventre River Ranch** in Moose (✆ **307/733-4138;** www.grosventreriverranch.com). Don't expect manicured landscaping or uniformed employees—these are all decidedly rural places, with pole fences and low-slung buildings and trophy elk heads mounted on pine-paneled walls. You'll dress casual and be on a first-name basis with the wranglers. And you won't be watching TV at night—not when you've got a sky full of stars and a crackling campfire for toasting marshmallows.

The ranchers have large herds and can carefully match horses to the riding abilities of the guest, usually giving you "your own" horse for the entire week. Even beginners catch on quickly, given that they're riding Western saddle and following a group along a well-marked trail (usually at an easy pace). When choosing a ranch, consider how its children's program is set up—at Triangle X, Red Rock, and R Lazy S, children have their own trail rides and separate meals, which significantly reduces your bonding time; there is an optional supervised kids' program at Heart Six Ranch, but children can join the adult trail rides if their riding ability passes muster with the wranglers. At Gros Ventre River Ranch, family togetherness is the norm on trail rides, but there is a rec room kids can escape to when their parents get too embarrassing.

✈ Jackson Hole.

WHY THEY'LL THANK YOU: Saddle sore and loving it.

Pony Trekking in Connemara

Ages 8 & up • Western County Galway, Ireland

West of Galway City lies a land of "savage beauty," in the words of Oscar Wilde, a vast bog-mantled, granite moorland sown with lakes, running north to stark mountains, the Maum Turks and The Twelve Bens. The Atlantic coastline is ragged with little inlets. It's a wild, tough, treeless countryside, sparsely populated since the famine of the 1840s—and that very wildness is what begs for exploration. There's no better way to do so than on horseback, preferably on the native sure-footed Connemara pony.

Horses need to be sure-footed to cross Connemara's plum-colored boglands, where unexpected marshy patches can plunge you fetlock-deep into water. The land looks flat, but each twist of the track reveals hidden gorges, streams, and lakes. Up close you see how gorse and heather, rhododendrons, and wildflowers soften the harsh rock-strewn land.

The Connemara pony—the only horse breed native to Ireland—is often raised in tiny fields with limestone pastures. With their great stamina and gentle temperament, they are ideal for children's riding. The inland crossroad of Maam Cross is famous as the site of the annual Connemara pony fair; in Clifden, Connemara's chief town, a **Connemara Pony Museum** (✆ 095/21699) has been set up in the old train station.

If pony trekking is the focus of your vacation, consider a weeklong horseback tour, beginning and ending in Galway City, with **Connemara and Coast Trails,** Loughrea (✆ 091/841216; www.connemara-trails.com), for experienced and beginning riders alike. Your luggage is transported from hotel to hotel and all meals are catered. For shorter excursions, **The Point Riding Centre** in Ballyconneely (✆ 095/38882) runs day treks around the area, as does the **Errislennan Riding Centre** (✆ 095/21134; www.connemara.net/errislannan-manor) up in Clifden. If splashing along the Atlantic beaches is your dream, the **Cleggan Beach Riding Centre** (✆ 095/44746; www.clegganridingcentre.com), in the seacoast village of Cleggan, organizes among other rides a 3-hour excursion at low tide across the shallow channel to Omey Island.

ⓘ www.irelandwest.ie.

✈ 🚆 Galway City, 80km (50 miles).

🛏 Three excellent local hotels have their own stables: the $$$ **Cashel House Hotel** on Cashel Bay (✆ 095/31001; www.cashel-house-hotel.com); $ **Glen Valley House and Stables** at the inland tip of Ireland's only fjord, Killary Harbour (✆ 095/42269); and $$$ **Renvyle House** on the coast in Renvyle (✆ 095/43511; www.renvyle.com).

WHY THEY'LL THANK YOU: Sturdy ponies, stunning views.

Stalking the Loch Ness Monster

Ages 8 & up • Drumnadrochit, Scotland

THE LOCH NESS MONSTER—or "Nessie," as she's fondly called—is one of the world's great mysteries. It's just about impossible to pass along the shores of this long lake in the Scottish Highlands without peering at its deep, dark waters and expecting a scaly snout or a sinuous, slimy hump to break the surface. Highway A82 runs along the north shore of the 39km-long (24-mile) lake, one of a string slicing diagonally cross-country between Fort William and Inverness—but why look out of a car window, when you could be on horseback, feeling the bracing Highland mist on your face?

Don't let monster mania distract you from the lovely scenery of this Highlands lake, where mossy Glen Urquhart runs down to Loch Ness's deep-blue waters. Even on a cloudy day—and there are plenty up here—the shifting play of light

on the wild landscape is dramatic. In the bucolic village of Drumnadrochit, 1.6km (1 mile) inland from the lake and 23km (14 miles) west of Inverness, the **Highland Riding Centre** runs 1- to 2-hour tours on horseback around a sprawling moorland sheep farm overlooking Loch Ness. Be sure to book in advance.

In the village itself, Drumnadrochit cashes in on Nessie's myth with the **Official Loch Ness Monster Exhibition,** on A82 (✆ **01456/450573**), centered on what purports to be a scale model of the creature. Chances are this is the best you'll do in terms of seeing her. Or you could try staring intently at the deep waters around the promontory of ruined **Castle Urquhart,** A82 (✆ **01456/450551**), 2.4km (1½ miles) south of the village; it's the spot where sightings have most often been reported.

The first recorded sighting of an underwater beast was by St. Columba in A.D. 565, and they've continued unabated ever since. Is it a sole survivor from prehistoric times? A gigantic sea snake? A cosmic wanderer? Everyone has his or her own theory. A team of scientists from Massachusetts has sonar-triggered cameras and strobe lights rigged up year-round, hoping to document Nessie's existence, but so far no luck.

ⓘ **Highland Riding Centre,** Borlum Farm (✆ **01456/450220**).

🚆 Inverness, 3½ hr. from Glasgow or Edinburgh.

🛏 $$$ **Polmaily House Hotel,** A831 3.2km (2 miles) west of Drumnadrochit (✆ **01456/450343;** www.polmaily.co.uk).

WHY THEY'LL THANK YOU: This could be the day Nessie comes up for air.

Loch Ness (and a well-hidden Nessie?).

France's Cowboy Country: The Camargue

Ages 8 & up • Camargue National Park, France

ON A MARSHY DELTA where two branches of the Rhône empty into the Mediterranean, the Camargue is France's cattle country. Here, black bulls are raised for bullfights in nearby Arles and Nîmes. The cattle are herded by *gardians*, French cowboys, who ride the range on small white horses said to have been introduced by the Saracens. This exotic corner of France, with its whitewashed houses, plaited-straw roofs, roaming Gypsies, and pink flamingos, can be explored by canal barge, bike, or jeep, but the best way to plunge into its rich interior is on the back of **camarguais horses**—proud white steeds whose cousins you'll see running wild through the salt marshlands, and whose hoofs are so tough they don't need shoes.

Descended long ago from Arabian horses, these sturdy little horses have distinctive long manes and bushy tails, which evolved over the centuries to slap the pesky, gluttonous mosquitoes who thrive in these wetlands. Two to three dozen stables (depending on the time of year) along the highway from Arles to Stes-Maries offer expeditions into the **park** (on D570 near Camargue's capital, Ste-Maries-de-la-Mer). Given the easy temperament and sure-footedness of Camargue ponies, these rides are recommended even for those who have never been on a horse before. On horseback, you can ford the waters to penetrate deep into the interior

where black bulls graze and wild birds nest.

The French cowboys of the Camargue live in thatched huts called *cabanes*, wear large felt hats, and carry long three-pronged sticks to prod the cattle.

With the most fragile ecosystem in France, the alluvial plain of the Camargue has been a national park since 1970, and exotic flora and fauna abound. Besides the wild horses, the bird life here is the richest in Europe—not only colonies of **pink flamingos,** but some 400 other species, including ibises, egrets, kingfishers, owls, wild ducks, swans, and ferocious birds of prey. The best place to see flamingo colonies is the area around **Ginès,** a hamlet on N570, 5km (3 miles) north of **Stes-Maries-de-la-Mer**—a perfectly preserved medieval walled town set amidst swamps and lagoons, long ago an embarkation point for the Crusades and well worth a visit.

ⓘ **Office de Tourisme,** place St. Louis, Aigues-Mortes (℡ **04-66-53-73-00;** www.ot-aiguesmortes.fr).

🚆 Aigues-Mortes, 1 hr. from Nîmes.

🛏 $$$ **Hotel Les Templiers,** 23 rue de la République, Aigues-Mortes (℡ **04-66-53-66-56**).

WHY THEY'LL THANK YOU: Playing cowboy with an exotic twist.

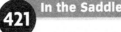

421 **In the Saddle**

Galloping through the Brazilian Pantanal

Ages 8 & up • Southwestern Brazil

WHEN YOU LIVE on the world's largest flood plain—a flat wetlands as big as France, stretching across southwestern Brazil all the way to Paraguay—you don't bother planting crops or laying down roads. Why would you, when it's all going to lie underwater from December through March? So in the Pantanal, ranchers graze their cattle in the dry season and retreat to higher ground in the floods; and when the waters spread, they simply splash around on horseback. This fertile land, ruled by the rhythms of its waters, is simply the best place in South America to see wildlife, better even than the Amazon. To see it at its best, make like a cowpoke and get up on a horse.

And what creatures there are to see—the Pantanal is home to capybaras, caimans, jaguars, pumas, marsh deer, anacondas, giant otters, colorful Hyacinth macaws, kites, hawks, and storks; there are nearly 700 species of birds alone, and 80 species of mammals. The Transpantaeira, a gravel road that was supposed to traverse the Pantanal, is one of the few roads here. Only the northern 89 miles were ever built, though, and today the Transpantaeira functions more like a nature trail, taking visitors into the heart of north Pantanal, where its roadside ditches are favorite feeding grounds for kingfishers, egrets, jabiru storks, and more than four varieties of hawks and three different kinds of kites. Beneath the many rickety bridges are small rivers or pools where caimans lurk by the hundreds.

Now that the secret is out, eco-tourism is on the rise, and many of the region's cattle ranches (fazendas) have created accommodations and gone into business as resorts, or at least as the Brazilian version of dude ranches. The stout Pantanal horses are accustomed to slogging through the shallow waters that engulf this treeless plain every wet season, and sitting in the comfortable Western-type saddles the local cowboys use, you can ramble far from settled areas, where the local wildlife wanders otherwise undisturbed. Rein in your mount and observe a flock of herons fishing in the rich floodwaters, then take off with a splash at a full gallop, startling alligators and snakes underfoot. While local lodges may offer short rides around their properties, you can also book entire tour packages based on exploring the flood plain by horse: Tour operators include **Pantanal Explorer** in northern Patanal (✆ **065/682-2800;** www.araraslodge.com.br) and **Open Door** in the south (✆ **067/721-8303;** www.opendoortur.com.br).

✈ Cuiabá in the north; Campo Grande in the south.

🛏 $$$ **Araras Eco Lodge,** Transpantaneira Hwy. (✆ **065/682-2800;** www.araraslodge.com.br). $$$ **Refugio Caiman,** near Miranda (✆ **011/3079-6622;** www.caiman.com.br).

WHY THEY'LL THANK YOU: Seeing a 20th capybara—or a first jaguar.

Chapter **13** On the Water

Paddling Away . . . 469
Swimming . . . 482
Snorkeling & Diving . . . 485
Beaches . . . 491

Snorkeling on the Great Barrier Reef.

Canoeing the Everglades
Paddling through a River of Grass
Ages 6 & up • Florida City or Everglades City, Florida, USA

THE EVERGLADES IS A BIZARRE ECOSYSTEM, when you think about it: a drawling grassy river that's rarely more than knee-deep, but spreads some 40 miles wide, harboring an exotic population of manatees, hawksbill turtles, water moccasins, coral snakes, panthers, armadillos, muskrats, opossums, river otters, herons, egrets, the roseate spoonbill, and the big black anhinga bird. It's the only place in the world where alligators and crocodiles live side by side. There's nothing like it anywhere else—and it might not be here much longer, given the encroaching development in southern Florida. Bring the kids here now, to dip a paddle into this River of Grass while it still flows.

While you can stick to dry land—driving or biking on the paved park roads, or walking short nature trails through jungle-like patches of forest—the whole point of this place is that it *isn't* dry land. What you really want is to feel the sway and lap of the park's waters, the lazy grace of its fluid meander through mangroves and cypresses and sawgrass prairies. Rent canoes at the **Gulf Coast visitor center** in Everglades City or the **Flamingo Lodge** by the Flamingo visitor center at the southern tip of the park. In a canoe you'll be incredibly close to the water level, casually coexisting with gators and birds as if you're part of their natural environment. That just won't happen on those powered airboats that offer Everglades tours just outside park boundaries. (They aren't allowed in the park proper.)

Everglades National Park's longest "trails" are designed for canoe travel,

and many are marked as clearly as walking trails. From the Gulf Coast, you can canoe 2 miles across **Chokoloskee Bay** to a mangrove island, or follow the **Turner River** 8 miles from freshwater cypress forest into saltwater mangrove swamp. From Flamingo, the **Noble Hammock Canoe Trail** is an easy 2-mile loop; the **Hell's Bay Canoe Trail** is 3 to 6 miles, depending on how far you venture. A guided canoe tour is a great idea, not only to find your way but to benefit from the guide's familiarity with the flora and fauna; contact **Everglades National Park Boat Tours** (✆ 800/445-7724) at the Parks Docks on Chokoloskee Causeway (Hwy. 29) in Everglades City, or **North American Canoe Tours** at the Ivey House (see below).

ⓘ **Ernest F. Coe Visitor Center,** Hwy. 9336 west of Florida City; **Gulf Coast Visitor Center,** Hwy. 29, Everglades City; **Flamingo Visitor Center,** end of Hwy. 9336 (✆ **305/242-7700;** www.nps.gov/ever).

✈ Miami International, 40 miles.

⇌ $$ **Best Western Gateway to the Keys,** 411 S. Krome Ave. (U.S. 1), Florida City (✆ **305/246-5100;** www.bestwestern. com). $$ **Ivey House B&B,** 107 Camellia St., Everglades City (✆ **239/695-3299;** www.iveyhouse.com).

BEST TIME: Dry season (winter or spring).

WHY THEY'LL THANK YOU: Gliding through the glassy, grassy silence.

An Everglades frog.

Way Down upon the Swanee River
Paddling the Okefenokee Swamp
Ages 6 & up • Southeast Georgia, USA

To start with, it's got a great singsong name—*Oh-kee-fee-noh-kee*, like something out of a Creedence Clearwater song or a Scooby-Doo cartoon—which means, in the Creek Indian language, "land of the trembling earth." To call this huge freshwater wetlands in southeastern Georgia a swamp is too simplistic: It's a fascinating mixed terrain of wet prairies, peat marsh, pine uplands, hardwood hammocks, small lakes and "gator holes," and floating islands, covering 650 square miles of wilderness. Paddling through its faintly creepy backwaters is an experience the kids will never forget.

There are a few developed park areas around the edges, but no roads traverse the wilderness itself—for that you'll have to get into a canoe (rentals, as well as maps, are available at all the visitor centers) and strike out on marked canoe trails over the tea-colored water. **Okefenokee Swamp Park,** GA 177, Waycross (© **912/283-0583**), on the northern edge of the preserve, is an easy place to start; there is an interpretive center, a boardwalk with observation tower, and a 1½-mile steam railroad tour included with admission. The swamp looks even thicker and more jungly at the southern end at **Stephen C. Foster State Park,** GA 177, Fargo (© **912/637-5274**), an 80-acre island park named after the 19th-century songwriter who was born in nearby Fargo. The Suwanee River of which he wrote flows through the swamp here, carrying much of its runoff. There are 225 miles of mirrorlike black waterways to

paddle through, delving into a sprawling forest of black gum and cypress; listen in the silence for the rat-a-tat-tat of a red-billed woodpecker or the agile slither of an otter. The **Suwanee Canal Recreation Area,** GA Spur 121, Folkston (© **912/496-7156**), on the eastern fringe of the wilderness, has a good set of park amenities—visitor center exhibits, a boardwalk to an observation tower, interpretive nature trails, bike paths—and it's also the place to go for guided canoe expeditions (contact **Okefenokee Adventures,** © **866/ THESWAMP** or 912/496-7156; www.okefenokeeadventures.com). If you're really hardy and want to head out on your own, staying overnight at campsites deep in the wilderness, make reservations 2 months in advance with the **U.S. Fish and Wildlife Service** (© **912/496-3331**). The paddling can be strenuous at times—you may have to climb out and push your canoe over peat buildups or shallow drafts—but then that's what being a backwoods explorer is all about.

ⓘ Rte. 2, Folkston (© **912/496-7156;** www.fws.gov/okefenokee).

✈ Jacksonville, FL, 50 miles.

🛏 $$ **Holiday Inn,** 1725 Memorial Dr., Waycross (© **912/283-4490;** www.holiday-inn.com). $ **Stephen C. Foster State Park,** Rte. 1, Fargo (© **912/637-5274**).

WHY THEY'LL THANK YOU: Gliding under the cypress canopy.

Canoeing in the Adirondacks
Pristine Waters of a Northern Wilderness

Ages 6 & up • Saranac Lake, New York, USA

THE 6 MILLION ACRES of New York's Adirondack State Park enfold no fewer than 3,000 lakes and ponds, connected by 6,000 miles of rivers and streams. Nothing could be closer to a canoers' paradise. You can choose a route where you slip along quiet rivers onto forested lakes; the only sounds you may hear are birdcalls and the dip of your paddle as it slices through the glassy water. Even first-time canoers are quickly hooked.

Saranac Lake is a smart base for canoeing, not least because there are two excellent outfitters in town: **Adirondack Lakes and Trails Outfitters,** 168 Lake Flower Ave. (© **518/891-7450;** www.adirondackoutfitters.com), and **St. Regis Canoe Outfitters,** 9 Dorsey St. (© **518/891-1838;** www.canoeoutfitters.com). You can rent canoes (or kayaks), paddles, life jackets, and camping gear; they'll also give you detailed maps and advice, or even provide a guide or a van to transport you. Another useful stop is the **visitor center** in the town of Paul Smith's, on Route 30 northwest of Saranac Lake.

Children too young to paddle can enjoy gliding along in the belly of a canoe, watching the shore slide past. Pull up to the water's edge whenever the mood strikes for a picnic, a nature hike, a swim, or an overnight stay (free campsites are plentiful along most of these routes). You may want to set out on the **Saranac lakes,** where several half- or full-day paddles are possible; a great starter trip for young children combines an easy 2-hour canoe excursion with a ride on the

Adirondack Scenic Railroad (© **518/891-3238;** www.adirondackrr.com), which runs between Lake Placid and Saranac Lake. Drive east on Route 3 to the Tupper Lake area, where there's a good continuous route along the **Raquette River,** with only one 1-mile portage. **Little Tupper Lake,** off Route 30 between the towns of Tupper Lake and Long Lake, is the area's largest motor-free lake.

The classic Adirondacks canoeing experience, however, is the Seven Carries Route through the gorgeous **St. Regis Canoe Wilderness** north of Saranac Lake. It's rare to find such an extensive stretch of water reserved solely for non-motorized boats. As the name suggests, there are seven portages along this route, as you visit all three of the St. Regis lakes and several secluded ponds. With so many miles of canoeing waters, you could easily spend 3 or 4 days up here, camping onshore every night. Closed in by woods on every side, it's possible to imagine yourselves back into the ages when Native Americans in their silent canoes were the only inhabitants of this wilderness.

ⓘ **Adirondack Regional Tourism Council** (© **518/846-8016;** www.adirondacks.org).

✈ Saranac Lake.

🛏 **Campsites** (accessible only to canoes) Saranac Lake Islands (© **518/891-3170;** www.dec.state.ny.us).

WHY THEY'LL THANK YOU: Pristine waters and peaceful wilderness.

Sea Kayaking in Acadia National Park
The Maine Way to Enjoy the Coast
Ages 8 & up • Mount Desert Island, Maine, USA

MAINE'S MOUNT DESERT ISLAND is home to spectacular Acadia National Park, a rich glacier-carved mound of rugged cliffs, restless ocean, and quiet woods. Mount Desert (pronounced des-*sert*) is surrounded by small bays and coast-hugging islands and nearly knifed in half by narrow, 7-mile-long Somes Sound, the only true fjord in the continental United States. Most visitors crowd onto 20-mile **Park Loop Road,** a spectacular drive that starts near the **Hulls Cove Visitor Center** and follows the rocky coast past picturesque coves, looping back inland along **Jordan Pond** and **Eagle Lake** with a detour to

Kayaking in Acadia.

Cadillac Mountain—a sort of greatest-hits tour of the island. But why spend your time poking along in traffic, staring out at the ocean, when you could be skimming along the water's surface, skirting the coast and exploring the coves in your own light and agile sea kayak?

Frenchman's Bay, where the island's main town, **Bar Harbor,** sits, is a great place for youngsters to learn how to kayak, sitting in the front seat of a flat, stable two-person kayak with a parent paddling in back. Head south from the bay and you'll reach Atlantic waters, where popular park sights include **Thunder Hole,** a shallow cavern where the surf surges boisterously in and out, and **Otter Cliffs,** a set of 100-foot-high granite precipices capped with dense spruce that plummet down into roiling seas. From your kayak you can also enjoy open views of waterside villages and the great shingled "cottages" of the wealthy elite—Carnegies, Rockefellers, Astors, Vanderbilts—who summered here in the island's late-19th-century heyday as a resort.

Outfitters offer a variety of options, from a 2½-hour harbor tour to a 7-hour excursion. **Coastal Kayaking Tours,** 48 Cottage St., Bar Harbor (*©* **800/526-8615** or 207/288-9605), has a 4-hour outing tailored for families with children as young as 8. Experienced kayakers can set out on their own with rentals from **Loon Bay Kayaks,** Barcadia Campground, junction of Routes 3 and 102 (*©* **888/786-0676** or 207/288-0099), or **Aquaterra Adventures,** 1 West St., Bar Harbor (*©* **207/288-0007**).

Frenchman's Bay is populated by seals, osprey, and other wildlife; in early fall, huge flocks of eider ducks can sometimes be seen floating just off the Atlantic shore. Summer boasts even more spectacular wildlife: humpback, finback, minke, and (occasionally) right whales, which migrate to cool summer waters offshore to feast on krill and plankton. For a closer look you can take an excursion with the **Bar Harbor Whale Watch Company,** 1 West St., Bar Harbor (℗ **888/533-WALE** or 207/288-9800; www.whalesadventures.com).

ⓘ **Hulls Cove Visitor Center,** Rte. 3 (℗ **207/288-3338;** www.nps.gov/acad).

✈ Trenton, just across the causeway from Mount Desert Island.

🛏 $ **Bar Harbor Campground,** Rte. 3, Salisbury Cove (℗ **207/288-5185**). $$$ **Harborside Hotel & Marina,** 55 West St., Bar Harbor (℗ **800/328-5033** or 207/288-5033; www.theharborsidehotel.com).

WHY THEY'LL THANK YOU: Skimming over steel-blue seas, swift as an osprey.

---

426 Paddling Away

Apostle Island National Park
Seeing the Great Lakes by Kayak
Ages 8 & up • Bayfield, Wisconsin, USA

THE OLD FRENCH EXPLORERS, the original *voyageurs* who paddled across North America in the 1600s seeking fur-trapping riches, probably would have used sea kayaks instead of canoes if they'd only known. A closed cockpit boat like a kayak is exactly what you want in order to venture onto the cold, often rough waters of Lake Superior, the largest freshwater lake in the world. Come here in the summertime and the waters aren't quite so cold, though the waves are still unpredictable. But you're snug in your kayak and you can ride it out just fine.

Apostle Island National Park.

Right off the northernmost tip of Wisconsin lies a scatter of 22 forested islands—on the map it almost looks as if the Bayfield Peninsula had sneezed them out into Lake Superior—and boaters have long found island-hopping in these frigid (but relatively shallow) waters an irresistible temptation. The Apostle Islands National Park headquarters lies on the tip of the Bayfield peninsula, but that's merely an anchor point—most of the park is accessible only by boat. Let the kids look at a map and choose day-trip destinations within easy kayaking distance—historic island lighthouses, shipwreck sites, abandoned brownstone quarries, a ruined one-room schoolhouse, inviting sand beaches. Red sandstone cliffs line the otherwise woodsy shore, with sea caves in their bases that only kayaks can explore.

Local outfitters offer rentals, kayaking instruction (usually in protected bays or inland lakes rather than Superior itself), and guided excursions, both day trips and overnights—unless you're already experienced kayakers, having a guide is a huge plus, allowing you to paddle directly to the most interesting sights. (The sea caves in particular can be treacherous to visit if you don't know the waters well.) Outfitters include **Living Adventure** (© **715/779-9503;** www.livingadventure.com), **Trek and Trail** (© **800/354-8735;** www.trek-trail.com), and **Whitecap Kayak Excursions** (© **800/933-7669** or 715/561-2227; www.whitecapkayak.com).

If your kayaking skills aren't enough to get you out onto the islands, never fear—you can always go there on narrated trips run by **Apostle Islands Cruise Service** (© **800/323-7619** or 715/779-3925; www.apostleisland.com), departing from the Bayfield city docks.

ⓘ **Bayfield Old Courthouse Visitor Center,** 415 Washington Ave. (© **715/779-3397;** www.nps.gov/apis).

✈ Hayward, WI, 75 miles. Bessemer, MI, 75 miles.

🛏 $$ **Bayfield Inn,** 20 Rittenhouse Ave. (© **715/779-3363;** www.bayfieldinn.com). $$ **Winfield Inn,** 225 E. Lynde Ave. (© **715/779-3252;** www.winfieldinn.com).

BEST TIME: May–Sept.

WHY THEY'LL THANK YOU: Feeling like a *voyageur.*

Paddling Away 427

The San Juan Islands
Going Down to the Sea in Kayaks
Ages 6 & up • Puget Sound, Washington, USA

IF YOU WERE TRYING to invent the perfect seascape for kayaking, you couldn't outdo the San Juan Islands. In the inland sea of Puget Sound, protected by mainland Washington State on one side and the Olympic peninsula on the other, lie hundreds of emerald islands, many of them accessible only by boat. Paddling around, you'll pass rocky islets where fat harbor seals nap, and reach isolated campsites no ferry passengers will ever use.

There are 175 islands in the San Juans that are big enough to be given names; another 600 or so smaller outcroppings punctuate the waters in between. Only four islands—San Juan, Orcas, Lopez, and Shaw—are served by Washington State Ferries, and only the first three have tourist accommodations; so make reservations before you arrive. The islands are a magnet for migrating wildlife, the biggest celebrities being **orcas** and **minke whales**—whale-watching expeditions set out from all the main harbors—which show up June through September, coinciding perfectly with school vacations. There's a good chance you'll see some orcas when you're out kayaking, especially if you hang around the west side of San Juan Island; at **Lime Kiln State Park** on the west coast of San Juan, you can even see them from the shore. But orcas aren't the only stars—out on the water you're also likely to spot bald eagles, osprey, Dall's porpoises, stellar sea lions, and otters.

To rent kayaks or join short guided paddles, in Friday Harbor check out **San Juan Safaris** at Roche Harbor Resort (© 800/450-6858 or 360/378-1323; www.sanjuansafaris.com) or **Outdoor Odysseys** (© 800/647-4621 or 360/378-3533; www.outdoorodysseys. com). Also in Friday Harbor, **Sea Quest Kayaks** (© 888/589-4253 or 360/378-5767; www.sea-quest-kayak.com/sanjuan. htm) has three-person kayaks that are great if you've got younger children. **Shearwater Adventures** (© 360/376-4699; www.shearwaterkayaks.com)

operates from Orcas Island's ferry landing. On Lopez Island, **Lopez Island Sea Kayaks,** Fisherman Bay Road (© 360/468-2847; www.lopezkayaks.com), offers a 2-hour sunset paddle that's great for families. If the kids are up for multiday tours, try **Crystal Seas Kayaking** (© 877/SEAS-877 or 360/378-4223; www.crystalseas. com), **San Juan Kayak Expeditions** (© 360/378-4436; www.sanjuankayak. com), or **Orcas Outdoors** (© 360/376-4611; www.orcasoutdoors.com).

(i) **Visitor information** (© **888/468-3701** or 360/468-3663; www.travelsanjuans.com).

✈ San Juan, Orcas, and Lopez islands.

🛏 $$$ **Lakedale Resort,** 4313 Roche Harbor Rd., Friday Harbor (© **800/617-2267** or 360/378-2350; www.lakedale.com). $$ **Lopez Islander Resort,** Fisherman Bay Rd., Lopez Island (© **800/736-3434** or 360/468-2233; www.lopezislander.com).

WHY THEY'LL THANK YOU: Paddling past a porpoise or whale.

---

428 | Paddling Away

The Okavango Delta
A Mokoro Ride through the Floodwaters
Ages 8 & up • Okavango Delta, Botswana

EVERY WINTER—which in Botswana begins in July—the Okavango River flows south out of the uplands of Angola, its waters swollen to bursting by the rainy season. By the time it gets to this vast bowl in Botswana, it's overrun its banks, spreading out throughout the delta. Crystal-clear pools, channels, and lagoons spring up everywhere, playing host to a rich diversity of wildlife, which flock here in grateful escape from the adjacent Kalahari Desert. Game lodges in the delta are classified as "wet" or "dry" according to whether or not they are surrounded by water during

flood season, but it's not as if being surrounded is a problem—it just means you'll do all your traveling around by **mokoro.**

No trip to the delta is complete without a ride in a mokoro, a narrow canoelike boat propelled through the water by a human with a long pole. The design copies a traditional boat hollowed out of a tree trunk, though nowadays most of them are made from fiberglass. These silent craft, ideally suited to the shallow waters of the delta, make it possible to get really close to birds and animals for wildlife viewing, and though they won't have the fun of poling it themselves, the kids will still be drawn intimately into the mysteries of life on the flood plain. As you glide along, the air is filled with the sounds of birds calling, frogs trilling, and antelopes rustling in the reeds. Wildebeest, hartebeest, buffalo, and zebra roam the islands before you; elephants wade across channels guarded by hippos and crocs.

Game camps in the Okavango are generally tented affairs, since the operators are required to make no permanent marks on the land, but some of these are quite luxurious tents indeed. Most of the camps are set within the **Moremi Game Reserve,** in the northeastern segment of the delta. Families with children are accepted, but generally required to book their own separate vehicle for game viewing, which works out just fine—that way the safari experience can be run at a softer pace.

Given the complexities of travel within Botswana, it's best to book your lodgings as part of a package trip through a safari specialist company such as **Abercrombie & Kent** (*(C)* **800/554-7016** in the U.S., 27/11/781-0740 in South Africa; www. abercrombiekent.com), or **Wilderness Safaris** (*(C)* **27/11/895-0862** in South Africa; www.wilderness-safaris.com). For a delta expedition exclusively by mokoro, contact **Okavango Tours & Safaris** (*(C)* **267/66-0220** in Botswana, 44/020/8343-3283 in the U.K.; www.okavango. com). All of these trips are pricey, but they're once-in-a-lifetime special.

✈ Maun.

BEST TIME: July–Sept.

WHY THEY'LL THANK YOU: Sharing the river with the hippos.

Paddling Away **429**

Torres del Paine
Kayaking on Glacial Lakes
Ages 10 & up • Puerto Natales, Chile

Rᴇᴀᴅʏ ꜰᴏʀ ᴀᴅᴠᴇɴᴛᴜʀᴇ? Then come to Patagonia, the extreme end of South America, where Chile and Argentina run side by side down the narrowing tip of the continent as if they're racing to the treacherous Cape of Good Hope. The most dramatic bit is Chile's Torres del Paine, a set of granite peaks and towers that soars from sea level to upward of 2,800m (9,186 ft.), but it doesn't stop there—surrounding the Paine Massif are vast glaciers and startling blue lakes (*paine* is the Tehuelche Indian word for "blue"), their waters turned milky turquoise by glacial melt. It's quite a challenge to get here—and to get around once you've arrived—but your reward will be mesmerizing glacier close-ups and an exhilarating end-of-the-earth feeling.

From Puerto Natales, the frontierlike gateway town to Torres del Paine, several boat tours head out to the glaciers, located in **Parque Nacional Bernardo O'Higgins,** but your goal is to do it yourself on sea kayaks. **Bigfoot Expeditions** (*(C)* **61/414611;** www.bigfootpatagonia. com), the main adventure-tour packager in Punta Arenas, leads kayak day trips onto the glacial fjord Ultima Esperanza; if the weather's right you'll get a view of the Paine Massif. Thrilling as it sounds, this is actually an easy paddle in cold but glassy protected waters. A 2-day version of this trip starts by riding the cutter *21 de Mayo* to Lake Serrano, then kayaking around Ultima Esperanza and camping overnight near Balmaceda Glacier; your second day is spent paddling around protruding

Torres del Paine.

icebergs in Lake Serrano, then returning on the *21 Mayo* back to Puerto Natales. Just be sure the kids dress warmly,

because there's a distinct deep-freeze element to this experience, even if you come in Chile's version of summer (Jan or Feb). Winters (July–Aug) can be cold but may be a better time to visit because the punishing Patagonian winds die down then.

If the view of Torres del Paine from the fjord wasn't enough, you can book a cruise on an open Zodiac boat past the glaciers Tyndall and Geike to the Torres del Paine entrance and on up the gnarly Rio Serrano to the narrow Serrano Glacier; disembark to walk upon the ice before boarding another boat for a 3½-hour ride back to Puerto Natales. **Aventour** (✆ **61/410253;** www.aventouraventuras.com) and **Onas** (✆ **61/412707;** www.onas patagonia.com) both offer this full-day expedition.

ⓘ www.patagonia-chile.com.

✈ Puerto Natales.

🛏 $ **Hostal Los Pinos,** Philippi 449, Puerto Natales (✆ **61/411735**). $$$ **Hotel CostAustralis,** Pedro Montt 262, Puerto Natales (✆ **61/412000;** www.australis.com).

WHY THEY'LL THANK YOU: The ultimate kayaking adventure.

430 Paddling Away

Nova Scotia: Riding the Tidal Bore

Ages 4 & up • Maitland, Nova Scotia, Canada

IN THE MIDDLE OF THE OCEAN, tides are no big deal—it's only when they get close to shore that you notice a difference in water levels. But when you funnel that rising water into a V-shaped bay that keeps getting narrower *and* shallower until it gets squeezed into the mouth of a river and hits the outflowing current—well, that's your recipe for an honest-to-goodness tidal bore. You can't see this natural phenomenon many places in the world, but you sure can see it up in Nova Scotia,

on the eastern arm of the Bay of Fundy. And when that surge of tidal water comes rushing up the Shubenacadie River, you and the kids want to be there, to ride it like a bucking bronco.

The top outfitter is **Shubenacadie River Runners,** who have the routine down to a science. Aboard 4.8m (16-ft.) Zodiac boats, fitted with powerful outboard motors, you'll lie in wait at the mouth of the Shubenacadie, admiring the forested cliffs on either side, waiting for the precisely timed tide to arrive. As soon as the first wave swells beneath the boat—it can lift anywhere from .3 to 3.3m (1–11 ft.), depending on water conditions—the boat is whisked on the powerful surge of the tidal bore upstream for half a mile or so, as the water keeps rising and rising. Then, as the tidal bore begins to dissipate, the boat slips off of its ride for a moment. Look up in the sky and you may spot bald eagles hovering overhead, scrutinizing the goings-on. The next part of the adventure consists of chasing a series of natural sand rapids, which develop in the river only at high tide—the convoluted pattern of sandbars, which normally lie above the water's surface, create rapids when they are submerged, but they don't last for long; you've got to time things just right.

The tidal bore hits the river at different times daily—consult River Runners's tides chart to find the right time for the dates you're looking at. You can also choose dates when the ride is expected to be wilder or tamer, according to tide conditions. Like I said, they've got it down to a science. And of course, this can be an educational experience for children, a virtual seminar in physical science and marine biology and all that. Sure. An educational experience, and *not fun at all*. Right.

(i) 8681 Hwy. 215 (© **800/856-5061;** www3.ns.sympatico.ca/river.runners).

A typical Nova Scotia view.

✈ Halifax, 177km (110 miles).

⇔ $$$ **Bellavista Bed & Breakfast,** 8029 Hwy. 215 (© **866/506-1414** or 902/261-2626; www.bbcanada.com/samcon). $$ **Captain Douglas Inn,** 8843 Hwy. 215 (© **902/261-2289**).

BEST TIME: May–Sept.

WHY THEY'LL THANK YOU: Riding nature's roller coaster.

Paddling Away **431**

The Delaware Water Gap
Tubing the Lazy River
Ages 6 & up • Bushkill, Pennsylvania, USA

SOME PEOPLE PREFER THEIR RIVERS LAZY, and I have to confess I'm one of them. The idea of floating downstream on a slow-moving current, with the water sparkling and the sun shining, suits me just fine. Tubing down the Delaware River? That's my idea of a laid-back summer's afternoon, and a great no-hassle way to bond with my kids.

When you see the dramatic vista of the Delaware Water Gap you might expect some white-water action. But what you'll find is a relatively shallow stretch of river with just a few riffles and quiet pools parting for tiny scrubby islands and drinking in tributaries along the way. The Delaware can take its time, because it's the last undammed big river in the East, though just barely—much of the land upstream from the Gap was once cleared for a planned hydroelectric project, which accounts for the absence of houses for 40 miles of riverbank in the Delaware Water Gap National Recreation Area. The government had to do something with the land it had already appropriated—and turning it into a park was the perfect solution.

Access points have been created along the river every 4 to 10 miles, which makes it ideal for short canoeing and kayaking trips; for inner tubes, which travel even slower, a trip of 4 miles or so is ideal (considering that the river only flows around 1½ mph). Local outfitters include **Pack Shack Adventure,** 88 Broad St., Delaware Water Gap (✆ **570/424-8533;** www.packshack.com), and **Chamberlain Canoes,** River Road, Minisink Acres Mall, Minisink Hills (✆ **800/422-6631;** www.chamberlaincanoes.com). They'll not only provide river maps and rent you stout inner tubes (with safety handles and two air chambers, so you can still float if one is punctured), but even rent you a cargo tube to carry a cooler and towels, so you can stop off at an island or river beach for a picnic en route. Wear Aqua Shoes or old sneakers so you can hop out easily. They'll drive you to your access point and pick you up afterward—all you have to do is slather on the sunblock and hit the water.

As you drift along, you'll have time to gaze at the forested ridges on either side, to see map turtles basking on rocks in the sun, to eyeball the bald eagles soaring overhead. A canoe or kayak may glide past you, but no jet skis will disrupt your idyll. Little sisters can keep up with their big brothers, because you can't go any faster than the river, and the river's in no hurry. Chill out.

ⓘ River Road 9 (✆ **570/588-2452;** www.nps.gov/dewa).

✈ Lehigh Valley International, Allentown, PA, 65 miles. Newark International, Newark, NJ, 70 miles.

🛏 $ **Delaware River Family Campground,** 100 Rte. 46, Delaware, NJ (✆ **800/543-0271** or 908/475-4517; www.njcamping.com/delaware). $$ **Shannon Inn,** Exit 309 from I-80, E. Stroudsburg, PA (✆ **800/858-8471** or 570/424-1951).

WHY THEY'LL THANK YOU: Gliding through the Gap.

---

432 Paddling Away

Guadalupe River: Tubing, Texas-Style

Ages 6 & up • Spring Branch, Texas, USA

DOWN HERE THEY CALL IT "TOOBING," and the Texas Hill country on the Guadalupe River north of San Antonio is a little livelier than the Delaware Water Gap (see above). Hill country Texas defies most outsiders' expectations of Texas—it's hilly, green countryside between San Antonio and Austin, where the local heritage is more German than Hispanic. The Guadalupe winds a looping southeasterly course through the hills down to the Gulf, and all those loops—not to mention patches of just-gnarly-enough rapids—make the tubing plenty interesting.

The Guadalupe River is well-known as a tubing spot, but what most people think of when they picture Guadalupe River tubing is the 18-mile stretch south of the Canyon Dam, near New Braunfels, Texas. New Braunfels's River Road is lined with watersports outfitters, and on a hot summer weekend afternoon the Guadalupe becomes like one big crowded frat party, where the tubes ride as close as bumper boats. You might as well be tubing at the New Braunfels water park, **Schlitterbahn,** 305 W. Austin (✆ **830/625-2351;** www.schlitterbahn.com), which claims to be the largest water park in the world, and I don't doubt it. Hey, we *like* water parks, but tubing on a natural river should be another thing altogether.

For families, the scene is a little calmer up above Canyon Lake, around **Guadalupe River State Park.** Along here the river is lined picturesquely with bald cypress trees, their huge roots exposed at the banks, as well as a couple of steep limestone bluffs. The kids are likely to spot deer, opossum, and armadillo browsing around the woods, and four natural

rapids make intriguing hiccups in the river, all of them relatively gentle. There are no tube rentals at the park, but you can get fitted out nearby at **Big Foot Canoes,** on the Weidner cattle ranch, FM 311 at the river, in Spring Branch (✆ **830/885-7106;** www.bigfootcanoes.com); the **Bergheim Campground,** 103 White Water Rd., Boerne (✆ **830/336-2235;** www.bergheimcampground.com); or **Rio Raft,** Canyon Lake (✆ **877/RIO-RAFT** or 830/964-3613; www.rioraft.com), all of which can arrange to drive you to your starting point and pick you up again wherever you choose to come off the river. Four miles or so should be just enough to splash off the summer heat.

ⓘ 3350 Park Rd. 31 (✆ **830/438-2656;** www.tpwd.state.tx.us/park/guadalup).

✈ ⊨ San Antonio **67**.

WHY THEY'LL THANK YOU: It's totally toobular.

Paddling Away **433**

The Flathead River, Montana
A First Taste of White Water
Ages 6 & up • Northwestern Montana, USA

FAMILIES ARE OFTEN SCARED away from whitewater rafting by its reputation as a daredevil sport. But plenty of rivers offer a toned-down version of the big thrill, where kids can get splashing wet and not fear for their lives. Riding the river, you become intimately connected with every bend and drop, every fallen tree and craggy boulder. And the moment when your child sees a doe and her fawns come to the riverside to drink, or even a mama black bear and her cubs—well, as the commercial says, that's priceless.

I can't think of anywhere better to let them dunk their first paddles into white water than Montana's Flathead River, which runs past Glacier National Park. The

North Fork, which flows down from Canada along the park's western border, rolls through remote wilderness, with sections so smooth that a raft ride is really more of a float than a proper white-water experience. Over on the busier **Middle Fork**—which forms the southern border of Glacier National Park—there are still placid stretches but also a few Class II–III rapids, safe enough for younger children but whooshy enough to give their older brothers and sisters a decent thrill, with gruesomely named rapids like Bonecrusher and Jaws. The waters are higher and faster in early summer, swollen by snowmelt off the majestic peaks nearby; come in July or August if calmer rafting is more your style.

One of the benefits of launching junior rafters on the Flathead is that it offers access points for **half-day excursions**—you can choose between tackling John Stevens Canyon, the heart-racing part of the Middle Fork, or the more easygoing canyon from West Glacier to Blankenship Bridge (even that has at least one mild rapid, at Devil's Elbow, to give kids a taste of the action). **Full-day trips** are also feasible; these begin with the quiet river and work up to the rapids later in the day, after young rafters have grown comfortable with the river. Longer excursions venture up to the North Fork, where the rafting party camps or stays in cabins overnight; expect mellow rafting through quiet wilderness the first couple of days, followed by a few rapids on the last leg of the trip, once you're in the swing of things.

Several outfitters, all of them based in West Glacier, Montana, organize a range of river rafting trips: **Montana Raft Company** (℡ **800/521-7238** or 406/387-5555; www.glacierguides.com), **Great Northern Whitewater** (℡ **800/735-7897** or 406/387-5340; www.gnwhitewater.com), and **Wild River Adventures** (℡ **800/700-7056** or 406/387-9453; www.riverwild.com).

ⓘ **Travel Montana,** 301 S. Park, Helena (℡ **800/847-4868** or 406/841-2870; http://visitmt.com).

✈ ⊨ See Going-to-the-Sun Road **22**.

BEST TIME: May-mid to Sept.

WHY THEY'LL THANK YOU: The surprise of that first splash.

The Snake River
White Water from Hell (Canyon)
Ages 8 & up • Enterprise, Oregon, USA

WHEN THE KIDS have to deliver the standard what-I-did-on-my-summer-vacation school report in September, there's an enormous coolness factor in saying, "I white-water rafted on the Snake River." It works even if all your family did was take a mild float trip along the Snake up in Grand Teton National Park. But now add this phrase: "I white-water rafted on the Snake River *through Hell's Canyon.*" Now they *own* that homeroom.

Hell's Canyon is the deepest gorge in North America, a full mile and a half deep, and it's gorgeous to boot. It curls along the border between Idaho and Oregon, as the river builds up a head of steam to pour into the Columbia River in Washington State. (One look at a map and the kids will agree they couldn't call this loopy river anything *but* the Snake.) The standard 3-day rafting trip through this steep-walled forested canyon covers about 36

miles, but it's not rapids all the way, not by any means—there are plenty of placid sections where rafters can relax and enjoy stunning views of the Seven Devils Mountains (another dynamite name) and the Summit Ridge. Technically, in fact, it can be classified as an easy run. What makes this white water so awesome is not the wildness of the waters, but how long the rapids go on, shooting through this relatively straight stretch of the river. And while they might be scary to those paddling a kayak (which may be an option for the daredevils in your party), if you're seated in a large inflatable raft it'll be a manageable thrill. Of course you'll get splashed and soaked, but that's part of the whole white-water experience.

When you're not rafting, there's plenty more to do along this stretch of the Snake River. Short hikes lead you away from the river to view Native American pictographs on canyon walls, or to find the abandoned cabins of early-1900s settlers. There are chances to try trout fishing, and also to swim in the surprisingly warm waters. Wildlife viewings may include bighorn sheep, elk, and eagles.

Long-established outfitters include **Northwest Voyageurs** (✆ **800/727-9977;** www.voyageurs.com), **O.A.R.S.** (✆ **800/346-7277;** www.oars.com), and **Zoller's Outdoor Odysseys** (✆ **800/366-2004** or 509/493-2641; www.

snakeraft.com). They'll handle all the details—supplying equipment, guiding the rafts, directing activities, setting up a very comfortable camp each night, and shuttling you to the starting point and from the ending point.

ⓘ 88401 Hwy. 82 (✆ **541/426-5546;** www.fs.fed.us/hellscanyon).

✈ Lewiston, ID, 125 miles.

WHY THEY'LL THANK YOU: Thrills, but hopefully no spills.

Swimming **435**

Swimming with a Million Tiny Lights

Ages 4 & up • Vieques, Puerto Rico

I THOUGHT PUERTO RICO WAS AN ISLAND—but how can an island *have* an island? Well, Puerto Rico has two, Vieques and Cule-bra, for years a well-kept secret among Puerto Ricans themselves, who come here to escape the tourists on the big island. Since the U.S. Navy in 2003 closed its installation on Vieques, though, much more land is available for vacationers, and Vieques is rapidly becoming known as an eco-friendly—and still charmingly scruffy—destination.

With some 40 palm-lined white-sand beaches, and reefs of snorkel-worthy antler coral off shore, Vieques—11km (6¾ miles) off the big island's east coast, only an hour by ferry—has an obvious appeal for sun-loving families. But one of the coolest things on Vieques has nothing at all to do with the sun. Just west of the main town, Isabel Segunda, lies **Mosquito Bay,** which has been renamed Phosphorescent Bay for the way its waters glow in the dark, thanks to millions of tiny bioluminescent organisms called pyrodiniums (translation from science-speak: "whirling fire"). They're only about one-five-hundredth of an inch in size, but when these tiny swimming creatures are disturbed (by, for example, a hovering tour boat), they dart away and light up

like fireflies, leaving eerie blue-white trails of phosphorescence. These pyrodiniums exist elsewhere, but not in such amazing concentrations: A gallon of water in Mosquito Bay may contain upward of three-quarters of a million such creatures. It's definitely worth letting the kids stay up late for once. Wear a bathing suit because it's possible to swim in these glowing waters, a sensation the kids will find incredibly eerie and cool.

Don't make the mistake of coming here on a full moon, however—the glow of the pyrodiniums is only discernible on a cloudy, moonless night. (**Warning:** Some tour boats go out to the bay regardless of the full moon—and you won't get your money back if you're disappointed.)

Island Adventures (✆ **787/741-0720**) operates 2-hour nighttime trips in Phosphorescent Bay aboard the *Luminosa,* though not during the full moon. If the kids are into kayaking, they can get even closer to those glow-in-the-dark waters on a kayak tour offered by **Blue Caribe Kayak** (✆ **787/741-2522**). In fact, Blue Caribe acts as a clearinghouse for all the island's watersports outfitters—it's a small island, and virtually everybody is related to everyone else. That small-town casualness is one of the things that still makes Vieques a great place for traveling families, hot spot or not.

ⓘ ✆ **787/721-2400;** www.gotopuertorico.com

✈ Vieques.

🛏 $$ **Hacienda Tamarindo,** Rte. 996, Barrio Puerto Real (✆ **787/741-8525;** www.enchanted-isle.com/tamarindo). $$$

Wyndham Martineau Bay Resort, Rte. 200 (✆ **787/741-4100;** www.wyndham.com).

WHY THEY'LL THANK YOU: Nature's night light.

436 **Swimming**

Blue Lagoon: Iceland's Tropical Oasis
All ages • Iceland

Oᴋᴀʏ, sᴏ ᴍᴀʏʙᴇ it is one of the most touristy things to do when you're visiting Iceland. But the bathers who frolic in this warm-water lagoon 40 minutes outside of Reykjavik include just as many locals as tourists—everybody wants to enjoy this great outdoor bathtub. Even when the countryside is covered in snow, steam rises from this huge pool of turquoise-colored water, and the very idea that you could have such a balmy swim in a place called Iceland will be irresistible to the kids.

Several local tour operators run half-day excursions from Reykjavik to the Blue Lagoon geothermal spa; in fact, it's so close to Keflavik airport that some travelers stop by for one last iconic Icelandic experience before boarding their flight home. The entrance fee isn't cheap (though kids do get in for half-price), but you can easily spend a couple of hours in this large pool sunk into a lava field, fringed by black-sand beaches and tumbled chunks of volcanic rock. It's not, in fact, a natural phenomenon but a by-product of the nearby power plant, where hot seawater is used to heat spring water, which in turn produces central heating for the houses in Reykjavik. The excess seawater is then pumped into this lagoon, for bathers to enjoy the curative powers of its salts and minerals (which do occur completely naturally). An ell of New Age-y modern buildings anchors one corner, where services such as a sauna and steam bath are offered; the sapphire lake

snakes away from the building, dotted with a few scattered black rocky outcrops and topped by wispy trails of steam.

Stepping into the lagoon, you'll notice how smooth its sides are—the result of high silica content in the water—and your toes will sink into thin soft sediment on the bottom, full of blue-green algae that gives the lagoon its distinctive color (as one recent visitor describes it, the exact color of Riptide Rush Gatorade). The water maintains a temperature of about

The Blue Lagoon.

40°C (that's 104°F), though as you swim about you'll find all sorts of vents and heat currents that make certain areas warmer than others. And as we all know, there's nothing a kid likes better than hovering by the place where hot water rushes into a heated swimming pool—well, the Blue Lagoon has dozens of such gushers to seek out.

Adults may want to spend extra on treatments such as a facial mask made of silica mud, but for the kids, just paddling around in this immense jewel-colored hot tub will be enough. Just another weird, one-of-a-kind thing about Iceland.

ⓘ 240 Grindavik (ⓒ **420-8800;** www.blue lagoon.com).

✈ 🛏 See Thingvellir **195**.

WHY THEY'LL THANK YOU: The mist rising off the waters.

Swimming

437

Floating in the Dead Sea

All ages • Israel

Tʜᴇ sᴇɴsᴀᴛɪᴏɴ ᴏꜰ ꜰʟᴏᴀᴛɪɴɢ ɪɴ ᴛʜᴇ Dᴇᴀᴅ Sᴇᴀ ɪs so freaky, you keep testing it again and again—releasing your body into that incredibly saline water and popping up to the surface, as buoyant as if you were weightless. It works every time, even for a novice swimmer. Such a simple thing, and yet utterly absorbing. The kids are likely to break out in fits of giggles—and then try it again . . .

Less than an hour's drive from Jerusalem, this is *the* saltiest sea there is, by a long shot, and the richest in minerals (magnesium, calcium, bromine, potassium). Not only that, it's the lowest point on earth, a remarkable 417m (1,368 ft.) below sea level. Water flows into the Dead Sea from several sources, notably the Jordan River, but it doesn't flow out, it just evaporates—at a rate so fast, the sea is shrinking year by year, so the sooner you get here the better. The air contains 10% more oxygen than normal, so just breathing makes you feel relaxed and energized. It's hot (up to 42°C/108°F in summer) but dry, and thanks to an extra layer of atmosphere caused by evaporation, the sun's UV rays are filtered, making it a fairly safe place to sunbathe. And there's sunshine 330 days a year.

The name is a misnomer, because this inland lake isn't truly dead—granted, no fish live in this salt-saturated water, but a certain green algae does just fine, plus lots of red archaebacteria. The water looks slightly greenish, and also milky from all the minerals; at rocky coves along the shore you can see encrustations of salt from evaporation. And although the desert ridges around the sea look sand-scoured and fierce, along the lakeside

Floating in the Dead Sea.

highway you'll find a few lush oases, many of them with sulphur hot springs.

Two main beach areas thrive along the Israeli shore. The first is at the ancient desert oasis **Ein Gedi,** where you'll find a rather crowded public beach, a kibbutz with a good hotel and spa, and a botanic garden planted with rare trees and shrubs from all over the world. Even nonguests can pay a day-use fee to use the hotel's spa or beach, which may be the Dead Sea's best for swimming. At Ein Gedi kibbutz, you can book a desert jeep safari, a Bedouin feast in a tent, or an hour-long cruise on the Dead Sea in an

eccentric wooden double-deck boat called *Lot's Wife.* Farther down the coast you'll pass the ancient fortress of **Masada 187**, and then reach **Ein Bokek,** where there are several hotels and free public beaches. The water is richer in minerals down here, and therefore said to be more curative. We won't argue—not if it gives us a chance to try floating again . . .

ⓘ **Tourist office** (ℂ 08/668-8808; www.deadsea.co.il).

✈ ⊨ See Masada **187**.

WHY THEY'LL THANK YOU: Doing the Dead Sea float.

The Great Barrier Reef
World's Biggest Marine Park
Ages 6 & up • Pacific Coast, Queensland, Australia

IT'S THE ONLY LIVING STRUCTURE on Earth visible from the moon; it's bigger than the United Kingdom; it's home to 1,500 kinds of fish, 400 species of corals, 4,000 kinds of clams and snails, and who knows how many sponges, starfish, and sea urchins. And snorkelers are in a prime position to see the Great Barrier Reef at its best—the rich colors of the coral depend on lots of light, so staying close to the surface maximizes your view of the brightest and richest marine life. Staring through your mask at green and purple clams, pink sponges, red starfish, purple sea urchins, and fish from electric blue to neon yellow to lime is truly a magical experience.

Even if the kids have never gone snorkeling before, there's no more rewarding place to start. Outfitters and resorts all along the Reef coast make it easy for you. **Day trips** on motorized catamarans head out from Cairns, Port Douglas, Townsville, Mission Beach, and the Whitsunday mainland and islands, with snorkel gear provided and marine biologists on board to explain all about the Reef. Each boat ties

up at its own private permanent pontoon, anchored to a platform reef. The pontoons have glass-bottom boats for passengers who don't want to get wet, but there's lots of instruction to ease novices into the water.

If a long boat ride puts you off, the coral cay of **Green Island** lies less than an hour from the city wharf at Cairns (ℂ **07/4051 3588;** www.tropicalaustralia. com), the town with the most direct air connections. The closest Reef site off Port Douglas, an hour north of Cairns, is the **Low Isles,** two tiny lushly vegetated coral cays where you can wade out to the coral right from the beach. The coral is not quite as dazzling as the outer Reef's, but the fish life here is rich, there are lots of seabirds, and you may spot sea turtles. From the lovely rainforest town of Mission Beach, south of Cairns, it only takes an hour to get to the Outer Reef, where shallow waters full of vibrant marine life surround the sandy coral cay, **Beaver Cay.**

If you base yourselves in the **Whitsunday Islands** (www.whitsundaytourism. com), of course, you're already out in the

You may spot a ray or a reef shark while snorkeling on the Great Barrier Reef.

Outer Reef, on rainforested islands surrounded by the waters of the Great Barrier Reef Marine Park. Just about any Whitsunday island has fringing reef around its shores, and there are good snorkeling reefs between the islands, a quick boat ride away. Most folks' favorite is **Blue Pearl Bay,** off Hayman Island; it has loads of corals and some gorgonian fans in its gullies, and heaps of reef fish, including Maori wrasse and sometimes even manta rays—and you can walk right in off the beach.

(i) **Great Barrier Reef Visitors Bureau** (✆ **07/3876 4644;** www.great-barrier-reef. com).

✈ Cairns.

🚂 See Kuranda's Scenic Skyways **35**.

WHY THEY'LL THANK YOU: Floating facedown in Technicolor wonder.

Snorkeling & Diving **439**

Snorkeling on Santa Catalina Island

Ages 8 & up • Avalon, California, USA

It's only 22 miles off the Southern California coast, yet oh, what a difference that distance makes. Santa Catalina Island feels like another world from the Los Angeles metrosprawl, a haven of clean air, untrafficked roads, and crystal-clear water. The water is so clear, in fact, that this is one of the West Coast's best snorkeling sites. Maybe you've seen the kelp forest in a tank at the Monterey Bay Aquarium **145**; on Catalina you can swim in a lush jungle of kelp yourself, watching fish wriggle and scoot around its undulating brown fronds.

Underwater visibility around the island can be 40 to 100 feet. Horseshoe-shaped Avalon, the island's main town, has three top locations for snorkeling: **Lover's Cove Marine Preserve,** off Pebbly Beach south of Avalon Bay; **Casino Point Marine Park,** located beside the round white Casino building, Avalon's most prominent landmark; and just offshore at

the **Descanso Beach Club,** a private cove around the point from the Casino. The Casino Point location has shipwrecks to explore, as well as artificial reefs to harbor additional sea life. To rent gear or take guided snorkeling trips, go to **Catalina Divers Supply** (✆ **800/353-0330** or 310/510-0330; www.catalina diverssupply.com) at Casino Point, or **Catalina Snorkeling Adventures,** at Lover's Cove (✆ **877/SNORKEL**).

You can also get a kelp-forest view on an Undersea Tour from **Discovery Tours** (✆ **800/626-1496;** www.visitcatalina island.com), a 45-minute cruise of Lover's Cove preserve in a semisubmerged boat. The same company also offers 50-minute nighttime trips to go out and watch schools of flying fish leaping above the water.

There are two ways to get to Catalina: by **Catalina Express** ferryboat (✆ **800/**

481-3470; www.catalinaexpress.com), hour-long trips departing from the Sea/Air terminal in San Pedro and the Catalina Landing in Long Beach; or by 15-minute helicopter crossings from **Island Express** (© **800/2-AVALON;** www.islandexpress.com, flying out of San Pedro or Long Beach. Arriving in Avalon, you'll notice swarms of golf carts in all colors of the rainbow—this is the only city in California authorized to limit the number of cars on city streets, so locals make do with golf carts. Near the dock you can rent your own, which the kids will find a blast. Take time to explore **Avalon,** which still bears the Art Deco look of Catalina's heyday as a pleasure resort developed in 1915 by

William Wrigley, Jr., the chewing-gum magnate.

(i) **Catalina Island Visitors Bureau,** Green Pleasure Pier (© **310/510-1520;** www.catalina.com).

✈ Los Angeles International, 45 miles.

⊨ $ **Hotel Catalina,** 129 Whittley Ave. (© **800/540-0184** or 310/510-0027; www.hotelcatalina.com/reservations.htm). $$ **Hotel Vista Del Mar,** 417 Crescent Ave. (© **310/510-1452;** www.hotel-vistadelmar.com).

WHY THEY'LL THANK YOU: Watching fish dart out of the kelp fronds.

440 Snorkeling & Diving

Biscayne National Park
Florida's Homegrown Coral Reef
Ages 8 & up • Homestead, Florida, USA

BISCAYNE NATIONAL PARK is one of the least-crowded parks in America's national park system, probably because its main attractions are kinda difficult to reach. It's not a question of being remote—it's so close to Miami, you can do it as a day trip—but more about being hidden from view. Aboveground, you'll see only a no-big-deal strip of mangrove shoreline and 44 barrier islands, most of them mere specks off of South Florida's east coast. But beneath the surface lies the world's third-longest coral reef, an aquatic universe pulsing with multicolored life. All it takes is strapping on a snorkel and fins for kids to be able to cruise around this tropical paradise, encountering bright parrotfish and angelfish, gently rocking sea fans, and coral labyrinths.

The clear, warm waters of Biscayne National Park are packed with reef fish, rays, moray eels, jellyfish, anemones, sponges, even sea turtles and dolphins—some 512 species, all told, in this 173,000-acre expanse. Not only that,

an **underwater trail** identifies five shipwrecks about 3 miles east of Elliott Key; mooring buoys point the way to the wrecks, with waterproof cards attached to tell the kids what they're seeing. You can rent equipment at the full-service dive shop at the park's mainland entrance at Convoy Point, and if you don't have your own boat, you can take a 3-hour snorkeling or diving tour operated every afternoon by **Biscayne National Underwater Park, Inc.** (© **305/230-1100**); you'll either stick to the bay or head out to the reefs, depending on the very changeable weather. Even beginning snorkelers will get a satisfying eyeful.

The mainland entrance is 9 miles east of Homestead, off U.S. 1; a small beach and marina is nearby, but the rest of the park is accessible only by boat, either your own or the park concession's water transport (© **305/230-1100**). Few of the park's islands are even open to visitors; the two most popular are Elliott Key and Boca Chita Key, which can be reached by launch from the visitor center. Both islands have campsites (call the park ranger at ℂ **305/230-1144** for information on permits and camping fees) and places to moor your boat; **Elliott Key** also has an interesting nature trail, and **Boca Chita,** once an exclusive haven for yachters, has some restored historic buildings.

If you prefer not to dive, take the wimp's way out and view the underwater sights on a 3-hour **glass-bottom boat**

tour offered by Biscayne National Underwater Park, Inc., departing from Convoy Point at 10am. Reservations are almost always necessary.

ⓘ **Dante Fascell Visitor Center,** at Convoy Point, 9700 SW 328th St. (ℂ **305/230-7275;** www.nps.gov/bisc).

✈ ⊨ See Coral Castle **92**.

WHY THEY'LL THANK YOU: Tropical colors and eerie shipwrecks.

Snorkeling & Diving
441

St. John
Snorkeling on the Trunk Bay Trail
Ages 6 & up • St. John, U.S. Virgin Islands, the Caribbean

THE FIRST PLACE MY KIDS ever put a mask and snorkel into the water was down here in the U.S. Virgin Islands, and I'm afraid it spoiled them for more ordinary snorkeling experiences. I still have photos of them standing on the white-sand beach at Cinnamon Bay, along with the five kids of the other families we were traveling with, looking like an invasion party of aliens in their rented snorkeling gear—eight breathing tubes sticking up like antennae, eight pairs of flippers shifting impatiently in the sand, and their masks making them look like eight frowning Cyclopes. We deliberately took forever getting that shot, just because it made them so antsy. Enough photos already, they wanted to get out in that turquoise water and *start snorkeling.*

Their snorkeling debuts took place where so many others have started out: at Trunk Bay, where the National Park Service has set up the **National Park Underwater Trail.** This 225-yard trail follows a reef where all the underwater features are labeled with signs 5 to 15 feet under the water's surface. Snorkeling snobs wouldn't be caught dead at popular Trunk Bay doing the trail—they prefer more remote places like Waterlemon Cay or Salt Pond Bay or Haulover Bay, where

the snorkeling's a lot more challenging—but with children, Trunk Bay is just the thing. The signs help to focus young snorkelers' attention and keep them going, and it was extremely helpful for them to learn the difference between various coral structures, between a sea fan and an anemone. As for the bright parrotfish flitting by, well, no sign can be attached to something that elusive, but since the signs had made the kids more attentive snorkelers, they spotted the parrotfish all right. They were hoping for sea turtles—hawksbills and leatherbacks are common in these waters—but the turtles sensibly kept their distance. With kids, we were also grateful for Trunk Bay's other amenities—flush toilets, a snack bar, and lifeguards.

We also just plain fell in love with St. John—with two-thirds of it protected as Virgin Islands National Park, it's remarkably unspoiled, with lots of dense foliage and hiking trails and unruffled quiet, surrounded by expanses of clear, sparkling turquoise waters. It's what we'd always expected the Caribbean to be—and now that we had the kids hooked on snorkeling, our island-hopping days could begin.

(i) **Virgin Islands National Park,** Trunk Bay (© **340/776-6201;** www.nps.gov/viis).

✈ St. Thomas, 45–60 min. by boat.

🛏 $$ **Cinnamon Bay Campground,** Cruz Bay (© **340/776-6330;** www.

cinnamonbay.com). $$$ **Westin St. John Resort,** Great Cruz Bay (© **800/808-5020** or 340/693-8000; www.westinresortstjohn.com).

WHY THEY'LL THANK YOU: Connecting the dots underwater.

Bonaire Marine Park
Diving Deep into Paradise
Ages 6 & up • Netherlands Antilles, the Caribbean

BONAIRE MAY BE A DRY, DUSTY ISLAND, but it's surrounded by rich coral reefs and incredibly clear water—visibility is often about 30m (100 ft.) or more. A couple of decades ago, as hotels first began cropping up along the ocean's edge, savvy Bonaire residents had the foresight to capitalize on this, their greatest tourism draw. By creating the Bonaire Marine Park, they ensured that this island would forever be known as a diver's paradise.

Stateside, you might ask someone his opinion about the best pizza place in town and spark some controversy. Here, ask a group of natives to name their favorite snorkel spots and the same sort of lively give-and-take begins. There's no consensus, but some of the more popular include Thousands Steps, Tori's Reef, Karpata (when it's calm), Andrea 1, and Windsock. The dive-shop pier by the **Divi Flamingo Beach Resort** is another starting point, relatively close to the cruise ship pier. The Marine Park plays no favorites, incorporating the entire coastline plus the tiny offshore island of Klein Bonaire. What it provides is permanent dive-site moorings (since anchoring on coral is a big no-no), rangers to police the reefs and enforce regulations, and services and facilities including a visitor center, the **Karpata Ecological Center.**

The reefs here are home to over 355 species, from beautiful parrotfish and damselfish to outsize groupers and

tough-looking moray eels. The variety of coral formations attracts a corresponding variety of fish: At 1m (3¼ ft.) you can find brain coral; at 3m (9¾ ft.) you begin to see staghorn and elkhorn coral and the graceful, swaying, feathery soft-coral "trees" known as gorgonians. Snorkelers only get to see the upper layers; it's divers who really get the best view of the island's 80-plus dive sites.

If the kids didn't take scuba lessons at home before you left, they can do so on the island. NAUI (www.naui.org) and PADI (www.padi.com) are the two most reliable certification organizations; both offer different levels of instruction, starting at age 5. Diving instruction takes time and commitment. Kids need to know that it's incredibly rewarding but it's also a serious endeavor.

Every dive shop has slightly different offerings; some of the better ones, that also rent snorkeling equipment, include **Dive II** (© **599/717-8285**), **Captain Don's Habitat Dive Shop** (© **599/717-8290**), and **Bonaire Dive and Adventures** (© 599/717-2229).

(i) **Tourist office** (© **800/BONAIRE;** www.infobonaire.com).

✈ Bonaire.

🛏 $$ **Divi Flamingo Beach Resort,** J.A. Abraham Blvd. 40 (© **800/367-3484** or 599/717-8285; www.diviresorts.com). $$

Sand Dollar Condominium Resort, Kaya Gobernador N. Debrot 79 (*©* **800/288-4773** or 599/717-8760; www.sanddollar bonaire.com).

WHY THEY'LL THANK YOU: Underwater, overwhelming.

Snorkeling & Diving

443

Feeding the Rays in Stingray City

Ages 8 & up • Grand Cayman, Cayman Islands

In the 1980s, fishermen just offshore of Grand Cayman Island cleaned their catch every evening in the shallow, sunny waters of North Sound, about 3.2km (2 miles) east of the island's northwestern tip. Over the years, stingrays began to gather to feast on the scraps, like a pack of dogs waiting to be fed. And while they still come, in droves, these days the fishermen have given way to snorkelers and divers, who allow these giant, gentle creatures to suck up bait up from their flat, open hands.

Grand Cayman's reputation as one of the best dive sites in the world means that you have a great number of solid, reputable dive shops to choose from, all of whom offer stops at Stingray City as part of their dive tour options. For kids who are comfortable snorkeling—and for kids who've just learned to scuba—Stingray City is a great spot, because the animals swim right over your shoulders or nudge your arms. Feeding them feels a bit like feeding a horse, except the mouths of the rays do create a fair bit of suction; it might frighten some kids if they're not forewarned. About 30 to 50 rays congregate here, in water that's about 4m (13 ft.) deep. They're as tame as any wild animal could be, and petting them is like stroking some wondrous newfangled silk-and-velvet fabric. The rays have occasionally harmed people who have mistreated them—*never* grab a stingray by its tail—but make sure your youngsters know to show a little respect and they'll be fine.

Divers sometimes find it challenging to balance in the water here, since it's relatively shallow. The only other challenge is to avoid the little bit of fire coral that lies along the ocean bottom. Boat captains go over safety procedures, though, before letting anyone in the water. The different companies are all in communication with each other and have planned in advance who gets to approach the site at a particular time; it's not unusual to see a few other boats waiting in line in a great half-circle. Operators include **Bob Soto's Diving Ltd.** (*©* **800/262-7686** in the U.S., or 345/949-2022; www.bobsotosreef divers.com) and **Don Foster's Dive Cayman** (*©* **345/907-9821**; www.don fosters.com). You can also opt for a

Swimming with the rays at Stingray City.

4½-hour catamaran tour that includes a stop at Stingray City and lunch offered by **Red Sail Sports** (☎ **877RED-SAIL** in the U.S., or 345/945-5965; www.redsailcayman.com).

Popular snorkeling spots in the clear, warm waters of the Caymans are **Parrot's Reef** and **Smith's Cove,** south of George Town, lush reefs abounding with parrotfish, coral, sea fans, and sponges. And of course, plain old swimming and sunbathing are fabulous at **Seven Mile Beach,** one of the Caribbean's best.

ⓘ **Tourist office** (☎ **345/949-0623;** www.caymanislands.ky).

✈ ⎘ See Booby Pond Nature Reserve **121**.

WHY THEY'LL THANK YOU: The whoosh and suck of a stingray, up close and personal.

---

444 Beaches

Cape Cod National Seashore
New England's Most Historic Strand
All ages • Chatham to Provincetown, Massachusetts, USA

Running for 30 miles along the Atlantic coast of Cape Cod, the Cape Cod National Seashore was set aside in 1961 to preserve the magnificent white sands and dunes of the Outer Cape. Here the Pilgrims first touched American soil (though they soon moved to Plymouth **219**); Thoreau meditated on nature; countless ships wrecked in the so-called Ocean's Graveyard; and Marconi's first transatlantic telegraph was received. The Seashore's real claim to fame, though, is its beaches—in reality, one long beach—with dunes 50 to 150 feet high.

Those awesome **beaches,** all well marked off of Route 6, include Coast Guard and Nauset Light beaches in Eastham, Marconi Beach in Wellfleet, Head of the Meadow Beach in Truro, and Provincetown's Race Point and Herring Cove beaches. This is the Atlantic Ocean, so the surf is rough and cold (if your kids aren't strong swimmers you may be better off choosing a town beach on the bay, like Mayo in Wellfleet or First Encounter in Eastham). Admission is charged to all beach parking lots, but there's a much smaller fee for pedestrians and cyclists, so we bicycle up the **Cape Cod Rail Trail,** which goes as far as Wellfleet, and walk onto the sand— that way, if we stay only an hour to enjoy the scenery, we haven't spent too much. Most visitors stay a full day, so parking lots fill up early. Tote along a cooler full of refreshments, as there are no concessions (which preserves the unspoiled feel of the open strand), and carry out all your trash.

The **Salt Pond Visitor Center,** just east of Route 6 in Eastham, has free exhibits and maps, brochures, and information. Several **nature trails** lead from the visitor center; our favorite nowadays is the Nauset Marsh Trail, but when the kids were younger they loved the Buttonwood Trail. Other free walking trails along the seashore include Fort Hill (off Rte. 6 in Eastham), a boardwalk trail through a red maple swamp; Great Island (on the bay side in Wellfleet); Pamet Trail (off North Pamet Rd., Truro), passing through a cranberry bog; and Provincetown's Atlantic White Cedar Swamp Trail, a rare stand of the lightweight trees prized by native Americans for canoe building. Five **historic lighthouses** also dot the Seashore, including Highland Light in Truro and Nauset Light in Eastham.

Though not officially part of the Seashore, the **Wellfleet Bay Wildlife Sanctuary,** off Route 6, South Wellfleet (📞 **508/349-2615;** www.wellfleetbay.org), is a natural add-on, a 1,000-acre refuge run by the Massachusetts Audubon Society. Nestled into a wooded site, the center offers 5 miles of trails through pine forests, salt marsh, and moors, as well as canoeing, birding, and seal-watching excursions.

ⓘ 📞 **508/255-3421;** www.nps.gov/caco.

✈ Hyannis, 25 miles.

🛏 $$ **Even'tide,** 650 Rte. 6, South Wellfleet (📞 **800/368-0007** in MA, or 508/349-3410; www.eventidemotel.com).

WHY THEY'LL THANK YOU: It ain't called the Great Beach for nothing.

Beaches **445**

Cape Hatteras National Seashore
Brave Barrier Islands
All ages • Outer Banks, North Carolina, USA

CAPE HATTERAS IS AN INFORMAL, barefoot hangout—you can easily beach-hop, pulling into the many beach-access parking lots, crossing a small boardwalk over dunes of sea oats, and plopping yourselves in the tawny sand. Yet lovely as it may look on a fine summer's day, this 70-mile strand of Outer Banks barrier islands is also "the Graveyard of the Atlantic," so named for its treacherous waters and shifting shoals. With the riptides and currents so strong, it's a place for dabbling in the surf rather than really swimming. But that's okay by me—I love the land's-end vibe of the Outer Banks, its edgy wind-scoured beauty and promise of drama.

North Carolina Highway 12 runs along the national seashore, linking its four long narrow islands—from north to south, Bodie Island, Hatteras Island, Ocracoke, and Cedar Island (a car ferry links Hatteras to Ocracoke and Ocracoke to Cedar Island). As you'd expect, each island has its own substantial lighthouse, three of which now house visitor centers with local history exhibits, nature trails, and frequent park ranger programs. Every summer night one of them offers an evening campfire program, where you and the kids can sit beneath the stars, snuggled under a blanket on the beach, hearing stories of shipwrecks and pirates and the German U-boats that battered this coast in World War II. The postcard landmark, of course, is the black-and-white diagonally striped **Cape Hatteras Lighthouse,** the tallest on the coast—its beacon can be seen for 20 miles—which you can climb up for an awesome view.

At the north end, on **Bodie Island,** guided walks along Coquina Beach explore this delicate ecosystem, home to blue crabs and sea turtles. Across the bridge on Hatteras Island, you can birdwatch on a nature trail at the **Pea Island Wildlife Refuge** (📞 252/473-1131); fish off a pier in Rodanthe, **Hatteras Island Fishing Pier,** 24251 Atlantic Ave. (📞 252/987-2323); windsurf or boogie-board at a

Birdlife on the North Carolina seashore.

spot called Canadian Hole (rent equipment at the **Hatteras Island Surf Shop in Waves,** (C) 252/987-2296).

On **Ocracoke Island,** ranger programs explore Ocracoke's colorful history (the famous pirate Blackbeard was captured here in 1718—legend says his treasure is still buried here) and visit the island's wild ponies. Yes, wild ponies, just like you'd find up the coast on Assateague Island **113**. Cape Hatteras is full of surprises like that.

(i) **Bodie Island Visitor Center,** 6½ miles south of Whalebone Junction

((C) 252/441-5711). **Hatteras Island Visitor Center,** Cape Hatteras Lighthouse, Buxton ((C) 252/995-4474). **Ocracoke Island Visitor Center,** Hwy. 12, Ocracoke ((C) 252/928-4531; www.nps.gov/caha).

✈ Norfolk International, 80 miles.

🛏 $$ **Cape Hatteras Bed & Breakfast,** 4223 Old Lighthouse Rd., Buxton ((C) 800/252-3316).

BEST TIME: May–Sept.

WHY THEY'LL THANK YOU: Beaches with stories to tell.

446 Beaches

Sanibel Island
Seashells, Seashells, Seashells by the Seashore
All ages • Sanibel Island, Florida, USA

I'M THE SORT OF BEACHGOER who could spend the entire day walking up and down the strand, searching for seashells, and I'm afraid I've passed this beachcombing obsession on to my children. So I owed it to them to fly down to the Gulf Coast of Florida, where a little apostrophe of coastal keys, attached to a long causeway to Fort Myers, offers the most amazing concentration of seashells I've ever seen. Sanibel and Captiva islands are superb beach destinations for other reasons too—their fine sugary white sand, the healthy stands of palm trees, the local curbs on high-rises and tacky development, the amount of land devoted to wildlife refuges—but it was the shells we went for, and they *did not disappoint*.

Some 200 species of shells can be found on Sanibel's wide, placid beaches. Prime time for shell hunting is February to April, or after any storm; low tide is the best time of day. Shells can be sharp, so wear Aqua Socks or old running shoes whenever you go walking on the beach. Just make sure the kids peer inside to check whether there are living creatures

still inside—Florida law prohibits taking live shells from the beaches.

Shoot, there's even a shell museum here: the **Bailey-Matthews Shell Museum,** 3075 Sanibel-Captiva Rd. ((C) 888/679-6450 or 239/395-2233; www.shellmuseum.org), devoted solely to saltwater, freshwater, and land shells. Shells from as far away as South Africa surround a 6-foot globe in the main exhibit hall, showing their geographic origins. Most important for our purposes, though, was the Wheel of Fortune–shaped case identifying shells likely to wash up on Sanibel.

To find really rare shells, you might need to head for the adjacent shoals and nearby small islands; **Captiva Cruises** ((C) 239/472-5300; www.captivacruises.com) runs shelling trips there from the South Seas Resort on Captiva Island, and several charter-boat skippers also will take guests on shelling expeditions (you can find them at the Sanibel Marina on North Yachtsman Drive, off Periwinkle Way east of Causeway Blvd.). But my kids were happy enough to fill their pails with the common shells—whelks, olives, scallops, sand dollars, conch—which lay scattered thickly on the sand.

ⓘ **Tourist office,** 1159 Causeway Rd. (☎ **239/472-1080;** www.sanibel-captiva.org).

✈ Fort Myers International, 14 miles.

🛏 $ **Palm View Motel,** 706 Donax St. (☎ **239/472-1606;** www.palmviewsanibel. com). $$$ **Sundial Beach Resort,** 1451 Middle Gulf Dr. (☎ **800/237-4184** or 239/481-3636; www.sundialresort.com).

WHY THEY'LL THANK YOU: The easiest scavenger hunt you'll ever do.

Beaches 447

Santa Monica Beach
The Golden Essence of Beachy California
All ages • Santa Monica, California, USA

Pʟᴀɴɴɪɴɢ ᴏᴜʀ ᴍᴏsᴛ ʀᴇᴄᴇɴᴛ trip to Southern California, my kids envisioned a classic white-sand beach with the Pacific Ocean sparkling blue-green beyond and a gentle white-fringed surf they could jump in to their heart's content. It was ridiculously easy for us to fulfill that fantasy with a lazy afternoon at Santa Monica State Beach (off the Pacific Coast Hwy.). What's not to like? Even on a summer Sunday, this wide strand was blissfully uncrowded; restrooms, yes, tacky food stands, no. We could even bicycle up here on the paved beach path from funky Venice Beach, where the vibe is edgier but the sand and surf not nearly so nice. Santa Monica Beach has big parking lots and nearby cafes. It's one of those cases where hunting for the exotic is a waste of time: Santa Monica Beach is easy to get to, free, and sparkling clean, an ideal place for a quintessential California day at the beach.

Just south of the beach you can visit the **Santa Monica Pier,** Ocean Avenue at the end of Colorado Boulevard (☎ **310/458-8900;** www.santamonicapier.org), one of the last of Southern California's vintage seaside piers. The Santa Monica Pier evokes the area's 19th-century seaside resort days, long before Los Angeles became La-La Land. Built in 1908 for passenger and cargo ships, the wooden wharf is now home to seafood restaurants and snack shacks, a touristy Mexican cantina, and a gaily colored turn-of-the-20th-century indoor wooden carousel (which Paul Newman operated in *The Sting*). A small amusement area perched halfway down, **Pacific Park** (☎ **310/260-8744;** www.pacpark.com), hearkens back to the granddaddy pier amusement park in California, Pacific Ocean Park; this updated version has a Ferris wheel, roller coaster, and other rides, right on the ocean's edge. Anglers head to the pier's end to fish, and nostalgia buffs to view the photographic display of the pier's history. This is the last of the great pleasure piers, offering rides, romance, and perfect panoramic views of the bay and mountains.

The fulcrum of a 60-mile beachfront stretching from celebrity-riddled Malibu to the Palos Verdes Peninsula, Santa Monica is prime real estate, with stylish oceanfront hotels, an artsy atmosphere, and somewhat wacky residents. We never come here without spending at least some time hanging out at the Third Street Promenade, a pedestrian-only outdoor mall lined with shops and restaurants; we dig the Fatburger, an outpost of a legendary Southern California fast-food chain. Might as well go for the total SoCal experience.

ⓘ **Visitor Information Center,** 1920 Main St., Suite B (☎ **800/544-5319** or 310/393-7593; www.santamonica.com).

✈ Los Angeles International.

🛏 $ **Best Western Marina Pacific,** 1697 Pacific Ave., Venice (📞 **800/786-7789** or 310/452-1111; www.mphotel.com). $$$

Hotel Oceana, 849 Ocean Ave., Santa Monica (📞 **800/777-0758** or 310/393-0486; www.hoteloceana.com).

WHY THEY'LL THANK YOU: Classic beach vibe.

448

Kauai: An Embarrassment of Riches

All ages • Kauai, Hawaii

WHEN IT COMES TO BEACHES, Hawaii has more beauties than any one state deserves; truth to tell, the garden isle of Kauai on its own has more stunning beaches than any state deserves. With its lush tropical greenery, soft golden sand, majestic ocean cliffs, and purposely low-key development—no building may exceed the height of a coconut palm—this island is a beach lover's dream.

I find it hard to resist the temptation of hanging out at popular **Hanalei Beach** on the North Coast—2 miles long, with relatively placid waters good for swimming, and all the restrooms and other beachfront facilities that are necessary when you've got kids with you. (And, I have to admit, I relish the opportunity to torture my children by singing "Puff, the Magic Dragon" over and over.) Sure, it's popular, with tourists and locals alike— you may have to walk a ways to find a spot to drop your towels—but in my experience, children *like* having other sunbathers around; making some new friends to help build sand forts is generally a plus. They don't place the same value on "getting away from it all" as we stressed-out adults (or canoodling honeymooners) do.

Still, for the best family beach on Kauai, my vote goes to **Poipu Beach,** on Kuaia's sun-soaked south shore. Developed but not overdeveloped, the whole Poipu resort area offers the requisite amenities, but you'll never feel crowded the way you might at Oahu's Waikiki Beach. Big, wide Poipu Beach Park is the place to hit the golden sands, equipped with restrooms and showers, a picnic area and restaurant. You can easily plant yourselves for a full day without getting restless; the beach is incredibly versatile—head to the left of the sandbar and you find a calm, child-friendly sandy-bottom pool protected by a lava-rock jetty; head to the right and you face an open bay of vivid turquoise water that attracts swimmers, snorkelers, and surfers. The curling waves here are enough to hang ten, yet small enough to bodysurf or boogie-board. Poipu Beach is an excellent place to learn to surf; lessons are available from numerous local outfits, the oldest and best being **Margo Oberg's School of Surfing,** Nukumoi Surf Shop, across from Brennecke's Beach (📞 **808/742-8019;** www.surfonkauai.com). Snorkelers can rent gear from **Snorkel Bob's Kauai,** 3236 Poipu Rd. (📞 **808/742-2206**), which also rents boogie boards.

ⓘ Hoone Rd., Koloa (www.poipu-beach.org).

✈ Lihue.

🛏 $$$ **Hyatt Regency Kauai Resort,** 1571 Poipu Rd. (📞 **800/55-HYATT** or 808/742-1234; www.kauai-hyatt.com). $ **Kalaheo Inn,** 4444 Papalina Rd. (📞 **888/332-6023** or 808/332-6023; www.kalaheoinn.com).

WHY THEY'LL THANK YOU: Riding that first wave.

Fraser Island: It's All Beach

Ages 4 & up • Queensland, Australia

FRASER ISLAND, off the Queensland coast south of the Great Barrier Reef, is the world's biggest sand island, so you'd expect it to have beaches—but to have an uninterrupted surf-foamed Pacific beach running the length of the island for 120km (75 miles), now that's something special. Only problem is . . . you can't swim there. The currents offshore are just too strong, and the shark population just too, well, *sharky.* But there's an easy way around that—go inland, where Fraser Island offers so many places to swim, it's like nature's biggest water park.

Set into the sand dunes of Fraser Island are more than 100 little freshwater lakes,

Fraser Island's *Maheno* shipwreck.

all of which have their own sandy beaches—whiter sand than the big Pacific beach, in fact. Some, like brilliant blue **Lake McKenzie,** sprang up when water filled hardened hollows in the dunes. Others, like emerald-green Lake Wabby, were created when shifting dunes dammed up a stream. Shallow, swift-flowing **Eli Creek** is as much fun as a lazy river ride—wade up the creek for a mile or two and then let the current carry you back down.

Of course you should spend some time on **75-Mile Beach**—it's actually a highway you can drive along with a four-wheel-drive vehicle (the only cars allowed on this island). A rusted wrecked luxury steamship, the **Maheno,** sits right on the beach (a rare chance for nondivers to see a shipwreck up close); just north of the wreck loom gorgeous erosion-sculpted ocher cliffs called the **Cathedrals.** Past the rocky outcrop of Indian Head, at the northern end of the beach, the kids can actually take a cautious dip in the ocean by sitting in the **Champagne Pools,** pockets of soft sand protected from the worst waves by a natural barrier of dark rocks. The bubbling seawater turns the shallow pools into miniature spas.

Fraser Island is a casual, no-frills destination for folks who love wildlife better than the wild life—there are no towns and very few facilities, apart from a couple of low-profile eco-tourism resorts. It's a place for camping out, for hiking through eucalyptus woods and rainforest and wildflower heaths, and for fishing. From August through October, you may even be able to see **humpback whales** returning to Antarctica with their calves in tow (book whale-watch tours, as well as dolphin or manatee-spotting tours, from local resorts). **Dingos** run wild here—what could be more Australian than that?

(i) www.fraserisland.net.

✈ Hervey Bay 15km (9⅓ miles).

🛏 $$ **Fraser Island Retreat** (mod), Happy Valley (*C* **07/4127 9144;** www. fraserislandco.com.au). $$$ **Kingfisher Bay**

Resort, west coast (*C* **1800/072 555** or 07/ 4120 3333; www.kingfisherbay.com).

WHY THEY'LL THANK YOU: Swimming on top of a sand dune.

---

450 Beaches

Antigua: Beaches, Beaches Everywhere

All ages • The Caribbean

ONCE, THE BRITISH COLONY of Antigua was known for its sugar plantations; today it's an independent nation known for a different kind of sugar—the fine white sand of its myriad beaches. Locals boast that Antigua has a different beach for every day of the year. Of course that's an exaggeration, but Antigua's indented coastline is fringed like a sea anemone with little bays and outlying coral reefs, and nearly every one of them protects a glorious sandy beach. Come here prepared to bask in the sun.

This is the sort of idyllic vacation spot you expect the Caribbean to offer, and it's worth experiencing it at least once. Antigua is an expensive island, with small, exclusive inns rather than high-rise package-tour resort complexes, but just about any hotel you choose will have doors opening right onto the ocean and sand. Usually vacationers plunk themselves down at the beach by their hotel and never move; truth to tell, there aren't many sightseeing attractions on Antigua to lure you from your hotel—not unless your children are *Master and Commander* fanatics who are keen to tour the restored Napoleonic-era dockyards 18km (11 miles) southeast of the capital, St. John's, Admiral Nelson's old Caribbean headquarters.

However, with such a wealth of beaches so close together, it's fun to hop from one to another, sampling each one's distinct character. **Dickenson Bay,** in the northwest—the side of the island with higher winds, breaking waves, and dramatic scenery—is favored by families with young children for its wide strip of powder-fine sand and blissfully calm turquoise waters. The swimming is quite safe, and all the amenities you need are close at hand—you can rent watersports equipment at the Halcyon Cove Hotel and slip inside for drinks and snacks at casual restaurants nearby. If you've got snorkelers in your group, just north of Dickenson Bay is **Paradise Reef,** a 1.6km-long (1-mile) coral garden of stunning beauty. On the more exclusive southern coast, it's worth a drive to gaze upon the strikingly blue waters of **Carlisle Bay:** Against a backdrop of coconut groves, two long beaches extend from a bluff, and you can actually tell where the calm Caribbean waters meet the more turbulent Atlantic. East of here, at beautiful **Half Moon Bay,** you can see that Atlantic surf kicking up, and watch windsurfers skim the waters out past its reef; the reef itself protects the waters nearer shore, making it good for a family swim.

(i) *C* **888/268-4227** in U.S., 268/462-0480 in Antigua; www.antigua-barbuda.com

✈ Antigua.

🛏 $$$ **Hawksbill Beach Resort,** Five Islands Village (*C* **268/462-0301;** www. hawksbill.com). $$–$$$ **Siboney Beach Club,** Dickenson Bay (*C* **800/533-0234** or 268/462-0806; www.siboneybeachclub.com).

BEST TIME: Nov–Mar.

WHY THEY'LL THANK YOU: The Caribbean formula: Golden sun, white sand, clear blue water.

Monte Carlo
Where the Sun Kisses the Riviera
All ages • Monaco

THE FRENCH RIVIERA can be baffling to children—you call these beaches? Many of the most famous strands aren't even sandy, but covered in pebbly rocks or gravel. And for American parents, sitting among topless sunbathers can be disconcerting. My kids scarcely noticed when they were younger, but as adolescents it made them terribly self-conscious. Still, this fabled year-round resort seacoast is a lovely sight to see, and an essential reference point for all other beach resorts. Plus, it's a really glamorous vacation memory to drop into conversations (". . . oh, yes, when we were down on the Riviera last summer . . ."). Ka-ching.

The French Riviera vibe ranges from hedonism (the Brigitte Bardot image of St-Tropez) to celebrity spotting (the film-star glitz of Cannes) to old-money snobbery (the F. Scott Fitzgerald aura of Cap d'Antibes). Nice is nice (sorry, I can never resist that one), but I think the best place to show children what the Riviera is all about is in **Monaco.** With its hilltop panoramas, tropical landscaping, and moneyed elegance, this tiny independent principality offers real sand beaches; the sand is trucked in, but who cares? The big free-of-charge public beach is **Plage de Larvotto** (✆ **04-93-30-63-84**), off avenue Princesse-Grace, fronting the blue Mediterranean waters just around a curve of coast from the yacht-filled Monte Carlo harbor. However, the chic option lies farther east, just over the border in France, where the luxe Monte-Carlo Beach Hôtel adjoins the long-established **Monte Carlo Beach Club,** 22 av. Princesse-Grace (✆ **04-93-28-66-66**). As is customary along the Riviera, there's a charge to use this beach, in this case a huge fee (comparable to a day at Disneyland), but you'll get amenities like changing rooms, toilets, a restaurant, use of a mattress for sunbathing, and two large pools, one of them designed for children.

ⓘ **Tourist office,** 2A bd. des Moulins (✆ **92-16-61-66;** www.monaco-tourisme. com).

✈ Nice, 20km (12 miles).

🛏 $$$ **Le Monte Carlo Grand Hotel,** 12 av. des Spélugues (✆ **93-50-65-00;** www.montecarlograndhotel.com).

WHY THEY'LL THANK YOU: Sunbathing à la James Bond.

The Calgary Rodeo

Baseball Hall of Fame
Shrine to the Great American Pastime
Ages 6 & up • Cooperstown, New York, USA

ADMITTEDLY MY FAMILY is crazy for baseball, but even when I look at it objectively, I'd have to say that the Baseball Hall of Fame in Cooperstown sets the gold standard for sports museums. The very word *Cooperstown* has become synonymous with baseball history, for legend (now discredited) claims that Abner Doubleday invented baseball here. Opened in 1939, the Hall of Fame has been around long enough to amass an unparalleled collection of sports memorabilia. You don't have to be a statistic-spouting baseball fanatic to feel moved by this homage to America's pastime.

The Hall's red-brick Federal-style facade looks as all-American as the game it represents. Laid down like a giant timeline, it walks you through the **history of baseball,** starting with the various European ball-and-bat games that were its predecessors. Recent renovations have added more hands-on and interactive exhibits for kids, including a 13-minute multimedia show and a special area for toddlers and preschoolers, but it's the **memorabilia** that really tells the story, from Ty Cobb's glove to Babe Ruth's bat. You'll see the ridiculous scanty protective gear catchers used to wear behind the

The Baseball Hall of Fame.

plate, the gradual evolution of the regulation ball and bat, a panoply of uniforms through the decades, the ever-changing look of trading cards. You'll learn about the Black Sox scandal of 1919 and how baseball survived World War II. Special galleries are devoted to topics such as the Negro Leagues and the women's professional leagues. Snippets of vintage broadcasts and video footage of historic games are played at the touch of a button. Sure, my kids gravitated at first to exhibits paying tribute to today's stars and teams, set in a replica major-league locker room, but the more they saw of baseball's storied past—the actual objects, worn and discolored from play—the more they got into it. We saved a

stroll through the actual Hall of Fame gallery for last, and by that time, those names on the plaques really meant something.

ⓘ 25 Main St. (☎ **888/HALL-OF-FAME** or 607/547-7200; www.baseballhalloffame. org).

✈ Albany, 75 miles.

🛏 $ **Best Western,** 50 Commons Dr. (☎ **607/547-9439;** www.bwcooperstown. com). $$$ **Inn at Cooperstown,** 16 Chestnut St. (☎ **607/547-5756;** www.innatcoopers town.com).

WHY THEY'LL THANK YOU: Baseball is more than a game, it's a window on America.

Fenway Park
Where the Red Sox Rule
Ages 6 & up • Boston, Massachusetts, USA

WHEN THE **Boston Red Sox** won the 2004 World Series—ending an 86-year dry spell—they may have lost their status as one of baseball's most beloved underdogs, but I haven't heard any members of Red Sox Nation complaining. Sure, the Yankees, their perennial American League East rivals down in New York City, have a higher payroll and more world titles. None of that matters to dedicated Red Sox supporters, and their numbers are legion. The 2005 movie *Fever Pitch* didn't exaggerate anything: Sit among them in the stands and you'll definitely remember that the word "fan" comes from "fanatic." But I for one never mind. You're watching ball in an intensely green place that's older than your grandparents, inhaling a Fenway Frank and wishing for a home run—what could be better?

My father was a Red Sox true believer his whole life, and though my family has committed the ultimate treason of

rooting for the Yankees, we still harbor a secret fondness for the Sox. So it is that from time to time, we take off our Yankees caps and visit Fenway Park.

It's a venerable stadium, though "stadium" seems almost too grand a term for this, the oldest park in the major leagues (built in 1912). Its quirks only add to the Fenway mystique: the narrow seats, the hand-operated scoreboard, the 37-foot-high left-field wall known as the **"Green Monster"** for its tendency to rob opposing hitters of their home runs. Those seats may be uncomfortable but they're gratifyingly close to the field, without the wide swaths of grass other parks have put between the fans and the players.

Compared with its modern brethren, however, Fenway is tiny, and **tickets** are both expensive and hard to get. Throughout the season, a limited number of standing-room tickets go on sale the day of the game, and fans sometimes return

Fenway Park.

presold tickets (especially if a rainout causes rescheduling). It can't hurt to check. Forced to choose between seats in a low-numbered grandstand section—say, 10 or below—and those in the

bleachers, go for the bleachers. They can get rowdy during night games, but the view is better from there than from the deep right-field corner.

We took a **Fenway Park tour** (conducted year-round; no tours on game days or holidays) that actually allowed us to peer inside the cramped space behind the Green Monster and walk out onto the warning track, stop in the press box, and visit the Red Sox Hall of Fame. Best of all, the guide's commentary was rich in team lore and highly entertaining.

ⓘ 4 Yawkey Way (ⓒ **877/REDSOX-9** for tickets, 617/226-6666 for tours; www. redsox.com).

✈ ⊨ See Boston Common **60**.

BEST TIME: Season runs Apr–Oct.

WHY THEY'LL THANK YOU: Baseball legends still matter here.

Wrigley Field: The Cubs' Den
Ages 4 & up • Chicago, Illinois, USA

THE CHICAGO CUBS HAVEN'T PLAYED IN the World Series since 1945 and haven't won the darn thing since 1908—when the Red Sox finally won a Series in 2004, the Cubs became undisputed holders of the crown for Most Beloved Losers. Chicagoans do love their Cubbies, champs or not, and there's no question that the team plays in one of baseball's classic venues, tiny Wrigley Field. Back in 1988 lights were finally installed for night play, but they're rarely used—the Cubs still play mostly day games. With its ivy-covered outfield walls, a hand-operated scoreboard, a view of Lake Michigan from the upper deck, and the El rattling past, it's old-fashioned baseball all the way, and our kids enjoyed every minute of their game there.

Built in 1914, Wrigley Field is the second-oldest venue in baseball (after

Fenway Park **453**), although the Cubs didn't move in until 1916 (a decade after their last Series victory!). Originally Weeghman Field, it was renamed in 1926 after the team's new owner, William Wrigley, Jr., the chewing-gum magnate.

No matter how the Cubs are doing in the standings, tickets go fast—most weekend and night games are sold out by Memorial Day. Your best bet is to hit a weekday game, where you'll be sitting alongside plenty of Chicagoans who called in sick to work and miraculously recovered by game time. Wrigley is small enough that every seat is a decent seat, and the place truly earns its nickname "The Friendly Confines"—every time I've been there, the fans around me were passionate, friendly, well-informed, and good-natured in the face of defeat. Riding the Red Line El to the Addison Street stop is part of the experience: You can look down into the park from the train, and hear the roar of the crowd as soon as you step onto the platform. During the regular season on non–game days, you can take a 90-minute **tour** of the vintage stadium, visiting the press box, dugouts, both visitors' and Cubs' clubhouses, and the playing field itself; these tours are popular, so book in advance (**☎ 773/404-CUBS**).

Just some of the **traditions** we love at Wrigley: Enterprising owners of surrounding houses have built stands on their roofs where they seat their own ticket holders; ground rules declare that if a ball

gets stuck in the ivy, it's a double; and a pennant is flown after every game with a big "w" or "L" to alert passersby to the outcome of the game (who needs the Internet?). When the opposing team hits a home run out of the park, somebody on the sidewalk outside picks up the offending ball and throws it back in. You've gotta love a ballpark where that happens.

ⓘ 1060 W. Addison St. (**☎ 773/404-CUBS;** www.cubs.mlb.com).

✈ ⊨ See Chicago **57**.

WHY THEY'LL THANK YOU: Watching a Cubs homer sail over those ivy walls.

Taking in a Game at Yankee Stadium

Ages 6 & up • The Bronx, New York, USA

Lᴏᴠᴇ 'ᴇᴍ ᴏʀ ʜᴀᴛᴇ 'ᴇᴍ, you can't deny that the **New York Yankees** are one of the world's most famous baseball teams, and their historic Bronx home is as close to a shrine as an active sports stadium can get. But it won't be active very much longer—the Yankees organization plans to build a new stadium right across the street, due to open in 2009, and though the intent is to reproduce the arched Art Deco facade as closely as possible, it won't be the old stadium anymore. See it while you still can.

New York's American League team plays 81 home games here every season from mid-April to early October—and on into the autumn if the postseason stars are aligned properly. It's great to see a game in person, a classic ballpark experience, with the live organ music and vendors hawking peanuts and Cracker Jack; subway trains rattling past on an elevated trestle over the bleachers; and an obligatory sixth-inning sweep by the ground crew that includes a choreographed routine to the Village People's "YMCA." Tickets can be ordered in

advance, or picked up at the stadium ticket office on game day, though availability gets tight toward fall if the Yanks are in pennant contention, which they often are.

The list of Yankee greats goes on and on—Babe Ruth, Lou Gehrig, Joe DiMaggio, Mickey Mantle, Roger Maris, Whitey Ford, Reggie Jackson, Roger Clemens, Derek Jeter. (One of the stadium's nicknames is "the House that Ruth Built," because its 1923 structure was paid for by increased revenues after the Sultan of Swat was acquired from the Boston Red Sox in 1920.) No other team even comes close to their World Series victories, including an astounding five in a row from 1949 through 1953. Even if you can't make it to a game, there are 1-hour tours, conducted year-round, that give you a great behind-the-scenes glimpse—seeing the view from the press box, learning how the scoreboard operates, peering into the bullpen where pitchers warm up, gazing upon the plaques in Monument Park—and, best of all, walking through the clubhouse where the players themselves actually suit up (provided there isn't a home game that day). Just show up several minutes before noon at the event ticket window near Gate 4.

(i) River Ave. and E. 161st St. (© **718/579-4531**; www.yankees.com).

✈ 🛏 See Manhattan **56**.

WHY THEY'LL THANK YOU: Hearing the sweet crack of a Yankee bat on a warm summer night—priceless.

456

Days of Grapefruit & Cactus
Spring Training Baseball
Ages 6 & up • Phoenix, Arizona, & Tampa, Florida, USA

IF YOU'RE A BASEBALL FAN, spring vacation means one thing: Baseball season is so close you can almost smell the hot dogs. With Opening Day drawing nigh, your favorite players have migrated to warmer climes to get back in shape—so why not follow them and get a jump-start on the season?

Spring exhibition games are a wonderful laid-back alternative to season games: Tickets are cheap, the fields are small so you can get close to the action, and the inconsistent level of play means you're likely to see a rusty shortstop bobble an out or an out-of-practice outfielder drop a ball—very reassuring to Little Leaguers. To protect their arms, pitchers stay in for shorter periods, meaning you won't sit through those agonizing pitching duels with no-hit inning after no-hit inning (which, frankly, are boring for youngsters).

If your major goal is simply to see as many teams as possible, the most efficient spot is Phoenix, where nine major-league teams train in March: the **Milwaukee Brewers** and the **Oakland Athletics** in central Phoenix; the **San Francisco Giants** east in Scottsdale, the **Chicago Cubs** farther east in Mesa, the **Los Angeles Angels** south of downtown in Tempe, and, northeast of downtown, the **San Diego Padres** and the **Seattle Mariners** in Peoria and the **Kansas City Royals** and **Texas Rangers** out in Surprise. In Florida, your best bet is the

Tampa area, where six teams train: The **Toronto Blue Jays** in Dunedin, the **Philadelphia Phillies** in Clearwater, the **Tampa Devil Rays** in St. Petersburg, the **New York Yankees** in Tampa, the **Pittsburg Pirates** in Bradenton, and the **Cincinnati Reds** in Sarasota.

Exhibition schedules include other teams who train elsewhere in the state, so expect a great variety of matchups. Spring training is no predictor of the season ahead: The teams that eventually dominate major-league action don't necessarily look their best in spring training, and teams who are hot in spring may fall apart by midsummer. But it is a great place to get close to baseball action, maybe even snare an autograph or fan photo—still flush with the enthusiasm of a fresh season, players tend to lower their anti-fan defenses in March. Get 'em while you can.

(i) **The Grapefruit League** (www.flasports.com). **The Cactus League** (© **866/705-4816;** www.cactusleagueinfo.com).

✈ Sky Harbor International in Phoenix or Tampa International.

🛏 $$ **Embassy Suites Phoenix North,** 2577 N. Greenway Rd., Phoenix (© **800/EMBASSY** or 602/375-1777; www.embassysuites.com). $$ **The Heritage Holiday Inn,** 234 3rd Ave. N., St. Petersburg (© **800/283-7829** or 727/822-4814; www.ichotelsgroup.com). $$$ **Pointe South Mountain Resort,**

7777 S. Pointe Pkwy., Phoenix (✆ **877/800-4888** or 602/438-9000; www.pointe southmtn.com). $$$ **Tampa Riverwalk Hotel,** 200 N. Ashley Dr., Tampa (✆ **888/**

625-5144 or 813/223-2222; www.tampariver walkhotel.com).

WHY THEY'LL THANK YOU: Practice makes perfect—even for professionals.

457

Summer Baseball on Cape Cod

All ages • Cape Cod, Massachusetts, USA

MY NEW YORK–BORN KIDS have been spoiled when it comes to watching baseball, with two excellent major-league teams right in town. But sometimes the slick perfection of those pro games obscures the heart of the sport. That's when we seek out **AA or AAA teams**—or, better yet, go to Cape Cod to watch some of the nation's best college players compete as unpaid amateurs in a summer season during which they hope to be spotted by major-league scouts.

It's refreshing to watch this level of baseball: Pitchers do not dominate batters, home runs are rare events, and pop-ups and outfield flies are often dropped. Games are held on grass fields on the edge of town, where families picnic, fireflies swarm, and local kids pop wheelies on their bikes in the parking lot between innings. They're a real community gathering, and admission is free, although there's often a request for a donation as you walk in (the league runs on a nonprofit basis). It's a small-town sort of experience that reminds you why baseball is America's game.

There are 10 teams in the league, each playing in its own Cape Cod town. Over the years, we've become partial to the **Kettleers** (so named because of the many kettle ponds in the area) and the **Commodores** (named for Falmouth's sea-captain heritage). Few players carry over from season to season, but we do try to remember the names of the most promising athletes, just in case they show up on pro rosters in a year or two. That's not such a long shot, if you look at the names of recent Cape Cod Leaguers who

made it to the majors: Nomar Garciaparra, Tino Martinez, Jeff Bagwell, John Franco, Barry Zito, J. T. Snow, Jeff Conine, Jeremy Giambi, Javy Lopez, Jeff Kent, and Jason Varitek.

Here's our routine: We warm up with a round of mini-golf in the late afternoon (Rte. 28 between Hyannis and Dennis is studded with courses, but our favorite is the Cape-Cod-landmark-themed **Storyland** at 70 Center St. in Hyannis (✆ **508/778-4339**). Then we find someplace local for a quick dinner (fried clams or pizza usually hit the spot; we love **Captain Frosty's** in Dennis, 219 Rte. 6A), and get over to the ballgame; starting times range from 4:30 to 7pm. After the game, we have to stop for ice-cream cones, at either **Smitty's** in Falmouth at 326 E. Falmouth Hwy., or **Four Seas** in Centerville at 360 S. Main St. This is the essence of a Cape Cod summer night, and nothing could be sweeter.

ⓘ ✆ **508/432-6909**; www.capecodbaseball. org.

✈ Hyannis.

🛏 $$ **Cape Codder Resort and Spa,** 1225 Iyannough Rd./Rte. 132, Hyannis (✆ **888/297-2200** or 508/771-3000; www. capecodderresort.com). $$$ **Red Horse Inn,** 28 Falmouth Heights Rd., Falmouth (✆ **508/548-0053**; www.redhorseinn.com).

BEST TIME: Season runs mid-June to late Aug.

WHY THEY'LL THANK YOU: Baseball gets back to its roots.

458

Home of the Green Bay Packers
Cheesehead Capital
Ages 6 & up • Green Bay, Wisconsin, USA

THE GREEN BAY PACKERS may not be the winningest team in NFL history—though surely they've had their day, especially in the Vince Lombardi era, when they won the first two Super Bowls—but in many ways they are the purest embodiment of American football. Founded in 1919, before there even was a National Football League, they've played in Lambeau Field since 1957, which makes this the longest-tenured stadium in football. Season tickets have been sold out for 45 years straight. All other NFL franchises belong to big cities, but the Packers thrive in a salt-of-the-earth Midwestern town of 100,000 people some 2 hours north of Milwaukee—and the local community actually owns the team, not some fat cat in a skybox. Late in the season, Lambeau Field gets so cold, it's been nicknamed the Frozen Tundra, but there's no sissy roof over the stadium. Okay, Lombardi did install soil-warming coils under the sod, but it is real dirt, holding real grass, not artificial turf. Like I said, pure football.

That's why a pilgrimage to Green Bay means something to every football fan. **Packer Fan Tours** (© 800/851-7225; www.packerfantours.com) offers a range of reasonably priced packages that include tickets, Green Bay lodging, autograph sessions, tailgate parties at the Brett Favre Steakhouse, and so on. Individual tickets may also be available at **www.eventusa. com**.

Year-round, you can visit the **Packers Hall of Fame** in the atrium attached to Lambeau field, which has interactive videos, mementos, an activity area for kids, and even a replica of Vince Lombardi's office. Any non–game day, hour-long stadium tours are conducted (© **920/ 569-7513**; tickets first-come, first-served), culminating in a walk through the concrete team tunnel onto the famed gridiron turf. Considering the Green Bay weather, however, you may prefer to come mid-July through mid-August, when you can watch preseason training sessions at Claire Hinkle Field, take the 1-hour Legends of Lombardi Avenue trolley tour around town (© **920/ 494-9507**), and enjoy the **Packers Experience** (1901 S. Oneida St.; © **920/487-5664**)—no mere video arcade, but an athletic activity gallery with stations like a 40-yard dash, bungee run, obstacle course, passing challenge, and cheese maze. Yes, cheese—this is Wisconsin, the Dairy State, and Packers fans are nicknamed Cheeseheads.

ⓘ **Lambeau Field,** 1265 Lombardi Ave. (© **920/569-7500;** www.packers.com).

✈ Green Bay, 6 miles.

🛏 $$$ **Hilton Garden Inn,** 1015 Lombardi Ave. (© **920/405-0400;** www.hilton gardeninn.com). $ **Microtel Inn & Suites,** 3031 Allied St. (© **920/338-9000;** www. microtelinn.com).

WHY THEY'LL THANK YOU: Being a Cheesehead for a day.

Notre Dame
The Holy Land of College Football

Ages 8 & up (Notre Dame), 6 & up (Hall of Fame) • South Bend, Indiana, USA

FROM NOTRE DAME STADIUM, you can see a 132-foot-high mosaic of Jesus on the side wall of the campus library—a mosaic shrewdly placed so that Christ, with upraised hands, is centered right over the north goal post. **Touchdown Jesus** is a fitting sight for this Catholic university in northern Indiana, which has had no fewer than eight national championships, seven Heisman Trophy winners, five number-one pro draft picks, and 171 All-Americans. You don't have to be an alum to be a rabid fan of Notre Dame football—you just have to love football, like my teenage son does.

Notre Dame has had a football team since 1887 (though its famous marching band is even older, the oldest in the country, formed in 1845). The red-brick stadium is vintage, built in 1930, the last year of famed coach Knute Rockne's

decade at the school. Rockne more than anyone is responsible for the nationwide Notre Dame fan base, for he actively sought far-flung matches and developed cross-country rivalries, with such schools as Michigan, USC, Navy, and Boston College. Notre Dame's popularity nowadays transcends regional loyalties; they're the nation's only football team, pro or collegiate, whose entire schedule is broadcast on radio coast to coast, and since 1966 there's only been one home game that wasn't sold out. But here's the catch: All 80,000 seats to home games are allocated to season ticket holders, alumni, students, faculty, and parents of current students, but somehow they do pop up on ticket services (at inflated prices, of course). Or work your connections—find a Notre Dame alum or parent who'll buy tickets for you. Otherwise,

The College Football Hall of Fame.

you'll have to be content with buying merchandise at the Irish Store in Eck Hall, or taking a 1¼-hour, free, student-led **walking tour** of the beautiful rolling campus (call ✆ **574/631-5726**), which doesn't go inside the stadium.

There is, however, another reason to come to South Bend. In 1995 the **College Football Hall of Fame** moved from King's Island, Ohio, to a new state-of-the-art facility in downtown South Bend. Built to look like a football stadium, with a green gridiron-lined outdoor plaza, the museum has, besides the honoree exhibits, plenty of interactive kiosks, a 360-degree theater where you can stand surrounded by the noisy blur of game-day action, and sizable interactive areas for testing your skills

against some of the greatest players in college football history.

ⓘ **Notre Dame Stadium,** University of Notre Dame (www.und.collegesports.com). **College Football Hall of Fame,** 111 S. St. Joseph St. (✆ **800/440-FAME** or 574/235-9999; www.collegefootball.org).

✈ South Bend Regional.

🛏 $$ **Comfort Suites,** 52939 State Rd. 933 (✆ **574/272-1500;** www.comfortsuites. com). $$ **Inn at St. Mary's,** 53993 U.S. Hwy. 933 (✆ **574/232-4000;** www.innat saintmarys.com).

WHY THEY'LL THANK YOU: Seeing Touchdown Jesus.

Pro Football Hall of Fame: Gridiron Glory

Ages 6 & up • Canton, Ohio, USA

To MY MIND, each of the pro sports halls of fame reflects the character of its sport—the Baseball Hall of Fame ④⑤② has a vintage intellectual appeal, the Basketball Hall of Fame ④⑥① has got a more jazzed-up and high-tempo game, and the Pro Football Hall of Fame is solid and down-to-earth, winning your interest a few dogged yards at a time. A bit off the beaten track—in Canton, Ohio, where the forerunner of the National Football League first formed in 1920—this NFL mecca caters to the true-blue gridiron fan. That's not me, but it sure is my sons.

You enter through an arena-shaped round building, with a white oblong protruding from its top like a giant football. Inside the front doors you're greeted by a bronze statue of Jim Thorpe (I won points for knowing the back story of this great Native American athlete, who was denied his Olympic medals because he had briefly played professional ball). In the rotunda, a century of **football history** is told in glass-case displays full of jerseys, balls, and scuffed cleats. There's a

historical display on each of the league's 32 teams, one gallery devoted to the history of the Super Bowl, another to African-American players, another to upstart leagues that rivaled the NFL. Fans who, like my older son, devour football stats will love the cases of artifacts representing current record holders' milestones. Each Hall of Famer (and there are over 200) is honored with a bronze bust in one dazzling wall. Three to six new inductees are elected every year by a team of sportswriters who meet the day before the Super Bowl. Players are eligible only 5 years after retiring, which means that kids recognize some names—Dan Marino, John Elway, Steve Young, not to mention ex-players like Terry Bradshaw who have found a second career as sportscasters.

Lest we forget that football is an action sport, the **GameDay Stadium** evokes the excitement of a live game in a rotating movie theater with an amazing Cinemascope screen; NFL action films are shown in another theater. And on the lower level beside the snack bar, museumgoers can get into the action themselves, with a football-passing activity, interactive trivia contests, and a Call the Play station where visitors take the role of quarterback, making snap decisions on how to run plays. Even non–football fans can't help but be engrossed by the museum by this point. I only regret that my football-fanatic dad never got a chance to take his

grandsons here—that would have been the ultimate bonding experience for them.

ⓘ 2121 George Halas Dr. NW (ℂ **330/ 456-8207;** www.profootballhof.com).

✈ Cleveland International, 50 miles.

🚈 See Rock 'n' Roll Hall of Fame **349**.

WHY THEY'LL THANK YOU: First down and goal to go.

The Basketball Hall of Fame
Hoop Dreams & Hardwood Heroes
All ages • Springfield, Massachusetts, USA

Iᴛs ᴏғғɪᴄɪᴀʟ ɴᴀᴍᴇ ɪs the Naismith Memorial Basketball Hall of Fame in honor of Dr. James Naismith, who invented basketball right here in Springfield, Massachusetts, in 1891. You can't miss it—there's a 136-foot spire twirling a 13-foot illuminated orange basketball on its fingerlike tip, and an immense titanium sphere (a globe? A giant basketball?) that's visible from I-91.

Inside the great sphere, glass elevators glide to the top (third) level, where visitors start at the circular balcony of the **Honors Ring,** detailing the biographies of the nearly 300 figures elected to the Hall of Fame. Along with familiar names such as Walt Frazier and Wilt Chamberlain, Bill Bradley and Larry Bird, Kareem-Abdul Jabbar and Magic Johnson, illuminated panels and memorabilia cases honor players, coaches, and other figures from the more distant past and more obscure realms of the game. One of the things I love about this museum is that it weaves in the stories of the women's game, high-school and college basketball, and the evolution of racial equality—not with separate galleries but as part of the whole Big Picture.

On the second floor, more excellent displays tell the sport's history in thoughtful detail. **Memorabilia** include everything from old peach baskets like those that Naismith's first team shot into, to the

red-white-and-blue balls used by the short-lived American Basketball Association; a huge case of team jerseys represents players old and new, including many current players not yet enshrined in the Hall. And here's the other thing I love about this museum, especially when you've got kids in tow: There are **interactive stations** everywhere. In the section devoted to The Players, you can compare your skills in a virtual one-on-one against various pro players; in The Coaches, you study great game plans and then test your own coaching calls in simulated court situations; in The Media, you see yourself on camera as a sports announcer. Video and audio clips run continually, adding texture to the experience.

The ground floor features the most interactive area of all: an almost-regulation-size hardwood court where frequent clinics and skill challenges are held. After listening to the echo of bouncing basketballs and overlooking the court from the top two floors, now your itchy hands can finally grab a ball and play. And, always with the youngest fans in mind, the Kids Court section has been built with hoops of varying heights. Sweet.

ⓘ 1000 W. Columbus Ave. (ℂ **413/781-6500;** www.hoophall.com).

✈ Bradley International, 20 miles.

🛏 $$ **Sheraton Springfield,** 1 Monarch Place (𝄞 **800/426-9004** or 413/781-1010; info@sheratonspringfield.com).

WHY THEY'LL THANK YOU: Hitting Center Court with a whole new sense of the game.

Olympia
Home of the Ancient Greek Games
Ages 6 & up • Olympia, Greece

LEGEND CLAIMS THAT Herakles (Hercules) founded the **Olympic Games:** After completing the last of his 12 labors, to celebrate he paced off 183m (600 Olympic ft.) and then ran the distance without taking a single breath. Whatever the origin, that distance became the length of the stadium at the religious sanctuary of Olympia, and for over a millennium, from 776 B.C. to A.D. 393, athletic contests were held here every 4 years.

Thousands poured into Olympia for the Games; much of the surrounding countryside was a tent city. (Women couldn't compete or even watch—any woman caught sneaking into the stadium was thrown to her death from a nearby mountain.) Events included footraces, short and long jumps, wrestling and boxing contests, chariot races, the arduous pentathlon (discus, javelin, jumping, running, and wrestling), and the vicious pankration (which combined wrestling and boxing techniques). The most prestigious event was the *stade,* or short footrace, for which the stadium was named.

Olympia's setting is magical: Pine and olive trees shade a small valley dominated by the conical Hill of Kronos. Make your first stop the **Archaeological Museum,** chock-full of statues (some of them world famous) as well as athletic paraphernalia from the ancient Games: stone and bronze weights used by jumpers, bronze and stone discuses, and even an enormous stone with a boastful inscription that a weight lifter had raised it over his head with only one hand.

The site itself is a jumble of foundation stones and toppled columns, marking various buildings around the ancient sanctuary. You'll see the ruins of **Roman baths** where athletes and spectators took hot and cold plunges; slender columns mark the site of the **gymnasium** and **palestra,** where athletes practiced footracing and boxing. Olympia was devoted to the worship of Zeus, so there's one **temple** devoted to Hera (Zeus's wife) and an even bigger one for Zeus, which once contained an enormous gold-and-ivory statue of the all-powerful god, one of the Seven Wonders of the Ancient World. Passing through a vaulted archway to walk onto the pavement of the old stadium, which could accommodate 45,000 on its sloped sides, you just imagine the roar of the ancient crowd. The Olympic flame is kindled here by sunlight every 2 years and then relayed by torch to the site of that year's Games.

The Museum of the History of the Olympic Games in Antiquity (𝄞 **26240/ 22-529**), up a steep path from the site, has a superb collection of artifacts: chariot wheels, musical instruments, statues of athletes, and all kinds of athletic gear.

ⓘ **Tourist office** (𝄞 **26240/23-100**). Closed Sun.

🚆 Olympia (change at Pirgos), 5 ½ hr. from Athens.

🛏 $$$ **Grecotel Lakopetra Beach,** Kato Achaia, Achaia (𝄞 **26930/51-713**). $ **Hotel Praxitelous,** 7 Spilliopoulou, Ancient Olympia (𝄞 **26240/22-592**).

WHY THEY'LL THANK YOU: Lighting the torch.

Olympic Glory Days in Lake Placid

All ages • Lake Placid, New York, USA

THE LAKESIDE RESORT town of Lake Placid, set in the middle of New York's Adirondack mountains, has the distinction of having hosted not one but two Winter Olympic Games, in 1932 and then again in 1980. While 1932 seems long ago, 1980 lives on in popular memory in two movies, *Cool Runnings* (the John Candy charmer about a Jamaican bobsled team) and *Miracle* (starring Kurt Russell, about the amazing U.S. hockey victory). Prime the kids with those movies to make their trip to Lake Placid especially memorable—and they'll watch future Olympic games with insiders' eyes.

While you're in Lake Placid, you can not only see sites where legends were made, but also try out your own skills on several of them. Begin in town at the **Winter Olympic Museum** in the **Olympic Center** on Main Street (© **518/523-1655;** www.orda.org), which sets the stage with a good history of the two Winter Games in Placid. Northeast of town, in winter downhill skiers can ski on the eastern U.S.'s only Olympic mountain, 4,400-foot **Whiteface,** Route 86, Wilmington (© **518/946-2223;** www.whiteface.com). Although it has the greatest vertical drop in the East, at 3,430 feet, there's lots of terrain for all levels—in fact, a third of the 65 trails are rated for novices.

If you prefer your skiing Nordic style, head for the cross-country center at the **Verizon Sports Complex,** 20 minutes west of Lake Placid on Route 73 (© **518/523-2811**), where Olympic athletes still train. You can have your own bobsled experience here on the bobsled/luge/skeleton track, where you'll watch athletes in training bomb downhill at breakneck speed. You can even strap yourself into a

bobsled and race down the half-mile track with a guide and brakeman—on wheels in summer, on even faster ice in winter.

Southeast of town, you can't miss the ski jump towers at the **MacKenzie-Intervale Ski Jumping Complex,** Route 73 (© **518/523-2202**), where athletes soar off the ramps December to March and June to October (in summer they jump into a pool); nonjumpers can get a vertiginous taste of the experience by riding the lift alongside the ramps and taking the 26-story elevator to the top of the observation tower. If that whets your kids' daredevil appetites, in the winter back in town you can toboggan down a converted ski jump right onto the ice of Mirror Lake, near the **Olympic Center** (© **518/523-2591**).

Wind up your Lake Placid visit by skating at night on the very rinks where legends like figure skater Sonja Henie (gold-medal winner in 1928, 1932, and 1936) and speed skater Eric Heiden (five gold medals in 1980) made history. At the Olympic Center (see above) you can skate outdoors in winter and on the indoor arena weeknights only in summer.

ⓘ **Lake Placid/Essex County Visitors Bureau,** Olympic Center, 216 Main St. (© **800/447-5224** or 518/523-2605; www.lakeplacid.com).

✈ Saranac Lake, 10 miles.

🛏 $$ **Best Western Golden Arrow Hotel,** 150 Main St. (© **518/523-3353;** www.golden-arrow.com). $$ **Hilton Lake Placid Resort,** 1 Mirror Lake Dr. (© **800/755-5598** or 518/523-4411; www.lphilton.com).

WHY THEY'LL THANK YOU: There's Olympic gold in these hills.

464

Siena: The Running of the Palio

Ages 8 & up • Siena, Italy

IN SIENA, a city of Gothic palaces, aristocratic mansions, narrow streets, and medieval gates, walls, and towers, you're transported back to the Middle Ages. It has one of Europe's oldest universities, founded in 1240, and an unforgettable cathedral. But as soon as I stepped into its historic Piazza del Campo, designed like a sloping scallop shell, my imagination leapt to the spectacle that takes place here each July 2 and August 16: the intense, colorful **Palio delle Contrade.** Part historical pageant, part horse race, it pits each of the city's 17 wards *(contrade)* against each other in a contest that has been going on since the 15th century.

Siena's Duomo.

For the 3 days before the big race, trial races are held, with the final trial the morning of the event. Though there are 17 *contrade,* Piazza del Campo holds only 10, so the wards are chosen by lot. Young partisans, flaunting the colors of their *contrada,* race through the medieval streets in packs. Food and wine abound on the streets the eve of the race. (You're likely to be invited along by the first local you befriend, but while visitors are welcome, this event is truly for the Sienese.)

Although tickets for seats are expensive, there's no charge for standing with the throng in the middle of the square. You'll have to get to Piazza del Campo *very early,* though, and expect to be trapped there for hours in a teeming crowd. (With younger kids, I'd opt for buying tickets, or else stick to the less crowded trial-race days.) On the big day, before the actual race, there's loads of pageantry, with colorfully costumed men and banners parading up and down. But the race itself is a deadly earnest competition, with each bareback-riding jockey wearing his *contrada*'s traditional colors. There have been kidnappings of the most skilled jockeys, and bribery is commonplace. Jockeys have been known to unseat the competition, although a riderless horse is allowed to win. Horses are sometimes impaled by guardrails along the track. In theory, riders are supposed to alternate whip strokes between their mounts and their competitors, but in practice anything goes.

The horses gallop three times around Piazza del Campo, and even though the Piazza is quite large, it doesn't take long. A blur of action, and then the race is over—time to start gearing up for next year.

ⓘ **Tourist office,** Piazza del Campo 56 (ⓒ **0577-280551;** www.terresiena.it).

🚆 Siena, 230km (143 miles) from Rome, 34km (21 miles) from Florence.

🛏 $$ **Palazzo Ravizza,** Pian dei Mantellini 34 (ⓒ **0577-280462;** www.palazzoravizza.it).

WHY THEY'LL THANK YOU: When horse racing takes to the streets.

The Kentucky Derby
Bluegrass & Red Roses
Ages 4 & up • Louisville, Kentucky, USA

As a kid, I must admit being disappointed that the grass wasn't bright blue in Kentucky bluegrass country, although it does have a bluish cast. Legend has it that this species of grass is the best for raising Thoroughbred racehorses. It must have some effect, because more than two-thirds of the winners of the Kentucky Derby—America's premier horse race—have been bred right here on Kentucky's splendid horse farms.

Louisville's **Churchill Downs** racetrack, its huge white frame grandstand topped by a distinctive pair of slim gray spires, opened in 1875, and the Kentucky Derby—originally patterned after England's Epsom Derby—has been run every May since then. It's the first in the Triple Crown, a trio of renowned flat races for 3-year-olds, and its traditions have become famous, from the prerace singing of "My Old Kentucky Home" down to the garland of 554 red roses draped over the winning colt's neck. Grandstand seats for the Derby must be

Racing at Churchill Downs, home of the Kentucky Derby.

booked months ahead and cost a fortune; a more casual option is to join the euphoric crowd picnicking in the 40-acre infield (you won't see much of the race but you'll have a fun party).

The **Kentucky Derby Museum,** open year-round just outside Gate #1 (✆ 502/637-1111), has videos and hands-on exhibits (don't miss the one where you sit on a saddle in a real starting gate).

Before you hit the track, though, I suggest driving around the countryside near Lexington, 100 miles southeast of Louisville, to see where generations of Thoroughbred champions have been bred. The most famous horse farm, **Calumet Farms,** doesn't allow visitors, though you can do a drive-by with Horse Farm Tours (✆ **859/268-2906**), which then visits other working horse farms. You can tour **Claiborne Farm,** Winchester Road, Paris (✆ **859/233-4252**), where Seabiscuit was born and Secretariat was a longtime stud stallion (his grave is on the farm), or **Three**

Chimneys Farm, Old Frankfort Parkway, Versailles (✆ **859/873-7053**), where Seattle Slew was the resident stud. The **Kentucky Horse Park,** 4089 Iron Works Pike, Lexington (✆ **800/568-8813** or 859/233-4303; www.kyhorsepark.com), has Man O' War's grave and a museum on horse history, but kids really have more fun walking through the barns, seeing shows in the equestrian arena (mid-Mar to Oct), and taking horse and pony rides.

ⓘ 700 Central Ave. (✆ **502/636-4400;** www.churchilldowns.com).

✈ Louisville International.

🛏 $$$ **Seelbach Hilton,** 500 4th St., Louisville (✆ **502/585-3200;** www.seelbach hilton.com). $$ **Sheraton Suites,** 2601 Richmond Rd., Lexington (✆ **800/262-3774** or 859/268-0060; www.starwood hotels.com).

WHY THEY'LL THANK YOU: And they're off!

Saratoga Race Course
Where Horseracing Goes High Society
All ages • Saratoga Springs, New York, USA

SARATOGA SPRINGS is not only the USA's oldest thoroughbred track, it is also the most beautiful, a place where smartly dressed socialites still quaff champagne as they cheer on the winners from their box seats.

With its sprucely painted white Victorian gingerbread and peaked green roofs, shady white-railed paddocks, and lush flower planters, Saratoga is an elegant place, where a dress code is strictly observed—forgo the jeans, shorts, and tank tops for your day at the races. During the **Spa Meet,** from the end of July through Labor Day, races are held here every day but Tuesday. There may be some seat tickets available on race day (buy at Gate A at 8am or at the Holiday Inn downtown the night before), but in general if you

want a reserved seat you should book ahead at ✆ **718/641-4700** (during race season, contact the racetrack directly—see below). Post time for the day's first race is 1pm; there are steeplechases as well as flat racing on either dirt or turf tracks.

Early morning before races is a great time to come out to the track. Expert commentary accompanies the thoroughbreds as they go through their morning workouts, and a buffet breakfast is served on the Clubhouse Porch from 7 to 9:30am. During the season, free tram tours are available from 8am to 9am. These include a stroll around the stables and a demonstration of the mechanized starting gate; at the interactive **Discovery Paddock exhibit,** children can dress

The starting gates at Saratoga.

like a jockey, "weigh in" on a scale, and hammer a mock horseshoe.

If you're here out of season, you can still visit the **National Museum of Racing and Hall of Fame,** 191 Union Ave. (📞 **518/584-0400;** www.racingmuseum. org), displaying trophies, memorabilia, artworks, and film explaining not just Saratoga's story but 3 centuries of thoroughbred racing in the United States. There's a Hall of Fame for the greatest names in the sport's history—horses like Man O' War and Seabiscuit, jockeys like Willie Shoemaker and Eddie Arcaro, and trainers from Tom Smith to D. Wayne Lukas. Interactive screens allow visitors to relive great moments in racing.

ⓘ **Saratoga Racetrack,** 267 Union Ave. (📞 **518/584-6200;** www.nyra.com/saratoga). **Saratoga Convention and Tourism Bureau** (www.discoversaratoga.org).

✈ Albany, 30 miles.

🛏 $$ **Adelphi Hotel,** 365 Broadway (📞 **518/587-4688;** www.adelphihotel.com). $$ **Holiday Inn,** 232 Broadway (📞 **800/465-4329;** www.spa-hi.com).

BEST TIME: Racing season is late July to Labor Day.

WHY THEY'LL THANK YOU: Glimpsing horse racing's elegant past.

Wimbledon: A Grand Slam on Grass

Ages 6 & up • London, England

Aᴌᴛʜᴏᴜɢʜ ᴛʜᴇʀᴇ ᴀʀᴇ ꜰᴏᴜʀ Grand Slam tennis championships, the Wimbledon tournament is the only one still played on grass. Some of the world's best tennis players compete here over a fortnight of elimination matches, spanning roughly the last week in June to the first week in July. Watching a match at Wimbledon is a tennis player's dream (the only thing better would be actually playing at Wimbledon—but there you're on your own).

It is possible to get **tickets** to the tournament, even one of those coveted center-court seats, which are awarded via public lottery. Send a request for an application form, along with an international reply coupon or self-addressed envelope (with U.K. stamps) to: All England Lawn Tennis & Croquet Club, Box 98, Church Road, Wimbledon SW19 5AE England. It must be postmarked by December 15 for the next summer's tournament, and the application itself must be returned by December 31. For more information, go to www.wimbledon.org, which also explains about same-day ticket sales at the gate. You'll have to stand in line for this limited number of tickets and you may wind up disappointed; but it's worth a try, especially early in the tournament, when even the outside courts have top players competing on them. For recorded ticket information, call ✆ 020/8946-2244.

Wimbledon's home is the **All-England Lawn Tennis & Croquet Club,** founded as a croquet club in 1868. In 1873, Major Walter Clapton Wingfield invented an outdoor racquet game, which soon became known as lawn tennis; by 1877 the croquet club was already holding an annual lawn tennis tournament—which grew into the championship we know today.

Outside of tournament time, visitors can soak up tennis lore by visiting the **Wimbledon Lawn Tennis Museum** on the club grounds. Displays include videos of matches and interactive exhibits, as well as historic trophies, racquets used by famous players, a costume gallery charting a century's radical changes in women's tennis clothes, and championship trophies. Museum visitors get a look at the fabled **Centre Court;** you can also book a behind-the-scenes tour, which takes in **No. 1 Court,** the **Water Gardens,** and the **Press Interview Room,** where all those post-match interviews are filmed. A visit to this lovely suburb makes a nice break from London sightseeing; you can get here via the Underground (District Line), and the tennis club is an easy 20-minute walk from the station.

ⓘ Church Rd., Wimbledon (✆ 020/8946-6131; www.wimbledon.org).

✈ 🚆 See London 🔢.

WHY THEY'LL THANK YOU: Wimbledon scores game, set, and match.

International Tennis Hall of Fame
Where Newport's New Sport Became King
Ages 6 & up • Newport, Rhode Island, USA

Miffed at fellow members of Newport's exclusive Newport Reading Room club, in 1880 *New York Herald* publisher James Gordon Bennett, Jr., launched a rival club called the Newport Casino. Determined to make it bigger, better, and more fashionable, Bennett hired McKim Mead & White—favorite architects of the Gilded Age New York elite—to produce a rambling shingle-style edifice of lavish proportions, with dark-green turrets and verandas and an interior piazza for games and social events. Along with archery and lawn bowling, space was provided for a new game called lawn tennis, which quickly took root among upper-class athletes. The very next year, the newly formed US Lawn Tennis Association held its first national championship at the

The Tennis Hall of Fame.

Casino's grass **Horseshoe Court.** Now known as the US Open, this tournament is played at Flushing Meadows, Queens, but the Casino still holds professional tournaments, as well as the U.S. amateur grass championship. The Horseshoe Court is a permanent grass court, one of few remaining in this hard-court age, and there's still a **walled court** for court tennis, one of only nine in the United States. And in the elegant former club rooms, the old Casino has, since 1954, housed the **International Tennis Hall of Fame.**

Even if you're not a die-hard tennis fan, it's fun to tour the Hall of Fame just to explore this landmark building. Exhibits explore how lawn tennis exploded in popularity, how professional tennis developed out of the amateur sport, and the growth of women's tennis. Honorees include American champions from Bill Tilden and Stan Smith to John McEnroe, Jimmy Connors, Billie Jean King, and Chris Evert, not to mention the African-American groundbreakers Althea Gibson and Arthur Ashe. The Hall of Fame doesn't play national favorites; you'll see plaques for such international talents as France's Rene Lacoste and Yannick Noah; Sweden's Bjorn Borg and Mats Wilander; Germany's Steffi Graf and Boris Becker; Australia's John Newcombe and Evonne Goolagong; Romania's Ilie Nastase; Argentina's Guillermo Vilas; and Czechslovakia's Martina Navratilova. Even a kid who's just picked up a racquet can feel swept into a grand old sporting tradition here.

(i) 194 Bellevue Ave. ((C) **800/457-1144** or 401/849-3990; www.tennisfame.org).

✈ ⊨ See Newport's Mansions **370**.

WHY THEY'LL THANK YOU: How a pastime of the privileged became a sport of the people.

469

St. Andrews: The Birthplace of Golf
Ages 8 & up • St. Andrews, Scotland

THIS HISTORIC SEA TOWN in northeast Fife, Scotland, was once an ecclesiastic hot spot filled with monasteries (St. Andrew is Scotland's patron saint). When Henry VIII dissolved the churches in the 1530s, St. Andrews seemed to have lost its claim to fame. What saved it was a little game invented a century-and-a-half earlier by a group of bored aristocrats knocking a stone into a rabbit hole with a driftwood club, something they called *gowff*. Though James II, III, and IV outlawed the sport, the ancient monks just kept right on playing. Today, the wind-scoured bluffs they played on are the world's most famous golf course.

The Old Course, Golf Place ((C) **01334/ 466666**), is a classic links course, meaning one beside the sea. Its fairways and greens have been kept emerald-green for centuries by devoted greenskeepers, but the surrounding rough shows what the local vegetation actually is—tall sharp-bladed grasses, heathery shrubs, and wind-stunted trees. Wind is always a factor when you're playing here, along with that treacherous deep rough, hidden pot bunkers, huge double greens, and devilish corrugations on deceptively flat fairways.

There are actually six golf courses in the town: the **Old Course,** the **New Course** (1896), **Jubilee Course** (1897), **Eden**

(1914), **Strathtyrum** (1993), and the 9-hole **Balgrove,** laid out especially for children in 1972. Encircled by all of them is the world's most prestigious golf club, the **Royal and Ancient Golf Club** (✆ 01334/ 472-112), founded in St. Andrews in 1754. You've seen its golden-stone exterior on TV, the memorable backdrop to the Old Course's 18th green, but sorry, you can't get inside to see its famous trophy room unless you know a member.

Anyone can play the New, Jubilee, Eden, and Strathtyrum courses; you can even book a tee time online at www. standrews.org.uk. It's a little trickier to get onto the Old Course, where club members have priority, but it's possible: Fill out a ballot card with the Old Course starter on Golf Place by 2pm for a chance at one of the time slots the next day, which are drawn by lottery. You must present a current handicap certificate and/or letter of introduction from a bona fide golf club.

Chances are the youngsters you're with, however, aren't ready to play the Old Course; they can still get a firsthand look at those mean bunkers via a 40-minute guided walking tour (daily every hour in summer); book ahead for a more comprehensive 2-hour version. You can all drive balls at the Golf Practice Centre, overlooking the Old Course, or putt around the Himalayas putting course by the Links Clubhouse. Also by the clubhouse is the **British Golf Museum** (✆ 01334/ 460046), with glass-case exhibits on the game's history.

ⓘ ✆ **01334/476-335;** www.standrews.com

🚆 Leuchars, 1 hr. from Edinburgh.

🛏 $$$ **Rufflets Country House Hotel,** Strathkinness Low Rd. (✆ **01334/472-594;** www.rufflets.co.uk).

WHY THEY'LL THANK YOU: For golfers, this is Mecca.

The Calgary Stampede
Great Rodeo of the Great North Plains
Ages 6 & up • Calgary, Canada

JOINING THE CALGARY STAMPEDE is not something you do at the last minute—for 10 days every July, this big friendly city on Canada's western plains lassos in as many visitors as its hotels and restaurants can handle, so plan several months in advance. But it's worth it: Of all the big rodeo events in North America, this is the one to see, not least because it happens in summer, when the kids are out of school and the nearby Canadian Rockies are at their most glorious.

Though Calgary has acquired a sky-scrapers-and-business-suits persona since the oil boom of the 1960s, at heart it's still a good ol' cattle town, and Calgarians get back to their Old West roots during the Stampede, putting on Stetson hats and

whooping and hollering. Their high spirits are infectious. Downtown is abuzz with pancake breakfasts, rope twirling, square-dancing, and horse-drawn wagon tours, but most Stampede action takes place in **Stampede Park,** a show, sports, and exhibition ground south of downtown that was built for just this purpose. Top billing goes to the rodeo events, the largest and most prestigious in North America, held in the 16,000-seat Stampede Grandstand. Over a million Canadian dollars in prize money is won by competitors from around the world, riding bucking broncos or Brahma bulls, roping calves, wrestling steers, and barrel racing. Nighttime events include the **Chuckwagon Races** and

Trying to stay in the saddle at the Calgary Stampede.

Stampede Grandstand, a huge outdoor extravaganza with a nightly race of old-time cook wagons thundering around the track, followed by precision kick lines, clowns, bands, and a skyful of fireworks.

Stampede Park has two other stages as well for **nightly concerts**—rock, alternative, and comedy as well as lots of country music—and the Saddledome, winter home of the Calgary Flames hockey team, hosts several indoor events day and night. Teens will gravitate to shows with stunt mountain bikers and exhibition skateboarding. A midway is set up with noisy lit-up rides whirling and swooping; you can wander around a replica Indian village or a re-created 1912 Calgary streetscape. Livestock shows, a food fair, crafts competitions, art shows, lectures, even a mini-casino make Stampede Park a whirl of activity even if you don't have tickets to any rodeo events.

While you're in town, there's one essential attraction the kids will enjoy:

Fort Calgary Historic Park, 750 9th Ave. SE (© **403/290-1875;** www.fort calgary.ab.ca), a 16-hectare (40-acre) park built around the ruins of the 1875 Canadian Mounties fort where Calgary began. Bit by bit, volunteers are building an authentic replica of the fort, and there are lots of role-playing activities for kids, along with videos and guided tours.

ⓘ Box 1060, Station M (© **800/661-1767;** www.calgarystampede.com).

✈ Calgary International, 16km (10 miles).

🏨 $ **Elbow River Inn,** 1919 Macleod Trail S. (© **800/661-1463** or 403/269-6771; www.elbowrivercasino.com). $$$ **Westin Hotel,** 320 4th Ave. SW (© **800/937-8461** or 403/266-1611; www.westin.com).

WHY THEY'LL THANK YOU: From pancake breakfasts to chuckwagon races, a place to play cowpoke all day.

The Highland Games: Olympics in Kilts

All ages • Various towns in Scotland

MEN WEAR KILTS, traditional flings are danced, and there's a continual skirl of bagpipes—it's the **Highland Games,** Scotland's version of the Olympics, and if these summer festivals seem more focused on clan traditions than athletic prowess, well, that just makes them more fun.

The Heavies, gigantic men who follow the circuit all summer, draw the most attention with their uncanny brawn. Athletic contests are mostly feats of strength such as tug of war, wrestling, the hammer throw, and a primitive kind of shot putting using round stones. Wellie throwing and haggis hurling are often thrown in for good measure. Perhaps the most famous and unusual events are the caber-tossing contests. A caber is a 6m-long (20-ft.) pine tree, stripped to its bare trunk, which is flung into the air in hopes that it'll land on a straight line. If you think it's easy, just try it.

If you're not picky about which games to attend, you'll be happy to know that there's a series of them, all across Scotland, the whole summer long—contact the **Council of Scottish Clans and Associations,** www.cosca.net, for a full schedule. In June, the Bearsden and Milgnavie Highland Games (✆ **0141/942-5177**) are held at Burnbray in the small town of **Milgnavie** (pronounced *mill*-guy),

6 miles north of Glasgow. **Inverness** holds its Highland Games in July (Highlands of Scotland Tourist Board, Castle Wynd, off Bridge Street ✆ **01463/234353**). In August, it's the turn of the western Highlands city of **Oban** (Oban Tourist Information Centre, Argyll Square; ✆ **01631/563122**), where pipe bands are a specialty. But the grandest of the Highland Games is the one in early September in the town of **Braemar** (Braemar Tourist Office, The Mews, Mar Rd.; ✆ **01339/742208**), at the eastern end of the Grampian Mountains. Braemar is conveniently near Balmoral Castle, and ever since the days of Queen Victoria these have been designated the **Royal Highland Gathering.** It's held in the Princess Royal and Duke of Fife Memorial Park, and the queen herself often attends. As a result, the whole Braemar locality is flooded with visitors, so book your lodgings at least 6 months in advance.

ⓘ www.cosca.net.

🛏 Contact local tourist offices or www.visitscotland.com.

BEST TIME: May–Sept.

WHY THEY'LL THANK YOU: Watching a kilted Heavy toss a caber.

NASCAR Classic: The Daytona 500

Ages 4 & up • Daytona, Florida, USA

LIKE MUCH ELSE IN FLORIDA, it all began with a beach: beautiful Daytona Beach, which runs for 24 miles along a skinny peninsula divided from the north Florida mainland by the Halifax River. In the early 1900s,

when "horseless carriages" were still a novelty, automobile enthusiasts discovered that Daytona Beach's uniquely hard-packed white sand made the perfect drag strip. A century later, the town has every right to call itself "The World Center of Racing."

Auto racing in Daytona outgrew the beach long ago. In 1959, a proper 2½-mile racetrack, the **Daytona International Speedway,** was built 4 miles inland, and stock car racing's premier event, the 200-lap Daytona 500, was launched. The National Association for Stock Car Auto Racing (NASCAR) is now based in Daytona, and over a million race fans come here for 9 or 10 major events a year. Big races sell out months in advance—tickets to the Daytona 500 in February can be gone a year ahead of time (✆ **386/253-7223** for tickets).

If you're not attending a race, you can still get a fair idea by visiting the **World Center of Racing Visitor Center** at the east end of the speedway. You can enter the stands to see the track, or take a 30-minute **guided tram tour** that visits the garage area, pit road, and so on. Speed freaks can pay a stiff fee to have the **Richard Petty Driving Experience,** run by seven-time Daytona 500 winner Richard Petty (✆ **800/237-3889;** www.1800bepetty.com; May–October)—a

three-lap ride around the tri-oval track in a real stock car, cruising at an average speed of, oh, say 115 mph. The kids, however, may prefer to spend your money on the phenomenally popular **DAYTONA USA** (✆ **386/947-6404** or 386/947-6800; www.daytonausa.com), also in the visitor center, where all sorts of state-of-the-art motion simulators, interactive activities, and IMAX films re-create the adrenaline-pumping experience of racing in Daytona.

ⓘ 1801 W. International Speedway Blvd. (✆ **386/253-7223;** www.daytonaintl speedway.com).

✈ Daytona Beach International.

🛏 $ **Old Salty's Inn,** 1921 S. Atlantic Ave., Daytona Beach Shores (✆ **800/417-1466** or 386/252-8090). $$ **Shoreline All Suites Inn & Cabana Colony Cottages,** 2435 S. Atlantic Ave., Daytona Beach Shores (✆ **800/293-0653** or 386/252-1692; www.daytonashoreline.com).

WHY THEY'LL THANK YOU: Banking the turn into the home stretch.

The Indianapolis Speedway
Home of the 500
Ages 6 & up • Speedway, Indiana, USA

THE AUTO-RACING WORLD has many battling factions—NASCAR versus Formula One versus Grand Prix versus Indy cars—but as a native of Indianapolis, I remain true to the greatest single-day sporting event in the world: The Indianapolis 500 Mile Race. Launched in 1911, it's a classically simple race: 33 cars trying to complete 200 circuits of a 2.5-mile oval track. "How could that be interesting?" friends ask me. But it *is* interesting; it's chock-full of maneuvering and heartbreak and human valor, with crashes and mechanical failures

laying waste to the best-laid plans of even the most seasoned racing teams. I still tune into the race every Memorial Day weekend, hooked for life on the death-defying spectacle of drivers hurtling around the track at speeds over 200 mph.

Out of season, you can visit the **Indianapolis Motor Speedway Hall of Fame Museum** inside the oval, where more than 30 winning cars are displayed. The bus tour around the famous track is eye-opening, because when you see the race on TV you can't imagine how steeply

Race Day at the Indianapolis Speedway.

banked those treacherous corner turns are, or how lonely that backstretch can feel, far from your car's mechanics in the pit area over by the grandstands. The track is nicknamed "the Brickyard" because originally it was paved in red brick; all the bricks have long been paved over with smooth asphalt, except for one yard-wide brick stripe at the starting/finishing line of the race. Here the official starter intones "Gentlemen (and ladies), start your engines" (no automatic ignition for these babies) and a black-and-white checkered flag is dropped 500 miles later as the winner whizzes past.

More than 400,000 spectators crowd into the Speedway every May to watch this race, either in the grandstands or in the big rowdy picnic of the infield area. Unlike the Kentucky Derby , another primo Midwestern sporting event, this one isn't over in a few tense minutes—you'll be here for hours, bonding with your neighbors, trying to keep track of the drivers' shifting positions, watching the field gradually whittling down to a few hardy contenders. Wear a hat and

sunscreen and pack the best picnic cooler you can. Traffic to and from the track is a nightmare, and you come home begrimed with burnt rubber particles and temporarily deafened from the persistent roar of the engines—but it's an experience you'll never forget.

If you can't make it to the 500 itself, try coming one of the 2 weekends before the race for the **time trials,** during which hopeful drivers try to post competitive times for shorter circuits of the track. The drivers who post the fastest times get to start in the front rows of the race ("pole position"), which is no small advantage. My first Indy outings were on time-trial weekends, not race day, and it's still an exciting day at the track.

ⓘ 4790 W. 16th St. (☏ **317/481-8500;** www.brickyard.com).

✈ Indianapolis International.

🛏 See Conner Prairie Farm ❷❸❼.

WHY THEY'LL THANK YOU: The whine of the engines, the gasps of the crowd.

The Grand Prix of Monaco

Ages 6 & up • Monte Carlo, Monaco

NOWHERE IN EUROPE is driving more exciting, even for the ordinary motorist, than along the French Riviera, with its precipitous climbs, breathless curves, and mountain-piercing tunnels. In movies like *Day of the Jackal* and *The Bourne Identity*, jet-setters whipping around those twisty roads in low-slung sportscars are part of the Riviera mystique: It was chillingly apt that Monaco's beloved Princess Grace would die in 1982 in a crash on the same hairpin turn she took at top speed in the Hitch-cock film *To Catch a Thief* (the film that brought her to Monte Carlo in 1956, where she met Prince Rainier). Perhaps the most famous road race of all is driven in Monaco every May—the **Monte Carlo Grand Prix.**

First held in1929, the Grand Prix covers a 3.3km (2-mile) route that daringly runs right through town, hurtling up a steep hill to the Monte Carlo casino, plunging back downhill, whooshing through a waterfront tunnel, then slicing sharply around the quays. Formula 1 race cars (similar to Indy cars) whir around this hair-raising route for 78 laps, negotiating turns and jockeying fiercely for position, with the possibility of a spectacular crash always imminent. Grandstands are set up for spectators along the quays, though viewing spots are hard to secure.

This densely built-up Riviera town—congested even in the slow season—becomes a madhouse at race time. You may opt to visit Monaco another time of year and simply drive the route, imagining the race cars and protective barriers and cheering crowds for yourselves. Stop in the **Formule 1 shop,** 15 rue Grimaldi (℗ **93-15-92-44**), where everything from racing helmets to specialty key chains and T-shirts celebrates the roaring, high-octane racing machines; then visit the **Collection des Voitures Anciennes de S.A.S. le Prince de Monaco,** Les Ter-rasses de Fontvieille (℗ **92-05-28-56**), which displays more than 100 vintage autos belonging to Prince Rainier III, including the 1925 Bugatti 35B that won the Monaco Grand Prix in 1929 and the 1956 Rolls-Royce Silver Cloud that carried Rainier and Princess Grace on their wed-ding day.

While in Monaco, don't miss the **Musée de l'Océanographie,** avenue St-Martin (℗ **93-15-36-00**), founded by Albert I, great-grandfather of the present prince. A passionate oceanographer, he himself collected most of the exotic speci-mens exhibited here, many of them previ-ously unknown.

ⓘ **Automobile Club de Monaco,** 23 bd. Albert 1er (℗ **93-15-26-00**).

✈ ⊨ See Monte Carlo **451**.

WHY THEY'LL THANK YOU: It's Mille Bornes come to life.

Adrenaline Rushes . . . 525
Carousels & Ferris Wheels . . . 532
Roller Coasters . . . 537
Theme Parks . . . 543

A roller coaster at Lake Compounce.

475

Summer Bobsledding in the Austrian Alps

Ages 14 & up • Igls, Austria

EVER SINCE WE SAW *Cool Runnings*, the 1993 film about Jamaica's 1988 Olympic bobsled team, our family's been fascinated with this particular sport, one that requires daredevil athletes to strap themselves into a low-slung sleigh and hurtle at breakneck speed down a chute of preternaturally slick ice. Now I personally don't plan to do any bobsledding ever, but if you've got folks in your family who do, I can tell you where to go: Innsbruck, Austria.

Innsbruck looks just the way an Alpine town is supposed to look, with narrow medieval streets; a jumble of turrets, gables, and dormers; and horse-drawn carriages clopping over cobblestone pavements, all tucked into a narrow valley beneath forested peaks. Innsbruck has been a winter sports magnet for years, hosting not one but two Winter Olympics, in both 1964 and 1976. The facilities built for those Games are still going strong—there are gleaming ice rinks in town, and the ski slopes in outlying Igls, only 5km (3 miles) north of town, are booked solid all winter. In the summer, of course, when the snows melt, this Alpine scenery is overrun by mountain climbers and hikers instead of skiers. But the state-of-the-art **ice chute** created for bobsled, luge, and skeleton events is still active June through September, and it's quite a kick to find yourself bobsledding in the middle of summer. Granted, in summer they use

a modified sled, but the adrenaline-pumping effect is the same, juddering downhill at speeds of up to 100kmph (62 mph).

Experienced professional bobsledders pilot you in a four-man bob down the track, which has 14 curves, one loop-de-loop, and sides banked as steep as 7m (23 ft.) high. The track drops about 100m (328 ft.) in altitude in the course of a run some 1,270m (.8 mile) long. You must be at least 14 years old to participate; in summer this thrill is only offered Thursday and Friday afternoons from 4 to 6pm.

While it pales in comparison, if you pass on the bobsled ride you can still get a little vertigo on the **cable car** from Pätsch (the next village up the mountain from Igls) to the top of the Pätscherkofel mountain, a peak 2,241m (7,352 ft.) high with glistening panoramas of the nearby Stubai Glacier. The cable car covers a distance of 4km (2½ miles) and takes 18 minutes one way.

ⓘ **Olympic Bobsled Run,** Römerstrasse (✆ 0512/338380; www.olympiaworld.at).

✈ Innsbruck-Kranebitten, 8km (5 miles).

🛏 $$ **Best Western Hotel Mondschein,** Mariahilfstrasse 6, Innsbruck (✆ 0512/22784; www.mondschein.at). $$$ **Sporthotel Igls,** Hilberstrasse 17 (✆ 800/780-7234 or 0512/377241; www.sporthotel-igls.com).

WHY THEY'LL THANK YOU: Speeding downhill like a demon.

Soaring over Mont Blanc in a Cable Car

Ages 8 & up • Chamonix, France

YES, IT'S POSSIBLE to burrow under the French Alps in 20 minutes by driving through the Mont Blanc Tunnel into Italy. But why go underground when you can see more of the mountains—and get a real adrenaline rush—by going over them in a cable car?

Nestled in an alpine valley practically at the junction of France, Italy, and Switzerland, **Chamonix** is the historic capital of Alpine skiing—it was the site of the first Winter Olympic Games, in 1924—with western Europe's highest mountain, **Mont Blanc** (4,734m/15,531 ft. high), as its irrefutably dramatic backdrop. Numerous cable cars and mountain railways stretch like a spider's web from Chamonix into the surrounding mountains. The most thrilling route by far is the one that climbs to the Aiguille du Midi and on to Italy—it's a full day's journey if you go the whole way, although there are various points where you can shorten the trip.

The first section, a 9-minute run to the **Plan des Aiguilles** at an altitude of 2,263m (7,425 ft.), isn't so alarming. But the second stage, to the **Aiguille du Midi** station at 3,781 meters (12,405 ft.), may make your heart leap, especially when the car rises 610m (2,000 ft.) between towers. At the summit, you'll be about 100 meters (328 ft.) from Mont Blanc's peak, with a commanding view of the aiguilles of Chamonix and Vallée Blanche, the largest glacier in Europe (15km/9⅓ miles long). From here you can gaze at the Alpine peaks of three countries: France, Switzerland, and Italy.

At this point, having survived the most precipitous climb, you can descend back to Chamonix, making it a half-day excursion. But if you have your passports ready, the next stage will take you to **Pointe Heilbronner, Italy.** Leave the tram station along a chasm-spanning narrow bridge to reach this third cable car, which swings you over the 12-mile Vallée Blanche glacier ski run and through mountain peaks, past jagged needles of rock and ice bathed in dazzling light. There's only one word for it: awesome.

From Pointe Heilbronner, which is roughly the same altitude as Aigulle de Midi, you can descend on three more cable cars to Pavillon, then Rifugio Torino, and finally to La Palud, a suburb of Chamonix's Italian counterpart, the ski resort of Courmayeur, Italy. From Courmayeur, you can catch a bus back through the **Mont Blanc Tunnel** (✆ **04-50-55-55-00**)—the way ordinary travelers cross the Alps.

If the trip up the glacier seems too scary for the children (or, admit it, for you), never fear—another cableway from Chamonix makes a more gradual 1½-hour round-trip up to **Le Brévent,** which, at 2,485m (8,153 ft.), still offers breathtaking views of Mont Blanc and the Aiguilles de Chamonix.

ⓘ **Compagnie du Mont-Blanc,** 35 place de la Mer de Glace (✆ **04-50-53-30-80;** www.compagniedumontblanc.fr/en).

🚆 Chamonix, 8 hr. from Paris.

🛏 $$ **Albergo del Viale,** Viale Monte Bianco, Courmayeur (✆ **0165-846712;** ww.hoteldelviale.com). $$ **Hotel de l'Arve,** 60 impasse des Anémones, Chamonix (✆ **04-50-53-02-31;** www.hotelarve-chamonix.com).

BEST TIME: The route to Pointe Heilbronner operates only mid-May to mid-Oct.

WHY THEY'LL THANK YOU: Feeling like you're at the top of the world.

On Camel Safari in India
Roughing It in Rajasthan
Ages 10 & up • Rajasthan, India

THE ANCIENT LAND OF THE PRINCES, Rajasthan is a sun-scorched desert province where magnificent forts and palaces once guarded trade routes of inestimable wealth—a perfect snapshot of the exotic essence of India, yet within easy striking distance of Delhi and the **Taj Mahal** 88. You can cross that perilous desert too, and do it the way the ancient traders did—on board a swaying camel, the traditional "ship of the desert."

While camel treks are popular in the sand-dune deserts of western Rajasthan, especially out of Jaisalmer (best known for its magnificent medieval Golden Fort), I'd recommend heading instead for **Shekhawati,** an arid semidesert area only 200km (124 miles) southwest of Delhi. Shekhawati is fascinating to explore, with a number of towns full of painted houses and temples, their elaborate exterior murals a status symbol for wealthy merchants under the British Raj. One of the better options is a 2- to 4-day safari with **Royal Riding Holidays** (© 0140/262-2949; www.royalridingholidays.com), based out of Nawalgarh. Going out for a few days allows you to explore a more varied terrain of semidesert, forests, salt lake, marshes, and flat grasslands, and includes visits to local villages and with passing nomads. You'll sleep in colorful striped Asian-style tents with chairs, beds, mosquito nets, and a full floor covering; toilet and bath tents are provided as well, and the expedition is fortified with a cook who spreads out a desert buffet at every meal. Expect to spend 4 to 5 hours in the saddle per day, covering 25 to 40km (16–25 miles). Horseback safaris are available as well.

For kids, just perching high on the camel's elaborate saddle will be a thrill, learning to rock along with the long-legged camel's loping gait. (Hang on for dear life when the camel heaves up from its knees after you've mounted and when it kneels down again at the end of the ride!) There are a saddle in front of the hump and another behind it, and a driver will pilot the beast from the front saddle while you cling to the back seat. If someone in your group doesn't care to ride, they can follow the safari in a jeep and still have the fun of sleeping out in the desert in those maharajah-style tents. Don't expect to bond with your mounts, though—camels are *notorious* grumps.

ⓘ www.indianvisit.com.

✈ Jaipur 160km (100 miles).

🛏 $$ **Desert Resort,** Mandawa (© 0141/237-1194; www.mandawahotels.com). $$ **Roop Niwas Palace,** Nawalgarh (© 0141/262-2949.

BEST TIME: Nov–Mar.

WHY THEY'LL THANK YOU: Sailing across the sands.

The Amalfi Drive
A Mediterranean Thrill Ride
All ages • Sorrento to Ravello, Italy

HUGGING THE COAST of the Gulf of Salerno, Italy's Amalfi Drive (Rte. 163) is the most beautiful and probably most treacherous seaside highway in the world, a heart-hammering series of narrow hairpin turns you'll share with reckless Italian drivers. There are few roadside railings as you follow the edge of a cliff top plunging straight down to a boulder-strewn coast. If you want to leave the driving to someone else, take the blue SITA public bus that runs between Sorrento and Salerno.

The drive begins in **Sorrento,** a luxury resort perched on high cliffs overlooking the bay of Naples. Shops along Sorrento's cobbled alleys and flower-ringed plazas sell exquisite items of embroidery, lace,

The Amalfi Drive.

cameos, and marquetry. If you have time, take a 45-minute hydrofoil trip to the island of **Capri** to see the **Grotta Azzurra (Blue Grotto),** a spectacular cavern where light refracted from an opening under the water turns everything a dramatic Mediterranean cerulean blue. The beautiful lighting will amaze the kids (although the way passengers are hustled in and out of their rowboats spoils the experience somewhat).

The first 24km (15 miles) of the drive swing around the tip of a rocky peninsula, with Capri lying out to sea on your right, to **Positano,** a Moorish-style town with a hillside cascade of pink and white villas. If you skipped Capri's Blue Grotto, make up for it by visiting the **Emerald Grotto** 13km (8 miles) east of Positano. From the coastal road, you take an elevator down to this eerie cavern, and then ride a boat past underwater rock formations saturated with dazzling colored light.

The next town, 5km (3 miles) farther east, is **Amalfi,** an important seafaring republic in the Dark Ages and today a posh beach resort. If you need a break, stop in at the cloisters behind its cathedral, with whitewashed Moorish-style arches and mosaic fragments. Heading east from Amalfi, you negotiate a wickedly curving stretch of road cutting through vine-draped hills that hem in the ominously named Valley of the Dragon. After 6km (3¾ miles) of this, you'll land in **Ravello,** a cliffside retreat for writers from Boccaccio to D. H. Lawrence to Gore Vidal. A few miles past Ravello, at Vietri dul Mare, you can turn (with relief) onto the A3 highway, which cuts back towards Naples on a considerably tamer inland route. You made it!

ⓘ **Sorrento tourist office,** Via Luigi de Maio 35, Sorrento (✆ **081-8074033;** www.sorrentotourism.com).

🚐 Sorrento, 1 hr. from Naples.

🛏️ **$$ Hotel Bristol,** Via Capo 22, Sorrento (✆ 081-8784522; www.acampora.it).

$$$ **Hotel Santa Caterina,** S. S. Amalfitana 9, Amalfi (✆ **089-871012;** www.hotel santacaterina.it).

WHY THEY'LL THANK YOU: Seat belts are a *good thing.*

Adrenaline Rushes

479

Ballooning over the Great Red Rocks
Ages 8 & up • Sedona, Arizona, USA

Hot-air ballooning is extremely popular in the Southwest—Albuquerque's annual balloon festival every October is the country's largest—and there are plenty of operators vying for your business. Beautiful as all these desert landscapes are, the one that's most thrilling to soar over, to my mind, is the red-rock country around Sedona, Arizona, with its wind-sculpted buttes and outcroppings thrusting up from the desert scrub, the rock glowing as if on fire.

These excursions are always early-morning affairs—you need still morning air to properly inflate the balloon and to ensure a stable takeoff. The entire outing may take as much as 3 hours, of which only an hour or so is actually in the air. But the kids will enjoy watching the limp

silk billow into shape as burners inflate the balloon and, once you've settled back to earth, having a breakfast picnic in the desert while waiting for the "chase team" to arrive, deflate the balloon, and pack it back into its sack. Gondolas suspended below the balloons carry up to seven passengers at a time, and the ride is surprisingly steady—instead of fighting wind currents, you're going with the flow. True, the pace is often slow and majestic rather than death defying. Still, you're high up and protected only by the wicker sides of the basket, which is thrilling enough. You're also at the mercy of the elements somewhat—pilots can't steer the balloons, they can only change altitude, but there's a certain skill in finding wind currents heading in different directions to

Hot-air ballooning in Sedona.

get you where you want to go. If the winds are right they may even be able to lower the balloon onto the surface of a river, slap the water lightly with the bottom of the gondola, and then lift back up into the sky.

Three Sedona-area operators are licensed to fly over the spectacular Cocomino National Forest: **Northern Light Balloon Expeditions** (© 800/230-6222 or 928/282-2274; www.northernlightballoon.com), **Red Rock Balloon Adventures** (© 800/258-3754 or 928/284-0040; www.redrockballoons.com), and **Sky High Balloon Adventures** (© 800/551-7597 or 928/204-1395; www.skyhighballoons.com). In flight, their pilots will chat with the kids about the landscape they're flying over and about the science and art of hot-air ballooning.

(i) **Sedona Visitor Information,** 331 Forest Rd. (© **800/288-7336** or 928/282-7722; www.visitsedona.com/).

✈ Phoenix, 116 miles.

🛏 $ **Don Hoel's Cabins,** 9440 N. Hwy. 89A (© **800/292-HOEL** or 928/282-3560; www.hoels.com). $$$ **Hilton Sedona Resort,** 90 Ridge Trail Dr. (© **800/HILTONS** or 928/284-4040; www.hiltonsedona.com).

WHY THEY'LL THANK YOU: Up, up, and away.

Adrenaline Rushes **480**

Flying over the Grand Canyon

Ages 8 & up • Grand Canyon, Arizona, USA

RUGGED, OUTDOORSY TYPES no doubt prefer to do the Grand Canyon the old-fashioned way, on foot or in the saddle, but there's no disputing that a bird's-eye view of this magnificent chasm is an awesome sight. Plenty of companies offer narrated airplane and helicopter tours out of the Grand Canyon Airport in Tusayan; some even offer excursions from Las Vegas, taking in Lake Mead and Hoover Dam 302 along the way. The truly heart-stopping moment is when you're looking down at the treetops of the Kaibab National Forest, and then you cross the North Rim of the canyon and—*whoosh!* the ground drops away suddenly beneath you, an effect more spectacular in person than any IMAX film could ever convey.

These small aircraft—fixed-wing Cessnas and quiet ECO-Star copters, carrying only half a dozen or so passengers at a time—soon seem as insignificant as bumblebees against the tremendous backdrop of this 277-mile-long twisting canyon. In the course of an hour or so, you can move through all four distinct climate zones the Canyon contains, ducking up into side canyons or tracing the course of the Little Colorado River, looking like a mere trickle down on the canyon floor. While I prefer the graceful swoop of a plane to the choppy sensation of riding in a helicopter, the helicopters do have one advantage: They can drop straight downward 4,000 feet or so into sections of the gorge, descending swiftly past the striated colors of the canyon walls, perhaps even setting down briefly on the canyon floor, and then lift directly back up above the rim.

Grand Canyon Airlines (© **866/235-9422** or 928/638-2359; www.grandcanyonairlines.com) is the granddaddy of scenic air tours out here, having been in business since 1927. Plane tours out of Tusayan are also offered by **Air Grand Canyon** (© **800/247-4726** or 928/638-2686; www.airgrandcanyon.com). **Papillon Grand Canyon** (© **800/528-2418** or 928/638-2419; www.papillon.com) operates both planes and helicopters, both from the

South Rim and from Las Vegas, a surprisingly short excursion that takes 2½ hours by helicopter, 3 to 4 hours by plane.

Tour operators claim that these flights have less of an impact on the environment of the Canyon than any other mode of exploration. True enough—if you don't count the noise they make.

ⓘ **Grand Canyon National Park** (𝄐 928/638-7888; www.nps.gov/grca).

✈ 🛏 See The Mules Know the Way **416**.

WHY THEY'LL THANK YOU: The drop over the rim.

---

481 Adrenaline Rushes

The Call of the Wild in Denali
Your Own Personal Iditarod
Ages 10 & up • Denali National Park, Alaska, USA

ALASKA'S DENALI NATIONAL PARK is about as pristine a wilderness as a national park can get, and in an attempt to keep it that way, the Parks Service permits no public access by automobile—there's only one gravel road through the center of the park, which you can travel on a shuttle bus that links rest stops and campgrounds and lodges and scenic overlooks. Disembarking at various points, parkgoers can then hike into the tundra as far as they wish, though most folks seem content just to ride the bus and look out the window at those incredible Arctic views. But there's another way to get even deeper into this stunning wilderness—by racing over the snowy backcountry on a **dog sled,** just as the park rangers do.

Two outfits have been approved to run wintertime dog-sledding packages into Denali, using their own rustic lodges as home base (guests sleep in private log cabins near the lodges). Both of these lodges are just outside the park, but so close that they feature views of majestic Mount McKinley, America's biggest mountain. **Denali West Lodge,** set on the shore of Lake Minchumina, is the smaller of the two operations (only 10 guests at a time), and so remote that you'll need to fly in on a little private plane. Its mushing expeditions are mostly day trips from the lodge. You can drive via Alaska Hwy. 3 to **Earthsong Lodge,** which runs 3- to 10-day dog-sledding camp-outs (using tents or outlying cabins), although itineraries can be tailored to guests' interests. Each guest 12 and over drives his or her own sled, with teams of four to six huskies. (Younger children may simply ride along on the sled.) Earthsong even offers an option for summer visitors to get a taste of the dog-sledding experience by driving a husky team with a wheeled cart.

It may sound as if you'd need special skills, but the proprietors of both lodges are longtime mushers experienced in training first-timers. You just need to be strong enough to hold on tight as the dogs surge forward, whipping you over the snowy track. Perhaps 4 or 5 hours of the day is spent mushing, covering on average 30 miles of terrain, across the snowy tundra, around lakes, through taiga forests and glacial river valleys. You're practically guaranteed sightings of moose, caribou, Dall sheep, foxes, lynx, wolverines, and beavers; your chances of running across other human beings, however, are practically nil. Nighttime camp-outs may be lit by the Northern Lights and serenaded by nearby wolves, howling in sync with the huskies. Now *that's* getting away from it all.

ⓘ Denali Park Rd. (✆ **907/683-1266;** www.nps.gov/dena).

✈ Fairbanks, 125 miles. Anchorage, 236 miles.

🚂 **Alaska Railroad** (✆ **800/544-0552** or 907/265-2494; www.alaskarailroad.com) runs trains from Anchorage (6½ hr.) and from Fairbanks (3¾ hr.) summers only.

🛏 $$$ **Denali West Lodge** (✆ **907/ 674-3112;** www.denaliwestlodge.com). $$$ **Earthsong Lodge** (✆ **907/683-2863;** www.earthsonglodge.com).

BEST TIME: Nov–Mar.

WHY THEY'LL THANK YOU: Bonding with the huskies.

Carousels & Ferris Wheels **482**

The Flying Horses

All ages • Watch Hill, Rhode Island, USA

THE OLDEST OPERATING CAROUSEL in the United States, dating back to 1867, is tucked away in the charming resort town of Watch Hill, the westernmost community on Rhode Island's coast. These Flying Horses really do fly, because they aren't mounted on a revolving platform—they're hung by chains from overhead sweeps, the only such merry-go-round in the country. Once the carousel gets going, they are a textbook demonstration of centrifugal force, swinging outward as you spin dizzyingly around the central post. The hand-carved wooden horses may be smaller than average, but they're real works of art, with horsehair manes and genuine leather saddles and bright agate eyes. Come here before your kids get too old, because only children under 12 can ride this landmark merry-go-round.

Watch Hill is a stunning beach town, but like many such enclaves it's more about insiders than tourists. So once we've done the carousel, we jump back into the car and head for the other end of Rhode Island (which, face it, is less than an hour's drive) to check out two more historic carousels in the Providence area, both from the 1890s. Notice advances in technology since the Flying Horses was built: These two have bigger, more elaborately carved horses mounted on poles, the majority of them prancing up and down as the platform revolves. The **Slater Memorial Park Carousel,** Armistice Boulevard in Pawtucket (✆ **401/726-1876**), throws in some more exotic animals like a camel and a giraffe and has lovely stained-glass windows in its enclosing pavilion, but the real showstopper is the **Crescent Park Carousel,** 700 Bullocks Point Ave., in East Providence (✆ **401/433-2828;** www. crescentparkcarousel.com), which the Looff Company designed as its showy sales piece: It glitters with beveled glass panels, glass jewels, and electric lights, and the band organ at its hub is covered with carved figures that move about in time to the music. Snazzy.

ⓘ **Flying Horses** (✆ **401/348-6007**). **Watch Hill** (www.visitwatchhill.com).

✈ Providence.

🛏 $$$ **Providence Biltmore,** 11 Dorrance St., Providence (✆ **800/294-7709** or 401/ 421-0700; www.providencebiltmore.com).

BEST TIME: Open mid-June to early Sept.

WHY THEY'LL THANK YOU: Developing the art of merry-go-round design.

The Flying Horses Carousel
Grabbing the Brass Ring
All ages • Oak Bluffs, Massachusetts, USA

HERE IN PICTURESQUE OAK BLUFFS, on Martha's Vineyard, the Flying Horses is the United States's oldest working platform carousel (the Flying Horses in Watch Hill, Rhode Island **482**, predates it but doesn't have a platform), and it does look suitably antique, almost like something out of a Grandma Moses painting. The first time we watched it, my children felt vaguely disappointed—why didn't the horses go up and down, like they do on all the merry-go-rounds they were used to? Then they looked longer and figured out the special thrill of riding this carousel: All the local kids know to stand up in their stirrups and lean outward as they pass one

point of the circuit, waving an arm wildly to swipe a metal ring from a dispensing arm. If the ring you grab is made of brass, you get a free ride.

Built in 1876 at Coney Island, and brought to Martha's Vineyard in 1884, this National Historic Landmark is now maintained by the Martha's Vineyard Preservation Trust. It's in a small seaside area of refreshment stands and arcades that preserves an old-fashioned innocence. The carousel itself is inside a building, but you can hear the joyful strains of calliope music a couple streets away. When they were little, my kids were content to glide smoothly along the painted horses, clutching their real horsehair manes, never making a risky stretch for the rings. But once you start participating in the **ring grab,** you never go back; you get obsessed. In between rides, take a moment to admire the intricate hand-carving and gaze into the horses' glass eyes for a surprise: tiny animal charms glinting within.

I have to admit, for years I used the Flying Horses to tempt my children onto the ferry from Cape Cod to Martha's Vineyard, just so I could prowl around **Oak Bluffs's Camp Meeting Grounds** afterward. This 34-acre circle with more than 300 gaily painted gingerbread cottages is a window onto the 19th-century past, when families flocked here for weeklong religious retreats; continual prayer services were held in revivalists' tents on the central green. My kids are outgrowing the carousel these days, but they still love the Camp Meeting Grounds. And someday I hope we'll be lucky enough to hit Oak Bluffs on whatever mid-August weeknight the community leaders choose (the date is kept secret beforehand) as

Gingerbread Houses in Oak Bluffs.

Illumination Night, when today's cottagers light up their homes with Japanese lanterns all on the same evening. That would be a special memory indeed.

ⓘ 33 Circuit Ave. (© **508/693-9481;** www.mvpreservation.org/carousel.html).

✈ Martha's Vineyard Airport, 5 miles.

🛏 $$ **The Dockside Inn,** 9 Circuit Ave. Extension, Oak Bluffs (© **800/245-5979** or 508/693-2966; www.vineyardinns.com).

BEST TIME: Carousel closed mid-Oct to mid-Apr.

WHY THEY'LL THANK YOU: Going for the brass ring.

Carousels & Ferris Wheels 484

Merry-Go-Round the West Coast
On the Santa Monica Pier
All ages • Santa Monica, California, USA

WITH SO MANY BIGGER-IS-BETTER southern California attractions to give it competition, this classic wooden carousel sits comparatively neglected on the Santa Monica Pier. Photo shoots and corporate events frequently use it as a setting, but on a summer weekday you'll hardly have to stand in line to take a ride. It's an underappreciated gem, a forgotten bit of Californiana.

The open-sided building covering the carousel is itself a historic landmark, a Byzantine-Moorish-California fantasy built in 1916 by Charles I.D. Looff, one of the great artisans of the Golden Age of wooden carousel design. The carousel inside was built in 1922 in Philadelphia, its ornate hand-carved wooden horses and chariots painted by German and Italian immigrant craftsmen. Inset mirrors and strings of light bulbs keep it bright and snazzy; romantic landscape panels sweep around the parapet.

The Santa Monica Pier was one of California's hottest attractions in the 1920s, back in the days when seaside amusement piers were all the rage. Times have changed, however, and the Pier just hasn't kept up. Today it offers a handful of other attractions—a small aquarium, a

games arcade, and **Pacific Park** (© **310/260-8744;** www.pacpark.com), which has 12 squeaky-clean amusement park rides including a moderately thrilling roller coaster and Ferris wheel. I admire the spirit of the city's intention to avoid a honky-tonk atmosphere—this is, after all, haute Santa Monica—but there's not quite enough to make it a tourist destination, and even local families often forget it's here.

Well, finding little windows onto an earlier era is part of my mission as a parent, and finding them in L.A. is a special challenge I embrace. As we circled around on these vintage prancing ponies, with the Pacific Ocean stretching to the horizon right outside, we took deep breaths of ocean air and were grateful for a bit of shade to let our sunburned skins cool off after a morning at the beach. And we were selfishly glad to have the place to ourselves; you can only stand in line at Disneyland so long.

ⓘ Santa Monica Pier (© **310/394-8042;** www.santamonicapier.org).

✈ 🛏 See Santa Monica Beach ④47.

WHY THEY'LL THANK YOU: Nostalgic nook on the ocean.

Wheeling around Vienna
The Prater's Classic Ride to the Top
All ages • Vienna, Austria

IN THE 1949 FILM *The Third Man,* set in a rubble-strewn post–World War II Vienna, Orson Welles and Joseph Cotten hold a clandestine meeting in the Prater, Emperor Josef II's old hunting ground and the official birthplace of the waltz (invented in 1820 by Johann Strauss, Sr., father of the "Waltz King" Johann Strauss, Jr.). And where do Welles and Cotten talk where no one can overhear them? In one of the enclosed cars of the Riesenrad, the Prater's giant Ferris wheel, where they lift high over the rooftops of Vienna, warily gazing over the ravaged city below their feet.

Talk about classics—the **Riesenrad** was built for the Universal Exhibition in 1897 (commemorating the 50th year of Franz Josef's reign) by British engineer Walter Basset. This "giant wheel" was supposed to be a temporary exhibit, but like the Eiffel Tower, which had been built for the World's Fair in Paris a decade earlier, it never closed. Heavily damaged in 1945, it was reopened in 1947 as a symbol of Vienna's rising from the ashes. At its zenith, the wheel is 67m (220 ft.) high; one revolution takes 20 minutes. Instead of sitting in small fixed cars, passengers stand in roomy wide-windowed cabins, where you can move from side to side, taking in fine aerial views of Vienna across the Danube canal.

The Riesenrad sits right near the entrance to the **Prater,** which has been Vienna's favorite outdoor gathering place since the emperor opened it to the public in 1766. The **Panorama,** an audiovisual exhibit in a set of replica Riesenrad cabins at the foot of the wheel, illustrates Vienna's history. An **amusement park** behind the wheel has typical attractions kids love—merry-go-rounds, go-karts, tilt-a-whirls, shooting galleries, and a couple of excellent roller coasters, one of them rising nearly as high as the top of the Riesenrad.

The Prater is charming at night, with tiny lights strung in the trees around open-air cafes and beer gardens, and the rides themselves decked out in colored light bulbs. From the top of the Riesenrad, the concentric rings of Vienna's city layout sparkle like strands of a diamond necklace. But we like it in the daytime too, when we can pick out Vienna's landmarks—the needlelike spire of St. Stephan's Cathedral, the massive complex of the Hofburg palace, the stately

Vienna's Riesenrad.

Kunsthistoriche art museum. Out here in the Prater, Vienna's sometimes-dour personality softens and relaxes into the dreamy rhythms of a waltz, and I remember why dowdy old Vienna is one of my favorite cities on earth.

(i) **Praterverband** (© 01/7295430; www.wienerriesenrad.com).

✈ 🛏 See Schönbrunn Zoo .

WHY THEY'LL THANK YOU: Spinning slowly in an old-world pleasure ground.

Carousels & Ferris Wheels **486**

The London Eye: Big Wheel, Bigger View

Ages 6 & up • London, England

As FERRIS WHEELS GO, they sure don't get any bigger than the London Eye. This is no mere amusement park ride—after all, what is there to see from the top of ordinary Ferris wheels? From the top of the Eye, you can take in a glorious view, the vast panorama of one of the world's greatest cities.

At 135m (443 ft.) in circumference, it's the world's largest observation wheel—to be precise, not a Ferris wheel at all (named after Pennsylvanian engineer George Ferris, who invented one for the 1893 Chicago Exposition; in England they just call them "big wheels"). A Ferris wheel has swinging, open cars hanging from the wheel; an observation wheel has enclosed cars fixed on the wheel's perimeter, which, for better or worse, make the ride less scary. Passengers are carried in 32 air-conditioned "pods" that make a complete revolution every half-hour, hardly a breakneck pace—at the bottom, the pods keep moving, but so slowly that disembarking is no problem.

From the top of the wheel, in clear weather you can gaze in all directions for some 40km (25 miles) over this famously spread-out metropolis, easily spotting not only the Gothic spires of the Houses of Parliament and Westminster Abbey across the river, but the British Museum, St. Paul's Cathedral, Nelson's Column in Trafalgar Square, Buckingham Palace, the Tower of London, Tower Bridge, and the green necklace of parks that runs through central London.

Since the restaurant and observation deck at the top of the BT Tower were closed in the 1970s, London has had no great vantage point for tourists. Well, they've got one now, and how.

(i) **Millennium Jubilee Gardens** (© 0870/500-0600; www.londoneye.com).

✈ 🛏 See London **55**.

WHY THEY'LL THANK YOU: This view of London isn't just for the birds.

The London Eye.

Boulder Dash: An Instant Wooden Classic

Ages 8 & up • Bristol, Connecticut, USA

THE NATION'S OLDEST continuously operated amusement park (opened in 1846), **Lake Compounce** has tidy New England–y landscaping and a traditional sort of family-friendly wholesomeness, but the rides are completely up-to-date. For fans of wooden roller coasters—a breed unto themselves—it's hard to choose between the two at Lake Compounce. Sure, the Wildcat is a vintage wooden coaster, built in 1927, an exciting double out-and-back with that jittery jolted-out-of-your-seat effect that wooden coasters are famous for. But the park's other wooden coaster is the one that's been winning all the awards, even though it's only been around since 2000: Boulder Dash, the only roller coaster that's actually built into the side of a mountain.

Boulder Dash hurtles along at speeds up to 62 mph, rising up a wooded slope to its first dramatic drop of 115 feet—a drop you can't anticipate because you can't look through the mountain to see what's coming ahead. From here on, the coaster whips over a course nearly a mile long, diving in and out of woods, crashing over and around a series of boulders, down to the nearby lake and back; the ride takes 2½ minutes. The height requirement is only 48 inches, which means this is an excellent ride for younger thrill seekers who still need to work up to the nerve rattlers I cover below.

As you'd expect from an outdoor New England site, Lake Compounce is open only seasonally, mid-May through early September (check schedule on the

The water park at Lake Compounce.

website before you go). Just as the name implies, it's set on a clear little lake, nestled into the wooded hills west of Hartford. The park also has a fairly extensive **water park area,** all part of the same admission. There's a good-sized **kiddieland** to occupy younger brothers and sisters, and a **vintage 1911 carousel** with hand-carved wooden horses and the original Wurlitzer band organ. A half-hour **cable car** ride glides gently to the top of

a mountain—the same mountain that you dive down from at top speed when you ride Boulder Dash.

ⓘ 822 Lake Ave. (ⓒ **860/583-3300;** www.lakecompounce.com).

✈ 🛏 See Mark Twain House **376**.

BEST TIME: Mid-May to early Sept.

WHY THEY'LL THANK YOU: Going over the cliff.

Roller Coasters **488**

The Cyclone
The Coaster That Made Coney Island Famous
Ages 8 & up • Brooklyn, New York, USA

BACK IN THE DAYS before air-conditioning, New York families flocked to the beach at Coney Island to cool off in summer, and it was a rite of passage to grow tall enough (54 in.) to be allowed on New York's most famous roller coaster, The Cyclone. Thrill rides may have advanced technologically since then, but this classic coaster, built in 1927, is still one of the best, plunging a heart-stopping eight stories from its highest peak.

The charms of Coney Island go well beyond the Cyclone, of course; for one thing, there's that dynamite location, right on a wide white-sand beach where Atlantic waters crash. **The New York Aquarium,** Surf Avenue and West 8th Street (ⓒ **718/265-3400;** www.nyaquarium.com), just a short stroll up the boardwalk, features dolphins, sea lions, seals, and walruses. Also clustering along the boardwalk are a handful of small private amusement parks, each selling their own ride tickets. At 12th Street, Demo's Wonder Wheel Park features the 1920 landmark **Wonder Wheel,** an ingenious double Ferris wheel of gargantuan proportions. For those

who like to stay closer to earth, there are bumper cars, tilt-a-whirls, spinning teacups, carousels, and kiddie rides, as well as satisfyingly cheesy arcades; the area also has mini-golf and go-kart concessions. Compared to huge plasticized theme parks like Disney, Six Flags, and Busch Gardens, the Coney Island amusements have a grungy midway glamour that older kids will appreciate—it's the Real Thing. (With kids, it's best to visit by day—and know where your wallet is at all times.)

The beach and boardwalk have been spruced up lately, though, and the beachfront souvenir shops and food stands have acquired a post-modern hipster gloss, with Brooklyn artists decorating their side walls with retro murals. Even the local freak show, tucked up a Surf Avenue side street near the parks, has the whiff of a performance art installation. The Stillwell Avenue subway station (last stop for the D and F trains) has been refurbished to a high sheen, and along the boardwalk to the east, there's a tidy baseball stadium for a popular Mets farm team, the **Brooklyn Cyclones** (ⓒ **718/449-8497;**

Coney Island's Wonder Wheel.

www.brooklyncyclones.com). But you can still get a reliable kosher frank at Nathan's famous open-air hot dog stand on Surf Avenue—some things never change.

(i) Surf Avenue and 10th St. (© **718/372-0275;** www.astroland.com).

✈ 🛏 See Manhattan **56**.

BEST TIME: Amusement parks open daily June to Labor Day, weekends April–May and Sept–Oct.

WHY THEY'LL THANK YOU: Atmosphere, atmosphere, atmosphere.

489 Roller Coasters

Millennium Force
Cedar Point's Record Setter
Ages 10 & up • Sandusky, Ohio, USA

WHEN IT OPENED IN 2000, the Millennium Force at Ohio's Cedar Point amusement park not only was the world's tallest roller coaster (310 ft.), but also had the longest drop (300 ft.), the steepest banked turns of any noninverted coaster (122 degrees), and traveled at the fastest speed (93 mph). It may climb up that 310-foot peak (taller than the Statue of Liberty) at a modest 45-degree angle, but when it plunges down the other side it's angled at 80 degrees. It whips through two tunnels, and covers more than a mile in length, speeding to its finish line in 2 minutes and 20 seconds, almost before you know what hit you. But no record is unbreakable. Within 3 years, the Millennium Force was surpassed—by another roller coaster at Cedar Point, of course.

There's no question that Cedar Point prides itself on its roller coasters—it has 16 of them, the newest being the **Top Thrill Dragster,** which debuted in 2003. Top Thrill accelerates like a dragster right out of the gate, taking only 4 seconds to reach 120 mph, then climbs *straight up,* perpendicular to the ground, to a height of 420 ft., the equivalent of a 42-story building. And what does it do next? It drops down just as steeply (again at 120 mph), throwing in a wrenching 270-degree twist. The **Wicked Twister** is another heart-in-your-mouth experience, a U-shaped suspended coaster that ping-pongs back and forth between two 215-foot-high towers, corkscrewing up and down each tower, three times forward and twice backward, reaching a speed of up to 70 mph. No wonder these two have a minimum height requirement of 52 inches, whereas for Millennium Force you only need to be 48 inches. Each of these coasters has its rabid fans, while others are passionate about the experience on **Magnum,** or **Raptor,** or **Gemini,** or **Blue Streak,** or any of the other innovative steel coasters at Cedar Point.

Like Lake Compounce above, Cedar Point is a vintage park, first opening in 1870 on a peninsula jutting out into Lake Erie, about halfway between Cleveland and Toledo. Cedar Point has 68 rides in all and that's not even counting the attractions at the adjoining 18-acre water park, **Soak City;** an indoor water park, **Castaway Island,** recently opened to extend the season (the outdoor areas are only open May to early Sept). Four resort

The Top Thrill Dragster at Cedar Point.

hotels on the 364-acre property are available for those who need more than 1 day to do all the rides.

ⓘ 1 Cedar Point Dr. (ⓒ **419/627-2350;** www.cedarpoint.com).

✈ ⛏ See the Rock 'n' Roll Hall of Fame ❸❹❾.

BEST TIME: May to early Sept.

WHY THEY'LL THANK YOU: That moment at the peak, before the drop. Multiplied 16 times.

Roller Coasters

490

Kingda Ka: Bigger Is Better in New Jersey

Ages 10 & up • Jackson, New Jersey, USA

AS SOON AS ONE ROLLER COASTER sets a record, another new coaster is built to break it. Recently, the crown passed from Cedar Point to **Six Flags Great Adventure** in New Jersey, where the Kingda Ka debuted in 2005. It's almost as if a

designer went down a list of stats from the previous record holder, the Top Thrill Dragster (see above), and nudged each one just a tick higher. At the time we went to press, this one held all the records.

Using hydraulic technology, the Kingda Ka launches from 0 to *128 mph* in a breathtaking 3.5 seconds, then climbs 458 feet at a 90-degree angle—nearly 40 feet higher than Top Thrill. Making a neat quarter turn at the top of its green steel track, the ride hesitates—just long enough for you to realize where you're going and wonder why you ever thought this was a good idea—then whooshes back down the whole 458 feet, torquing into a 270-degree spiral. This is followed by a fast-paced camel hump and a banked left turn, before you glide back to the start, shaken if not stirred. The whole episode lasts less than a minute—50.6 seconds, to be exact—and you probably stood in line an hour to do it. And you'll probably do it again.

For those who prefer wooden coaster action—where the heights may be less but the sensation more intense—Six Flags Great Adventure was scheduled to open **El Toro** in 2006. This out-and-back wood coaster will drop at a record-breaking 76 degrees on its first 188-foot hill, followed by three more hills in rapid succession (112 ft., 100 ft., and 82 ft.), all at a speed of 70 mph.

As you'd expect from this homogenized theme-park franchise, the New Jersey Six Flags has an overwhelming number of top-class rides—wood coasters, steel coasters, dark rides, soak rides, free-falls and flumes and a Ferris wheel, many of them with licensed-character tie-ins (Batman: The Ride and Superman Ultimate Flight are two of the most popular). There are a cable car, a large section of rides scaled for younger kids, and plenty of pocket-emptying food and souvenir stands. Lines are a fact of life, and it doesn't come cheap—but for East Coast roller coaster addicts, this is an essential visit.

(i) Off I-195 (© **732/928-1821;** www.six flags.com).

✈ Newark, NJ, 67 miles. Philadelphia, PA, 60 miles.

🛏 $$ **Freehold Gardens Hotel,** 50 Gibson Place, Freehold NJ (© **732/780-3870;** www.freeholdgardens.com). $$ **Ramada Inn,** 2373 Rte. 9, Toms River, NJ (© **800/ 5-HOTELS** or 732/905-2626; www.ramada. com).

BEST TIME: June–Aug; weekends Apr–May and Sept–Oct.

WHY THEY'LL THANK YOU: Saying they rode the biggest.

491 Roller Coasters

Dueling Coasters at Islands of Adventure

Ages 10 & up • Orlando, Florida, USA

FOR KIDS WHO'VE GRADUATED to the top of the thrill-ride chain (that is, those who can pass the 54-in. height requirements), no trip to Orlando is complete without tackling The Incredible Hulk Coaster and Dueling Dragons at Islands of Adventure. Both were opened in the same year, 1999, almost as if Universal Studios Florida—the theme-park mega-corporation that's given Disney such a run for its money in Orlando—knew it was setting up a duel. Coaster addicts can't go home without riding both, investing a serious chunk of line-waiting time—no matter how early in the day you get here, you can only stand in line for one at a time, which means that by the time you hit your second coaster, the line is already snaking around the block.

Dueling Dragons was the world's first inverted dual coaster, running two intertwined coasters (the red Fire Dragon and the blue Ice Dragon) through loops, rolls, corkscrews, inversions, and . . . oh, yes, at each other (don't worry—you'll miss your oncoming foe by about 12 in.). As green as its comic namesake, **The Hulk** coaster is a steel-framed thriller that pulls the same G-forces as an F-16 fighter jet, includes seven inversions, hits speeds of up to 60 mph, and (much to the delight of kids) glows at night.

So, who wins the battle between the Hulk and the dragons? Both rides offer good themes and preattraction queue areas: You tour Bruce Banner's lab as you wait to climb aboard the Hulk; over at Dragons, you wend your way through a medieval castle and get briefed by Merlin. The Incredible Hulk Coaster offers a more dramatic launch (from a dark tunnel out into the sunlight) and a smoother ride than Dueling Dragons, but for pure thrills, the front seat of the Fire Dragon (which tops out at 60 mph, 5 miles faster than its Ice counterpart) gets my vote as the best rush in town.

Once you've tackled both coasters, Islands of Adventure offers plenty of other adrenaline-pumping options. Take an 85-foot plunge on the amazingly detailed **Jurassic Park River Adventure**

water ride; get swept up in a tangle of 3-D action and special effects on **The Amazing Adventures of Spider-Man** ride, perhaps the best themed ride in all of Orlando; or nose-dive in a log flume at 50 mph over **Dudley Do-Right's Ripsaw Falls.** Though there are rides for younger kids (especially in the delightfully whimsical **Seuss Landing**), Islands will appeal most to the over-10 set.

(i) (C) **800/711-0080** or 407/363-8000; www.universalorlando.com.

✈ Orlando International, 25 miles.

⊨ $$ **AmeriSuites Universal,** 5895 Caravan Court ((C) **800/833-1516** or 407/351-0627; www.amerisuites.com). $$$ **Royal Pacific Resort,** 6300 Hollywood Way ((C) **800/232-7827** or 407/503-3000; www. loewshotels.com).

WHY THEY'LL THANK YOU: Action, action, and more action.

Roller Coasters **492**

Catching Airtime Along the Strip
Las Vegas's In-House Thrill Rides
Ages 8 & up • Las Vegas, Nevada, USA

THE STRIP IN LAS VEGAS already looks like a carnival midway, with hyperbolic dazzle on all sides competing for your attention. So no one should be surprised to learn that Las Vegas has its own set of roller coasters and thrill rides that dance in and out of the casinos. For me, that kitschy incongruity is exactly what makes it a sure bet for kids.

The New York–New York property uses its roller coaster almost as a decorative flourish, highlighting the fake Manhattan skyline atop the casino, and for many gamblers that's all it will ever be, a bit of scenery. But this **Manhattan Express** does in fact offer coaster hounds quite a respectable 3-minute ride, hitting speeds of up to 67 mph. It begins by climbing 203 feet, dropping 75 feet, then surprising you with a second vertical drop of 144

feet. (Somewhere in here you careen past the Statue of Liberty's torch, but who's paying attention to the scenery?) Next comes the coaster's trademark "heartline" twist, a barrel-roll inversion that hangs passengers upside down for a terrifying instant before diving under its own track again. A series of bunny hops atop the skyline repeatedly lift you off your seat, followed by a second inversion and a 540-degree spiral drop for a finale.

At the Sahara, **Speed: The Ride** is a stellar example of a shuttle coaster, that is, a ride that goes to the end of its track and then makes the return trip backward (as in not-being-able-to-see-where-you're-going backward). The ride begins in the NASCAR Café (where there are also several race-car simulators), blasts through a

Manhattan Express Roller Coaster in Las Vegas.

hole in the wall, dips through a tunnel under the Sahara's sidewalk, whirs around a vertical loop, rattles through Arabian-fantasy arches in the hotel's marquee, and shoots straight up a 224-foot tower—yep, at a 90-degree angle—where it hangs for one gravity-defying moment before crashing backward and repeating the whole course in reverse, loop and tunnel and all. You do this at 70 mph and see how wobbly your legs are when you get out of the car.

ⓘ **Manhattan Express,** New York–New York Hotel & Casino, 3400 Las Vegas Blvd. S. (✆ **702/740-6969;** www.nynyhotelcasino. com). **Speed: The Ride,** Sahara Hotel & Casino, 2535 Las Vegas Blvd. S. (✆ **702/ 737-2111;** www.saharahotelcasino.com).

✈ ⊨ See Las Vegas **46**.

WHY THEY'LL THANK YOU: Loop-de-loops over the Strip.

493 Theme Parks

Playland's Retro Rides

All ages • Rye, New York, USA

REMEMBER IN THE MOVIE *Big,* when a creepy fortunetelling machine granted Tom Hanks's younger self a fateful wish to become big? That scene was shot at Playland, a nostalgic throwback of an amusement park set in a leafy seaside suburb conveniently close to New York City. This old-timey collection of rides and games is what amusement parks used to be like before they went on steroids and became big, overhyped, commercialized mega–theme parks.

But it's no mere rinky-dink midway—Playland is actually listed on the National Register of Historic Places. Playland opened in 1928, right on Long Island Sound, and has been kept up beautifully ever since, with neat landscaping, landmark Art Deco buildings, and old-fashioned charm: striped awnings, painted wooden fences enclosing the rides, and festive-looking ticket booths.

Kids 5 and under should be steered straight to **Kiddyland,** which has rides tailored to their size like The Kiddy Whip, Kiddyland Bumper Cars, and the Demolition Derby. For older kids, the most thrilling rides (which of course require the longest waits in line) are probably the **Hurricane Coaster,** the **Crazy Mouse, Power Surge,** and the vintage wooden **Dragon Coaster**—tame by Busch Gardens standards, but enough to make me lose my lunch. My favorites, however, are the more retro rides: the **Ferris Wheel,**

the **Whip,** and, best of all, the one-of-a-kind **Derby Riders,** a circular track where you plunge forward on steel horses that race twice as fast as carousel nags. I'm embarrassed to tell you how many times in a row I've ridden that one. Plan on several hours here; your kids will insist on it.

To make a full day of it, in addition to the rides, Playland offers a beach, a pool, an ice rink, mini-golf, and a lake for boating, which are open seasonally.

(i) Playland Pkwy. ((C) **914/813-7010;** www.ryeplayland.org/).

MetroNorth ((C) **800/METRO-INFO** or 212/532-4900; www.mta.nyc.ny.us/mnr), 1 hr. from Manhattan.

✈ 🛏 See Manhattan **56**.

BEST TIME: Open May–Sept.

WHY THEY'LL THANK YOU: A kinder, gentler notion of what it takes to have fun.

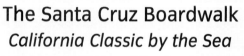

Theme Parks **494**

The Santa Cruz Boardwalk
California Classic by the Sea
All ages • Coast between Monterey & San Francisco, California, USA

ONE OF THE FEW old-fashioned amusement parks left in the world, the Santa Cruz Beach Boardwalk is California's answer to Rye Playland **493**. Situated next to Santa Cruz's lovely mile-long public beach, the boardwalk is a half-mile strip of rides, shops, and restaurants, harking back to an era of seaside innocent fun. It's the sort of classic site you don't necessarily expect on the West Coast.

The park has 34 rides, two of them national landmarks. **The Carousel of Delight,** built in 1911 by Charles I.D. Looff, boasts hand-carved wooden horses, a 342-pipe organ band, and one of the few brass ring grabs left in existence; snatch the brass ring as your horse whirls past the post, then throw it into a painted clown's mouth to win a free ride. Looff's son,

Arthur Looff, designed the park's other landmark, the red-and-white 1924 **Giant Dipper** roller coaster, which offers great views of Monterey Bay from its peaks—though few riders manage to take them in while being hurtled up and down at 55 mph. They have a split second longer to enjoy the views from the top of the 125-foot-tall Double Shot drop tower. A host of other thrill rides trade on speed, with names like Hurricane, Typhoon, and Tsunami; indoor "dark rides" include the Haunted Castle and Ghost Blaster, though I prefer the 1961-vintage **Cave Train,** where glow-in-the-dark prehistoric characters pop out. There is a section of smaller-scale rides for the under-36-inch crowd as well.

Although there's no admission fee to get onto the boardwalk, the individual ride

Santa Cruz Boardwalk.

tickets can mount up fast—an "unlimited rides" bracelet, which at first doesn't seem cheap, could end up saving you money. The beach boardwalk keeps seasonal hours, open daily from Memorial Day weekend to Labor Day but only on weekends and holidays throughout the spring and fall.

(i) ✆ **831/426-7433;** www.beachboardwalk. com.

✈ San Francisco International, 77 miles.

🛏 $$ **Fern River Resort,** 5250 Hwy. 9, Felton (✆ **831/335-4412;** www.fernriver. com).

WHY THEY'LL THANK YOU: Screaming from the top of the Giant Dipper.

---

495 Theme Parks

Disneyland
The Theme Park That Started It All
All ages • Anaheim, California, USA

I WAS A DISNEYLAND BABY—my parents took me there the summer it opened, in 1955, when it was still surrounded by sleepy orange groves. I went again in 1967, 1989, and most recently in 2005, the amusement park's 50th anniversary year. And although I'm not a theme-park fanatic, I will always have a deep and abiding love for Disneyland. My skeptical 13-year-old, having heard it dubbed "The Happiest

Place on Earth," spent his entire day in the Magic Kingdom looking for people who weren't happy—and he failed. Happily.

Smaller than Walt Disney World, Disneyland feels truer to the childlike enthusiasm of founder Walt Disney. Originally Disneyland was divided into four "lands"—Adventureland, Fantasyland, Frontierland, and Tomorrowland, symmetrically arranged around the iconic **Cinderella's**

castle, where fireworks still scintillate every night. As the 1950s Wild West fad waned and Sputnik-era optimism went sour, Frontierland and Tomorrowland shrank and new areas were wedged in: Main Street USA, an old-timey-America shopping area; New Orleans Square; Critter Country; and Mickey's Toontown, a Roger Rabbit–inspired section for younger children. In the process, the park's layout has become a little more confusing; we were constantly consulting the free park map we got at the front gate.

Every kid will have different **favorite rides,** but these were my kids' (remember, this is from a teenager and two preteens): Mr. Toad's Wild Ride (Fantasyland), Pirates of the Caribbean (New Orleans Square), Tom Sawyer's Island (Frontierland), Peter Pan's Flight (Fantasyland), Davy Crockett's Canoes (Critter Country), the Jungle Cruise (Adventureland), It's a Small World (Fantasyland), and Innoventions (Tomorrowland). And what they liked about them was the storytelling—not heart-skidding vertical drops, not flashy laser light effects, just scrupulous artistic detail and wry humor. Hurtling into a cartoon hell with naughty Mr. Toad—that alone made the whole day worthwhile.

Long lines are a fact of life at Disneyland, especially on weekends and all school vacations. Don't be suckers for them—my kids decided that 5 minutes of watching huge ceramic Dumbos fly around flapping their ears was more fun than waiting 45 minutes to ride them. If you must, arrive early and make a beeline for the most popular rides, which are generally the

Dumbo at Disneyland.

adrenaline pumpers—the Indiana Jones Adventure, Star Tours, Big Thunder Mountain Railroad, Splash Mountain, the Haunted Mansion, and Pirates of the Caribbean. But I'm philosophical about lines: What's so bad about 30 extra minutes of unplanned conversation with a child?

(i) **Magic Way** ((C) **714/781-4565** or (C) 714/781-7290; www.disneyland.com).

✈ Los Angeles International, 33 miles. John Wayne Airport in Santa Ana, 15 miles.

🛏 $ **Candy Cane Inn,** 1747 S. Harbor Blvd. ((C) **800/345-7057** or 714/774-5284; www.candycaneinn.net). $$$ **Disney's Grand Californian Hotel,** 1600 S. Disneyland Dr. ((C) **714/956-MICKEY** or 714/635-2300; www.disneyland.com).

WHY THEY'LL THANK YOU: The one, the only, original theme park.

Theme Parks

496

Legoland
Constructing a Fantasy, One Brick at a Time
All ages • Carlsbad, California, USA

I SUPPOSE IT HELPED that both my boys were fanatical Lego block builders in their younger days; they felt immediately at home in an environment that's all primary colors, right angles, modular components, and imagination. I haven't visited

Legoland.

the sister Legoland parks in England, Germany, and Denmark, but I'm told they're more or less the same as the one in the United States (what a Lego-like concept—interchangeable parts). All I know is that the one we visited gave us a supremely happy day indeed.

Legoland is by no means all built of Lego blocks: The Southern California park is beautifully landscaped with 1,360 bonsai trees and other plants from around the world, and features more than 50 rides, shows, and attractions. While a few coasters and rides have a higher thrill factor, these are tame compared to the Six Flagses and Busch Gardenses of this world, making Legoland an ideal place to bring younger children. Kids are encouraged to be physically active—instead of a perpendicular drop tower where riders are randomly jerked up and down, Legoland's **Towers of Power** challenge children to haul themselves up to the top on pulleys if they want to get the maximum plunge. They can take part in a joust at the **Knight's Kingdom,** dig fossil replicas out of the sand, and maneuver their own Lego-replica boats or cars. While the Jungle Cruise at rival Disneyland 🔵495 has realistic hippos and gorillas cavorting

around, **Legoland's Fairy Tale Brook** boat ride has storybook characters that look like Lego figures, calling on the children's own imaginations to turn them into Little Red Riding Hood or the Three Little Pigs. There are plenty of hands-on displays here, including an **Imagination Zone** where you can build virtual Lego creations on computer terminals, or get busy with the blocks themselves.

But to my mind, the most amazing thing at Legoland—make that one of the most amazing things I've seen anywhere—was the obsessively accurate models of several American cities, built out of real Lego blocks by real Lego Master Model Builders. To build a Washington Monument out of Legos is one thing; to make the ribbed Capitol Dome is quite another, and yet there it was. The colorful Victorian townhouses of San Francisco's Alamo Square, the streamlined Art Deco sleekness of New York's Rockefeller Center, the lacy wrought-iron balconies of New Orleans's French Quarter—all of them were there, made out of Legos, and looked completely authentic. We must have spent an hour studying those cityscapes, and I could have stayed longer.

ⓘ 1 Legoland Dr. (ℰ **877/534-6526** or 760/918-LEGO; www.legoland.com).

✈ San Diego, 34 miles.

🛏 See San Diego Zoo ⑬.

BEST TIME: Closed Tues–Wed Sept–May.

WHY THEY'LL THANK YOU: Piecing the world together and pulling it apart again.

The Mall of America
Minnesota's Mega-Mall Amusements
All ages • Bloomington, Minnesota, USA

WHAT NERVE IT TOOK to build a shopping center in suburban Minnesota and call it The Mall of America. And yet there is something iconic about this over-the-top shrine to consumerism. Subscribing to the all-American bigger-is-better philosophy, the mall could hold seven Yankee Stadiums or 258 Statues of Liberty; walk one circuit around a level of stores and you've clocked nearly a mile. There are over 520 stores at this huge retail center 20 minutes south of downtown Minneapolis,

stacked on four brightly lit levels around a central glass atrium—not only that, but 14 movie screens, a food court, 20 sit-down restaurants, half a dozen attractions, and even a wedding chapel. You've got to see it to believe it.

The main attraction is **Camp Snoopy,** America's largest enclosed theme park, which covers 7 ground-floor acres in the immense central atrium with 30 rides, including a kiddie roller coaster that loops around large planters full of trees. This will

Underwater Adventures Aquarium.

thrill toddlers and young grade schoolers; kids who've outgrown those tame rides will still enjoy the **Underwater Adventures Aquarium,** where 4,500 sea creatures swim around in tanks on a subterranean level. Between the virtual submarine ride and the "shark encounter"—a glass tunnel that walks you through a shark tank—it's like a mini–Sea World. At the *mall.*

For teens or preteens (and, admit it, adults too), the **A.C.E.S Flight Simulators** let you play virtual pilot on an F-18 Hornet jet or a WWII-era P-51 Mustang. An even bigger deal is the **NASCAR Silicon Motor Speedway,** where anyone over 52 inches tall can get behind the wheel of a rigged-up stationary stock car and spend 20 minutes stepping on the gas, banking on the turns, and stomping on the brakes (there's a passenger seat where kids age 4 and older can ride shotgun on this virtual race).

While not strictly a theme attraction (no admission charge, for one thing), the four-story **Lego store** is as good as a ride, with some 90 life-size Lego models to marvel at; the **Build-a-Bear Workshop** is another store that offers plenty of entertainment. So what if most of the other shops are the usual gang of chain stores? It's called the Mall of America, dude—so who's expecting snooty high-end retail? It's supersize, it's commercial, and it caters to the masses—and there's nothing more American than that.

(i) 60 E. Broadway (www.mallofamerica.com).

✈ Minneapolis/St. Paul International, 10 miles.

🛏 $ **Best Western Kelly Inn,** 161 Saint Anthony Ave., St. Paul (✆ **800/780-7234** or 651/227-8711; www.bestwestern.com). $$ **Doubletree Park Place,** 1500 Park Place Blvd., Minneapolis (✆ **800/222-tree** or 952/542-8600; www.doubletree.com).

WHY THEY'LL THANK YOU: Looking down from Level 4 to see Camp Snoopy below.

---

498 Theme Parks

Parc Asterix
'Toon Time in the Paris Outskirts
All ages • Plailly, France

EXPLAIN ME THIS: Why would an American family who took the trouble to fly all the way to France ever go to Disneyland Paris? You could just as easily go to a real French theme park that's just as much (if not more) fun: Parc Asterix. Families I know who've done both definitely vote for the homegrown French park—its *joie de vivre* is the real thing.

Granted, English-speaking children may not be familiar with these comic book characters. But you don't have to read *Asterix* comics to get the gist of the thing; it's enough to know that the characters are goofy Gauls living under the rule of the Roman Empire, which gives the theme park an excuse to haul out images from Roman mythology, Viking lore, even the Druids. There's definitely a sense of humor at play—when you stand underneath the giant statue of a thunderbolt-clutching Zeus that presides over the top-rated roller coaster, look up under his toga and you'll see he's been provided with spotted underpants (providing a photo op that few parkgoers pass up). Parc Asterix's

Parc Asterix.

autoroute ride cracks me up: Nationale 7, where children drive Model-T-style jalopies along a replica of the French highway that's famously choked with holiday traffic every summer weekend. So what if it doesn't tie into the Asterix theme—they couldn't resist the joke.

This spick-and-span, smartly conceived amusement park, open seasonally, offers some 30 rides, for all levels—everything from a tiny **kiddie carousel** to the **Towers of Zeus** (Europe's biggest wooden roller coaster) and the exhilarating **Goudurix,** a speedy coaster with no fewer than seven loop-de-loops. Themes are not just tacked on, they really enhance the rides—like the swing ship shaped like a Viking longboat, the scramble ride with a many-headed Hydra dragon sprouting from the center, or the inner tube ride that swoops down the Styx river, the mythological entry to Hell. The kiddie section is designed like a Druid forest (or at least a cozy Smurf-esque Druid forest); the stage shows are in a pseudo-Roman arena, with an aquatic Poseidon's Theater added for dolphin shows.

Your vision of touring France with your family may be all about Versailles and the Louvre, but the children may eventually clamor for something more . . . well, *fun.* In that case, you can feel good about giving in to the Parc Asterix option: In its own way, it is a little slice of French culture, something you could never do back home. Yet it's about the same distance from Paris as Disneyland: 35km (22 miles) north of Paris, easily within day-trip range (you'll need a connecting bus from the Roissy train station if you don't go by car). *Pourquoi pas?*

ⓘ Off the A1 (✆ **03-44-62-31-31;** www.parcasterix.fr).

✈ ⨭ See Paris ㊴.

BEST TIME: May–Sept.

WHY THEY'LL THANK YOU: It takes a lot of Gaul to have this much fun with history.

Europa-Park
The Grand Tour, All in a Day
All ages • Rust, Germany

FROM THE COUNTRY that brought you the Porsche and the autobahn, you'd expect the rides at Germany's largest theme park to be high-tech and speed-obsessed. And yes indeed, Europa Park does have Europe's highest and fastest roller coaster, the **Silver Star,** which climbs to 240 feet, travels at 79 mph, and (here's a plus) delivers a ride that's a full 4 minutes long. But though there are seven dramatic roller coasters at Europa Park, this place is not just about the rides. It's a clever **microcosm of Europe,** with shops and restaurants and shows as well as rides in miniversions of 11 different countries. Corny as it may sound, it works.

Sound familiar? Yes, Epcot in Orlando originated the pocket-nation idea, and Busch Garden Williamsburg jumped on the same bandwagon—but Europa Park covers more European countries on its 160-acre site, from Scandinavia to Greece, from Portugal to Russia, and does so with an attention to architectural detail that puts the other parks' stage-set streetscapes to shame. From the replica of England's venerable Globe Theatre to one of Russia's Mir Space Station, it hits all the cultural highlights; the **Panorama Train** that circles the park lets you drink it all in for an overview, but immerse yourself in each section and you'll be engrossed. If thrill rides aren't your thing, well, Europa Park is fun, even without taking a single ride.

But when it comes to the rides, attention to creative detail again makes all the difference. The folks who designed this park clearly have scoped out the competition—if they can't have Mad Tea Party spinning teacups, they'll put **spinning Delft coffee cups** in the Holland section; instead of a Haunted Mansion, they have a **Ghost Castle** in the Italy area; and let's just call Pirates in Batavia, in the Portugal section, an "homage" to Pirates of the Caribbean. But these aren't cheesy imitations, they are every bit as well-executed as the Disney originals, and just as much fun.

Although Europa Park isn't open year-round—that pesky German climate—they manage to have at least part of the park open most of the time, with a Halloween-themed experience in October and a December Christmas theme; even though several of the bigger outdoor rides are closed in the off-season, there's still plenty to do. See the website for details.

(i) Europa-Park Strasse 2 ((C) **0180/ 5776688;** www.europapark.de).

🚂 Freiburg, 2 hr. from Frankfurt.

🛏 $$$ **Colombi-Hotel,** Ritteckring 16, Freiburg ((C) **0761/21060;** www.colombi. de). $$ **Park Hotel Post,** Eisenbahnstrasse 37, Freiburg ((C) **0761/385480;** www.park-hotel-post.de).

BEST TIME: May–Sept.

WHY THEY'LL THANK YOU: Fjord-rafting and splashing in the Mediterranean, all in a single park.

Tivoli Gardens: Copenhagen's Jewel

All ages • Copenhagen, Denmark

THOUGH IT'S BEEN AROUND FOREVER—since 1843—and is as much a simple pleasure garden as it is a thrill-ride attraction, Copenhagen's Tivoli Gardens still regularly appears on 10-best lists of amusement parks. Profuse flower beds, fantasy pavilions, tiny twinkling lights illuminating it at night—the entire fairy-tale effect is magical, just what you'd expect from the homeland of Hans Christian Andersen **381**. This place is as classic as it gets—and kids still love it.

Perhaps even more so than its Vienna counterpart, the Prater **485**, Tivoli Gardens is woven into the life of its city. Tivoli is right in downtown Copenhagen, between the city hall and the central railway station. While much of Tivoli is devoted to gardens, restaurants, theaters, and a tiny lake for pleasure boating, there are **25 fanciful rides,** spangled with lights day and night. The kids can try out a merry-go-round of tiny Viking ships, a Ferris wheel with cars shaped like hot-air balloons, a set of dragon boats, and the Flying Trunk, where you wheel past wooden-doll scenes from Hans Christian Andersen stories. There are a fun house, a couple of auto-drives, and not one but two drop rides, one of them scaled for toddlers—two-thirds of the rides, in fact, are suitable for younger children. For older kids, the new steel roller coaster here, the **Demon,** is the biggest in Denmark, and though it only goes 49 mph, it does have three vertical loops; there's also an exciting wooden coaster, the **Rutschebanen.** The **Star Flyer** is Europe's tallest swing ride, bedazzled with stars and planets in tribute to the great Danish astronomer Tyco Brahe.

Between the rides, just strolling around Tivoli is delightful. An Arabian-style palace, with towers and arches, houses more than two dozen **restaurants** (including a Hard Rock Café!) in a range of prices. Try to time your visit to coincide with the parade of the red-uniformed **Tivoli Boys Guard,** looking just like toy soldiers, on early weekend evenings (also Wed); their regimental band gives Saturday afternoon concerts on the large open-air stage at the center of the gardens, where at night you can see tumbling clowns, acrobats, and aerialists.

ⓘ Vesterbrogade 3 (ⓒ **33-15-10-01;** www.tivoligardens.com).

✈ ⊨ See Elsinore Castle **358**.

BEST TIME: Mid-April to mid-Sept.

WHY THEY'LL THANK YOU: Speaks to the child in all of us.

Tivoli.

Alphabetical Index

Abraham Lincoln Birth-place National Historic Site, 430

Abraham Lincoln Presidential Library, 431

Acadia National Park, 472–473

Acre, 224–225

The Acropolis, 190–191

Adirondack State Park, 471

Agate Fossil Beds, 168–169

Ajanta, cave temples of, 366

Akeley, 108–109

The Alamo, 292–293

Al-Aqsa Mosque, 349–350

Alaska Marine Highway System, 43–44

Alberobello, 98

Alcatraz Island, 103–104

Alcott, Louisa May, 416–417

Alexander Keiller Museum, 182

The Alhambra, 407–408

All-England Lawn Tennis & Croquet Club, 516

Alpine Museum, 38

Amalfi Drive, 528–529

Amana Colonies, 264–265

Amana Heritage Museum, 265

The Amazon, 49–50

American Civil War Museum, 290

American Museum of Natural History, 317–318

American Museum of the Moving Image, 395

Amish Country, 265–266

Amish Farm and House, 266

Amsterdam, 59–60

Anasazi Heritage Center, 178

Andersen, Hans Christian, House, 424–425

Angel Falls, 126

Angkor Wat, 368–369

Anne of Green Gables country, 421–422

Ano Nuevo State Reserve, 134–135

Antebellum Plantation, 106

Antigua, 497

Apostle Island National Park, 473–474

Aran Islands, 210–211

Aransas National Wildlife Refuge, 131–132

Archaeological Museum (Crete), 194

Archbishop's Palace, 227

Arches National Park, 83–84

Arizona, USS, Memorial, 308

Arizona-Sonoran Desert Museum, 133

Arles, 202

The Armory Museum, 235

Arran Island, 459

Art Institute of Chicago, 379

Assateague Island, 128–129

Astronaut Hall of Fame, 331

Athabasca Falls, 86

Atlantic City, 52–53

Atlatl Rock, 179

Australian Butterfly Sanctuary, 41

Australian Memorial, 295

Auvergne, volcanoes of, 95

Avebury, 182–183

Avenue of the Giants, 3

The Aviary, 41

Avonlea, 421–422

Ayasofya, 362

Bad Blumau, 117

Bailey-Matthews Shell Museum, 493

Ballooning, Arizona, 529–530

Baltimore Inner Harbor, 300–301

Banff National Park, 35

Barcelona, Gaudí buildings in, 361

Bar Harbor, 472

Baseball Hall of Fame, 500–501

Basilica San Zeno Maggiore, 426

Basketball Hall of Fame, 509–510

Bath, 206

Battle Road Trail, 285

Bayeux Tapestry, 222

The Beatles, 385–386

Beatrix Potter Gallery, 423

Beatrix Potter Home, 423

Běijīng, Forbidden City, 408–409

Beechwood, 413

Belcourt Castle, 414

Bemidji, 109

Ben & Jerry's Ice Cream Factory, 339

Ben Nevis, 440–441

Bergen, 46

Bergsteigerzentrum, 452

Berlin Wall, 313–314

Berlin Zoo, 153–154

Betsy Ross House, 72

Betws-y-Coed, 451

Billy Bob's Texas, 268

Biltmore, 414–415

Birmingham, 276–277

Bisbee, 268–269

Biscayne National Park, 487–488

Bison, Custer State Park, 132

Black Forest, 453

Black Heritage Trail, 271–272

Blaine Kern's Mardi Gras World, 76

Blists Hill Open Air Museum, 334–335

Blue Ice Grotto, 452

Blue Lagoon, 483–484
Blue Mosque, 362
Blue Mountains, 92
Blue Ridge Parkway, 22
Blyde River Canyon, 96–97
Bobsledding in Austrian
    Alps, 525
Bodleian Library, 224
Bonaire Marine Park,
    489–490
Booby Pond Nature
    Reserve, 136–137
Book of Kells, 220
Borobudur, 369–370
Boston Common, 69–70
Boston Red Sox, 501–502
Boulder Coastal Park,
    140–141
Bowfin, USS, 308
Brainerd, 108
Bran Castle, 401–402
The Breakers, 413
British Museum, 204–205
Brontë Parsonage
    Museum, 422–423
Bronx Zoo, 152
Brookfield Zoo, 147–148
Brooklyn Bridge, 16–17
Brown v. Board of Educa-
    tion, 279
Bruges, 227–228
Brussels, 55–56
Bryce Canyon National
    Park, 446–447
Buckman Tavern, 285
Buda Palace, 100–101
Bunratty Castle & Folk
    Park, 241–242
Bunyan, Paul, 108–109
The Burren, 94–95
Butchart Gardens, 42
Bygdoy peninsula,
    295–296
Cabinet War Rooms,
    305–306
Cable cars, San Francisco,
    79–80
The Cabot Trail, 22–23
Caen Memorial, 309
Cahokia Mounds, 174–175
Calgary Stampede,
    518–519
California Gold Rush,
    270–271
California Mission Trail,
    269–270

The Camargue, 466
Cambridge, 45–46
Camel safaris, 527
Canterbury Cathedral,
    356–357
Canyon de Chelly,
    176–177
Cape Breton Highlands
    National Park, 23
Cape Breton Island, 22–23
Cape Cod, baseball, 505
Cape Cod National
    Seashore, 491–492
Cape Hatteras National
    Seashore, 492–493
Carlsbad Caverns,
    121–122
Carver, George Washing-
    ton, Birthplace, 274–275
Castel Sant'Angelo, 61–62
Castelvecchio, 426
Catacombs
    Paris, 98–100
    Rome, 97–98
Catedral de León, 360
Cave temples of Ellora and
    Ajanta, 366
Central Park, 65
Channel Island Military
    Museum, 307
Charles Towne Landing,
    248
Charmouth Heritage Coast
    Centre, 172
Cheddar Gorge, 122–123
Chedworth Roman Villa,
    206
Chester, 221
Chesters Roman Fort and
    Museum, 205–206
Chicago, 66, 379
Chicago Cubs, 502–503
Chichén Itzá, 213–214
Chihuahua al Pacífico
    Railway, 36
Chincoteague, 128–129
Chinkana, 7
Christ Church, 223
Churchill Downs,
    513–514
Church of the Holy
    Sepulcher, 350–351
Church of the Nativity,
    351–352
Cincinnati Zoo, 149
Cirencester, 206

Cité des Sciences et de
    l'Industrie, 326–327
Cliff Palace, 178
Cliffs of Moher, 8–9
Clonmacnois, 357–358
Coalbrookdale Museum of
    Iron, 334
Colleen Moore's Fairy
    Castle, 321
College Football Hall of
    Fame, 508
Cologne Cathedral,
    359–360
Colonial Williamsburg, 246
Colosseum, 198–199
Columbia Icefields, 85–86
Columbia River Gorge, 5–6
Columbia State Historic
    Park, 271
Como, 47–48
Concord, Battle of,
    285–286
Connemara, 464
Conner Prairie Farm,
    263–264
Constitution, USS,
    298–299
Coolidge, Calvin, State
    Historic Site, 431–432
Copacabana, 7–8
Copper Canyon, 36
Coral Castle, 106–107
Corinium Museum,
    206–207
The Corn Palace, 111
Coskata-Coatue Wildlife
    Refuge, 454
Country Music Hall of
    Fame and Museum, 389
Covered bridges, Vermont,
    15–16
Cowtown Coliseum, 268
Crater Lake, 458
Craters of the Moon
    National Monument,
    84–85
Crayola Factory, 340
Crazy Horse Memorial,
    109–110
Crescent Park Carousel,
    532
Crystal River, 129–130
Cuevas de Artà, 123
Cuevas del Drach, 123
Culloden Battlefield,
    284–285

The Cumbres & Toltec Scenic Railroad, 33–34
Custer State Park, 132–133
Cutty Sark, 301
The Cyclone, 538–539
Dachau Concentration Camp Memorial Site, 310–311
Danube River, 48–49
Daytona 500, 520–521
Dayton Aviation Heritage Park, 329–330
D-Day beaches, 308–309
D-Day Museum, 299
Dead Sea, floating in, 484–485
DeKlomp Wooden Shoe & Delft Factory, 107
Delaware Water Gap, 478–479
Delphi, 193
Delta Blues Museum, 387–388
Delta Steamboat Company, 43
Denali National Park, 531–532
Deutsches Museum, 327–328
Devil's Tower, 82–83
Dexter Parsonage Museum, 277
The Diamond Treasury, 235
Dinosaur Valley, 167
Dion, 195
Disneyland, 545–546
Djemaa El Fna Square, 101–102
Dog-sledding, Alaska, 531–532
Dolgellau, 451
Dolphin Discovery Centre, 144–145
Dome of the Rock, 349
Doolin, 384
Drumnadrochit, 465
Dublin, Vikings in, 238–239
Dublinia, 238–239
Dude ranches, Wyoming, 463
Dun Aengus, 210–211
Dune walking in the Sahara, 447–448

Durango & Silverton Narrow Gauge Railroad, 32–33
Dutch Village, 107
Easter Island, 186–187
Ebenezer Baptist Church, 276
Edinburgh Castle, 406
Edison National Historic Site, 335–337
Edo-Tokyo Museum, 243–244
Effigy Mounds, 175–176
Eglise St-Ouen, 227
Egyptian Museum, 187–188
Eiffel Tower, 62
Eispalast, 452
The Elgin Marbles, 204
El Greco, 375–376
Elkhorn Slough Wildlife Reserve, 162
Ellis Island Immigration Museum, 71
Ellora, cave temples of, 366
El Morro, 260
El Portal Tropical Forest Center, 135
Elsinore, 400
El Teleférico, 39–40
El Yunque, 135–136
Enchanted Doll Museum, 111
Ephesus, 197
Epidaurus, Theatre of, 391–392
Europa Park, 551
The Everglades, canoeing in, 469
Experience Music Project, 391
The Exploratorium, 322–323
The Fairy-Tale Road, 30–31
Fenway Park, 501–502
Field Museum, 318
Fitzgerald Marine Reserve, 134
Fjords, Norway, 46
Flanders Field, 294–295
Flathead River, 480–481
Flinders Chase National Park, 145
Florissant Fossil Beds, 169–170

Flying Horses Carousel, 533–534
Fontainebleau, 409–410
The Forbidden City, 408–409
Fort Calgary Historic Park, 519
Fort Mackinac, 456
Fort McHenry, 301
Fort Raleigh National Historic Site, 261
Fort Scott, 266–267
Fort Ticonderoga, 286–287
Fort Worth Stockyards Arena & Livery, 268
Foula, 142
Frank, Anne, House, 425–426
Franklin Institute, 320
Fraser Island, 496–497
Freedom Trail, 70
Frigate birds, 136–137
Fukagawa Edo Museum, 244
Funen Village, 425
The Galápagos, 138–139
Galleria dell'Accademia, 373
Gateway Arch, 77
Gaudí, Antoni, 361
Geffrye Museum, 240
German Military Underground Hospital, 307
German Occupation Museum, 307
Gettysburg National Park, 289–290
Ghibli Museum, 397
Ghost Ranch, 170–171
The Giant's Causeway, 9–10
The Glacier Express, 38–39
Glasgow Science Centre, 325
Glenmont, 336
The Globe Theatre, 392–393
Going-to-the-Sun Road, 25–26
Golden Gate Bridge, 19–20
Golden Hinde, 296
The Golden Temple, 365
Gold Rush, California, 270–271

Goya, Francisco de, 376
Graceland, 386–387
Granada, 407
Grand Canyon, 462, 530–531
Grand Ole Opry House, 389
Grand-Place, 55–56
Grantchester, 45
Grant's Farm, 77
Grapevine Vintage Railroad, 267–268
Grauman's Chinese Theatre, 396
Great Barrier Reef, 485
Great Cotswold Ramble, 450
Great Ocean Road, 31–32
Great Smoky Mountains, 444–445
Great Sphinx, 189
Great Stupa of Sanchi, 211–212
Great Wall, 236–237
Green Bay Packers, 506
Greenfield Village, 251–252
Green Gables, 421
Green Island, 485
Greenwich, 341–342
Griffith Observatory, 343
Grindelwald, 452
Guadalupe River, 479–480
Gù Gōng, 408–409
Haarlem, 460
Hadrian's Villa, 399
Hadrian's Wall, 205–206
Haleakala Crater Road, 28
Half Moon Bay, 27, 134–135
Hampton Court Palace, 403–404
Hanalei Beach, 495
Hans Christian Andersen Museum, 424
Hastings, Battle of, 283
Hawaii Volcanoes National Park, 89–90
H.C. Andersens Barndomshjem, 424
Hearst Castle, 415–416
Heidelberg, 232–233
Hellbrunn gardens, 117–118
Helldorado Town, 269
Henry Bridge, 15–16

Henry Ford Museum, 251–252
Herculaneum, 201
The Hermitage (St. Petersburg), 377–378
The Hermitage (Tennessee), 429
Heyward-Washington House, 248
Highland Games, 520
Highway 61, 387–388
Hill Top, 423
Hinchman House Natural Science Museum, 342
Hiroshima, 311–312
Hoedspruit Research and Breeding Center for Endangered Species, 97
Hohenschwangau, 412–413
Holland, 107–108
Hollywood, 396
Hollywood Walk of Fame, 396
Homosassa Springs Wildlife State Park, 129–130
Hong Kong, 67
Hoover, Herbert, Homestead, 432–433
Hoover Dam, 337
Hopewell Culture National Park, 173
Hopi Reservations, 256–257
Hôtel de Ville, 55–56
Housesteads Fort and Museum, 205
Howe Caverns, 119–120
Huffman Prairie Flying Field, 330
Hundertwasser, Friedensreich, 116–117
Hundertwasser Haus, 117
Hundertwasserkirche, 117
Huntington Library, 380–381
Icefields Parkway, 35, 85
Iguazu Falls, 125–126
Imperial War Museum, 305–306
Independence Hall, 72
Indianapolis 500 Mile Race, 521–522
Indian City USA, 254–255
Inner Harbor, 300–301
Innsbruck, 525

The Inside Passage, 43–44
International Tennis Hall of Fame, 516–517
Intrepid Sea-Air-Space Museum, 304–305
Iona, 358–359
Irish National Heritage Park, 240–241
Ironbridge Gorge Museums, 334–335
Islands of Adventure, 541–542
Isle of Arran, 459
Istanbul, 362, 411–412
Jackson (Wyoming), 463
Jackson, Andrew, The Hermitage, 429
Jamestown, 246
Jasper National Park, 35
Jefferson National Expansion Memorial, 77
Jersey City, diners, 105
Jerusalem, 349–350
Jewel Cave National Monument, 133
Jewish Museum Berlin, 309–310
Joan of Arc, 226–227
Johnson, Lyndon Baines, Homestead, 435–436
Johnson Space Center, 332–333
Jorvik Viking Centre, 239
Joshua Tree National Park, 439–440
Judisches Museum Berlin, 309–310
Juliet's House, 426
Jungfraubahn, 452
The Jurassic Coast, 172
Kailashanath Temple, 366
Kangaroo Island, 145–146
Kansas Aviation Museum, 334
Kansas Cosmosphere, 333–334
Kauai, 495
Kawaguchiko Trail, 442
Kennedy Space Center, 331–332
Kentucky Derby, 513–514
Kerry Bog Village Museum, 29
Kilauea volcano, 89–90
Kilimanjaro, Mount, 441–442

King, Martin Luther, Jr., 275–276
King Center, 276
Kitty Hawk, 328–329
Knife River Indian Villages, 255
Knossos, 194
Knossos, Palace of, 194
Knowth, 184–185
Kon-Tiki, 295–296
The Kremlin, 235
Kruger National Park, 141–142
Ksar Ghilane, 447–448
Kuranda, 40–41
Kyoto, 237–238
La Brea Tar Pits, 171
Lafayette, Mount, 443–444
Lake Compounce, 537–538
Lake Placid, 511
La Mina Falls, 135–136
Landmannalaugar, 449
La Sagrada Família, 361
Lascaux, Caves at, 180
Las Meninas, 375
The Last Supper, 373–374
Las Vegas, 53–54, 542–543
Laura Ingalls Wilder Museum, 420
Legoland, 546–548
Leonardo da Vinci, The Last Supper, 373–374
Les Calanches, 10
Les Puys, 95
Lexington, Battle of, 285–286
Liberty Bell, 72
Lincoln Boyhood National Memorial, 430
Lincoln's Boyhood Home, 430
The Lincoln Trail, 430–431
Linlithgow Castle, 406
Little Rock Central High School, 280–281
Livestock Exchange Building, 267
Loch Ness monster, 465
Loines Observatory, 342
London Bridge, 31
London Eye, 536
Louisville Slugger Museum, 338
Louvre Museum, 374–375
Ludwig II, 412–413
Lyme Regis, 172

Machu Picchu, 216–217
MacKenzie-Intervale Ski Jumping Complex, 511
Mackinac Island State Park, 456
Mack Truck assembly plant, 340
Magnolia Plantation, 248
Majorca, 123–124
The Mall (Washington, D.C.), 73–74
The Mall of America, 548–549
Mammoth Cave, 120–121
Mammoth Hot Springs, 445
Manatees, 129
Manaus, 49–50
Manhattan Express, 542–543
Marangu Trail, 441
Marble House, 414
Marienplatz, 54–55
Marshall Gold Discovery State Historic Park, 271
Martel Lake, 123
Martin Guitar Company, 340
Masada, 208–210
Mashantucket Pequot Museum, 253–254
Mauna Kea, 345
Mawddach Valley Nature Reserve, 451
Maya, ancient, 213–216
McDonald, Lake, 25
Meiji Jingu Shrine, 68
Mendenhall Glacier, 44
Menil Collection, 381–382
Mérida, 39
Mesa Verde National Park, 24, 177–178
Metropolitan Museum of Art, 378
Michelangelo, 61, 199, 353, 373
Michoacán, monarch butterflies, 139–140
Millennium Force, 539–540
Mini-Americana Barn Museum, 265
Miniature World, 42
Minute Man National Historical Park, 285
Mississippi River, 42–43
Missouri, USS, 308

Mitchell House, 342
Mokelumne Hill, 271
Mokoro rides, 475–476
Moldavia, 363–364
Monarch butterflies, 139
Monk's Mound, 174
Monongya Gallery, 256
Monroe School, 279
Mont Blanc, 526
Monte Carlo, 498
Monte Carlo Grand Prix, 523
Monterey Bay Aquarium, 161–162
Monteverde Cloud Forest, 91
Montgomery, 276–277
Monticello, 428–429
Montréal
    bicycling, 457
    underground zone, 60–61
Mont-St-Michel, 355–356
Monument Valley, 2
Moremi Game Reserve, 476
Mosquito Bay, 482–483
Mount Palomar, 344
Mount Vernon, 427–428
Mozart, Wolfgang Amadeus, 382
Mundo Perdido, 216
Munich, 54–55
Musée d'Orsay, 374–375
Musée du Débarquement, 309
Musée National Auguste Rodin, 375
Musée Picasso, 375
Museo della Tortura, 231–232
Museo de los Momias, 118–119
Museo del Prado, 375–376
Museum Haus am Checkpoint Charlie, 313–314
Museum Het Rembrandthuis, 376–377
Museum of Afro-American History, 272
Museum of American Frontier Culture, 262
Museum of Anthropology, 259
Museum of Indian Arts & Culture, 257

Museum of Medieval Stockholm, 56
Museum of Science and Industry, 321
Museum of Television and Radio, 395
Museum of the Gorge, 334
Museumplein, 376–377
Mystery Park, 115–116
Mystic Aquarium, 156–157
Mystic Seaport, 302–303
Naismith Memorial Basketball Hall of Fame, 509–510
Nantucket, 342, 454
Napipiri Reindeer Park, 115
Nashville, 389
National Air and Space Museum, 330–331
National Aquarium, 157–158
National Archaeological Museum (Athens), 192
National Archaeological Museum (Naples), 200–201
National Civil Rights Museum, 278–279
National Constitution Center, 72
National Mall, 73–74
National Maritime Museum, 302
National Museum of Emerging Science and Innovation, 68
National Museum of Natural History, 319
National Museum of the American Indian, 252–253
National Museum of the United States Air Force, 330
National Park Underwater Trail, 488
National Science Museum, 68
National Tom Sawyer Days, 420
National Voting Rights Museum, 277
National Zoo, 151
Natural History Museum (London), 324–325
Natural History Museum (Iceland), 144
Nazca Lines, 185–186

Nazi invasion of England, 306–307
Neuschwanstein, 412–413
Newark Earthworks, 173–174
New England Aquarium, 155–156
Newfound Gap Road, 444
Newgrange, 184–185
New Orleans, 76
Newport, 413–414
New River Gorge, 455
New York Aquarium, 538
New York Yankees, 503–504
Niagara Falls, 74–75
Nikko City, 367–368
Normandy American Cemetery, 309
Normandy Battle Memorial Museum, 309
Norsk Sjofartsmuseum, 295
Northern Lights, 346–347
Northern Plains Indian Culture Fest, 256
Northumberland National Park, 205
Notre Dame, 507–508
Notre-Dame, 14, 354–355
Ocean Park, 67
Ocracoke Island, 493
O.K. Corral, 268
Okavango Delta, 475–476
Okefenokee Swamp Park, 470
Old Hundred Gold Mine, 33
Old Ironsides, 298–299
Old Sturbridge Village, 247
Old Town State Historic Park, 249
Olympic Games, 510
Omaha Beach, 309
Onizuka Visitor Center, 345
Orchard House, 416–417
Orkney Islands, 183–184
Orléans, 227
Osaka Aquarium, 164–165
Oxford University, 223–224
Pacific Coast Highway, 26–27
Pacific Park, 494, 534
Pacific Undersea Gardens, 42
Paestum, 199–200
Painted Desert, 86–87

Palace of Holyroodhouse, 406
The Palace of Knossos, 194
Palazzo del Popolo, 231
Palio delle Contrade, 512–513
The Pantanal, 467
Pantéon y Museos de San Isidoro, 360
The Pantheon, 199
Paper Mill Village Bridge, 15
Parc Asterix, 549–550
Paris, 62–63
Paris Opera, 383–384
Parque Nacional Bernardo O'Higgins, 476
Parrot Jungle Island, 159
Parthenon, 190, 191
Peace Memorial Park, 311–312
Pea Island Wildlife Refuge, 492
Pearl Harbor, 307–308
Pella, 195
The People's Place, 265–266
Petra, 207–208
Petrified Forest, 86–87
Petroglyph Canyon, 179
Petroglyph Point Trail, 178
Phang Nga Bay, 11–12
Phantom Ranch, 462
Philadelphia, 72
Piazza del Duomo, 231
Piazza delle Erbe, 426
Pietà, 353
Pikes Peak State Park, 176
Pilgrim Hall Museum, 245
Pinnacles National Monument, 88–89
Pirates of Nassau, 44–45
Pisa, Leaning Tower of, 230
Playland, 543–544
Please Touch Museum, 320
Plimoth Plantation, 244–245
Plymouth Cheese Factory, 431–432
Plymouth National Wax Museum, 245
Plymouth Notch Historic District, 431
Pointe du Hoc, 309

Poipu Beach, 495
Polar Nights, 346
Polynesian Spa, 93
Pompeii, 200–201
Ponsi Hall Visitor Center, 256
The Ponte Vecchio, 12
Pont Neuf, 14
Porta Nigra, 203
Portsmouth, 299–300
Potter, Beatrix, Home, 423
Powerhouse Museum, 323–324
The Prado, 375–376
Prague, Jewish Quarter of, 233–234
Prince Edward Island National Park, 422
Pro Football Hall of Fame, 508–509
Public Garden, 70
Puffins, Vestmannaeyjar, 143–144
Puget Sound, 41
Punting on the Cam, 45
Puy-de-Dôme, 95
Pyramid of the Sun, 181
Pyramids of Giza, 188–189
Québec, whale-watching, 130–131
Queen Mine Tours, 269
Rainbow Forest Museum, 86
Rainforestation Nature Park, 41
Ramesses VI, tomb of, 190
Rapa Nui, 186–187
Redwood National and State Parks, 3–4
Redwood National Park, 27
Reina de las Columnas, 123
Rembrandt House Museum, 376–377
Rheinisches Landes-museum, 203
Rhodes, 225–226
Riesenrad, 535–536
Rijksmuseum, 376
Rim Drive, 458
The Ring of Kerry, 29–30
Roanoke Island, 261
Robert Gould Shaw Memorial, 272
Rock and Roll Hall of Fame, 390

The Rocky Mountaineer, 34–35
Rocky Mountain National Park, 461–462
Rocky Ridge Farm, 421
Roman Army Museum, 205
Roman Baths (England), 206
Roman Forums, 199
Romeo's House, 426
Roosevelt, Franklin Delano and Eleanor, homes, 433–434
Rosa Parks Library and Museum, 277
Rose Center for Earth and Space, 317–318
Rosecliff, 413
The Rosetta Stone, 204
Rotorua, 93–94
Rouen, 227
Royal British Columbia Museum, 259
Royal Navy Submarine Museum, 299
Royal Observatory, 341–342
Royal Palace, 56
Royal Shakespeare Company, 394
Rushmore, Mount, 109–110
Ryman Auditorium, 389
Saguaro National Park, 87–88
The Sahara, 447–448
St. Andrews, 517–518
St. Basil's Cathedral, 364–365
St. John, 488–489
St. Moritz, 38
St. Peter's Basilica, 352–353
St. Regis Canoe Wilderness, 471
Salzburg, 382
San Antonio River Walk, 78
San Carlos Borromeo de Carmelo, 270
Sanchi, 211–212
Sanctuary of Apollo, 193
Sanctuary of Asklepios, 392
San Diego Zoo, 146–147
San Gimignano, 231–232
Sanibel Island, 493–494

San Ildefonso Pueblo, 257
San Juan Capistrano, 269–270
San Juan Islands, 474–475
San Juan National Historic Site, 260
San Juan Pueblo, 257
San Juan Skyway, 24–25
San Pietro in Vincoli, 61
Santa Barbara Mission, 270
Santa Catalina Island, 486–487
Santa Cruz Boardwalk, 544–545
Santa Elena Cloud Forest Reserve, 91
Santa María de Regla, 360
Santa Monica, 26, 494–495, 534
Santa's Village, 114–115
Santiago de Compostela, 229
Saranac Lake, 471
Saratoga Springs, 514–515
Schloss Hellbrunn, 117–118
Schönbrunn Zoo, 154–155
Schwarzwald Hochstrasse, 453
Science Museum, 324
Seal Bay Conservation Park, 145–146
Seal Cove Beach, 135
Seaquarium, 159
Seatown, 172
Sea turtles, Costa Rican coast, 137–138
Secret Caverns, 120
Sedona, ballooning around, 529–530
Selçuk, 197
Selma, 276–277
Sequoia & Kings Canyon National Parks, 4–5
Sewers, Paris, 98–100
Shakespeare, William, 392–395
Shedd Aquarium, 160
Shelburne Museum, 250–251
Sidmouth Museum, 172
Siena, 512–513
Sierra Madre Express, 36
Silk Road Bridge, 15

Sistine Chapel, 353
Site Préhistorique de Regourdou, 180
Six Flags Great Adventure, 540–541
Skansen, 298
Skara Brae, 183
The Skellig Experience, 29
Skyline Drive, 21–22
Skyline Skyrides, 93
Skyrail Rainforest Cableway, 40–41
Slater Memorial Park Carousel, 532
Snake River, 481–482
Snowdonia National Park, 37, 450–451
Southern Plains Indian Museum, 254–255
Space Center Houston, 332–333
Speed: The Ride, 542–543
Springfield, 431
Spy Museum, 314–315
Stanley Park, 162
Stargazing, 341–347
Statue of Liberty, 71
Staunton, 262
Stax Museum of American Soul Music, 386–387
Stephen C. Foster State Park, 470
Stevenson, Robert Louis, cottage, 417
Stingray City, 490–491
Stirling Castle, 406
Stockholm, 56–57
Stockyards National Historic District, 267–268
Stonehenge, 182–183
Stone Mountain National Park, 105–106
Stratford-upon-Avon, 393–395
Sturbridge, 247
Sun Records Studio, 386
Sutter Gold Mine, 271
Suwanee Canal Recreation Area, 470
Swanee River, 470
Swiss Open-Air Museum, 242–243
Sydney Aquarium, 19, 163–164
Sydney Harbour Bridge, 18–19

Sydney Observatory, 323–324
Taj Mahal, 102–103
Taos Pueblo, 258
Tataouine, 448
Temple Mount, 349–350
Teotihuacán, 181
Terra-cotta warriors of Xi-ān, 212–213
Te Wairoa, 93
Thingvellir, 219
Thórsmörk, 449
Tikal, 215–216
Titicaca, Lake, 7–8
Tivoli Gardens, 552
Toei Uzumasa Movieland, 238
Tokyo, 68–69
Tombstone, 268–269
Toronto Zoo, 152–153
Torres del Paine, 476–477
Tortuguero, 137
Tower Bridge, 17–18
Tower of London, 17, 402–403
Tremezzo, 47
Trier, 203
Tromsø, 346–347
Troy, ancient, 196
Truman, Harry S., Home, 434–435
Tulum, 214–215
Turtles, Costa Rican coast, 137
Twain, Mark, 418–420
Uffizi Gallery, 372–373
Uluru, 6
Underground Railroad Freedom Center, 272–273
Union Station, 77
Universal Studios Hollywood, 396
Unstan Chambered Tomb, 183
Uros islands, 8
U.S. Capitol, 74
USS *Arizona* Memorial, 308
USS *Constitution* Museum, 299
Val-Kill Cottage, 433–434
Valley Forge, 287–288
Valley of the Kings, 189–190
Vancouver Aquarium, 162–163

Van Gogh Museum, 377
Varenna, 47
Vasamuseet, 297–298
The Vatican, 352–353
Veldheer Tulip Farm, 107
Venice, 57–59
Verdun, Battle of, 293–294
Vergina, 195
Vermont Covered Bridge Museum, 15
Vermont Teddy Bear Factory, 339
Verona, 426–427
Versailles, 410–411
Vestal Street Observatory, 342
Vestmannaeyjar, 143–144
Via Appia Antica, 97
Vicksburg, Battle of, 290–292
Victoria Butterfly Gardens, 42
Victoria Falls, 124
Vienna, 535–536
Vieques, 482–483
Vikingskiphuset, 295
Viking Splash Tour, 238
Vindolanda, 205
Wailing Wall, 349
Waiotapu, 93
Wall Drug, 111–112
Warren Bisbee Railway, 269
Warwick Castle, 404–405
Washington, Booker T., Jr., Birthplace, 273–274
Washington, George, Mount Vernon, 427–428
Wasserfelle Gutach, 453
Watch Hill, 532
Waterloo, Battle of, 288–289
Waterside Theater, 261
Watts Towers, 112–113
The Wayside, 417
Wellfleet Bay Wildlife Sanctuary, 492
Wentworth Falls, 92
Western Wall, 349
Westman Islands, 143–144
Westminster Abbey, 64
Wet Tropics Rainforest, 40–41
Whakarewarewa Thermal Reserve, 93

Wheelwright Museum of the American Indian, 257
Whiteface, 511
Whitney, Mount, 4
Whitsunday Islands, 485–486
Wilder, Laura Ingalls, homes, 420–421
Wimbledon, 515–516

Winchester Mystery House, 113–114
Wind Cave National Park, 132–133
Windmill Island, 107
Wookey Hole, 122–123
World of Beatrix Potter, 423
Wright Brothers National Memorial, 329
Wrigley Field, 502–503

Xi-ān, 212–213
Yankee Stadium, 503–504
Yellowstone National Park, 445–446
Yorktown, 246
Yosemite National Park, 438
Ypres, 294–295
Zealand Falls, 444
Zoo Atlanta, 150

Geographical Index

Alabama, 276–277
Alaska
  Denali, 531–532
  Inside Passage, 43–44
Antigua, 497
Argentina, 125–126
Arizona
  Arizona-Sonora Desert Museum, 133
  ballooning, 529–530
  Canyon de Chelly, 176–177
  Cumbres & Toltec Scenic Railroad, 33–34
  Grand Canyon, 462, 530–531
  Hopi Reservations, 256–257
  Monument Valley, 2–3
  Petrified Forest & Painted Desert, 86–87
  Saguaro National Park, 87–88
  Tombstone & Bisbee, 268–269
Arkansas, 280–281
Australia
  Blue Mountains, 92
  Dolphin Discovery Centre, 144–145
  Fraser Island, 496–497
  Great Barrier Reef, 485–486
  Great Ocean Road, 31–32
  Kangaroo Island, 145–146
  Kuranda, 40–41

Powerhouse Museum, 323–324
Sydney Aquarium, 163–164
Sydney Harbour Bridge, 18–19
Uluru (Ayers Rock), 6–7
Austria
  the Danube, 48–49
  Hundertwasser's architecture, 116–117
  Riesenrad, 535–536
  Salzburg, 382
  Schönbrunn Zoo, 154–155
  summer bobsledding, 525
  The Wasserspiele, 117–118
Belgium
  Bruges, 227–228
  Brussels's Grand-Place, 55–56
  Waterloo, 288–289
  Ypres, 294–295
Bethlehem, 351–352
Bolivia, 7–8
Botswana, 475–476
Brazil
  the Amazon, 49–50
  Pantanal, 467
California
  Alcatraz, 103–104
  California Mission Trail, 269–270
  Disneyland, 545–546
  The Exploratorium, 322–323

Golden Gate Bridge, 19–20
Gold Rush Country, 270–271
Griffith Observatory, 343
Half Moon Bay, 134–135
Hearst Castle, 415–416
Hollywood, 396
Huntington Library, 380–381
Joshua Tree, 439–440
La Brea Tar Pits, 171
Legoland, 546–548
Monterey Bay Aquarium, 161–162
Mount Palomar, 344
Old Town State Historic Park, 249
Pacific Coast Highway, 26–27
Pinnacles National Monument, 88–89
Redwood Forests, 3–4
San Diego Zoo, 146–147
San Francisco cable cars, 79–80
Santa Cruz Boardwalk, 544–545
Santa Monica Beach, 494–495
Santa Monica Pier, 534
Sequoia & Kings Canyon, 4–5
snorkeling, 486–487
Watts Tower, 112–113
Winchester Mystery House, 113–114
Yosemite, 438

Cambodia, 368–369
Canada
  Anne of Green Gables
    Country, 421–422
  British Columbia's
    native peoples, 259
  Cabot Trail, 22–23
  Calgary Stampede,
    518–519
  Columbia Icefields,
    85–86
  Montréal, 60–61, 457
  Niagara Falls, 74–75
  Nova Scotia, 477–478
  The Rocky Mountaineer,
    34–35
  Seattle-Victoria Ferry,
    41–42
  Toronto Zoo, 152–153
  Vancouver Aquarium,
    162–163
  whale-watching in
    Québec, 130–131
Cayman Islands, 44–45,
  490–491
Chile, 186–187, 476–477
China
  Forbidden City, 408–409
  Great Wall of China,
    236–237
  Hong Kong, 67
  Warriors of Xí-ān,
    212–213
Colorado
  Durango & Silverton
    Narrow Gauge Rail-
    road, 32–33
  Florissant Fossil Beds,
    169–170
  Mesa Verde, 177–179
  Rocky Mountain
    National Park, 461–462
  San Juan Skyway, 24–25
Connecticut
  Boulder Dash, 537–538
  Hartford, 418–419
  Mashantucket Pequot
    Museum, 253–254
  Mystic Aquarium,
    156–157
  Mystic Seaport,
    302–303
Costa Rica, 91, 137–138
Crete, 194
Czech Republic, 233–234
Denmark, 400, 424–425,
  552
Ecuador, 138–139

Egypt
  The Egyptian Museum:
    Cairo, 187–190
England
  Battle of Hastings, 283
  Beatrix Potter Country,
    423–424
  British Museum,
    204–205
  Brontë Parsonage
    Museum, 422–423
  Canterbury Cathedral,
    356–357
  Cheddar Gorge &
    Wookey Hole, 122–123
  Chester, 221
  Geffrye Museum, 240
  The Golden Hinde,
    296
  Greenwich, 301–302,
    341–342
  Hadrian's Wall, 205–206
  Hampton Court Palace,
    403–404
  Ironbridge Gorge,
    334–335
  Jorvik Viking Centre, 239
  The Jurassic Coast,
    172–173
  Liverpool Beatles Tour,
    385–386
  The London Eye, 536
  London sights, 63–64
  The Nazi Invasion,
    306–307
  Oxford University,
    223–224
  Portsmouth, 299–300
  punting on the Cam,
    45–46
  Roman Britain,
    206–207
  The Science & Natural
    History Museums,
    324–325
  Shakespeare's Globe
    Theatre, 392–393
  Stratford-upon-Avon,
    393–395
  Tower Bridge, 17–18
  Tower of London,
    402–403
  Warwick Castle,
    404–405
  Wiltshire, 182–183
  Wimbledon, 515–516
  World War II in London,
    305–306
Finland, 114–115

Florida
  baseball, 504–505
  Biscayne National Park,
    487–488
  Coral Castle, 106–107
  Crystal River, 129–130
  Daytona 500, 520–521
  the Everglades, 469
  Islands of Adventure,
    541–542
  Kennedy Space Center,
    331–332
  Miami Seaquarium, 159
  Sanibel Island, 493–494
France
  Arles, 202
  The Bayeux Tapestry,
    222
  The Camargue, 466
  The Caves of Lascaux,
    180
  Cité des Sciences et de
    l'Industrie, 326–327
  Fontainebleau, 409–410
  Joan of Arc sights,
    226–227
  Le Pont Neuf, 14–15
  Les Calanches, 10–11
  Mont Blanc, 526
  Mont-St-Michel,
    355–356
  Notre-Dame de Paris,
    354–355
  Parc Asterix, 549–550
  Paris for art lovers,
    374–375
  The Paris Opera,
    383–384
  Paris sewers and cata-
    combs, 98–100
  the Seine, 62–63
  Verdun, 293–294
  Versailles, 410
  volcanoes of the
    Auvergne, 95–96
Georgia
  Dr. King's Legacy,
    275–276
  Stone Mountain
    National Park, 105–106
  Swanee River, 470
  Zoo Atlanta, 150
Germany
  Berlin sights, 153–154,
    309–310, 313–314
  Black Forest, 453
  Cologne Cathedral,
    359–360
  Dachau, 310–311

Deutsches Museum, 327–328
Europa-Park, 551
The Fairy-Tale Road, 30–31
Heidelberg, 232–233
Marienplatz, 54–55
Neuschwanstein, 412–413
Trier, 203
Greece
The Acropolis, 190–191
Alexander the Great, 195
Ancient Theatre of Epidaurus, 391–392
Delphi, 193
National Archaeological Museum, 192
Olympia, 510
Rhodes, 225–226
Guatemala, 215–216
Hawaii
Haleakala, 28
Hawaii Volcanoes National Park, 89–90
Kauai, 495
Mauna Kea, 345
Pearl Harbor, 307–308
Hungary, 48–49, 100–101
Iceland
Blue Lagoon, 483–484
Landmannalaugar, 449–450
puffins, 143–144
Thingvellir, 219
Idaho, 84–85
Illinois
Brookfield Zoo, 147–148
Cahokia Mounds, 174–175
Chicago sights, 66, 160, 318, 321, 379, 502–503
India
Ajanta & Ellora, 366
camel safaris, 527
Golden Temple, 365
Great Stupa of Sanchi, 211–212
Taj Mahal, 102–103
Indiana, 263–264, 507–508, 521–522
Indonesia, 369–370
Iowa, 175–176, 264–265, 432–433
Ireland
The Book of Kells, 220
Bunratty Castle & Folk Park, 241–242

The Burren, 94–95
Cliffs of Moher, 8–9
Clonmacnois, 357–358
Doolin, 384
Dun Aengus, 210–211
Irish National Heritage Park, 240–241
Newgrange, 184–185
pony trekking, 464
The Ring of Kerry, 29–30
Vikings in Dublin, 238–239
Israel
Acre, 224–225
Church of the Holy Sepulcher, 350–351
Dead Sea, 484–485
Masada, 208–210
The Temple Mount, 349–350
Italy
The Amalfi Drive, 528–529
Beehive Houses of Apulia, 98
canals of Venice, 57–59
catacombs of Rome, 97
Colosseum and Pantheon, 198–199
Hadrian's Villa, 399
Lake Como, 47–48
The Last Supper, 373–374
Leaning Tower of Pisa, 230
Paestum, 199–200
Pompeii & Ercolano, 200–201
Ponte Vecchio, 12–13
Rom sights, 61–62
San Gimignano, 231–232
Siena, 512–513
Uffizi Gallery, 372–373
The Vatican, 352–353
Verona, 426–427
Japan
Edo-Tokyo Museum, 243–244
Ghibli Museum, 397
Hiroshima, 311–312
Kyoto, 237–238
Mount Fuji, 442–443
Nikko, 367–368
Osaka Aquarium, 164–165
Tokyo, 68–69

Jordan, 207–208
Kansas, 266–267, 279–280, 333–334
Kentucky, 120–121, 338, 513–514
Little Cayman, 136–137
Louisiana, 76
Maine, 20–21, 472–473
Maryland, 157–158, 300–301
Massachusetts
baseball on Cape Cod, 505
Basketball Hall of Fame, 509–510
bicycling on Nantucket, 454
Black Heritage Trail, 271–272
Boston Common, 69–70
Cape Cod National Seashore, 491–492
Fenway Park, 501–502
Flying Horses Carousel, 533–534
Lexington & Concord, 285–286
Little Women House, 416–417
New England Aquarium, 155–156
Old Ironsides, 298–299
Old Sturbridge Village, 247
Plimoth Plantation, 244–245
stargazing on Nantucket, 342
Mexico
Chichén Itzá, 213–214
Chihuahua al Pacífico Railway, 36
monarch butterflies, 139–140
Museo de los Momias, 118–119
Teotihuacán, 181
Tulum, 214–215
Michigan, 107–108, 251–252, 456
Minnesota, 108–109, 548–549
Mississippi
Highway 61, 387–388
Vicksburg, 290–292
Mississippi River, 42–43

Missouri
The Gateway Arch, 77
George Washington
Carver's Birthplace,
274–275
Harry S. Truman's
Home, 434–435
The Mark Twain Home,
419–420
Monaco, 498, 523
Montana, 25–26,
445–446, 480–481
Morocco, 101–102
Nebraska, 168–169
The Netherlands
Amsterdam's Mu-
seumplein, 376–377
The Anne Frank House,
425–426
canals of Amsterdam,
59–60
Haarlem, 460
Netherlands Antilles,
489–490
Nevada, 53–54, 179, 337,
542–543
New Hampshire, 443–444
New Jersey, 52–53,
104–105, 335–337,
540–541
New Mexico
Carlsbad Caverns,
121–122
The Cumbres & Toltec
Scenic Railroad,
33–34
Ghost Ranch, 170–171
Santa Fe, 257–258
Taos Pueblo, 258
New York State
American Museum of
Natural History,
317–318
American Museum of
the Moving Image, 395
Baseball Hall of Fame,
500
the Bronx Zoo, 152
The Brooklyn Bridge,
16–17
canoeing in the Adiron-
dacks, 471
The Cyclone, 538–539
Fort Ticonderoga,
286–287
Howe Caverns & Secret
Caverns, 119–120
Hyde Park, 433–434

Intrepid Sea-Air-Space
Museum, 304–305
Lake Placid, 511
Manhattan, 65
Metropolitan Museum
of Art, 378
Niagara Falls, 74–75
Rye Playland, 543–544
Saranac Lake, 417
Saratoga Race Course,
514–515
The Statue of Liberty &
Ellis Island, 71
Yankee Stadium,
503–504
New Zealand, 93–94
North Carolina
Biltmore Estate,
414–415
Cape Hatteras National
Seashore, 492–493
Kitty Hawk, 328–329
Roanoke Island, 261
Skyline Drive & Blue
Ridge Parkway,
21–22
North Dakota, 255–256
Northern Ireland, 9–10
Norway, 46, 295–296
Polar Nights & Northern
Lights: Tromsø,
346–347
Ohio
The Cincinnati Zoo, 149
Dayton Aviation Her-
itage Park, 329–330
Millennium Force,
539–540
National Underground
Railroad Freedom
Center, 272–273
Newark Earthworks,
173–174
Pro Football Hall of
Fame, 508–509
Rock and Roll Hall of
Fame, 390
Oklahoma, 254–255
Oregon, 5–6, 458,
481–482
Pennsylvania
Amish Country,
265–266
Delaware Water Gap,
478–479
Franklin Institute, 320
Gettysburg National
Park, 289–290

Moving Down the
Assembly Line, 340
Philadelphia, 72
Valley Forge, 287–288
Peru
Lake Titicaca, 7–8
Machu Picchu,
216–217
The Nazca Lines,
185–186
Puerto Rico, 135–136,
260, 482–483
Rhode Island
The Flying Horses, 532
International Tennis Hall
of Fame, 516–517
Newport's Mansions,
413–414
Romania, 363–364,
401–402
Russia, 235, 364–365,
377–378
Scotland
Arran Island, 459
Ben Nevis, 440–441
Culloden Battlefield,
284–285
Foula, 142–143
Glasgow Science
Centre, 325
The Highland Games,
520
Iona, 358–359
Loch Ness Monster, 465
Orkney Islands,
183–184
royal castles, 406
St. Andrews, 517–518
South Africa, 96–97,
140–142
South Carolina, 248
South Dakota
The Corn Palace, 111
Custer State Park,
132–133
Mount Rushmore & The
Crazy Horse Memorial,
109–110
Wall Drug, 111–112
Spain
The Alhambra, 407–408
Barcelona, 361
Catedral de León, 360
Majorca, 123–124
Museo del Prado,
375–376
Santiago de Com-
postela, 229

Sweden, 56–57, 297–298
Switzerland
  The Glacier Express, 38–39
  Grindelwald, 452
  Mystery Park, 115–116
  Swiss Open-Air Museum, 242–243
Tanzania, 441–442
Tennessee
  Graceland, 386–387
  The Great Smoky Mountains, 444–445
  The Hermitage, 429
  Highway 61, 387–388
  The Nashville Music Scene, 389
  National Civil Rights Museum, 278–279
  The Skyline Drive & Blue Ridge Parkway, 21–22
Texas
  the Alamo, 292–293
  Aransas National Wildlife Refuge, 131–132
  Dinosaur Valley, 167
  Guadalupe River, 479–480
  LBJ's Texas Homestead, 435–436

The Menil Collection, 381–382
San Antonio River Walk, 78
Space Center Houston, 332–333
Stockyards National Historic District, 267–268
Thailand, 11–12
The Bahamas, 44–45
Tunisia, 447–448
Turkey
  Ancient Troy, 196
  Ephesus, 197
  Istanbul, 362, 411–412
U.S. Virgin Islands, 488–489
Utah, 83–84, 446–447
Venezuela, 39–40, 126
Vermont
  Calvin Coolidge State Historic Site, 431–432
  covered bridges, 15–16
  Shelburne Museum, 250–251
  Waterbury & Shelburne, 339
Virginia
  Assateague, 128–129
  Booker T. Washington Birthplace, 273–274

Frontier Culture Museum, 262
Jefferson's Monticello, 428–429
Mount Vernon, 427–428
Skyline Drive & Blue Ridge Parkway, 21–22
Williamsburg, Jamestown & Yorktown, 246
Wales, 37, 450–451
Washington, D.C.
  National Air and Space Museum, 330–331
  National Mall, 73–74
  National Museum of Natural History, 319
  National Museum of the American Indian, 252–253
  National Zoo, 151
  The Spy Museum, 314–315
Washington state, 41–42, 391, 474–475
West Virginia, 455
Wisconsin, 473–474, 506
Wyoming, 82–83, 445–446, 463
Zambia, 124
Zimbabwe, 124

Photo Credits

p. 82, bottom: © Jack Brink; p. 83, bottom: © Lauren Etting; p. 85, bottom: © Jack Brink; p. 87, top: © Jack Brink; p. 88, top: © National Park Service; p. 90, top: © Margot Weiss; p. 92, bottom: © Copyright BlueMountainsTourism/Photographer Richard Powers ; p. 93, bottom: © Margot Weiss; p. 94, bottom: © Tourism Ireland Imagery/Nutan; p. 96, bottom: © Margot Weiss; p. 99, top: © Paris Tourism Bureau Photographe: Henri Garat; p. 101, bottom: © Peter Bobrowsky; p. 103, top: © Margot Weiss; p. 104, top: © National Park Service; p. 108, top: © Michigan Economic Development Corporation/Vito Palmisano; p. 110, top: © Jack Brink; p. 114, top: © Lauren Etting; p. 116, top: © Mystery Park AG, www.mysterypark.ch; p. 119, bottom: © Photo by Peter Jones for Howe Caverns; p. 121, top: © National Park Service; p. 125, bottom: © Nehiel F. Rojas; p. 127: © San Diego Zoo; p. 128, bottom: © National Park Service; p. 131, top: © Groupe Dufour ; p. 134, top: © Arryn Bronson; p. 137, top: © Frank Roulstone, National Trust for the Cayman Islands; p. 138, top: © Caribbean Conservation Corporation; p. 139, top: © Jack Brink; p. 140, bottom: © Alexis Lipsitz-Flippin; p. 142, top: © Alexis Lipsitz-Flippin; p. 146, top: © Tourism Australia; p. 147, top: © San Diego Zoo; p. 148, top: Jim Schulz, Staff Photographer. © Chicago Zoological Society 2005. ; p. 150, bottom: © Atlanta Zoo/Courtesy Adam Thompson; p. 157, top: © Courtesy of John Anderson/Mystic Aquarium & Institute for Exploration/© Jack Brink; p. 158, top: © The National Aquarium in Baltimore © JamesWest/JWestProductions.com; p. 161, bottom: © Shan Carter; p. 163, bottom: © Sydney Aquarium; p. 166: © Jack Brink; p. 168, bottom: © National Park Service; p. 169, bottom: © National Park Service; p. 172, bottom: © Jack Brink; p. 175, top: © Jack Brink; p. 177, top: © Bill Brink; p. 178, bottom: © Photo by Tom Stillo/CTO; p. 182, bottom: © Jack Brink; p. 186, bottom: © Jack Brink; p. 187, bottom: © Jack Brink; p. 189, top: © Jack Brink; p. 191, top: © Greek National Tourism Organization; p. 198, bottom: © Lisa Monsees; p. 201, top: © Lisa Monsees; p. 204, top: © Jack Brink; p. 207, top: © Suzanna R. Thompson; p. 208, top: © Peter Bobrowsky; p. 209, top: © Courtesy State of Israel, Ministry of Tourism; p. 213, top: © Jack Brink; p. 213, bottom: © Theodore W. Thompson; p. 217, top: © Mike Spring; p. 218: © Old Sturbridge Village photo by Thomas Neill; p. 223, bottom: © Suzanna R. Thompson; p. 225, top: © Courtesy State of Israel, Ministry of Tourism; p. 228, top: © Toerisme Brugge; p. 231, bottom: © Melinda Quintero; p. 232, bottom: © Heidelberger Kongress und Tourismus GmbH.; p. 234, top: © Margot Weiss; p. 236, bottom: © Jack Brink; p. 245, top: © Photo Courtesy of MOTT; p. 247, bottom: © Old Sturbridge Village photo by Erika Sidor; p. 250, bottom: © Shelburne Museum; p. 253, top: © Photo by Jeff Tinsley © Smithsonian Institution; p. 263, bottom: © Courtesy of Indiana Office of Tourism Development; p. 264, bottom: © Amana Colonies Convention and Visitors Bureau © 2005; p. 268, top: © Fort Worth Convention & Visitors Bureau; p. 270, top: © Robert Thompson; p. 273, top: © Collections of the National Underground Railroad Freedom Center; p. 275, top: © Missouri Division of Tourism; p. 277, top: © Alabama Bureau of Tourism & Travel/Photographer Karim Shamsi-Basha; p. 278, bottom: © State of Tennessee; p. 280, bottom: © AR Dept Parks & Tourism ; p. 282: SACVB/Michael Giordano; p. 284, bottom: © Jack Brink; p. 286, top: © Photo Courtesy of MOTT, Jim Higgins, photographer; p. 288, top: © National Park Service; p. 290, top: © Dell Bleekman; p. 291, top: © Photos courtesy of the Mississippi Development Authority/Division of Tourism; p. 292, bottom: © SACVB/Robert W. Bone; p. 297, bottom: © www.imagebank.sweden.se/Richard Ryan; p. 298, bottom: © Photo Courtesy of MOTT; p. 300, top: © Jack Brink; p. 302, top: © Visit London 2004; p. 303, top: © Jack Brink; p. 304, bottom: © Courtesy Intrepid Sea, Air & Space Museum; p. 306, top: © Visit London 2004/Andy Lane; p. 312, top: © JNTO; p. 313, bottom: © Margot Weiss; p. 314, bottom: © courtesy of the International Spy Museum; p. 316: © Photo courtesy of the North Carolina Division of Tourism, Film and Sports Development. Bill Russ, photographer.; p. 317, bottom: © Margot Weiss; p. 321, bottom: © Scott Brownell, Museum of Science and Industry; p. 322, bottom: © The Exploratorium/photo credit

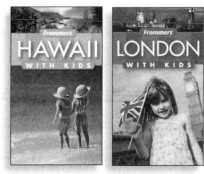